The Final Colossus
In the Light of Her Majesty
AD 2013-2015

by
William L. Roth
Timothy Parsons-Heather

The Morning Star of Our Lord, Inc. is a nonprofit, tax-exempt religious and charitable organization incorporated under the laws of the State of Illinois. It has been established for the dissemination of a miraculous body of work received through the supernatural intercession of the Blessed Virgin Mary under the titles of the Morning Star Over America and the Final Colossus. This organization is solemnly dedicated to all the principles delineated within these written texts in union with the spiritual catechesis of the Supreme Pontiff of the Roman Catholic Church, the Vicar of Christ on Earth. It is the intrinsic role of this Corporation to evangelize the Gospel of Christianity and provide pastoral consolation to those lacking in faith, the infirm, homebound, incarcerated, deprived, dejected and those who are otherwise suffering-humanity for the sake of the Glory of the Kingdom of Jesus Christ.

The Morning Star of Our Lord, Inc.
Springfield, Illinois
www.ImmaculateMary.org

Published by The Morning Star of Our Lord, Inc.
Used with permission.

Copyright © 2019   Timothy Parsons-Heather
All rights reserved.   William L. Roth

Publish Date: October 13, 2019

ISBN: 978-0-9793334-5-3

Our Marian Consecration

We hold our Holy Mother's gracious favor as the most precious and sacred thing that we could have ever had deposited into our hands, noting that we receive the Eucharistic Body of Jesus upon our tongues. One of our strictest intentions is to never allow the thought to arise in the Most Blessed Virgin's mind that Her words and intercession are not the most welcome and appreciated gift that we could ever have received in our lives. We accept all that we have been given as mankind's treasures, as if we were all humanity receiving Her. She loves us. We want Her to feel loved in return. No sorrow will arise in Her thoughts from any lack of receptivity of Her mystical grace on our part. This is our commitment. This is how we want our lives to be recorded in the Book of Life.

When Our Lady gazes across the world looking for love, we want Her to immediately see us. We will venerate everything from Her, even if we are the last two standing. We will respond to Her with the fullest measure of our strength and devotion. Our faculties and lives are in Her service. We will obey Her every request and progress on every path She points out to us, even if it is to our own cross. The flesh may be weak at times, but we are determined that our spirit will always be strong. We will hold in infinite regard all that She dispenses and will protect it with our integrity and honesty until we meet Her in Heaven face-to-face. And there, we will thank Her again. And, all of this is because of Her Son whom we love in our unity.

The Final Colossus
In the Light of Her Majesty
AD 2013-2015

Historical Introduction

Prologue
30 Questions
1

Anthology of Messages

AD 2013
195

AD 2014
357

AD 2015
525

The Final Colossus
In the Light of Her Majesty
AD 2013-2015

"Rejoice, O' brothers and sisters, for we are Christians! The darkness cannot find us now; we can scoff at our predators' lies, we are foreign to the netherworld, and we are immune to the curses that befall those not of our kind."

- William L. Roth

Historical Introduction

On June 24, 1981, the Blessed Virgin Mary began daily appearances to six young children in the small Catholic parish of Medjugorje in Bosnia-Herzegovina, an uninterrupted mystical phenomenon that continues to the present day. Tens of millions of men, women, children, bishops, priests, and other religious from all over the world have made pilgrimages to experience this Marian event to engage their discernment, petition their needs, accent their faith, and to advance their journey of conversion and sanctification through the Immaculate Grace of the Queen of Peace in communion with the Revelation and Traditions of the Roman Catholic Church.

In the fall of 1989, two men who had been best of friends since the mid-1970s traveled to Medjugorje, and during that pilgrimage were called from a crowd of hundreds to receive a private blessing through the simultaneous laying on of the hands by Medjugorjian visionary Vicka Ivankovic. Touched deeply, the two men expressed gratitude, completed their pilgrimage and returned to their lives in the United States of America, adhering to their newly-awakened faith and exercising the requests that the Mother of God was making to humanity worldwide through Her intercession there.

Just over one year later in the early morning hours of February 22, 1991, on the Feast of the Chair of Saint Peter and the 60th anniversary of Our Lord's appearance to Sister Faustina who transcribed a mystical Diary bearing the message of His Divine Mercy, the Most Blessed Virgin Mary augmented Her beautiful intercession through these two men in the Roman Catholic Diocese of Springfield in Illinois, thereby initiating another diarist body of work under the title "Morning Star Over America."

From the very first moments on that early winter morning over a quarter century ago, these two sons of the Church sacrificed life as they knew it and committed to recording the Virgin Mother's mystical relationship with them and the heartfelt conversations that they exchanged with the Hosts of Heaven during almost daily transcensions. Their cloistered relationship of prayer with Jesus and the Virgin Mary has now spanned over 28 years, and thousands of pages enshrined in fifteen public works that archive one of the most spectacular effusions of Marian grace ever recorded in the history of the Catholic Church, all in the heart of the United States of America.

The initial period of the Virgin Mary's intercession spanned the six years from February 22, 1991 through February 22, 1997, and was composed of spiritual acclimation to the mystical, mentoring, tutoring, purification, tempering, dedication, sacrifice and the assaying of their commitment to proceed with Her to the Triumph of Her Immaculate Heart through prayer of the Holy Rosary and faithfulness to the Church. A meticulous diary was recorded during this period of time that is nearly 1600 pages in length, titled "In Our Darkest Hour - Morning Star Over America." In this diarist transcript is recorded the personal unfolding of the events and the innocent faithfulness the two men engaged in response. It documents the parables, miracles, prophecies, lessons and conversations with the Queen of Heaven that solidified their allegiance to Heaven's calling, two bonded as one in their commission to evangelize the Gospel of Christ the King.

After publication of the original diary in 1999, Our Lady set upon assisting them in the completion of six specific thematic works describing true faith, religiosity and spirituality to our contemporary secular world, highlighted by a spectacular rebuttal in "White Collar Witch Hunt" against those who have unjustly assailed the Roman Catholic priesthood and the Hierarchy of the Church over the last two decades.

At the dawn of the millennium on January 2, 2000, Our Lady elevated the magnitude of Her intercession by initiating Her anthologies of "New Millennium" messages. The revelatory strains that She imparted are bold, beautiful, deep, and revealing of the relationship that She wishes to have with Her children, while leading us to the foot of the Cross. She opened Her Immaculate Heart publicly for nine more years until December 28, 2008, the Feast of the Holy Family, pouring out a Marian River of Light that is arguably unmatched in the annals of Christendom. She wishes us to awaken to the reality of God and take, imbibe and savor Her grace and unassailable wisdom.

The official deposit of the revelation of Our Lady under the title Morning Star Over America is contained within the first twelve published works, spanning the message dates of February 22, 1991 through December 28, 2008. The authors testify that the deposit of revelation under the title Morning Star Over America possesses an inclusive character whereby the Most Blessed Virgin manifests a conveyance to Her side through the work, thus gathering all Her children around

Her in prayer before the Cross of Her Son Jesus Christ, under the paternal auspices of the Roman Catholic Church. The Morning Star Over America revelation is a "private revelation" in accordance with the definition prescribed by the Roman Catholic Church. It holds no requirement of binding assent even in the case of its authenticity. Yet, the Holy Spirit beckons us to accept it so that the world may benefit from our Heavenly Mother's guidance through the authentic witness of the graces subsisting within the Catholic Church. These works are not to be confused in substance or stature with the official Public Revelation and Deposit of Faith sanctioned within the authoritative catechesis of the Church of Rome. The published works of the Morning Star Over America neither add to, supersede nor supplant, either in part or in toto, the official Deposit of Faith of the Roman Catholic Church.

They are a grace of explication through the power of the Holy Spirit, given to assist and focus our understanding of and commitment to the Public Revelation of Jesus Christ. Morning Star Over America exists as a subordinate outpouring of grace that subsists beneath the official Deposit of Faith; a particular animation of the Holy Spirit through the benefits of the Sacrament of Confirmation. These works are an organic, maternal flowering generated as a product of obedient acceptance of that official Deposit of Faith.

Any messages or portions of messages in subsequent works dated after December 28, 2008 or other content, parables, lessons or spiritual treatises related to messages that are not recorded in the original twelve works, are likewise bound under the definition of private revelation, and at present, do not reside beneath the Morning Star Over America revelation until such time that they may be specifically elevated by the Church as an addendum to the original work. The Church holds the power to magnify Our Lady's work in this regard through the "sensus fidelium" and its authority to bind.

The affirmation of the inclusive nature of the Morning Star Over America revelation reflects an explicit welcoming by the Matriarch of Heaven for all people to unite with Her through the special grace of the works and gather with Her in prayer and faithfulness to the Roman Catholic Church. Her presence as the Morning Star Over America is not simply a limited grace of significance only to Her two obedient sons. She reveals that She comes to speak to all of Her children with equal emphasis, and with the same maternal authority and motherly compassion; and She petitions our obedient acceptance of Her wise counsel in return.

The subsequent record of Our Lady's continuing relationship with Her two sons after December 28, 2008 is currently recognized by them as a personal gift that remains within the intimate privacy of their personal relationship with the Holy Virgin that can be disclosed or remain secret in perpetuity at their discretion in union with Her guidance. The Virgin Mother wishes to emphasize that She should not be required to cease any relationship as a precondition for Her to be given venue so that the faith of the Church may be strengthened by the vested recognition of Her motherly guidance as the Morning Star Over America. We are encouraged to remember Matthew 5:13-16.

Each work in succession upon completion has been submitted to the sitting Bishop of the Roman Catholic Diocese of Springfield in Illinois, beginning in 1999 with the original diary. While the process has been cloistered and private, the fruit has been fully revealed and laid respectfully at the feet of the apostolic successors of the Church. The burden of discerning mystical intercessions is truly light, only requiring the love embodied in a simple "Fiat" when faced with undeniable grace. The Mother of Jesus asks everyone to imitate Her example to the Archangel Gabriel. This is the sacrifice my brother and I offered to Her on the morning of February 22, 1991.

"How many words have I said to you in almost two decades? It is nearly unimaginable. You should be pleased with yourselves, even righteously proud, for caring enough about your brothers and sisters to help Me convert them to the Cross. There are moments in history that account for thousands of years of change, and your lives here in this place are filled with those times. What humanity will see the most on this side of the veil is not the dailiness you have invested, but the earthshaking product of that investment. While you have lived hours at a time, they will see an eternity of beatific grace. Why? Because they could not have lived your agonies. Someone had to be called. A certain soul or two had to be touched by the miracles from afar, where the Angels tread and Saints repose, and you and your brother are these fortunate and yet unfortunate souls. Your sorrows have been real, your burdens toilsome, your suffering intense, but your hopes remain alive.

There is a new beginning for everyone who lives, those who are addicted to drugs, they who have given their past to the pleasures of the flesh, the many who cannot see because they choose to remain blind by their own callousness, hatred, and unmitigated arrogance and greed. Again, I say to you, the key to this change is 'response.' React to the intercession of God, and He will guide the lot of you to the peaceful ravines where you can be brave again, where you can draw a new breath, take a fresh drink, sit on your tired breeches and look into the skies with a wholly new arrival again! Respond! Respond! Is this not, too, the essence of prayer? There are no endings to the countless years during which a homily would continue that reveals the newness of Life in the Love of My Son. There is only the unrivaled destiny of wholeness anew, a way to escape, a means of protection, a model for flight, and a change for the best! If it is only one 'I am sorry' away for those who cannot bring themselves to accept, please get down on your knees at the feet of your brother and beg his pardon in advance! Tell him that Jesus is alive in you, that the Holy Spirit is prostrate at his side and begging him to consider your soul as having been refreshed, absolved, and enlightened, and that you wish for him to join with you there!

My little ones, I impel and implore the nations to turn themselves over to Jesus, the Son of Man, for everything required to set the world aright. There is no poverty in this that cannot be explained by the tenets of His Word. There are no reasons to defer to any future age the responsibilities that have fallen upon you. Your ancestors and forebears handed you a world with unlimited potential to do good, to see Light for what God made it to be, and open the future far beyond the horizons you see with your eyes. They passed to you a torch of spiritual vision that cannot be supplanted by the brevity of crescendoes by which you spend the hours. They saw in you what you refuse to see in yourselves. They recognized that you were more than capable of seeing the conclusion of Earth's realities in the Resurrection of the Messiah, faced and devoted to the purification of every man, woman, and child who would inhale the world to come."

- The Blessed Virgin Mary

Prologue
30 Questions

Question 1
After the passing of nearly 30 years, how do you personally envision the preeminent existence of God as the determiner of the fate of humankind?

I once saw a horse race as an 11-year-old child. It was the last race of the storied Triple Crown which was run at Belmont Park in New York on June 9, 1973. A great thoroughbred named Secretariat had come from behind to win the two previous races of the series at the Kentucky Derby and the Preakness, and was the beloved national favorite to capture racing accolades if he were to succeed again this third time in successive races. In a field of five horses at the Belmont Stakes, Secretariat broke from the gate and moved to the front along the rail against a single worthy competitor who together left the other competitors behind in the mile and a half race. Then on the back stretch, it happened. Secretariat thundered into the realms of legend. I was transfixed to the television screen on that day as an aura engulfed me. With the backdrop of the announcer and the screaming crowd, and even as a child, I knew I was watching something beyond the boundaries of the ordinary. It was as if a mighty dam between the possible and the impossible was collapsing before my eyes. It started as just a small trickle of daylight between two horses on a back stretch. Then, the daylight grew wider and wider with each second, the breach between horses opening as the euphoria of every spectator began to crescendo in synchronization to the expanding separation between them. The breach in the dike of ecstasy finally burst wide open with a realization that "It was finished," as Secretariat was exploding away from his competitors in a way where the announcer exclaimed to all those listening that this tremendous machine would be impossible to catch. The race was still in progress, barely half run, but in the story of human spectacles, it was already finished before the victory could ever be celebrated. For another sixty seconds, those present and watching by television experienced the bonds breached as Providence poured forth its equine definition of victory which expanded into realms that transcended the imaginations of this blessed segment of humanity who looked on. Secretariat processed alone as an elegant wonder down the final home stretch striking a thunderclap of revelation that awestruck the sensibilities of every man, woman and child who was blessed to witness his domination. And, I saw it happen as it happened, forty-six years ago. This impeccable creature of God, a beautiful chestnut thoroughbred, exceeded the story of his animal nature with a definition of victory that will never be matched by his kind. The point is not that he won by 31 lengths ahead of his nearest competitor while shattering the world-record time, or that according to every stopwatch he was still accelerating at the finish line after running one and a half miles. It is that 70,000 people in attendance and millions on their television screens witnessed the Providence of God imprinting a paragon upon the Earth, an image of Himself in one of His creatures. God not only lifted up this mighty stallion from birth in a stable, but gave him a heart thrice normal size as an imprint of His Trinity. The Father ordained the circumstances that brought the revelation of His own greatness in one of His creatures. Our Creator captured the attention of millions, choreographed the unfolding drama, primed the expectations of every person who would witness His work, nurtured hope in the minds of millions of men, women and children; and, He also blazed a beautiful day where it would all take place. Then, He obliterated the boundaries of expectation in every mind and heart with a triumphant vision, pulling back the veil, leaving everyone wondering whether they had in fact just witnessed a supernatural event from their God. It was soiled by nothing. Human pride was left in awe. All competitors were left heeled and humbled. Antagonistic opponents bowed in respect. Prognostication was vanquished. Spectators wept in overwhelmed emotion. Seasoned racing veterans stood speechless. Announcers and newsmen were lost for adjectives to describe it. And, not a single sinner could lay claim to the accolades. Even the rules of the realm had been respected, leaving no human decisions that mattered. It was not a come-from-behind win by a nose at the tape. It was an ethereal definition of absolute dominion, alone and supreme of that day, a beatific aria of triumph that was complete from the moment the great Secretariat was born. Destiny played its part in ushering this creature to its glory. God's signature is even in his name: Secret-*aria*-t.

    Whenever I attempt to describe my vision of the preeminence of God, my heart supersedes my words in just such a way. My vision bursts; my everything, my faculties and thoughts, my comprehensions and articulations all transcend human boundaries, prescriptions and descriptions. Words fail, leaving me only the frail faculties of allusion and parable to deflect the hearts of men into the heights of these mystical perceptions so they may see. This moment of grace by Secretariat is one of those parables. This race in the spring of 1973 on a spacious New York racetrack is the culminating point where the venerable tides of history and possibility met in a spectacle where everything was said. On that auspicious day, Providence Himself reached into our world and gouged His testament into mankind's lore. It would have been monumental if humanity would have been prescient enough to say after that race, "Let us never race horses again that we not obscure what we have seen here today." My friends, it is not that he won. Many horses and other athletes have claimed victory in their time. Rather, it was how he won. It was in the "exceeding" that defined the moment; the transcending of every rational thought, parameter and expectation that could have possibly been conceived by man that day. Many thought the great Secretariat would win; multitudes wagered on that hope, but no human dared to imagine what they witnessed. It was an "exceeding" without diminishment that became a preeminent definition by which things are forever measured. And, through this "exceeding" one can contemplate in the direction of gazing upon the Son of God on Mount Calvary in the ethereal spectacle of His Glorious Death. The Messianic Triumph is finished. Creation has been imprinted and defined by the Paragon, the Infinite One, He who did not just achieve a mortal victory, but "exceeded" all histories, eras, ages and epochs and the triumphs that have flourished from their storied records. Indeed, The Christ exceeded the origin of Creation itself, the breathtaking instant where a universe burst forth into being at His loving command and roared across time seeking its destiny in Him. Jesus Christ claimed the realms, vaults and pantheons; and inscribed the sanguine definition by which all things shall be weighed, measured, judged and saved. All the accomplishments of men; all the thoughts, hopes, sentiments and dreams of the mortal ages now defer and kneel to Him. We can only pray to run as a Christological Secretariat in our time, His instrument and progeny, leaving something of sacrificial remembrance, surrendering to the charge of our opportunities and engaging our race with grace so as to be identified with the Savior of the world for all the ages; so that mankind may see Him who was crucified and rose in His Eternal Triumph in how we lived, moved and poised our being. The awestricken gasp of Jesus' Original Church sighed at Calvary, "Let us never sin again that we not obscure what we have seen here today." And, this has been the conviction and daily testament of the Roman Catholic Church for the last 2,000 years in the liturgical celebration of the Holy Sacrifice of the Mass. One day soon, all humanity is going to see again that small trickle of daylight in the race of human life, that separation among competitors, between good and evil. And, that Light will begin to grow wider with each passing second as we watch, and the streams will turn into cascades; our emotions will burst into tears that will flow, then the cascades will become torrents as the veil of the vaults is ripped at its seams. Glory accompanied by its legends will pour forth from the skies. Victory will come flooding into Creation before every eye; the dam holding back ecstasy will collapse as on that day in 1973. Then, beyond our minds having the capacity to understand, the Eternal Light will burst into the Beatific Vision of the Crucified Christ, still alive as Conqueror, Savior and King. A beatified realization will then overwhelm every man, woman and child from all ages; and the full realms of human consciousness will acknowledge and adore that which was "finished" long ago, before the final revelation of Eternity ever stared us in the face.

Question 2
Can you describe the definition of Deific Love in the way that you understood it for your first 28 years of life, and how that compares with your present vision?

I have attempted to give constructive perspectives about this comparison in many places of my writings, knowing that they can never be an end-all to such a question. Imagine if you were blind and someone described a car that was next to you. They told you that the car belonged to you. You could touch it, take a seat in it, and maybe listen to it run. But, could you ever take either full enjoyment or ultimate utility in the car in any way that would respect its actual purpose? Now, imagine being given sight. Not only would your eyes take in all the exquisite styling, its appointments and comforts, but you would marvel at your reflection in the mirrored finish of the paint, the powerful engine beneath its hood, and how the steering controlled the direction of the wheels. You would realize the reason for the layout of the seats and the windshield, the gauges, switches, and mirrors. You would understand why the passengers sit forward-facing so as to see the path leading them to their destination as it came into view. You would see the world through the windshield, and the past in the rearview mirror. I now see the Roman Catholic Church as it consecrates Deific Love on the Altar of Sacrifice in the way the blind man was given sight to engage the full use of his car. Before, I interacted with it as if I was blind. And, even if I could have seen it, I did not know how to start it, steer it, or drive it. I could not propel the vehicle of my conversion or evangelization before our Blessed Virgin Mother showed me how.

Another example would be the water faucets in all the homes of a city. When one thinks of drinking water, our mind might develop a mental picture of the small stream that pours from the spout of our kitchen sink. And, we would savor its sparkling refreshment on a sultry summer day in order to quench our thirst. But, consider if our vision was expanded beyond our comfortable homes. What if we were lost in the desert near death from dehydration when suddenly we stumble upon a reservoir of crystal clear water being fed by a massive waterfall pouring into its basin; a reservoir that we suddenly realize supplies each of our homes in the far off city. The thundering roar is so loud that we are not able to converse with our companion standing right next to us. At this point, we not only dive into the water to soothe our sun-baked skin, but we open our mouths to gulp in directly the water we are floating in. Now, the transposition is this: If we merely think of water in terms of the tiny trickle of water from our faucet in our home, do we not miss the thundering grandeur of the Living Waters from its original source?

When I attend the Holy Mass, I do not see the individualism of a single water faucet; a single congregation, a single parish family, or a single day of worship and praise to God. I see Creation from its inception; all the ages and times, and the people who steered and defined those ages with their heartfelt sacrifices and devotions. I see all the sunsets painted upon the canvases of the millennia and the mountain ranges over which they set, sculpted throughout the epochs by the forces of the planet. I see the travelers in each generation who climbed those mountains to see the day's closing from their peaks. I see the lonely places where some of them died in their quest to strive for greater heights closer to God where most men never go. I see every waterfall that has poured itself into bays below for millions of years, and every meadow with its deep green grass softly swaying in the breezes. I see every companion from the Church-Triumphant who hoped for me to join them within the realms of Truth as an individual droplet in the thundering turbulence of God's saving grace which has deafened humanity with the spectacle of His refreshment that has cascaded into our times. I see the billions of babies birthed, from hovels to hospitals, in cabs and family vehicles, all those who greeted this exile, flailing their arms and whimpering their separation from Heaven into an exile they did not choose. I see the Glory of the ages from its source. I see the Roman Catholic Church from its very conception in the Mind of God, from His very lips as He said, "I will give you this sign…" I see its successive march from the Birth of God in human flesh to its triumph at His Second Coming. I see the Creator who came into His own Creation to bestow Eternal Life upon His beloved creatures. And, I realize that someday I am going Home into all this Glory. It is all for Love, which is who He is. Before, I just saw a water faucet filling a glass from my kitchen sink.

The thought that I would like to express is that we risk being locked into a conscripted rhythm of darkened misery inflicted upon us by the constrictions of sin in this exile. Our minds and hearts have the capacity to conceive and contemplate stupendous glory and ethereal majesty. But, what dominates and dictates our thoughts and perceptions instead? How enslaved are our minds to depletion and death? The definition of Deific Love is a beautiful thing for each of us. Every person's relationship with God is a very sacred matter, filled with possibility, light, ecstasy and unending happiness. It is not of this world, but thrives within it. Jesus' Crucifixion is the ultimate, the greatest thriving of Divine Love in the history of the universe, the zenith of human grandeur robed in the power of God. It sustains the universe in a way scientists have not even pondered. Our Savior asks for our unity with Him in this Love through our lives immersed in His Holy Sacrifice on Calvary. Our hearts have the capacity to enter into His Sacred Heart as He hung upon the Cross, and contemplate why He remained there and did not come down to confront the jeerers with almighty power. We were doomed had He not fulfilled His Sacrifice. Every newborn baby's cry is in His Heart. Every flash and flourish of earthly beauty, whether in heart or landscape, is an imitation of His Glory which flatters Him. He is devotion for the most unpopular, but worthy cause. He is strength after every hero's courage has failed. He is glorious power eons beyond every titan's greatest achievement. He is victory before any two human beings ever thought to compete, or if all decided to level a challenge at once. And, He commands with such merciful understanding that it leaves even the most gentle mother in tearful astonishment that grace could be so tender and convalescing. Is this what we imitate? Is this what we allow to define our thoughts? Is this what we hope to be the definition of our lives? If we would do so, to what heights would the human species ascend? What acts would mankind invoke then? What courses and agendas would we set our convictions upon? Indeed, we live in darkness where a Great Light ignited and still burns. It shines upon faithful hearts beckoning Him to come again to judge, redeem or condemn. Our cultures are being dominated and dictated by hordes of people who have no vision of Deific Love, and they have locked the train of earthly destiny upon the tracks of distraction, darkness, greed, immorality, and worldly influence that will be stripped from them the instant their bodies break and their eyes are pried open by judgement upon their deaths. It is then they will sense just how long Eternity truly is, and they will realize in that ominous timelessness that they never prepared themselves to reside with Jesus in His Kingdom. It is then they will see the definition of Deific Love, as I have so inadequately tried to describe it in all my writings. There the comparison between all they did and believed and the beauty of the Sacred Heart of the Lamb of God will leave them aghast at the failure they wrought with their lives. They will be left languishing in their miserably inadequate legacies which will be thrown down and trampled under the feet of the mighty Archangels. Is it any wonder why we need Our Lord to show us Divine Mercy? Would we have ever been able to transform our vision into the glorious realms had Jesus not come to save us? Our contemporary world proves that we could not because we reject Him still. Therefore, let us begin by lifting our eyes into the heavens from whence comes our strength to be a people honored and set apart because we sacrificed to be so beautiful for Him.

Question 3
Discuss what it means for the people of the Earth to become absorbed in the Divinity of Jesus Christ, and what this state of grace looks like in the course of our lives while we tend to the matters of mortal life, i.e, rearing children, maintaining a household, providing material goods, and the like.

I see the entire concept of being absorbed into the Divinity of Jesus Christ defined in one word: Sanctification. Imagine our interior constitution as a matrix, or a maze, or collage. It is dynamic; it conceives, fluctuates, mutates, molds, guides, directs, responds and impedes. It is a manifestation of the powers of the soul. It is subject to our free will which can influence and shape it, but at the same time can itself be enslaved by the tides and turbulence that are thrust upon it. Some Saints have described it as interior castles, while others have referred to it as being a playground for all kinds of ill will and evil intent. But, above it all is the soul which is the perfect identity of our being that God conceived at our creation in Himself; an identity He is trying to redeem and save through His Son Jesus. And, this soul has a spiritual heart which is both the intrinsic knowledge of itself united with its Creator and its character of perfect conception. The process of sanctification is the reorientation, cleansing and maintenance of this interior constitution so that it reflects, comports, mirrors and obeys the heart of the soul. One image is that sanctification aligns our interior matrix into the formation of a ladder that reaches from the highest peaks of perfection, the deified human hypostasis of our soul with God, downward throughout the many facets of our interior constitution to the basest instincts of our human will to act. This ladder rarely looks like a symmetric step-ladder, but rather an interconnected rope-ladder that you may see servicemen climbing during their military training. Consider perfection transcending from the heart of the soul as being Light illuminating darkness where nothing impedes it; and the matrix being a lens that becomes so focused that a clear image can be seen through it when we look into the highest vaults of our heart. Sanctification is the state where the perfections of the heart of our soul flourish downward unimpeded throughout our being; through our instincts and will, informing them, supporting them, and interpreting them, in order to make holy every thought, action and possibility that the powers of our soul could generate and reflect through its communion with God. In this sense, we are perfectly sanctified into union with God as in the beginning, and our identity as children of God is regained and made manifest. The culmination of sanctification is when we come to exist perfectly and permanently in union with the original conception of our soul in the Mind of the Father which was immaculate in the beginning, and remains so. It is an immaculate nature that can be lost forever if we do not accept Christ and proceed on the path of sanctification. This perfection illuminates everything below it with the Light of God [Ephesians 5:8-9].

Our conception by the Father was good, meaning perfect and without stain. The conception of our soul is immaculate in God in the beginning. Our Lady told me that our soul was conceived first outside of time, and that our mortal body was manifested materially as we know it upon our entry into exile. Our conception actually occurred outside of time in the Mind of God who has always known each of us. Our Heavenly Mother said the human soul in its sinless entirety is as timeless as God Himself. The soul's connection to Divine Love had no timely beginning, just as it will have no end. She said that we must not be deceived by the element of sequential time. This is not the way that Heaven sees human souls. God's capacity to conceive things does not mean time can bind Him as doing so at a particular point. There is not a "time" when He conceived us, as difficult as this is for us to understand. He already possesses every thought, word, execution of will and conception in its entirety, and they are all perfect. He already embodies every event, consequence, option and outcome. Everything, all conception, the generation and completion of everything has always been completely present in Him in both its initial and final state. We have already breathed in His grace, just as a fish swims in an ocean, before we were ever exiled to this world. This is a difficult perception for sinners who are yet confined in exilic time. Many theologians deny what they define as the pre-existence of the soul before its incarnation in the womb of a mother. Our Holy Mother said, "Please tell them that the Mother of God is saying that they are not being consistent. How can a gift of the human soul be perpetual if it somewhere had a beginning?" There has never been a time when God has not been present to our soul, although He conceived each of us whereafter we were given a body and entered physically into the exilic realms of earthen time where sin corrupted our human nature and blinded our soul, which we can lose forever if we deny our sanctification in the Blood of Jesus Christ. It is a mystery as deep as the oneness of the Three Persons of the Most Holy Trinity.

His perfection traversed unimpeded from the heights of the timeless conception of our soul to its manifestation in the bodily existence of our beings. Then, our timeless existence became subject to the consequences of Adam and Eve's sin where we inherited conscription in the time-bound exile of the material world to be sanctified and redeemed through Christ's Holy Sacrifice. As we entered the exile of this world, the matrix, our interior constitution, became overwhelmed by the consequences of the absence of God's full Light throughout our beings. Exile began its obscuring phenomenon. We became subject to other forces impacting and influencing our matrix. I would say most of the composition of our interior constitution is a darkened consequence of simply being in a world where we cannot see God outright. For example, the very thought that tells us that God is not present is a result of this darkness, along with all the other decisions, deductions and beliefs that our confused rationality may posit from that first mistaken premise. There is a cascade of delusion that ignited the moment we entered the exiled world from our mothers' wombs. It is like being thrown into a pool of freezing water where your entire constitution is shocked with the singular thought of the frigid sensation. Before that, we only knew the warmth of a loving embrace. Our exile was the immediate splash of sequential recognition of our separation from God in each successive tick of the clock. We are living the consequences of the very first human sin where the unimpeded thoroughfare of grace between God and man became obstructed, needing reconstruction by a Savior. This is what I saw clearly the first instant Our Lady spoke to me. An amazing enlightenment cascaded through my interior constitution that rearranged, clarified, ratified, eradicated and reorganized the perspectives, logic and conclusions that had been constructed in me since birth. My soul experienced the original Light of heavenly warmth. Holy Light pierced my exile and allowed me to see past all the interior commotion and disorientation to gaze upon my true identity as a child of the Most Blessed Virgin Mary. I recognized someone intimately whom I thought I had never met. I could see and recognize my own being from the purer frame of reference which She brought as Her gift. Being reborn in the spirit, indeed!

So, the question is how is sanctification effected in our daily lives; how does this Light come; what does the original creation of our soul look and feel like? Well, God's conception of our soul looks like Jesus, but with our own unique person still intact that He might be the firstborn of many brothers and sisters [Romans 8:29]. Thus, sanctification means transforming our interior constitution through the process of converting, conforming and blessing our matrix; our constitution, by the power of the Holy Spirit that it becomes cleansed, healed and restored into its original image before the fall of man. Then, we have the power to dictate and shine the glory we had at our conception. Sanctification means the reconstruction of the thoroughfares of grace between our soul and its revelation as a child of God in the earthen realms [Roman 8:19]. Our existence must reflect our soul in its finest hour in Christ.

And, that finest hour is the Crucifixion of the Messiah where He brought the power to cleanse and make straight the constitution of every man. Sanctification unveils to our recognition what the soul actually is. Our mortal existence, from conception in the womb until physical death, is the arena that our soul traverses for its sanctification, restoration and redemption. We engage the sanctifying power that comes from Jesus' Life, Death and Resurrection in the Sacred Mysteries that are preserved within the Roman Catholic Church. Without Him and His Church, there is no power capable of the sanctification of humankind. There is nothing for man to grab onto. There is nothing to influence a realignment of our matrix. When the identity of humanity fell from the perfection of the Garden, that state where we openly recognized our unity with God, our identity became damaged, culpable and then deranged through the myriads of deceptions that cascaded throughout the interior constitution of every man. We collectively became vulnerable and thereafter began our cooperation with things opposed to our original image in the Father. Our physicality became vulnerable, and everything related to it. We became subject to death where we previously would have only known eternal life. Moreover, our frame of reference, our matrix, the collage within us that would inform us about the path of our restoration, became corrupt, leaving us disoriented, while being impressed by things that were not true. Our interior subliminal hierarchy of influence became debased, blemished and disorganized. Choices began to have terrible consequences; and a human history filled with suffering and death has been the result. Humanity did not know how to return to perfection because our understanding failed, while one generation of misstep piled upon another waiting to take its place. We became burdened by what the Church calls "concupiscence," which is a longing for things generated by our base human instincts that run contrary to the beatific reason of our soul. Flesh began to dominate the spirit of man.

Try to imagine the things that are thrust into the human mind based simply upon the fact that the body is vulnerable and will someday die. Think of the things that would have never entered the mind of men if no human being could ever get sick or die. Jesus brought the conception of overcoming death into the minds of men in John 11:26 when He said that everyone who lives and believes in Him will never die. Never had the concept of the binding of death been broached as a true reality in the minds of men. And, it disturbed His hearers. This supreme intelligence, prescience and protection of the Father was obscured from our perceptions, thoughts, intuitions and decisions, and thus our thinking became tainted by influences that were not of Him. We became blind where we succumbed to being led by others who themselves could not see. The traditions of exile flourished from Adam and Eve. In addition, the fallen world received Satan and his demons, hellish spirits who were also thrown to the earth to roam amongst sinful men for the engagement of the battle for Redemption [Revelation 12:7-12]. They hate us, and wish only to maintain our derangement so we will not stand again in the beauty of our soul and make our way back to the Paradise from which they were forever cast.

So, not only could humanity not see our path home, we also became vulnerable to demonic spirits who deliberately intend to lead us away from our return to God. They blow the satanic smoke of distraction, disarray, desolation and death. Anyone who believes that Satan is just an allegory used to describe the idea of evil is speaking delusion. Our Lady said that Satan and his demons are real and will never be in Heaven, and that we should stop contemplating theological scenarios where we feel it might be possible in the end. Theologians who do so harbor derangement in their thinking about Satan that needs to be sanctified by the Truth of the battle they are evidently losing. Absent the protection of God and the limits He has placed upon this world, Satan could, and would, kill any human being just by looking at them, just as Our Lady laying Her gaze upon a child can sanctify them in holiness and bring life. This is how our Holy Mother can heal. It is a manifestation of sanctifying power granted by God through Her immaculate soul united with the soul of one of Her children. She opens the thoroughfare to allow the perfect conception of our soul to once again overwhelm our existence in human flesh which rescinds the derangement, and the flesh thereafter conforms to its original conception united with the soul. Any impediments that Satan instigates to obscure this transmission of grace are obliterated by Her pure power. She unites with the soul of Her child and augments the grace of God past all barriers that impede its flourishing into our existence. Love does what love does; it restores and heals. The soul is a child of perfect love which comes from and is united with God; and healing flows from it. Is this not what the Bible means when it says 'Physician heal thyself?' It means sanctification of the interior constitution, the matrix, granting a new frame of reference to everything in our lives. It prescribes that we become oriented and informed by the perfections of our soul that still exist in their original conception because God is always united with the soul to sustain it. Our conception was spotless while our entrance into exile effected the blemish. We not only need to be sanctified in the ethereal intangibles such as the virtues, but in everything that sustains our existence in the flesh. Not that our flesh becomes impenetrable or would possess attributes beyond its purpose, but that it becomes of service to our soul, and in defense of it, in every way it was intended at our conception; although, there are properties that even the flesh takes on when sanctified in the supreme grace of God. Is not good health maintained through sanctified habits that flow from the realization that we are temples of the Holy Spirit? Consider when the human flesh of a possessed person exhibits horrific paranormal phenomenon. Have we not also seen ecstatic radiance emanate from the faces of visionaries whose flesh cannot be burned by a flame while gazing upon the beauty of Our Lady? We do not understand the bodily, intellectual, contemplative, and spiritual properties of a creature in a state of beatific sanctification. What does Jesus' Transfiguration on Mount Tabor tell us about sanctified humanity and the flesh? What does Our Lady's Assumption tell us? Others who have approximated this optimum state are a few of the recognized Saints. Remember the sanctification of Moses and the radiance that emanated from his face in Exodus 34:29-35. Or, Saint Francis of Assisi stripping naked and lying down in a burning hearth as if reclining on a comfortable bed and not being consumed by the flames, all to convert a prostitute who had propositioned him. Many have exhibited very explicit manifestations of holiness in the flesh as evidence that their sanctification was manifest, present and maintained. They were in union with their original soul in the image of God, '...in the image of God He created them' [Genesis 1:7]. Our Lady says there are Saints who never personally sinned, but only needed Baptism to remove the original sin of Adam. Imagine what those lives must have been—sheer beauty in the sacrifice of mortality that they endured. Their souls were identical to their conception in the Mind of God, although they were asked to remain exiled in mortal flesh for their lifetimes as reparation for the sins of all other men.

From these previous insights, it may seem that sanctification is too herculean a task to ever accomplish. We must instead ask ourselves whether that thought itself is part of the derangement that needs to be sanctified, for the Bible says the yoke is easy and the burden light. Our Lady says love is the easiest thing to do. Love brings the sanctification. This is the description in Luke 7:47 where the woman bathing Jesus' feet with her tears brought Him to invoke the great salutation that her sins were forgiven. She brought the transforming cross of repentance to bear within herself which allowed the perfections of her soul to become present in her love. She received Christ. And, Jesus ratified her act of faith by confirming to her the restoration of her image as a child of God. He said, "Your sins are forgiven,...Your faith has saved you." She dared to believe that the love in her soul would be found pleasing to this Messiah whom she loved. It is not about great efforts to sort ourselves out intellectually or exerting gargantuan labors of consistent discipline that we not impede our truest selves. It is about the sacrifice of our old selves and donning the new in hundreds of different moments each day; a restoration of our frame of reference within us so that we know from which direction to draw the perfection at every breath of our lives. A single beam of light becomes a glowing radiance throughout. The Bible speaks of the new wine skin supplanting the old so that a fresh new wine may be poured into it. If you pour the grace of God into an old frame of reference, it will burst everything about it, and you will lose everything that you tried to contain there. This is why people fight against the new world to come. This has reference as well to Jesus' parable about sowing seed on rocky ground as opposed to a fertile tilled field, and how thistles can choke. But, if God finds the floodgates open to the thoroughfare of a new wine skin or a fertile field, the perfection sweeps through our beings and enlightens our perceptions so that our sacrificial love becomes a sweet chariot—and our sins will be forgiven.

> Swing low, sweet chariot,
> Coming for to carry me home.
> Swing low, sweet chariot,
> Coming for to carry me home.
>
> I looked over Jordan, what do I see,
> Coming for to carry me home.
> A band of angels coming after me,
> Coming for to carry me home.

Christ is the Love that restores through the Holy Spirit, which then animates our constitution in the image of Jesus. We leave it to Him because He is always in communication with a penitent heart, and He is present within each of us at every moment to offer His Wisdom and guidance. He wipes away the stain of sin that impedes the flourishing of His grace from our soul into our human experience. But, we must do our part as well by learning how not to re-erect obstacles that He has torn down by His Holy Sacrifice. Jesus said to the woman about to be stoned, "Go and sin no more" [John 8:11]. Do not re-erect the obstacles. For some people, God sees them treating Him as an outlaw in their world as if they were its Creator instead. They are huddling behind all the town's furniture, chuckwagons, stagecoaches, tables, benches and water troughs piled in the street to impede His coming into their presence. This is what their interior constitution looks like to Him. Thus, our frame of reference, our matrix, must be destroyed, wiped clean, and reconstituted according to His Life and teachings. Born again, indeed. We must open the main street, clear the thoroughfare, raise the bunting, and call up the bands for the procession of Christ the King to commence in us. And, that Life and those teachings which reorient us, opening both the byways and the interstates, still exist in their full clarity in the Roman Catholic Church and in the lives of its esteemed Saints. When you touch the Original Apostolic Church, you touch the night our Savior was born; you become present on the evening of the Last Supper, you live standing beneath the Cross on the day He died, you gather in vigil before His sealed Tomb, and you are blinded at the third day's first light when He came forth in Power and Glory from death to live again. The Roman Catholic Church is the only church anchored in the actual presence of these moments through a succession of Pontificates, 266 and counting. Therefore, our frame of reference must become perfectly united with the Original Apostolic Church. We must become its newest legacy in our time. Its facets and expanse of genius are enormous through time in its Dogmas, Traditions, Sacraments, Liturgies, Hierarchy and Saints. In fact, the Traditions and Dogmas of the Catholic Church recorded in the Catechism are the "matrix of genius" flourishing through time where we unite as one Body through our communal obedience. This Church provides the new wine skin, the reorientation that our frame of reference requires for the thoroughfare to be restored between our original conception and all that we see ourselves as being in presence, thought, action and future.

So, being absorbed in the Divinity of God at every moment simply means being prepared to defer our constitution to love at every moment, through every action and thought as did the woman who bathed Jesus' feet with tears. Our will is attached at thousands of points throughout our matrix. Thus, if our sinful nature, our misconfigured matrix, is to be sanctified, we must engage the crucifixion of those attachments of will which are influenced by concupiscence; our lower base instincts absent beatific reason. Our old wine skin will burst when its supporting attachments of will are severed, whereby a new wine skin may be given to us. This is why Jesus' Crucifixion is our restoration and redemption because the grace to accomplish this in ourselves, to return to our original image and to allow it to flourish, rests in the grace He gives us in His Holy Sacrifice, transmitted to us through the Most Blessed Sacrament of the Altar. He forgives, makes straight and sanctifies our matrix, and says, "This is who you truly are. This is who I made you to be," as our interior eyes fall upon the timeless beauty of our soul for the very first time. Our original immaculate conception can be seen as in the beginning. It is a nuptials in a beatific sense. It is a hypostatic deification of the child of God. This is why Jesus says whatever we do to the least, we do to Him. He is the Perfection who is in complete communion with the souls we might offend, including our own. There again is the Crucifixion of the Lamb of God. We are to love our neighbor as ourselves. Our Lady says that we are sometimes reticent to remember the latter. So, let love flow freely from the soul, but maintain a well-ordered and reasoned matrix, reflective of the reasoned intelligence of the Christian virtues harbored in the Roman Catholic Church.

Then comes prayer from the heart. Prayer allows us to transcend the darkness of our exiled constitution. It reaches into our being past the commotion and distraction to unite our conscious awareness with the beauty of the heart and soul. Then, we recognize how God communes with our soul and holds it in His Love. Prayer is sanctifying and gives us true vision because the Holy Spirit responds to bring the perfection. This vision is the eye that Jesus speaks about in Matthew 6:22-23 where He says, "If your eye is sound, your whole body will be filled with Light." And, He also says, "And if the light in you is darkness, how great will the darkness be." There can be a deceptive pseudo-light. There can be false reason. If we never elevate our vision to see from the plateau of the heart, we surrender our vision to be possessed by the base instincts of our sinful nature, influenced by all things diabolical. Derangement reigns. Our powers of conception conceive disorientation. Our lesser selves command. Exile becomes permanent, and hell a certainty. Therefore, we must be humble in our prayers for them to have elevation where God can effect reorientation within us. The truth we are searching for through prayer will bring Light that will confront the errors in our constitution, and demand that they change. Our conscience can be a pretty tough taskmaster when God is allowed to inform it. Our humility is the only thing that will allow the transformation of our constitution because God will not violate our free will if we are intent upon damning ourselves. If we do not invoke humility and accept the Cross, the Light will be repelled by our pride, which is quite fond of our base instincts and sensual nature. The final effect is the mirror where our entire being, including the shape of our constitution, becomes polished and conformed where Jesus looks at us and sees Himself.

I suppose this has been a long-winded treatise to what was expected to be a simple answer. For this I apologize. The way to become absorbed in the Divinity of Christ: Accept that you are a child of God, recognize what Jesus has done for you, then pray and love. Pray to understand what love truly is. Pray to love what should be loved, and diminish the rest. Jesus must increase while we decrease. Let the Light come up in your interior house and allow Jesus to take the stage of your heart. Change whatever He wants you to change, no matter the cost. Revere the Roman Catholic Church and defend it, for this is where the matrix is restored. Accept the Holy Sacrifice of the Lamb of God as your reason for living. And, tell the truth. Then, your constitution will become restored, and Light will fill your whole body. Our Lady said that life is meant to be lived in a human way, but also a saintly way. Remind yourself of the virtues and take time to pray. Pray, pray, and pray some more. Take the Most Holy Rosary into your hands, call your Heavenly Mother to pray with you and begin. Remember humility over pride, kindness softening envy, abstinence starving gluttony, chastity extinguishing lust, patience outlasting anger, charity deflating greed, and diligence shaming sloth.

"Whatever is true, whatever is honorable, whatever is just, whatever is pure, whatever is lovely, whatever is gracious, if there is any excellence, if there is anything worthy of praise, think about these things."
Philippians 4:8

A final thought about truth. There are a multitude of Christians who generate excuses for every occasion of sin and instance of wicked conduct that they witness other people committing. Their minds immediately engage a plethora of imaginary hypotheticals and mitigating possibilities to keep anyone from responding with merciful admonishment and correction. They strain every realm of credibility to the breaking point in order to generate imaginary perspectives, oftentimes with no evidence, in order to diminish the culpability of anyone plying outright evil works; and they believe it is mercy they are displaying. This illusion of mercy is a complete contradiction to the Spiritual Works of Mercy. They douse holy admonishment with their chiding retorts at every turn. I made this mistake in the beginning, and Our Lady corrected me. I once tried to envision an excuse for someone who was acting very unholy, thinking I was manifesting mercy toward them to our Blessed Mother. She counseled me to instead speak the truth of what I was seeing. She thought there was no excuse for such conduct, and that these people needed to be corrected, even at the expense of their ego and my own suffering if they retaliated. She said the Saints endured more than unsavory parting glances from those they admonished. They crucified Jesus for the same reason. Look again at the spiritual works of mercy. None of them say, "Excuse all sin, never admonish anyone," or "Maybe they had their reasons for doing this, don't cause a stir." Holy admonishment has gone extinct in our current age because most people now believe that admonishment is an offense against mercy and love. This derangement has come through the ideology of humanism. The self-glorification of the human instead of the divine has blinded humanity to the courage of speaking the truth. Making excuses for evil conduct believing it is mercy is part of the darkness.

Question 4

Has the Virgin Mary ever spoken specifically to you about Her role in the everyday lives of ordinary men and women who are not Roman Catholic?

The answer is yes. Our Holy Mother's entire revelation as the Morning Star Over America is to unveil and communicate Her role in the lives of each child of God, especially those who do not yet know who She is. She has demonstrated through the lives of my brother and myself the very definition of that maternal role. She wants us to worship Her Son Jesus with great thanksgiving so that we will be prepared to embrace Him without shame and enter Heaven when we are called from this life. I believe the most primal questions that each person asks are, "Who am I?," "Where did I come from?," and "Where am I going?" Those who never ask these questions of themselves truly never live. They simply navigate the shoals of a shallow existence that they never really understand. Our Lady responds to the questions we may have, but it requires our faith to receive and accept the answers She gives. Our Virgin Mother possesses great confidence and poise. She does not get all that disturbed by those who are on wayward paths because She knows that She has the power to touch each of them any time She wishes. She simply ponders whether it would do any good before She throws Her pearls. I heard Her say to me one time, "I know where each of My children is. They believe they are hiding under a table. But, they do not realize that it has a glass top, and I can see their every move. They are too little to outrun Me." All life is a preparation for each successive opportunity that will be sprinkled onto a person's path to know Jesus and ask for His Absolution through heartfelt repentance. Our Heavenly Mother spends each day praying that we accept Her grace, that we remain protected from crossing the bridge too far for our confessions to bring us Home.

The Most Blessed Virgin wants no child to be lost for Eternity, and desires that we move into our greatest place of protection at Her side in the Heart of the Roman Catholic Church. Not that we are simply parked in a pew on occasion, but that we would partake of the wisdom, power and protection that thrive in the Providence that Jesus willed into His Original Apostolic Church. The Church exists to sanctify us and unite us in a premonition of the Heavenly Kingdom, awaiting His Triumphant Return in Glory. Of course, there have been churchmen through the ages who have failed miserably, whereafter Christ's enemies have leveraged these human weaknesses to slander and assail the Church entire in their pursuit of worldly power. These slanderers are losers because in the midst of it all still stands the Truth of the Ages in the millions of great Prelates, priests, religious and laity who stand in Heaven as its Saints, and on

Earth at its sacrificial Altars. The Lighthouse of Salvation will never be snuffed out or grow dim in the fog of any man's sins or the calumny of the ages. It stands calling, not convicting; soothing, not assailing; healing, not perpetrating offense. But, it tells the Truth without apology. It asks its onlookers to accept it and drink from its waters of everlasting life. It is a crucifixion to acknowledge or a revelation to learn, but surely an ecstasy to embrace. Conversion must meet the pardon, and adoration greet the Holy Sacrifice.

Our Lady simply asks that each of us begin to pray the Holy Rosary because it orients us in the realms of the Holy Spirit and portrays the greatness of Jesus' Life in our contemplations of His Sacrifice. His Life is the origin of all genius and the source of all perfection. The Most Blessed Virgin Mary sees Her role as being Mother to God's children. It is difficult to help a person acknowledge something that has been in their life all along which they have failed to recognize. They are acclimated to not seeing the truth that is openly apparent. It is like handing a tiny child a million dollars and trying to convince them they're rich. They look at you inquisitively, wondering why you are so excited by a stack of paper that resembles no toy they recognize, thereafter reaching for the sparkling metal change lying on the table that tinkles when they shake it between their little palms before they put it in their mouth. They function by a completely different set of enticements. And, attempting to take the change out of their hand so you can get them to focus on the millions....good luck. You will have a fight of colossal proportions on your hands. Nonetheless, Our Lady wants each of these children to know that greater things than we have ever dreamed lie within our reach when we are ready to listen and understand. But, She asks, is it going to take being deprived of all that God does for us before we recognize how generous He has been and how much protection we were previously under? One way to cure someone of not recognizing their blessings is to rescind them. Beware the chastisements.

Question 5

What do you have to say to those who maintain that the Almighty Father has no gender? How do you support your position?

First, I am not inclined to support my positions as if I am required to defend them before any sinner. Our Lady is offering a loving opportunity, not a requirement. I do not receive my dignity through anyone agreeing with me, and surely, the Truth can stand on its own. "How do you support your position," is a challenge to a sinners' duel. Arguing is highly overrated. Intellectualizing nearly always breeds hubris, division and contempt. So many contrarians thrive in the banter and swell with accomplishment upon sustaining their own radicalism in a debate. While I hope that everyone comes to faith in Jesus Christ, the sacrifice to believe belongs to those who do not. No bearer of the truth is required to grovel in subservience, hoping someone will take their words seriously as if being held hostage by their obstinance. There is far too much intellectualizing, pontificating and bantering as it is. If someone does not wish to accept rational conclusions based in Christ's Life, the language of Creation, and the witness of the Church, then I say, walk on to your destiny. It will be yours alone. The story of your faith will be written as you choose. I have no power to make this choice for anyone. A person's conversion and sanctification belongs to them, singly and solitarily. I can only hope they humbly choose for Christ and His Church, then radical distractions such as gender discussions will be seen to be as irrelevant as they are.

Secondly, I try never to make the determination of what God does not have or cannot do as this question suggests. He can be and do anything He desires, and He does not require my analysis of Him as exploitation for any cause. Notwithstanding, He obviously desired to create gender in the beginning. Gender is a prescription describing our physical bodies in the material world as He created them. The language of Creation and our DNA tell us this. Male and female, He created them. This is the sum total discussion about gender. Yet, there are radicals who have hijacked the definition of the word 'gender' in order to control the term and force legitimacy of that which is illegitimate. This is no more than an attack upon wisdom itself. We come to know God's intentions and motivations more deeply by recognizing the things He has done and what He has revealed. We cannot go farther than that without direct supernatural revelation from Him. And, even in that, for any subsequent private revelations to be deemed authentic, they must be in harmony with what He has already revealed through the Roman Catholic Church. God is not some chaotic entity who is unhinged from order and peace. But, we must also remember that just because someone is lettered, esteemed or maybe wears a red hat does not mean everything that they theologically deduce or personally believe is a reflection of wisdom and truth. There is heresy being proposed by many representing Catholicism, deranged progressives who believe that the great Traditions of the Catholic Church are outdated to their modernist ways of surrender to the secular void. They have contorted themselves into all kinds of heterodox deceptions, then they pontificate and pressure Holy Christendom to deliver its ethereal wisdom to their dysphoria. Their pluralistic utopia is actually a dystopian nightmare.

In answer to the question asked, one cannot definitively say that the First Person of the Most Blessed Trinity, as uniquely revealed and identified theologically, has never donned a specific gender because no one yet alive has seen the Father as He is. But, we do know that human bodies are in Heaven; both Jesus and the Virgin Mary through His Ascension and Her Assumption. No one knows how the Father maintains Himself in His Eternal Kingdom, other than by way of the descriptions of Jesus calling upon Him as "Father" which natural law recognizes as male, in the Catholic Catechism which tells us He is Spirit, and in the visions of the Book of Revelation as He whom the Ancients surround in worship. Jesus did not lie or employ an obfuscating euphemism by recognizing the Father's Paternity as His hearers would understand. But, since we do know that gender is an attribute in the material world, we can ask what might be the Father's gender if He were to come to Earth. Then, by recognizing what He has already done, we see that He came to Earth in the Person of His Son who was, and is, a Man by gender, who has returned through His Ascension to oneness with the Most Holy Trinity as a Crucified Man in the flesh. God gave flesh to Himself in His Son who is one in being with Him in the Godhead. Jesus' Flesh is God also, and this too we receive in the Most Blessed Sacrament of the Catholic Altar as the Bread of Life [John 6:51]. The Father took on human flesh in the Person of His Son because they are "one" in every way, consubstantial our Creed tells us. God has never become Incarnate in the flesh of a female in any way recognized by the Church or human history. There has been no revelation of an Only-Begotten Daughter as a Person of the Most Blessed Trinity. In addition, the Father has never revealed that He has incarnated Himself as female in Heaven. But, if He did, that woman would be the reflection of the Most Blessed Virgin Mary who is the embodiment of all feminine perfection in the flesh of the female gender. She is the summit of feminine perfection. She is the "perfect deified human hypostasis," united with the Most Blessed Trinity, who is called the Mother of God. She is the Immaculate Conception. Still, our Holy Mother has told me directly that She is not a Person of the Most Holy Trinity. She is not God, but His Immaculate Virgin Mother.

Another point to be made is that nearly all gender discussions throughout our culture have their origin in the rebellious spirit of Eve. This is where they originated and from where this contagion spreads. Gender discussions are about mortal flesh that is headed for the grave. They were spawned through the radical ideology of feminism whose basis is in the wholesale rejection of the paternity of the Father revealed by Jesus Christ. Our Lady said that these sinners will bow to no man, including their Savior. The origin of feminism is in a poorly disguised agenda of misandry which has cloaked itself in a deceptive halo of victimhood, thinking there is no man with the courage to counter their wailing typhoon of character assassination, should any of these men speak the truth. At the inception of radical feminism is selfishness and hatred for God becoming man, instead of a woman. It is about lust for power and the misappropriation of identity. Our Lady told me that the New Adam will not eat of the fruit being offered by the sinful Eves of this world. Our Lady is not a feminist in any sense of the word, but is rather the Paragon example of the female gender as God wishes His daughters to become. The Most Blessed Virgin gives glory to the Father alone through Her Son Jesus Christ. She is the Servant of all servants to the paternity of the Godhead. She asks all of Her little girls to be like Her, and to stop their fight against what their Creator asks them to be and to whom they must humbly submit in the hierarchy of His Kingdom. Feminism is about self-elevation and self-glorification, and not about sacrificial love. Feminism craves for worldly power and control, even by forceful intimidation if necessary. It is the incubator of harridans. It is not about the strength of a pure spirit that animates meekness, purity, self-control and the ability to sacrifice and support the hierarchy of God's creation, especially in His Church. It lusts over every seat of influence that it can identify. It screams for liberation from its sacrificial responsibilities, most glaringly in its claims to own its own body, while dismembering children in the womb and selling their body parts. It seeks to define the orders of life so as to ingratiate itself in the temptations of the devil that Jesus endured in the desert. It does not matter that its motivations are couched in the language of victimhood or a great supposed movement of female dignity. There have always been liars and snake-oil salesmen who have sold their wares in deceptive ways for personal gain. It remains a mind-set absent of Light that makes demands that are selfish under a veneer of false-righteousness. The question is, if power were equated with sacrificial love unto martyrdom, how many of these women would seek it then? They seem not to even be able to accept the premier sacrifice of bearing children into the world for the propagation of the human species, let alone empty themselves so as to become the image of our Crucified Savior. They do not see their scaling of the ramparts of the priesthood as being about selfless service and sacrifice at all, but rather about control and the gaining of power to activate their will. If becoming a priest meant your horrific martyrdom, how many of today's feminists would be so eager to don a Roman collar? If there were no congregations filled with adoring parishioners, no social influence to wield, no great churches with open chairs of veneration or waiting ears to satiate the ego; what if no eyes were on them; imagine only the Cross staring them right in the eyes every day. How many would be demanding their allotted portion of Jesus' Crucifixion in defense of this omnipotent Patriarchy? You do not see feminists selling everything they have and beginning a life in imitation of Saint Mother Teresa. Our Holy Mother says that they should start there if they wish to influence God and become clothed with His power.

    My brother and I have tried to remember this wisdom during the sacrifices of the past thirty years. Our Holy Mother has encouraged us to remain dedicated in silence before the world, all the while hoping that the example She has built with our lives would transmit the wisdom dispensed to us. We have hoped that this path would render a far more powerful witness than if we had scratched and clawed for venue, demanding that we be heard and respected. Laudatory respect from other people is ultimately fragile and temporary. The respect offered is hinged upon a person's capacity for sustaining their devotion to the truth amidst the trial, such as Jesus experienced Palm Sunday turning into Good Friday in the short span of a week. Where was the crowd's laudatory respect of Palm Sunday when the dawn broke on Good Friday? It vanished because they had no devotion to the truth that could withstand the eclipse of the Light and the suffering that was to be inflicted. If we are worried about who respects us, or bothers to listen to us, or who rejects us, we are not prepared to experience Jesus' prophecy, "If they hated Me, they will hate you," on our path of proclaiming the Holy Gospel. In fact, we will avoid the sacrifices that will make this Scripture true in our lives, and little Light will shine from us. We will not keep our hand to the plow because we will always be looking back for followers. Each of us falls by the wayside in compromise absent this single-hearted commitment. One who is looking for stature, influence and worldly power is on a treacherous road. Power comes from the Passion of Jesus Christ and how we join Him in that desolation. He bestows it where He wills. We cannot claim it in any fashion, nor demand it as our entitlement. It is a product of the sanctification of our soul and our familiarity with suffering and sacrifice at the expense of every affirmation. In the final analysis, the discussion of gender is a corrupt social phenomenon of the secular void that is irrelevant and a waste of our precious time that would be better spent proclaiming Jesus Christ, "The Man," the Only Son of God who testified to the Patriarchy of His Father over all Creation.

Question 6

Has the Virgin Mary ever spoken to you about the masculinity of God, not in an anatomical way, but by comparison of the fathers of the Earth?

Yes, Our Lady has spoken to us about the paternal affections and resolute love possessed and displayed by the Father for the children He created. She made specific comments about this subject in Her conversations with me on April 6, 2013. Roman 1:19-20 states, *"For what can be known about God is evident to them, because God made it evident to them. Ever since the creation of the world, his invisible attributes of eternal power and divinity have been able to be understood and perceived in what he has made."* God's greatest creation is man whom He conceived in His image and likeness, and who was given dominion over the Earth and its creatures. Genesis 1:27, *"God created mankind in his image; in the image of God he created them; male and female he created them."* Therefore, if we wish to ask the Father to make Himself known to us, could we not begin in these Scripture declarations, and then contemplate the Creation where His "invisible attributes" may be "understood and perceived?" In addition, we recognize from Scripture that Jesus Himself prayed to God in Heaven as His Father, intending to reference His relationship with the God of Heaven within the filial bonds of the masculine relationship that all His hearers would understand. All those who heard Him knew the privilege of the firstborn son of a father, along with the scriptural prophecies that Salvation itself would transcend to them through the male lineage of the God of Abraham, Isaac and Jacob.

Our Lady has directed my understanding toward the masculine attributes of earthly fathers in their finest hours of sacrifice and love as reflections of the Father Himself. Our Heavenly Father is not a being that is incomprehensible, eccentric or alien. He created man in the image of Himself, and maintains dominion over our beings in protection, guidance and support, very much like an earthly father over his beloved children. When we contemplate things such as the qualities of stature, composure and strength that fathers display from their lionhearted existence, we are witnessing the Father truly present in His own grace, communicated to His earthly sons by the power of the Holy Spirit. When we see hardened warriors holding newborns in their calloused hands and their eyes beaming with pride from their battle-scarred faces, there is the Father. If we were to see a father sitting inconspicuously in the back row of the bleachers watching with great pride as his son succeeds in dominating an athletic event, knowing his nurturing, support and inspiration flourished his offspring's success, there is the Father. On each Sunday, as elderly priests walk across the thresholds of their sacristies onto the altars to perform their sacred duties, and even when no one from their congregations recognizes their decades of loneliness, sacrifice, satanic attacks, and penance in the service of human redemption, there is the Father.

Women would do well to realize and admire the manifestation of grace displayed by Christian men throughout the ages. We were created physically strong in most cases, masterful in disposition, dominant for the subduing of the wild nature of the world, courageous and enduring for the triumph over the worst of evils, and spiritually intelligent enough to know what our God expects of us. No wild gender or animal has any authority to intimidate us into following any other path than what our God inspires us to be when we remain united with Him. If God commissions us to lead in the orders of His Mystical Body, then He has also given us the faculties and wisdom to lead. But, can you imagine a world of males unrestrained by Christian virtue who are absent the wisdom to guide the pilgrimage of humankind peacefully through time? Imagine a race of men where concupiscence dominates the will with no chance for wisdom and light to be granted influence over them. We need not look very far, as there are examples of regions of the world in this state. Therefore, when we see men of piety, prayer, devotion, self-control, heroic in sacrifice and motivated by a deep love for humanity, especially within the bonds of their families, there we are seeing the Father glorified in His sons. He recognizes the Sacrificial Lamb in the person of each of them, and honors that character so impressed and manifested. It is a horrible vision to imagine a world where men are unrestrained by Christian virtue, who recognize no vision of a loving and sacrificial Heavenly Father, who see no heroism in the Crucifixion; who are enslaved by animal passions and directed by the lies of the devil who prowls in their midst; who would subdue women for their physical enjoyment and slaving labors; a time when no woman could raise her head, say a word without permission or dream of anything that would respect her dignity. Indeed, in that radical world of anti-Christian demonism, women would barter away the beauty of their souls and their capacity to birth the progeny of the human race for the only thing of any currency. They would surrender their flesh for momentary social power and attention. Their cravings for attention and love would escalate their sensuality to obtain it. Radical feminists in their battle to stave off this horror should reevaluate the course they are set upon, because if they succeed in extinguishing the paternity of Christian virtue, the resultant barbarians will unleash their concupiscence matched to their strength and intelligence to fight for supremacy as in the worst of pagan times. And, these masculine barbarians will win in a complete dominating enslavement of the female gender. Women will then have no power other than what these heathens allow them to have. This is not about effeminizing our young boys so they will not fight, but rather instilling in them the character to realize what they must fight for. We must lift up the masculinity and paternity of the Father in the hopes that all men will imitate it to the subduing of the inordinate passions of the fallen world. Little boys must grow up to be heros of sacrifice, not indoctrinated into being effeminate metrosexuals who are too cowardly to engage the darkness assailing the story of humankind. Adam must not partake again of the fruit that Eve is offering.

Our Lady is the most powerful example of the only future with any hope. Every single man would throw themselves down before Her, even the barbarians, and beg to give their lives in Her service if they were to see Her just one time. The Bible reveals that husbands must love their wives, and wives must be subordinate to the paternity of their husbands, to be fruitful and multiply. It does not mean that they cannot aspire to anything else as a sacrificial contribution to humanity. But, 'having it all' is not a definition of a sacrificial life in the image of Jesus. If women would imitate Our Lady in grace, men would elevate them with all their strength to the highest pinnacles of respect and happiness in Creation. This is what our Holy Mother has done for me. I love the Woman She is. She is the true Lady of Creation with all grace and perfection. She is filled with power and is so easy to love, even when She is asking for the sacrifices of the Cross from me. She has lifted up my soul into heroic strength and has instructed me in the paternity of the Father as the omnipotent guiding power in the world in whose stead Salvation rings through the King who is Her Son. And, in this is the Father. Salvation from our God is not a negotiation for His approval upon our wiles, but rather a submission to His prescription for our ascension into perfection as He conceived us...in the beginning.

Question 7
How has the Most Blessed Virgin taught you to discern the great social problems of our time and the appropriate courses of action regarding worldly issues like immigration, legalized abortion, political acrimony, acerbic rhetoric, demonization and character assassination, the influence of mass media venues, the secularization of culture, and all the other issues the Church must grapple with in guiding its members along the path of truth?

I would begin by saying that those immersed in the secular void do not realize how lost they are, and how close they have become to being lost forever in eternal death. First and foremost, there is no discernment required for the scourge of abortion. Abortion is a diabolical killing machine that surpasses in depravity all the murderous horrors in the history of mankind combined. Why? Because we know better, as well as it being directed toward the most innocent life on Earth. It is an attack upon the origin of human life through a complete self-absorption that is in the realms of demonic possession. This is not hyperbole. People in our country, indeed throughout the world, are slaughtering babies. Sixty million is the number in the United States, and 42 million worldwide in 2018 alone. Think about those numbers. The tragedy is that there are also nearly sixty million women in our country who are defending this wickedness because they have been participants in it. Their psychology demands that they defend it, lest they be required to admit the horror they have wrought upon human civilization. They must come to realize that they can be forgiven and their lives can be saved from eternal death, but they must repent of this evil or they will never see the Kingdom of Heaven. This also includes all of its advocates in the media, pop culture, religious sects, and government. If you are for the choice, you are for the act, and are, therefore, a participant in this hideous psychology of killing before the sight of God. You serve the beast of hell. Only in the vacuous realms of secular relativism do people believe evil to be a valid choice that must be defended. Nothing governs the arena of their thinking toward virtue, moral principle and truth. Atheistic relativists surrender Creation to the most deranged despots that appear, and the destabilization and collapse of civilization is the fruit they thrust upon us all.

Everything alluded to in this question is related to our fallen nature and the rejection of Jesus Christ. I believe most everyone is finding it difficult to know how to set in motion the collective restoration of the integrity and character of a nation that possesses the potential of the United States of America. Numerous factions seem determined to advance agendas and announce alliances to bring about their version of ideological change, and they are employing tyrannical intimidation and secular punishments against those who do not comply with them. This is where the national media companies have become such scurrilous instruments of cultural immorality. They profit from sowing seeds of division and magnifying wickedness, believing they will never be held accountable for corrupting our nation and its children. Millstones await them all. They are sowing shadows of iniquity in people's souls, and are delivering us into a nightmare conjured by people who serve the father of lies. Our Holy Mother has never instructed me to join, accommodate or give approbation to any of these supposed justice movements of cultural manipulation. None of them proclaim Jesus Christ Crucified or the conversion of humanity to His Cross. None of them ask others to bear their souls in repentance before the Crucifixion of Jesus Christ.

Our Blessed Virgin Mother has taught me to be very simple in my discernment of our culture; to not be deceived by celebrity pontifications, monetary stature, secular prestige or the politics of secularism. None of them have any standing before God. We should look instead to their motivations and detect the contortions they generate in opposition to the truth that She teaches — a Truth that will last beyond the ages and judge us all. I compare everything I see with Her immaculate grace and the Holy Gospel of Her Son. It is somewhat different for my brother and me compared to others because we personally know what our Heavenly Mother believes about these things and how we should address them. We know Her Immaculate Heart. It just seems that rare few wish to listen to Her. She has spoken to us at length, and across the world, about human holiness over the past three decades. I always keep ever present in my interior perception the reasons why we are here, and where each of us is going. What is to be our ultimate fate? Our appearance before the Throne of God could occur before the sun sets tonight. We could be called to stand before Jesus Christ at any given moment to give an accounting of our lives in light of His Crucifixion and how He asked us to live. In fact, we are actually standing there now and do not realize it yet. My frame of reference informs me this way at every moment. Our country is overwhelmed by the idea of pluralism, which is a false belief if one is striving to be recognized as a child of God. Jesus Christ owns everything we see, and allegiance to Him is the only pathway to eternal glory.

I believe it is beneficial for everyone to recall how serious the Holy Spirit was when the man and his wife lied and held back the profits from the sale of their possessions before the early Christian community. The Holy Spirit dropped them in their tracks [Acts 5:1-11]. I have seen the devil deceive people two ways amidst the secular squabbles. Satan misleads people into blindly adopting supposedly righteous positions on the micro level so that he can destroy on a macro level beyond their sight once he has distracted them. He also incites people to be sanctimoniously proud of their rhetorical righteousness on the macro level, while he causes great destruction on the micro level of people's lives because the righteousness never arrives. Then, everyone wonders how such destruction could possibly be happening when so much righteousness is being proclaimed. It is the phenomenon of believing the darkness within us is actually light. Satan mimics the Spirit of God, then begins twisting perceptions and generating false justifications to bring corruption to our frame of reference, while maintaining the veneer of virtuosity when no sacrifice was ever present. For example, he will demand that the faithful show him great charities on the smallest levels so that he can obliterate Christian civilization on the continental level. He will cry with the sound of compassion in his voice for humanity to let his deranged followers have access to peaceful domains so that he can sow his seeds of wholesale destruction. Satan advances an agenda that destroys from the inside whenever possible, while never relenting in his siege from the outside. Don't we ever wonder how he gets in? He enters the door of our Christian charity by feigning being a beggar. Then, we forfeit our expectations of discipline and truth, give away our stabilizing wisdom, and he then ransacks the house and destroys it because he has no intention of adopting the virtues of Christ. The way to know whether it is the Spirit of God calling to us is to implement the call for Christian conversion and sacrifice, and discern whether there is respect for that call in the one who is knocking. Are they asking in the Name of Christ? Surrendering our charities to thieves who have no intention of petitioning us in the Spirit of Christ is a misplaced act of our Christian character. These charlatans are not the neighbor found beaten by the side of the road that God asks us to care for. They instead are the highwaymen who beat and threw our neighbor in the ditch who should face the justice of God. The devil never compromises with Christ; and if he says he will, he is again lying.

Both the Gospel and the Catholic Catechism acknowledge that it is not improper to recognize disciplined domains in a world of sinners in order to protect sovereign realms from anyone who would enter and destroy peace, civility, and human life from within. Would Jesus condone His Church as an institution to be infiltrated and ransacked by someone demanding that we show them Christian charity? Indeed, He would not. Huge groups of protesters have left the Church through the ages because the Holy Spirit would not concede to their demands. Jesus Christ allowed their departure so that those who would destroy His Church from within would exit its sacred domain of their own free will; thereafter to convert and be regained into His fold through the Sacrament of Reconciliation, if these prodigal sons and daughters should so choose to return to the Father's house. The most unfortunate consequence of history's religious revolutions is the collateral damage to the lives of innocent people who had nothing to do with the rebellions stirred at different points in history. Imagine the Christian unity that could have been present to squelch the horrors of the 20th century had Christianity remained united as one heart. The posture of a truly united Christianity would have been enough to stave off these chastising events from ever happening. This composure has been fractured, but Our Lady is attempting to repair it as we speak for the first time in five centuries. We should not be trying to downplay the requirement of sacrificial conversion in order to create a situation where we allow others to remain in an unfocused imitation of Christian faithfulness through simple ecumenical comradery. No acceptance of Jesus' Sacrifice is ever manifested in this duplicity, and the authentic Bread of Life is never received. Now, all of these principles come down to wise, but courageous, pastoral implementation because Jesus is not a harsh dictator, but a loving Savior and spiritual Father who is beckoning everyone to rise to their fullest perfection in the unity of His Original Apostolic Church in order to be saved. All those outside the Roman Catholic Church must realize that we will treat them as the father treated his prodigal son upon his return. But they must return for the feast to be proclaimed and the fatted calf slaughtered!

As the story of deliverance plays out, huge numbers of people are beginning to realize what is wrong, but the simple truth seems to be impossible to accept because it cannot be poured into an old wine skin. The frame of reference of hundreds of millions is corrupt, leaving it difficult for them to embrace the truth that Our Lady has come to tell them. The truth has to wander through all the rhetoric, feelings and attitudes, the secular propriety and intellectual etiquette, the ecumenism and theology, the political correctness and thorny agendas, the mediocrity, the compromise, and the debates. And, all it would take is one miracle to wipe out this entire landscape of distraction and misdirection. I believe that discerning the current movements of our society is relatively easy if one has embraced the Gospel as the most faithful Roman Catholics understand it. In the face of Christ Crucified, the selfish concept of entitlement is dead. But, charity must flower, especially from the rich, or they will be searching like prospectors with gold-fever for the thoroughfare of a needle's eye on the final day. Christian charity is not a commodity that can be demanded, nor should it be deployed upon those immersed in the deadly sin of sloth. Our goods and the fruits of our sacrificial efforts cannot be extorted by people who have contributed nothing to society but the silage of their sinful lives. The prodigal son was stripped of his sense of entitlement before he returned to his father to offer his repentance and ask to be treated as a hired hand. A self-possessed thief does not have the stature to approach us and demand anything but our absolution, should he be offering repentance. God has said the idea of stealing and coveting our neighbor's goods, wife, success and blessings is an outrageous offense against justice and is represented by not one, not two, but three of His Ten Commandments. Entitlement is the mantra of the slothful in our day. It is the same ideology that brought communism to leave a path of destruction across the last century, and which is hollowing out country after country in our modern day. We would never condone or respond to a group of atheists walking up to a Catholic Cathedral and saying they do not have a cathedral, but we have many, and thereafter demanding they be given the building and everything in it to prosper their godless religion. They have no claim to make of our sacred places secured by the sacrifices of the Saints. We must remember that the vineyard belongs to Christ Jesus, and we must be wise stewards and not allow the fruit to be stolen and the arbors trampled and burned. Brigands and slouches truly have no claim to make of any parcel of the Earth for it belongs to the meek as the Beatitudes say. Indeed, secularists and their irreverent posterity shall not inherit the Earth. Progressive social justice warriors have no concept of the justice of God or the responsibilities of His Holy Gospel. They are wolves whose clothing is scriptural sound bites. There are actually Christians who would say that we are required to surrender our great treasures to these reprobates out of Christian love to profane as they see fit. This is the lie that has nearly brought America to its knees and corrupted the very idea of Christian conversion. Our excellence, integrity, and sacrificial nature have been forfeited to mediocrity, irresponsibility, self-indulgence and pleasure-seeking, while squandering the moral inheritance of a nation. Our Lady told me that the way American children are scandalized is an outright abomination. She reminds us of the punishment for anyone who leads the little ones astray. The hip-hop culture is a wasteland of mortal sin. Our youth are being brainwashed and imprisoned beneath their depraved cadences, grooming the children of our nation for destruction in a cauldron stirred by the Prince of Darkness himself. Christian civilization is being destroyed right in front of our eyes because liberal progressives are engaging demonic fantasies, while trying to sell the illusion that they are giving glory to God, when in fact they reject everything His Cross stands for. Now, the caveat brings great responsibility because we are required to care for the poor and less fortunate. We are required to assist those who have stumbled. There is no argument about this from any true follower of Jesus Christ, and no amount of invective hurled against us can alter the truth of our sentiments. I am prepared to declare that our love must be great enough to bring dignity to anyone whom life has brought to their knees. But, our society seems to be having a problem determining just who the poor and less fortunate really are, especially when the gravy train of entitlements pulls into the station and hordes of sluggards have no shame in picking every railcar clean. It is the same phenomenon as when particular disastrous events occur and people break down doors and windows to storm local businesses to steal their contents as if an enormous free giveaway had just been declared by the forces of nature. God sees this as nothing more than the violations of His Seventh Commandment that no one should steal the possessions of another.

If there is one thing that might assist our addressing this entire body of difficulties, it is to come to the realization that there are people who serve the Antichrist who are trying to force an atheistic relativistic utopia upon us using self-assumed powers based in the destructive ideology of socialist politics. They are selling their revolution as a reflection of national obligation. They don the rhetorical confections of Christianity out of convenience; and with the intent of manipulation, portray moral standing, almost as if they are priests of a secular religion. And, in order to be successful, they must assail Jesus Christ and His Catholic Church into irrelevance because they neither know nor heed the Ten Commandments of God. He has not given them any authority to create a world that ignores His Divine Revelation. The godless and those who claim to be spiritual, but otherwise eschew the Original Apostolic Church, are flailing about because they sense victory in the instabilities arising in our nation. They wish to exploit turmoil to gain power to inflict their vision as any tyrant throughout history has done. They are portraying the descent of our nation as being caused by everyone but themselves, hoping to become its secular saviors for the sake of power. These misguided individuals are trying to bring about a hypnotic movement that promises salvation without the demands of the Cross. There are even many supposed religious leaders who have been deceived by the Christian confections that Satan sprinkles on his works. They have succumbed to the metronome of distraction being waved back and forth before the attention of our countrymen. And, they all tout how supportive they are of Jesus' Gospel in the process. Wolves in sheep's clothing indeed. They are liars and hypocrites with no foundation in true Christian sacrifice. Did Jesus lack compassion when He saw the crowds chasing after Him, realizing they only wanted to get their bellies full? [John 6:26] He was clear-sighted about this phenomenon because He wanted something far greater from them. He wanted their belief in Him as the Bread of Life, knowing that He would become their eternal nourishment.

Liberal academics throughout our country snobbishly believe themselves to be the oracles of human civilization. The rest? Merely ignorant minions of lesser sophistication, deserving of mockery, ridicule and public shame for their traditional sentiments and honorary customs. The ideologues who suborn chaos never build anything worthy of being remembered because they do not possess the vision to dream nor the heart to construct upon noble foundations. Renegades absent virtue remain blind to the nobility of contemporary existence, the hallowedness of human destiny and the breathtaking eternity in a Kingdom where a mansion would have otherwise been built for them. Rancor, revolution and rot are the plague of their motivations, and all that could have been dies lonely in the wreckage of the world they pass through like locusts in a seventeen year nightmare. Their smug arrogance is colossal, and their sin a lie against the Holy Spirit. They hail before their peanut galleries of socialist partisans, none of whom can see the forest for the trees whose knotholes they have their snouts stuffed into. The tides of history are screaming at them, but their pride has rendered them deaf. They refuse to either contemplate or engage the difficult path of sacrificial love and personal virtue that will make us a better country; and for this reason, fate will perfect us all. But, be not deceived, the holy and good will be the only thing left standing at the resurrection of our nation's honor in the final hour. The legends will rise again and rebuke these blind guides into whose hands the reins of our country fell. Progressive secularists are obscuring and distorting the truth in so many ways. Major segments of the American media act almost as if they are crime families, ideologues who have coopted enormous national megaphones who believe they are the only legitimate voice of the republic. It is like a toddler walking into a room waving a loaded handgun as if it were a new toy. The national media are dominated by people who hone their venues to manipulate the American consciousness according to their personal ideological bent. If Satan intended to compromise the American culture with his lies, would he not groom his secular minions, place them in the profession of journalism, and do exactly what we are seeing in nearly every broadcast? And, why would he do it? To influence minds and hearts in order to destroy the moral foundation of people's souls and create a new world order that serves him in the realms of death. He hangs tantalizing fruit in the boughs of the tree of communication, and proclaims how great the world would become if everyone ate their daily meal from his table. Journalism seems to have been a more noble profession in decades past. This was the case because moral character was more intact in the cultural fabric of our nation and its people. Journalists informed the public of the truth from a Judeo-Christian frame of reference that had been dominant in our country from its founding. Then came secular relativism and the rise of atheistic thought masquerading as enlightenment. Moral perspective has been under siege for over 60 years through the secular fruit we have been offered. As our countrymen lost their moral beings reflective of the great truths of Christianity, journalism too has become the propaganda arm of every radical ethos that can be conjured, including every evil that can be dreamed up. There is no distinction in human actions and no hierarchy of truth left to moderate human conduct. Wisdom is gone from their ranks. The liberal media owners make themselves associates to any agendum of radicalism that seeks to disobey any rule, soil any tradition or violate any moral norm, thinking it is progress for a nation. They barrage the national consciousness with each new abomination until it is ratified as a legitimate exception requiring societal approbation, lest all deniers be cursed as bigots in the public stockades of social communication. They extort concessions in support of any immoral agenda from those who were charged to defend the legacy of our sacrificial countrymen who provided them a country of such moral stature. And, they do it in the names of multiculturalism, diversity, freedom and choice. The exception then wipes out the disciplined order that was the foundation of these rules, traditions and moral norms, and poverty, desolation and death are the result. No wonder Our Lady says we are allowing children to be scandalized. We are destroying their future by giving them nothing to nourish their hearts or their relationships. They are being raised in a nightmare, and are too naive to dream otherwise. Progressive radicals hate objective moral truth. They hate the sacrificial lives of the great Catholic Saints, while boasting that they are overflowing with compassion they feel to be greater than everyone else combined. They cannot be reoriented because their arrogance knows no shame. Their cynicism is boundless, and they adopt a utilitarian view of manipulation of the entire hemisphere and its people. While thinking they are prescient, they are blind. In truth, those they supposedly care about are only tools for the sustaining of their authoritarian secular power. Their mantra of social justice is driven by a vast dictatorship of relativism wrapped in the contemporary attire of false victimhood and entitlement. They function by the conflict theories of Karl Marx, hoping to bring about change through their destabilization of Christian civilization which they know to be a Rock in their path. Make no mistake, they hate Jesus' Original Apostolic Church and only engage it to either punish it, disparage it, or force concessions from it. Saint John Paul the Great gave his life in the battle against radical ideologues such as these. And, he won; and so will Our Lady in the Triumph of Her Immaculate Heart. But, until then, let no one be fooled. Our national nightmare is upon us. In our darkest hour, Morning Star Over America, indeed!

Secular atheists have been playing a continental game of Jenga with the moral foundations of our great American nation through every judge who unilaterally overturns the will of a moral people, every politician who caters to fiscal irresponsibility, every ideology that brings diminution to our traditions, every rogue who contravenes our stabilizing laws, every person who defends the slaughter of the unborn, every activist screaming for socialist revolution, every globalist harvesting the world for profit, every artist who profits from vile debauchery, every educator who is ideologically indoctrinating their students, every news person whose religion is politics, every moral leader who stands silent, and every person who no longer takes a moment to acknowledge their Creator every day and follow in the ways of His Son. There will be consequences just as every game of Jenga ends with a collapse into a pile of chaos. But, there will be no laughter and no victory for those who have done this to our nation. In that smoldering chaos to come, only Jesus Christ will rise triumphant through the hearts of those who believed. We will throw our fists in the air and say, "You lose!" Only a miraculous transformation of biblical proportions can stop our country's asteroidal impact against the floor of hell. Why? Because nothing short of the reprobates seeing face-to-face their destiny in the eternal flames of Gehenna will encourage them to reevaluate their existence. It is then that we all hope they will begin to pray and seek their redemption in their obedience to the Son of Mary.

The forces of darkness are disparate, but possess much synergy amongst them. For example, the concept of Christian charity is being distorted as a method of manipulation by the enemies of Christ. Charity cannot be extorted from the Christian soul and then used as an accessory to this descent. Charity is a gift from the heart that glorifies Jesus' Sacrifice. No one could look at God the Father and say, "If you claim to be love, then I demand you sacrifice your Son so that I can come back to Heaven. I'm entitled to Paradise." Really? I believe every sacrificial Saint and Martyr has something to say about that. There is justice in the Heart of Almighty God. In our age of relativism, the government has no soul, and it has no charity to give unless it steals first at the hands of politicians in the name of their secular powers. Our politics, and therefore our government, are manipulated and orchestrated by sinners for reasons having nothing to do with the Gospel of Jesus Christ. Its motivations are none other than securing ever-increasing worldly power and influence. The problems throughout the world are colossal and are being socialized on the macro scale for the profits of an elite few. And, with this socialization comes ideological and material slavery beneath the same elite cabal. Every social anthropologist worth his salt would tell us that this approach is not sustainable. Socialism has failed at every step and brings with it tyranny, destruction and death. Socialism destroys human freedom because "We the people" no longer decide our future. The social debt presently incurred through these failed ideologies and their wasteland of immorality are catastrophic to the stability of any culture because greed dictates handily to a godless materialistic world. Secular socialism will destroy human civilization and crucify Christianity with it, just as it has always done. We are being made slaves as we speak as a result of socializing the costs of dereliction, recklessness, irresponsibility and immorality, while doing almost nothing to demand responsibility, virtue and right conduct from those who are causing such liabilities throughout our culture. Our countrymen of the United States are paying to support putrescent immorality without having any voice as to the true solutions prescribed by Christianity. Jesus Christ, the King of kings, is told to take a back seat in silence, while sinners in the place of Saints define the meaning of progress into the next generation. The worst of politicians are buying constituencies with demagoguery, trying to convince everyone from whom they are stealing just how magnanimous they are. We have corporate profiteers and media moguls illicitly generating, financing and propagating corruption, vice, slander and sin under the guise of news and entertainment. They are masquerading their deceit in the protections of the First Amendment to our Constitution, while trying to take away the ultimate insurance provided to the masses enshrined in the Second when culture eventually falls into chaos after having rejected Jesus Christ altogether. Our country is dying because we have forsaken the wisdom of Christ the King and the disciplines of human holiness that the Catholic Church has been proclaiming for 2,000 years on every land mass of the world.

So, what is the solution? Remember that prayer is power. Sacrifice in the image of Christ is earth-changing. Imitation of the Sacrificial Lamb is the meaning of life. Confronting evil is heroic. Love is the reason why we live, move and have our being. Truth must be spoken and lived. Justice must be implemented mercifully, fairly and firmly. And, abortion must cease. Unity at the expense of morality cannot withstand the test of virtue. Therefore, we must unite in the center of virtue at the Holy Sacrifice of the Mass in our Catholic churches throughout the world. There is no other place where it flourishes so clearly. Only there will our collective frame of reference be molded once again and ratified in the realms of holiness with our sanctification finding both its origin and its completion in Jesus' Divine Mercy. Then, and only then will our country be united and healed. Our eradication of abortion from the United States of America will be our testament to the world that this nation wishes to survive the Divine Justice of God. Sixty million is the death toll.

Question 8

Discuss the reasons why you believe that the Roman Catholic Church is God's "chosen" faith, and share the reasons why you believe that the Holy Father is the Vicar of Christ.

Our Lady would have us begin by realizing that no one truly believes that the Roman Catholic Church is God's chosen faith except through an act of faith, notwithstanding their review of history. God has yet to appear visibly hovering over Saint Peter's Basilica testifying to the Seat of His chosen faith in a way where every eye would in fact see their confirmation, although He surely has done so mystically throughout history as the power that sustains its 2,000 year old procession through time. But again, that must be believed through faith. As a side note, I am amazed that the entire Protestant world did not humble itself when St. Peter's tomb was actually found directly beneath Saint Peter's Basilica at the Vatican during archeological excavations after World War II. But, such was not the case because too many egos could not make the sacrifice to accept the prophetic Truth that God revealed to them at that revelation. Jesus said in Sacred Scripture that upon Peter would His Church be built. And, there lies his tomb beneath the great Basilica of the Seat of Roman Catholicism. Prophecy fulfilled because there she stands as witness to her authentic foundations.

Now, the question being asked is rooted in the reasons why one would believe that the Roman Catholic Church is the Repository for the Original Apostolic Faith that Jesus wished to be propagated for making disciples of all nations. Our beloved Savior articulated rather specific wishes and commands which would testify to our acceptance of His Sacrifice on the Cross and our conversion into a likeness worthy of His gift of redemption into Paradise. He said that if we do what He commanded, we would become His friends. Humankind is required to "do" something. So, reason would dictate that these wishes and commands would require transmission through the ages. This would imply that they be protected from the manipulation of human beings and evil spirits bearing agendas to manipulate the multitudes for gaining power. We see these sentiments had begun to flourish even in Jesus' day. His Holy Spirit cautioned His flock not to be seduced by people who would spread any other gospel. He said that He is the Way, the Truth and the Life, and that no one comes to the Father but through Him. Think about this in this age of pluralistic multicultural humanism. 'Through Him' means through our obedience to those commands that He said would make us His friends. It means living in a spirit of communion with His Sacred Heart. Our existence is not a salvific free-for-all that God allows sinners to define. It is not about fraternity based in whimsical feelings, masquerading as some flavor of love. The Apostles stated similar sentiments in their evangelizing travels. We see even today the many factions who wish to redefine for everyone else what is truly necessary to fulfill Jesus' commands, and what they believe His words actually mean. Where is the integrity of the Truth when left to the hubris of sinners? Hence, reason, wisdom and prudence rang like a clarion that His New Testament go forth in a state of anchoring. But, anchoring in what? Many today would reply by saying their anchoring is in the Bible. This is true. But, is that actually where the anchoring originates? Simple logic tells us that it is not the origin because the truth existed before the Bible was written. I would respond by asking which Bible version and who authorized the creation of that version amongst a world of sinners and their tendencies to fillet and fry interpretations? What sinner are we all to trust with something as precious as the tenets of our salvation? Do we believe the integrity of a particular Bible simply because it's old and contains peculiar language we no longer use? Does not the Bible now have numerous versions edited by multitudes of sinners with differing persuasions and agendas? Which Bible versions have Satan's followers edited? If I were Satan, I would take the Bible and have it edited for my purposes too, in order to obscure the authentic one. He is not hard to anticipate. It is common historical knowledge that many versions of the Bible at the time of the Protestant Reformation were riddled with new progressive translations of the time, edited to justify the revolutionist theological interpretations of particular factions, indeed Protestantism itself. Every legitimate biblical scholar concedes this. All those protesting interpretations were at war with themselves at the time, clawing for an authority that to this day they have never owned. Today, some radicals are removing all masculine pronouns; some self-acclaimed historians believe they are more enlightened about Jesus' times than the original writers; some are even beginning to use the Gospels to justify all manners of sexual abomination in direct contradiction to its revealed testament. Some are even advancing the idea that the great Prophet Isaiah never intended to speak of the Virgin with Child, and are reinterpreting the words of the Old Testament to obscure the Queen of Heaven. Simply look at the King James version of the Bible as an example of what I am referring to. The writings that were ultimately contained in the Catholic Bible thrived for over 1,400 years before the final translations of the King James Bible even existed. Now, was Jesus prescient enough to expect this would be the case at the hands of sinners down through history? Surely, He was. We would have anticipated as much. And, was He not wise enough to implement an anchoring that would protect His testament to humanity that His Church founded upon Saint Peter might never fail? No doubt. Then, where is the anchoring?

The Holy Spirit inspired the Roman Catholic Church, indeed the only Christianity that existed, to organize the earliest writings of the Apostolic Age into the first Bible at the Council of Rome in A.D. 382. Scripture testifies in 2 Peter 1:20, "Knowing this first of all, that no prophecy of Scripture comes from someone's own interpretation." So, where is the authority that gave the Prelates of the Catholic Church the right before God to interpret and compile the writings of the Apostolic Fathers into that first Bible for all Christendom for all ages? Where does the anchoring of authority originate that would guarantee the integrity of the original testament of Jesus' Life, Death and Resurrection? What was Jesus' method to preserve the archetype of faith against man's meddling sinfulness, progressive tendencies and wilful agendas? It is in the power dispensed at the sanctifying event of Pentecost as the Holy Spirit was imparted through tongues of fire. Scripture states in Luke 24:49, "And [behold] I am sending the promise of my Father upon you; but stay in the city until you are *clothed with power from on high.*" This is the declaration of the "anchoring of authority." Protestantism was neither present nor represented at that great supernatural dispensation. Furthermore, the propagation of that unified authority into future ages is testified to in those same Scriptures. Acts 1:24-26 states, "Then they prayed and said, 'Lord, you know everyone's heart. Show us which one of these two you have chosen to take the place in this ministry and apostleship from which Judas turned aside to go to his own place.' And, they cast lots for another, and the lot fell on Matthias; and he was added to the eleven apostles." The propagating mechanism of the original "anchoring of authority" is testified to in this Scripture passage by the Holy Spirit. And, from this comes the Apostolic Succession of Pontificates and the birth of the Magisterium.

Now, if we go back to the original question, how do we know that the Roman Catholic Church is the "chosen faith" of God? We should accept that Jesus imparted the Truth of His Testament to the original Apostles to fulfill the prophecy that His Church founded upon Peter would never fail. It is obvious that they, along with the Most Blessed Virgin Mary, were the first human beings in Creation to know the Messiah best. No one can legitimately challenge this supremacy and authority. If they were resurrected into our presence today, every theologian and biblical expert would fall silent in veneration. Anyone disputing with these great Saints would be seen as a fool. Jesus revealed Himself to them in a special manner where He said in Matthew 13:10-11, "Because the knowledge of the secrets of the kingdom of heaven has been given to you, but not to them." The Apostles are whom Jesus chose for the propagation of the sacramental graces of Salvation to a sinful world walking in darkness. And, Our Lady is the Heavenly Mother whom Jesus gave all the children of God. From this original dispensation, the Truth would remain undiminished and untarnished on the Earth until the last day of the world. His Original Church would not fail, but would remain intact as clear as on the day He died to every generation thereafter.

Therefore, it is truthful to look upon the unbroken chain of successive Pontificates and the priestly vocations that have prospered from each of Christ's successive Vicars as being a manifestation of Acts 1:24-26. This spiritual genealogy is our "motive of credibility" that the propagation of the "anchoring of authority" lies in this chain of Pontificates in union with the Hierarchy that each manifests, much as each season of fruit appears on an orchard's trees. The spiritual DNA from the original Tree is in every piece of fruit. The Roman Catholic Church is the original tree with no equal and no replica because Her founder is Christ Himself. And, in this "anchoring of authority," the Holy Spirit has implanted, secured and protected the Gospel of Salvation and its interpretation into a world of sinners for each succeeding generation. We are not at a disadvantage in the twenty-first century by not being able to hear the authentic voice of Jesus Christ and His message of Salvation from His own lips, for the Roman Catholic Church speaks! Saint Peter is speaking; Saint John is speaking; the Holy Virgin is speaking. The Voice of Roman Catholicism is Christ's Voice through the succession of ages. The fruit of Salvation comes from this tree. And, this "chosen church" that was lifted up in the beginning speaks from Her own Cross in the image of Her Savior, just as Saint Peter witnessed to his allegiance to the Messiah in his own inverted crucifixion in Rome. There again is the Father! All the cerebralizing by theologians, philosophers and historians obscures their capacity to shed tears of devotion and veneration over it. Tears well in my eyes right now because I love the Roman Catholic Church so much, what She stands for, what She is, what She has sacrificed to preserve the original Annunciation of the Archangel Gabriel of the Savior of the world. The Holy Spirit has no use for protestors and their pride; no use for intellectuals and their mentalism, and no use for atheists and their sanctimonious hubris. They can stay in the darkness, pontificating their pride for all the heavens care. There will be no lifeline thrown to them on the last day. They will have to swim to outrun the flames on the day of Salvation as the mighty ship of Christendom steams toward the horizon of Glory. Their cerebral antics and faithless self-justifications are blasphemous. They are separated from grace, not realizing their vanity would be vaporized if Jesus allowed them to see how they are crucifying Him. It is only His Divine Mercy that precludes this mortifying vision of justice from being administered to them by Saint Michael the Archangel. It is Christ's generosity that He allows them to remain in their error, granting them the possibility for conversion before He sets the eternal record straight right in front of their eyes. He knows none of these people really want to have the final picture of their lives testify that they refused every opportunity to accept His chosen faith from the depths of their hearts.

Question 9

Do you believe that people who have never been exposed to supernatural miracles are as capable of living as holy a life as the seers who experience them?

The simple answer is "yes," although I would submit that the question begs an errant bipolar understanding of life in exile. The action of receiving miraculous intercession is not necessarily a sign of a holy life. Remember the grace bestowed on Saint Paul on the road to Damascus. This event did not come because he was holy, but rather because God wished to use his fearless determination to confront the pagan world. He needed a messenger with intrepid conviction who would obey Him unto death, knowing He would be required to provide the holiness. Miraculous intercession is a unilateral dispensation from God executed through the supreme generosity of His divine will, notwithstanding the composure of the recipient. But, the paradox is this. Living a holy life can present God a great thoroughfare to portion miraculous intercession in extraordinary ways that He will take advantage of because of the love that a soul has for Him, and He for humanity. We see this in many victim souls, most conspicuously in the life of Saint Padre Pio. He was sacrificially holy before he received the stigmata. Miraculous intercession is often a fruit of a very holy life where God is granted opportunity for supernatural engagement through a person's faith and capacity to suffer for Him. We must remember that the invocation of faith makes miracles possible. The actual sign of a holy life is suffering in union with Christ; and usually those who receive miraculous intercession suffer excruciating private burdens so the world may receive these gifts. Our Lady says, "Mystical gifts come through the diminishment of the flesh." Hence, those who make themselves celebrities in popular culture with supposed paranormal gifts, who receive wealth, prestige and accolades, risk being sideshows who are personally delusional, diabolically inspired, or are abusing their authentic gifts altogether. If we see miraculous intercession without the suffering unity with Christ, beware! Thus, we should realize that supernatural phenomenon are not required in order to suffer for Jesus' sake. So, being holy is more related to sacrifice and suffering. Our Holy Mother says that suffering for Jesus is a manifestation of supernatural grace all in itself. Therefore, holiness does not require supernatural miracles, per se, but holiness is the manifestation of the supernal grace of God where they may be recognized. No one saves themselves or performs any act of goodness without the assistance of divine grace. So, mystical gifts and supernatural phenomena are great actions of the Holy Spirit that manifest and function in the midst of our communion with Jesus' Sacrifice, but this communion is in our suffering with Him as a sign of our love for His Mystical Body and lost sinners. The Church says none other than this, although many misguided people pervert this logic to deduce that everyone should ignore miraculous intercession altogether because, "We don't have to believe that." Those six words are a bane to Catholic evangelization. These people would better realize that God is trying to say something to them through every miracle and instance of miraculous intercession, and that their brothers and sisters are oftentimes suffering horrible diminishment so that doubters, such as themselves, can receive graces of conversion which they are summarily dismissing. For instance, God rebuked Balaam through his donkey who spoke in a human voice [Numbers 22-24, 2 Peter 2:16]. Even the donkey was responding to the miraculous intercession of the angel who appeared in his path. Was that donkey actually more faithful than we are? I can empathize with that little burro's beatings sometimes as I try to encourage everyone to go in the way Our Lady directs through Her miraculous intercession. Ignore anyone who tells you to dismiss Our Lady's miraculous intercession. They are speaking under the influence of the Antichrist.

A question we should ponder is whether we allow ourselves to become recipients and beneficiaries of miraculous intercession. Do we want our Lord near us? Do we give Him reign? What can He do that will matter? Do we mean it when we say, 'Come Lord Jesus?' Do we welcome this relationship by invoking our faith when He does? Jesus said in Matthew 13:58 and Mark 6:5 that He could not work miracles in His hometown of Nazareth because of their lack of faith. He wanted to give Himself to them to bring healing and ignite faith. Possibly one of the most profound sentences in all of Scripture is Mark 6:6, "He was amazed at their lack of faith." Think about that. The 14th chapter of Saint John states, "Whoever loves me will keep my word, and my Father will love him, and we will come to him and make our dwelling with him." Is not Jesus' revelation of Himself to a person the ultimate miraculous intercession we are talking about? Our contemporary secular wine skin is telling us that miraculous intercession is a fanatical aberration, instead of realizing that Roman Catholicism is flourishing with the Divine Intercession into the lives of the faithful from all the hierarchies of Heaven. We invoke them in every Mass and through our every prayer. My goodness, if people would just attend the holy day liturgies of All Saints Day and allow their souls to be overwhelmed with our calling litanies sung to the vaults of Heaven, it might make sense that our Holy Mother would descend to us in happy tears. '...all you holy men and women, pray for us.' Why are we shocked when they respond? Because it requires our faith. It is a challenge to our wine skin that we sense must burst. The prayers of the parishioners of the Roman Catholic Diocese of Springfield in Illinois invoked the Morning Star Over America into their midst. These faithful people called to their Immaculate Mother, and She came. This Catholic Diocese, consecrated to the Immaculate Conception, has lifted prayers and sacrifices to which the heavens have responded. The lives of my brother and me stand upon generations of faith brought to us by some of the most sacrificial people to have ever appeared in America. The messages of the Morning Star Over America and Final Colossus are resultant relics of a miracle of faith that everyone can see with their eyes, just as much a sign as the miraculous tilma of Our Lady of Guadalupe. Is the miracle only in personally being allowed to see the mystical mechanics of their transcension into recorded form through sinners such as my brother and me? What person alive can now say that they have never been exposed to miraculous intercession after seeing these works of the Mother of God? The question should be rephrased—'Do you believe that people who have never "accepted" supernatural miracles are as capable of living as holy a life as the seers who embrace them?' I am not so sure they can. If one cannot accept the supernatural action of the Holy Spirit, their faith may be in trouble. Nonetheless, anyone can be just as holy, even if one walks away disbelieving, because they can suffer for Our Lord just as adequately. But, Our Lady said that this is not the best use of one's faith. Suffering will come for every person who wishes to be admitted to Heaven, but She hopes that our discomfort does not come because we had to suffer for our own sins. Sanctity is rising to holiness, and then offering our lives as a sacrifice for others.

Humanity's love for Jesus seems to be very weak in these modern times because faith has been characterized as a commodity for only weak-minded people. Faith has gone dormant in the motivations of secular men, and also terribly atrophied in the souls of many professing Christians. Faith simply means theology to the intellectuals. They believe they are conquering Heaven with their compendium of acquired knowledge. Sacrifice for the sake of love is being mocked and impugned. Christian love is the entire superstructure of a holy life whose many rooms contain the atmosphere where Jesus reveals Himself to us. Many lives we see are veritable walking examples of miraculous intercession by the Holy Spirit, even though in observing them we may not see a healing, hear an audible message, witness an ephemeral angel or be thunderstruck by the appearance of our beautiful Heavenly Mother hovering over them. But within them, the healing of the soul has occurred; they speak with God and His Angels in their prayers, and they most assuredly know their Heavenly Mother who hovers in protection above them. Indeed, every sacrificial Saint was calling out to humanity through their devotion. Saint Teresa of Calcutta invoked thunder in the consciences of the people she met. She was intimidating to titans and could admonish without uttering a word, although she often did. She spoke the glaring truth of the atrocity of abortion directly in the face of those who supported it politically, and was cheered by the faithful as the reprobates looked on. She was more concerned about pleasing God than she was about offending unrepentant sinners. The fruits of miraculous intercession have been fully present in Saints such as this tiny lady. In fact, nearly every person has been the recipient of miraculous intercession interiorly through the scents and sentiments of the Holy Spirit, even though most assumed it was just their own conjuring imagination because the Holy Spirit found no faith that could be kindled into a blaze. Authentic locutions are not all that uncommon. God calls to us all the time through our conscience, if it has not been rendered deaf by the din of sin and distraction. This is why we pray.

In the early days of Our Lady's intercession, She told my brother and me that She was going to intercede into the life of another person of our prayer group as a gift to help us magnify Her presence. She instructed us to announce this to everyone present so that each person might prepare for the possibility in their life. As the weeks moved forward, no one recognized this intercession manifesting itself, which inflamed terrible doubts among many people about the authenticity of our mystical claims. I was grieved to the bottom of my soul because I recognized the growing conflict between Our Lady's perspective and that of the doubting members of the prayer group. Why were Her words not fulfilled, they wondered. Finally, She instructed my brother and me to tell everyone that after repeated attempts, the next person She had chosen refused to open themselves to receive Her. She said they were filled with doubts that they refused to set aside. I asked Her how I could possibly tell the group that She could not come to the next person because of their lack of faith. She responded by telling me this was exactly the point that I was to relate to them—each person in the group realizing that it might have been them. I obeyed our Heavenly Mother as difficult as it was to do, and especially because I knew what was to be the outcome. As you can imagine, this incident caused a terrible fracturing within the prayer group, and from that day forward nearly all who previously stood beside us separated themselves from our presence. I watched how it was possible for Palm Sunday to transform into Good Friday in the span of a week. Then, the persecutions began. But, it bore the graceful cloistered atmosphere of peaceful protection where my brother and I could complete the works of the Morning Star Over America without doubters assailing us at every turn. Does not this disciplinary occurrence bear the answer as to why we might not see miraculous intercession flourishing more profoundly? Jesus rarely, if ever, reveals Himself exceptionally to those who are not disposed to accept Him. He will not work miracles where there is no faith. Would Scripture not be violated if God just threw miraculous gifts before a willful humanity that refuses to prepare itself to receive Him? Pearls before swine, indeed! Incidently, a short time later, a very humble woman from our original prayer group, who always sat quietly in the back of the room, related to my brother and me personally that she had an interior mystical experience during the time of these chastening events. She related that Our Lady had appeared to her interiorly, but she never told anyone at the time. She was not in attendance the night when it was related that our Heavenly Mother was going to reveal Herself to another person. She had no idea what was prophesied to occur. So, our Heavenly Mother's prophecy was fulfilled nonetheless in this faithful soul. This sequence of events is very revelatory of the many lessons that our Holy Mother has engaged with my brother and me over nearly three decades. Everyone can see the challenge leveled by faith, and the consequences in our response, or lack thereof. It also shows that our Heavenly Mother is unconcerned about whose ego is offended. She has no part in that. These people offend themselves. If everyone would move closer to Jesus and obey Him, He would adjust our collective recognition and reveal Himself to all humanity. Then, no one would ask whether we can be just as holy without miraculous intercession. Mankind cannot be holy without being united with the King of kings on the Cross. From this perspective, there is no line between holiness and miraculous intercession. The Holy Spirit has always been miraculous. The reception of the Sacrament of Confirmation is miraculous intercession into the lives of each recipient.

Question 10

How do you see the environment of discernment by Church leaders and individual people who are faced with claims of miraculous intercession such as what you are personally describing or in places such as Medjugorje? What does discernment mean to you, and how do you feel it should be engaged?

I believe it is a paradox for human judgement where the extension of faith provides the only reconciling path to both the elevation and protection of the truth of Divine Revelation in all its manifestations. It is certain that the Deposit of Faith must be protected from being deposed or transmuted by the devil through those who serve him. This is the sacred responsibility borne in the Succession of Pontificates and the seasons of the Magisterium who serve in obedience to the Dogmas and Traditions of our Faith. All the same, each successive generation of Prelates has also been required to maintain a faithful posture that is responsive to the Holy Spirit. They must guard themselves in sacrifice so as to not surrender the operations of this custodial protection to stagnant stubbornness, ecclesial hubris or progressive pride. The leaders of our Church are required to have faith too. The paradox is this: While the Magisterium has the responsibility to protect the Deposit of Faith, it means they must extend their faith in order for it to be protected. It is not just a defense of theology or having been bequeathed the custodial care of a building. The truths in the mystical intercessions of the Holy Spirit are a majestic component of this protection, while also being a mystical facility dispensed by God for the conversion of lost souls. Why do I say this? Because God does not extend His power for no reason or without dispensing responsibility. "*Yet even if Revelation is already complete, it has not been made completely explicit; it remains for Christian faith gradually to grasp its full significance over the course of the centuries...It is not their (private revelation's) role to improve or complete Christ's definitive Revelation, but to help live more fully by it in a certain period of history*" [Catechism of the Catholic Church 67]. Our Lord Jesus advances the work of His Holy Spirit to explicate the Truth and defend His Church so that it can succeed in its salvific purpose. This is why the gates of hell will never prevail against it. The Holy Spirit brings clarity and attention to the message of human salvation, and dispenses life-sustaining protection to the vehicle of this message, which is His Mystical Body. The Church becomes weak when the faith of men grows cold, and thereafter the pathway to salvation becomes obscured to the detriment of human souls. People lose the mystical sense of Immanuel — "God is with us." Pope Emeritus Benedict XVI recently stated in a personal treatise:

A paramount task, which must result from the moral upheavals of our time, is that we ourselves once again begin to live by God and unto Him. Above all, we ourselves must learn again to recognize God as the foundation of our life instead of leaving Him aside as a somehow ineffective phrase. I will never forget the warning that the great theologian Hans Urs von Balthasar once wrote to me on one of his letter cards. "Do not presuppose the triune God, Father, Son and Holy Spirit, but present them!"

Indeed, in theology God is often taken for granted as a matter of course, but concretely one does not deal with Him. The theme of God seems so unreal, so far removed from the things that concern us. And yet everything becomes different if one does not presuppose but present God. Not somehow leaving Him in the background, but recognizing Him as the center of our thoughts, words and actions.

(2) God became man for us. Man as His creature is so close to His heart that He has united himself with him and has thus entered human history in a very practical way.

He speaks with us, He lives with us, He suffers with us and He took death upon Himself for us. We talk about this in detail in theology, with learned words and thoughts. But it is precisely in this way that we run the risk of becoming masters of faith instead of being renewed and mastered by the Faith.

I believe this excerpt speaks to the motives of credibility of our Faith where the Holy Spirit reveals the Father and Son in our lives through our mystical sense of miraculous intercession, and how we have become disinclined by intellectualism to respond and take comfort in these revelations of their mighty presence. These are "moments of the Faith" seeking to renew and master us; "...to help (us) live more fully by it in a certain period of history." Our Lady through Her miraculous intercession forces us to deal with God, because She does not presuppose Him, but "presents Him" as this great Pope states. Everything that God manifests before our awareness in the realtime of our lives with Him bears a responsibility upon us at our judgement because we will hold ourselves accountable for any lacking in perfection or openness to Him during our lives, especially if we were faced with extraordinary intercessory gifts and shunned them. "*Afterward He appeared to the eleven themselves as they were reclining at the table; and He reproached them for their unbelief and hardness of heart, because they had not believed those who had seen Him after He had risen*" [Mark 16:14]. I believe this Scripture passage encourages us to beware of unbelief, while instructing us as to how Jesus wishes us to approach the mystical operations of discernment in the face of miraculous intercession. It was no different for the original Apostles than it is for us. If an extraordinary mystical event is authentic, verily our God expects us to heed it and its message, and most definitely He gives us the grace to do so. Lack of humility and human sin are the reasons we do not. Does God grant leeway for every unbeliever to ignore without consequence the evangelists He raises up? Of course not. At the very least, He sees every evangelist who is not believed as a missed opportunity by unbelievers, albeit not one that definitively closes the final door to their conversion and ascent to perfection that they will one day wish they had embraced and displayed with passion. Only our death closes the final door, although some exist in a state of mortal sin that God already knows is going to be unbreachable. It is man who closes the door and holds it shut, not God. But, do we ever wonder when our last chance will come? Is Morning Star Over America the last chance for the United States of America?

If we wish to speak about the environment in which discernment takes place, would we not be correct in saying that in order to discern the truth, we must do so in the sacrificial light of our greatest faith? The problem is, great darkness has descended upon the environment where the Church is presently stationed in exile. Faith has not only grown cold, but the courage to display it has been overwhelmed by the concessions demanded by the dictatorship of relativism. Everyone can sense that this is happening. Yet, the differing ideological persuasions are seeing neither its cause nor its remedy as being in the same direction. It is difficult to generalize the causes in any way that will matter because each is the father of a thousand consequences that generate distractions to a common remedy. Wild progressive arrogance will not make the sacrifice to humble itself, and those with a deferential sense of the traditional tides of history and its human frailty are trampled in the stampede of immorality which is being justified. Most seem to be concentrating on doctoring the consequences to the advancement of their ideologies, while being completely oblivious to the causes they themselves have created. Obedience to divine law is out of the question, and reasonable spiritual deduction that would respect natural law is banished by whimsical feelings dictated by the flesh. We have no idea what to do with obstinate sinners who wish to be accepted, but refuse to do anything to make themselves acceptable to a community of faith and sacrificial commitment. In the midst of this ideological turmoil, the mystical nature of the Roman Catholic Church has been eclipsed. Everything mystical and miraculous that the Church is and believes has been pummeled and plundered for decades and centuries, but no more aggressively than in the years since the Second Vatican Council. Again, most everyone senses this, but those with a vision of the course set out by Our Lady are excoriated by offended liberals if we attempt to delve into its causes. The question is, how deep will we dig?

    The magnification of Satan's voice of distraction has been colossal in our contemporary age because we have given him a seat at the table within our midst through a false sense of respect. An accelerated progression of descent and destabilization has occurred due to the seats of power of the modern world having fallen into the hands of outright wickedness and their advanced technologies for evangelizing the masses. Secularism is an atheistic religion whose pulpits are the mass media and social platforms of the nation. Narcissism is its credo, and hedonism is its rituals. They have their scriptural manifesto blaring into the senses of every person with a cell phone at every minute of the day and night. Likewise, relativistic mind sets surrendered to worldliness have entered the Church and are bantering it into subservience. These people are swept up in the tides of atheistic secularism and its fanciful fraternity in multiculturalism that has no foundation, unity, or cohesion in divine truth. Further, faith has died on the vine in many who are exhausted from the fight being leveled against them by the secular void, and few leaders of the Church are anywhere to be found in creating a defense for them in which to seek refuge. Hear me now, Our Lady is the Refuge! The progressive disease of humanistic relativism has been feasting upon the Sacred Mysteries of the Original Apostolic Church in the name of the "spirit of the Council" since the heady days of progressivism in the early 1960s. Vacuous radicalism has run rampant throughout our sectarian culture of academia, religious orders, media, conferences, conventions, and publications with no winnowing mechanism which would protect the clarity of our Faith. Now that the Church has been nearly emptied of sacrificial conviction, progressives believe we must double down on their methods in order to encourage everyone to come back. But, they refuse to proclaim the Calvarian Cross that stands waiting at the door. They have forsaken the call for holiness and replaced it with a simple invitation to a fraternity party where no one is required to bring the gift of sacrificial conversion to the Sacred Altar.

Satan took advantage of the generosity of the Catholic Church and seized the opportunity to bring corruption and compromise to the table of Roman Catholic discernment. The doors were thrown open and human arrogance walked right in, sat down and began to dictate the "new church" into being. Evangelization of the Original Apostolic Church and its Sacred Mysteries was beaten back into obscurity by these ideological members of the Church. At the slightest wisp of criticism or correction of the ecumenical fraternity-building, absent the Holy Sacrifice of Jesus, the orchestrators pushed with all the force of divine authority, claiming any disapproval against their agenda was somehow damaging our attempts at pluralistic Christian unity. The sour fruits of their tree have proven them to be wrong. After nearly sixty years, everyone can see the shambles of the vineyard that has ensued, while the revolutionaries belch their satisfaction after having eaten the grapes that should have been turned into wine by our evangelic sacrifices. The human ego has been unleashed. Narcissism abounds. Effeminacy flourishes. The flesh is worshiped. Sinful Eve is deified. Secular pop culture is raising our children. Hedonism is our feast. And, our children are being wrapped in sexual depravity through catchy rhythms and salacious conduct which are being sold to them as maturity and expression. And, parents who should be defending the virtue of their daughters seem more concerned with their social popularity and that they somehow triumph over little boys at every turn. Cynical? The evidence proves otherwise. The most thriving strains of sacrificial devotion in the Church are from those who never conceded to this banality, those who remained at Our Lady's side beneath the Cross; our great matriarchs and patriarchs who are wondering what happened to their beloved Church and the country they built with their sacrifices. And, they go to their graves as our intercessors, begging God to give us the peaceful Light of virtue once again. Rare little remains of the mystically holy to nourish the interior strength of people's hearts. The pastoral decision to extend a conciliatory hand to our detractors in response to the Council has backfired like half-spent gunpowder into our faces. We have done nothing more than legitimize blasphemy, heresy, division and error, while being forced to become relativists to maintain some semblance of ecumenical fraternity. Our Lady, the Communion of Saints and all the spiritual mysticism of the Roman Catholic Church that would challenge unbelievers to the deeper truths of Jesus' Original Church were retired to the rear as intangible impediments to the progressive intellectual sophisticates and the parishioners who had become protestantized through their proselytizing agendas. Our Lady was shuttered in Her chambers like an old maid simply because Protestants refused to believe Heaven has a Queen. "Why not concentrate on our common goals of social justice instead," they said, "and leave those triumphant Catholic things behind? They are all so divisive." Sacrificial conversion to Christ was repudiated and replaced by ecumenical platitudes absent any true sacrificial oneness with the Cross. The aggressive license illicitly spawned by opportunists after Vatican II successfully bantered the front lines to yield their mystical armor in order to prepare for an acceptance that would never come. All spiritual weapons of Roman Catholicism's great history of sacrifice were surrendered, and a stand-down order was issued to the faithful, while the Church's enemies coaxed our Prelates from the saddles of their war horses and road away with legitimacy that was never given to them by Christ. Everything it meant to be a Roman Catholic was effeminized by radicals in their attack on the Patriarchy of the Father at the same time the American cultural leftists began their assault on every facet of traditional stability, purity and morality enculturated into our institutions of religion, education, politics and entertainment. The derangements of homosexuality flooded the priesthood like twenty-one year old boys being invited to live in a sorority house, while the secular culture exploded with unrestrained sensuality which coaxed tens of thousands of religious to declare divorce decrees from their Master, leaving vocations to holy and religious orders dying in the wreckage. They all believed humanity had found a better way to live, unfettered from unity with Jesus' Crucifixion. All that was needed was for the old order to be torn down and hauled away that they might reign instead.

This is the diabolical deception that has been crescendoing throughout the world since World War II. And, we are seeing the sorrowful result in the social and moral collapse of nations, as well as a tragedy of faith within the Church. One need look no further than the crash of weekly Holy Mass attendance since the 1950s for the evidence. It has cratered because of everything I am speaking about. Our Lady of Fatima intimated that this was going to happen if we did not heed Her instructions in 1917. This has all flowed from neo-Marxist conflict theory as the vehicle for the destabilization of the culture and the destruction of Christian civilization. While we were waiting for an offensive war of tanks, missiles and bombers with communism, the evil that spawned it destroyed us from the inside by gutting us of moral principle and replacing it with the atheistic entitlement of the proletariat revolution. No revolutionary could have succeeded in convincing humanity outright to surrender the wisdom of Christ. Therefore, Christianity had to become the target for a surreptitious transformation into something completely worldly, humanist and relativistic. And, it happened through our surrendering of the miraculous for temporal reasonableness because we thought the unconverted could never really understand a mystical kingdom of the heart. The ultimate apostasy is upon us — Fraternity with no conversion to Jesus Christ through the Cross – and no Bread of Life. A new worldly religion is being constructed right in front of our eyes. Satan is offering the bargain to humanity of world peace among all its members if we will surrender the authority and teachings of the Roman Catholic Church which stands calling for a completely different world.

In the aftermath of this temporal transformation, the flesh has begun its reign in place of the Holy Spirit. The great compromise of our faith has left relatively little to inspire conviction after it was given away. Honor is mocked to near extinction. Purity is laughed at. Sacrifice and self-denial have been replaced by self-glorification. Discipline and order are stampeded by creative anarchy. Both Catholic architecture and sacred music have been stripped of their mystical grandeur. And, the great lights of saintliness that would edify us have been all but extinguished or concealed beneath bushel baskets of compromise all across our culture. Indeed, '...his tail swept a third of the stars out of the sky and flung them to the Earth' [Revelation 12:4]. The great moral courage, heroic sacrifice, unyielding rectitude, princely nobility, ferocious conviction and intrepid sanctity lost their apparent examples for our children. The rebuke of evil has been silenced at the calling of the demon of diversity. For example, Venerable Archbishop Fulton Sheen edified a nation for decades proclaiming the Gospel and describing the times to those who were blessed to hear his voice for fifty years beginning in the 1930s. This great Catholic Prelate was a household name because of his conviction, eloquence and the truths he spoke with such fearlessness. Where did his voice go? Where is his vision? Who has risen to take his place in such a way, with such courage and truth? Fulton Sheen would be thundering at the progressive leftists who are injecting such venomous evil into the veins of our country, especially our children in nearly every university in our nation. He would be telling millions not to be deceived by these charlatans. He would have spoken while there was still time to do so, realizing that these radicals are simply the newest incarnation of the demonic socialist ideology that he rebuked with such courage. Marxism is not a version of Christianity. Socialism is predicated on theft, which veritably leads to slavery, dictatorship, destitution and destruction. It is not about Christian charity at all. It lies to everyone by donning the fleece of the Lamb, but an insatiable wolf resides beneath its coat. It does not care about the less fortunate as it claims. It seeks power alone by violating the seventh, ninth and tenth Commandments as part of its conflict credo which comes from its father, who is the devil. Archbishop Fulton Sheen knew this, and he also knew this evil was responsible for the deaths of tens of millions, for the tyranny and desolation of continents, and that it would also rear its head under many sophisticated titles if Christ's redemptive Sacrifice were not proclaimed. Who will rise and tell the truth to the nations walking toward the abyss? Who will challenge this onslaught of evil?

"The refusal to take sides on great moral issues is itself a decision. It is a silent acquiescence to evil. The tragedy of our time is that those who still believe in honesty lack fire and conviction, while those who believe in dishonesty are full of passionate conviction.

Modern man has so long preached a doctrine of false tolerance; he has so long believed that right and wrong were only differences in a point of view, that now when evil works itself out in practice he is paralyzed to do anything against it.

It is characteristic of any decaying civilization that the great masses of people are unaware of the tragedy. Humanity in a crisis is generally insensitive to the gravity of the times in which it lives.

Men do not want to believe their own times are wicked, partly because they have no standard outside of themselves by which to measure their times. If there is no fixed concept of justice, how shall men know it is violated?

Only those who live by faith really know what is happening in the world; the great masses without faith are unconscious of the destructive processes going on, because they have lost the vision of the heights from which they have fallen."

- Archbishop Fulton Sheen

Saint Fulton Sheen, please ask God to give us a Saint like unto yourself. Saint Michael, raise up sons of thunder and give them venue and miraculous faculties at your side! Hear our intercessory prayers. Is this not what Our Lady is attempting to bring to its feet through Her miraculous intercessions, both here and abroad? Is Her miraculous presence not a wake-up call to a drunken world lost in its glittering estimation of itself? Of course it is, but most are loath to admit the times we are in and the abyss we are staring into. We refuse to summon the courage and the wisdom to hear God's voice and respond with all the conviction of Martyrs. We have intimidated the voice of truth into a state of muted cowardice. We are obsessed that no disturbance be caused. Thus, it remains very difficult for most people to discern the truth of God in a world veiled with such deception, darkness and falsehood with no light allowed to be seen. We hear few prominent voices of leadership which would unify us to battle back this darkness. And, the ones who do are attacked by their own. Beware you evangelists, your enemies will be those of your own household.

Nonetheless, the truth presents itself before us, just as Christ taking on human flesh. But in our disoriented state, it only takes the option of deception, not true deception, but the option of its possibility to obscure the reality of our Heavenly Mother's presence and the seriousness of Her call. Think about it. What stirs us not to believe when faced with these instances of extraordinary visitation? What causes us not to claim the opportunity to ride upon a tsunami of maternal grace? Is it not simply the option of deception, even when there may be none occurring? Thus, the question remains, 'Is mankind always going to crucify messengers?' Will there ever come a day when one will be believed? God could work any number of miracles for us, and all Satan has to do is drop the whisper of the option of deception. Thereafter, 'Fiat' is challenged, consumed and extinguished in most people. The evil one can then walk away because his work is complete, knowing fearful antagonists will do the rest. He plants his seed of doubt to stir us away from our joyful, euphoric abandonment to God and our enraptured interaction with Him in our lives. The devil causes us to reject our Heavenly Mother. We claim if God is for us, who can be against us? Jesus said that His sheep know Him and they heed His voice. He said that the Holy Spirit would come and teach us. He said that He would reveal Himself to us. He would not leave us orphans, and He would come to us. Over and over, He told us that He would care for us and guide us. He counts the hairs on our head and will provide for us. Well, if there is such overwhelming protection, assistance, knowledge and grace spread over us, why are we terrified when the mystical and miraculous flourish from the realms of the Holy Spirit? Our Holy Mother says it is because we fear to have faith, and we do not realize that the temperature of truth in the secular void has plummeted to the freezing realms of Dante's ninth circle of hell. We find our security in our tethers to worldly reasonableness, which we do not realize is being dominated by atheistic darkness that does not believe in God. We need to stop worrying about whether there is fraternity in diversity. This is only relativism by another name. Our Lady says that the secular void will not be allowed to define either Jesus' Church or His Kingdom. Secularists have a choice to make. Do they want to go to Heaven, or not? Therefore, how does it make sense for anyone to stir fear of Our Lady's miraculous intercession when She so much wants to assist them?

"The United States of America holds the greatest potential to manifest God's Kingdom and live as an example of how humanity should grow. This potential has been realized to exponential degrees because of the freedom of worship that has been built into its framework. Now, however, you are seeing American citizens and government representatives who are declaring their freedom from the capacity to embrace the Lord on a national scale. It used to be true that the righteous pride of the American people was well placed because of their focus on the spiritual good. This was a patriotic sense of moral accomplishment. Now, however, the entire prospect of being patriotic is demeaned as being a way to practice only prejudice against other people. It is now seen as appropriate to embrace foreign ideologies whose mission is to destroy the American democracy. Terms like 'nationalism' are abused as propaganda to describe an alleged movement by white European Americans to hold a grip on the civilized western mind-set of hard work and self-sufficiency. And, this in itself, is considered a dangerous movement toward the eradication of diversity and inclusion, which they believe must be fought against. Imagine this, the spirit that has founded a nation has been determined to be detrimental to the sustaining of that nation. The hundreds of thousands of war casualties who have protected the right of people to speak have opened the door for those speakers to denounce the very homeland for which those casualties died. You are seeing a new cohort of leftist representatives attempt to destroy the legacy of those who gave them the opportunity to come forward. It is the same concept of an animal growing to its fullest size and killing its elderly parents who are still trying to teach it right from wrong.

My Special son, this is the approach that American patriots should denounce in their reflections about your country. What would seem to be a benign movement of human and civil rights is actually an underhanded attempt to destroy the fabric of America. They will say that the same thing was declared about the civil rights movement, but they are wrong. In this new century, the movement has gone past equal rights and into the realms of marginalizing and destroying the race of people who allowed those rights to be granted. You and your brother are likely not surprised that the Mother of Jesus would speak to you about a matter that seems to have such secular overtones. I will refer again to the civil rights movement. You know that the call for equal rights in the 1950s and 1960s was based on the promises of a country that claimed to believe in God. Today, however, you are seeing a movement from leftist elements who are claiming equality while using an argument that contradicts nearly everything that God has said to humanity. My Special son, this represents a stark departure from the civil rights movement that met with such success during the years of your youth. It was a righteous movement back then, but this new declaration of independence by those who would destroy America is not about safeguarding its laws and proper ways of life. It is about diluting the goodness and propriety of a nation that stands, in itself, the lone beacon of human freedom. You are seeing the convergence of rancid spiritual ideologies with the tenets of the United States Constitution. You are also seeing representatives from the leftist media in the United States being paid billions of dollars by liberal activists who would rather see God removed from any mention in the government of nations. One would think that a script could not be written that would align so many elements in opposition to institutional honor and virtue. The entire definition of freedom on a secular level must find its nucleus to be the righteousness of the Church. These are among the many things for which we pray. My messages have come to you here as the Morning Star Over America because I am the Patroness of the Americas. I am the Lady of Wisdom who has come to speak to the wise about sharing the genius of God with those who have the greatest ability to transmit it. You will find in the decades to come and long after you and your brother have come to Me and Jesus in Heaven that you have participated in a movement of love that has meant the world to God."

- The Most Blessed Virgin Mary

Give me a world of sacrificial martyrs and mystics, visionaries and messengers; a world of Christian evangelizers, instead of a sect of theologized intellectuals. Tear down your ivory towers, pick up a Rosary, take to the streets and cooperate with the Mother of God if you want your life to have meaning. Give me little children who love their Heavenly Mother and the Son perched in Her arms. Our Lady has never in thirty years taken my brother and me into any more complex web of thought than a child could understand, but we know Her as well as any theologian, perhaps better. Our Holy Mother is gentle when telling theologians that they may not be the exalted gatekeepers to God they risk believing themselves to be. They are simply practitioners of mental frameworks constructed by other sinners which cannot confine the Almighty Trinity. Theology is not a cage for Christ our Lord, and neither was the Tomb. This does not mean that some of these frameworks do not maintain great truths amidst their scaffolding. It simply means that the Holy Spirit does not need to be audited and dismissed. He is not a Dove in a cage lined with the latest theological propositions. He knows what He is doing, and so does His Spouse, the great Mother of Jesus. She told me that She could have given me the greatest theological treatises in the history of man, but most theologians would have done nothing more than haggle over Her works, spread sparsing disarray, then dismiss them as irrelevant for a century, whereafter their progeny would have pored over Her gift for another five hundred years before they ever asked themselves why She had even interceded to dispense them. She rhetorically asked me what good it would do for the conversion of the lost in our time which we are running out of? She is here to touch the hearts of humble children who will listen, not titillate anyone's intellectual pride or throw pearls before swine. And, She cares not about the opinions of any celebrated sinner who claims everyone can simply ignore Her. The road to unity with God is not through radical intellectualism, but in the Holy Sacrifice of Jesus Christ and the Confirming Spirit coming amongst men. Then, comes the sacrifice which is pure action in the Holy Spirit guided by Heaven. Evangelists have authority by virtue of the truths they speak. There is no sacrifice within intellectualism that the Sacred Heart of Jesus recognizes. He knows the impediments to obedience that mentalism brings. Can we see the hubris that intellectuals generate if they have not been bridled by the great sufferings of Christ? Let he who wishes to know Christ embrace the Cross in all its desolation first, then he will have something to teach the world. How many intercessions of Heaven's Queen have theologians claimed the authority to reject? They have no such authority. They reject the Mother of Jesus Christ at their own eternal peril. Intellectualism has nothing to do with our hearts or our obedience to God. It is the arena of the gnat-strainers who are rejecting Her miraculous assistance altogether. People such as these believe that She is an extraneous option whom they fear is going to somehow overshadow Jesus and damage their ecumenical designs with people who have no use for Her anyway. So, their expedience calls them to retire Her to the far chambers of the Church, and only to be talked about as an accessory to Redemption. What kind of discernment is this? Jesus would tell them that His sinless Mother is not a stumbling block to any ecumenism that matters. The Angels and Saints look at them, puzzled by their lack of sense. It is ironic that they are not paused by the millions who flock to Her miraculous shrines and convert into great states of faithfulness — Hardened sinners falling to their knees like meteor strikes on the rocky hillsides of Medjugorje, weeping decades of repentant tears at the feet of Heaven's Queen. Nothing ominous comes over the intellectuals at seeing this.

It is just a peculiarity to them that they must guard against for fear of losing the power they believe they have and every listening ear that they have subordinated to themselves. I tell you, God will take it all away from them and give it to others. They fail to recognize and obey their Heavenly Mother when the perfect opportunity arises in front of them. This will be their earthly legacy. It is as simple as this. They do not consider surrendering themselves to the agenda of God through Her Queenship — a Woman clothed with the Sun and the moon under Her feet. It is a coming Apocalypse of the Eagle, indeed!

I know how our Holy Mother changed me, and how She helps me to remain changed each day. If She had not come, I certainly would have continued my reading of the Saints as I do now, imbibing in the example of those whom God blessed with the mystical friendship of the Holy Spirit in extraordinary ways. I would have always wondered what they did to be blessed with such deep relationships so that I could imitate them, even if a miracle never came. I would have remained faithful to the Catholic Church in which I was baptized and made every effort to build it up and not tear it down. But, I would have continued to be nagged by a particular sense. I could not have believed, even in all the great theological scholarship, for all the intellectualism developed throughout the ages, that modern men would ever know Jesus better than Peter, James and John who were exposed to none of our contemporary scholastics. They had three years, Mount Tabor, the Crucifixion, Resurrection and Tongues of Fire. And, they also had what my brother and I have; they had Jesus' Mother. They believed in the power of their Master like children, and great prodigies proceeded from their faith in Him. Even from early in my childhood, I was mesmerized by what Jesus said about asking in prayer and it would be done for you. *"Amen, amen, I say to you, whoever believes in me will do the works that I do, and will do greater ones than these, because I am going to the Father. And whatever you ask in my name, I will do, so that the Father may be glorified in the Son. If you ask anything of me in my name, I will do it"* [John 14:12-14]. This is a tremendous commitment made to us by our Lord. But, in my innocence, I always asked, 'If this is true, where is the miraculous? Where are the healings? Where are the risings from the dead? Where are the angels?' Greater works than these you shall do, He said. Nevertheless, I began to ask in His Name as just a little boy kneeling and praying with the 'Lovely Lady dressed in Blue.' I asked Her to 'teach me how to pray.'

My father read us the Bible stories of all the miracles and God's great power, and he taught us of our Holy Mother's intercessions, not as an afterthought, but as centerpieces of God's Love. And, in my prayers, I pondered not seeing this great power of God manifested in our day when it was so needed.

It was always storied blessings from centuries past. I speculated that if I was not seeing the mystical prodigies processing from faith in our time, then maybe I was not seeing true faith at all in the places it claimed to be. Whereupon, he came. I saw the colossal spiritual mightiness of Saint John Paul the Great, and verily our Heavenly Mother's actions accompanying him in our time. A great cathedral bell rang within me and continued to resonate. My spirit screamed, 'Yes!' Thereafter, he swept across the globe with great pontifical mysticism, and the Mother of God came to Medjugorje in 1981 just days after his great sacrifice of being wounded by an assassin's bullet. One decade later, She transcended unexpectedly to my brother and me in February 1991 on the Feast of the Chair of Saint Peter to complement the passion ignited in our Medjugorjian pilgrimages of 1989. She opened the pathway of mystical vision as opposed to intellectual mentalism. My brother and I did not have to climb, we were raised. If the theologians could see Her one time, everything they are cerebralizing over would have a flamethrower taken to it, which leaves me wondering what would survive the refiner's fire. It reminds me of a process where an artisan has a figurine over which they apply a dull paint. Then, they place the figurine in a flaming hot kiln and fire it for a short period of time. When the figurine is extracted from the fire, the dull painted surface is transformed into a smooth high-gloss finish that exhibits a reflective beauty that it never possessed before. Theology is the dull paint at best, the application of an initial state waiting to be transformed by the purifying fires. Two things possess the fire to make it beautiful. Prayer and suffering. They are the kiln that sustains the inferno to bring the beauty. Our Lady's miraculous intercession is one of the greatest accelerants in that kiln. But, She gives us the opportunity for our kiln to transform us by prayer, instead of suffering.

When Our Lady came to my brother and me, we chose to walk a path of belief until we were proven wrong so as not to offend grace. Here we stand almost three decades later as subjects of discernment, holding great opportunity for the world. For my part, I did not take the stance of rejecting until I understood all things and had each proven to me to be right. The imitation of Our Lady's Fiat was my example, not the disbelief of the Baptist's father. I believed in trusting God more than that. I reached out and cooperated to the fullest measure of my childlike faculties. I believed in a patient assessment of the extraordinary, not a fearful fleeing out of cowardice. I generated an absolute loyalty to the integrity of my brother out of fraternal love. God would never throw anyone into hell for honestly trying to understand and cooperate with something they were convinced came from Him through miraculous intercession. This is an authentic example of what Saint Thomas Aquinas would describe as obeying the Spirit-infused conscience which cannot be denied without sin. I put up no walls to challenge the Queen of Heaven. I have never been afraid after the initial moment She came to us. I knew in my soul that it was Her. I did not travel the road of intellectual comparison or sifting of anything. I did not scour history to determine any precedent for the graces my brother and I were being given. I simply accepted each moment as it came; I accepted every word She said and obeyed every request that She made, anticipating each day how I should respond in accordance with the faith I had been taught since my baptism. My heart knew what love is, and I knew I had been thrown into the kiln of the Sacred and Immaculate Hearts, and the fire was raging. What sinner's opinion can honestly compete with that, indeed, even my own? I did not raise my head to decide anything. I tested the spirits who attempted to convince me in worldly ways that I was embracing deception; and there were many who tried. The demonic attacks that Satan leveled against my brother and me were heart-rending to us. We were all alone, defending the opportunity for Our Lady to transmit grace into the world through our faith for the sake of the conversion of men. The evil one attacked my heart with any piece of the world that held comfort for me by ripping it away. My brother and I were assailed mercilessly by the devil, both psychologically and physically, for years. And to this day, he takes aggressive swipes at us as punishment for loving the Immaculate Virgin so much. But, we have been stable enough in our faith and in the mystical assistance that we have received to remain steadfast as witnesses that our detractors have all been mistaken. Our Lady protected and strengthened us with mystical graces all along the way. I have recognized deception when it arose because I have known that my soul is attached to the eternal truth of the events being shared by the Mother of God, and that my brother and I had been called to serve Her cause. The first thirty messages of 1991 were enough to bring my obedience to Our Lady into a state of permanence. In the beginning, I tested myself by asking why would I return to doubting as did those who stood in fear asking why we did not doubt as they did. They wanted to be comforted by seeing a crack in the armor of our certainty because they could not make the leap of faith themselves. Our unyielding witness convicted them. They were intent upon testing our spirits by battering us in order to prove we were wrong. Time has proven that they failed. No one's derision or defamation can outlast the Spirit of Truth. Untruth is too fickle and has no spirit behind it that can maintain its longevity and consistency. Our Lady said that if one is looking for Satan, this beast will create the perception of evidence that they are looking for. He is a deceiver from the beginning. He is always going to tell your doubts what they want to hear if it means keeping you from embracing greater faith. He wishes to keep humanity enslaved in doubts and worldly distractions, causing great turmoil in the intellectualism of men.

All discernment is for the purpose of the conversion, purification and sanctification of every soul without exception. I always remember that God loves us, protects us and truly wishes for us to know Him in every personal, human, mystical and miraculous way. I am now convinced the Holy Spirit works just as powerfully in our contemporary era as is described in the Sacred Scriptures. But, I also believe that sinners have the same difficulty accepting graces from God in our day as they did when Jesus walked the Earth. Fallen human nature has not progressed all that much, despite motives of credibility abounding for twenty centuries. What seems not to be prevalent among those who discern is the recognition that they can be just as sincere, but just as wrong to reject Our Lady's miraculous intercession as those who rejected every miraculous thing Jesus ever did. And, they do so for the same reasons. By the power of Beelzebub, they said. Isn't that the approach taken to Her miraculous intercession by most people these days? Discernment is as frail today, and obedience is left languishing in its stagnant backwater. Why did so few recognize Jesus as the Messiah, despite all the miraculous good He did? We must realize that our perceptions might be just as clouded due to original sin, while also believing we have expansive clarity to our vision and judgement.

There is also the issue of true humility. Sometimes I wish God would generate universal clarity in a very simple way for everyone to understand how corrupt and convoluted the intellectual arena where discernment takes place has actually become. Narcissism abounds in those who refuse to make the sacrifice to comply with Our Lady. Then, these narcissists join into collectives beneath mantles of authority thereafter to support each other in their darkness. And, authority claims many faces. Satan thrives in this arena of pride. The great gift of Fatima should have been enough for humankind to awaken and avoid the horrors of the 20th century. Why was this not the case? Why did such destruction and death overwhelm the Earth when She appeared in 1917 to help us avoid it? Well, the Holy Spirit found nothing combustible to set a fire upon the Earth. Too many who had the obligation to magnify their Immaculate Mother shirked their responsibility and decided to tell everyone else She was not necessary. It is the devil who tells people this. And, this phenomenon increased in intensity as the 20th century crescendoed in its godlessness. It has always been very difficult to convince any pride-filled intellectuals of anything, and courageous leadership is very difficult to convoke when the Cross stands on a hilltop looming. Most do not consider that their intellect is not their capacity for faith. Faith is about the sacrificial heart united with the Sacred Heart of Jesus in the Crucifixion. Intellectuals spend their lives creating and meandering through mental frameworks, while rejecting everything they feel does not conform to the pattern that composes their frame of reference. The question is, who gets to their frame of reference first? They are unprepared to grant any room for the spontaneity of the Holy Spirit on His own terms. They flee from any sacrifice too sour for their ego to taste. They fail to meet the challenge of God testing their faithful obedience to Him, and dismiss the opportunity to convert millions if they would simply comply. They have no idea how to fix our broken world while in such a state of spiritual lethargy, but tell everyone to ignore Our Lady and follow their dispassionate ways instead. I ask, where do they think they are going? Where are they leading humanity? Are the blind truly leading the blind? They believe their frame of reference is ratified by God, and the end of all ends, and they will bow to nothing mystically sacred. They have conceptual faith, but none that functions for the conversion of the world. I have always contended that there is not an intellectual in history whose mental framework could have withstood the Sacred Mystery of the Crucifixion on the day when it occurred. Intellectualism was the enemy of faith on Mount Calvary. Each of today's proud thinkers would have either run at the horror of it or stood by pontificating that they were justified in opposing such a blasphemer, at least until the earthquake of that afternoon hit. Judas stumbled for the same reason. The intellectuals who rejected Jesus actually believed His Death would solve the problems He was causing for them. He admonished their frames of reference and dared to tell the world not to follow their examples. Our Lady says this as well. The religious leaders who sent Jesus to His Crucifixion presumed without any veritable allegiance to the Most High that they spoke for God. The temptation to do this is just as prevalent today. I say again, religious leaders are expected to have faith too. And, many of them do. Everyone knows who they are because they shine like beacons, and are attacked because they do.

Our perceptions must be tempered to recognize the intellectual, hard-edged, ego-driven mentality of most people in the developed world. If you disagree with any of these people, secular or religious, they immediately recognize you as someone who is not affirming them. They feel the abrasion and that your unity with them has been fractured. And, since they believe they sit at the center of truth in their worldview, you must be the one who is no longer united with reality, not realizing that it is themselves who are actually separated from the truth through their pride. In the religious sense, they believe the separation is a sign that what you are saying is not of the Holy Spirit, and then they trot out demands of obedience to crown their willful pride. Criticism of faithlessness is not an offense against the Holy Spirit, no matter who it is directed toward as an edifying act of mercy. Those who refuse to believe never seem to ask themselves whether they should. They rarely consider that it may be themselves who are not in perfect alignment with the Holy Paraclete, and they believe surely you cannot be. They only recognize something as being of the Holy Spirit if you approach them and grovel to them, affirming everything they think, say, do and decide. Humbling themselves to listen and reevaluating the direction of their spiritual composure is usually out of the question. It is a rare messenger from God who can ever penetrate their estimation of themselves. If you call them to sacrifice, they will reject it. This is classic human pride.

The opinions of sinners about mystical things are actually no more than that. Unsanctioned discernment is littered with faithlessness, aggressive derision and dispersion. For example, simply because a multi-millionaire may have the money and time to raise a personal voice of doubt about our Holy Mother's miraculous intercession in Medjugorje does not bestow any authority upon him at all. Merely having the ability to write a book, create a website, appear on a television program, obtain a college degree or travel like a politician to sow seeds of slander does not mean one's vision has been sanctified in order to discern correctly the works of God. The arenas of cultural power are filled with cordial people of worldly influence who are, for the most part, lost; many of them headed for the fires of hell. And, like a fussy old English teacher, their going in search of unorthodox linguistic sentences in mystical messages that seem not to have been conjugated according to their view of contemporary systematic theological styles is no way to convince God that one is anything more than a strainer of gnats. Our God is not interested in checking any sinner's boxes of validity before He invokes His expectations that we exercise our faith and obey Him when He calls, especially through the extraordinary presence of His Immaculate Mother. Who could He send that we would listen to if not for Her? Name that person.

Why does our Lord give mystical gifts through His Spirit? What would any of us do if we gave a miraculous gift to the world which possessed the power to convert billions to Christ, but find so little kindling to set any appreciable fire? "Oh, not me," they say; "I am not going to place my credibility on the line for some sideshow." Jesus' contemporaries thought as much about Him when He appeared in their midst. This sounds more like those who said, 'Let us send this man to crucifixion to see if God will save him. Then, we will believe in him.' Should we not learn the lessons of wisdom from the necrology of our great Saints and how they were treated? Almost every person at Saint Joan of Arc's trial in 1431; Cardinals, Bishops, priests, theologians and nuns, sanctimoniously believed they were in complete conformity with the Catholic Church and the

Holy Spirit as they searched for Satan in this heroic Saint in order to burn her at the stake. Contemplate the deception that thrived even in these consecrated members of the Church itself. Jesus Christ was nowhere near their trial, except in the heart of a valorous French maiden who sat before them hoping to avoid their decree of execution. Yes, execution, because each of them knew and approved the inevitable consequence of their edict, just like pro-abortion politicians are responsible for the deaths of millions. Beware rejecting a beautiful Maiden coming to help you! I believe members of the Church should have a soul-searching conversation, and maybe a conversion, about this mentality because it thrives even now. We risk outright faithlessness being enshrined as prudence simply because Our Lady did not manifest Herself personally to the deciders. She asks what kind of faith does that require if She were to do that. No one has yet been found worthy to bring forth a message from the Queen of Heaven that matters, according to the discernment of many. I would say that the Church has been decimated in my lifetime, but the word 'decimated' only means ten percent. In fact, much of our collegial discernment in the Church is crippled by those with the weakest measure of faith who have surrendered to the highest degree of compromise with the secular and Protestant worlds. The Holy Spirit is beckoning us to rise and walk, listen and hear, and open and proclaim. If all must move together in unity, who are we waiting for to make the collective leap to trust our Heavenly Mother and obey Her? No one should wait until everyone believes before they move; rather, one should move so that everyone else is drawn to belief. There is a lost world out there. Unity never precedes evangelization in a world of pagan sinfulness; it is really quite the opposite. God draws people to Himself one faithful heart at a time, and sometimes there are people who will never come. So be it. Should we wait to manifest our saintly obedience to the Queen of Heaven until everyone converts from their stubbornness? Those filled with the Spirit of God have always led the rest in wisdom, sacrifice, self-denial and evangelization. Our Lady said that manifesting the collegial wisdom of the Communion of Saints is nearly impossible in a world of sinners because progress will be handicapped by the most stubborn sinner in the college. And, if Satan clandestinely enters those synodal ranks, he will stifle obedience to God and squelch the spreading of the truths of the Gospel, then lie about his prudent discretion and more progressive vision. Synodality does not work if saintliness in the image of the Crucified Messiah is not the composure of those ranks. However, Our Lady says that a single man filled with the Spirit of God can bend the course of history through his sacrificial obedience to Her. He can drag the rest kicking and screaming to the doorway of sanctification, even as the rest plot to deliver him to the Cross. These are very sacrificial statements that I am making, but they are the truth that needs to be contemplated. However, they must be tempered by the acknowledgment that the Roman Catholic Church is sustained by an honorable contingent of heroic Prelates and priests who are of great faith, and who would give their 'last full measure of devotion' to Christ and His Mother in the blink of an eye. You, saintly Prelates and priests, we hail you! Each of these brothers of Christ grieve deeply over the disarray caused by those in their midst who have forsaken the traditions and teachings of the Church, who have surrendered their sacred responsibilities to secular ideologies, Marxist politicism, expedient approaches, and sins of the flesh. They personally recognize the great gift of our Holy Mother's miraculous intercession in the world. Hundreds and thousands of them have shown their devotion and witness in visiting our Holy Mother's miraculous shrines. But, they know they do not possess the power or the venue to convoke the universal collegiality of the Church and lead the response of Roman Catholic Christendom in magnifying the wishes of our Queen as they might passionately desire. Only those Bishops who oversee episcopates in which Our Lady manifests Her miraculous intercession have the unilateral power to convoke this magnification, like a lens focusing the rays of the sun to set holy fire upon the Earth. So, we pray for the day of opportunity where clarity comes and heroism ascends to the Crucifixion because there are legions of faithful followers who are consecrated to the Most Immaculate Heart of Mary and the Sacred Heart of Jesus who will rise beside these saintly Prelates when the battle to end this age commences.

Remember that most any person who claims miraculous intercession has been condemned at the drop of a hat by the ego-stricken people I have frankly admonished. Our Lady once told me that those who are looking for evidence of Satan will find him because the evil one will plant the evidence amidst their frail discernment in order to skew their perceptions away from the truth of Her grace. They approach Our Lady's miraculous intercession by meandering around saying, "I know Satan's here somewhere, and I am going to find him; just give me a century or two." God presents the clarity, but Satan tells the observer it is really too good to be true. Some people are terrified that the devil may be lurking clandestinely in every place of miraculous intercession. Well, of course, he is. That's what he does. He is always prowling. This is why we invoke the powerful intercession of Saint Michael the Archangel. Saint Michael came with Our Lady on Palm Sunday 1991 in a great sign in the sky at the commencement of Her intercession to my brother and me. Our prayers to this mighty Archangel are not hollow wishes. He is our invocation of protection upon everything holy we do, and He stands at our side. But, under the arena of Her authentic intercession, it is the first doubter that allows Satan entrance who becomes his instrument, and our collegial response as the Body of Christ disintegrates from there. The devil and his minions launch their mission to stir doubt and fear any time God exposes extraordinary intercession from the heavenly Hosts in the realms of men.

Let us engage a contemplative scenario. Suppose Our Lady initiated an actual authentic intercession to show Her love, granting us the opportunity to encourage hundreds of millions, perhaps billions, that Heaven is real and wants something from us. She petitions everyone to sacrifice their agendas, then listen and obey so She can guide us all, knowing that the measure of our collective response is proportional to the power that will effect the magnitude of Her converting intentions. What should discernment look like in this authentic situation? How should discernment serve the Most Holy Trinity? What does perfect faith look like? What does collegiality mean? How does God want humankind to respond to Her? The truly humble soul recognizes Her voice, invokes their faith, moves into a path of obedience and rejoices at having a Mother so beautiful. Then, they tell the world the grace they have come to know. Their perfect response is 'Fiat' in imitation of their Heavenly Mother. Their discernment is instantaneous in their faith, simplicity and humility, and they act. They act! Their response is full. Jesus said, "My sheep hear my voice, and I know them, and they follow me" [John 10:27-28]. Those who respond like children invoke a direct reciprocity, unmediated by the pride-filled snares of intellectualism. But what of the others? Their discernment does not originate in faith, simplicity or humility. It originates in their intellectualism, untempered by the humility and innocence of a child. This goes to the heart of the question about whether faith is predominately an intellectual construct or if it is a relationship in the heart with our living God whom we commune with at every moment through our sacramental Communion with Him. The most intellectually-challenged person in the world may be the greatest saint, just as the widow who placed two small copper coins in the temple treasury gave more than all others combined. What happened to intellectualism on the day of Pentecost? Usurped and obliterated by miraculous intercession. Do we know Christ and His Mother well enough to recognize them when they dispense extraordinary grace to us? We should. And, if we recognize them, are we not obliged to respond? Does not the responsibility in our age fall upon us? The intellectual construct of faith is simply a description, as best can be generated, of the mystically-driven Sacred Mysteries which are beyond the descriptions of human intellectualism. We must live in the latter, while not dismissing the former. Reception of the Most Holy Eucharist gives us more than everything that has ever been contemplated and written about it. We must unite in the Mysteries, not stand around mulling over the descriptions and bantering over theological interpretations. Jesus addressed this same misalignment when He confronted the Jewish leaders of His day. They functioned in the intellect with rules, regulations, tenets and commandments. And, none of them were able to recognize the Author of those Commandments who stood before their eyes, while Our Lady responded to the miraculous intercession of the Archangel instantaneously, and Saint Joseph believed Her from the depths of his soul, but only after he experienced the miraculous intercession of an angel in his dreams.

What our Heavenly Mother would like everyone to see and realize is the storm of thoughts, attitudes, perspectives and responses that we as human beings invoke upon being presented with anything that tweaks us to look at ourselves more honestly. It is truly like a thundering tornado with projectile debris filling the air. This is no way to convene discernment. How does the Dove of the Holy Spirit fly in a tornado? It seems to be so easy for Satan to obscure our Heavenly Mother's miraculous intercession. He can defer its benefit to the world for a century with the bat of his eye due to the traditions of skepticism that he has anchored in the orders of discernment. God is not inclined to blast away this faithlessness just yet, knowing He will be triumphant at the last with a revelation that will leave us grasping for a reason why we would not listen. He knows that He has done His part in repeated ways in every century. He simply hopes we will contribute our part because chastisements are descending upon our contemporary world if this is the only way He can get us to come to Him. He can take away the distractions of Satan in one fell swoop. Our Lady echoes the Gospel, "Do not persist in your unbelief, but believe."

Question 11

How would you respond to people who would say that you are arrogant and often harsh in your assessment of individuals and secular American society? Are you afraid that you are projecting a lack of humility or charity that is impeding your message and causing people to doubt the authenticity of your claims of the Most Blessed Virgin's intercession?

There is a phenomenon that Satan is leveraging to maintain his reign of darkness. It is characterized as "smile and keep on coming," because contemporary Christians like smiles over virtuous truth. Satan is using the accusation of arrogance and lack of humility against us to dull, and effectively silence, Christian opposition because we are afraid of being accused of being unChristian, which is a definition he wishes to control. He has coopted our culture of relativism to arrogate a position of ideological standing that he claims must be respected. Our Lady thinks differently. She asks us to remember our baptismal promises. The father of lies chides people to throw away the hierarchy of reasoned morality at the same time he is demanding that everyone be required to respect the hideous ideas that he foments. Are secularists in America even slowing down to recognize that God reigns supreme? Do they honor and obey the King of kings? Satan wants to be indulged, as do those who serve him. And, if you proclaim the narrow path of Christianity, he will accuse you of being rigid, vitriolic and divisive. There is a difference between being arrogant or harsh compared to being uncompromising in the call to holiness. We need to do better. We must do better, and we must realize it, or there is no future. For those who wish to doubt all that is of God, there will always be a pedestal of reasons for them to rest their skepticism upon. And, even if the authenticity of claims such as those of my brother and me were proven to be undeniable, the most stubborn of men will resort nonetheless to personal attacks upon the messenger by claiming some perceived character flaw so their consciences can dismiss them from responsibility to their Heavenly Mother who is calling them. They realize we are calling for an end to their relativism in the Name of Jesus Christ. Are we to pander to those who reject this call? Her messengers are not jesters who are required to entertain the mercurial pride of insolent worldlings. The humble believers in those crowds are a blessing to themselves and the Mystical Body of Christ, and we love them immensely as our brothers and sisters. So, no, I am not afraid of those who are dismissive of our Holy Mother's grace because there is nothing for which I am going to be held responsible related to anyone's refusal to believe in this moment of Her visitation. I will be held accountable if I do not speak firmly and clearly what I have been asked to relate [1 Corinthians 9:16].

Imagine if you had the mystical gift of hearing the Communion of Saints cheering when you spoke, and knowing by their response when you spoke well. Would you ever care about the howling of dissenters who jeer at your words? Conversion is not about patronizing anyone's armor of feelings which they strategically don to defend themselves from accusations of depravity. It is not about being respectful or generous to relativism and granting it undeserved leeway to distract and destroy souls. It is rather about confronting it, overcoming it, superseding it and eliminating it in the glorious unity of our relationship with Jesus Christ and His Mother. They love us. Those who wish to make this sacrifice are beautiful to God; those who reject it are ugly and unsightly, and possibly doomed. Our Lady has told me that the invocation of faith is a sacrificial act that belongs to each person. No one has the capacity to actually force another person to believe anything, even at the tip of a sword. If one is truly concerned about mental oppression by an aggressor or the forcing of ideas upon a group of people, why do we not admit that it is actually atheistic secularists who are executing psychological warfare against the citizens of the United States, as well as the parishioners of Jesus' Original Apostolic Church? Through the force of intimidation, they demand respect for abomination through their diabolical authoritarianism. For the record, they are now legislating the outright killing of newly born babies. In the face of this wickedness, no one has the right before God to demand silence from a Roman Catholic because they do not like what they are hearing. Our Lady has told me to be unfazed by those who reject and turn away with scowls on their faces. The Saints and Martyrs endured far worse than unsavory parting glances. My brother and I are simply to play the part assigned to us.

If I knew a shape that I could assume so that every person would believe what our Holy Mother has dispensed to my brother and me, we would attempt to take that shape. We are doing it now. It is the shape of nearly thirty years and twelve books proclaiming the Morning Star Over America, with further personal messages and works that are ongoing. It is a configuration of sacrifice absent marital love, family comforts, children, material opportunities, successes, and worldly accomplishments that we could have rightly secured through our educated faculties instead. It is a single-minded Marian consecration to the agenda of the Final Colossus. It is a constellation of stars above the head of Revelation's Woman clothed with the Sun; stars that testify to our conformity to Jesus Christ in His Life and Death, leaving our resurrection to Him alone. If the Cross does not convince a soul of the Truth of the Gospel and the reality of sin, then that soul is damned. What more could a loving Messiah do that would matter? But throughout the ages, He has tried and tried again through the Sacred Mysteries of His Church and the faithful people who have surrendered in unity to its sacrificial wisdom. Additionally, He sends His Immaculate Mother from the Heart of His Church, along with Angels and the Communion of Saints, into our realms to intercede and explicate His Divine Revelation in mystical ways where He hopes everyone would listen from their heart, be enlightened and convert. "Peace on earth and goodwill toward all men..." This is the hope heralded by heavenly angels 2,000 years ago. Those strains still ring today in the hearts of Christians who have been commissioned by the Christ Child to speak the truth, admonish, counsel, forgive, love, seek reconciliation and evangelize those who despise us for the beautiful story we relate and the responsibilities we ask them to accept. The story is about sacrificial conversion into unity, not prosperous fraternity in diversity at its expense. All in all, Christians should be better acclaimed for their witness to the virtues of Christ than being worthy of ridicule for things that other sinners unilaterally determine to be momentary failures. Jesus gave the Sacrament of Reconciliation because He knew that we would all need it. The question is, do we respect the purifying grace of the Sacrament that is imparted in those confessionals? Do we allow our brothers and sisters to be redeemed there, or do we just continue to caricature them as unredeemable sinners bearing no voice of legitimacy whatsoever? So, enough with the gratuitous attacks upon faithful Catholics who take seriously the evangelization of the lost.

The main point is that there is no perfect medium of communication between hearts until we arrive in Heaven without faith being invoked. Its conduit is in the faith to love our neighbor as ourselves in the Spirit of Christ Crucified. It is sometimes disappointing to realize how difficult it is to communicate with others in this modern day. Even these words are difficult to compose in a way which actually gives dimension and clarity to my heart which generated them. No one seems to own the meaning and intent of their own words and gestures any longer. Under the guise of discernment, debate, analysis and rebuttal, a person's intentions are dismantled and reconstructed by adversaries who are flush with personal agendas and arrogant hubris pertaining to every subject imaginable. There seems to be no such thing as humble acceptance based in faith and truth that respects the nuances and degreed complexities involved in most issues, especially the miraculous intercession of Heaven's Queen. We function along a bipolar spectrum of partisan sound-bites that have no more depth or clarity than a mud puddle. Our Holy Mother does not want us to analyze Her, but to obey Her. Indeed, what kind of person believes they have the capacity or authority to critique Her? It is the very definition of radical audacity, pride by any other name. She has given enough and does not deserve humanity's pursed faces. Yet, She continues to be generous in the dispensation of Her great charm for the sake of the holdouts, knowing they have no future unless they listen. Dishonest special interests are all too willing to hijack honest declarations, contort them beyond recognition, reassign their meaning, magnify their own personal misinterpretations of them, and impale the speaker as either a bigot, lunatic or demoniac with the false evidence they have illegitimately conjured. As an example, our political affairs are bloated like a dead corpse with mistrust, demagoguery and acts of outright lying, cheating, and stealing that are masquerading as simply "professional politics" that must be engaged. Character assassination, slander, deception, falsehood, duplicity, hypocrisy, treachery and manipulation of the masses are the order of our secular government, with the garnish being a brash, naive, socialist twenty-something with no historical perspective and a Twitter account who garnered enough votes from her minuscule district to pontificate and prevaricate to our nation as an official member of the United States House of Representatives. The official levers of governance are weaponized against political adversaries, and the ideological arms of the partisan media complex are full-on sycophants manipulating the menagerie to maintain viewers for profit. The shame is the suffering of the embedded good people in their ranks who have no true power, but who surrender to the partisan line of their superiors to maintain a career in order to care for their families. The political machines are not filled with people who respectfully disagree with one another while holding common moral goals for our societies. Most have no morals, nor any goals for spiritual integrity. They function through expedience in the maintenance of their secular power. Our government is dominated by fanatical sects who deeply hate one another and do not make a move unless advantage is gained for their personal ideological agendas or utter humiliation is inflicted upon those who oppose them. This is not cynical; it is the truth.

The modes of communication between people have always been imperfect mediums. Sometimes I wish God would just allow each person to read every other person's heart, much like some of the Saints were capable. Then, no one could hide their deceptive agendas behind any false pretense or stature. No one could lie about another person's motives or intentions. Having the capacity to intimately know the origin of another person's thoughts in order to better understand them would be very revealing. But, look how others, especially media personalities and partisan comedians, assume the power to define the origin, character and motivations of every other person's body of communication, yet completely overlook their own wretchedness. Beams impaling eyes, while they search the world for splinters! In truth, they have no such power to assume, just temporary worldly force which in due season will come crashing down upon them at their eternal judgement. Their lies and condemning conduct will be part of the indictment that will be announced against them at their judgement. Only the Holy Spirit gives the gift of discerning power. In His absence, these people make themselves nothing but thieves of human communication who steal the truth from others, then accuse their victims of being the burglars.

Have we also noticed how people are triggered by the adjectives that are used in other people's speech and writing? Egos hate adjectives used by other people. Think about it. When an adjective is used to describe a noun, it implies that a person has made an observation and value judgement regarding something about which they are communicating. Adjectives hint at the elevation and value of something in a hierarchy of influence. For example, one could innocently say,

'People will go to Heaven.' But, if you are someone who adds a clarifying adjective, '*Some* people will go to Heaven,' it immediately invokes an impression of a decided quantity which presents a target for radicals because you have added a limitation on who will get there. It offends their relativism, their autonomy, and their self-acclaimed authority to define Creation for everyone else. Many in our radicalized culture believe no one has the authority to evaluate existence and attach any adjectives to "their" world without their approval. These tyrannical ideologues believe they are the arbiters and enforcers of our cultural parameters and how each person may speak, think, decide and act. This is the extremist residue of the fascistic authoritarianism of the 20th century which seems to be innate to human sinfulness. We should ask ourselves who bestowed any authority on these rebellious provocateurs? The answer – no one; not even God Himself. It is Satan who gives them the force they wield because they have rejected the Commandments and conceded to the same temptations that he thrust upon Jesus in the desert. They believe they alone are authorized to decide the adjectives according to their ideologies, and they do so to either obscure or tear down the structured traditions and norms of divine grace erected over the last 5,000 years, the descriptive elements that characterize the stability of human civilization as the Holy Spirit brings it to maturity. They do not want to hear that only "some" people will go to Heaven because they know they are in the group that is doing nothing to get there. Even our Christian orthodoxy is guilty of this compacted authoritarianism at times. Our evangelization seems to be stuck in doing nothing more than regurgitating the generic orthodox prescriptions of our faith that are repeated over and over and over ad nauseam from textbooks as if from people who are suffering from some autistic abnormality like "rain man." They refuse to let Love speak. We talk from our brains and not our hearts. Then, Our Lady arrives and floods our world with mystical adjectives describing Her vision of Her Son, and the religious intellectuals are thrown off-guard wondering how someone would dare tamper with their sentence structures. They did not even know adjectives existed. We should instead be telling the world how much we love Jesus and His Mother, and using every adjective that we can think of to do it. Our Lady's miraculous intercessions are God's great adjectives that He has adorned about the Church to bring clarity and amplitude to the nouns and verbs of the Deposit of Faith. Most are saying, "The horse runs," when our 'secretarial' God is thundering through the maternal amplifiers of Creation, "He is running like a tremendous machine!"

Unfortunately, we now live in a country that has had the faculties of human communication moved into perpetual attack formations through partisan media outlets and social communication platforms which are overrun by infantile nitwits who could not care less what another person may be honestly trying to relate, let alone respecting the First Amendment to their own secular Constitution. But, Our Lady says, 'Let them come! Let them tell the heavens who they are! Let them announce their final words before they greet the Son of the Most High!' They have enshrined the meaning of analysis as being synonymous with the marginalization of opponents. Hamstringing the truth with lies is an actual political strategy that most stripes of consultants and public servants have perfected to the demise of everything truthful about interpersonal communication. Integrity? It seems that none know what it is because it has been thrown out along with the bath waters of baptism. Politics is a demonic wasteland of some of the most egregious liars, deceivers, charlatans and manipulators that the world has ever seen. They would yell fire in a sold-out public movie theater just to get a seat. Controlling the sound-bite is a manipulative scheme and actual strategy because the political communication experts realize that only a minuscule few are actually paying attention so as to be in touch with the deeper motivations that are simmering in their quest for power. They are pandering with quips and retorts to their peanut galleries who are, for the most part, oblivious to any moral truth or the practical outcomes of their atheistic progressive politicism. Maybe we should consider applying slander and libel laws to both our politicians and news media, and allow any citizen to file suit. They might then call a truce because none of them wish to expend their fortunes on lawyers battling each other and the nation's citizens in courts of law; but we might all be the better for it. Make no mistake, these groups I am referring to are headed for the fires of hell for their sins, as well as condemned in the historical refrains of our country for having destroyed the moral fabric of the greatest nation ever to have been seen on the Earth. This is factually what they have wrought. Their work is nearly complete and ready for the onslaught of Saint Michael the Archangel. They have driven the moral character of the United States to its knees and flat on its belly to heave the dirt of secular demonism. I can only hope that my mode of communication is clearly understood as containing the seriousness and truthfulness that Our Lady intends. Someone has to proclaim the spiritual dimensions of the eternal truth. It is not a joke that the Queen of Heaven comes to help us; it is ominous of the Great Reckoning which She says to be swiftly approaching.

Our beloved Virgin Mother has spoken very gently and meekly to six visionaries in Medjugorje every day since June 24, 1981. She ponders why so few of the world's leaders have listened. Why is it only the little children who seem to care? God is willing to provide different approaches and tones to His intercession, hoping to penetrate the secular roar and ecclesial hubris. And, that penetration brings the confrontation between the droning ideologies of the devil and the mystical Truth of Almighty God who is reaching into the world to save us. Has the final separation of the sheep from the goats actually commenced? One might ponder whether it has begun as we look at the fractious culture wars that are being waged. The audacity of evil is crescendoing. Our Lady speaks from a position of great power and authority. None of my forthright descriptions should be received as if any depression or weakness is being portrayed by them. My words are a warning of the triumph of righteousness and truth that is going to fall from the heavens in a blizzard of authority. I am not going to grieve on that day. I am going to scream in jubilation as the unrepentant wicked are heaved into hell, and the Light burns its gaze upon the history of man. There is no futility to be found in the cultural stature of the faithful because the overwhelming victory belongs to Christ who will wield our deliverance as the mighty King. I say, woe to those who do not listen during the time of our Holy Mother's mystical visitation. Reaping and reckoning by the Archangels is on its way. The politics of today will be torched and all its participants sifted for anything left that might be salvageable for the realms of Paradise. The chaff will then be discarded into the inferno to the glee of the Saints and Angels.

But, let us speak of the opportunity for holiness instead of the inevitability of punishment. Our Lady has told me many wonderful things about Her children in the United States. She says that we are a special breed of self-assuredness. Our forebears displayed a titanic will as a nation that has taught the generations of Americans to engage anything, challenge everything and stare into the face of destiny with courage, resolve, determination, and a good measure of brash audacity. There is a reason that this nation was brought to its feet in so many good graces and spiritual powers; and those seeking entrance into it should revere what God has impressed into our American spiritual identity and learn from it, not hold it in contempt or seek to depose it. The composure of Christian civilization which radiates from the Seat of Christianity in Vatican City touched the New World in the founding of the United States of America. God has attempted to preserve the liberty of human freedom in His grace in a very pinnacle way through the rising of our country and its people. He raised it to such might, wisdom and presence as a firewall to the great evils that would come, and to give the world a chance for His Kingdom to be manifested in peace. We have been bequeathed a legacy that has molded us with an almost impenetrable expectation for the future. We expect to define human civilization; we demand to be its stewards. For most of our history, we have done our best to respect the rule of law and the Eternal Lawgiver. We have subdued and elevated the capacities of the human will to unleash unimaginable achievement. This has come through hard work, sacrifice, common purpose, love of homeland, moralized human freedom, suffering, devotion and a desire to know and defend what we believe to be our right to define our lives. We have been gifted with amazing confidence in ourselves that seems almost surreal to anyone who would observe us from the outside. We fully expect without doubt that our potential shall bear the fruits of our will to survive, prosper and revel in human accomplishment. We throw off opponents to our progress as if batting away trifles. There is nothing we will not do to guarantee the success of civil liberty. This is how we live. Our Lady simply wishes for us not to see Her Son Jesus as one of these opponents. She wants us to remember that there is no true freedom without Him, and certainly no salvation into the heavenly Paradise we are now seeking in such materialistic and worldly ways. Somewhere amidst our steely convictions and independent idiosyncrasies, She says we must carve out a respectful softness and pliability that allows us to be led by the wisdom of the Holy Spirit. This is where Jesus and Herself are finding it very difficult in these modern times. They feel that their whispers of gentleness are being deliberately lost in a typhoon of combative secular wilfulness. Our countrymen are primed, locked and loaded for any battle that confronts them, including the spiritual one. God sees us as not respecting the gentle voice of His Holy Spirit where we would be encouraged to remain on noble paths. So, what is He to do? Punish us? Destroy us? Level our institutions and raze our great cities to the dust? ·Well, not yet, although September 11, 2001 was an ominous message. He believes that we must be reminded in ways that impact our realization, yet still respect our capacity for faith. If we are not willing to listen to the gentler side of God and obediently respond, He becomes more than willing to increase the volume of His righteous Voice. He will let nature speak for Him in its most aggressive tones. He will bring the reign of justice to men's battlefields. He will engage the ultimate confrontation between Light and the night. He will lift commanding authority to its feet in anonymous men, those who will invoke their faith and be obedient enough to grab the reins of destiny from the despots leading a nation as great as America to its demise. And, the irony? It has little to do with assuming the command of political or material systems. It is about either purifying them or preparing them for their defeat. It is about crushing the demonic spirit with prejudice. It is about capturing hearts and busting them open to the Light. It is about getting the big things right, and cleaning up the splinters in the aftermath. It is about the transformation of a dimming flashlight into a laser beam that can cut steel at fifty miles. It is about throwing down the

Rock of Truth into humanity's path without apology, but with such devotion and sacrifice that lost souls will wonder what just shook the ground beneath their feet. Then, the earthquakes of nature will stand aside in peace, knowing that men will finally proclaim their Crucified Savior who created them. We must become tempered by the cardinal and theological virtues of prudence, justice, temperance, courage, faith, hope and charity. And, since we are a special breed of such intense will, they believe a frontal assault is not altogether inappropriate if Americans will not listen to, nor respect, the legacies of the Church Triumphant who have loved them and provided them such a beautiful country. Saints cannot allow their loved ones to travel the road to eternal doom without warning them. If they have to hurl stones into our path, they will most assuredly do so.

All the same, the questions above are very good for any Christian evangelizer to ponder, realizing as well that Jesus was the full spectrum of the human person perfected. He is neither an effeminate wimp, nor remotely a metrosexual. He is a King of such masculine qualities as to be worshiped. Do we think Jesus could drive out demons because of His gentleness? Why did demons cower before Him? He did not try to convert them; He banished them at the leveling of His word. His restraint in not destroying evil outright is only temporary and merciful. He is not a wallflower; far from it. He has the power of eternal command. He challenges everyone with blanket authority and blatant impartiality. His blunt altercations with the thinkers and gatekeepers of His earthly day were numerous, and now biblically legendary. Read the New Testament. His rhetorical exchanges would get Him killed even today, and for the same reasons. In this age of rampant atheistic relativism, both high principle and objective truth have been usurped by those who betray an offensive sense of self-importance, and have claimed an authority they do not own. So, Our Lady would ask who the arrogant ones really are? Why is God asked to grovel before sinners, lest He be accused of offensive arrogance in His efforts to save them from the eternal fires of hell? A question could be asked as to what does the American character look like wrapped in the grace of God and brought to its feet. What legacy will the contemporary American Saints of the Catholic Church leave to the story of the ages? If our entire cultural disposition, aptitudes and soul could be wrapped in the grace of Jesus Christ, imagine it! What might the United States rise to be at the calling of the ages, if we would but listen to Our Lady as the Morning Star Over America?

The Mother of Jesus told me that each Saint has in their time brought their own witness to bear, while attempting to evangelize the Gospel with their lives. She said that not every one of them was a diminutive piccolo or a waving harp.

Some were trumpets calling for conversion through their blaring reports. Others were kettle drums that beat a marching cadence of daily duty and suffering. Still more were the angelic voices of accompaniment that sang their sacrificial arias in harmony with the melodies resounding around them. Many were warriors commissioned to defend the Church Militant across God's earthly estate. And, some were unobserved mystical ships passing in the night that steamed to a destination that they alone would seek out. Some of them conquered the intellectual domain and organized it in the realms of grace; others were as challenged by academia as fence posts, but as esteemed in Heaven as the heralded Aquinas himself. Nevertheless, all were giants of the heart in their unity with the Spirit of God in the Holy Sacrifice of the Altar. Our Holy Mother said that we must always remember that none of them were shrinking violets. The Prince of Peace also thundered, but could lay the gentlest hand upon anyone wishing to repent and seek His blessing. Have we ever wondered why the planet quaked at the moment of His Death? Was it because of His inflated self-importance as the Son of God? Hardly. It was rather the crack of His dominion upon a kingdom of darkness that He had just uprooted, leveled and destroyed. Where were the arrogant wagging tongues at the moment of that rock-bursting apocalypse? They were running in terror like cockroaches to hide themselves from the justice of Almighty God for what they had done. And, that Justice still lives. Look at Saint Paul compared to Saint John. Both were unique reflections of Christ in His power through their acceptance of the Holy Spirit in their era and circumstances. But, while the Bible depicts St. John with a seraphic meekness complementary to the Most Blessed Virgin whom he would care for, St. Paul was a spiritual warrior who got himself abused, mocked, beaten, stoned, and martyred because of his glaring convictions and fearless confrontations. He threatened his presence upon the wolves who worked to disperse the flocks he had gathered. He spoke directly and forcefully to his opponents. He had the faculties to confront everyone, including Saint Peter himself. This is what the Holy Spirit commissioned him to do, and we now revere him as one of the Pillars of the Church who stands beside that Proto-Vicar, both of whom have spread the Kingdom of Christ to the far corners of the globe. Dear God, please place pillars atop these faithful fathers and build your Church to the heights of your Celestial Kingdom!

Declaring someone arrogant is usually nothing more than a subjective opinion from someone who does not like what they are hearing. Their frame of reference is being impacted, and they do not like it. Our Lady has characterized it to me as them saying, "How dare anyone talk to little ol' me like that?" Instructing the ignorant, counseling the doubtful and admonishing the sinner are definitive responsibilities of mercy, for there is eternal judgement approaching like a tsunami's wave the height of ten thousand Mount Everests. Being confident in the Truth and declaring the obligations of our faith has nothing to do with arrogance. It is about Salvation. It is our sacred commission. It is mercy. It is a confrontation with the lie of relativistic pluralism. In a country filled with people nurtured in individual pride to the point of abject narcissism, how low does one have to grovel to avoid piquing at least some of these overtly-sensitive consciences? They are the ones who cry arrogance first, which is nothing more than projection and deflection, while they stampede through Creation, dominating it with their own will. We have baptismal promises to keep. Do you reject Satan, and all his works, and all his empty promises? If you do, then you have to reject secularism because it is his vomit. As it stands, we seem not to have the courage to reject anything unholy, while having the temerity to kick Holiness in the teeth, right before escorting it to the curb and running it and its companion Virtue completely out of town. We are compromising with those who are peddling lies and bringing great suffering to bear upon the innocents with their immoral debauchery. What unity is possible with any person who believes in the slaughter of a child in the womb? I reject what they do and the beast they serve. Jesus did not say go out and "hint at the Gospel" to all nations. He said to proclaim it, even from the housetops. "And He said to them, 'Go into all the world and preach the gospel to every creature. Whoever believes and is baptized will be saved, but whoever does not believe will be condemned" [Mark 16:15-16]. Based on a simple observation of our culture, there seems to be quite a measure of condemnation looming. And, the swift retort from the guilty is that I am not their judge. Our Lady told me to respond to them confidently, "No, I am not your judge, but I am to tell you how you will soon be judged."

Now, do we employ aggressive declarations and strident retorts at every turn? Of course not, because the spiritual state of our audience matters. But, Our Lady says, 'there comes a time.' We must be ready to give reason for our faith and defend the reign of God Most High. Our opponents are not shrinking violets either. Roman Catholics must not take another step back for the sake of the outcome of the world and our ultimate accountability before the Crucified One. What have we gained by remaining silent as a satanic abomination has swept across our nation since January 22, 1973 when the slaughter of this nation's innocents was enshrined in secular law by the U.S. Supreme Court? Those seven Supreme Court justices have answered for their crimes before the Throne of God, each and all. Can we imagine the fire of Truth they stood in? They failed the United States of America and sixty million of its children who had the right to life, liberty and the pursuit of happiness. Our Lady told me, as well, that if there had been even a modicum of organized opposition convened against abortion, the media companies would have cooperated to outlaw it by now. The days of hunkering down in cowering defense are over. What sacrifice will we make so the Gospel may be heard? What darkness will we confront? What Cross will we accept? What Light will we bring? What leaders will lead? How big of an offensive will we raise?

The greatest sacrifice is to tell humanity the Truth of Jesus Christ in His Roman Catholic Church. It will take you to the Cross in this relativistic age of religious pluralism. The enemies of Christ have expanded the narrow path into a twelve-lane meandering interstate freeway paved with sin, mediocrity, and compromise. In the economy of Salvation and the propagation of the Holy Gospel, unrepentant sinners will always hear arrogance in the voice of Catholics who are advancing the supremacy of the Original Apostolic Church in their domains, while the Church Triumphant will weep at hearing the Voice of Christ resounding in the world once again. The frame of reference within each person determines how the Voice of the Holy Spirit is interpreted and embraced. The wine skin of the Scribes and Pharisees interpreted the Voice of Jesus Christ as being the most blasphemous and arrogant that they had ever heard. 'Who does He think He is speaking to us this way? Is He not merely the carpenter's son from Nazareth? Where does He get all this? How dare He proclaim Himself to be God's Son. How dare He think He can forgive sins.' And, they killed Him for it, thinking it would silence The Word of I AM. Then came the earthshaking, rock-busting power of the third day, and they stood horrified, unable to do anything more than conjure lies to cover their deeds. Is this the way worldly powers act in every age? Our Lady hopes not.

I have always contemplated many situations and what would be my response if those things were to happen. This is what I ponder. How would we act if Jesus came to each baptized member of the Catholic Church and commanded that each of us convince one hundred people of the beauty of our Faith within the next month or we would never see the Kingdom of God? How might we evangelize the Faith then? How might we beg for the conversion of others? What sacrifices would we engage, knowing then, the wisdom that begins in the fear of this great Lord? With what conviction would we go out into the world knowing that our own eternal salvation might be hanging in the balance? Now, this is not the case, unless you believe Mark 16:15-16 might contain that responsibility. But, what is it going to take to motivate us as Catholics to fulfill our commission of evangelization of the Truth we own? We are to be more than 'happy accomplices of worldliness' to others. Jesus said that we would be His friends only if we do what He commanded us. Our Lady is giving us a reason to become His friends, for if we do not, the threshing floor awaits us. The Morning Star Over America stands asking. She is trying to motivate us as Her evangelists to proclaim the Gospel of human Salvation in the Cross of Her Son, while there is still time; and She has given us a weapon in Her miraculous intercession and the message texts She has dispensed. She is saying, 'Be united. Be faithful. Be one body. Be Roman Catholic.' One only risks arrogance if they do not possess the justification and authority for the high pronouncements they declare.

Question 12

About the Sacraments. If someone who receives the Sacraments does not believe in their powerful Grace, does this mean that their soul does not receive them in full? (i.e, the Sacrament of Extreme Unction, Confession, reception of the Holy Eucharist, etc.)

Each of us probably possesses some measure of deficiency in our belief in the powerful grace of the sanctifying Sacraments; and this is not a sin, but simply a state of weakness or vulnerability. Our Virgin Mother taught me a lesson about this early in 1991 when I asked Her "how" Jesus is present in the Eucharist. She, in effect, responded to me by saying that my question indicated doubt on whether I actually believed the consecrated Bread and Wine from the Altar had actually become the Body, Blood, Soul and Divinity of Jesus. She finally said, "Do you see Jesus when you look at the Most Blessed Sacrament?" I said yes; then She responded, "So do I." Nevertheless, there is a discussion to be had about what it means to "receive" the graces. For instance, when we take the Most Blessed Sacrament onto our tongue and consume it, we "receive" the Infinite in its completeness, but our intellectual understanding and the state of purification of our frame of reference affects our recognition of "becoming one with" that divine Person. So, it is not about "receiving," because we receive in full. It is rather about the flourishing and incorporation into our spiritual character of this fullness that may be affected, especially within our intellectual composure. We must remember that our intellectual belief is the most rudimentary plateau of our faith. It will always fall by the wayside in the heights of divine revelation. Engorging ourselves with intellectual knowledge does very little to actually effect our "mirroring" of Christ; it is prayer and suffering in union with Him that conforms and enlightens the soul. Our Lady says that faith and belief are two separate things. Belief can ebb and flow. Faith is constant. The Faith confirms that powerful graces are received through the reception of the Sacraments. Belief is accepting what happens to us at their reception.

Oftentimes, it is like throwing a bucket of water on someone, and then they look at us and say, "Missed me" as they stand soaked to the skin. They are wet no matter what they believe. And, in the case of the reception of the Holy Eucharist from the Catholic Altar, God overwhelms our soul with His completeness. The great blasphemy is to lie to God and Creation by saying Jesus' Sacrifice did nothing for them. Ultimately, God will allow their declaration to be true as they plummet into hell, although they may have consumed the Bread which gives Life during their mortal life. God's dispensation of grace is unaffected by our response. He is loyal, even if we are not. "If we are unfaithful, he remains faithful, for he cannot deny himself" [2 Timothy 2:13]. Every grace that is received through the Sacraments has already been imparted to the world in Jesus' Crucifixion. There has never been any take-backs. When someone receives a medicine, do they not receive the full dose each time, although it may take several courses to be fully healed? The medicines are applied in their most propitious course with the intention that the body will ultimately be stimulated to comply with the healing agency. The Sacraments of the Catholic Church serve the healing, reorientation, sanctification and salvation of the soul. Life is that sanctifying process in action where we receive the healing Sacraments in their proper course. And, the more our beliefs become one with the Faith and everything that flows from it, our conversion and transformation become perfect. We become an animated creature in spirit, thought, and action that is the successor to the First Born of all Creation, our Lord Jesus, He who has many brothers and sisters. This is the same succession that is alive in the Pontificates of the Roman Catholic Church over the past 2,000 years.

Question 13

Discuss your relationship with your non-Catholic friends. Are people open to your discussion about the Roman Catholic Church, the Virgin Mary, the Pope, and other Catholic issues in places where you go, e.g., restaurants and cafes, your workplace, taverns, athletic stadiums, and other secular places?

To the question, 'Are people open to our discussions about the Roman Catholic Church,' the answer is, 'not as Our Lady would wish.' And, it is not solely their fault, as most everyone we meet, especially the millennials, have been surrounded and indoctrinated with godless secularism and humanistic narcissism, accompanied by a pluralistic vision of human dignity, where the concept of objective truth has been replaced by individualistic relativism and self-glorification. Now, I know this is a rhetorical mouthful, but true nonetheless. Most younger people are simply reacting to the cultural environment that is lying to them at every moment. They have fallen into the morass of believing falsehoods. It is like one blind man talking to another, and both accepting the 'fact' that there is no such thing as light. They are convinced of it. But, the fault belongs to those who should have taught them better from the times they were children, along with those who have militantly placed the Christian heritage of our country under siege. I often ponder how these progressive revolutionaries are going to judge themselves seeing the destruction they have wrought. The moral collapse of the 1960s has come of age where nearly all seats of power in our country are now occupied by people who have no sure-footed bearings in moral truth. As a nation, we are submerged in greed-based humanism as the pinnacle of aspiration. It is an ideology that attaches an overriding importance to matters of the flesh and our sinful humanness rather than our divine spiritual origins as children of God. Corrupt humanity is worshiping itself. Truth is touted as being what anyone happens to think it is at each given moment; and when these individual convictions conflict among the cultural powers, it is the group who can congregate the largest lynch mob through the national and social media and other public accommodations who dominate the culture as fascists would do. Force, intimidation and authoritarianism — these are the sad fruits of relativistic immoralism. But, this does not mean that all people who struggle in the secular void are evil or unredeemable. Our Lady would say that most of them have simply been misguided and now find themselves in a deep dark forest, not having the foggiest notion of needing to be saved from it. They are in a fight for dignity and survival when they do not even know what they mean.

The vision comprising our culture has been inundated with lies that vast multitudes believe to be the truth. Indeed, if the light inside you is darkness, how deep the darkness actually becomes. We are experiencing a cultural death, and the killing of babies upon being born is the approaching midnight of our darkest hour. This is why Our Lady has revealed Herself as the Morning Star Over America. She is a person hailing of Divine Authority who is providing a glaring contradiction to what the thinkers of the world deem to be important. And, that vision is both chastening and indicting to them. It is difficult for those who think they own the truth when the Mother of all Truth makes Her appearance. It is like a squatter in a house opening the door and staring into the eyes of the homeowner who has just returned. Our Lady's grace is confronting their paradigms of thought and their estimation of how insightful they believe themselves to be. Secular intellectuals have to deal with what the Queen of Heaven is doing because it is becoming too apparent that She is convicting them of being blind. There is nothing they can do about it; history has already recorded their delusion and that their conversion is necessary, or else. They must respond or lose all credibility as philosophers and oracles of the human domain. They are a voice that is growing more hoarse by the moment, and are destined to become mute. At present, they mock, dismiss and slander Her miraculous intercessions as fanciful aberrations that only deluded impoverished people would believe, much like the derision they heap upon the Catholic Church itself as being filled with a bunch of weak-minded parishioners who refuse to accept their so-called progressive ways. They should be far more worried about how Jesus intends to protect the dignity of His Mother from their blasphemy. He may decide that He will never allow them to see either Himself or His beautiful Mother...ever.

In our interaction with this cultural phenomenon, Jesus told us that He would give us what to say in our engagement with the world. Each person we meet is an individual unique soul that God is hoping to fill with Light. There is no cookie-cutter approach to these encounters. Meeting each person is a discernment process that occurs in conjunction with the fruits of the Holy Spirit that we employ toward any child of God whom we are asked to love. Many of them are our brothers and sisters who have spent their lives interspersed among wicked souls who are lost and will never see the Kingdom of God. The fruits we employ are love, joy, peace, patience, goodness, kindness, faithfulness, humility and self-control. Each person has a unique frame of reference and interior constitution, a matrix, that in our contemporary day is usually in a state of unfocused understanding related to who they are and how God loves them. My approach is described in the motto: Lift them up! People know whether you care about them or not. Each person has a simple, tender heart inside which is oftentimes buried beneath great suffering and sin, and sometimes struggling with tremendous guilt, oppression and evil. But, our Holy Mother told us never to be complacent by believing that Satan cannot come and stare us right in the eyes and smile like our most dear friend. Our mission is not to be liked, but to deflect humanity toward the Truth of God's High Kingdom and the true meaning of their lives.

So, it is a mixture of approaches, words, conversational subjects, and opportunities. I rarely attempt to theologize intellectually with anyone, nor do I get into scriptural parsing with Christians who protest the Catholic Church. It is usually a waste of time. I simply ask them to be honest and read the earliest Church Fathers, and then ask themselves whether those leaders of Jesus' Church nearly 2,000 years ago believed as they do now. Then, I ask them to explain our Immaculate Mother's miraculous intercession throughout history and in our time. Usually the conversation ceases at this point because they are not remotely prepared to honestly engage the mysticism or the historical integrity of the

Church of Rome. They know that one of the hallmarks of the Roman Catholic Church is the veneration of the Most Blessed Virgin Mary. They just do not know why. Most others I try to take to the source of who they are, and how great they can be with just the innocent intellect of a child. Sometimes opportunities take years to cultivate at the expense of great sacrifice. And, sometimes what we start is completed far in the future by others. We are never to audit someone's response as to whether they have listened or if there is compliance on their part. Should evil be admonished? Most certainly, but we rarely waste time stoning the devil's dogs. Foremost and at a minimum, we encourage others in a way so as not to instigate their evil actions, if they may be looming. Most conversions happen while people are alone in their rooms when face to face with the mightiness of God in their thoughts, and maybe what we have said to them. The greatest thing they can draw upon in those silent moments is that we thought their soul was beautiful and created for infinite happiness. If they accept this, they will make heroic sacrifices to convince themselves and others. And, this occurs through the strengthening of their faith through their own sacrifices and prayers. Sometimes someone only knowing that you take your faith seriously and attend Holy Mass each week, or perhaps daily, is enough to crack the door of their faith. They compare, as people most often do, their conduct and beliefs to that which you take comfort in. They are looking for meaning. Stature, poise, compassion, understanding and simple good-heartedness are effective qualities in creating a moment of unity with another person.

Then, there are those who are arrogant, outright destructive, vocal, evil, aggressive and have no intention of being open to the Spirit of God, although they may have great capacities for intellectualism and fraternity in diversity. These are the people I reserve for my greatest poignancy. Satan wraps great crowds of ne're-do-wells around himself who do his bidding. They will hover around you and feign friendship to exercise their intellectual autonomy over you. They like the psychological jousting, as if their faithlessness matters to God. They like sparring with your attempts to impress a change in them. They pine inside for you to try to convert them. After every encounter, they swell with a sense of pride and power that they were victorious in the argument and did not succumb. They are deluded to believe they have actually achieved something by holding the truths you speak at bay. They feel power over you by withholding any compliant faith, while they watch you grovel trying to convince them. They are the lot of humanity who use their time in the service of the devil to destroy. They mock and slander, deride and conscript others into their heresy and blasphemy behind your back. They want to know your approach to souls so they can create new defenses against any newer avenues of grace that they may have yet to encounter. It is ominous for them when they discover that they have no worthy defense when faced with our Heavenly Mother's miraculous intercession. They simply dismiss it with a wave of the hand, which is of no intellectual honesty at all. And, them getting close enough to engage any honest discernment of Her works? Forget about it. My brother and I never cower from these people, but are keenly aware of who they are and their capacity for inflicting physical harm and secular punishments. They will punish and penalize you with every force they can wield, given the opportunity. A soul who is undisciplined and filled with this evil intent is an easy target for Satan to use to cause great disturbance and violence. We do not have to engage a manifest sinner if we are aware that it is Satan begging us to engage him to generate an even greater atrocity. Our Lady's approach when confronted with people such as this is to turn and walk away from them, leaving their supposed power broken as the beauty they were always looking for turns its back to them. Tell them that you have no message 'for them,' that your words are only meant for those who will be redeemed, and that you do not care whether they believe anything you say. Tell them to go to their destiny. Kick the dust from your feet in testament against them. In fact, this is the final thing they are ever going to see at their final judgement—God turning His back and saying, "Go your way into hell." Pride gets us nowhere but damned. Yet, many a sinner has been converted because of an evangelizer's stern rebuke. It echoes like thunder bouncing off the walls of the barren canyon of their conscience. Cowards run around in the underground trying to avoid the law. Heroes search inside themselves as to why there is the law.

Another important perspective to remember is patience. Some people force a lifetime before they will convert because they lack childlike humility. It sometimes takes many seasons of cultivation for the seed even to be planted within them, let alone grow into a field of grain. We must not be afraid of the strong nature of evangelization that is required sometimes, as the Holy Spirit prompts. Jesus will let us know when it is appropriate to dispense the stronger inflections of His Spirit; and no one has the authority to admonish us otherwise when the Holy Spirit calls for our engaging witness. It is the cultivation that busts up the soil. Many people in the Church abhor anyone standing up strongly for the Truth or admonishing sinners in reprimanding ways because of the disturbance that usually ensues. Those reprimanded nearly always cry their victimhood, and the lukewarm believe it pushes people farther away from the Church. Our Lady says this is not true. It actually reveals where they truly are, and gives them the opportunity to move closer someday. The spiritually timid profess their instability and cowardice before the evangelic demands of Christianity. This is not Woodstock, microbuses, and flowers in our hair, while all wallow in the happy fraternity of mediocrity and sin. It is the seminal battle for souls in the realms of the eternal Spirit. I have often pondered that if I would leave this life hated, but the result would be that everyone would finally accept Christ and His Mother because I spoke, it would be a sweet life indeed. Is this not what Jesus Christ really did and what the Crucifixion was all about? When lukewarm people see cultivating engagement in its due season, they most always run to the sinner being admonished with consoling words that the true disciple was not acting like Jesus at all. What these people do not see is the smile that comes across the interior wickedness of the one whom they are consoling at finding another gullible Christian who will compromise their faith and waste time groveling before them out of respect for their pride. There is also satisfaction in these wicked hearts that they can use this "consoler" to assault the courageous disciple who would not put up with their blasphemy. I am convinced that each of these "consolers" would have run to the Scribes and Pharisees to commiserate against Jesus after witnessing His thundering rebukes in the Temple during His cleansing tirade. Our Lady would say, "*Oh, give Me a band of brothers who will stare down the evil of this world. With the Cross, shame it, mock it, dethrone it. Take up My weapons. Launch your salvos. Tell the Son of Man you are on the move with your swords of truth and breastplates polished. Release the captives and call upon Saint Michael to throw the demons to their everlasting doom.*" My friends, fear no one walking away because you spoke the truth loud enough to be heard. Let them go, do not flinch in your convictions, and stare into their eyes as they look back over their shoulder wondering what kind of power they just faced. Admonish sinners and rebuke evil, but console those who wish to take up the sacrifice. Invoke the spirit of Saint John Paul the Great announcing "Solidarity" in the face of the demonism that sought to kill him in his youth—"from the housetops!," he said in Cherry Creek State Park in Denver, Colorado in 1993.

If we think about this in the terms I related before about the matrix of man's interior constitution, these strong altercations of the Truth of God are nothing more than an opposite procession of grace through the faculties. Instead of perfect grace flowing through an open thoroughfare from the soul into their existence through faith, it is blocked by the matrix of their old wine skin. They are actually incarcerated and require someone to break the lock that Satan has put on the door. Our act of mercy is an assault on their matrix from the outside in, from our heart to theirs through everything separating those two hearts. We dig deeply into their misguided beliefs in an attempt to gouge out a place for

Christ, if not puncture all the way to their eternal soul itself. The worst impediment to the converting of a soul is when an admonished person comes looking for re-affirmation of their error, whereupon they approach a marginal Catholic about the conscience ringing in their soul, and the Catholic comforts them by extinguishing the voice of their conscience and saying the admonisher was not being Christlike. The sinner finds affirmation for their previous state and returns to it with approbation and reinforcement from the marginal Catholic. Does not Scripture say that once a demon is cast out and the house is clean, given the opportunity, he will come back with more demons worse than himself, leaving the final state worse than the first? [Luke 11:26] This is an example of it.

All the rest, those who are suffering the misfortune of never having been told of the beauty of Christ and His Mother; they are the beautiful children who just need to hear the great stories of devotion and intercession, of the legacies of saintly conviction and heroic sacrifice so they can come to know how special they truly are. Again, 'Lift them up!' If our Virgin Mother's miraculous presence is ever given venue universally by Roman Catholics as a body of faithful Christians, beauty and comfort will sweep across the meadows and bring soothing relief to those who labor in darkness. It is a phenomenal moment when one actually realizes that God is real and that we are loved in ways we always dreamed.

Question 14

What makes you believe that the apparitions that you claim to have experienced and the locutions you say have been given to you are authentically from God, and not the deception of the evil one?

This question is asked by one who admits that they are not able to recognize Jesus Christ and His Mother. For if they did, they would readily see the work of Jesus' Mother in the Morning Star Over America. They admit that they do not know Christ well enough to accredit His works, although the evidence is abundant right before their eyes. Jesus said that His sheep know His voice and they follow Him. Therefore, we must not harden our hearts when He does speak through actual graces that He wishes to be communicated. The answer is really very simple and harkens to Sacred Scripture. All authenticity is rooted in our communion with the Holy Sacrifice of Jesus Christ and our faithfulness to the Roman Catholic Church. And, faithfulness to the Church does not mean being submissive to the personal, whimsical or worldly perspectives of every religious intellectual with a few letters behind his name. The ticket for entry into Heaven is not a diploma. The evil one will ask you to sacrifice nothing nor convert to anything. He instead promises rewards of worldly esteem and power, freedom from responsibility, material riches, and satiation of the flesh. He will encourage your pride and ego to run according to your own will and your own glory. He promises that the world will love you if you follow him. And, you will never be questioned about the authenticity of your mission should you do so. In others words, do the mystical experiences encourage you to succumb to the temptations that Jesus faced from the devil while in the desert? Or, do they call you to the Cross and its sweet sacrifice? In addition, does the message flourish in harmony with the Roman Catholic Church and its 2,000-year tradition of virtue through its Communion of Saints? Obviously, someone who would demand that we prove our claims is really more worried about the sacrifice they will have to make, should they admit the truth in them. They see obedience and say, "I will only serve on my terms." So be it.

In regards to the revelation of the Morning Star Over America, each person will ultimately decide for themselves. Our witness rests before humanity as a reflection of the Gospel itself, that each person may discern whether they see and hear the challenge of the Cross echoing from this witness in our time. In the end, it does not matter how many times my brother and I declare our Holy Mother's work to be authentic or that it is as real as real can be. That proof will come in time, but it will be too late for the holdouts, doubters and skeptics who could have so profited from it. We pine for people to accept, but the assent of faith that each person invokes is their act, not ours. It is their cross that they must assume in order to cooperate with their Virgin Mother in these ominous times for our homeland. Our Lady has simply been allowed to provide the opportunity for us to be elevated into greater realms of beatific grace when the only other option before us is unimaginable desolation, darkness and death. My brother and I, along with the many who do believe, have tendered our allegiance to everything our Beloved Mother wishes to accomplish as the Morning Star Over America. We will be vindicated for our faith at the Triumph of Her Immaculate Heart. The rest will simply stand wondering what it was that kept their vision so darkened, realizing then that they never truly knew how beautiful and powerful She really is. They will one day wish they would have believed. This is a prophecy that will come true.

Question 15

During your conversations with the Virgin Mary, does she ever preempt your questions by addressing issues about which you have yet to mention? Does there seem to be a particular time period that she will speak with you that she will not allow to increase? In other words, does she speak to you as long as you pray, or do you stop praying when her messages are through?

My relationship with our Virgin Mother, as well as my brother's, is expansive across decades, and has taken on many extensions and alterations. It is authentic, dimensional and maturing with each day. Her conversations with us are influenced by many things, just as our conversations with our friends are seasoned by our experiences and the events in our mutual lives. For example, if you met a friend whom you knew just had a baby, how could you not bring it up? She often speaks in themes and inflections that are influenced by the liturgical calendar of the Church which She respects and uses as anchors to many of Her devotional instructions. She addresses personal experiences that my brother and I have faced, the troubles that She senses we are dealing with, joys that have impacted us, and of course, the particular teaching or facet of wisdom that She wishes to impart to us on any given day for our communication to the greater world. On most every occasion when She transcends to us, She speaks privately to us about certain subjects; few of which are recorded in any of our writings, or ever will be. She anticipates many things intuitively, but also prophetically. She accompanies our lives, just as your friends or family might accompany yours. I am very respectful in the questions that I place before Her, while She nearly always asks whether I understand Her words and if there is anything that I would like to discuss with Her personally. I revere the sanctity of Her presence and kind attention by not asking curious questions about irrelevant things. I would rather listen to Her than have Her listen to me. And, if anyone asked Her about speaking with any of Her children, She would graciously say, "I would rather listen to your heart than do all the talking." She would prefer to listen to Her children profess their love for Jesus and the heavens than reiterate things that She wishes we already knew. I try to never purposely take advantage of any privileged position to belabor Her about future things or hidden knowledge that would diminish my life of faith or my sacrifice in the flesh. I do ask about the progression of our work in the world at times, and She might give me information of what is occurring beyond my sight on occasion. She says that She does not want to diminish my joy by preempting my surprise of things to come. She wishes my brother and me to live our lives as would any other person, even while She is generous in sharing knowledge, even of the future, that might help us maintain our perspective and composure as Her sons. But, it nearly always comes through Her motherly initiative because I rarely pry. The times that I have asked for specific information that is behind the veil, She will query me first on my purpose for wanting to know the information, then She will teach me some lesson about it before answering. Sometimes, She teases me with comical responses if She feels I have asked something inappropriate. One day, She was teaching me about the mind-set of our financial culture and I asked for specific information about what a certain secular individual was thinking at the time. She deflected my question with the statement, "Did I just discern a hint of insider trading?," then She giggled, but I understood.

One thing we would profit from realizing about Her revelations of the future is that we have the ability through prayer to influence, change and choreograph the future that we may ask about. Hence, She is very cognizant of our free will that She not damage our life of faith, although She has been rather dramatic in Her revelations of future things to us, indeed to the world in previous and ongoing appearances. We should also realize that Satan acts in different ways according to what Our Lady might reveal. He is a vile beast who has the ability to act with a free will. He wishes to both make it appear that She is wrong and to impede Her plans in any way She might advance, if he comes to find out what they are. He will hone in on particular events and people, and manipulate the consciousness of his legions to fight against anything She might say. Every person still has free will, whether for good or evil intent, and each can be tempted to evil or inspired to holiness. She is careful to say in timelessness what men can manipulate in time. We must realize that She will always be right, but sometimes it takes a lifetime for us to believe it. Although prophecy is a true spiritual gift, its utterance, even from Our Lady, very rarely locks in any predestination where the free will of mankind is rendered moot. When She speaks of chastisements to come, it is nearly always with the caveat, "...if men do not convert their hearts," and our discernment should realize that this is implied, even if it is not spoken outright. We always have the free will to convert and avoid chastisements. Then, there is always the point of no return when it is apparent that men will not change where She may state unequivocally that particular events will come to pass or when God will intervene through His own Divine Power. It is a form of protecting us from Satan that She reveals things in very prudent ways. She protects Her work this way. Yet, She often blesses us with knowledge that we would not ask for ourselves. If I am burdened, She knows it, and offers Her compassionate Heart if I wish to speak with Her specifically about unknowable things. It seems to be nearly impossible for Her to speculate about things as would a friend because She knows in fact everything about the subject you approach Her with. There is no speculation for Her. Hence, She will ask many questions of me in these situations to help me through dilemmas, instead of definitively offering Her knowledge of the actual answers. So, our personal conversations are somewhat different than ones we may have with our friends or family members. She guides my path, at times, by way of spiritual deduction through the prescience offered by the Holy Spirit.

She spoke with me at length in the earlier years about the dimensions of things that we were experiencing and the impacts that our hearts were enduring. It was a very difficult time for my brother and me. She has been there for us all throughout our maturing years to where we are now. Although I believe that our Virgin Mother would tell me anything I wished to know about the future of humankind, there is not much that I am interested in knowing. I always ask myself whether it would be of benefit to souls and ponder what good it would do. If I thought anyone would listen without mountains of skepticism, I would beg Her to let me chronicle the closing ages of history, minute by minute. But, contemporary evidence tells us a completely different story as most of the world has summarily rejected nearly everything She has said so far. Why would any more prophetic knowledge of the future be looked upon any differently? Scripture says as much in the parable of Lazarus and the rich man when Abraham said that "...if they do not listen to Moses and the prophets, they will not be persuaded even if someone rises from the dead" [Luke 16:31]. It is amazing to realize what it takes to convince anyone of anything. God could prophetically reveal through His Mother every detail of what will come in this 21st century, and it would be rejected, and the tragedies would come nonetheless because humanity loves the darkness. It seems that only the remnant of faithful little children will accept Her revelations and prepare themselves. They are the ones who are already on the Ark. Just as in the time of Noah leading up to the great flood, so will it be again. "For the coming of the Son of Man will be just like the days of Noah. For as in those days before the flood they were eating and drinking, marrying and giving in marriage, until the day that Noah entered the ark, and they did not understand until the flood came and took them all away; so will the coming of the Son of Man be" [Matthew 24:37-39].

Another dimension also exists in our conversations with the Hosts of Heaven. The Dominion Angels have been allowed to speak to us and assist my brother and me with direction and edification. They are angelic beings of unique spiritual character whose example is not seen in this world. There are thousands of them at work beneath God's reign. The Bible says myriads and multitudes. Our Lady has introduced us to several of them by name so that we would know them personally and call upon them faithfully, including the name of their leader whom I love dearly. I have not revealed these names because I recognize the possibility for confusion in the Church which rightly discourages anyone "naming" an angel. They already have beautiful names given to them by God. We should not, in effect, give them nicknames that are not worthy of them. But, it is different when those names are directly revealed to us either in Sacred Scripture, or through authentic private revelations, which has happened in our case. Anyway, the Dominion Angels giggle in unison like tiny children of great innocence and playfulness but, at the same time, are mastered geniuses in eloquence, statesmanship, negotiation of creation, and prescient anticipation. They portray impenetrable happiness that is wrapped in serious potency. Their mystical presence is a posture of complete power. Humanity has rarely conceived being faced with total dominion that does not care about what any sinner personally thinks. The demands of political correctness have no effect on them. They are only defined and driven by the righteousness and truth of God. They are unfazed by the opinions of sinful creatures and respect none of us, yet they love us in the Holy Spirit of the Most Blessed Trinity who created them. Many people define love by whether someone agrees with their demands. The heavens define love by whether we agree with the Sacred Heart of Jesus. There is not a deferential bone in the spiritual bodies of the Dominion Angels toward any sinner, and they cheer when any sanctifying suffering comes upon us. They can shred and destroy the enemies of Jesus Christ in the blink of an eye, and laugh in victory while doing it. They are so happy to see the world cleansed. They have instructed us how to engage our enemies many times, and taught us not to flinch in our holy admonishments. I feel so sorry for those that the Dominion Angels become focused on for engagement, for I know their reckoning is on the way. They can invoke a form of medicinal justice and make any reprobate answer for their crimes at any moment. I have marveled as their discipline has unfolded upon our enemies too many times. They can remove roadblocks with a puff of their breath. I affectionately call them the "wrecking crew" at times. They can destroy falsehood in a blinding flash without a whiff of apology. No man or beast is any match for them. They command too many circumstances and effects, and possess too much powerful wisdom. Even while resembling the tiniest of children in their mannerisms and demeanor, they exhibit monumental power and dominion, and can convoke consequences like battle-seasoned warriors, whereupon they giggle while executing their disciplinary actions. I find it odd watching grand atheistic intellectuals pontificating in debates and interviews on the television at times, knowing just how vulnerable and delusional they are, while failing to realize it. One Dominion Angel incarnate sitting beside them on one of those panels could humiliate them where they would crawl back to their closet and hide themselves for the rest of their lives. These people do not know into what weakness and enslavement their pride has taken them. They are merchants of destructive intellectual fabrication and fallacy. Their self-delusion is colossal and will meet its imminent doom. Our Lady said that Christopher Hitchen's pride met this fate, while the prayers of Saint Mother Teresa and the Roman Catholic Church, both whom he hated, obtained Purgatory for him to his ultimate joy. This is Divine Mercy.

The Dominion Angels are not preferential to my brother and me when it comes to obedience. It is ironic to us that they can take such joy in our experiencing uncomfortable consequences after dismissing their advice, thinking we might have somehow known better. They see these consequences as healing us, after we did not choose the better path of loving obedience to them. They are not bashful when giggling in unison, "We told you so," when my brother and I ultimately face the discomfort they were counseling us about. As a primitive example, in their efforts to protect us, they have on occasion warned us not to eat particular foods from the refrigerator, or during our dining in some restaurant we may frequent. Imagine being famished and before you is one of your favorite foods that you were pining all day to eat, fully prepared and piping hot, and the Dominion Angels say, "Don't eat that." Not only is your ego frustrated that you are being told not to eat it, but there is no evidence to you that it is bad other than their word. It is even more difficult when they withhold their warning until after we have gone about the effort to prepare it, just to have it thrown away. Or, imagine ordering a fully prepared meal from a restaurant and have the waitress place it before you, and having to tell her you cannot eat it, having no proof that it is bad, but paying for it anyway. It is an act of faith and a sacrifice of obedience to comply. Imagine this happening in the company of others at a table, and the invocation of faith that must be generated to comply in those moments when no one else understands what has just happened, and you cannot tell them. Can we see the scope of self-denial and obedience in this, and also the benefit that the sacrifice allows? This is one way they have strengthened our execution of faithful obedience. It has been a great gift because every time we have not obeyed in these circumstances, we were usually sick from the food being unfit to eat. Will they always protect us this way? I do not know. It depends on whether Jesus will ask us to endure those sufferings in reparation for the sins of the world.

The Dominion Angels have protected us to the measure we have allowed through our obedience to their word. But, it usually takes the overcoming of our ego as a sacrifice to comply. My posture is, they ask it, I do it. They say it, I believe it. They want it, I ask when. This interactive relationship has many dimensions related to numerous subjects. They assist, but not without our sacrifice. It is a continuous, 'Do I believe in this moment? Do I immediately surrender my will?' Every single time that my brother and I may have wondered how their words could possibly be accurate and having no proof other than their word, our pride was later humiliated and we suffered the consequences if we did not obey. Before them, we know nothing contrary to their word. This has helped me realize the sheer magnitude of prideful pontificating among people who have no idea that their willfulness is meaningless, and is a bit audacious before God. The world suffers so many debilitating consequences because people refuse to obey the Holy Spirit in the moment. How long does our Heavenly Mother have to appear and speak before we obey Her? Who is it that says we do not have to believe Her? The consequences will come for the deniers and skeptics, just as consequences came when we did not take seriously the counsel of the Dominion Angels regarding our appetites.

Back to the point, Our Lady's conversations come through our union with the suffering of Jesus Christ Crucified. She has said that mystical gifts come through the diminishment of the flesh. As a contemplative exercise, imagine that God would allow the Most Blessed Virgin to appear and speak with you, but you would experience suffering commensurate with the heights of the revelation during the length of time that She was actually speaking. Imagine the devil inflicting terrible human suffering to your body during the length of Her conversations as punishment for your faith. How long would you allow Her to speak to you each time? If Satan overtly blistered you with torment in a hundred different ways as punishment after every mystical encounter with the Queen of Heaven that you embraced, how many times would you kneel to pray for Her to come again? If for every book that you wrote and released to the world, Satan would lambaste you with misfortune, harassment, indignity, sickness, physical injury and mental oppression, how many books would you write and publish for Her? If you do good, the devil will come after you like a fanatical pitbull to the measure of the effect you are having in damaging his sinister reign. But, fear him not. Tell him to bring it on because the Cross is your destination and Jesus is your Glory. Every spiritual gift that is given to this world comes through our union with the suffering Christ. This is also one of the scents of authenticity within miraculous intercession, but it is sometimes difficult to see because the recipients often hide these dimensions.

Question 16

Isn't it a pretty big leap for you to ask non-Christians to believe that you are interacting with a "God" whom many of them have either never heard-of or have already rejected as irrelevant in the ongoing nature of everyday life? If not, why?

Is it a big leap for tiny children to believe what their mother tells them? It is no leap for them at all. They giggle in excitement at what's next. Tell us more, they say, as they lie on their pillow enraptured by the voice of their mother regaling them a story of honor before they fall asleep. Truth has its rightful and natural place within them. Non-Christians and unbelievers who are hardened by a secular life are often more like teenagers who believe they have outgrown bedtime stories and disregard every morsel of wisdom anyone tries to impart to them. What is the difference between tiny children and those who do not believe what their God does to touch them? People should see their lives more as an unveiling process rather than a static exercise of experiencing each day which has already been defined for them. The question should be, am I more than I was yesterday? What is my heart seeking? Anyone who approaches life this way will eventually come to realize that Jesus is the Messiah and Savior of the world through their own honest conclusions. Conversely, those who seek out nothing more than an epicurean identity which devours sensible satisfaction will remain as deniers and skeptics without any elevation of their soul into what they could have become. What evidence do the deniers and skeptics have that the words of my brother and me are not true? The answer is they have no such evidence, just their own frail opinions detached from reason, evidence and revelation. They should better realize that their worldly opinions do not matter to God or Our Lady, nor do they matter to us. These people are in the untenable position of being separated from the wisdom of their Creator. And, consequences loom which they will endure on the day the Truth is finally revealed where their pride can no longer be sustained. They will find that they were wrong, and that they forfeited what life could have been. They will see that the truth was trying to penetrate their lives the whole time, while they rejected it with impunity and prejudice at every step. They will see what they could have become and the glory they might have secured. Yet, Christians have hope that each of them will be the laborer who took to the field in the later hours to gain their full day's wage [Matthew 20:1-16]. God wishes us all to accept His Only Begotten Son now, in these times when it is easy to discover Him, in these times when it is like tiny children playing hide-and-seek with their father. The father goes to hide and the toddler peeks around the house looking for the one they love, knowing he is there somewhere. Then, the little one opens the closet door where the father is hiding, and the tiny child squeals with delight at seeing his face as he scoops them into his arms and twirls them around in joy. Any person who does not know that a game is being played also does not expect anyone to be behind the door. They believe they are in the house all alone. But, when they open the door and suddenly see someone standing directly in front of them whom they do not know, are they not startled in great fear? God wishes us to be like tiny children looking for Him throughout the house, instead of being an adult who is suddenly brought to terror because an unknown intruder is found to be in their closet.

Faith is a true entity that initially presents itself to us in our minds as a concept or idea that has huge dimensions and implications. It is the original mustard seed. We become aware of the "idea of faith" and what it asks us to accept, believe and do. It is as simple as this in the beginning. It may come to us from any number of directions and present itself in any number of forms. It may be a mere mention by a friend, or the knowledge that they are Catholic and go to Holy Mass every Sunday. It may come in the passing of a loved one and our wondering where they have truly gone. It may be that we are touched when witnessing the most beautiful sunset we have ever witnessed and wondering how something so grand could be merely an accident of nature. It might be the miracle of innocence in a newborn child. It might be in the first inspiration to open the New Testament and read its words the first time. Do we ever wonder where that first tiniest inspiration comes from, or how many times we might have pushed it away? In Truth, those tiny inspirations are the voice of God. They are the actions of His Holy Spirit. They are graces. And, when we hear someone who is encouraging us to learn more, or encounter someone asking us to attend them to Holy Mass, or find ourselves in tears at a vision of beauty, or happen upon someone who is showing us that their faith truly means something to them, that is the voice of God also. Our Holy Mother would tell everyone that it is easy to believe because it is the only life where happiness is found. We really do not have to give up all that much once we realize there is no comparison between the things that we hold on to compared to the power and glory She offers through Her Son. Faith is power. Sacrifice is Glory because there is no Glory without the power of faith in the reasons why we sacrifice. Acceptance of faith is the first sacrifice where we compare our doubt to Christ on the Cross and realize that our reservations can no longer compete. They are defeated, nailed to the Cross in Christ's salvific Flesh.

There are many groups of people who maintain differing degrees of separation from the Truth. Many non-Christians have simply never been told of the greatness of Jesus Christ and His coming Kingdom. Nor have they been acclimated to the power of the Holy Spirit within them and what their lives could actually become in the midst of His grace. They might know of the idea of a god, but have yet to truly meet He who is. Saint Paul spoke to the Romans of this same idea when he proclaimed to them that the Person of Christ is truly the "Unknown God" that they worshiped unawares. There is very little difference in what is occurring now in our contemporary day. People say they are spiritual, but not religious. They are the modern day worshipers of the God they do not know. For if they did, they would flock to be part of His Original Apostolic Church and receive His Flesh and Blood as real food. Of course, Jesus' Church is an enduring institution across two millennia. This is self-evident. How could it be otherwise when He said that His Church would not fail? People shy away from this great supernaturally-instituted religion because they see the sacrifice and refuse the contribution of their faith to the Mystical Body of the redeemed. We must realize that God is the great choreographer behind all human existence. He is in control of His Creation whether we want to believe it or not. No one will be able to arrive at their final day estranged from the Truth of the Gospel and be able to say that they were never told. Christ as the determiner of human fate makes sure every soul is given the opportunity to accept Him. So, for all those who have yet to recognize the Savior of the world, please give Him a chance to love you because the Salvation that He grants is beyond your capacity to even dream. He will dispense to you an eternal happiness that will gush over you and lift you upon a tide of deliverance to mountaintops of ecstasy where you will experience creative power, freedom, and a love that will embrace you throughout the eons of Eternity.

Question 17

How has your personal temperament been changed by your experiences with the Blessed Virgin Mary? Is your demeanor different? Do you become frustrated when other people do not believe you? Do you feel forsaken, alone, or abandoned by your friends when they tell you that they are not required to believe in the substance of your claims?

I believe that I am still the same person that I was before Our Lady came to us. My soul has a particular identity. I do not believe that I have outwitted my genetics or my personality or memories from youth, although I now see them from under the reign of the Morning Star Over America. I am as much a Roman Catholic as I was before February 22, 1991. I have always said that I was awakened to a mystical reality that was already the foundation of who I was. I did not have to convert once Our Lady came to me and confirmed the truth I already knew. I did not have to be wrenched around toward a different direction of understanding. Mostly, I am more at peace with myself because I know my thoughts are ratified by the heavens, and I also know when they are not. It does not matter to me what anyone else may say about them, although I am inquisitive toward the spiritual insights of other deeply holy people. They comfort me and bless me with insights from their mansions. My childhood feelings of insecurity are greatly diminished, while my patient perspective is more enhanced. I also know what to be patient about so that I do not fall into an anemic state of indifference, malaise or outright cowardice toward our responsibilities to advance the Great Commission two by two. All evangelists have their companions. My brother has been with me for nearly 50 years as my best friend and confidant. No one on Earth has loved me more or stood by me so faithfully in a brotherly way. What a gift! I will say one time for the historical record and in rebuke to all the character assassins. Our relationship has never envisioned, contemplated, or touched the sin of homosexuality. We are repulsed by this abomination. We are united in our consecration for the sake of the Immaculate Virgin Mary. It began through God's Divine Providence decades before our Holy Mother's first appearance to us. Although I recognize that few of our childhood friends or family members are close to my brother and me at present in our service to the Mother of God, I understand that the unfolding of this mystery is prescriptive of God's Providence.

Among the greatest things that Our Lady has given me is an amazing confidence in my standing before Her as Her adopted son. She loves me with a power that is incomprehensible, Her approval is tantamount to salvific Glory, and I live in that affirmation at each moment. I never stand alone having to contend for the legitimacy of what I know to be the truth, no matter who disagrees. I compete with no one, but do not see my soul as superior to any other, although my thoughts reflect all that She has taught me which transcends what millions of people believe instead. Knowledge of something does not make one superior to anyone. The sacrifice defines our stature. There are literally hundreds of thousands, perhaps millions, of intellectuals who are veritable geniuses in human knowledge, and even theology, who are vagrants before the wisdom of the heavens. And why? Because they do not have any stature in sacrifice for the Son of God and His magnificent Queen. Their will has never been violated as a sacrifice for their King. Nothing that I am or believe is built upon or resting atop any sinner's beliefs, interpretations or understanding. I stand upon Saints! I rest in the perfection of the Queen of Heaven who supports me, while the Saints are my companions in their image of our Savior. I came to know them through the Catholic Church, and now I commune with them in the mystical realms of my contemplative prayers, as well as my daily interactions of faith. My responsibility is to maintain my balance in the sanctifying graces of the Church and the supernal action and motivations impressed into my soul. I do not recognize any shifting sand under my feet in my present composure, nor do I require approbation from any others, although I am comforted when moments of approval and acceptance arrive. Unity and companionship in the sacrifice is always sweet. This comfort is not really a personal benefit to me; it is a happiness borne to me by they who offer it, knowing how radiant is our Holy Mother's joy in them. I have always said that I love to see people win things. I love to see their joy and happiness when their good fortune pours over them. I would rather see it for them than experience it for myself. I remember a young female friend in college who used to nearly become ecstatic at the smallest good fortune. If she found a penny on the ground, her eyes would light up and she would squeal with delight that something out of the ordinary had occurred. This does not even begin to describe the NCAA basketball tournament pool each year where I believe she actually won one year without knowing a single thing about college basketball. I think she picked which uniforms she liked. It was such a great feeling seeing her so happy. When anyone finds the Triumph of our Virgin Mother, it must be shared and savored, hence I share their joy with them. I do not feel envy seeing someone blessed, nor do I ponder why it could not have been me. And, I don't remember ever being any other way in life before Our Lady came to my brother and me so prolifically. I am aware not to covet my neighbor's goods, but to be thankful they live fulfilled. Our Holy Mother has filled my cup to the brim and overflowing. What more could I ask for? I simply want to see the world wake up to the blessing of God's Glory. I want to see everyone win. I want the suffering of so many to stop. This is what I pray for every day of the world. The only victory I want is for every soul to know Jesus and our Heavenly Mother the way I do. They deserve to be loved. Then, our Heavenly Mother in fulfilling Her commission will place a seal atop our unity as we follow Her to the Catholic Altar to receive the authentic Bread of Life that we may be bathed in Jesus' Blood and live forever. Then, He will come again!

  I rarely become frustrated anymore when people do not believe the things that I try to relate to them personally. Neither do I give much thought to how rapidly might be the acceptance of our work. Our Lady knows that timing, and the openness of men's hearts. Does She wish it to be as immediate as Her Fiat? Of course, but it is men who must decide their destiny and station in Heaven. This is applicable to pagan, publican, parishioner and Prelate. The highest seats in Heaven for all Eternity are for those who merit it by the faith they displayed, the sacrifices they made, and the sanctity they achieved. In the early days, being slandered and derided for our claims impacted me to a greater degree, simply because I did not want to be ostracized and alone. Matthew 10:34-39 is the Word of God. Now, I see we have already won; the Morning Star Over America was not stopped and has made its appearance in the world through our obedience to our Heavenly Mother. Her intercession has succeeded on an entirely different plane of time and existence. We were victorious from the first moment on February 22, 1991, but I did not know it then. Her intercession had to play out in time for me to come to know what actually occurred in that first moment. It is much like Redemption being complete at the instant of Jesus' Crucifixion. Human history has already been imprinted with these works of Our Lady, and no one has the power to remove them. No one can reverse time and keep Morning Star Over America from unfolding as it did through our faith. No one can rescind our acts of obedience to our Most Blessed Mother. Our witness is secure in the Eternity of God. Our Lady told me that even if our work's credibility was annihilated on Earth and in history, every soul will read its every page nonetheless in the fullness of its truthful testament before they enter Heaven. Every soul will know that She graced their day, and tried to help them. This, my friends, is the indomitable work of God. This is Triumph everlasting!

So much happens at the particular judgement of each person outside of time. In fact, every soul now standing at their judgement is witnessing the work of the Morning Star Over America as it has happened, is happening now, and will happen hereon. I am so happy for them because the beauty is overwhelming for them; the grace is mitigating the errors they set into time by their sins, and they are in the merciful embrace of the greatest Gentleness in all Creation. They see that I loved them which is all I ever wanted each of them to know. They are each sitting on Our Lady's lap as She has the book open before them, pointing Her finger to each word of the story of Morning Star Over America as She tells them about each day we spoke. I was somewhat lacking in understanding in the beginning about others not being able to accept what was unfolding through us as it occurred. I kept thinking that it was my fault in some way, that I was not holy enough to be believed. But, I now understand the sacrifice that is required for anyone to believe is theirs alone. I understand how hard it is for God to penetrate the human will and its fortress of perceptions. There is a great convincing veil of darkness spread over us that separates us from true vision. I speak about frames of reference and our subliminal interior hierarchy of influence. I have tried to describe a matrix composing our perceptive being. I always remember that the most despicable person might have grown to be far more holy than myself if they had been chosen to receive Our Lady in these times as the Morning Star Over America. My brother and I have simply done our best. I am sorrowful only for the pride-filled, aggressive and obstinate, especially those who are Catholic, in that they are not disposed in these moments to receive their Heavenly Mother's great graces when they would be so advantageous to them for their sanctification and in their evangelization of the world. I am sorrowful, for them, not myself. Our Beloved Mother wants to touch them, but they say no or are looking another way, distracted by the things of the world as She comes to engage them. She sees them as no more than tiny children in highchairs shaking their heads vigorously and batting away a spoonful of peas with grimaces on their faces. She says that their path of acceptance is their journey to make; it is their hunger that will come upon them. And, it is their rejection that will be their suffering to endure. When I encounter someone who tells me they are not required to believe, I know that I am looking at someone who is not a tiny child as God would wish them to be. In the face of such an immense confrontation between Salvation and damnation for the souls of men, they have not assessed the strength of those they oppose, nor recognized their maternal ally in the fight. Luke 14:31 says, "Or what king marching into battle would not first sit down and decide whether with ten thousand troops he can successfully oppose another king advancing upon him with twenty thousand troops?" I recognize that our Beloved Virgin Mother in Her miraculous intercession is the forefront of the vanguard of Saints who bring assured victory in this battle. Her heel crushes Satan. We should ask, what composes Her heel?

Another aspect of my demeanor that is more strengthened is the willingness to engage the battle and hold the line marked out by the sacrifices of the Saints. I am not going to insult this great Communion of the Church-Triumphant by surrendering without a fight and relinquishing what they secured for us through heart-wrenching suffering and sacrifice in their times. Roman Catholics are not a people of compromise with things that are not of God. Satan is positing the lie to humanity that if we would just "wash-out" the great anchors of Truth of our Catholic Faith and concentrate upon everyone simply being treated equally that he will provide the "diversity of equality and inclusion" that will bring happiness and justice to the world. He is a liar. He is seducing everyone possible to accept that all beliefs are equal, and that each of them must be protected, magnified and respected. I do not respect either him or his works. Hear me now, "I reject Satan and all his works, and all his empty promises!" He is diluting the Truth of Christianity so that it becomes so weak in its evangelization that he can ultimately extinguish Roman Catholicism altogether from our culture, or at least, create a massive battle of ultimate destruction that will close out the ages. For Satan to destroy the world, he must diminish and bring extinction to the Roman Catholic Church by overwhelming it with such atheistic secularism that people will wonder where virtuous faith ever went. The devil is saying, "If you and your fusty old traditions will just go away, the world will become united and filled with brotherhood under my guidance. You are the cause of disunity in the world; you and your so-called institutional religion." This is the voice that has abused the Second Vatican Council. What this has led to is that anytime a Catholic stands up for the truths of Jesus' Original Church, the Catholic is pummeled by not only the secular world, but by marginal progressive parishioners as well, for a supposed lack of charity. They have decided that being united with the traditions of historical Christendom is too divisive for them. We are out-of-touch with their new, more sophisticated ways, they say. Well, they are lost—so sayeth the Mother of God. And, the secular world moves into allegiance with them and magnifies anything that would soil the reputation and legacy of the Original Apostolic Church. Multitudes have already bought into these lies. Too many Catholics are scandalized by the Cross. They reject Scripture that says, "If they hated Me, they will hate you." But, the caveat is apparent; only if you testify to the truth loudly enough to be heard. Too many are trying to avoid anyone hating them than encountering the wood of the Cross for the proclamation of the Gospel. They are trying to avoid the inevitability of its prophecy by surrendering their witness to Christ for a faithless fraternity in a false peace that will ultimately consume them in death.

Question 18

If you were to lay-out ten (10) of the most important things that the Holy Mother has ever spoken to you about, what would they be and why?

Our Heavenly Mother has spoken to my brother and me for nearly thirty years, and it has not been an exercise in repetition. It has been a mystical manifestation of dimensions, hierarchies and choirs. There have been themes and sequences, cadences and chronology, and prophecy and poignancy according to the unfolding times and the maturation of our hearts. She has spoken to the limits of what my brother and I could accept and understand; and even sometimes beyond those limitations, while leading us by the hand to realms and elevations closer to Jesus and Herself. Timothy and I each brought our natural gifts, strengths and aptitudes to this consecrated relationship. We surrendered our interior motivations, loyalties and devotions into a communion with Her as our beloved Virgin Mother. It is an authentic and vibrant relationship encompassing over 10,000 days of wisdom, guidance and insight delivered by the Messianic Truth-Bearer Herself. Christians have been engaged in a mission and commission since the Church's infant christening to pierce the veil of sin and caress the hearts of God's children, while guiding everyone to prepare for the judgement of the ages and our worthiness to reenter Paradise. I somehow never lose the hope that each person would experience the lightning strike of mystical revelation in their hearts. Oh, that each person would come to truly know that God is real, Jesus is the Messiah, and the Holy Spirit is knocking on the door within them. Our Holy Mother as the Morning Star Over America is taking the United States of America, indeed all humanity, to the door. My brother and I have been speaking directly to the very Lady whose life-story graces the sacred pages of the ancient Scriptures, from the Annunciation of an Archangel to a barren stable at the Incarnation of God in human flesh, through a life of perfect grace in that glorious Son to His horrific Crucifixion, culminating in His triumphant Resurrection from the Tomb and Ascension into Heaven. Thereafter, She was assumed into Heaven body and soul and, verily I can attest, speaks to us now, in person, across the expanse of the ages through Her mystical intercessions. If one can contemplate for just a single span of moments that our testament is authentic, the dimensions of the gift of the Morning Star Over America would exceed their greatest dreams.

Consider the breaching of time in Her presence with us; and the life of Heaven that will never die. Here, on this day, in these times, is the crackling concussion of the continuity of revelation given as a motive of credibility of the Roman Catholic Church. The Most Blessed Virgin Mary is alive and speaking of Her Son to all of us. That is the door. Everything She has intimated, revealed or declared to be important is fully apparent and present to us through the Holy Gospel and the Traditions and Teaching of the Original Apostolic Church, still alive, vibrant and flourishing in our time. This is what She testifies. She is the maternal instrument of Jesus' Church in the realms of conversion and sanctification. Her purpose has been two-fold. She wishes to remove the veil of darkness that is blinding us from the realities of Heaven; and secondly, to augment our spiritual capacities by elevating the sacred wisdom of Roman Catholic Christianity within us so that we would share it with the world, that all may be saved within its beautiful Sacrificial Communion. The Truth brings Light; the Truth is Light. It makes us strong, and it saves. The guiding questions to which the Mother of Jesus provides answers are how does one come into communion with the full clarity of the Truth; how is one elevated in strength to maintain that clarity; and how does one magnify that clarity to the rest of humanity walking in darkness? Conversion, sanctification, and evangelization is the Great Commission bestowed by the Savior of the world upon His disciples which effects the answers to these questions. And above all else, the reason the questions even exist is the Love of God in Jesus who is the Way, the Truth and the Life. No one comes to the Father except through Jesus Christ.

The following ten (10) topics are my initial list of the most important things that the Immaculate Virgin has communicated to my brother and me. I could probably speak to a dozen more that are integral and embedded within these that I mention. Something is not left out or not important just because we cannot speak of everything at once. Our Lady did not personally specify this list. It is the first ten things that rose in my heart based upon how I have gleaned Her wisdom and recognized the things that She has concentrated on in Her lessons and relationship with my brother and me. These things are more about the relatable adjustments that we should implement as opposed to unveiling deeply spiritual foundations which will inevitably come as a result if we but comply with Her. They are like a synthesis of allusions, priorities and preferences that She has spoken to that She would be happy that I relate.

I. *Slow down, be patient, and always extend the best you have to offer.*

II. *Pray from the heart so as to contemplate the Most Sacred Heart of Jesus so you may love and imitate Him.*

III. *Make your life a sacrifice in union with His for the conversion of men.*

IV. *Never hate anything or anyone, while declaring sin as the enemy of humankind.*

V. *Repent, forgive, and never make excuses for sin.*

VI. *Never compromise with those who wish to obscure or diminish the truth. Stand your ground!*

VII. *The Most Blessed Sacrament of the Catholic Altar is the authentic Bread of Life. There is no other.*

VIII. *Defend the Roman Catholic Church and its priesthood.*

IX. *Obey the Most Blessed Virgin Mary as the Morning Star Over America.*

X. *Love people enough to tell them the Truth.*

I. *Slow down, be patient, and always extend the best you have to offer.*

I would begin by offering this short sentiment as one of the ten most important issues taught to me by Our Lady because it requires no religion or great mystical advice from seer, sage or swami. Even in a secular world, it is completely relevant and unassuming. It should be a matter of simple insight in anyone's quest for peace between their neighbors and coexistence among peoples. Our burdens are many in the elemental matters of survival and sustenance, and it is difficult striving together when the destinations in our lives are often in diametrically opposing directions. I have often referred to our frame of reference, interior constitution and subliminal hierarchy of influence. Our interior environment is like a riled ocean, and our person is like a scuba diver who is swimming through our perceptions of existence. We have seen on television where a diver can become too rambunctious underwater near the ocean floor, and the turbulence he generates can stir up so much silt and debris that he can no longer see to navigate his exploration. Many a diver has lost their lives as victims of such treacherous phenomena. Most people are already in this stirred-up, turbulent state in their lives where they are not only obscuring vision for themselves, but for everyone near them. Our Lady wants the debris and distractions of the exiled world to settle to the bottom so that our vision can become clear again. Many in the secular world understand this principle already. Numerous are their attempts to resolve their cluttered and stressful lives through trendy and cultish novelties, such as life coaches, meditation providers, relaxation techniques, relationship counselors, and even psychiatrists. These are all sought out because a person knows the turbulence in their frame of reference and that they cannot see their path to peace.

Our Lady taught me from the outset in 1991 about the concept of "motion," as She called it, and how it is related to the interior peace of the Holy Spirit. She said that I must slow down. There were many practical disciplines that She employed to help me understand. For example, back in the days before more advanced technologies, I would read a copy of the newspaper delivered to my front porch every morning. As part of perusing its content each day, She asked me to slowly count to five as I turned each page, instead of ripping to the next page as if I was running out of time. Likewise, Her main discipline with both Timothy and myself was teaching us to eat more slowly, instead of gulping down our food. She said that She would not allow Her sons to eat like wolves who were unappreciative of the food that has been given to them each day by God. These simple disciplines helped us to be aware of what is happening in the moment, rather than storming through life at a torrid pace as if we were an unconscious machine whose internal governor was our worldly appetites. It was an effort to detach us from the world which ultimately enslaves us.

She also helped us understand the value of patience that can be invoked in many situations. Quite a lot of impatience is generated because our vision has been obscured by the turbulence we experience inside. Even our genetics can contribute to this turmoil without our realizing it. Some people are blessed to have genetically docile spirits at the outset where they were never disturbed during their physiological, psychological and spiritual formation as children. Others have not been so fortunate, either genetically or in the environment that has made turbulence a seemingly natural part of their interior constitution. So many children have spent an entire childhood cringing from the suffering around them almost as if experiencing electrical shocks. Our Lady says that oftentimes it seems as if a foreign entity within us is dominating our lives where we become slaves to demands that are not truly our own. This foreign entity is not necessarily the presence of the devil, but he takes every opportunity to instigate the turbulence, hoping we will respond with impatience and a lack of peace, hoping to bring suffering, darkness and even death in the process. Every daredevil and extreme sports enthusiast is a victim of this uncontrolled interior turbulence which drives them to risk the great gifts of their life, health and safety for nothing more than momentary stimulations of the flesh, financial gain and celebrity. Our Lady says that this is such a waste of a life. Their actions and endeavors are not a prayer to God. No temporary rush of euphoria is worth the sin that is being committed and the danger that is being created. If not for the merciful grace of God upon their lives, He would allow Satan to accept the challenge, and their "daring of the devil" would result in unimaginable suffering or death for each of them. Does God have to allow this to happen in order for them to recognize how they are offending Him? Yet, the crowds are entertained and roar with approval. Patience allows the dregs of our interior constitution to settle to the bottom as sediment to be discarded, leaving us clear vision to what God would have us see instead. We must realize that most marketing and television programming are meant to stir turbulence into impatience so that we will not summon greater wisdom and prudence in the expenditure of our lives and resources. If we learn to be fluently patient when it is appropriate, we will be able to slow down. Or, if we consciously slow down, we will find that patience has a fighting chance. Then, our lives and the forces that influence us will become more clear to us so that our free will can be administered in more beneficial directions. Our heart has a tiny voice. We should live so we can hear it at all times.

Finally, when distractions fall away and our hearts become clear, and we are not prodded by the interior turbulence to become impatient, we will realize what is best for ourselves and those around us. Wisdom will take on newer, more expansive dimensions and our hearts will tell us how to best contribute to the lives of those we love. This clarity will also expand our awareness of what and whom we should love. Knowing how to give our best always leads to personal sacrifice. But, our best sacrifices are not necessarily what we might consider them to be. If we are worldly and materialistic, simply giving a few dollars to a cause is not truly the best that we have to offer. Merely surrendering money is oftentimes not a personal sacrifice at all. The widow's mite should tell us this. What is best about ourselves is that which is most valuable to God, and what is best is the moment when we can reach into ourselves and summon the image of Jesus and unite with Him in His Crucifixion for the sake of the salvation of the world. I was marveling at Saint Mother Teresa's loving sacrifice one day, and mentioned to Our Lady that it was nearly unimaginable that this simple woman chose a life of poverty lasting well over a half century. Our Virgin Mother simply replied, "Why did she have to?" I was startled by this response. I had never thought that there might have been an option where Mother Teresa would not have had to suffer in abject poverty amongst the poorest of the poor for nearly seventy years. She did so because no one came with the resources, talents and attention to help her change it. Rare few reached into themselves to sacrifice as she did to rescind the suffering. She gave herself to God's children out of love and vowed to remain with the least of them until the day that their suffering would be no more. She is still with them now through her intercessory power. When we give from the Cross within us, we are surrendering the best of who we are. Love gives of itself. Hence, when we always give the best that we have to offer from this frame of reference, we transmit and magnify love into the world. We actually magnify our own spiritual presence throughout Creation which will be recognized for Eternity in Heaven. This is why two homeless people sharing of a morsel of food between themselves is a more titanic manifestation of the best that they are as human beings than a millionaire becoming well known for supporting a food bank and having his name engraved on the side of the building. What is the value to a homeless person of the other half of his only food for that day? We know what this means because we conceptualize it in the great themes and depictions of our arts and entertainment all the time. The grand devotions, the monumental self-giving, the great love, the most heroic sacrifices are emblazoned before us in our stories, our cinema and our cultural impressions where they cultivate our hearts so our own personal renditions may be encouraged from our brief moments of life in this world. Our Lady told me that a rich person performing generous acts usually only comes after they have denied everyone else first in order to get rich [James 5:1-6]. She also said it does not do any good to be charitable with your wealth after you pass into death. It is not a sacrificial act of love at all to refuse your charity until after your money is no longer of any value to you. A very simple example might illustrate the point. If you had two pieces of fruit and one was more fresh and appealing, without blemish compared to the other, which would you extend to a stranger? If a person asked for your help, would you go with him the second mile instead of just the one? In these moments are the opportunities to give the best that we are as a loving sacrifice, even if these occasions are as simple as those of a pauper.

II. *Pray from the heart so as to contemplate the Most Sacred Heart of Jesus so you may love and imitate Him.*

The only key to unlocking the soul from the darkness wrought by sin is communion with the Sacred Heart of Jesus Christ. Without Him, it is not possible to escape the bonds of darkness and death. Man has no hope without the Messianic Savior of the world. This is as definitive, unequivocal and permanent as can be. Relativists and religious pluralists somehow believe otherwise. There is one pearl of great price that leaves all other riches worthless. What does it profit a man to gain the whole world and suffer the loss of his soul? [Mark 8:36] Since this is true, what is it then about the soul that is of such great worth, even greater than all the world at our feet and its riches piled in our storehouses? Does anyone really want to remain forever in this world that we see every day, with its trials and tribulations, its suffering, its corruption and greed, its lying and cheating, its frustrations and impediments, and our vulnerabilities and fears? Imagine if someone told you that you would never die and had to go about your everyday routines of survival from sunrise to sunset for the rest of endless time in the midst of other clawing beasts and greedy despots. Imagine losing your health, but never dying. Consider being vulnerable to repeated plagues, diseases and disasters, never able to find lasting comfort or peace. Most people are mentally and emotionally exhausted by the time their retirement comes, after being pummeled by a lifetime of sacrifices, misfortunes, mental torments and responsibilities thrust upon them by others just to survive. This does not even begin to describe those lost in desolation, poverty and ill health. Does not a Savior make perfect sense in the treacherous orders of this worldly domain marked by such deprivation and sin? Every person is already looking for some way to be saved from it all. But, most are not looking for the Lamb of God. They are instead seeking their deliverance in wealth, power, control, worldly stature, fame, and a whole host of other dominating venues and personality characteristics, hoping to outrun their own share of the Cross. Our Lady says that the focus of this generation must change to recognize its true Savior or it will not be redeemed and saved. It is as simple as this.

Now, the problem is not necessarily clear to us as black and white, although it should be. People are in differing states of recognition and surrender to the Savior of the world. Millions of people attempt to sell a compromise to themselves where they believe that they can hold on to this world, and at the same time, convince themselves that they are devoted to Jesus and His ways of everlasting life. Prosperity preachers are hideous liars. The celebrated rich who adorn themselves with popularity may speak of their spirituality and recognition of Jesus as their Savior, but they also love their exalted positions in society too much to ever give the best of themselves. Everything they surrender to Jesus is merely window dressing from their opulent lives. But, as they might deliver up the curtains from their windows, everyone else can see inside that they have not paid the light bill and that they live in darkness, trying to sell the deception of progressive sophistication to everyone else, marketing the lie that they are something more than actual paupers. They rarely, if ever, reach into the fiber of who they are and make a sacrifice of their wealth, worldly esteem and power for Jesus because they love the things of this world more than their Savior. If they were able to be this honest, they would tender their fealty to their true salvation, sell their worldliness, purchase the pearl of great price, and come to realize how precious their souls truly are; the souls they are losing by trying to maintain their grip on the material world instead. Jesus would love to have command of the resources of the world in order to bring us all to Paradise.

These previous sentiments are simply a backdrop to an environment of deception that keeps many people from being united with Jesus in a way where He might save them from eternal darkness. The light does not come on within us all by itself. It is the same principle as if we wish to get warm on a frigid blustery night. We must move closer to the fire. Wealth and material contentment are not signs that we are close to any flames other than maybe those of hell. We must realize that nothing in the universe matters, except the Fire of the Holy Spirit inflamed within us. Everything that we hold on to in this material world, whether it be money, fame, opportunity, aptitudes or the constructions of a material legacy, are all temporary and returning to the dust. On my first birthday, September 20, 1962, the Port Authority in New York announced the selection of Minoru Yamasaki as lead architect and Emery Roth & Sons as associate architects of the World Trade Center complex and the building of its skyscraping twin towers. [*Esterow, Milton (September 21, 1962).*

"Architect Named for Trade Center." The New York Times.] Not one person in the crowd of financial titans, dignitaries, politicians, businessmen or the public present realized at its ribbon cutting ceremony on April 4, 1973 that those towers would lie in smoldering rubble within a short span of just 28 years. As an aside, might we ponder whether it is a coincidence or the fingerprint of Providence that the public announcement of the lead architect of the Trade Center Towers, which were destroyed in one of the most conscience stunning events of American history, occurred on the birthday of a Marian seer, with the addition of the associate architects being the namesakes of that same messenger? Each and every one of our worldly accomplishments and material successes, while apparent in their secular grandeur, are temporary, fragile and finite. They all arrive at the point of being meaningless at the threshold where our consciousness realizes that we are transcending from this life into our deaths. Consider the following choice. Suppose someone approached you at age 18 and said that they would give you 500 billion dollars to do with what you will, and all the fame and adoration you could take in, but at age 50 you would be required to surrender everything back to them and that they would own you forever to do with whatever they pleased. Another person comes to you at the same age and asks that you belong to them, serving them and their cause with daily sacrifice and loving devotion, and then at age 50, they will make you 18 again and give back to you every moment of time that you spent in their service, bestow upon you infinite wealth, and declare you free forever to live untold lifetimes in worlds you would have the power to create. And, you would be loved and esteemed infinitely forever amidst it all. Which would you choose? Which covenant provides an open eternity of glory and power? Conversely, which dispensation guarantees a future of chains? Can we see that there are multitudes of people who are making the pact with the first deal maker, instead of the second? And, why do they do it? Because, they cannot see past age 50, and they do not trust the one who is asking for their sacrifice.

So, why is prayer from the heart and contemplation of Jesus' Most Sacred Heart one of the ten most important issues that our Holy Mother has spoken about to us, indeed throughout Her many appearances? Because, Jesus is the second deal maker. Our ability to fulfill our portion of the salvific covenant is in our continual renewal of our union with the intentions of His Most Sacred Heart. And, to be in union with His Heart, we must know Him. This intimate relationship is nurtured through prayer, meditation and contemplation of His Sacred Heart as He experienced life for us in His Passion, Death and Resurrection as recorded in Sacred Scripture. When we pray and meditate upon the reason why He came into the world and what power originates in His Sacred

Heart, a dawning occurs within the human soul as to just how special we truly are as children of the only God. The Most Holy Trinity is re-sanctifying Creation from whence it fell by asking for our union with the Sacrifice of the Messiah on Mount Calvary. And, that union is certified in realtime through the Holy Sacrifice of the Mass in the Roman Catholic Church.

Prayer is an actual present conversation with this Blessed Trinity who will speak to us in ways that will bolster our sacrifice for Jesus and secure our seat at His Feast Table in Heaven. Is there comfort in prayer? Of course. Is there peace? Most definitely. Do our perspectives become more refined through the deific frame of reference invoked in prayer? Surely they do. Will the Holy Spirit come upon us? Undoubtedly. This is where wisdom comes out of the fog of worldliness. She processes in elegant beauty into the life of every man from the altar of his heart, across the apse and down the nave of the soul into the vestibules and piazzas of our identifiable demeanor and actions. And, what does this wisdom tell us? We are loved with the mightiness that created the universe spectactularly arrayed. And, that Creator came into the world to suffer with His own because He loves us, and that we might be saved into the Paradise from whence He came. That thought, if believed, is shattering to the entire worldly composure of the human constitution. Our minds are left ringing, "How could something so beautiful be happening for me?" The entire universe exists for the singular purpose of our God not condemning us to oblivion after the first sin of Adam and Eve. He could have, like any inventor, tossed the idea of human creatures en masse into the trash bin of the ages as a failed experiment of human free will and never thought of us again. And, He would have glorified Himself by taking out the trash to the incinerator, just as He banished the demons to the infernos of hell. But, He loved us so. He saw the beatific potential that would be forfeited. He anticipated the vulnerabilities of free will exacerbated by the demonism of a fallen angel. Hence, from the beginning, He envisioned this universal exile to convoke the grand plan of His power to remake His Creation, endow His creatures with knowledge of Himself once again, and clothe them in the power of His Calvarian Sacrifice in order to save the idea of a perfect Creation of human children who were His image and likeness, whom He could congregate around Himself in love for all Eternity. He said corruption would not have the last word. Only He is the Alpha and Omega.

I remember when I was in kindergarten and all the children had made a simple art project of colorful paper and glue that depicted a birdhouse. I was very small, but that art project was very special to my childlike sensibilities because I had made it and proudly brought it home to show my parents. It was one of the "first things." It hung by magnet on the refrigerator for quite some time. One day, I was helping my father carry the trash to the barrel for burning in the back yard. He started a roaring fire and was tossing the trash from each can into the burning incinerator when in a flash I saw my bird house fall down into the flames and begin to curl as it ignited. I screamed and pointed as I saw it burning. My father saw immediately what was happening and plunged his arm into the leaping flames, singeing his hair to the elbow to save my simple creation. He quickly patted the fire out that was still charring my work and handed it back to me. I was saddened looking at it, damaged as it was. It was blackened around its edges, but I was so happy to have it back. The thought of it being destroyed pierced my heart. After completing the burning of the trash and without saying a word, my father returned to the house, collected some colored construction paper, sat down with me and repaired my art project as if it were new again. Now, fifty-one years later, I still remember it as if it were yesterday. I saw the salvation of my work in my father. My father was Jesus for me that day, saving my creation and restoring it to its original likeness. And, I believe the Father's Heart was as innocently pierced as mine when Adam and Eve sinned and headed for the fire. But, we have been saved by Jesus and recreated by the Holy Trinity through a Sacrifice so horrific, and yet of a power beyond the imaginations of history's greatest poets; an imagination that could only have come from the Mind of God himself.

Jesus appeared in the world as the First Born Son of the Father. To know Him is to know our true identity. Prayer to Him reveals that identity to us. The stories and sacred liturgies of the Church propagate and honor His identity. The Saints imitated His identity. And, the Holy Sacrifice of the Mass confirms His identity in each of us. If we are to live 70 years and more in our contract with the Son of God, it behooves us to communicate with Him during our tenure here. We are the deciders of the mental arena within us. We can think about anything we wish. We can place our thoughts into any dimensions we please. Unfortunately, we can also surrender them to demonic spirits that cross our paths. The question is, where do we place our thoughts? What do we consider within us? If someone never places their thoughts into the arena of any field of study, will they ever know anything about those specific realms? Of course not. Then, how are we to learn anything about the Father, the Son and the Holy Spirit if we do not voluntarily place our thoughts into the mystical arena of our prayers? The answer is suffering. We learn through involuntary suffering in the absence of voluntary prayer. Suffering places the human heart into the arena of the Crucifixion so that we may contemplate firsthand the Sacrifice of our Savior and the conversion for which He asked. The deceptions of worldliness do not matter much when we are in the throes of agony. Suffering goes on in the world, seemingly without cessation, because men do not know Jesus Christ. The farther mankind is away from the Most Blessed Trinity, the more suffering will crescendo because, absent the wisdom of the Father, there are far more people shortsightedly grasping the first deal, instead of investing in the second. It is no more complicated than this.

Finally, we might consider what God will do if we give ourselves to prayer and communicate with Him. What do we suppose that He will bestow upon us? What greatness and possibility will grow in the human heart and mind through the power of the Most Blessed Trinity inebriating us with heavenly wisdom? What will we create then? Do we suppose the greatest healing knowledge might be one of His gifts for all those enduring sickness and disease? How many suffering people are waiting for that to happen? Might we see advances where no child will ever know what it means to starve? Could we cross a threshold into a future age that does not know what the word "war" even means? God would wish us to smelt our spears and swords into cultivating graces, but it seems the enemies of God are not yet ready to cooperate, thus they require us to expend resources in defense of the truth and the peace of our societies. But, they remain possibilities nonetheless because these visions lie readily apparent in our contemplative dreams through the power of the Holy Spirit. Jesus Christ is our Salvation into these glorious realms. We are simply the distance of our sacrifices away from convoking them in Creation. We have a loving God who is pining to dispense these things, if we would but turn to His Son in great faith and be remade into His image and likeness by opening the perceptive spiritual brawn of our hearts to His ways of sanctification and perfection. Then, we will be ready for His Triumphant Return in Glory where we will be released from every impediment that ever confronted the dreams in our hearts. The dealmaker will say, "Be 18 again because you are loved!"

III. Make your life a sacrifice in union with His for the conversion of men.

The next step in Our Lady's revelation of our path into the Kingdom of Heaven is that each of us would be the one who will repent, convert and change, even if no one else in the world will follow suit in our time. It is a personal decision unaffected by anyone else. We cannot hold out our sacrificial conformity and participation in imitation of Christ's Life until everybody else decides to join us at the foot of the Cross. It would be nice if everyone were moving to congregate at the Altar of the Calvarian Sacrifice, but we are not there yet. Therefore, those with faith and the strength to sacrifice must lead the rest as part of the Great Commission that Christ Jesus commended upon those who would believe. I previously mentioned the idea of always giving the best that we have to offer; and the "best" is also founded deep within us where the Cross is implanted in our soul. Let us consider a line of association through a progression of ideas, much like if we would say rain feeds starving people. Some might say that rain is water, and starving people cannot live on water. They require food. But, if you asked people in the desert what they most need in order to live, they say water, whether it is from wells beneath the ground or rain from the sky that fills those wells because water upon their fields provides them their food. For Catholics, we understand a very beautiful and powerful line of association between our initiation in grace and the starving hearts of those who do not know Christ. At our Baptism, the waters of everlasting life pour over our heads, giving us our first sensation of the beatitude of the Savior of the world. Our Lady told me that even the smallest infants realize that a sanctifying transformation has taken place within them. She said they may not be able to articulate it, describe it, or even remember that original moment in any intellectual form later in life, but each infant knows that God has embraced them as His own through this sanctifying Sacrament. There is a mystical sensation granted to every person who receives the Sacrament of Baptism in the Original Apostolic Church. This is the original point in the line of association with Jesus Christ, leading to our engagement with lost souls. From this moment, any evil forces launched against this baptized soul manifest the "Suffering Beauty." Everything leveled against this glowing innocence is like a hammer pounding a mystical saber into a weapon of Light with sparks flying in all directions with each strike. God the Father sees His sacred child smelted in His grace, having separated out the sin, and now being forged by His Divine Power into an instrument for His conquest and restoration of human souls. Baptism is the calling of the union of God upon His creature once again, the garment unstained donned about a soul, dignity arrayed that will remain impenetrable throughout the everlasting ages. The soul tastes its immaculate conception.

Imagine if in all the innumerable billions of light-years of the universe and the seemingly endless ages of time that there were only two human beings remaining, male and female. Imagine all humanity snuffed out in the universe as if the planet Earth had endured a fatal holocaust, and nary remained but two human creatures in the aftermath on its desolate smoldering plains. Now, envision the moment where these last two stand facing the end of their kind, the extinction of humanity forever into the backwater of oblivion. What and who do these two represent in that moment that will never be seen again? With no future to come, what dignity would this male and female possess in those closing moments of the age of men? Everything that humanity ever was in all the ages and eras, the history, the accomplishments, the inquisitive exploration, the evolution of dignity, the knowledge that matured, the wisdom that was pondered, all the laughing and joy, the songs sung, the smiles shared, the babies that laughed, the courses that were charted, the ponderings of devotion and sanctity, the greatness of heart and soul, the epochs of the world that were built, the kingdoms that came, the cataclysms that renewed, the movements of vision, happiness, suffering, triumph, and creation manifested from each heart of the billions who had ever lived, all resting as an image within these last two—yes, these last two souls. Can we imagine; can we grasp who those two would be and what they would embody? At the precipice of extinction, the priceless existence of human nature married to the Divine, the entirety of the ages of the history of man right before our eyes standing in dignity ready to breathe its last forever. This is Christ and His Mother when He was born in the manger in Bethlehem. Jesus was the last perfect human male who became the first, both the Alpha and Omega, who embodied the entire history of beatific Eternity that had been snuffed out by the sin of Adam and Eve. And, through the New Eve who ratified obedience to God once again through an Archangel, He came into the world with the power of Sanctification and Resurrection, confirming that the Last would become the First of a resurrected world! Born again, He said! While all the forces of sin had aligned to quench the flame of the human race and the history of man, this Redeeming Savior brought the power to live again through water and fire [Matthew 3:11]. How ironic! These two perfect creatures of the human race stood as the last of their kind, holding in their possession the Resurrection of humanity from the holocaust of sin and death. A burned out world was to be given Life again. A superior race birthed in the divinity of God was to come forth as Lazarus would be called from his tomb. The Last Two became the First, the King and Queen in the dawning of the new Kingdom of God. How could this Salvation be more beautiful? How could extraterrestrial aliens who might have looked upon the tragedy, along with the Angels of Heaven themselves, not have wept in thanksgiving at seeing it all saved, all brought back from the precipice of extinction and given an Eternity to go on once again. All of it retrieved from the fires of desolation, death and damnation at the scream of God's Heart. The Son said to His Father, "I will go! I will breach the bonds into the flames. I will launch the crusade into humanity's exile and bring them home. If it is a Cross I must endure, let that Cross be the Monument of that future Kingdom!"

    The waters of redemption flow from the spigot of Jesus' Sacrifice, and the fire is His Holy Spirit. When we begin to understand His Sacred Heart in our contemplations, we are then drawn to be like Him because His beauty is so breathtaking. We find all comfort there. It is like loving someone so much that you would walk into a fire where they are being consumed –consummation–and never give a thought about the flames. This is what our sacrifice in union with His is all about. Walking into the flames of His Sacred Heart by sharing the Sacrifice He bore. And why? For the same reason He gave His Life on the Cross–so that men may be converted and saved into the Kingdom of Eternal Life. All of the intellectualism of Christianity is scaffolded upon this first revelation in the human heart. Jesus is the Eternal Love that came to the Earth. Our sacrifice unites us with His Crucifixion, and in it, not only are we saved, but we become the reflection of His love in human form that all other men may be drawn to the unity we share with Him.

IV. Never hate anything or anyone while declaring sin as the enemy of humankind.

Hatred, angst, animosity, hostility, antagonism, violence and all the rest against our fellow man have no standing in the story of human redemption into the Love of Christ. Everyone would acknowledge that no one enjoys suffering. But, while the family of humankind is in such a state of sinful disunity, not only in our organization and execution of the physical machinations of life, but in our hierarchy of understanding and the clarity of our collective frame of reference, we impact one another in ways that stir ripples of discomfort that sometimes rise into tidal waves of human misery. Then, we respond against our brothers and sisters whom we believe to be the origin of the suffering, and sometimes rightly so. Those who are the origin of the disturbance offer their excuses for doing the things they have done, which usually reveals they are simply trying to outrun their own suffering as well, albeit in shortsighted ways. There is an entire spectrum of human reasoning filled with justifications that comprise the scaled interpretations and responses in each and every person. The problem is that humanity is not passionate about nurturing a universal frame of reference that reflects the excellence of the Divine Love of Jesus. He is the frame of reference who bears perfect clarity and wisdom to every soul. He is the only reference frame. Sin is anything that distorts, impedes, obscures, blinds or destroys that perfect vision. If we have any honesty within us, we would concede that we live as if believing the beatific state I am describing is merely a pipe dream from a person who does not have a grasp on the realities of life. I too confess that most of our society seems lost to a sufficient knowledge or experience of Christ's love. And imitating it, that is a whole other dimension of difficulty.

Now, let us make a distinction between the emotions and animations that I listed above in relation to declaring sin as the enemy of humankind. The conflict that our interior constitution experiences when confronted with anyone or anything that oppresses us, brings our recognition of it and our response to it. In that interior sphere of recognition, our soul tastes the offense against Love. Our soul senses the distortion from the perfect vision of Christ, and sorrow is felt for what Jesus is required to suffer once again. This arouses our response. The mechanics of our responses are all the same, no matter whether a person is lost or a great Saint. Our responses originate after the recognition that an occurrence has impacted our frame of reference. What we should consider is the state of our frame of reference when it is impacted and the formation of the response that is generated. Everyone is trying to incorporate what impacts them into their frame of reference in a fluently peaceful way. It is our wine skin. But, it can work one of two ways because there is a deceptive dichotomy that can occur. A person who is fluent in evil is mechanically impacted by holiness in much the same way that a Saint is impacted by wickedness. A truly wretched person can actually experience euphoria when torturing another human being because their frame of reference is completely oriented to accommodate evil acts into their perceptions without the impediment of conscience. When they encounter holiness, they feel the repulsion against holiness generated within them by Satan who owns their frame of reference. Conversely, a person of holy heart would generate sorrow, indignation and righteous anger witnessing these evil acts because their frame of reference is in communion with Jesus' Sacred Heart. This is what prompted Jesus to assail the corruption of the moneychangers and marketeers in the Sacred Temple of His Father. And, if we become like Him, and further realize that we are temples of the Holy Spirit, our actionable sentiments will become just as stern in the face of abomination. So, can we see that the orientation of our frame of reference matters?

    The dilemma for most people is in being aware of what hatred actually is. Hatred is the repulsion of Divine Light. It arises from the severing of ourselves from love, life and redemption. It is a state of corruption in our frame of reference which becomes fertile ground for all manifestations of wickedness as our response without the recognition that what we do is evil. For evil works to be exterminated, our frame of reference must have the "shape" of life and love preserved within it. This is why abortion is a damning tragedy to the soul which brings great acts of evil into human existence as if they are no more than a simple legitimate choice or a benign medical procedure. There is no life in the frame of reference of a person who supports the slaughter of a child in the womb. They cannot enter the Kingdom of Heaven because their souls are separated from it due to the hideousness of their sin. Their frame of reference is repulsing of the Kingdom of Heaven. Jesus chose to remain hanging on the Cross until death because He knew it was the ultimate answer to how the hearts of men could be broken open, healed and sanctified. He knew that it was an impact to the human frame of reference that could not be superseded. If He would have come down, He would not have given sinners a chance to crucify Him again, and He would have been victorious with not a sinner possessing the power to stop Him. But, that purifying holocaust would have been at the expense of the souls He loved from the beginning. Some might ask why the Father did not intercede for Adam and Eve when they disobeyed Him. Why did He not reveal to them how much they had hurt Him so they would repent and return to their union with Him? The answer is, He did respond. He did act. The Father's pain flushed out into Adam's fallen existence in the Crucifixion of Jesus Christ who would initiate the reunion that the Father so desired. The Father said, "If only My wayward children could see the Love of My Heart and how it suffers for them, they would love Me again and come back to Me." The Most Blessed Trinity suffered in the fall of man from Paradise. In the Crucifixion, Jesus manifested His unity with the Father's pain. This is where the veil was rent. They suffered together, the Father at seeing Adam and Eve disobey Him in the Garden, and Jesus through the wickedness of men's sins. Are they not the same? Adam and Eve's fall brought a horror of suffering and anguish to the Father consubstantially united with the Crucifixion of His Messianic Son. The Crucifixion is the manifestation of the Father's pain at the first moment of Adam and Eve's sin. Jesus and the Father are one in the Paradisian Fall and the Crucifixion which restored fallen Creation. The Father was crucified in the Paradisian Fall, and Jesus was crucified because of the Paradisian Fall. When you see Jesus on the Cross, it is the clearest vision of the Father because Christ visibly revealed Him in their suffering unity, and that they are one and the same Being. Jesus' passionate cry upon the Cross, "My God, my God, why hast thou forsaken me," are the words of Adam in the Garden after he was exiled. Jesus completely entered exile, not just physically through His Birth, but into the spiritual depths of Adam's deprivation where he and the Father became one again in the forgiveness of his sin by the Christ.

  Let us further contemplate this unity between the Father and the Son. Might we approach our contemplation of the Most Holy Trinity through an allusion to this great Sacred Mystery? Imagine a perfect man standing in front of you, embodying the consummate attributes to be and do anything; intelligent, masculine, handsome, perfect genetics, wise, visionary, virtuous, confident, ecstatic, virile and powerful. This perfect being before you is everything that is ultimate as a man. Suppose this 'man' generates the desire to bring forth children which he has the right and power to do. He acts, which results in the succeeding manifestation of himself as 'father.' This is why we say a man 'becomes a father,' but he has always been, and remains, a man. So, the man and the father are one in the bringing forth of children. In this, the man reveals two distinct identities or "persons"— man and father, while at the same time existing as one 'being.' Then, at the birth of children, the father who is still the man, manifests once again as 'provider' for his children — a third identity or person, while not conceding the other two. So, we have the man, the father and the provider; or three distinct manifestations or persons, but all the same being, completely one and inseparable. The capacities and substance of each are in all as one. The man becomes the father as he conceives children in union with the actions of the father and the longings of the provider. The act of bringing forth children is the distinct characteristic of the father that is shared by the man, whose mutual act of bringing forth children provides the object of love for both the father and the provider. The provider's distinct characteristic is nurturing the children of the father who are also progeny of the man. Both the man and the father reciprocally provide the object of love to the provider so he can act as the nurturer. The man bestows upon the father the capacity to bear children because he gives their conception to the father from his conceiving power. And, the man and the father bless the provider with the fruit of their persons which was manifested to fulfill the longing of the provider, which inspired them to bring forth the act of creation. The man's distinctive characteristic is realizing that he is conceiver, father and provider in the union of the three as one in being.

Now consider this as a simile to the mystical relationship of the Persons of the Most Holy Trinity. Since the Father, Son and the Holy Spirit have always existed as God, the progeny of the Father have always existed in Him through His conceiving power. His acts of creation are always acts of "bringing forth that which is already in Him." Therefore, there has never been a time when He did not know us. The proof? We exist. Everything that exists has always been present in God. And, we are present in God in the image of our perfect conception which is His likeness [Genesis 1:27]. The likeness of humanity is in the Image of the Son, the First Born of His conceiving power. The Father created us through Himself in the Revelation, or "extension," of Himself as the Second Person of the Most Holy Trinity, in much the same way as the man becomes the father in the conception of children. Everything the father is has always been the man. The Second Person of the Most Holy Trinity, the Son, was eternally begotten by the Father as a "person" of Himself for the creation of humanity in His likeness. And, since every conception of the Father already exists in Himself, both humanity and the Son have always existed as well because the Son is the eternally begotten First Born image of humanity. Otherwise, how could there be the distinct persons of the Son and Holy Spirit without the humanity conceived by the Father? How could the man be father and nurturer without children? This is why all humanity which unites with the Son is His Mystical Body. Again referencing our simile, if there are no children, there is no father, and there is no provider because there are no progeny to nurture. Only the man as a single person would have been present in his being, and he would have been no less because he still would have been the ultimate man possessing everything the father and the provider would be. This is where the Son and the Holy Spirit existed as one with the Father before He acted in the genesis of Creation. They were a single God who rested in peace, poised to act through the manifestation of distinct Persons, just as the man was poised to be father and nurturer upon the initiation of his conceiving desire for children.

What is God from all Eternity? Anything He wants to be. And, in this complete liberty and power, He could manifest Himself as a thousand Persons in His ability to conceive and convoke His will. And, every Person would be Him, just as surely as Jesus is God, and just as the man becomes a father through a pro-creative act of conception. God can become, because He is becoming of all possibility, already existent in His omnipotent being. Just as there has always been a Most Holy Trinity as one God, there has always been children of the Father that were created in the image of the Son who would come as His First Born to redeem and save [John 1:3]. This speaks to the eternal nature of every human soul. God extended Himself as Three Distinct Persons as an act of Divine Revelation to, and of, humanity as the precedent to His conception of man, whose conception always existed in His Being. Hence, the Most Holy Trinity as Three Distinct Persons has always existed as one God — Father as the Creator of the human race, Son as Image and Savior of the human race, and Holy Spirit as the Sanctifier of the human race. The Father conceives, the Son brings forth life and saves, and the Holy Spirit nurtures and sanctifies. So, the analogy of man, father and provider becomes Father, Son and Holy Spirit, all One as God. This Almighty God reveals Himself as the Most Holy Trinity through the conception of children with free will whom He knew would fall to the realms of sin, who would then be saved by the Son and sanctified by the Holy Spirit with the cooperation of man through that same gift of free will. In a sense, Jesus Christ, the original Image of humanity in the Godhead, was conscripted into the realms of exile at the fall of Adam. The Second Person of the Most Blessed Trinity was cast into exile in the Image of humanity which was falling. God sustained His unity with humanity in the Fall from Paradise by allowing His perfect human Image to be cast into exile as well. Cast does not mean responsible for the sin, but cast into exile due to the unity with humanity that would sustain salvation. Jesus was validating His very Person by accepting His condescension into exile. Humanity itself was falling from the Divine nature, but Jesus would not let go of Himself. He remained united with the sacred image of humanity in order to preserve its restoration. Jesus conserved the original conception of humanity which He would redeem and enhance in a perfect new conception defined by His Calvarian Sacrifice. When He saw His Image plummeting into exile as if in a mirror, He did not shed the humanity of the Second Person and toss it into the descent so He would have no part of the sin. He became sin by remaining united with humanity in order to redeem it. He clung to human perfection as perfectly united in the Most Holy Trinity and followed His brothers and sisters into exile as an avenger who would battle the serpent who caused them to lose the luster of their divinity.

In the Passion of the Son's Crucifixion, the Father was completely present and united in the Sacrifice which was caused and necessitated by the offense of Adam and Eve whom the Father conceived. The Father's Heart was pierced to the depths of the death of His Son on Mount Calvary at the instant Adam and Eve rejected Him in the Garden. And, He reconfirmed His Love for humanity through His Son so that we might once again be born into Eternal Life. Forgiveness has been eternally present in God in the capacity of the Most Blessed Trinity to suffer. If there was never to be forgiveness, God would never have begotten suffering in His Sacred Being at losing humankind to the serpent of the Garden. Jesus would never have entered the realms of exile. Nor would He have spent Eternity lamenting the loss of a creation of human beings that wished to be corrupt and separated from Him, just as He will not manifest regret or sorrow for the souls who will choose the fires of hell. The Most Holy Trinity suffered knowing that forgiveness cohabitated in their Persons. God chose to accept suffering because He had begotten forgiveness. But, He knew that it would take time, and it would take the love of His Son; the time in which we are living until the Messiah comes again as the Just Judge and Merciful Redeemer. In conclusion, we must remember that this meditation is only an allusion bearing its own deficiencies because the Most Holy Trinity supersedes our contemplations of Him. It has simply been a meditation to help us think more deeply that we are truly united in the Most Holy Trinity in the Image of the Son, as progeny of the Father. Hence, we should never hate any conception of the Father in His Creation, while declaring anything that separates us from that image as being the enemy of humankind and Creation itself.

Therefore, our thoughts should be to concur with His two millennia of patience, and desire to unite in the suffering of the Most Blessed Trinity through the Sacred Heart of Jesus because that suffering is union once again with the

Father who created us and said we were good. It is the redemption that God wishes us to propagate throughout His earthly Kingdom so that men might be saved. We do not hate anyone whom we hope to convert; and we do not hate anything about the world that is serving its purpose in bringing about the uniting of man and God. Nevertheless, evil should be put on notice that it will not be allowed to own, influence, or expect safe harbor in the vineyard left under the custodial care of His followers. The custodians have a responsibility. The impediment to this cleansing action is that people are afraid to declare sin as the enemy of humankind because they have been badgered by Satan's followers into believing that their telling of the truth is somehow an act of hatred toward their friends who are living sinful lives separated from God. Our Holy Mother told me never to be cowed by threats of someone walking away because I spoke the truths that She asked me to relate. She said they did as much to Jesus, and He never relented. Ultimately, they crucified Him for it. We should remind ourselves of the times in the Bible where Jesus was very clear, perhaps blunt, in His confrontations with those He was trying to impress with His wisdom. He was very poignant with those who were seated around Him at tables. He was forthright with the woman at the well. We too often act as if we must handle demons with satin-lined kid gloves, just because their egos have rubbed their feelings raw. Satan claims all kinds of deference. If someone wants to defend stripping tiny babies from their mothers' wombs and selling their body parts, "Get out! Do not dare live such a lie and approach the Altar of Sacrifice while defending such monstrous evil." Jesus merely removed moneychangers, for Heaven's sake. Is there any sacredness that we will defend with conviction?

All human suffering is related to sin. One cannot lament human suffering without looking at the offending sinners and asking them to stop sinning, convert their hearts and live holy lives. The problem we have is that humanity does not see the connection between personal sin and worldwide suffering because it is oftentimes not directly correlated in the material realms. Sin inflicts human suffering across the spiritual realms more prolifically than through material avenues. For example, almost no one has seen an abortion occur, but this horrific sin has darkened the conscience of our entire nation and brought unimaginable spiritual grief, moral derangement and suffering upon us. You might ask how. Well, where do we believe respect for human life went as we watch the glorification of murder, mayhem, drive-by killings, mass school shootings, delinquency, divorce, and pornography? They all crescendoed because we allowed abortion and destroyed our national devotion to human dignity. We cannot instill a respect for the children of our nation by allowing millions of them to be slaughtered because it was convenient to someone's materialistic way of life. This damning sin creates human suffering by sending waves of accommodating darkness to infiltrate the innocent hearts of those who do not yet know Christ well enough to defend their souls from being impressed by such wickedness. Sin is the enemy of humankind. Abortion is Satan's sacrament of death. Abortion is the destroyer of human life. Those who defend it serve the beast of hell. Those who are its purveyors and propagators will hear Christ say, "Get out!" [Matthew 7:23] This is not hate, it is love for suffering humanity to tell sinners to reject sin and accept the Cross of Jesus Christ or risk being damned forever. Salvation and damnation is zero sum. What is gained by the one is lost by the other. Sin and human suffering is also zero sum. Humanity suffers because of human sin. When you see a suffering soul, know true that you are seeing the effects of sin committed by someone in the world. And, if you wish to see this suffering cease, you cannot be indifferent toward human sin. The conversion of any soul is the eradication of suffering in the world. In the midst of this choreography of eternal redemption, it is the Saint who says, "Dear Lord, let me suffer for the deliverance of your children, both the sinner and the sufferer. I offer to you sin's impact upon me, and ask you to extend merciful Light and healing to us all."

As evil attempts to propagate from the origin of sin in the world, its mysterious waves of influence impact hearts who possess the frame of reference of God. A "Planned Parenthood" sign hanging on a building is the diabolical profanity of darkness in the world. But, where the vision of those signs meets holy souls, the darkness is consumed by Light. Those waves of evil perish as they meet virtue. Hatred no longer propagates. Disordered understandings meet clarity, and are restored. Darkness meets Light and is annihilated. Roman Catholics declare, "Here, no farther!" And, the Father in Heaven hears these suffering convictions as deafening thunder that is calling for His divine lightning. Every sin is calling to the heavens for redress, reform, restoration and recreation. And, if that grace is not accepted by sinners when it is dispensed, sin calls for the vengeance of God and its own annihilation. If you love humanity, you must realize that sin must come to an end.

V. *Repent, forgive, and never make excuses for sin.*

In the midst of all holy conviction and the recognition of human sin, we must always maintain the crown jewel of realization that each human soul is a miracle. Every human soul possesses a dignity that must be saved from self-inflicted extinction; its story of life preserved; its eternal longevity defended. The parameters of life from conception in the womb until physical death are the story of its mortal existence; its presence as a creation; the time allotted, its opportunity to be saved into glory. Each soul possesses a destiny which will be respected for Eternity, if it is deemed worthy of Heaven. God is hoping each one will choose to be part of His family and unite with the image of His likeness. So, each person has the potential to become one of our family members forever. We should care about that. Hence, we must be prepared to forgive every penitent heart. And even more, we must tell God that we are "at the ready" with prefigured forgiveness for anyone who has offended us who does not yet know how to extend repentance. This is the consuming nature of the Cross, taking sins upon oneself in reparation.

We must remember that forgiving sin does not mean making excuses for sin. Repentance removes sins, excuses do not. Many people are very good at overlooking and making excuses for people who have offended someone else, thereafter chiding those who have been offended that it wasn't such a big deal. Very few ask God to allow the evil person to offend them instead. They never ask God to make a very difficult person their friend. Christians must ask themselves why Jesus said, "If they hated Me, they will hate you." How does the call for goodness and mercy make people hate us? It is not the goodness and mercy, it is in telling the world that it is separated from goodness and mercy unless it repents and believes in the only Name by which we might be saved. And the world says, "What...little ol' me? How could you talk to me like that? Don't judge me." Then, the hate starts its process of crescendo. Jesus was very direct. "I am the Way, the Truth and the Life; no one comes to the Father except through Me" [John 14:6]. He seemed to challenge everyone in oftentimes very blunt ways, at dinners, outdoors at wells and gathering places, in temples and around porticos, with the ultimate challenge of a Cross on the day of the eternal earthquake. He threw down a gauntlet of Sacred Life on the day of the eclipse of the Light. "Surely this must be the Son of God!," a pagan centurion exclaimed. Christian evangelization has become a dance around human egos who are loath to repent and change their ways. Our steps on that dance floor must return to having patterns prescribed by the Life, Death and Resurrection of Jesus. The heavens are concerned that the call for repentance and conversion has been replaced by a relativistic, cafeteria-style approach to a secular humanist utopia, instead of to complete conversion to the Savior of the world who is trying to deliver us from an eternity in the flames of hell. Secularism is a demonic aberration built on the foundations of atheism; and the flow of its machinations are being defined by Marxist conflict theory which rained a swath of desolation, darkness and death across the 20th century.

Recently, Our Lady asked me what I believed was missing in humanity's frame of reference that would cause Americans not to take inventory of their lives and how they live them. I told Her that I believed people do not grasp what it means to be given the vision of their life passing before their eyes and having to someday answer for every moment of it. She said I was absolutely correct. Remember again how our perceptions can completely invert in an instant through a change in circumstances. Our frame of reference, if not rooted in the wisdom of God, can be shattered in the blink of an eye, leaving us gasping like a fish thrown onto the bank. Our passing from this life into the Presence of God brings the ultimate revelation of circumstances — our Eternal Judgement — each moment of our lives laid bare before the scrutinizing gaze of the ages in the actual instant of it occurring. We will not only see our actions and what we were thinking in each of those moments, but we will see all the consequences thereafter impacting the hearts of each person, and the impressions they have had upon nature, creation, and spirit through time. For example, each of the seven Supreme Court Justices who voted so haughtily to enshrine abortion into America's laws have seen, just as they happened, the actual procedures of each of the 60 million babies that have thus far been slaughtered in their mothers' wombs as a result of their decree. They have witnessed the pain and feelings of each of those children as they were being slaughtered. They have seen all the good each of them would have done had they been allowed to live, every smile, every warm thought and feeling, each act of happiness and love, the children they themselves would have conceived, the family lines of human life that would have flourished, and the life each would have lived for Jesus. They have witnessed all that they snuffed out by their wicked decision. I tell you, these Supreme Court Justices have already drank their horror. And, I tell you, none of those jurists was ready to gaze upon the Truth of that diabolical holocaust that they raised. Fortunately, they saw every thought of love, every gaze extended into Heaven, every sentiment of compassion, every prayer that was ever said for them, and every sacrifice of reparation offered for them, as well. Do we believe enough reparation has been made to blot out the condemnation they are staring at even now? Can we not hear them pleading with God saying, "Please make it stop so that our condemnation may cease." You see, we will have an opinion about ourselves that will turn into an eternal judgement. Right now, reading this, you will see and recall every thought you are having at this moment. You will also know then whether the seed that is being cultivated in you now by the Queen of Heaven fell on fertile soil, rocky ground or was lost in the briars of life. When we experience our judgement, there will be no impediments to memory. All will be real and present as in its original moment. The question is, what frame of reference will we possess when our judgement impacts us? Jesus said that unless we become as a little child, we will not enter the Kingdom of Heaven. Jesus also said, "For as you judge, so will you be judged, and the measure with which you measure will be measured out to you" [Matthew 7:2]. Everyone must realize that we are, in effect, standing in the circumstances of our judgement at this very moment. Our conscience knows it; this is why it calls to us as if a sentinel giving notice. This is why each moment of our lives matters. As I write this sentence, I know that I am also outside of time at my judgement before the Throne of God, watching the words being composed from my heart right now. My future self and I are one in this recognition. I not only write to share the things Our Lady wishes me to communicate, but I try to write in a way that I will not be ashamed when my present self has its perception transformed into Glory and becomes one with my future self who is watching me now. What transforms our perception into Glory is the mighty presence of the Most Blessed Trinity whom we will see in the Light of our judgement. The Holy Trinity will accompany the judgement of our lives with the Divine Mercy of Jesus Christ. At the same time we are seeing our lives in an omnipresent review, we will also be overwhelmed by the vision of the Crucifixion of Jesus Christ and its every impact through human existence, nature, creation and time. What a glorious moment awaits us! What excuses for sin are going to matter at that moment? What good will it have been to have glossed over and made excuses for sins which crucified Jesus, instead of having assisted repentance and conversion? Repent, forgive and make no excuses for sin. No one can be healed by placating their sins. Healing comes through the Divine Mercy of Jesus Christ heaped upon any soul who loves Him.

VI. *Never compromise with those who wish to obscure or diminish the truth. Stand your ground!*

Let us speak about compromise for a moment. Compromise is a way of addressing an impasse between people of conflicting persuasions so that the impasse may be overcome and progress made by either party toward their particular goals. It entails a negotiation where one or both parties concede to a less than desired option in order to remove the obstacle creating the impasse. Many compromises have nothing to do with the parties advancing in a common direction. Despots throughout history have deployed the olive branch of compromise in order to strategically advance against the party with whom they are shaking hands. And, history tells us that no good is served conceding to those who would drag you toward evil either in enormous leaps or hidden increments. Nothing is gained by compromising with wickedness, except that portion of the truth you surrender believing that you can satisfy the ravenous appetite of the devil's minions. Compromise presupposes that each party has convictions toward their own particular outcomes and goals, apparent or clandestine. Therefore, wisdom must be employed because the process of discernment about the parameters of a compromise can be very difficult. For example, in the Scriptures, Jesus was approached to adjudicate a dispute, and He replied, "Friend, who appointed me as your judge and arbitrator?" [Luke 12:14] Now, this was a message to the people about greed, but it is also a warning about our compromising and how we discern whether to even enter into the discussion. Jesus was not going to dignify a search for a compromise about how to adjudicate greed because He did not recognize greed as having any standing to demand terms. Jesus' Crucifixion is another epic testament that there are eternal convictions that are beyond negotiation. For example, loyalty to Jesus is beyond any compromise to lessen it for any reason. The Deposit of Faith of the Roman Catholic Church is beyond compromise because Jesus' Life must not be diminished by any corruption. Everyone understands the principle of there being limits where compromise is not an option. Certain things are of supreme value and require protection or we inevitably surrender ourselves into the spiral of irrelevance, self-destruction and oblivion. We must remember that dying in defense of the truth is not the worst option. Imagine if someone said they would not go to Holy Mass unless we paid them to attend. Many people execute their Christian evangelization this way. They surrender away every manner of holiness and tradition so that those who have no intention of converting will stick around for awhile. They purchase false fraternity by surrendering the treasures of our Faith to the ultimate diminishment of the Kingdom of God on Earth. This is how we have arrived at the blase pluralistic Christianity that has lost the evangelic voice of the Martyrs. Fraternity without conversion to the Truth of Roman Catholicism is meaningless.

Most of the mantras dominating our contemporary American culture are reflective of our wholesale embrace of secular relativism, or atheism by another name. It is a void of sinister darkness where vast multitudes of our citizens no longer respect any of the stabilizing principles, virtues, convictions and traditions that informed and supported our nation from its foundation. Much of this has come to be because the generations of children since the 1960s have been betrayed. Of course, our forebears have not been perfect, which ones have? Many a sin has been committed for which forgiveness has been required. But, there has always existed the open and apparent search for truth by a righteous contingent who tried to get it right out of respect for the ages of Truth that were bequeathed to them. Many have been just little obscure people whose simple efforts had great effect in the shaping of the conscience of our history. Christianity is the sole voice that speaks about conviction in virtue, warning against chastisement, and the seriousness of Eternal Judgement. No worldly voice even pretends to tread in these realms, so they marginalize and ignore them as irrelevant, then replace them with their version of self-advancing expediency that they sell as secular righteousness. Everyone alive knows that they will someday pass from this world in death. But, those without faith in Jesus Christ have no authenticity to their comprehension as to what they are going to face just past that veil. They are unprepared to greet Eternal Glory. They are in a position of ignorance where the Truth is going to take them by surprise as it stares into their eyes for the very first time, asking for an accounting of their lives in Light of Jesus' Crucifixion.

So, this leaves us with very important questions. Do we care whether each of our brothers and sisters is prepared for a glorious reunion with their Savior? When ignorance abounds, do not those who know the Truth bear a great responsibility to bring clarity to the rest who are traveling the road to eternal death? Why would we not warn them of their future if we love them? Why would we not fulfill the commission Our Lord gave to us? It is like a physician having the cure for a deadly disease but refusing to offer it to a hospital filled with dying patients because none of them like doctors. As an analogy, what would be the result if a group of people effectively lobbied that it was an offense against the freedom to choose to require primary and secondary education of our youth? What if every child was given the choice about whether to attend their schooling? What overall ignorance and darkness would prevail upon our societies then? Every achievement and advancement of civilization would wither and die away, leaving the world to fall into chaos, darkness and death. Children must be taught virtue and holiness in order to become something more than pack animals when the evil forces of the world come against them. Would we compromise with these lobbyists knowing that our cultures would slip back into the darkest times of pagan holocaust? We should not compromise with those who wish to diminish or obscure knowledge of Jesus Christ and the meaning of His Holy Sacrifice on Calvary because He is the very foundation of wisdom that makes all human intelligence operable in every noble way. This is why we must teach our children about the Savior of the world and that the Holy Spirit surrounds them at every moment, offering great light for every step of their lives and how they will create, engage, experience, suffer and conquer. And, they must be disciplined, self-sacrificing and informed that they will see Jesus in all His Glory immediately after their passing from this life. This is the greatest knowledge that can ever be imparted into the human mind, and it must be obscured by nothing and believed because it is the truth.

Our Lady has never compromised the truth with my brother or me. And, I do not suppose it would be any other way with anyone else. She is not intimidated to speak about anything She wishes with whomever She pleases. She does not possess the ability to be intimidated. As ferocious as Satan displays himself to be, it was profound the first time She said, "I care not what Satan thinks or what he demands." That is having your heel on his throat! She is not deceived by feigned devotion or lukewarm commitment, which She believes to be no commitment at all. Her presence is so overwhelming and impenetrable. For all the people who believe that their mind and will could match Her determined convictions, 'you got another think a comin',' as my father used to say. She is standing in the doorway of Glory calling all to come in. No one outside that doorway has any real power. She does not have to engage a battle with anyone on the outside using any force, manipulation or intimidation. As powerful as anyone might believe themselves to be in resisting, rebuking or rejecting Her, their minds have not realized the eternal power of whom they are opposing. But, they will when the moment arrives where She steps back inside the door and Her Son peacefully closes it forever. It is then that all these titans will hear the bolt of the lock slide into place; that deafening gentle thud of a door kissing the jamb and its lock engaging the final security of Heaven, which will leave them in a shock of horror where they will wail and grind their teeth forever. A new perspective of terror will flood their beings. Utter helplessness will overwhelm them. The meaning of 'it is over' will rattle like thunder in accompaniment to the hideous squalls of all those who joined them in eternal damnation. Their own arrogance will shriek at them in condemnation forever. And, they will realize that their pride was their doom from the first instant they reared their head saying, "I will not serve." Our Lady knows where She stands. She knows the power She possesses. We must gather the world while the door is open. Nothing else matters. What does compromise with any other persuasion even mean?

VII. *The Most Blessed Sacrament of the Catholic Altar is the authentic Bread of Life. There is no other.*

This point is perhaps the single most important thing that the Most Blessed Virgin Mary has ever confirmed to me. The Most Blessed Sacrament of the Catholic Altar is the source and destination of human perfection. It is the summit of allegiance to Jesus Christ, the pinnacle of faith, and the origin of the unity of Heaven. It is the Alpha and the Omega. It is the complete, authentic expression of Jesus' Sacred Word from the Bible. He is the Bread of Life which comes down from Heaven for us to eat as real food. It is not a symbolic allusion to something only spiritual. It is the keystone that maintains the entire edifice of the Gospel that He shed His Blood to transmit to the entire world and the ages of men. The Doorway of Glory is the Roman Catholic Church from which this Bread is given to humanity. The one Table of Faith is in this sacramental mansion. There is no other authentic Bread of Life outside the Roman Catholic Church or the places She recognizes as being in Her Communion. Our Lady stands in the threshold of the Church of Rome where Her beloved Peter took to its pagan streets to lay the foundation of Her Son's earthly Kingdom. This is factual history, according to the Most Blessed Virgin, that still stands at its epicenter in Vatican City. Our Lady cares not about any other voice or force that claims or encourages otherwise. She cares only that the truth be told because it brings the possibility for peace on Earth and goodwill to the men who believe what She is saying. The center and summit of the authentic Church established by Jesus Christ nearly two thousand years ago is the Most Blessed Sacrament of the Catholic Altar. Jesus said at the Last Supper before His Holy Sacrifice on the Cross, "Do this in remembrance of Me" [Luke 2:19]. Jesus' Original Church is doing what He asked in our celebration of the Holy Mass offered each and every day of the world by our Catholic priests. And, what is the "this" that Jesus was talking about? It is the consecration and reception of the Bread of Life about which He said no one would have life unless they ate of it. Every time a Catholic receives the Most Blessed Sacrament at the Holy Mass, we are actually united with the night of the Last Supper and the salvific events of Good Friday in every way of grace. We are still 'doing' in perpetuity until He comes again what we were commanded to do in unity with Him and the Faith of the original Apostles, His Mother and disciples.

Everyone believes and respects the authenticity in an historical lineage that is present in a chain of successors. Secular atheists respect as much with any possession they hope to acquire. Do they not fawn over any item when its origins are found in the uniqueness of a celebrated master? One could go to an antique store searching for an artifact, but, if two of the same artifact were resting on a table and the proprietor presented you with an historical chain of evidence that one of the artifacts actually belonged to Christ, while the other did not, which would be most worthy to possess? Imagine that artifact being the actual Cup, the Holy Grail, from the Last Supper. I am sure that the makers of those Last Supper dinner vessels might have made more than just one, which they then sold to multiple customers to sustain their commerce at the time. If another cup had survived into the present day and was resting beside the actual Holy Grail on that antique store table, which one would you want? Which one possesses the dignity of Our Lord's hands having blessed it and having drank from it? Consider the breathtaking realization of something so fragile surviving the millennia through the protection provided by the people who cared for it down through the ages so that it not be broken. That artifact is the Faith and Traditions of the Roman Catholic Church in all their integrity, and the verifying historical lineage of authenticity is the unbroken Succession of Pontificates. Jesus said at the Last Supper, "Do this in remembrance of Me." He said as well, "Unless you eat of the flesh of the Son of Man and drink his blood, you will not have life in you," and "My flesh is true food and My blood is true drink." Embodied in this is the mission of His Original Apostolic Church. Everything the Catholic Church does services this original intention. Jesus prayed that we might all be one in Him, and that He would draw all things to Himself after He was lifted up. He spoke repeatedly about unity in love and oneness in Him. The Bible speaks of receiving the one bread at one table of faith. The Bread of Life discourse in the Holy Bible is beautiful and true as you read it. The contortions of protestors through the ages and the manipulations of revolutionaries in their most fervent rebellions have not placed a scratch in the sheen of the truth it states. The Bread of Life is indelible in the True Faith and is a signpost to the Church's final destination and magnification in the Glorious Return of Jesus Christ. Our Lady appeared in our midst on Sunday, May 5, 1991 in the majestic Saint Martin de Porres Catholic Church in Peoria, Illinois. It was just over two months after She began Her miraculous intercession to my brother and me. In recounting that event, everyone present was offering prayers of Eucharistic adoration to the Most Blessed Sacrament of the Altar through the recitation of the Holy Rosary. As part of our time of prayer, we celebrated the traditional "May crowning" of a statue of our Blessed Mother. The 5-foot tall statue was resting immediately beside the altar where the Bread of Life was enshrined in the Monstrance. The children processed with their crown of flowers and placed it atop the head of the statue of our Immaculate Mother. At that, She appeared in an apparition to my brother Timothy with the children's crown of flowers on Her head. Now the purpose to this story. The Most Blessed Virgin Mary turned and bowed in humble adoration of Her Son—in the Monstrance—where He rested on the Altar that day as the Most Blessed Sacrament. If the heavens ever gave a message to the people of the Earth, this was it.

Our Lady wishes not for anyone to feel chagrined by having it revealed to them that they may not understand the Bread of Life as well as they might think.

There are all kinds of demons who are trying to keep the Heavenly Father's children from returning to Him through His Son in the Great Sacrament of the Altar. Entire theologies have been constructed by the devil over the last 500 years in order to deny the actual Flesh and Blood of Jesus in the Most Holy Eucharist. One of the greatest spiritual impediments to any person is bearing the burden of ideas and convictions from those who formed their frame of reference first. I have said before that most of us are impeded by either who influenced us first or offended us last. The Roman Catholic Church and its great Saints have formed mine, and the Most Blessed Virgin has confirmed to my brother and me that it is what She believes as well. The problem throughout the world is that we are so worried about who might be offended by the truth that we rarely speak it anymore in a voice loud enough to be heard. We hint at it, hoping our hearers might decipher our mysterious intentions. We only present it as just another option in a world of egalitarian religious intellectualism. The Truths of the Faith have become relative to what any sinner might despise about them. And, what a shame this is. It defies logic to believe that the world can do anything but collapse into chaos after the great moral truths have been dragged down from their stately thrones, stripped of their esteem and crucified before the sight of all men with the indignity befitting a criminal.

The Most Blessed Sacrament through the Sacred Liturgies of the Catholic Church is the uniting element for all Christendom in the Eternal Life of Salvation. It is the restoration of all things beautiful and holy. It rescinds the anarchy of sin. My message is to ignore anyone who tells you otherwise because they are speaking under the influence of the Antichrist. Yes, people who believe themselves to be good and well-intentioned can be lost and cooperating with the darkness of the devil. There are legions of proud dissenters who together decide every day of the world to make skeptical arguments about Scripture passages referring to the Bread of Life. Our Lady asks, "What authority do they believe they have?" Her answer, none. They refuse to accept what Jesus said in John 6:52-59, "For my flesh is true food and my blood is true drink." This declaration offended those surrounding Our Lord in His time because they knew exactly what He meant, and neither their minds nor their faith could grasp it. The only reason dissenting opinions are conjured is because the protestors know they must maintain opposing perspectives to the Dogmas of the Catholic Church in the centuries-old battle that their forebears instigated. Talk about being offended last and influenced first. None of them seem to consider that they are preparing themselves as the last to be offended when the truth of the Bread of Life stands inviolate at their eternal judgement. Our Lady asked me, "What will they protest then?" It is ironic to realize that if the Catholic Church did not exist, these dissidents would be claiming the position of the Original Apostolic Church because the words of Scripture are so clear. Their generational opposition to the Catholic Church is their impediment to actually understanding the Gospels and uniting as One Body at One Table of Faith.

So, let us go to the origins of our succession of credibility—our motives of credibility. If modern men cannot agree on what Scripture states in our modern day some 2,000 years out from actual events, then let us ask ourselves what the original followers of Jesus believed about this scriptural subject. To do this, we need look no further than to Saint Ignatius of Antioch who lived from A.D. 36-108. He knew Saint John personally who was the writer of the Gospel passages in the Bread of Life discourse which is under critical scrutiny. Saint Ignatius also knew both SS Peter and Paul, and was the third Bishop of Antioch where Sacred Scripture says the followers of Jesus were first called "Christians." Pretty impressive credentials, wouldn't you say? He is one of the great "Apostolic Fathers" of the Christian Faith from the days of its initial flourishing. Should he not know what Jesus meant when He spoke of the Bread of Life and His Flesh and Blood? Did he not surely hear the truth from Peter and John who were actually present at the Last Supper? Saint Ignatius heard the story of human salvation firsthand from members of the original Twelve who actually witnessed the unfolding of the Sacred Mysteries of Christianity. There is, perhaps, no other more authoritative confirmation of the correct interpretation for the articles in question than in these men who knew Jesus and each other personally. Saint Ignatius composed a particular letter on his final travel to Rome where he would be martyred for his faith. In it, he wrote:

> *"Pay close attention to those who hold wrong notions about the grace of Jesus Christ which has come to us, and see how contrary their opinions are to the mind of God… They abstain from the Eucharist and from prayer, because they do not confess that the Eucharist is the Flesh of our Savior Jesus Christ, Flesh which suffered for our sins and which the Father, in his goodness, raised up again. They who deny the gift of God are perishing in their disputes."*
> — Letter to the Smyrnaeans, Ch 6

There you have it. What modern theologian two thousand years removed from events can compete with the words of this Apostolic Father? The answer again is, none. It is like someone from the South scandalizing Civil War history by saying that Abraham Lincoln never visited Gettysburg while holding the Gettysburg Address in their hands which reads in part, "We are met on a great battlefield of that war. We have come to dedicate a portion of that field..." The Holy Spirit is speaking to the world in Ignatius' Letter to the Smyrnaeans.

As our Heavenly Mother has spoken to my brother and me over the past three decades, She has repeatedly confirmed that the Bread of Life received at the Catholic Mass is actually and truly the crucified Flesh and Blood of Her Son Jesus. She told me that those outside the Catholic Church who believe they are receiving the Bread of Life in their communion services actually are not, even as well-intentioned as they might be. They are not fulfilling Jesus' scriptural command. She likens it to the difference between an actual cow standing before you compared to looking upon a picture of a cow. There is no animation or life in their communion bread, just as there is no milk in the picture of a cow. This She is confirming to them through we who are Her messengers. Protestant communion services may be configured and choreographed to look like a Catholic Eucharistic celebration, but the Flesh and Blood of Jesus as the authentic Bread of Life are not present. Their bread is not the Bread which comes down from Heaven, although their gathering in prayer is a blessed petition for God to give them the knowledge to know Him better. Our Lady does not wish any of these children to feel chided or inferior, but we should not be silent about the truth because their pride might be offended. All is for love. Our Heavenly Mother has the commission as their Matriarch to teach them the truth. She is not afraid of them hating Her because She knows Her love is spectacular enough to win them over at any time She desires. She knows they will one day see Her and fall in love with Her. But, before then, She wants them to come into full communion with Her Son's Original Apostolic Church so that their final reunion with the heavens will be graced by an unstained, seamless garment of unity with perfect Truth. The Truth must be told for them to even have a chance of being rewarded with this joy. She wants them to be front-row, center stage when the curtain of Eternity opens, not distracted in some distant mezzanine where they might find they missed the show altogether. She says that protesting against the unity for which Jesus is calling is no way to complete a life.

I wish to say something about the accusations of being condescending which are leveled by others when certain truths are proclaimed. First, Cardinal Joseph Ratzinger said in a homily to the conclave immediately before being elected as the Supreme Pontiff upon the death of Saint John Paul II, "We are moving toward a dictatorship of relativism which does not recognize anything as for certain, and which has as its highest goal one's own ego and one's own desires." This phenomenon of a dictatorship of relativism has a direct impact on our frame of reference and how we interpret the concept of condescension. Condescension implies that there is a difference between two ideas, one which is recognized as being of a higher order than another. And, in recognition of this difference, a discernment process ensues as to each idea's position of subordination in the hierarchy of truth. And, from this discernment and subordination comes order and peace. But, what assists us in creating and maintaining a hierarchy of truth where we can begin ordering a world of peace? For those with no faith, they could begin by observing the things that God has made and how the universe functions. Regrettably even in this, we see they would rather attack the definitions of biology instead. When faith is granted and accepted, one can begin to recognize the hierarchy of authority propagating from the Supreme Authority of God who created the universe that gave us a first taste of His peacefully ordered intentions. This speaks to Saint Thomas Aquinas' explication of eternal, divine, natural and human law. Now, the dictatorship of relativism is manifested by people who reject the Author of Life, and thereafter make themselves the destroyers of the hierarchy of truth that they know exists. The reason they know it exists? Because they fight against it. The reason? They do not wish to be subordinate to the hierarchy of truth whose Author is God. They wish to be God, which is the original sin of pride presented by the Serpent in the Garden. Therefore, they attack the idea of discernment according to the truths of Creation and its Maker. They squelch the authentic conscience and replace it with the voice of their misguided will. And, they do this by maintaining that there is no difference in any two things or one being of greater virtue than another. The essence of truth becomes relative to the interior wilful authority of each sinner. And, the problem is, that interior will can be filled with darkness and guided by outright demonism when it becomes separated from the vision of divine beatitude. Then, when the supremacy of the truth is presented to them and they realize that it will not give way to their pride, they reply, 'You are so condescending thinking your ideas are the only way to think.' This happens no matter how gentle your presentation of the truth may be. For all the pontificating by relativists that the truth is decided by what each person thinks it is 'for them,' they can never answer the question, "What makes history's despots wrong in your view of the world? Weren't all of them doing what they believed to be right 'for them?'" There must always be an outside agency which confirms the interior authority of man in what is right and good. Virtue is real. And, that outside agency cannot claim authority if it contradicts itself. The moment it becomes divided within itself, it cannot stand. Democracy in a world of sinners cannot have either internal or external consistency without Christ.

So, when someone makes the claim that a person is being condescending, are they not simply recognizing that someone is making a declaration of a difference between two things, and they are testifying that one of those things may possess a more elevated stature in the hierarchy of truth? Now, the great truths of Catholic Dogma make it easy to avoid the charge of condescension because they are impenetrable and permanent in the hierarchy of truth, and always will be. Man has no legitimate say in this, just as we have no say about whether the sun exists in the sky at midday. They are the "outside agency" revealed by God. In contrast, the simple perspectives engendered in the life of Christian grace seem to be more difficult avenues to navigate. Oftentimes, opinions are no more than that, and should be recognized as such, even though we may feel they are great anchors to our individual spiritualism at any given point in time. We should have a hierarchy of the great truths of Roman Catholicism within us into which all other perspectives of our lives, including miraculous private revelations, must be fitted in individual positions of subordination. This is the construction of our optimal frame of reference from which all other things are discerned. So, the point is, our accusations of someone being condescending may be nothing more than our legitimate recognition that we are being faced with a greater truth than we are willing to accept. And, this truth, which may be subordinate to nothing, finds it has no home in us if the disease of relativism has imploded our hierarchy of truth into a smouldering pile of rubble. There is no elevation to a relativistic hierarchy. In fact, it has no hierarchy at all. Relativists believe everything must lie flat in a heap of diversity on the ground, breathing the noxious effluent of the most notorious sinner's mind. Nothing can stand in beauty in their world. Nothing reigns supreme. No great universal truth can be spoken. No tradition of purity is defended from spoiling. Finally, they believe no one has the authority to tell them anything because they are the creators of their own truth. They do not realize how wrong they are.

    I wish to say something about the concept of conscience, which vast numbers of people enlist to defend the evil they wish to propagate and participate in. Our Lady says that if their conscience is not in unity with the Truth of Her Son Jesus, they have no conscience at all. They are making a claim based upon a foundation that does not exist; one that will collapse beneath their feet. A house built on shifting sand, indeed. There is no grace in an interior voice that has no unity with the Truth of Jesus Christ. At best, it can be utilitarian in support of a mortality which is dying. At worst, it will condone and guide great evil, such as abortion. Conscience is more than our interior voice which makes assessments in adjudicating our human condition. It is a dead corpse until it is given life by God through faith in His Son. The Bread of Life from the Catholic Altar is one of the Supreme Truths of the Hierarchy of God's Wisdom. There can be no compromise with anything that obscures it or diminishes it in the minds of those who wish to be saved. This is why no one who supports abortion should be allowed to touch the Most Blessed Sacrament until they repent. They should not even be allowed into the sacred confines of a Catholic Church. They are walking death, harboring the great lie. If someone feels that this is condescending or divisive, so be it. Political correctness will always howl until its beastly nature is put down. Our Lady said that there is no difference between an unrepentant sinner's hand reaching into a Tabernacle and an abortion doctor reaching into the womb of a mother to kill a child. We must remember that the Bread of Life came down from Heaven. Jesus condescended to humanity, bringing the Truth in order to save us. This is the condescension that sinners recognize when confronted with the truths of the Bread of Life written in the Holy Gospel that the Roman Catholic Church declares.

Lastly, the station of the Blessed Virgin Mary in the Kingdom of God is defined by great dogmatic declarations in the hierarchy of truth. They are pinnacle beliefs. These Marian Dogmas are of the same essence as those enthroning the Bread of Life in the Christian conscience, our frame of reference and our interior hierarchy of truth. Of course, Our Lady is subordinate to Her Son, but only to the level of being His Queen and Mother. But, do we ever consider that Jesus has dimensions of subordination to His Immaculate Mother even still, She whom the Commandments of His Father tells Him to honor? And, just as it is ordered for us to recognize and respond to the manifestation of our King as the Bread of Life on the Catholic Altar, so too is it ordered that we give attention, allegiance and veneration to the manifestations of His Queen in Her miraculous intercessions. Her miraculous intercessions are Her venues granted to Her by the Holy Spirit. They are integral operational manifests of Her universal Motherhood of the redeemed through time. This may be a condescending idea to those who feel they can ignore Her miraculous intercession with impunity. I tell you, someday they will wish they had not. I would ask any person who claims they do not need their Holy Mother's intercessory assistance, "Are you perfect?" If you say yes, I would respond, "God bless you, please pray for me. I need more grace, I'm not there yet." If you say no, then I would ask you, "What is it then that you do not need?"

VIII.   Defend the Roman Catholic Church and its priesthood.

The previous thoughts about the Most Blessed Sacrament of the Catholic Altar being the authentic Bread of Life is the reason behind the defense of the Roman Catholic Church and its priesthood. The Sacrament of Holy Orders received by Roman Catholic priests is the propagating mechanism for the Bread of Life through the Original Apostolic Church until the Second Coming of Jesus Christ. Catholic priests are given the power of Consecration of the bread and wine to be transformed into the Body, Blood, Soul and Divinity of Jesus at every Holy Mass. This is called Transubstantiation. This is how Jesus is giving His Flesh and Blood for the life of the world through time. The power of Consecration which is given to His Catholic priests upon their ordination has come directly from the Last Supper through the Succession of two hundred and sixty-six Pontificates.

Our Lady has spoken to me at length about the facets and dimensions of defending the Roman Catholic Church and its priesthood amidst the turmoil of darkness generated by the secular void. We must remember that the teachings of Jesus are going nowhere. His Church can be beaten, scourged and led to death, but its King will respond with power once He has seen enough. And, woe to the plunderers. No revolutionaries are going to change anything in the eyes of God. The malcontents are spitting into the wind of the Holy Spirit who will throw every fleck of phlegm back into their faces because He does not care what any sinner believes. If a man does not want to be saved, then he will be damned into hell forever. Justice is indelible and will prevail. The expectation of receiving Divine Mercy means that we must extend it to those who repent, while moving at every step to preserve the justice of love which sustains forbearance and forgiveness, yet expects the rise to perfection. We must be very clear to ourselves that sin will not be incorporated into perfection in the name of mercy. It will be purged. The concept of condoning sin in the name of mercy is a lie. It is just and reasonable to be merciful because all are sinners who are justifiably condemned unless Jesus Christ shows us mercy. So, what are we to do when our speaking in defense of the Church generates backlash from those who revel in the momentum they have generated for their ideologies, hoping to permanently anchor in history their modes of transformation and reformation of a Church they feel to be out of touch with their progressive ways? Well, simply knowing and speaking about the truth behind closed doors does little to defend the Church or evangelize the Gospel. But, if the truth is brought into the open as Jesus manifested it before the eyes of men, the Cross looms. Our Lady says fear it not. The enemies of Christ are predictable in their grievances. There seems to be nothing to bring them down from their stratospheric plateaus of rage. They are people who do not possess peace or love in their hearts. And, they will inflict their spasmodic fury on anyone who brings them light because they love the darkness. The Bible speaks of them. This is why it is very sacrificial to speak the truth regarding the attacks against the Church and its priesthood. Most people attempt to find common-ground phrases and themes of self-flagellation as their response to those who are hurling their accusations against the Church of Rome. It grieves us all when a leading Catholic Prelate who rocketed to the pinnacle of the Church hierarchy is found to have repeatedly committed sinful acts of licentiousness with young boys. But, are the horrible acts and agendas of a dozen evil men in the Church deserving of the crucifixion of the entire Faith-Church which is the spiritual heart of over a billion people, and the only hope of the rest?

We must come to understand a spiritual dynamic that is in effect in this world. It is applicable to both the seen and unseen realms. Satan will attack that which is good, while granting great benefits and forbearance to those who are content in their distance from the truth. He will leave lost souls, institutions, agendas and societies in their worldly contentment, but attack, subdue, antagonize, punish and destroy anything which can do damage to his kingdom of darkness. He hates the light and is terrified that the world will reach the blinding brilliance of high noon truth. If Satan knows someone is stagnant in the mediocrity of the morning twilight, and knows they have no intention of rising to high noon, he will leave them alone until they begin to move. In this twilight, he has so many minions and abundant opportunity to destroy these souls. If someone is content in sin and error, then Satan is happy in their state of malaise and will reward them. But, if someone is devoted to their relationship with Jesus and living as He commanded, the beast will bring unimaginable suffering and disruption, if he can. Therefore, if we wish to recognize where the high noon of truth really exists, all we need to do is observe what is attacked and marginalized with the most intensity. That place is none other than the Roman Catholic Church and everything for which She stands. Satan has spent twenty centuries attempting with varying degrees of success to claim influence in the highest reaches of Jesus' Church in different eras. So, it should be no surprise that a Catholic Prelate might fall to terrible sins of the flesh. For what purpose, we might ask? Not necessarily to lead an individual sinner astray, but rather to destroy the integrity of the Mother Church of Christianity before the eyes of the world. He wants to obscure the origin of the only Redemption mankind will ever know.

The Roman Catholic Church through the propagating faith in its holy priests is the high noon brilliance of the Truth of Jesus Christ. These holy priests of Christendom possess the strength to extinguish the night with the full day brilliance of Jesus' Sacrifice. And keeping with his modus operandi, the devil attacks the strength he sees and the capacity he knows will destroy his kingdom of darkness. The wholesale assault upon the institution of the Catholic priesthood and its integrity is a clear and present attack by Lucifer against the

Original Apostolic Church founded by Jesus Christ using the sexual sins of a few as his pretext. How could it be more obvious? What is the truth regarding the integrity of the Catholic Church and its esteemed hierarchy? There were 109,694 active priests in the United States from 1950-2002 [John Jay Report]. According to the most detailed documentation, there were 105,302 priests from this overall number who lived their vocations with sincerity, who testified to their Savior with devotion and distinction to the best of their courage, and who made noble contributions to American society that secularists did not have the heart to engage. That is 105,302, some 96% of all Catholic priests in America in the second half of the twentieth century. Show me any institution with these numbers of sacrificial devotion. These men lived, and still live, attempting to maintain the high noon of truth to a world that desires to walk in darkness instead. Is it not a horrible injustice to impugn the lives of these 105,302 men and relegate them to being no more than collateral damage of the secular fanaticism that is tearing through society like a tornado? Of course it is, but zealous lynch mobs and scarlet letter brigades dominate and distort the proportional implementation of justice – the true implementation of justice – making themselves instruments of Satan in the process through their excesses. Once again, their discernment has failed them in the midst of the secular nightmare they created. Legitimate grievances regarding the terrible actions of certain sinners are being used as pretexts by Catholic-haters to inflict a definitive attack on the Roman Catholic Church in the hopes of extinguishing its influence in the world. No one should be deceived into believing it is anything less. It is the work of the father of lies. Look at what these worldlings and their progeny have done to our country, indeed the world, since 1950. They have driven God out of everything through any means they could effect, except in the hearts of faithful Christians led by the faithful men that Our Lady defends. One hundred and five thousand, three hundred and two men have served honorably in their commission to lift high the Cross as the Messianic beacon to all who would invoke the wisdom to follow them. Too bad the rest of the nation did not, because the priestly sexual scandal would never have occurred. The Queen of Heaven defies anyone who assails the honest efforts of this great body of devotion. Our priests are the consecrated shepherds of Her Son who rely on His help daily, who need our prayers of support, and who humbly petition the grace to administer their authority to forgive sins in His name and dispense the Bread which grants Eternal Life every day of the world. Have there been wolves among the sheep? Of course, but those wolves are progeny of the libertine atheistic secularists who have tempted, cajoled, prodded, assailed, mocked, impugned, enticed and have now scandalized several generations of children, families, towns, states, and ultimately, our nation through their attack on Christian moral truth since the 1950s. It is a miracle what these 105,302 men have heroically stood for in the midst of the moral implosion of our nation, indeed the world that is failing. We have not seen true horror yet, but it is coming if we do not return to God through His Son at the calling of the Mother of Jesus and through the Bread from these priests' hands. Our Holy Mother said that the secular enemies of Jesus sowed corruption and unleashed licentious abomination, and now sanctimoniously scream that a monster is on the loose. She said that it is their monster. They have conceived and reared this beast which has infiltrated into Her beautiful Church and attacked its purity from the inside. Hear me America! Hear me you assailants of the Roman Catholic Church! The Immaculate Mother of the Savior of the world stands with complete devotion, power and gratitude beside each man who has faithfully worn the Roman Catholic collar. She is also prepared to receive to Her breast through the Sacrament of Reconciliation each who may have fallen to Satan's temptations. They will receive the Divine Mercy of Jesus Christ through Her Immaculate Heart. She will repair anything they may have damaged by their weaknesses. Those who refuse to forgive are in danger of the fires of hell. My beloved fathers, each of you bears within yourself the rewards deserving of a king. Stay the course! You are warriors in the midst of a gruesome battle that you did not choose, but was thrust upon you. Know true that you cannot lose. The victory of your sacred identity and your holy convictions is in the Triumph of the Immaculate Heart of Mary who loves you and is poised to intercede for you. You are wrapped in the raiment of the Son of God. You are united with Him in His Crucifixion, and your souls shine like high noon. Your grace and beauty are blinding to the heavens. Let Satan rage against you. He is a secular demon who will be thrust into hell at your command. Stand tall, stand proud and proclaim the Gospel to humanity with the courage of Martyrs.

  No one should be under any delusion that the attacks against the Catholic Church will be mitigated before they are superseded by something far more glorious, miraculous and breathtaking, because the imprint of hatred for the Catholic Church impressed into the hearts of secularists is profound. These people do not know the way out of their nightmare because Satan has achieved an angle of perception through the failures of a few religious leaders, which is having the extraordinary effect of defining a false frame of reference that he controls through the inordinate passions of these lost souls. Most of these people have hated the Catholic Church from the beginning. Now, they believe they have the ultimate justification for doing so. They feel vindicated in their hatred, and nothing of this world will convince them otherwise. I say again, nothing of this world can change their minds, but they have not considered the power that is not of this world; the power of God that comes to Earth from the heavens. What will they think when that overwhelming revelation arrives? They will stand horrified and naked. They will run to the Rockies, pleading for the mountains to cover them from the arrival of Divine Justice. Until then, all the angst and unrest throughout our culture is being consolidated into organized frontal attacks against the foundational pillars of civilized society. The very idea of justice is being lampooned and destroyed right in front of our eyes through highly-placed principals who hold megaphones of public influence through which they spread their ideologies of corruption. The evil one is the master of incitement, self-righteous manipulation, and the debasement of virtuous restraint which leads to fanatical manifestations of human action. This is from where violence, revolution, terror and war ultimately flourish. This description is reflective of the disorientation of people's frames of reference that have become unhinged from the beauty of divine truth that wishes to speak to their souls instead. Entire textbooks could be written about the pandemic of public mania that has swept across our culture like a deadly contagion. Will writing about it do anything to defuse or eliminate it? Probably not. Why? Because the maniacs are self-possessed, if not possessed outright; their frameworks of reference are owned by Satan; they are his property and they serve him with passion that grows by the measure of their rage. They have lost all moral bearings, reject humility and reason, refuse to pray for wisdom, believe the darkness within them is light, and are fueling fanatical indignation based in a hypocritical partiality that consoles their ideologies. For example, it is easy for a progressive who does not like the ancient traditions of the Church to join in attacking its episcopal leaders who represent and are charged with protecting those same traditions. They are in the mode of tearing down, and have been since the Second Vatican Council. If they see a bulldozer happening by, they do not care if it might be driven by the devil and his minions as long as it attacks the Patriarchy of the Church. It suits their collective progressive agenda to join in the vehicle of the attack. It is a bandwagon of disaster, so sayeth the Mother of God. She asks what is going to be left if they succeed in bringing the Catholic Church to its death? Darkness would cover the Earth with nothing to prevent the final holocaust. Do we actually believe that the world is going to be governed peacefully by leaders who have overseen 41 million abortions worldwide in 2018 alone without a twinge of conscience? Whom will they assign to be killed next? The Roman Catholic Church is the only thing that is holding back this tidal wave of ultimate human annihilation, and there are hordes who are screaming for its eviction from the world. Jesus Christ is being crucified by this generation.

Our Holy Mother wishes every Christian to know that She is the Refuge of sinners who appears to bring clarity to what is occurring so that we might find our path to conversion, sanctification and peace. She is the Protection of Christendom, the Defender of the Church and the Consoling Mother of the holy priesthood. She can invoke the flaming intercession of Saint Michael the Archangel any time She chooses. She is the Destroyer of all heresy and the Throne of Wisdom. The Woman clothed with the Sun is present and shining. The Book of Revelation rings! She wishes Her loyal Catholic children to not take another step back in compromise with the secular void. Advance on them with all the approbation of Heaven. Tell humanity the truth. If there is to be a confrontation between the light and the darkness, then let us fight in the daylight of high noon where Jesus Christ reigns. This Mother loves and defends the Church instituted by Her Son nearly 2,000 years ago. She stands with Roman Catholicism. She has no intention of abandoning it now. She does not recognize the opposition as having any true power, and She believes that those who oppose Her are deluded to believe that She would ever accept any of their hollow terms for Her surrender. Mercy is the order of Her Immaculate Heart, but She knows the inevitability of Divine Justice that will fall and obliterate all the opponents of Her Son's Church. She wants them to be saved, but She will not shed a tear if the Archangels are required to eject them from the Banquet Feast into the fires where they will wail and grind their teeth forever. The horrible events that we watch throughout the world every day are the Father's vision of mercy being shown to us, because if God had no mercy, He would not stand for what He sees occurring. Nonetheless, the fateful day is coming sooner than what any human being realizes; it will catch evildoers by surprise just as the Scriptures state occurred in Noah's time.

IX.   *Obey the Most Blessed Virgin Mary as the Morning Star Over America.*

Obedience presupposes that two and perhaps more directions, paths or courses of decision and action are present. In addition, the Truth is always present in the soul because God would have it no other way. He did not leave us orphans. Our Lady asks for obedience to the path that She is prescribing as a unifying gift from our Most High God. The mystical phenomenon that She be allowed to openly communicate in such a way with we who are in mortal flesh is, indeed, an astounding mystical gift of Her Motherhood. Millions have been the people who have taken to their knees petitioning the heavens to respond to the secular darkness that we see engulfing the minds of men and the societies of nations. She asks that we trust Her, then listen and obey. The problem is, people believe that they need to trust my brother and me first, which causes them to pause, knowing that we are as vulnerable as anyone to misstep and confusion if we do not remain sacrificial in the grace of God. Truth is, my brother and I are not requiring anyone to trust us. We are simply proclaiming the reasons why you can, and maybe should. We do not believe that anyone cannot grow to know Our Lady as we do, even if they chose to bypass everything we ever said or did. Although, we wonder how that would be possible, knowing the amount of selflessness and suffering they would have to embrace to get there on their own. From our position, we understand Jesus a little more personally when He faced the same stubbornness in John 10:37-38, "If I do not perform my Father's works, do not believe me; but if I perform them, even if you do not believe me, believe the works, so that you may realize [and understand] that the Father is in me and I am in the Father." Now, we are not claiming a hypostatic union with the Almighty Father just yet, but we are sharing an immaculate relationship with His Queen. This is why my brother and I say, "If you don't believe us, read the books that you may come to know and believe your Heavenly Mother." We have never personally offered anything as profound as Her words. And, if you never believe a syllable that we have personally uttered, even in all the prefaces and prologues we have written, please read Our Lady's messages contained within the works. My brother and I could not, and would not, have conceived their content on our own. Consider where we started, and how long ago. Imagine what we have been doing every day for nearly 30 years, compared to most every other person in the world. We have not been doing it alone. We do not think anyone could have. What we have experienced and have attempted to record, and the responsibility that the Holy Spirit has placed upon us, is the answer to the prayers of millions who have been asking God to show us a sign, give us a miracle, bring us Light, and change the world. I understand what our Holy Mother means when She says that She can do very little without our help. Neither can my brother and I do anything more than what She has assisted us in doing. We have only one life to give to Her. What is it that neither ourselves nor the great Queen of Heaven can do? Force someone to believe the Good News that we announce and the events we are sharing. Each person's faith is their gift to Jesus Christ. We must remember though, that God is intent upon cleansing and converting the Earth through one of two things: Human suffering or the Faith of Saint Peter, he whose convictions become our own faith when we believe and obey what he set out into the pagan world to proclaim. I do not mean merely intellectual faith, although that should be incorporated into our steps of conversion. I refer to the strength to recognize God calling from within ourselves, believing in our stature as His children, and exhibiting the confidence and humility to see the path on which He would guide us. We must have the courage to contradict our comfort and engage the sacrifice to advance to the front lines of His Passion. It is the ability of the Martyrs to walk as confidently as Saint Polycarp to the fires.

Everyone should see that Christian civilization is failing and that we are caught in the tyrannical riptides of the end of the age. Evildoers applaud this. God is not going to unilaterally save us from this descent if He cannot find the righteous ten who will invoke their faith. The Kingdom of God on Earth has been spread through the faithful convictions and actions of men from the beginning. Every sinner who has converted their lives from sinfulness to saintliness has believed someone, going all the way back to the original Apostles believing the Messiah. Millions of Saints throughout the ages have passionately contributed their portion of the Cross to subdue the bestiality of men. So, what has happened to us in this age of post-Christian modernism? Our collective social identity has become complacent in the plush material prosperity of our technologically advanced age. Sacrifice for the Kingdom of God and the salvation of men has become foreign to us, replaced by the lie of creating mere fraternity in multicultural diversity at the expense of the call for Christian conversion. We do not have His Mind, while trying to create some global convocation of sinners without the need for a Savior. Many believe their comforts in life are going to transfer into comforts after their passing. The discomforts of the Saints are anathema to the sensibilities of secular materialists. Why? Because they do not understand the meaning of their existence, the sanctification of their souls or the Triumph of the Cross. They have not contemplated well enough their eternal judgement and the threads of their clothing in order to be presentable at the wedding feast of the Lamb, although the Gospel speaks with seriousness to the requirements of our preparation.

We must remember that the obstinance of humanity can never win. Mediocrity is a coward's path of leisure. Do we care that we might perish in our sins forever and be doomed by the greatest mistake of our lives? The Bible says it is a narrow path which leads to salvation, while the secular utopia is advertised as an expansive thoroughfare. We must stop thinking that we are too precious a creature for God to throw us to eternal damnation. When we are thrust by death before His Glory, our entire discerning constitution will be suddenly transfigured, and everything I am trying to say here will become as clear as crystal in an instant, and consequences will loom. Our Holy Mother changed me to see this. Priorities were upended. Passion exploded up from the crevices as if light were streaming up out of the cracks in the ground. My hierarchy of truth was permanently imprinted with a divine order. And, my love for the truth began to move as if having no intention of stopping for anyone or anything that wished to impede it. God has allowed the Most Blessed Virgin the opportunity to reconstruct humanity's framework of reference through Her miraculous intercession as the Morning Star Over America, if we will listen. Her purpose is to clear the slate within us as if a standing field of rotting grain is cut down and prepared as silage on which the beasts would feast. Then, She wishes to lay new patterns of righteous thought and virtuous possibility within us through Her parables and lessons. Even the cadence of Her words and the tenor of Her sentiments bring reflections of how the heavens think, how special we are, and the seriousness of the apocalyptic times in which we live. Jesus is preparing to enter the world a second time to deliver those who loved and obeyed Him. The rest will meet their fate.

X.   *Love people enough to tell them the Truth.*

Every person who wishes to spread the truths of the Gospel must realize the collision generated between the Good News and the darkened reference frames of sinners. When light comes into the darkness, people squint their eyes to deflect the glare. Those who have lived longest in darkness are sometimes nearly blind when brought out into the day. There is a measure of discomfort in nearly all who move into greater light. The exception may be in those whom life has broken, sending them to their knees and opening them to any redemptive word or perspective. Once one comes to recognize that everything they are is useless in bringing them deliverance from their desolation, they are ready to accept anything their hidden God might tell them. They could see a match struck at twenty miles looking for grace. There is not a mountain they will not attack, scratching and clawing for its summit. But, from those who have yet to be broken by the repetition of days and the failing of their bodies, the Truth must confront their monsoons of obstinance and error. So, we must be prepared to be repulsed, rejected, slandered, hated, attacked, marginalized, persecuted and even killed because these are the methods and tactics that the unrepentant employ to continue imbibing in their paths leading to their ultimate destruction. We must love them nonetheless. We must love them enough to tell them the truth, while time for them still exists. It is the very heart of the Great Commission and the spreading of the Gospel to all people. This tenth concept probably has the shortest description because it is the underlying basis beneath everything that I have attempted to elaborate on in concepts one through nine. Everything is for Love. All the clarity, all the organization of thought, the hierarchy of truth, the frames of reference, our motivations, the conception of our visions; all of it is for the manifestation of the final destiny of humankind in the Sacred Heart of Jesus. We love humanity when we spread the Gospel and hold the line on the parameters of sanctification required by Jesus Christ, especially in our own lives. Jesus did say to make sure that we pick the beam out of our own eye before addressing the splinter in our brother or sister's eye. But, He did not say that we should never address splinters simply because we are all vulnerable to sin. It means don't be a hypocrite. Love others as you love yourself, which means tell yourself the truth with the same message you impart to others. This speaks to prayer and our daily examination of conscience; and further, our reception of the Sacrament of Reconciliation when needed.

We should consider how much love is required of us to engage the places where Light needs to be shined and shared, knowing it is going to hurt both our hearts and maybe our reputations. How many wayward children bring desolation and sin into their families under the license of being a family member, believing they are entitled to the affirmations deserved by saints while contributing nothing but the darkness of reprobates? How many great holiday feasts must have ground rules because worldliness and materialism invade these sanctified gatherings and instigates pandemonium if challenged? It is not cliche that at family gatherings the discussion of religion or politics brings on the confrontations. Usually it is a battle between the Light and the darkness. In a world gone cold and comfortable in sin, it is very sacrificial to cut against the grain of human understanding and carve out Christ's rightful place in our midst. Our Holy Mother offered a very profound statement one day as She addressed the supposed gatekeepers when She said, "They should get off the throne and let the real King sit down." The message of Christianity has been diced, filleted, quartered, minced, and ground up to mean nothing more than go along and get along. And, since evil will always throw a fit when confronted by the truth, we have been conditioned to avoid bringing the truth to the fore because we shy away from any environment of potential conflict. Then, Satan claims that we should be more merciful and not cause such a commotion. What audacity! Allowing wickedness to have the run of the house unchecked is not a display of mercy. Being silent through a false sense of maintaining peace is misguided. Our Lady would say that this type of peace is what is false, and any fraternity not based in the Holy Sacrifice of Jesus cannot maintain a cohesiveness in the truth with enough strength to withstand the deceptions of the devil. All will collectively fall into the pit. This is no Christianity at all. It is a truth that is loving enough to tell. Do we have the love in our hearts to bring humanity the only knowledge that matters, that of our Lord's Death and Resurrection, why He came into this world and what He will expect when He comes again? All roads lead to God, but not all of them lead to Paradise. We will stand to be judged upon the sanctification of our lives. Lastly, if you do not know what to say as part of your message of evangelization, Our Lady says, "Tell the world to read the Morning Star Over America."

Question 19

Regarding the nature of human sin, has Jesus or the Virgin Mary ever spoken to you about its inevitable nature? Has Our Lady ever told you that there will be a time before the Return of Jesus in Glory when no one alive on the Earth will ever sin again?

Our Lady says that, except for the original sin of Adam, no sin is inevitable, and we should stop believing that it is. She wishes there to be no sin on the Earth right now. Humankind simply needs to stop sinning and seek absolution in the confessionals of the Catholic Church. It is we who must choose Jesus' Mercy and convert our hearts, and we have every capacity and capability to do so. She knows that our lives exist in this world in a state of vulnerability to sin because we have the gift of free will that is susceptible to many influences, both good and bad. Yet, our will is free and sovereign. There is nothing that has power over our ability to decide the direction of our intentions, and our hearts united with Jesus will always tell us the way. Nevertheless, Satan and his demons roam the Earth seeking souls whom they can agitate, lead astray and make his instruments to destroy. Jesus Himself came into this vulnerable state bearing the overwhelming capacity to render the vulnerability extinguished through His will united with the Father as One in Being. Jesus' presence within the exilic realms of vulnerability is why Satan even bothered to attack and tempt Him at all. He saw a New Adam come into the fallen domain, and he was arrogant enough to believe that his manipulation of the vulnerable state might overpower the deific free will of the Christ as Man, just as he had done with Adam. And, if nothing more, he would have the latitude to make the Christ suffer to generate the illusion that he was more powerful. He was deluded enough to believe that he could succeed again as he had in the Garden with Adam and Eve. What audacity! It is a mystery that the devil did not give up and flee to the farthest corner of Creation, never to be heard from again. His evil attempts at sabotaging the redemption of man were futile from the first instant of Jesus' Incarnation in the flesh. In fact, it was destined at the instant our Virgin Mother uttered Her Fiat to the Archangel Gabriel because neither could Her pure will falter. Two perfect Creatures; one a God, the other, His perfect Mother. One an omnipotent Creator, the other His Immaculate Conception.

Then, there are the rest of us. For as much as theologians and thinkers have pondered and argued over the nature of grace, the occasion of sin and the completion of sanctification, none of these intellectuals know the individual amounts, moments or finalities in any soul. For all the talk of affective and effective love, actual grace, sanctifying grace, natural grace, supernatural grace, habitual grace, preventing grace, cooperating grace, sufficient grace and the discussion of intrinsic energy and extrinsic efficiency, still no man can see the origin or operation of any of these within any particular soul, nor can they definitively judge their presence or action. None of these analyzers know the timetables of maturation, the dispensations of intimate revelation or the motivations that cause God to favor a soul at seeing how they pine for Him or what they wish to suffer for Him. Neither do they know the state that the soul possessed upon its initial entrance into exile, notwithstanding the stain of original sin. Our Lady said every soul spoke with God in the beginning before its entrance into this world; and the tenor of those conversations is reflective of the lives many of them are leading, Saints and hellions alike. The best one can do is recognize the fruits that would indicate what tree has been borne there, and then hope our soul is clear enough in its own discernment to have recognized the fruits correctly. There are blind theologians who have been misleading, harassing and condemning other people with their scholastic interpretations for centuries. This is why the Congregation for the Doctrine of the Faith matters. Even the Church refuses to judge the ultimate state of a soul, while it attempts to make clear the prescriptions of holiness and describe the concepts of mitigating circumstances and levels of culpability that reveal how vulnerable we actually are in discerning God's works. And, in the midst of all of this, the Mystical Body of Christ still confidently declares the singular Truth of human Redemption in one Crucified Messiah.

Ironically still, it seems that our intellectualism more ponders the vulnerabilities of human sinfulness than recognizing the colossal power in the grace that God dispenses upon His repentant children through the Cross of His Son Jesus Christ. He dispenses the grace of kings and conquerors, while our discernment of miraculous graces is afflicted with an ecclesial bar of official recognition being set so high that our habitual refusal to acknowledge these graces has become entrenched as pastoral tradition that seems to have reached the heights of dogma. God is manifesting His presence with us and in us, guiding us to the deepest reaches of sanctification and union with Him through His Immaculate Mother, but most trumpet nothing more than the tired mantra, 'Well, we're not required to believe that.' How did we pervert the simple recognition that the Deposit of Divine Revelation is complete into a rejection of most everything this Deposit mystically generates by saying it is something we do not have to believe? There is a complete disconnect between the theories of theologians and the lessons taught by actual grace. This harkens to Our Lady's comparison between a cow and picture of a cow. I am sure there are innumerable theologians who would desire to set me straight with their hair-splitting intellectualism. But please remember, nearly every one of them rejects in practice and veneration the miraculous intercession of the Queen of Heaven whom they would rhetorically claim they love. And, a rare fraction of them will fulfill Her requests that they spread Her messages. Why? If we cannot be thankful for the manifest graces flowing from our Dogma, what are we thankful for? What does Eucharist even mean? It is false humility to reject that God may be far more in union with our thoughts of Him and our actions for Him than we have the faith to accept. Do we actually think that all the good we see, the virtue we pursue, the sacrifices we make, the knowledge we avow, the conversion we witness, and the love we display is solely our own doing? It is the revelation of the presence of grace sanctifying us; creatures communing in oneness with their God, even if only in those moments. This leads to the salvific manifestation of our reception of the Most Blessed Sacrament from the Catholic Altar, the true Bread of Life, the Body, Blood, Soul and Divinity of Jesus Christ. But, that Communion does something to us.

Many like to quote Saint John who said, "If we say that we have no sin, we deceive ourselves and the truth is not in us" [1 John 1:8]. This is done as a way to exact a wholesale judgement against every man throughout every moment of their lives until death, implying that we can somehow never remove the original stain on our soul or escape the fate of sinning every day. I might ask these same people if they believe the Sacrament of Reconciliation wipes away our sins at the invocation of a priest's absolution in the Name of the Crucified Christ? Or, is there always "some little bit" that everyone remains guilty of until we close our eyes in death? Where can thanksgiving arise for the Sacrament amidst defeatism such as this? Do we believe a newly baptized baby is not a perfect creature lying in their mother's arms right in front of our eyes? Saint John's call in his letter was to a world which he was trying to convince with the facts to come to the saving Christ who would wash away their sins and grant them stature as a new creation. He said everybody requires the absolution of Christ; and he was right. He was implying that there was no one among them who did not need the saving Blood of Jesus Christ, but that we could live together in absolution before His purifying Cross in a state of sanctification, should we accept the Man who died upon it. Thereafter, it is through the fortifying power of the Holy Spirit in which we must remain immersed that our free will is strengthened by sanctifying grace to remain above the vulnerable state of the exiled world, just like Jesus. In effect, the indomitable power of His will becomes our own as we invoke it in His Name. We must remember that Saint John also said just two chapters later, "No one who is begotten by God commits sin, because God's seed remains in him; he cannot sin because he is begotten by God" [1 John 3:9]. A very interesting passage, indeed.

Now, this does not mean that any man should proclaim throughout the world that they are perfect in perpetuity for the endless ages. This is not the best use of our voice. The story of our lives is not yet complete. No mortal man can claim "I AM" from an eternal state of declaration because we are still in the time of vulnerability. Jesus said it because He was God throughout time and Eternity, and He knew His every act and intention forever was in complete unity with the Father. He spoke a truth that He knew intimately because He spoke from the Mind of God which was His own. "No one has gone up to heaven except the one who came down from heaven, the Son of man" [John 3:13]. We do not have the knowledge to declare this beatitude just yet, although we may in fact be in a sanctified state now where we will declare later our seamless unity with the Most Holy Trinity at this point in exile. Even still, we must proclaim where sinlessness is granted, while remaining in a humble posture that recognizes the state of our vulnerability. And, if one is proclaiming their sinlessness, although it may ultimately be found to be accurate, they are poised in a more vulnerable state because their cautious oversight of their soul is being distracted. Satan will come with great force to convict them as a liar. But, in the same balance of our soul, we must be confident in what our God has done for us when we leave the confessional and receive the Most Blessed Sacrament. There is something to defend upon receiving the Sacrament of Reconciliation. We must recognize the ultimate measure of perfection granted to our soul according to our honest confession, while acknowledging that if any other stains remain of which we are not aware that Jesus would lead us to a lesser state of vulnerability, until perfect sanctification is our permanent state. Did Jesus not say to the woman about to be stoned, "Go and sin no more?" He was not mocking or taunting her about something that was futile, like holding a treat too high from your pet just to see how high he can jump. Sin is not inevitable, and it can be forgiven and wiped away, and avoided forevermore. Cleansing our souls to perfection and maintaining this state of sanctification is the expectation of our Savior. But, absent divine revelation to us directly from God of the state of our soul, no one will know where they were at any given moment in their lives until they see Him Face-to-face, although there is always a sense of the conscience and how it convicts or exonerates. If your conscience is clear, hold it as a special gift and defend it with your purity. Thus, we are left to ponder, even ecstatically, the immediate moment after our reception of a great Sacrament of the Church where sanctifying grace is imparted upon the soul. The moment of a baptized child; the moment of absolution of a penitent, the ordination of a new priest, the creation of unity in a marriage, the anointing of the sick, the Most Blessed Sacrament touching our tongues, and the affirming blast of spiritual maturity in Confirmation. These all bear the "I AM" to our soul. And, they all come through the Sacred Mysteries of Christ's great Calvarian Sacrifice in the Liturgies of the Roman Catholic Church.

Our Holy Mother explained it to me this way. There is a difference between believing one must scale the mountain of holiness while being told repeatedly one can never achieve it, compared to defending the summit through time after God places you upon it through His sacramentally-divine power. Mankind is caught believing the former instead of realizing the latter, and the parsing intellectualism of the theologians has barely helped the matter. Although many attempt to legitimize this defeatist narrative, everyone does not have to achieve the intellectual heights of Saint Thomas Aquinas to embody perfect holiness or know Jesus and His Mother personally. No theologian can declare the exclusion of anybody for not being inebriated in the systematic scholastics they worship. Their intellectual prowess is as frail, faulty, and temporary as anyone else's. The Church would be advancing the same ultimate truth of Jesus Christ had Saint Thomas Aquinas never been born. But, what a blessing he was. There are many children who have surpassed him in the Wisdom of the Father and the grace of the Son; and he sits in his exalted place in Heaven joyful that this is true. How did they do this? They were more childlike than Aquinas. We must realize that much theology was generated simply as a defense against heathen intellectualism throughout the ages. But, what if there would have been no heathens who thought they knew better? Would Christianity have been less? No, it would have flourished in the simple genius and tender purity of the Queen of Heaven and Her Child, much like what happens through Her shrines of miraculous intercession. We must see the battle for redemption as being in our defense from being torn from the heights as opposed to fighting the devil and his minions while trying to scale the perils of a treacherous mountainside. The Roman Catholic Church, in union with its loyal children, is defending the summit. And, that summit is simple holiness in reflection of Jesus and His Mother. Multitudes are living perfected lives, acceptable to the Father, and are in a sustained state of sanctifying grace that they will maintain until the final breaths of their earthly existence. Some people do not sin every day, and it is not presumptuous to recognize this fact. We may not be able to definitively identify who they are, but the evidence is apparent in many people. Many will never go to Purgatory, although most in our day probably will because of the general lack of acceptance of the Gospel and its prescriptions. We live in great darkness. Nonetheless, multitudes will hear, "Well done, My good and faithful servant," the instant their eyes fall upon their Savior. Great numbers will be found to have polished their souls to an impeccable sheen where their gaze at Jesus will be like looking at themselves in a mirror, just as Christ will look at them and see Himself. They will have proven to Him that they cared enough to live as if to allow themselves to believe that they achieved His personification. Suffering throughout the world by so many precious people united with the Original Faith of the Apostles is the sign that what I am saying is true. Spiritual martyrdom abounds; sacrifice is as deep and wide as the oceans. And, the love of the Mystical Body of Christ is ringing like a cathedral bell at every second somewhere on the globe. Our Lady says the possibility exists that the Earth could be so pure that every sin will have been forgiven, and every soul as clear as crystal, before Christ returns the second time. She so pines for this, and is working diligently to accomplish it through holy means that include the revelation of Herself as the Morning Star Over America. Is this not why the Catholic Church prays for the souls in Purgatory—that each of them be cleansed and found perfect at the Second Coming? Is not the Church's daily offering of the Holy Mass the petition to the Father for this perfection to be sustained among its people, and that the rest of the world join us in this perfection that we celebrate in preparation for His encore appearance in Glory? Everyone will be present at the Second Coming, not just those who are still in mortal flesh at the time.

Spiritual perfection does not take decades to obtain. It merely takes a lifetime to sustain. It does not take great outward feats of eccentric sacrifice or penances. It takes patient conviction, selflessness in the way of grace, humble compliance, steely devotion and sacrificial vision. How deep and passionate can a prayer be said? How far can the heart reach into the sufferings of the world? How hard is it for us to obey the teachings of the Church and participate in its liturgical worship and mutual disciplines? It simply requires a clear vision of the Cross, an acceptance of the magnitude of Jesus' love for us, and a realization of the power of the life given to us in Christ where we pine to unite in His Crucifixion in any way He might wish so that Creation may become one in Him. Yet, a person can become the greatest saint before God in the final seconds of his life. The transforming effects of the Sacraments in those moments are enormous. Consider a person living the life of a lost soul their entire lifetime. How tremendous must be their authentic invocation of faith to accept Christ at the last, to overcome everything they otherwise proved themselves to be in life? Oh, how much of the Crucifixion must they experience in one fell swoop? Imagine the mountain to be scaled through a sheer act of faith, and how strong in virtuous conviction that soul must be to overcome eternal death in those final moments. Whatever hole has been dug must be crawled out of. Sometimes Saints climb the Everests and scale the precipices and peaks of eternal death in one great heroic ascent on the last day that leaves the heavens in tears–'the more rejoicing in Heaven,' as it were; a massive self-annihilating sacrifice of being that some of the most pure never have to invoke with such immediacy because they sustained their sanctification in small steps throughout a lifetime. Of course, the latter is how Jesus wishes we would engage life because Saints should not dig holes they will have to crawl out of. But in addition, Jesus truly does not wish us to suffer so intensely in that final decisive moment that many wait for instead. Nor does He wish us to face the risk of being unable to make that unimaginable ascent. His compassionate desires are that we not suffer the purgative grief of having to convince ourselves that He loves us even so. The question remains, what do we have to accept to make low these mountains and straight these paths? Well, we are loved, and our success is to overcome the vulnerability not to love. Our Lady described a sinner's return to Christ at the last as their life being attached to a rubber band being held by Jesus. The farther they move away from Him in life, the greater the force of return that is generated when they see Him Face-to-face at their judgement. They either step farther away and break the rubber band and are lost, or they release their grip on rebellion and snap back with a tremendous force commensurate with the distance they were away. Those who are at great distance, but not lost forever, experience an impact with the Truth of Jesus' Sacrifice like someone would snap us with an enormous rubber band pulled as far back as possible. But, it is as colossal as two gigantic planets colliding before our eyes in the heavens as if the angels fired a heavenly body at our solar system with a galactic slingshot from a thousand light-years away.

Question 20

What is the "mystique" about human prayer? Since God knows everything we will ever need, why is it so important that we somehow "cast our petitions" in the direction of a Throne of Eternal Dominion that we cannot even see?

I would answer this way. Why do we educate ourselves? Since we know how to eat and where to go to be protected from the elements, why seek out any other knowledge? It is because we aspire to the limits of human potential, even though we do not know the heights of those vaults. Do we ponder what the human person is yet capable of? Five thousand years ago, or maybe just a millennium ago, what did human beings think about themselves? Surely some of them were pride-filled enough to believe they possessed the pinnacle of all relevant knowledge. But, even these could not have begun to imagine the things that posterity has become and the works we have generated. If you were to thrust any man into the present day from those ancient societies and displayed before them a giant airliner, an aircraft carrier battle group, any of our skyscraping towers in our great cities, our medical technology, the orbiting laboratories, lasers, artillery, mechanical automation, space shuttles or Apollo moon rockets, our planes, trains and automobiles, would any of them ever ask, "Why should we educate ourselves, we are surviving just fine?" as they pound flint into points and dig motes around their castles. We are much like those simple men from millennia ago. We neither recognize our potential or from where our great works have flourished; and we have no vision of what is to come. Generations of faithful Christians have in their time embraced their transition into greater potentials of the human species. This is the elevation and sanctification that we engage to ascend into the realms of our spirit where the wisdom of the ages is portioned to us by divine design. Prayer to God is the engagement with our potential that is personified in Jesus Christ. Our true identity as children of an Omnipotent Creator is revealed in the "mystique" of our communion with Him. And, the communion between ourselves and our Creator was bestowed when the Son of God entered the world to extend His loving embrace to all His creatures who were wandering the Earth in darkness. Prayer is not only about obtaining things we need. Prayer is about revealing and becoming everything God created us to be. Prayer initiates the transformation of the human person into the being of Christ.

We live in this world that is a combination of realms. There are the material realms in all that we see and engage each day. Then, there are the spiritual realms that are invisible to our physical eyes, but give life to our existence, and substance and animation to everything we consciously engage in the moment. There is Spirit behind everything, holding it in existence and providing it with poise, purpose, direction and ultimate outcome. Even the stars and planets in the sky are performing their reason for existence. They are obeying the paths set out for them by their Creator. They are harmoniously fulfilling the will of God, and they rejoice in it. Yes, the heavens rejoice and the Earth be glad! None of them manifest free will in opposition to God where they will do anything other than fulfill the reason for their presence in the Creation conceived by their Creator. Yet, they obeyed when Jesus quieted them [Matthew 8:27]. Man often displays something quite different. Our soul has been endowed with the power of free will in the image of God, which is an amazing sovereignty. We can decide whether we will be united with our Creator forever in Paradise, or be separated for Eternity in regret and horror that we did not choose to obey the commands of His Son.

The mystique of human prayer is that it is unique to each person. We have our own unique voice which God recognizes. Each soul is a precious singular beauty conceived by the Father. Human prayer brings about the communion of each individual soul with its Creator in a divine sanctuary of mystery within. The human soul was created for the Infinite; it was created from the Infinite, and will not find fulfillment and peace until it rests in union with God who is the Infinite Source of all things seen and unseen. Proof of this is in the visions and dreams inside us that will never see the light of day in this world. We have visions within us that are not of this world and that we do not have the power to bring into being. Yet, we never ask why they are there or where they come from. We do not have the power to create something from nothing, but we have the capacity to envision anything within us, including images of the vaults of Heaven. Lack of fulfillment originates in our not having the power which comes from God. We are conscripted within boundaries defined by sin and death. Thus, we must acknowledge that we are not in the place where our visions become reality. We are somewhere else; and that somewhere is in the exile of the material world, confined in a body which will succumb to death. The question above posits that if God knows everything that we need, why petition Him for anything; He will take care of us nonetheless. It is true that He will take care of us in many ways to sustain our fragile existence in this world, just as He does the flowers of the field and birds of the air. He maintains the world in which we now exist. Scripture states that even the hairs on our head are noticed by God and counted. In my case, He does not have to count as high as He once did. But, there is a purpose. We are here for a reason, not simply to be born, live out a sense of existence, then die, passing into nothingness as atheists boast in their brazen ignorance. We were born into exile as an act of God's Mercy so that our lives here can bring about our great return to the infinite realms of Heaven. Jesus revealed that not everyone is allowed entrance into Paradise once they pass from this world, but only those He finds worthy. The question then becomes, how can we become worthy? This is a recognition in which we have a part to play. Commands have been given by our God in order to obtain the reward of Eternal Life.

I believe that the basic hurdle for anyone to get over is the most important. Nearly everyone who does not pray sees no need for it. They anticipate no benefit for themselves because God has never previously revealed Himself to them, even though in their non-existent prayers is where He would have done so. How ironic! It is like someone saying they are poor, but seeing no benefit of a job because they presently don't have any money. Our interior contemplative world is precious. It is the foundation of our being and the originating arena of our decisions and actions which compose our state of life. From that arena flourishes everything good that we could ever be, if it is illuminated by the Light of Heaven. If people are not thoughtful and reflective about themselves, and open to the wisdom that the Holy Spirit brings, they do nothing more than portray what miserable people they are. There is no light in that arena that would allow them to see their way. Individuals like this never draw forth any beauty from within themselves because they are constantly distracted, overwhelmed and blinded by the harshness of the world that they battle every day of their lives. They may lie in their beds at night and ponder the feelings they have and the anxiety they are attempting to keep at bay, but without moving their thoughts into a prayerful relationship with Jesus who is the Way, the Truth and the Life, light will never be invoked in their thoughts to provide a path out of the heaviness that grows and ultimately consumes them in desolation and pain. It is like being sick and lying in our bed every day thinking about nothing more than the next set of sheets you are going to have to change when you could be calling the doctor who could provide you with the medicine to be healed. It is a rather mysterious phenomenon when people have descended into horrible conditions in their lives, but seem not to possess the ability to ask the question, 'How did I get here?' And, even if they ask it of themselves, how many times are they too beholden to their attachments to the world to admit that those same attachments are the 'how' that caused the terrible conditions of their life? These are the "juncture moments" that prayer transcends to bestow life to the soul. Prayer brings the lights up in the interior arena where the thoughtful flows of our lives begin to be dictated, driven and directed by our God whom we cannot yet see with our eyes. But, does not our soul see His Light? Do we not become a new being whose interior identity is illuminated with previously unknown possibilities? It is like an advertising agency placing new billboards all across the nation for a company that wishes to rebrand itself and its product offerings. The interior arena of our being is our personal "company." We decide how it acts, what it produces and how it makes deliveries out into the world. When we pray to Jesus, He is the advertising agency that begins to place billboards all across our interior contemplations that rebrands us as His children and testifies to the world that we have something completely different to offer.

    The mystique of human prayer is synonymous with the wondrousness of the interior arena, which is none other than our recognition of our soul, our spirit, and the presence of God within, if we but call out to Him. Our interior arena flourishes with a compendium of many thoughts and visions, oftentimes with only the mere mention of a single thing to us. It is like throwing a rock into a pond that sends out ripples and impacts across the body of water. Anything floating in that body of water is rocked, no matter how slightly, by that original stone that is tossed. Sometimes it may be a large boulder that is thrown into our arena. And, sometimes the universe has wayward asteroids heading our way. This principle of "making waves" has been studied deeply by physicists in the realms of the material world. This is why I used a body of water as symbolic of our interior arena. Consider the idea of sound and how it relates to the idea of waves. A sound is a wave of vibrations through the air that strikes our ear drum which detects and interprets them. Languages such as english, french, or spanish are nothing more than very complex systems of sound waves that have been further recognized as having meaning when they are generated in particular sequences. Stupendous qualities are added to human life by our ability to translate sound into modes of communication between people. What would have ever been accomplished in the world without one person being able to understand the visions from another person's interior arena? Our languages are nothing more than our ability to communicate that which is in us that no man can see. Let us go further. Sound has also been recognized and organized into frequencies, much like languages have been, that provide amazing qualities that people have manipulated and sequenced to create beautiful and uplifting strains of music. Think of all the different musical compositions throughout history; refined, organized, and reflected for the purpose of communicating what was once only in someone's heart. Within the frequencies that compose the spectrum of notes, from the low registers to the high, there are what we call harmonics where sound waves of a particular type complement and reinforce each other to produce resonance, or standing waves. In other words, two sound waves can work together to produce something "resonant" between them that they could not produce on their own. One example is when a particular note of sound is projected at a glass and it shatters. The sound wave projected at the glass matches the interior vibrational frequency of the glass in such a way as to magnify the waves produced between them, which destabilizes the structural integrity of the glass that breaks. Another example is when a large vehicle may have passed our house and we notice the door jam or windows begin to hum or buzz with the same frequency as the sound from the passing vehicle. This is called "harmonic resonance." Why do I give this simple physics lesson about the material world? Because it is a parable that describes our interior arena.

Scripture states that God can be understood in many ways by contemplating how He constructed the world.

Just as there is harmonic resonance in the material world related to sound, there is spiritual resonance with God that occurs in the human soul when the sound of His voice is called upon. When the sound of His voice reverberates in the human soul, it creates standing waves of grace in its unity with our conception that have powerful and harmonic effects that magnify grace. These harmonic effects are love, and other souls know when the resonance matches the heart of their soul. People know when they are loved. They also know when they are being told the truth, which is often a bitter impact. The problem throughout the world is that there are rogue, chaotic spiritual frequencies projected from the disordered interior arenas of sinners. It is like they are sitting down at a piano and hammering up and down the keyboard with their fists, not having even the basic notion of what they are pounding on. They have no harmonic resonance either with God or any other soul. The racket they create is of no value and unbearable to anyone listening. They are not in harmony with the great pianist; and they destroy the spiritual harmony between the hearts of humanity. So, not only do we need to enter into the mystique of human prayer to hear the beautiful sounds of God, but we must stop generating the horrible, out-of-tune noise that destroys the harmony that God wishes would resonate within us instead. There is no relativism in the harmonies of the heart. Sinners do not get to decide what is resonant with God. He has already played the basic tones of Eternal Life that resonate with His Divinity. He plays in the beatific key of the Crucifixion of His Son. This is the key by which the Roman Catholic Church resonates and scripts its scores.

Therefore, the mystique of human prayer is, first of all, to stop the noise of the human will. Human prayer is initially for the recognition, repentance and conversion away from the noise of attachments that are discordant, jarring, and grating against the sound of the Light of Christ. Sin generates discordant noise in the soul. Therefore, we must search for peace within us by seeking repentance and absolution for the sins within us. Once we begin this silencing in earnest, then the new melodies begin in the human soul which resonate in their harmonics with the Spirit of God. Along with these new melodies is the accompaniments of the Angels and Saints who sing in choirs of happiness that Heaven is finally being amplified into the mortal world through a beautiful human heart. Jesus spoke about this in the parable of cleaning the house and not allowing evil to return. This cleaning is the silencing of the noise. It is like evicting the death metal band and the rap artist from the house. Our Lady says that the sound generated by these people is nothing but noise that violates the peace of the Almighty Father. All should enter into the interior arena in silence and call upon the melodies of Heaven instead.

Question 21

Regarding the Saints you have discussed in your other books who have received the stigmata, what do you suppose God's purpose is in giving it to certain people? The point of this question is, what are the common attributes of people that seem to be prevalent in those who have received the sacred stigmata? How can it be true that someone who is not a Roman Catholic priest would receive it? How do you explain God's dispensation of this phenomenon?

Let us take Saint Padre Pio, for example. It is not so much that the world would see that he embodied mystical phenomena that he received the stigmata, it is the vision we will have of him at our judgement outside of time and in Heaven that is revelatory and significant. Wait until everyone sees the hidden heart of Padre Pio at each moment of his life of suffering. Wait until we see his heart from the inside and the sacrifices and sufferings that he endured for us over a half century without respite because of his great love. The power of his hidden heart is colossal. We have not yet seen Saint Padre Pio. This is where the blazing light of his life will be venerated in the blinding of the universe. This is where the power of his life will be made manifest. We think we honor him now with an ecclesial title or salutary devotions. Just wait! The sacrifices of Saints such as him are capstones that seal the pits of the fiery abyss. They fill and seal cavernous pits of sin. They are like the doors which seal intercontinental ballistic missiles in their silos, those instruments of death and destruction, that they never reach out into the lives of men. The stigmata inflicted on particular Saints is a revelatory sign of their divine union with the suffering Christ. It is a particular mode in which Christ reveals Himself in a soul that suffers with Him. The attributes of those who endure the stigmata are their passionate sacrificial love for Jesus, their love for the souls of humanity, and their obedience to the Holy Spirit. It is on a scale that is outside the dimensions of their earthly existence. We never truly see the attributes in the souls of these sacrificial victims. Therefore, it is nearly impossible to interrogate and discern them. Again, we have yet to see Padre Pio.

A dimension that I have experienced related to this subject is that our Heavenly Father pines to protect us from any harm and unhappiness. He desires the Earth to be like Heaven in complete joy and comfort right now. So, if God can be in any way conflicted, it is in His allowance of one of His children to experience the sufferings of His Son Jesus, even for the purpose of providing graces that the world be saved in His Son's Sacrifice. I believe the reason that we do not see instances of the stigmata more frequently is related to Jesus asking the Sons of Thunder whether they could drink the cup that He was about to drink. It is counterintuitive to His desire to bring us into heavenly beatitude that His children suffer so. I believe this is one of the reasons why you see very few people asked by God to endure the stigmata in their flesh. Yet, there is another dimension that has two manifestations. There are those who generate such love in their hearts, who have crucified the world within them to such an extent, that they live completely for God whereby their love demands unity with Jesus on the Cross in the same way that Jesus drove toward Calvary as His purpose in the world. Jesus knows that they will not find ultimate happiness in Heaven unless they suffer with Him on Earth to the spiritual degree of the Crucifixion. The other manifestation is souls who are so little and vulnerable, so unsuspecting of the depths of suffering, whom Christ finds so pure that He unites Himself with them and asks them to suffer with Him, even though they may have only pined to simply do well for Him in life. Of course, they say yes because their hearts are not shaped to count the cost. So, there is the reflection of pure obedience to beatific reaches, and also the reflection of passionate yearning for unity in the Cross. Man can ask to suffer with Christ, or God can make the request.

As to the question of how a person who is not a Roman Catholic priest could receive the stigmata, no person is excluded from sharing in Christ's suffering. All are called to assist in the conversion of sinners. Roman Catholic priests share a particular vocation, or responsibility, whose primary purpose encompasses the administration of the Sacraments of the Church. This is a great responsibility of discipline in the life of the Mystical Body of Christ. They secure and maintain the framework of reference through which God acts in any way He chooses. No priest is the decider on how the Holy Spirit chooses to work within this framework of reference. They are responsible to comply with all facets of the grace of God, and give affirmation to His works in cooperation with the Holy Spirit so they may flourish to their intended effect. But, they are not personally the adjudicators of God's graces. They maintain the anchor of all Christians in the Seven Sacraments from which all graces flow. It is like setting off fireworks. They are technicians who set the match to the fuse of a rocket which they have not created. They do not decide how the explosive contents are placed in the rocket at its construction or what beautiful pattern of lights splays across the sky at its detonation in the heavens. Yes, some try to do this. Some tell God which fireworks displays they like, and which they do not. This is why the miraculous intercession of the Virgin Mary which is launched into the world by the Sacraments is discarded so routinely. The stigmata manifested in any person is ultimately the concussion in the flesh of the fireworks of the Most Blessed Sacrament. The discernment that is necessary is that the devil can manipulate flesh and sometimes imitate the effects. But, God never allows this without countering the deception. The devil cannot duplicate the mixture of ingredients, the rocket, the concussion, nor the beautiful display in the skies. His display is always aberrant. He cannot launch his own fireworks. But, he can manipulate flesh and the perceptions of men who are watching the effects unfold. Usually the devil is simply waving around diminutive sparklers and throwing them into the air because this is all the power he has. He has so many sparks flying around these days that those who discern believe they are watching a July 4th fireworks celebration. Then, when Our Lady starts detonating aerial bombs of grace through Her miraculous intercession, sinners become completely confused wondering how Satan threw his sparklers so high into the air. Then, fear sets in because they are terrified that Satan may have gained so much power to deceive. The deception is thinking Satan has anything to do with these sky-bound displays at all. All the while, simple little children ooh and aah with devotion at everything their Holy Mother does. So, let us go back to the stigmata. We must venerate any heart who bears the authentic stigmata and pray for them because it is one of the fireworks displays that has detonated in the skies of Heaven. A soul has embraced the concussion of the Crucifixion in their being, which is accompanied by great suffering and purification. It is a great communion of love between Jesus and one of His children for the sake of the conversion and salvation of souls. It is a beautiful thing to behold.

Question 22

How do we know when the Blood of Jesus Christ has washed our soul clean of sin? Is this something that is metaphysical in nature? Do we feel anything? Is it something that we can discern with our emotions or inherent psyche? And, once we have given ourselves to the Blood of Jesus on the Cross, what happens if we change our mind?

Our Lady says that faith becomes knowledge to those who serve. So, there is the concept of faith becoming knowledge in our intellectual senses. And, for us to know "when the Blood of Jesus Christ has washed our soul clean of sin," we must have faith first. Knowing this, we then ask ourselves where we can obtain faith. This leads us to search for its origin, which is admitted in the question as being "the Blood of Jesus on the Cross." Hence, the knowledge of when our souls are washed clean always leads us back to the origin of Christ's redemptive Sacrifice on Calvary. From this source of Salvation, the entire framework of reference of Christianity "scaffolds" itself, giving us the knowledge that propagates from its anchoring of authority in Saint Peter whom Christ declared to be His Rock. Propagating within this great framework is the Roman Catholic Priesthood which is ordained to steward Christ's Gospel to humanity throughout time until Jesus' Second Coming. Part of this ordination is the power to forgive sins in the name of the Most Blessed Trinity when each person enters the confessional to offer their repentance and receive absolution for their sins. The "particular when" for our soul being washed clean is at the priest's intonation of the words, "I absolve you from your sins in the name of the Father and of the Son and of the Holy Spirit." Our faith united with the ordinations of the Original Apostolic Church brings us the knowledge of the "particular when" when our sins are forgiven. The reason that I say "particular when" is because the Crucifixion of Jesus Christ was a timeless act of the absolution of all humankind who would confess their sins and believe in Him. It is we who are constrained by time that manifests the "particular when." The washing of sin from our souls actually occurred on Mount Calvary in Jesus' great Sacrifice on the Cross as His Blood poured down. But, redemption requires the individual confessions of men through time whereby we accept His Death and Resurrection in order to be saved. Each confession occurs in time, at the "particular when" when we repent and seek the gifts of His Sacrifice in the Sacrament of Reconciliation. The Crucifixion is truly present in the Sacrament of Reconciliation. And, Jesus' Blood from that one Crucifixion washes us clean of sin in the confessional at the instant of the intonation of the priest's words of absolution. Our souls become pure as the driven snow. "Cleanse me with hyssop, that I may be purified; wash me, and I will be whiter than snow" [Psalm 51:9].

    The next part of the question relates to our acceptance of the cleansing graces that we are offered there. Let us recognize two aspects of the human person. First, there is the soul with its definition of our perfect being at its conception in the Mind of God. It is our endowment from our Creator when He envisioned our being. The soul in every man is made in the image of God; it is His conception of everything that we could ever be. It is infinite in its origin in God; and it is eternal. This is what John envisions in his first Letter, verses 1-3, "See what love the Father has bestowed on us that we may be called the children of God. Yet, so we are. The reason the world does not know us is that it did not know him. Beloved, we are God's children now; what we shall be has not yet been revealed. We do know that when it is revealed, we shall be like him, for we shall see him as he is. Everyone who has this hope based on him makes himself pure, as he is pure." The second aspect is the condition that John says renders us unable to see that which has yet to be revealed—'...we shall be like him.' This second aspect is overcome through a sanctified framework of reference within us that rises up and flourishes from the independent powers granted to our soul. This framework of reference is like the many scenic vistas throughout our country intertwined amongst the national highway system that allows us to travel past them to take in their beauty. The framework of reference manifests the revelation of the soul outwardly. It ultimately informs and guides the motivations of our thoughts, intentions and actions. Our framework of reference has a spiritual shape that was distorted upon being placed in exile, which rendered our vulnerability to sin. We see through our reference frame, but it can become a very corrupt lens. The Bible says we see now indistinctly [1 Corinthians 13:12]. Faith, prayer and sacrifice reshapes our frame of reference into conformity with God's perfect definition of our soul. Faith gives our frame of reference the correct embodiment for our soul. It clothes us in the garments of the children of God. Our raiment radiates light just as Jesus revealed His Being on Mount Tabor. For example, remember the child's toy that has different shaped holes in it, such as a circle, square, star, triangle, oval and several others. As part of the child's play, they have a pile of plastic or wooden blocks shaped the same as the holes in the toy. The little one then attempts to place the correct shaped block into each hole so that it falls through, sometimes using a small hammer to pound the shaped object into their lap. This is how God looks at us. He has the shape of our perfect soul and has sent Jesus into the world to show it to us, hoping we will allow our faith in Him to shape our frame of reference so that He can escort our true identity to our understanding, just like the child pushing the shaped block through the toy. Our soul has the powers of flourishing a frame of reference and bringing the shape of sanctity to our identity through the power of faith. But, our free will can be seduced into creating all kinds of other shapes that are not in conformity with God's perfect definition of our soul, just as Adam and Eve were seduced by the serpent to invoke their will separated from the identity given to them by God in the Garden. It becomes like God trying to push a cross-shaped block through a square-shaped hole. Adam and Eve changed their shape unilaterally, and thus their identity, where they were no longer united to their original conception and the perfect definition of their souls. Light and understanding no longer flourished within them. They blinded their vision of their original identity by corrupting their frame of reference through disobedience. The distortion was made manifest. And, that distortion became both their exile and ours. Thereafter, they were unable to re-assume the shape that would allow them to transcend back into the Paradisial Garden. Sin defined their frame of reference. They could not overcome the knowledge that they had disobeyed God. Sin became their knowledge. They created the rock upon which their exile was founded. This is the consequence of the original sin they committed; and humanity was thereafter destined to live by this rock. It does not require faith to see it. Sin can see itself. Humanity can see its corruption. And conversely, faith becomes knowledge to those who serve God where love can see itself once again. And, in the course of human events, God sent His Son to establish a new Rock upon which Salvation would be built and clarity would be reestablished in the hearts of men to recognize who they are — to become children of God.

When Jesus washes away our sins, He creates a new reality; a new redeemed creature in the image of Himself, where we are allowed to see once again without sin corrupting our frame of reference. A new definition is conceived. Our souls are restored to match the identical shape in which He first conceived us. It is like God handed His children a new toy that matched the shape of all the little blocks. Our soul is reestablished into unity with Him. I said that "we are allowed to see once again," but it does not mean that we do. Our faith tells us that our sins are washed away, but do we allow our faith to reshape our frame of reference as an affirmation of this gift? If faith is weak, usually this reshaping takes place in small repeated installments of contrition and repentance because we seem to fall over and again. We can always be confident that the Roman Catholic Church is impenetrable because it is the frame of reference given by Christ and sustained by His Mystical Body of believers through the Holy Spirit. Its vision does not fluctuate in and out of distortion and corruption. It is clear, consistent and strong as the definition of faith throughout the ages. It is the new Rock, the Divine Faith that becomes knowledge to those who embrace its wisdom and serve its great commission. The final question referenced is, "...what happens if we change our mind?" This phenomenon is nothing more than the frame of reference fluctuating between faith and doubt. It is like clouds passing overhead on a sunny day. Someone who changes their mind has had a change in their frame of reference, or is divided within themselves by a competing one. If doubts about our faith come upon us, we should ponder why. We are either having our interior clarity reinforced at every moment through our daily prayers and holy habits, or we are allowing ourselves to be seduced by the lies of the world which obscure our inner clarity. We must remember that the knowledge carried to us by faith is eternal and invincible. It will always remain throughout eternity, while our doubts will experience a final confrontation with this infinitude of certainty. Which do you think will win, your doubts or the Truth?

Question 23

Speak to the subject of those who complain that God does not work enough miracles in their lives. What do you have to say to the thousands in the world who have given everything they have ever owned to Him in exchange for His blessing upon their lives, only to find that their fate and future seem to be much like they were before they ever invited Him into their hearts and minds?

Our Holy Mother said to me one time that we should not think that a God who asked His perfect Son to suffer will not ask sinners to suffer as well in the economy of their salvation. This does not mean that the Father is a sadistic overlord who demands that His creatures endure pain or grovel before Him. He loves us beyond all imagining, but has motivations completely different from our desire for material comforts and worldly blessings. He wants us to be united with Him. For the record, God does not want us to have to experience suffering in even the slightest way, but we will while in an exile that exists in a state of violation against His Kingdom. The world is filled with sin and sinners. For example, God wishes that no one would ever experience starvation again. But, is it a lack of blessing on His part that certain people starve? No, it is because sinners will not feed their brothers and sisters from their surplus. Sinners withhold God's blessings from those who are in need. What then is God to do? But, it becomes even more complex. What if someone is starving because of their own sloth and dereliction, after dismissing every opportunity for progress the Father ever extended to them? Do they deserve to eat from our abundance? Saint Paul said in 2 Thessalonians 3:10 that if a person is not willing to work, then they should not eat of the blessings of others. This does not say that the incapable or incapacitated should not be cared for.

As far as anyone complaining that God does not work enough miracles in their lives, it depends on what miracles they are asking for, and for whom. The Most Blessed Virgin asks the Father every day for miracles for us; and we receive them no matter whether we recognize them or not. The Bible states that we often do not receive what we are asking for because we ask wrongly. Indeed! It is also difficult to accept that there are thousands who have given everything they have to Jesus, but still do not see His blessings in their lives. I believe that statement to be a fabrication used for rhetorical effect with no evidence to support it. Giving ourselves to Jesus is not a barter for His blessings. Giving ourselves to our Savior is an act of loving Him unconditionally; an act of surrender with hope for His bringing us to the glory of Heaven, no matter what. Many times, it is not the world that changes as a fruit of our prayers, but it is our being that changes in that we become more Christlike and able to present ourselves in Christ before the Father in reparation for the sins of the world. Then, the world changes through our sacrifice in union with His. Everyone who has truly given their lives to Jesus receives the blessings inherent in this communion. All receive the gifts of the Holy Spirit.

Most people do not realize that faith is maintained for everyone by God, even in those who directly experience particular dimensions of His miraculous assistance. This may be hard to believe, but people like Padre Pio in all of his mystical experiences was required to maintain a huge capacity for faith. Many believe that since he experienced so many mystical occurrences and conversations from the Heavenly Hosts that his faith was not required to be as strong. It is actually quite the opposite. Many never answer the question, 'How could he sustain the sufferings of his life otherwise?' In the case of my brother and me, there is a continuous circle of faith as a living entity between him and myself in union with our Holy Mother. I believe him, he believes me, and we both believe Her with the Dominion Angels and Saints adding additional dimensions of faithfulness—all for Jesus' Glory. Her miraculous intercession spans this entire arena where the mystical occurrences flourish.

Within the transcending aura of the Holy Spirit, it is much like a Mount Tabor moment where faith somehow remains intact, while we may be disoriented from our exilic frame of reference. Were not Peter, James and John disoriented from their normal perception at the Transfiguration? Many instances of miraculous intercession are recognized as such simply because of this disorienting effect; and these instances can be very simple manifestations in the lives of each of us. This is why we often recognize grace-filled "coincidences" as signal graces. There is often a character of disorientation in them. Although one could say facets of faith are suspended in visionaries because we have seen and experienced dimensions of things most often only described by faith, it becomes fully reinstated, almost as if being placed back in time at a point before the occurrence so that the exilic perception of our judgement can continue as before. We are left to observe the event in retrospect through faith, just as everyone else, although it has definitively imprinted our frame of reference in a special way. This is why we observe the phenomenon where people say, "Did you see that?," after having seen something directly that was beyond their linear or sequential comprehension. These events do not burst mortal reality in a definitive enough way to effect a complete replacement of our exilic frame of reference, but they do leave a mystical imprint. Miraculous intercession does not burst our exile for us, nor does it damage our ability to continue in faith. It merely expands our frame of reference much like a balloon being inflated an amount more. Of course, God can do anything He wants if He chooses. Miraculous intercession sometimes has the dimensions of suspending the progression of exile, whereafter it continues as before with your intellect realizing that your experience no longer fits in the continuum of time and exilic human experience. Then, your base intellect responds, "Did I really just experience that?," while the halo of grace surrounds your frame of reference much as a warm blanket until the world invades again. This is Our Lady's mantle that we can truly feel. Miraculous intercession is usually not something that you can grasp to incorporate into the physical world. And, even if you could grasp it and pull it into exile, such as Our Lady's messages or Juan Diego's tilma, it is not the original transcension, just its relic or its fruit. People must believe in the origin of the messages for them to impart the benefits of their actual grace. They remain in the realms of faith, but encourage the heart to reach for the origin. Does it not require faith from bystanders to believe Our Lady's words actually came from Her through a visionary, while they stare directly at the text that came by way of miraculous intercession? The words would not exist had She not placed them mechanically into existence through the translational faculties of a visionary. The responsibility of the Church is to assess the frame of reference of the visionary to determine whether the intercession came through with its shape intact, much like the function of the child's toy previously mentioned. And, this assessment really has nothing to do with any Prelate or theologian's personal opinion. The shape by which we discern has already been given by Jesus Christ in His Life, Death, Resurrection and Descent of the Holy Spirit.

It is an amazing perspective sometimes for a messenger to see the distance between their perception and those of others who may be skeptical, while looking at the same miraculous gift. We see the message artifacts in a completely different way because they are part of the original relationship for us. We know the tree they were picked from. For us, they are still a fruit from that original tree whether on it or off it. Every visionary would love to have others believe as they do, and accept to the depth of their soul the transmission of grace in the words that are passing before their eyes. Faith allows this if it is invoked with enough intensity. Every time I review our Holy Mother's messages, I hear Her voice in an original way that is more than just memory. Her words and relationship are timeless to me. Recipients of miraculous intercession also can experience the phenomenon of feeling, 'Did that actually just happen?' as a recognition of the breach that the Holy Spirit generates. It is really not a breach for the Holy Spirit, but only for us because our frame of reference has not yet been completely refined, purified, expanded and released from exile. I felt this breaching in much more pronounced ways in the early years of the 1990s. Now however, there is more a sense of acclimation and fluency to such graces because my faith is stronger, my frame of reference more pure, and my vision wider to recognize the Holy Spirit and accept His supernatural presence in my life. It is like the rusty gears of my frame of reference have had oil applied to them where my perception moves more freely when impelled by the grace of Our Lady. My balloon was expanded by Her miraculous transcensions each time they occurred, which would deflate to a little larger composure after each experience. Now, my balloon has taken on a permanent state of being expanded where it no longer deflates to the smaller proportions I possessed before She came to us. The miraculous stature of the Holy Spirit has become more fluently incorporated into my being where my frame of reference better mirrors the eternal composure of my soul. Our Lady has brought my brother and me very close to Her Immaculate Heart. We know that She is our Mother. We know that She is always with us. This has led us to even deeper levels of faithful surrender that we could never have touched if we were still trying to move our old perceptions out of the way or grousing in astonishment about whether a simple locution or message was from Our Lady as skeptics would do. Skeptics have very tiny balloons and rust encrusted gears that are encased in colossal pride and self-possession, which will not allow them to expand or move. Faith grants the expansion which allows the balloon of our frame of reference to begin expanding and contracting as if it were breathing. This is how the breath of God breathes in a soul.

Imagine a wall separating you from a great vision of beauty. The wall has consistently been part of your perception your entire life. You are told what is behind the wall, but you have never seen past it with your physical eyes in any way you realized. Now, imagine someone telling you to stand with your face six inches from a wall with your eyes open. Then, they ask you to extend your arms out in front of you. Your hands bang up against the wall as you try to raise your arms. This person then tells you to close your eyes, and raise your arms again. This time, you lift your arms straight out in front of you as if no wall is there. You place your hands back to your side and open your eyes, still standing with your nose to the wall, whereupon you reach up and touch the wall, finding that it is as impenetrable as before. Indeed, 'Did that just happen?' Consider everything that would fly through your mind as you tried to reconcile this inconsistency in your intellect. This is the kind of inconsistency that has overwhelmed my intellectual constitution as a result of Our Lady's intercession to my brother and me to the point that I am not disturbed at the occasion of these dimensions being manifested. The wall in this allegory is inside of us, and it can be permeated when we close our eyes to the corrupt frame of reference impressed upon us by this exile. Prayer reaches past the wall. Our hearts can permeate the wall. Many supposedly religious thinkers believe the wall is required in order to maintain faith, so they reject miraculous intercession because it violates their concept of an impenetrable barrier. Miraculous intercession causes their wall to seem a little too thin for their frame of reference. They do not realize that faith renders the wall irrelevant. Our Lady said that faith can become so strong that we would not realize our passing from this life into the next. It sounds much like Her Assumption, does it not? You can live as if there is no wall, with spiritual eyes that see past it all the time. Your heart can exist on the beatific side of the wall at every moment.

For faith to actually be breached, not only do we have to witness something that transcends our frame of reference, but it also has to render the old reference frame non-existent, creating a new one that is not of this world. The reason we are in exile is because we have an exilic frame of reference that we cannot fully escape until we pass from our mortal lives. This is why faith will always be required in exile until the Second Coming of the Son of Man. Our frame of reference is composed in part by the spirit being married to the flesh in exile with death being the wage for sin. That is part of the definition that conscripts the frame of reference. But, faith must be allowed to empower our frame of reference completely so as to give us vision into the coming new world. We must die to the impulses and influences of the flesh. Miraculous intercession goes a long way to assist that empowerment. The miraculous intercession of Jesus' Mother provides the opportunity for great sanctification of our being. She assists faith by impressing anchors to belief in our frame of reference and forces conversion into our intellects by the expansion of the mystical into our lives. If we do not rearrange our intellects to accommodate these extraordinary graces, they just rest there like abrasive inconsistencies, beckoning us to deal with them. But, the inconsistency is actually between the Truth and the imperfections in our frame of reference. Fatima, Lourdes, Rue du Bac, Knock, Beauraing, Banneux, Guadalupe, Medjugorje, the Morning Star Over America, and all the rest are not going away. They can only be ignored by the force of pride. They are marginalized by being categorized as private. They are far more than that.

Faith can do everything that miraculous intercession accomplishes for the conversion of men. But, with our Heavenly Mother, we do not have to do it alone. When faith becomes strong and impressive upon our reference frame, we all see as mystical visionaries. Beatific mysticism then inflames as a sanctifying fruit, whereupon our perfected soul shines through. It is called seeing through faith, which becomes our knowledge of that for which we hope. This is what allowed Saint Paul to be so confident in his professions of a crowning destiny. He had seen Christ through miraculous intercession. If someone spoke like Saint

Paul today, most would wonder what kind of arrogance and audacity they were facing. Verily, how can and when will men extend their faith to this degree if not encouraged by miraculous intercession to do so? Our soul can sense the workings of the Holy Spirit when we encounter them. This is where discernment meets miraculous intercession and is forced to concur, lest the haunting of denial wracks our soul. This is where faith meets the Most Blessed Sacrament and says, "My Lord and my God!" It all comes to light in the process of the sanctification of the soul.

God works miracles all day long. Just because a disordered frame of reference does not allow one to recognize any of them does not mean they are not occurring. Look at Medjugorje for nearly forty years; apparitions, messages, mystical phenomenon, healings, heraldry, conversions, confessions, prayers and sacrifices; and still the world refuses to collectively humble itself to thank Jesus for the gift of His Mother's appearances and guidance. Look at the time that has been wasted stumbling around in so-called prudent discretion. What is God to do; burst our exilic frame of reference altogether and blast away our faithlessness, holding us to account? Well, the miracles of Medjugorje are prophesied; and they are coming. But, it will be too late for the skeptics, just as Our Lady has said. All the hemming and hawing is going to be burned to the ground in the throes of their suffering. The visionaries of Medjugorje will be vindicated for every message they have suffered to receive, not just the initial seven appearances. The tables will be turned on those who have refused to believe, and each person will realize their pride and what could have been accomplished had their faith reciprocated the succoring kiss of the Queen of Peace.

The second question asked above is related to the gift of human suffering. For those who have experienced great anguish in their lives, I ask you to see it as a great gift, as hard as that may be. I am proud of you in what you have endured for the purification of the world, and so is your Heavenly Mother. The Saints of Heaven admire you. What we see now is not how we will see later. I promise. When we meet Jesus and see the surreal giantness of His loving Sacrifice, the only thing the soul will wish to say is, 'Did I suffer enough with You?' We know our unity with Him is in the sacrifice that we share with Him. While enraptured in unimaginable awe at seeing He Who Is, the Crucified One, our humility will say amidst our tears, 'Did I love you enough?' Those who surrendered life to Him will find they gave Him everything, and in exchange will hear Him reply, 'Oh, most assuredly! Oh, how I love you. My pride swells that you have loved Me so. Thank you for loving your brothers and sisters so much as to embrace the suffering they heaped upon you.' This is why Scripture states, "Whoever seeks to preserve his life will lose it, but whoever loses it will save it" [Luke

17:33]. Our sacrifice of life is our gift. It is the meaning of life. Understanding our lives is bound up in understanding His. We are being prepared for the moment of Redemption at the Final Judgement where we will see ourselves as we are, and have been, in His Light. We will see our lives there from a frame of reference released from the physical body, but a frame of reference we possessed all along through our faith. The balloon will burst and our confinement rescinded. Our infinite spirits will revel in the eternal vision of the Truth. We will acknowledge that we were not here in this world to see what we could materially create, or what we could experience to stimulate our senses or flesh, or who could die with the most worldly accomplishments or toys. What a failure it is for one to live their great gift of life this way. Can you imagine what this kind of person experiences at their meeting with the Crucified and Resurrected Christ? They answer their own question, 'No, I did not suffer enough for You.' And, they either damn themselves or enter Purgatory so that they may suffer in a condition of expiation for their deficient love. We have life in this exile to make it Home, to be returned to the Kingdom of Heaven. If we saw Heaven as it is, then were returned to the Earth, we would live a wholly different way. All those who are blessed with a glimpse of Heaven do this. Why? Because their balloon experiences its expansion into realms to which it always seeks to be re-inflated. Faith becomes our knowledge, and our entire frame of reference is transfigured into a completely different universe of purpose. God knows this, so He sends manifestations of Heaven to us by allowing His Virgin Mother to dispense miraculous intercession to impress our frame of reference in a way our frail faith and meager sacrifices are not capable. Then, faith finds its ascension and expansion in these anchors of revelation, and mystical knowledge penetrates the wall and bursts upon us. Beatific vision, indeed!

Finally, if we serve God, we will suffer because Satan will make sure we do. He hates us and goes wild with pungent fury when we unite ourselves ever more closely with our Savior. Our obedience to the Most Holy Trinity makes Satan go lathered in hysteria because he knows his doom is resounded in each soul that embraces their sacrifice in union with Jesus on the Cross. In that united Sacrifice at the Altar, the Light grows exponentially in the world, driving Satan into forgotten realms where he will be confined forever. Satan drove Jesus to the Sacrifice on the Cross which destroyed evil. How ironic! It is the same in the sacrificial soul. When we suffer, truly know that it is for a salvific reason. Faithful souls suffer so that wicked souls may be converted and saved from the fires of hell. The suffering of some also relieves the suffering of others who are weaker. We are a family, each doing our part, that all may be redeemed. No prayer or petition is without its answer. Sometimes God withholds all comfort and satisfaction from a sacrificial soul to dispense it to souls who are spiritually dying, or who otherwise need comforting support from their brother or sister. This sometimes leaves the praying soul wondering why God is not answering their prayers. Saints never wonder why. All are actually living sacrificial lives in the image of their Savior who gave His life that all may live. God knows that the sacrificial soul will be ecstatic at having been given the opportunity to suffer in these ways for Him. He is making us happy forever, even though we might not understand now. When we feel our prayers are going unanswered, proclaim, 'I believe in You, O Lord. Give my merits to Thy Divine Will and change the world. I will suffer with You until You come for me. I shall greet You then in thanksgiving that You allowed me to share the sweetness of Your Cross.' This is where Jesus retrieves pearls that He wishes to throw. He is consumed with the Fire of God within Himself. And, that Fire is Love for the Creation of His Father. He wants to save it at all costs. And, that cost was the Life of Jesus offered in the Sacrifice of Calvary so that His Mystical Body would be saved into Eternal Paradise.

Question 24

Please explain your opinion about why God would place a human soul in children who are conceived in laboratories outside the womb of a woman. If He is so against this kind of conception, why does He give it His overt approval by placing a soul there?

God is faithful, even if we are unfaithful. He gave the mechanics of creating human life into our hands, and the language of Creation tells us how those mechanics should be employed. Our Lord is concerned about how to save the souls of those who are abusing these mechanics. They are damning themselves. Our Lady said the power of God will always meet the challenge of evil and destroy it. These rogue scientists who are running headlong down the path to condemnation do not realize that the children they are manipulating into being in their test tubes will ultimately rise up and destroy their life's work, convicting them of heinous crimes, as they reset the Creation of life on its intended path. The work of their own hands will rise up to condemn them. Are not the children who have miraculously survived being aborted the flaming denunciation of the entire ideology of the culture of death? These children have the power to single-handedly end abortion. They speak for 60 million aborted infants in a voice that cannot be challenged or refuted. What about children afflicted with Down Syndrome speaking to the nation's leaders about their right to life when the culture of death is trying to convince everyone they should be winnowed from society? But, what happens? They are stubbornly dismissed, ignored, rejected and silenced in every way possible by the esteemed secular giants who think they know better. Those who reject these voices are damned. You cannot agree with and defend abortion and enter Heaven on the last day. Millions are on the pathway to hell.

Likewise, scientists and doctors who abuse the process of conception are simply another incarnation of those who kill children in the womb. They are manipulators who are tinkering, while using misguided women as their laboratory subjects and children as their victims. Strict doctoral and religious ethics should be wrapped around these techniques and technologies to prevent them from being abused in the commission of great sin and the manifestation of abomination. The problem in our contemporary era of secular godlessness is that there are barely a few ethicists whose spiritual depth and wisdom you can trust. They are just another group of intellectuals who in many cases fail to recognize the mystery of God in a newly conceived child. Everyone should start with the basic principle of truth that an embryo is a child from the first moment of conception who has rights before God and man. Life has rights by its veritable existence. Creation has taken place. It is the presence of a human soul. Any offense to that conception is a mortal sin which is punishable by the eternal fires of hell. It is just this simple. All of our discussion about right and wrong related to that child must start at the recognition of its conception. Our seriousness about the recognition of human dignity originates in our protection of life at its very inception. If we concoct justifications that allow us to manipulate the fruit of that conception, which is in any way detrimental or harmful to that conception, we will concoct justifications for manipulating and damaging any life from conception until death. Our claims of respect for human dignity will be proven to be false. This does not mean that there may not come a day where our medical knowledge will allow us to be of benefit to the human conception itself, while respecting its infinite worth, but I do not believe that day is here yet. We should be as horrified by the killing of an embryo as we are by the slaughter of a one year old child. We should have the same passion for that conception as a mother who would give her life that her newborn infant be protected for a lifetime.

Question 25

Regarding the nature of evil, how do you differentiate between evil acts and evil people? Is it true that there are certain individuals who are absolutely unable to become open to the possibility that they will ever live in Heaven? Have such people already given-up on ever being saved to the point that they feel that they might as well commit evil acts and enjoy the pleasure of seeing other people suffer at their hands?

Jesus said you will know the tree by its fruits. In order for a person to cooperate with evil, they must surrender their free will, which makes them slaves to the sins they are committing and the darkness they are entering into. Our ability to invoke our free will to do good in the image of Jesus is a manifestation of the eternal life of the soul. People who surrender their free will to the forces of evil intentions forfeit the life of their soul. They become locked into a world that no longer conceives the idea of redemption because they believe they no longer need it. The direction of our will can be influenced by many things because our frame of reference can be manipulated by the devil, tempted by matters of the flesh, and formed by human experience that has not been tempered by the guiding influences of virtue well practiced. For example, a person who has never practiced self-denial will easily succumb to any force that entices their senses. They are dupes who can easily, and perhaps innocently, be led into all kinds of evils, suddenly finding themselves in miserable predicaments, wondering how they ever got there. This is why Jesus spoke about loving the Light to those whom He knew would love the darkness instead. Do certain people become so submerged in worldly darkness and evil works where they give up and simply ingratiate themselves in the pleasures of the flesh? Of course, we see these people everywhere we look. Do they realize they are lost and heading to judgement? Not in the slightest. People of faith are backward little rubes to them. Yet, in the face of this phenomenon, the possibility always exists through Jesus' Divine Mercy and the reparative prayers of the Roman Catholic Church for each of these souls to return to the Light and be saved. The Holy Mass has saving power seen nowhere else in Creation because it is Jesus' Sacrifice on Calvary made manifest.

Now, it is obvious that many people have surrendered themselves to Satan and do his works willfully with adequate knowledge that what they are doing is outright evil. The defense and commission of abortion is one such example. There are no excuses left for defending this murderous abomination. Its defenders know exactly the death they are perpetrating and that babies are being slaughtered. Their legacy of human carnage and complicity is nearly unimaginable. It screams for the justice of God. This is why they are soon to face the judgement of the Almighty Father where none of them would survive if it were to occur today. They now revel in the pain, blasphemy and abomination that they perpetuate because the sacrifice required to enter into the Light is repulsive to them. The yoke and burden are too heavy because they love the things of this world more than they love either God or themselves. They never seek true happiness because they have no comprehension where happiness is found. The leap to this knowledge is across a chasm too far for their selfishness to ever transcend. They know not sacrificial faith. They desire not eternal life in Heaven. They wish not to worship the Maker of Life. In the case of the killing of unborn children, there is no difference between evil people and the evil acts. They are one. Nonetheless, Our Lady says that even these do not fully comprehend what they are doing because the deception consuming them has been so great. They have not tasted sweetness yet. But, if they have, and then reject the sweetness so as to willingly choose the darkness, they are in grave danger of losing their souls forever.

Sin brings its own darkness where all bearings of moral judgement become lost and new anchors of deception are erected creating a false travel guide to our lives, which leads to sorrow, desolation, and eternal death. Just because a person has been deceived into great sin does not mean they are not responsible for the evil they generate once they get there. Ignorance is not bliss in many cases. There is deception written all across what Satan does to mankind. People do not see the back yard of ultimate responsibility when they are being greeted by the demons at the front door and are welcomed into the great party of depravity. Yet, when they finally arrive in the back yard of realization, they see the wreckage of the house where their debauchery took place and the homeowner standing in the livingroom with the angels of justice who are seeking the assailants. It will be then that they will decide their fate with nothing from their lives to assist them. The question is, will their pride destroy them? Will repentance rise in them? Will atonement be made? Will reparation be offered? Their judgement will be their moment of Truth whereupon they lived a lifetime of lies. In addition, Our Lady said that the souls who will be damned, outside of time, have been damned from the beginning because damnation is as eternal as Salvation. They never truly belonged to Jesus Christ. He has always known who they are. This is not predestination, just an eventuality they have manifested from the beginning. We see those who are currently manifesting their own damnation. The question is, will there be any of them who will repent and convert before they are damned forever? We must realize that outward professions are sometimes only that. God knows the interior state of each person and the sources of our motivations. Religious hucksterism, feigned piety and pretentious devotion do not validate an acceptance of Christ Jesus. Sometimes words are not enough. Giving Jesus half-hearted allegiance so that we can indulge in decadence with the other half of our devotion is a terrible approach to engaging a life. Only the origin validates spiritual perfection in the Holy Spirit. All else can be a deceptive imitation; nothing more than vaunted window-dressing. Sacrifice is the valedictory poise that flows from integrity in the Holy Spirit. In the end, no man can lie his way into the narrow gate of Heaven because each person knows in the depths of their soul whether they accepted Jesus' Crucifixion or whether they flew in the face of God's Commandments as reprobates their entire lives, however clandestinely they may have hidden their wickedness from other men. No one can lie to God. Everyone knows whether they placed their hand to the plow at one time, then rejected the Son of Man because they loved the darkness more than the Light.

There are also those who are never approached with the story of Salvation in any substantive way, who may have stumbled through life, but nonetheless, lived the best they knew how, reflecting on the righteousness of the heart. Even these may jump into Jesus' arms as they see Him for the very first time at their judgement because they do not have the impediment of actually and willfully rejecting Him. And, they will be forgiven and accepted into the Divine Kingdom as a result of the prayers of the Roman Catholic Church and its worship of Jesus' Holy Sacrifice throughout the ages. God will answer the prayers of His Church that they be granted Divine Mercy. These are the people that Our Lady says were never told. But, once anyone has been told and has accepted the dimensions of conversion in even the smallest of ways, they will hold themselves accountable at the Throne of God. It is then that the determination of rejection looms. This is why Roman Catholics who have rejected the Original Apostolic Church, and thereafter disparage it as if they are authorized critics, are in terrible danger of eternal damnation. They are assaulting Jesus' Bride. How do they think the Bridegroom is going to respond? As would any, we might imagine. Catholic politicians who have condoned, defended and suborned abortion will most likely enter the fires of hell. Why? Because their lives are proclaiming their own judgement. Their arrogance renders them incapable of generating the repentance that will allow them to forgive themselves once they are forced to accept what they have done; and their excuses will be incinerated like straw in a campfire on a windswept evening. They do not understand such helplessness after living lives of such worldly power. Likewise, Prelates and priests who betray the integrity and Traditions of the Roman Catholic Church will be judged in such harsh terms as to be unimaginable — because they knew better and were given extraordinary graces and stature to defend the Truth for the sake of human souls. Lukewarmness is not the way to live a Christian life. Scripture says as much. Anyone who engages their existence through such miserable dimensions will wish at their judgement, as if in a burning fire, that they had lived some other way. Multitudes, at their judgement, do not call upon or generate a belief that Jesus could, would, and will forgive them, and they enter the fires of hell immediately, cursing and screaming at the Lamb of God and His Mystical Body. For those who do find repentance, Purgatory is engaged as a process of purification before entry into the vaults of Glory. We must realize that our judgement is not a station stop where our ticket is gratuitously punched before we walk through the turnstile into the heavenly entertainment venue. Our lives are the ticket. They testify whether we are allowed entrance. We will not be able to simply say, "Jesus, I'm sorry," whereafter He says thank you and moves us along through the narrow gate into Paradise. Reparation must be made by those who generated and advanced evil in this world, which might be centuries of prayer and suffering. Centuries of prayer from the Church-Triumphant and centuries of suffering from these poor souls in Purgatory. Our contemporary understanding of Christian mercy advertises redemption to the point of insulting Jesus' Crucifixion. People do not realize that every last scintilla of sin has been accrued as if we have dug a hole, and we will account for it. Life is not only about not digging a hole in sin and living in it, but crawling out of the one we have dug, and filling it in so others may not fall into the pit our sins excavated into the world. Many people arrive at their judgement standing in a cavernous pit where they do not have the strength to ascend out of it. We see people throughout our country, indeed, vast numbers in places of authority and prestige, who have no fear where they stand or how they will be judged. They realize it, they revel in it, and they will rue it. They will have gained the whole world, and will suffer the loss of their souls forever. The great merciful dimension to this mystery of human deliverance is that we have the ability to help people crawl out of their pit, and to fill in the holes they have dug. Our prayers and sacrifices fill those holes, even as horrifically dark and subterranean as they might be. This is why we pray and sacrifice for them. But, if they reject our gift of reparation for them at their judgement, we will cheer their ejection from Creation into the languishing darkness of hell where they have always belonged. We can almost sense this inevitable horrific end in the smugness of politicians and hubris of Supreme Court Justices who defend abortion. They who do not respect the goodness and truth of Jesus Christ while in life usually do not respect it in their deaths. It is possible to sense who will be damned for eternity. They have a miserable stench of arrogance that reeks from them. They are self-justified in abomination and derangement. They pride themselves on being intellectual and smarter than anyone else around them. While rejecting the consequences of their beliefs, they are impenetrable to argument, impossible to convince, and inebriated in the collective derangement of their partisans. Sophisticated and intelligent, they use their faculties to maintain aberrations that secure their power and influence. They reject the Cross and refuse to submit to the sensus fidei—the sense of the faith—while also rejecting the logic of natural law that might lead them to their redemption through the language of Creation. It takes no soul searching to realize that you do not slaughter children in the wombs of their mothers, and that you will be held accountable at the Throne of God. They know exactly what they are defending, believing no one will ever have the power to hold them accountable. How wrong they are. Creation is near its climax of evil, and God Himself is preparing to act in order to cleanse the world of evildoers. As in the days of Noah, so shall these times unfold. But, there is hope if each person repents and seeks the Divine Mercy of Jesus Christ. This is why Our Lady has appeared as the Morning Star Over America. She wishes to give each person a chance to listen to Her, if they will not listen to anyone else.

Question 26
When people fall into deep mortal sin, such as lustful acts, committing abortions, getting an abortion, murdering someone, (and the like), how on Earth could the Holy Mother's statement be true in Her May 2, 1997 message that says,...I am at your side at all times.(?) Does She actually see these things and do nothing about it? Does God allow Her to see the worst of human corruption, even though She is in Heaven? How does this reflect Her May 9, 1997 message that says, "...I will not allow evil to tear the love from your hearts."(?)

I wish to relate something that I do not believe I have divulged anywhere in my writings. It was the early 1990s during the early years of our Beloved Mother's miraculous intercession. I experienced a mystical transcension one evening. I was trans-located to the day of the Crucifixion and was allowed to be present at Calvary as Jesus died. Even to this day, it is now a memory in my mind of having experienced an actual event like any other worldly memory that I have, and it oftentimes brings me to tears to think about it. The mystical experience was conscripted within parameters that contained the revelation into a bounded perspective. I was standing on Mount Calvary as if my back was to the Cross. I did not see Jesus hanging in agony as part of this firsthand experience. I was instead allowed to look into the actual faces of those who were gazing past me at Him hanging behind me. Each of these people was individually and completely apparent to me, the tears, faces grimaced in grief, the begging that it not be so, the crying, the helplessness of those who loved Him. There was no wailing, just utter devastation in human thoughts and emotions. I saw the Crucifixion in their faces and the throes of love pouring from them as if I was staring directly at the Cross myself. I saw Jesus' death as a perfect reflection in them, while knowing exactly what was happening behind me. They were a mirror of Christ's Sacrificial Death to me. It was shattering to my soul to see such pain in those who loved Him. I will never forget it. I saw only the sinners. Even though She was standing at the foot of the Cross, I did not see the Most Blessed Virgin. Somehow I believe it would have been an invasion of the beatific sanctity of Her soul in those moments for me to be a spectator to the Sacred Mystery unfolding in Her Immaculate Heart. I did not notice the environment that surrounded me. I did not have a sense of any disinterested bystanders. I saw only they who loved Him as they looked upon Him in grief and sorrow.

We must realize that the Mother of Jesus has already seen the most grotesque and horrifying event of human history. Her perfect femininity, motherhood and immaculate disposition were offended totally to their depths by the Crucifixion of Her Son. She possessed the capacity and composure to witness it and be assaulted by it, but without diminishment in any of Her faculties or perfections. Thus, there is nothing less that can touch Her beauty in any way. She has conquered the pinnacle of human devastation. It is not difficult for Her to remain at the side of any of Her children after remaining steadfast in the Crucifixion of Her Son on Mount Calvary. We should never worry that we have done something that would make Her run from us. It is not possible. It may be a shock for us to realize, but we don't have that much power. She is not afraid of Satan or anything he can do. She knows that the King of kings surrounds Her, and that the evil one cannot touch Her now. It is true that our Heavenly Mother sees most everything we do and have done in our lives. We are Her children. Yet, She said that there are certain atrocities that Her Son does not allow Her to see in order to defend Her dignity, although it is usually instances of Satan biting himself amongst the horde of demons who are all destined forever to hell. Her children receive Her presence and grace in every way we will allow. She does everything that She is allowed to do in our lives. One thing that each of us will be shocked in seeing at our judgement is just how much assistance we actually received during our lives, but did not realize it. Our Holy Mother is helping us all the time. She asks whether She should rescind Her heavenly assistance so that we would realize what grace we were previously under once it is gone. We must realize that our conversion and sanctification is our work to do. It is composed of the daily sacrifices that we are charged to make. Our Lady cannot do these things for us, but She does ask us to realize that She understands what sacrifice is because She too lived a lifetime of sacrifice so that we could receive heavenly grace.

The final point is this. Our Heavenly Mother will not allow evil to tear love out of our hearts because She always resides there. Our souls have not yet been separated from our bodies in death. She cannot be driven out by evil. There is nothing that She will run from. She simply asks to be noticed within. She desires that we come to realize how close She is to us, and recognize how much we are loved. We can feel this within ourselves. By faith, we can be convinced to the point of perfect knowledge of Her maternal overwatch within us. And, from this, we will draw strength to stand amidst the gales of life just as She stood beneath the Cross. Our perspective will then expand to realize that our Heavenly Mother does not just provide moral support. She has the capacity to address changes in our time through our faith. It is not coincidence when prayers are answered. The protection where we would thrive is not just a happenstance of the environment. Blessings abound the more our faith is given eyes to see the greatness of our God. Ask and you shall receive, seek and you will find, knock and it will be opened to you. These are not hollow commendations. They are filled with revelatory power, but one must believe.

Question 27

It is obvious that the Holy Mother is not shy about proclaiming her own Divinity in her messages to you at the same time that she proclaims the Supremacy of the Blessed Trinity and defers to the Crucifixion of Jesus as the expiation of all human sinfulness. If she is so humble and selfless, why does she say such things that appear in her July 25, 1997 message of, "...all access to Salvation is granted through My sinless love."(?)

There it is! There are the words! Those ten beautiful words—'All access to Salvation is granted through My sinless love.' Those ten words are the Holy Gospel. Those ten words glorify the Incarnation of Jesus Christ in the flesh, the incorrupt fruit that came from the perfect tree. They are the same words spoken by the angel to the shepherds through the Virgin's Maternity, "For today in the city of David a savior has been born for you who is Messiah and Lord" [Luke 2:11]. It is amazing that sinners do not consider their words before leveling a veiled accusation against the Queen of Heaven such as, 'If she is so humble and selfless, why...." as if She is required to submit to the scrutinies of those who are responsible for the death of Her Perfect Child. This logic ultimately leads to no one glorifying Jesus Christ because if the Mother of God is not allowed to sing the origins of Salvation, then who can? It is just that She gets to do so in a very unique way as His Immaculate Mother. Those ten words are none other than, "...the Almighty has done great things for Me, and holy is His Name." Is the Mother Most Pure to be accused of lacking in humility because She states the fact that all Glory and Salvation came to Earth when the Messiah was born from Her Fiat and Womb? Is this Salvific Communion of Mother and Child worthy of no merit? Has it no Voice? Remember that She is a perfect Creation of God, never having been tainted by sin. She defended purity upon the Earth. Can She not thus declare Her cooperation with human redemption as a matter of fact? Does Her great act of faith not require veneration from every soul who wishes to be saved? A sinless Virgin prophesied by Isaiah brought forth by Her Surrender the Divine Son of God to save a cabal of questioning reprobates of which She was not a participant in any shape, form, fact or function. Her being is the birthing source of the deliverance for this rabbling group of renegades. Are not the words, 'All access to Salvation is granted through My sinless love,' the origin and echo of the words, "No one comes to the Father but through Me?" [John 14:6] The historic procession of the story of human deliverance is stark. She is credited for all Eternity for responding to the Archangel Gabriel with Her faith-filled affirmation. She did not have to, and would have been no less in perfection and would have been assumed into Heaven nonetheless. She was not coerced in any way to respond with Her Fiat. Nothing was hanging over Her head. Can you imagine if She had not? What access to Salvation would mankind have had then? Sinners doomed to the netherworld would have had no access to Redemption; no access to Divine Mercy by any person. Our sins would have remained, and eternal punishment would have been the result of God's justice. Our exile would have been forever. Her entire life was one great selfless act that embraced the Crucifixion of Her innocent Son for the sake of sinners.

As far as whether Our Lady is shy or not, what does shyness tell us about a person? Does it signify lack of confidence, insecurity or being unsure of one's beliefs, a lack of command of the facts, being afraid of making mistakes or laughed at for them, or maybe a deficiency in self-worth recognizing no contribution worthy of merit? None of these describe the Immaculate Mother of Jesus Christ. Shyness does not apply to Her. Why would She not speak gloriously about Her role in the redemption of the world? She is the greatest woman ever to have breathed air in human history, and look at how few words She has actually spoken during Her earthly life and throughout the millennia. This is monumentally humble and selfless. But now, it is Her time to speak in order to set the record straight in these final times at the doorstep of the Reckoning. She will not be quieted by any sinner who presumes to believe that

She should not have the right to speak. And, when She does, Her words glorify Her Son, and the integrity of His Incarnation that proceeded from Her. Indeed, all access to Salvation is granted through Her sinless love!

Question 28

In the same message of July 25, 1997, Our Lady said, "...you live many days in the peace of this Truth, with others fumbling over their own curiosity." What type of 'fumbling' is Our Lady referring to? How do you believe that the Blessed Virgin Mary actually sees you? Has she ever referred to you as being immature, lacking in ecclesiastical discretion, self-righteous, zealous, bellicose, or unwittingly arrogant? Keep in mind that some of the Medjugorje seers have been widely regarded as being arrogant. Why do you suppose this is the case? And, does it also apply to you?

When I am faced with a series of questions like this, I sometimes do not know where to begin. I know that these queries are usually based in unwarranted and illegitimate scrutinies by people who oftentimes do not know what they are asking. People are always going to think what they think, rarely holding themselves accountable to the standards by which they measure others. They judge by appearances whose interpretations are built on their frail frame of reference as sinners themselves. They never consider that they do not have the ability to judge a soul. Saint Paul stated, *"It does not concern me in the least that I be judged by you or any human tribunal; I do not even pass judgment on myself; I am not conscious of anything against me, but I do not thereby stand acquitted; the one who judges me is the Lord. Therefore, do not make any judgment before the appointed time, until the Lord comes, for he will bring to light what is hidden in darkness and will manifest the motives of our hearts, and then everyone will receive praise from God"* [1 Corinthians 4:3-5]. My intentions are to always give thoughtful answers when appropriate, and be silent when no answer would matter. Our Lady told me that I am not required to engage people's curiosities if I sense intentions of scandal. For example, She has told me to beware of any interrogator who seeks to meet with my brother and me who has never read our books. Not just one of them, but all of them. If they read our books, they will not have to discern any further as to whether it is actually Her who has been speaking to us for nearly 30 years. They will be left with no other possibility.

As I contemplate the scope of an answer in this case, my thoughts invariably seem to expand into numerous dimensions which all deserve attention. I think I would begin by recalling everyone's attention again to the concept of frames of reference characterizing the interior constitution within each person, and how it can be shaped with differing states of competition between coherence, logic, and truth. I believe that Our Lady sees me, in the first order, as Her child who needs Her to keep my frame of reference in union with the Deific Wisdom of Her Son. She loves me, and I love Her; and in this is Wisdom found. The soundness of judgement that She possesses originates in Her Son Jesus; and His Light restores clarity to our soul, allowing anyone to relate their sentiments clearly and an interrogator to comprehend them accurately. But, does not the interrogator require the same communion with Her in order to understand both who they are actually scrutinizing and the answers they are given? We can see in these times that cultures and peoples are having a terrible time with interpersonal communication amongst themselves. A person of righteous intent possessing Jesus' Wisdom finds it nearly impossible to relate any moral truth coming from this Light without entire lynch-mobs of unreasonable fanatics screaming for their destruction, either financially, socially or politically. In other dimensions, historical entrenchment in godless ideologies by lost barbarians who bring destruction and destabilization to humankind is prevalent, and great human suffering is the result, while our efforts to remedy the nightmare bring the hauntings of war in response. In fact, if one possesses true wisdom, they would see that those on the progressive, secular left who are most wailing about the specter of fascism are the ones who are using fascist tactics to force their ideology upon the nation. Our Lady has nurtured me from a place of incoherence to a sanctuary of communion in Her Immaculate Heart, and has aligned my frame of reference into a fortress of conviction sustained by the wisdom of the Holy Spirit. Am I perfect?—I don't think so, but that does not mean I do not see the Light clearly as Our Lady informs me. She has never admonished me, as I remember, about any of the aforementioned states posited in the question; immaturity, a lack of ecclesiastical discretion, self-righteousness, zealousness, or bellicosity. But, the phenomenon is this. It seems that anyone who is not lettered as an esteemed theologian, who moves to evangelize, will nearly always be accused of being immature if they begin to be successful in any way that might be interpreted as unorthodox by the more self-possessed gnat strainers. Our Lady's miraculous intercession is unorthodox to these people, yet She accomplishes more in one day than they do in a lifetime. In addition, anyone who admonishes members of the Church to be of more courageous conviction will be accused of lacking in ecclesial discretion. One who transforms the message of the Gospel into words and actions that show loyalty and devotion to Christ the King will be accused of being self-righteous and overly zealous by those who have grown lukewarm. Thousands of Saints were assailed for their righteousness. Multitudes were accused of arrogance for standing firm in their convictions. For goodness sake, even Saint Teresa of Calcutta was attacked as being a fraud in her spirituality and saintly efforts. And, if one declares the Gospel unyieldingly and loudly from the housetops as Saint John Paul the Great encouraged, they will most assuredly be accused of being bellicose by the brash egos who do not want to hear it. So, it comes down to whether someone has the capacity to determine actual excesses in another soul, or should they? One perspective overrides everything that any person could believe or say about me, and it is this. 'I know what Jesus and the Queen of Heaven think of me,' and nothing else that any sinner says matters. Saint Paul would have said as much. As for myself, I care almost nothing about anyone's judgement of me, except what my Bishop counsels. And, I hold suspect any opinion of a priest who is not in respectful union with him.

Human beings are proficient at leveling accusations about anything and everything when they have no authority to do so. We must remember that each of the previously mentioned fronts of accusation require an objective reference point for any of them to have meaning. Most people believe their unique, personal frame of reference is the anchoring source of all truth, which in most cases harbors the original deception that has generated their questioning. Those who are lost judge things based upon their worldly perspectives, and then assail those who bear any clarifying truth to them. For example, the determination of immaturity requires an objective reference point. Tiny children cannot be said to be immature because they execute their optimum maturation level for their age, even though in any false comparison with their older siblings, they might fail the subjective maturity test. God does not expect to see the mature genius of Saint John Paul II as Pontiff in a small child. Would that not be a miracle? Nonetheless, that very genius was embodied and made manifest in Jesus as a Baby. The point is, sinners should be wary of creating false reference points which then produce unjust comparisons, and ultimately unjust condemnations. A child can be perfectly mature for their age, but not if someone unfairly compares them to an adult, or even another child who has been the recipient of greater gifts. Our Lady does not have false reference points, but She has verifiable expectations of each of Her children at every station of their lives. Her frame of reference is all one and coherent. She relates to all of us as Her little children because that is where we are in relation to the final state of our soul when we will see God as He is. "Beloved, we are God's children now; what we shall be has not yet been revealed. We do know that when it is revealed, we shall be like him, for we shall see him as he is" [1 John 3:2]. There is perfection in a newly baptized baby, and that perfection may be just as large in that initial sacramental moment as when that child may grow to be the most sacrificial of Pontiffs. Love for Jesus is the same whether we are six years old or ninety.

Man's intellect has very little to do with magnifying our soul. Sacrificial love has no reference point in levels of intellectualism. This is why we hear some say that age is no presumption of wisdom, while Jesus spoke about becoming as the little child. This should be a sobering thought to theologians everywhere, not to mention a warning to critics who have no idea what Jesus might have commissioned an evangelizer to accomplish in His Name. If dirt clods could speak, we should expect that they would not be very happy after a farmer has roughed them up preparing the soil for planting. The souls of men are the same. Dirt clods should stand proud on the day of harvest, no matter what God asks them to endure.

The second state, 'ecclesiastical discretion,' is nothing more than prudent love for the Roman Catholic Church, the Mystical Body of Christ, amidst a world of heckling sinners who are determined to crucify it. We must remember that Satan roams the Earth seeking the destruction of souls and the Church. Jesus asked us to be shrewd as serpents and gentle as doves, but He does not expect us to be silent so no one is disturbed by the truth. We must remember that He told some whom He gifted to not share their healing experiences, which most seemed to do anyway. He did not want them to suffer due to the graces He had bestowed. It was an act of love for them that He asked them to be quiet. It was His attempt to teach discretion to souls who would become victims to vulnerable circumstances, knowing His enemies were legion. Criticism often comes from envy, which the Church teaches us to combat with humility. But, can Jesus be accused of lacking humility and discretion when thundering the Truth in His Father's house? Was He accused of being self-righteous, bellicose and immature then? Most likely He was, but the accusations of these sinners were not sustained in Heaven. It is in this we see that the seemingly roving reference point must always be secured in the highest wisdom. And, while in that anchoring, no man will stand convicted in the Court of the Saints for defending the King of kings and advancing His message of conversion anywhere in the world he desires. He will be hailed as heroic. Our Lady has never done anything but affirm my love for Her Son's Original Church and how I may defend it and advance its commission. Her intentions are for us together to stare down the world with as much grace and Truth as She can sustain within Her Catholic children. She does not kowtow to insolent sinners. She knows that I have loved the Church from my baptism and have never breathed a word against its stature, authority and genius, even if human failures requiring admonishment have occurred within its hierarchical ranks. Discretion implies a point of reference because the Truth has much to say about the present anemic state of the professed body of the faithful, while recognizing the sea of reference frames and states of development. We must take into consideration the "spiritual age" and the levels of rebellion of those whom we are engaging. For example, I never let disparaging attacks on Roman Catholic priests stand without my rebuke of those accusers. Evangelizers cannot be accused of being the offenders simply because someone finds themselves offended by the truth that is spoken. The Truth is the truth in and out of season. Man cannot curse a rock that he himself stumbles over. Our Lord alluded to this when thundering at those who claimed they see, while offering succoring defense of the broken who may have known little of the law.

The determinations of self-righteousness, zealousness, and bellicosity also require their point of reference. If Jesus were to appear in our day and not reveal His true identity, would He not inevitably be accused of these? Surely He would because accusers are numerous and their reference frames would not be in union with His. This is also why Jesus rebuked Peter, telling him to stand behind because he was not thinking as God thinks. This is why Jesus was driven to Mount Calvary and crucified. Consider self-righteousness. Righteousness was embodied in Him, and He displayed it to the point of saying, "I AM." Zeal—not only in the clearing of His Father's house, but in the single-minded conviction to save the world that He would seek out Crucifixion in order to destroy death itself. And bellicosity—He was routinely engaging, confronting, and admonishing others to the point of His enemies' hatred. If He embellished His words with serious emotion, so be it. Every one of His opponents thought our Lord was aggressive in His convictions simply because they felt the impact of His words. Read the four Gospels and ponder our Lord's fearless engagements. Look whom He challenged openly at dinners, in courtyards, in synagogues and on the street; look at the challenges to human egos; and His followers loved Him for it because He was the Shepherd whom the sheep recognized. Our Holy Mother once told me that it should be no surprise that Jesus was not a very well-liked little boy. She said He was constantly engaging His companions to do right by the God of Israel, even to the point of coming home from His play with scrapes and black eyes after being assailed. But, She said that He walked in the door with great joy and a smile on His face at having been faithful to His Father and engaged as a human being with His childhood friends whom He loved. A boy of twelve confronting the Elders in the Temple. This did not just happen on a whim. He was not seeking their wisdom, but rather engaging them with His, asking them questions to probe their reference frames whereby He would pierce them with Light. "Amazed at his understanding and his answers" [Luke 2:47]. This is confident audacity. This could have been considered a lack of ecclesiastical discretion in His time. He was on a mission seeking out the hearts of men. I would love to have been privy to that entire conversation with the Elders. The Holy Spirit in some private revelations has hinted that He was challenging them all as no one had ever experienced, even to the point of prophesying to them His own coming reign. He left the impact of His Divinity upon them, leaving them all wondering about the boy who had just faced them. Could He possibly be? We have been sold a modernistic narrative about Jesus that is not in conformity with the Gospel accounts. In our contemporary world, any strident conviction in defense of the Kingdom of God is met with ferocious rebuttal by those who are walking in the darkness of their relativistic mediocrity. And, on occasion, those misguided rebuttals come from fellow Catholics, even priests and Bishops. While it is possible for anyone to be guilty of each of these overages, it is not worldly judgement that matters. Are not these behaviors more identifiable in those who are impeding the propagation of the Gospel, those who are hurling epithets of self-righteousness, zealousness and bellicosity against those who are speaking to the refinements of human conversion? Our Lady sees it this way. Jesus prophesied that they would do as much. 'If they hated Me, they will hate you.' Why? Because they know you are confronting them with the truth that they are unwilling to profess because the sacrifice is too great.

A spiritual tragedy has occurred in the last 60 years. Catholic evangelization at many levels has undergone an illicit shift in its frame of reference. It is failing by nearly every statistic. Roman Catholicism surrendered spiritual supremacy after Vatican II, and bowed to pluralism. Traditional catechesis was thought backward and non-ecumenical. Christian mysticism and the supernal realms were replaced by psychology, intellectualism and ecumenical relativism. Love for all that the Church had been for 2,000 years was attacked from within and without. Faithfulness to the Church was wiped out by a plague of compromise with secular reasonableness. Only a remnant of Roman Catholics remains who possess the perspective of our Virgin Mother. We are presently living in a world that believes that since we have all been sinners, no one has the authority to speak the truth to anyone, let alone hold anyone accountable to it. Vast throngs seem to believe that in order for Catholics to validate their Christianity, they are required to retire to their closets and remain in somber silence with their faces to the ground when confronted with monumental atrocities being perpetrated in God's vineyard. Our Lady said that Jesus did not live life this way, and neither should we if we wish to imitate Him. Jesus did not retire into silence when He came into the world. His Word thundered from the Manger with audible Light that is heard to this day. Even when He knew His enemies intended to kill Him, He marched to Jerusalem with righteous determination. Had Jesus retired to a cave in the desert, He knew that everyone would have ultimately been standing at the entrance to His dwelling. He also knew that religious authorities would have been just as irrate that their subjects had left them to imbibe His grace in the desert. And, upon finding them, they would have hauled Him out of His cave and crucified Him nonetheless. But, He did not seek out the cave. He confronted them head on in their soiled sanctuaries and secular marketplaces. In the center of their religious world, there He came. And, His Apostles have done the same. See how courageous they were upon going to every region of the pagan world and proclaiming the truth of the forgiveness of sins in Jesus Christ and declaring all men must convert. And, it was Jesus who advanced upon the world in them.

Satan's weapon to silence the truth in our time is two-fold. First, he inspires the arrogance of men to be offended, then he lies to Christians by telling them they are the offenders; and they believe it. Thereafter, evangelization dies away because we think more of comradery in sin as opposed to conversion into holiness. Christians accept the false accusation of being self-righteous and thereafter modulate their witness into silence in response. This is cowardice. The only admonishments acceptable in our time are leveled against courageous Christians, and it is occurring through their fellow faithsians who chide them to not cause such a stir. It makes me think of the old game show, "Make Me Laugh," where contestants attempt to sit stone-faced before comedians who try to make them laugh. If the contestant maintains their composure in the face of the humorist, they win money. Christians seem to have accepted the same disposition. We believe we are on a game show where feigned holy silence brings us success. We believe we are proving our virtue and self-control. What is really happening is that we do not want to feel the pain of confrontation, so we forsake our responsibilities in the Gospel. We think that we are being Christlike if we can maintain our silence in the face of overwhelming blasphemy and heresy, while the Holy Spirit is doing everything He can to encourage us to proclaim the Truth. We remain silent in a false humility so that we won't be accused by rabble-rousers of causing the commotion that their obstinance initiates. We think it is a great virtue to become patently mute. The spittle of abomination, slander and persecution are ejected into the Face of Christ, and we think it is a violation of virtue to respond in defense of Him. All the while, the Christian world collapses in front of our eyes. And, when we do raise our voices and testify to the truth, entire galleries hail that we are hypocrites who are not imitating Jesus like we claim. Imagine that, unrepentant sinners chiding the faithful that they are not holy enough. This leads us to the accusation of arrogance. 'Who do you think you are? You are a sinner like everyone else. Sweep before your own door. Pick the beam out of your own eye.' And, on it goes. This is the only strain of Scripture that reprobates seem to be aware of, as if they believe themselves wise enough to grab our own weapons and shoot us with them. Who is truly arrogant here—the one who advances the Gospel without apology or the one who expends their brief moments of life impeding it? One who senses arrogance in another is simply saying that their reference frame is encountering something that is challenging their ego and causing them discomfort. The little voice of ego inside says, "Who do they think they are, talking to little ol' me like that?"

The 'fumbling' that Our Lady was referring to in Her message is our stumbling around trying to come to grips with the implications of our Catholic Faith. She is trying to get us to stand up in grace as Her children. If the world needs to be converted, who is going to do it? Who is going to stand for the redemption of humanity? Who is going to tell the Truth? Who is going to relate the requirements of salvation? Who is going to confront atheistic secularism? We should be far more confident in our possession of the True Faith. We have something to both preserve and advance into the final generation of mankind. Christ is the only hope for the world, and we should never apologize for knowing Him. Let the world rage at our witness. We must stop cowering. Those who will be saved will listen. The rest will wish for eternity they had. The manifestation of the fruits of the Holy Spirit in our lives is our constant goal—Love, joy, peace, patience, goodness, kindness, faithfulness, humility and self-control. But, they are not a cave that we reside in as evil consumes the Earth. If there is a battle to be waged, then let us prepare for the conflict. There was a Crucifixion that occurred in public, before the full view of history. I cheer in my heart the great Prelates in their finest hours of admonishment. It is then that I see the Father. I see Saint Peter at the first Pentecost, speaking to the crowds about the Messiah whom they had just crucified. He was not worried much about any of their feelings then. This is how the Holy Spirit speaks in His finest hours of revelation. Read Saint Peter's words at Pentecost. He pierced them to the soul because he was trying to save them, and thousands were converted that day as they stood listening to this Lion. O' dear Jesus, give us those thousands in our day.

There is one thing that brings clarity and responsibility to our frame of reference and our discernment of anyone's Christian witness. Realize that every innocent child born with deformity and disability bears this Cross because of humanity's sins. Every sickness, disease, misfortune, accident, torment and grief is the consequence of sin committed by humanity. Every city and town destroyed by the forces of weather and planet, the suffering endured, the routines upended, and the lives lost is because of sin condoned. Every terrorizing attack upon human beings, each military conflict and any political squabble; all this occurs because mankind sins. Now, why would anyone chide another to come down from the housetop in proclaiming Jesus Christ Crucified so that these misfortunes may stop? Our Lady asks, why?

Question 29

Our Lady has told you things such as, "...I tell you these things because they are true." In other places, she has said, "...if this were not true, I would have told you." Does this not seem to you to be like stating the obvious? Why would the Mother of God tell you something, and then ask you to believe that it is true? Does she not understand that everything she tells you is accepted by your soul, mind, and heart as being the irrevocable Truth? In other words, does such added literati seem to you to be nothing more than just 'filler' for the time during which she is speaking to you? What do you suppose her speaking in this manner implies for our relationship with Jesus Christ, the Holy Gospel, and the Kingdom of God as a whole?

The types of quotations from our Heavenly Mother referenced as examples here harken to Her oneness with Jesus when He said in John 14:2, "*In my Father's house there are many dwelling places. If there were not, would I have told you that I am going to prepare a place for you?*" Can Jesus be accused of being redundant or "stating the obvious," in the way this question alludes? Why did Jesus speak this way? I would go back again to the idea of our soul, our frame of reference and all succeeding thoughts, perspectives and actions. It is not true that everything the Most Blessed Virgin says is accepted by the mind. All Her deniers prove this. Millions of people have minds and intellects that are dismissing Her miraculous intercession, even among the religious. Their intellects are deformed. When our Holy Mother says something, the heart and soul know it, but our mind is not always united with the heart and soul. The conformity of everything below the highest state of our soul must concur with the heart of our soul and everything below it to be complete in our being. While the soul unequivocally knows the truth, our will must concur to be one or we find ourselves divided within us as Scripture warns. Therefore, She says things to me such as, "I tell you these things because they are true,' or 'if this were not true, I would have told you,' as ways to reinforce and anchor the assent of my mind with what my soul already knows. She also asks me routinely, "Do you understand?," to which I am required to respond verbally. Obviously, She already knows whether I have grasped the things She says, but She wishes me to hear my own response as a reinforcement for my faith. It is the same as when

She asked me not to "think" my questions toward Her. She said that if God was going to allow Her to speak with me, then I should converse with Her openly within the dimensions of the gift. This entire dynamic is an example that our relationship as Mother and son is as authentic as any relationship we would have with friends or family. It cannot be diminished to merely being some imaginary conversation with ourselves or hearing words out of the unknown as many people would presuppose. These people are simply looking for an excuse so as not to have to admit the truth. Too often, we spontaneously conjure perspectives that are wholly inaccurate upon hearing of our Blessed Mother's miraculous intercession. We try to interpret their dimensions and implications using our incomprehension and disordered frame of reference as our foundation of discernment. It is like trying to understand a sunny beach in Hawaii when we have been living in the arctic our entire lives. We have no frame of reference of the climate of a paradise island. Unfortunately, we live in a world where there have been examples of unbalanced people who have declared to others that God is speaking to them when they are doing nothing more than attributing their own interior mind streams and imaginary delusions to the Son of God or His Saints. We can have all kinds of seemingly "ah-ha" moments that we believe come from God when they are no more than newer perspectives generated amidst the idiosyncrasies of our mortal frame of reference. We must realize that if our frame of reference is disordered and cluttered, those newer perspectives may be just as disordered as what produced them. This is how people can have the convicted realization that a woman's right to choose supersedes the life of the child in her womb. These people believe they are such sophisticates when they are actually embracing diabolical delusions straight from the bowels of hell; and it is nearly impossible to convince these doomed individuals that this is the case. Likewise, when many try to make sense of claims of miraculous intercession by the Most Blessed Virgin Mary, their frames of reference usually attempt to understand it by attributing it to being simply an intellectual, imaginary event in the visionary's mind. They are unfamiliar with the idea of a Saint or Angel from the realms of Heaven ever actually transcending and speaking directly to someone, even though the Sacred Scriptures accurately testify the possibility of these actual graces. The Protestant mind-set is very susceptible to distortion in judgement regarding the Blessed Virgin Mary. They have 500 years of error fortressed against Her statuesque dignity and station in the Kingdom they hope to enter someday. Most of them live in a state where they fully disdain Jesus' Original Apostolic Church, and they believe their great stubborn rejection is the power of the Holy Spirit informing their judgement. It is actually quite the opposite, but their frame of reference is too distorted to allow them to recognize the truth, even after the Virgin Mary appears in the world, trying to get them to listen. This is why nearly every Protestant immediately disparages the idea that Jesus' Mother would appear to anyone; or if She does, it does not apply to them. They know the Roman Catholic Church loves Our Lady, and always has. They realize that She is a hallmark of the Original Apostolic Church whom they cannot allow to rattle their unity in their protesting frame of reference. Therefore, they give Her mere lip service, if they do not scorn Her altogether. If She is ever allowed in, She would convert every one of them with Her immaculate grace and bring them to the Altar of Sacrifice to receive the True Bread of Life, which they are presently rejecting. They are not receiving the True Bread of Life in their communion services, and never have.

So, Our Lady's personal interaction with my brother and me in conduct and conversation is another way that She gives dimensions to Her intercession that do not fit into the spontaneous perspectives of those who doubt Her. She gives evidence repeatedly that does not conform to the doubters' narratives. In other words, She is destabilizing the sand under their feet that they believe to be concrete pavement. This is why I have always said that if the world could see Her just one time, the world as we know it is over. The frame of reference of the entire world would be recreated into a purified image just as at Pentecost. The Roman Catholic Church would be seen as She is. But, consider the psychological implosion that would occur first; imagine the carnage in the perceptions of men that will occur should God grant that grace. Right now, unbelievers are shameless in their error, and proud that they are. Our Lady believes that She can help them in Her gentle ways, but they must humble themselves enough to listen for the briefest of moments and allow their perspectives to be kneaded into a purer form of understanding. If they do not, the reckoning will eventually arrive and purify them anyway. Victory for God! In the grand context of our sanctification, Jesus wishes us to become a new creation fit for our return to Paradise. I believe everyone can admit that we are not there yet. Therefore, it would be beneficial for each person to ask what it is within them that must change where their mind would begin to testify in communion with their heart. And, for us to know our heart, we must begin to pray as Our Lady asks and allow Her to guide us into the Sacred Heart of Jesus.

Question 30

In your diarist writings, you relate that Our Lady asked you to read a brief testimony that you had apparently written previously. You indicate that she has had you read other scripted themes to her as well, as if you were asked to walk to a podium where all the heavens were listening. Why does she do this when she already knows their content? Does she ask you to read them aloud? What could possibly be the purpose in your reading passages that have already been recorded? Is this an aspect of her method of teaching that you have yet to tell the rest of the world?

I get so excited when questions like this are asked because I know the person is pondering deeply into our Holy Mother's thoughts and actions. Each of these questions is such a great seed for the growth of our perspective and understanding. I know that the one asking the question is at the doorstep of having their visionary faith taken to different dimensions. These were simple acts of faith that our Heavenly Mother asked me to engage obediently, but they were a testament to actual mystical dimensions that are beyond what most people would understand or accept. I can illustrate what I am saying. Using the example of this question as it was stated, my response to Our Lady was characterized by the questioner as being, '...*as if* you were asked to walk to a podium where all the heavens were listening.' A metaphor was employed because the questioner was not ready to accept his own metaphor as being the true reality. In fact, the metaphor is the actual truth. She told me on March 15, 1997 - "I have elevated you to the podium, at the lectern from which you may speak the Truth to the world." That was 22 years ago. Our body of works is the lectern. And from this dais, She has great hopes that Her children will listen in droves so that conversion may cascade through our lives and Jesus may have all things drawn to Himself at the Altar of Sacrifice in the Roman Catholic Church.

Our Lady's approach to my learning throughout the years has been through my obedience to lessons and teachings which I could have declined, and simple practices that She asked me to ponder. She encouraged me daily to accompany Her in disciplines such as this, then She would explain the way She would see me and why She had asked for such things. Sometimes She would dispense mystical phenomena to punctuate Her impressions into my perception to assist my faith. Humanity cannot imagine what She would reveal if we would just obey Her. Everyone who says 'no' does not realize the door they are closing. One thing that I have recognized that is rather ironic about our Heavenly Mother is that She can actually not know something if She wishes. Although I mentioned previously that She does not speculate when I speak with Her because She knows everything about which I may be speaking, Her perception can be altered where

She does not know something. For example, there have been times during our relationship when She did not call upon Her prescient knowledge of things in order to be able to guess something that I was approaching Her with. Someone who has access to all knowledge would usually not possess the ability to guess because guessing implies a lack of knowledge. This speaks to the power of the Sacrament of Reconciliation which renders Her not susceptible to recall any sins that we confess there. She does not have lingering memories of our sins that we have confessed, and neither does Heaven, because it would be a lie against the Holy Spirit to testify to something that has been wiped away and no longer exists.

Everyone should begin to sense that we live in a world of deception and distraction. Our vision is obscured by things conjured through sinful perspectives that are not true. We are lost without divine light. It is as if a group of people who were one day on a hike in the wilderness became disoriented and were unable to find their way home. After a time, they setup a community in the wilderness just to survive. As the decades go on, families grow and the original members of the group die, whereafter their children simply come to accept their community in the wilderness as being normal life. The posterity of the original group loses the realization of their state in the wilderness. They no longer possess the sense of being lost. But, they are still confused and without hope because they no more know the way home than did their parents. When Our Lady came to my brother and me, I recognized Her as my Heavenly Mother whom I have always known. I had an immediate recognition of the deception and distraction which flourished about our lives. I knew I was in the wilderness with the rest of humanity, but suddenly I knew the way home. My difficulties now are to get everyone uprooted from their perceptions and pack their belongings because we are going home. The search parties of Heaven have shown up. Much of what is described in this question is related to how Our Lady maintained my spiritual perceptions and kept them free from my old wine skin. It was Her way of molding me in the parameters of the unseen world that flourishes around us. They are the search party that is shining the light into our wildwood and beckoning us to come out to our salvation. She has always wanted me to never forget that I am surrounded by divine grace that is poised to assist me in every way that I allow. This means that our lives must be in communion with the sanctifying grace that God wishes to dispense upon our soul. And, for this grace to be dispensed upon our soul, we must be in communion with the font from which it pours. The font is the Sacramental Liturgies of the Roman Catholic Church. If we do this, every prayer, petition, or soliloquy that our hearts wish to raise will be heard by the heavens because we are veritably standing atop a podium, which is the heart. From that rostrum, we speak our loyalties to the Church-Triumphant who are rapt in attention at the beauty of our every word. Can we see why Our Lady says that prayer is power?

The Final Colossus
In the Light of Her Majesty
AD 2013

"I am uncertain how to describe these messages to you here, but even without doing so, I am sure that you realize their magnitude. These thirty-six months of messages will do everything that you could ever expect them to accomplish. And, remember here again, these messages are being published only because you have asked. They are your private revelations that are additional to your original deposit of works. There will not be a search for reasoning as to why I spent so many hours pouring accolades upon you and your brother's souls because of the lifetime investment that you have made in fulfilling your mission with Me. After all, how would any critic or detractor complain that you did not invest a sufficient amount of effort on behalf of the Church to accomplish what we set out to do?

My Special son, you live in a fragile world where things tend to break. Believe it or not, one of the simplest things to shatter is the will of uncertain minds. No one can stand in the bedrock of himself and claim that God will never judge him. This is the essential doubt that is implanted in creatures that are brought to life beyond their own doing. We have spoken about the hubris that it requires for a man to say that he does not believe in God. It is worse than the pride that felled Adam from the Garden."

- The Most Blessed Virgin Mary

Saturday, January 5, 2013
3:47 p.m.

Holism – the belief that an entity is greater than the sum of its parts.

"Spiritual Holism"

"My dearly beloved sons, it is true that your spiritual light shines brightly here in the land of darkness, and Satan is trying to douse your flames for Jesus. Evil has been lurking and ferociously attacking you because of the progress you have made toward your united accomplishments. I have told you that you must live one day at a time. However, if you continue in your penitential successes, a miracle so profound will occur that this city, and the world, will be shaken into consciousness. I have entered your presence today with the gentleness of Jesus; you are hearing Him speak more prolifically around the globe, even in places like Medjugorje where His voice is rarely heard. These are the things of the year 2013. I have said that an automobile is not an automobile unless it is moving. If it is standing still, it is simply a collection of assembled parts. An example of holism is when these parts work together to transfer passengers or property. The automobile becomes a vehicle of conveyance, and this is functionally more than the summation of its parts. This is the metaphor that I wish for you to internalize when thinking about the segments and moments of the days, weeks and months. You are creating a holism that you cannot yet see because you are working closely on each individual aspect of your lives. It is impossible to think two thoughts at the same time. Each of your thoughts and actions unite as in a picture, one that I also once told you that you are too close to see. Each thought and action that you generate is deposited into a hopper-like receptacle that Jesus fashions into the triumph of your lives. This is what you must know, that you are trying to see as one image many and multiple facets of this image that are timeless and multi-dimensioned. You become frustrated when you cannot see where you are going. *"At times, it is like running through a room in the darkness."* My Special son, your analogy is correct; it is as though you are running through the darkness, much like you remember your tiny nephew scurrying uncontrollably toward the concrete wall at the Marian Conference in South Bend some years ago. You must know that this is not something that will bring you harm if you instead travel carefully and thoughtfully. Recklessness comes when you do not remain self-composed in your thoughts and actions. It is not reckless to question the motivations of God, but you should realize in faith that these motivations are absent the element of time, but not its consequences. Therefore, your brother's sister has become a perfected person in her suffering. Everything about her that was not acceptable in the eyes of God died in the December automobile accident. Her soul is clean; her heart is pure, and her life begins anew. You can sense it when you ponder her alone in the car after the crash. She tasted the Cross and has become a new creature. As backward as it may sound, this is a good day.

All those who find themselves in lives wayward from the Truth will ultimately discover this awakening. They cannot escape it. They will never outlive its imminent occurrence. I have told you time after time that human conversion comes at the will of the sinner, and the human will comes around once the value and validity of life itself is placed on the line. My Special son, these are part of the 'consequences' that you have spoken about, while I remind you to pause the administration of your sword until the Lord announces that He has finished with these souls. You have known all along what His justice entails. The sacred justice that unites exiled men with The Christ involves the diminishment of the self in oftentimes horrible ways. The Cross is emblematic of the unification of humanity and God. This life here, for all who will live and die in Jesus, is for your assimilation into the Cross. Some people take their whole lives of 80 and 90 years to get there. Others are four and five years old. But, the time comes, the moment arrives, the awakening begins, the transition occurs, and the communion takes hold. My hopes and prayers are fulfilled when I see a soul break through the obstacles of this world and hand themselves to Jesus unafraid. I do not like catastrophes and tragedies any more than anyone else, but they have a redemptive effect. Most times it occurs to good people who suffer for the conversion of the wicked; other times the wicked themselves are the victims. All in all, the lives of men are handed to the Father through awful winds of torture and torment, and He makes new life out of them. Brokenness is the infancy of sainthood. I come to you and your brother during this new year to continue My witness for the preservation of human dignity amid the egregious negligence of lost sinners. It is like picking the low-hanging fruit for Jesus to take into His arms the innocent ones who suffer for the sake of the Church. I have said this previously to you. It is easy to make Saints of the despised and persecuted. For others, they must be shaken from their lives of sin; they must see, feel, smell and touch the Blood of the Cross in more temporal ways. My Special son, I sense the fragrance of victory in the air. It is somewhat akin to the days to which I harken when I was on Earth and the miracle of Jesus' Resurrection occurred. I ask for you to remember that you need not be apprehensive when speaking truthfully and critically about the condition of the world and the fate of humankind. You lose your sense of peace when your confidence wanes. I ask you to conduct your affairs and your conversations with a mature and surefooted heart. You have the Angels and all the heavens on your side, so what is to worry over? Speak like Me. You are part of Me. You have My poise and intelligence. You have My patience too, if you would only realize it. You are seeing the transition of the material world into a living hell that only the righteous will survive, and then, only the righteous who are confident in the Providence of the Father. Your faith has been given to you as was handed to millions before you, to all the Church-Militant, to individuals and societies, to little girls and boys, and to the masses who shout in acclamation that their destiny ends in God. I envy you because I have seen your future. And, Satan knows a lot about your future too; this is why he attacks you at every turn. It is not because you do not pray that he lurks, it is because you pray fervently.

These are the strains of the pending glory that will come to you in this life, even before you shall walk the streets of Heaven. Neither you nor your brother have learned everything you need to know about standing with confidence on the battlefields of human redemption. You are yet somewhat uncertain and unclear what lies in the offing. This is natural; the most uncertain in your lifetime was Saint Pio. And, look what he did! We have come so far in advancing the mission of the Church through your lives here in this home and this city that its revelation is being felt in universes incalculable distances from here. I ask you to believe what I am saying. And, this same distance is reflecting holiness back onto the Earth like the shining of the sun to light the way for the lost to find their peace in the Cross. One cannot be awakened unless he is asleep. He cannot be resurrected until he dies. There are spiritual-logical facts that you have known, but they have found themselves in the recesses of your thoughts instead of their fore. I am elated to come here to this place where so much good is being done. It seems that everyone in Heaven knows it; the stars and Moon know it, everything and anything that is of God in the supernatural realms knows it, but you and your brother are unaware. This is why I am still here. I am trying to tell you something. I am asking you to believe that the dailiness of your lives and the sacrifices you are making mean something greater than the sum of their parts. They are initiating and facilitating the victory of the Cross, the hope of the ages, the gold in the cup, the winds from the west. Your love for God is life and light; it is the food for the paupers everywhere who need the Father more than they need food in their stomachs. This is My message for this day. Your friend Michael is in Heaven with all the Saints; today would have been his birthday. And, you are aware of the tremendous surge of power that you are given every time you pray the Most Holy Rosary. I ask you to remind your brother that he should rest when he can and work when he must. He is stronger than he was a year ago. You both have vision and perseverance from the first days of My messages. My gratitude is strong, and its evidence is unfolding as we speak. I see that your bronchitis is nearly gone. This is because you are covering your mouth when you go outside into the cold air. Please remember to pray for all who are far from God, for the millions who will come to know the deficits in their faith that will be filled by their realization that they have yet far to travel. They will see soon; they will undergo an epiphany of their own that will take them deeply into the land of suffering. I promise, however, that Creation has a happy ending."

Sunday, January 13, 2013
9:41 a.m.

plaudit - *(n)* an enthusiastic expression of approval, a round of applause

"The man who burns with the fire of divine love is a son of the Immaculate Heart of Mary, and wherever he goes, he enkindles that flame; he desires and works with all his strength to inflame all men with the fire of God's love. Nothing deters him – he rejoices in poverty; he labors strenuously, he welcomes hardships, he laughs off false accusations, he rejoices in anguish. He thinks only of how he might follow Jesus Christ and imitate Him by his prayers, his labors, his sufferings, and by caring always and only for the glory of God and the salvation of souls."

St. Anthony Mary Claret (1807-1870)
Feast Day October 24

"This is the Day of the Lord. Let us rejoice and be glad. My little ones, you have come so far beyond the failures of this world that even you are yet unaware. Please remember what the Angels told you this week. Human morality does not come in a measurable mass; it comes in fibers. And, these fibers compose the moral fabric that covers the Earth in the Lord's grace. Each person who follows and practices the teachings of the Gospel is a fiber; each one tethered to the next, the one beside and intermingled with all the rest. You must realize the intervention of The Miraculous in your everyday lives. You should by now know the Providence. Indeed, you do. My little sons, your awakened state of consciousness is where I am trying to lead all My children. Your place of 'being' and your appreciation for the greater good must be taken to the dark corners of the world. Indeed, it will get there. You are seeing in the faces of the poor, the brokenhearted, the suffering and the innocent the presence of the Most

Blessed Trinity. Proof of the existence of God is not needed by those with faith, but such evidence in the lives of those about whom Saint Anthony Mary Claret spoke is there nonetheless. My little sons, do not permit this world to shake you from your confidence. Please do not allow the hollowness of the secular void to draw you into any unhappiness. I ask for your full joy in everything that Saint Claret mentions, especially in his autobiography. We need all the Saints to be your advocates and the Holy Spirit to be your refreshment. Your hearts are opened-wide to receive the gifts that the Lord is dispensing with tremendous measure around the globe. You have already seen the fruits of your labors. You have written and published an arsenal through your diary and books that can flatten the evil forces of this world in a single second. Indeed, they will do so. I yearn for the day when you will see these things with your own eyes because I already have. Therefore, it is with tremendous thanksgiving that I come to pray with you today. The entirety of My mission here is about prayer. (*My stomach began to growl very loudly.*) My Special son, please have a glass of milk. The whole of My existence revolves around My desire that all creatures come to fulfillment in the Kingdom of My Son. You will tend to extreme measures before that occurs; you will deal with the devil's worst. You will witness crises and catastrophes. You will lower your heads in mourning and raise them again in hope. This is the way of mortal life; this has always been the path toward righteous enlightenment. It is the Way of the Cross.

So, when I speak about human morality not being a measurable mass, I am saying that divine love is not an inorganic object positioned somewhere. It is fluid and ever-present. This love is always and forever. It cannot be contained. This is the reason that your spiritual hearts are incapable of being imprisoned by anything you will ever see or experience. When I speak about sublime awareness that surpasses all understanding, I am referring to this. All your worldly systems must be dealt with in this context. The role of bearing children, educating the young and the old, awakening the spirit of triumph, protecting societies from murderers and thugs – all these things must be viewed through the perspective of the infinite power of the human heart. This is the product of faith. It is its harvested crop. You know more than you know! You know more than you know! This makes you one and united with the perpetuity that I am celebrating here today. For many years, I have collected My children at My feet. I have asked them to be mindful of all the benefits of Christian conversion and the fruits of pureness and goodness. These words will never be lost on anyone. Everything I have ever said to you through the years will be heard by the Church, except your private thoughts and questions, and My private responses. Even as you are seeing and hearing what I am saying now, all this will fall on the ears to whom the Father is directing it. You are messengers, participants, witnesses and also spectators of some of the greatest genius that is being bestowed upon the ages. It is not important right now who takes-up your cause. We are still building; we are still erecting and righting what must be constructed, what must be assembled so that all humanity can be led to The Kingdom. I am not saying that your work is incomplete. I am saying that we are building it up as Jesus is elevated before the world. This is the mission that is still ongoing. And, the process feels mighty and good.

    My dear sons, I take glory and jubilation in hearing the Angels and Saints issue their plaudits for you. Although this is just beyond your hearing, it is deafening to Me. Every time you say a prayer or think about the way the world ought to be, your followers in the upper realms of Heaven cheer for you. They throw their fists in the air and shout-out your names from the higher decks. They toss roses into the arena here in this land where the Great Emancipator once walked to lend you their love. Wherever you go and whatever else you might think about the silence of God, know deep in your hearts that your advocates and colleagues are with you just past the veil. You need not hear them to know that this is true, in fact hearing would be counterproductive. Inability to see does not preclude the ability to believe. Your hearts and souls know; your dutiful consciences know, and your hopes and dreams that pattern themselves from your confident faith keep you strong and vibrant throughout the years. This is not an unending chore! Vast multitudes of people come to Heaven every day. Further multitudes more are born from the womb. What happens between the latter and the former determines the composure of the ultimate ages of men. These are the years to which all eyes of Paradise are turned because they have been told about the presence of the Child. Maturity has come; the Man-God has staked His claim on this place through you. This is why you are the chosen and elect. You are commissioned to feel at ease by what you have always known would come in your day. If your day transcends the years that you will live in exile, then your day will proceed with you into Heaven. All in all, it does not matter which it will be. The outcome will be the same. All the emotions and physical jubilation that you can know here in this life are capable of superseding life and death. You belong to God, and His Creation belongs to you. My Special and Chosen sons, you have been good stewards not only of this place, but of the Wisdom that has been transmitted to you by the Power of the Cross. You are innately wise and transforming because of your faith in Jesus. Victories on top of victories cannot begin to describe what you are seeing. You are blinded by the trials, tribulations and responsibilities of everyday life here in America from seeing what I am saying. This is the same task that was borne by all your predecessors; it is not unique to you. I only ask that you live in peace, knowing that you are walking the path of righteousness with dignified poise. My Special son, I ask you both to take life one day at a time here in this home, at your workplace, and during your brother's studies at his school. Let Me say this with feeling. Thank you for believing in Me! Thank you for handing Me your hearts with unfettered trust. Thank you for knowing Me in the way of Saint Anthony Mary Claret. It means all and everything that you have placed your lives in Jesus' hands as I hold Him in My arms. You are living a blessed conveyance on your journey to the Promised Land. I ask you both to assist My prayers for the safety of all who are in harm's way, and especially for the mental and physical healing of the confused and broken. Violence comes from the gap between love and hatred. Yes, let us pray for these blessings."

Saturday, January 19, 2013
10:05 a.m.

"Managing Peace"

"Yes, dear children, I have seen the awesome wonders of your works here on Earth glorified before the Father. Just like those foundations that you just formatted into being, I have witnessed the towering heights of your labors in the Lord's vineyard come to fruition in your time. You must not be discontented with the setbacks schemed by the devil because your own internal peace can overcome them. It is clear that you have seen this before; you have called upon your own sense of logic and determination to stay the course. My Special son, when you saw your brother's sister from the hall at the hospital, you saw the beginning of the refurbishing of the world. If you place your suffering and that of your brother in that context, you will see what I mean about categorizing the contributions of humanity to the conversion of lost sinners. You are playing an equal part as your brother's sister in your own way; your problems and difficulties are different, but they have the same outcome. Today, I have come to speak briefly because this is sometimes what I do. I wish that your brother's work was not so time consuming, but this is the way of his chores right now. He must concentrate and work hard because the weeks are fleeting. His work will be accomplished soon. I wish to speak to you again about the virtues of peace. Is peace something that must be managed? Can it be procured? Is its outcome the complete alliance of all the nations? I have told you that Peace is like a dove that lights where there is comfort and silence. Do you remember? *"Yes."* It is rightfully yours to decide what you believe peace to be. To Jesus, peace is in knowing that humanity is being cleansed. He finds peace in watching the cultivation of the Church and the conversion of the world to the diminishment of secularism. This is the way you feel when you see pretty sunsets and vibrant rainbows. We have spoken about these metaphors before. However, if you were to spiritualize the presence of a rainbow, you could describe it in terms that are comprehensible to the human soul. The way an image makes you feel is the transformation from sight to sensation. Seeing the Crucifixion was the same way for Saint John and all the witnesses. New Creation implies that everything existing before an event is transformed into an entirely new essence of itself. You are aware of the Transfiguration in this sense as well. The whole perpetuation of Messianic Truth was seen in different dimensions by Peter, James and John. This is what we have been trying to do here for so long; it is what I was saying in Fatima and Lourdes. It was what I meant when I said that redemption comes through the diminishment of the flesh. Peace must be justified by the determination of men and women to live the purity mandated in the Holy Gospel. It is clear that you saw one of millions of like example that occur every day around the globe. But, where is the peace? This is what I mean that peace must be managed. Peace must be invited and nourished. It must be cultured into a framework of good intentions. You and your brother have always stood on the confidence that you are accorded by the power of the Holy Spirit. This same sense of peace is given to all who allow peace to enter. Managing peace is not the same as manipulating peace. The Peace of the Lord cannot be manipulated. However, it is managed in such a way that people open doors and create environments where peace can prevail. This is the same concept that God had in mind when He told the first souls to have dominion over the Earth and its creatures. It is in the power of humanity to have and hold peace, to manage peace for the good of the Church. Situations where peace can flourish can be established by peace-loving souls all around the globe. This is the proper management of peace. I tell you today that 2013 has unfolded with new wars and suffering for precisely the reason you gave last evening. There are too many tyrants, despots and ne'er-do-wells in the exile of men for conditions to improve. We will stop them. I will stop them. This is no empty promise. When Jesus told Creation on Good Friday that everything was finished, He meant that the outcome of all you ever hope to see was then and now assured. Jesus will remold, remake and rebuild the Earth in the likeness of Heaven from the ashes of all the turmoil. Part of this restructuring is for you to help your brother when visiting the hospital where his sister lay broken. The driver of the other vehicle has made victims of his entire family who grieve for her."

Saturday, January 26, 2013
2:27 p.m.

"God is not unjust; he will not forget your work and the love you have shown him by your service, past and present, to his holy people." (Heb. 10)

"In the Glory of God the Father, I am with you on this special day to pray for the conversion of the world. My little sons, awesome are the moments when we ask My Son to heal the brokenhearted and send peace to warring places. My message today is about the gratefulness of the Lord for your lives, for your deep devotion to the Church, for your loyalty to Jesus, and for your years of dedication to humanity. In a manner of speaking, your hearts are in Heaven and simultaneously here on Earth. My Special son, we have much more praying to do because of the issues that are confronting the nations, not like they were before, but the new and even more damning conduct that erodes the morality of the world. When your brothers and others speak about globalization and all its benefits, it must be mentioned that these progresses have brought the infiltration of evil works where they would otherwise not be permitted to enter. I have spoken to you for many years; I have addressed the needs of My children for centuries to other visionaries, but still the problems remain because human nature is the same from one millennium to the next. It is not that men and women are reluctant to accept the teachings of the Church as much as it is that those teachings are not enforced by the Church Hierarchy. In how many more centuries and across how many more generations are the Bishops going to turn their backs? We have always known that leadership implies shepherding one's flock toward the narrow gate with conscience and without fear. Therefore, we pray as always before; we ask Jesus to tend to the tenders. I have said in My Medjugorje messages that My children should always support the shepherds that Jesus has chosen, realizing that they are sinners like their flocks. In most cases, priests and religious who violate their vows are not so much unholy as they are weak. They are not unwilling, they are simply unprepared for the changes that are rapidly coming through this new century and the ferocity of the demonic forces waging war against the Gospel. The insults against the dignity of anyone who supports the mission of the Church come from those who are not aligned with its teachings. For example, the woman who criticized the Catholic Church in her newspaper letter is a member of the feminist movement. She has said privately that the priesthood should be open to women and male priests who are allowed to marry. These are decisions for the Holy Father in Rome to make. The whole idea that these types of transformations can come from people writing letters to the secular editor seems utterly misguided to Me. Prayer is always the answer. Prayer is the way to speak to God about concerns involving the weaknesses of other sinners. The secular media are as hungry as wolves to find this kind of dissension on their tables when they arrive at work in the morning. Do you remember long ago when I told you that all this would be taken into account during the Final Judgement? *"Yes."* This woman who wrote the newspaper editorial letter and all who condemn the holiness of the Catholic Church, its mission, its eternal station, and its elegance and majesty will be forced to rescind their blasphemy against Jesus' Holy Body before they will be allowed into Heaven. I watch these things from My purview in Heaven and here on Earth with eyes wincing. I bend down as if to take a knee and look into the faces of these souls and wonder why they believe that they are sinless. This 64-year-old woman has never written a letter to the newspaper condemning abortion. Does this not say a great deal more about her than it says about the Roman Catholic Church? I say yes. Who needs enemies when you have these kinds of friends; this is the old saying. Hence, our prayers are not only for those who are far from God, but for those who believe they are close to Him while standing-out in criticism when seeing the few who fail. Imagine what the tremendously holy priests of this Diocese and around the world think when they see their vocations impugned by slander from their own parishioners.

    I began our message today with a verse from Hebrews to tell you that the Lord will long remember the gifts you have given to Jesus, but He will also long remember people such as those who publicly attack His Original Church. Secular populists and media operatives went out of their way to ensure that America's Muslims were not condemned because of the terrorist attacks by their radical counterparts in September 2001. But, let a single priest make a mistake, and these same seculars believe that the whole Catholic Church is a manifestation of the devil. You have seen this kind of hypocrisy before. It is the same gutter-wash that Jesus will flush in His time, when you believe that it may be at its worst. Do not fret, and do not worry. It is clear that you recognize what must change; and this change is at hand. Never mind the passing of the years; this change is nigh. And, when you speak about the Bishops being silent in the face of criticism; when they look the other way when popular leaders and public figures preach against the teachings of the Church, they condone these offenses. You have said it correctly; they must be thundering against the enemies of the Church with pen and staff. I pray that you begin to realize that all the promises that I have made are now extremely close. I ask you to live calmly and with peace; you will know inside your heart when the moments are at hand that will determine the configuration of the final battles. I ask you and your brother to be confident. Reassure each other about your station before the Cross. Do not feel pressured to surrender to sorrow or embarrassment. You are beneath My Holy Mantle where I placed you at the moment you were both conceived. Tomorrow will bring another anniversary of your brother's birth. He prefers to let it pass without any particular commencement, so shall it be. I am pleased that you have stayed with him and he with you. How many more blessings can the Earth possibly procure through your unity and friendship? This is the continued miracle that has already enlightened the Church through My Morning Star messages. It is only a matter of time. *"Thank you for all the lessons that you've given us."* You are welcome. You must remember at the same time that My messages are your gift to humanity, the Church, and the Kingdom of God! I can do none of this without My children. You are loved, cherished, venerated and embraced because of your faith and service."

Sunday, February 3, 2013
3:39 p.m.

"Lord Jesus, hold us close during our struggles to meld our lives with yours. Make your Sacrifice our lighthouse to the shore. Dispense to dying men a wisdom too true to deny. Share your hidden secrets; reveal what must be done to overcome the demise of this world. Prepare us for your reckoning, and drive our faith so deeply into your Kingdom that we will never once look back. Crush our enemies with catastrophic tempests of your beatific love. Give us peace in our day, and lead us gently down the pathway of our mortality, that we may rise again in you. We ask this through Christ, Our Lord. Amen."

- William L. Roth

"My little children, Jesus crushes your enemies' heads to make way to their hearts. It is the Lord's way of emphasizing the Spirit-world over the frameworks of the human intellect. Welcome again to the harbor of My Immaculate Heart. It is here that I have found My purpose. You are aware of all the messages that continue to be dispensed around the globe because the world is in turmoil. Your Bishop is correct; it is all about the tragedies of sinful men. We have here in this place a bastion of peace and joyfulness because we have one another in Jesus. I am dependent upon you because you are My messengers to the outside world. You have the ability to change the face of the Earth because you are imbedded there, and you are on the outside working through the Church in places where My apparitions are considered of abhorrent origins. Imagine what would happen to a boy or girl of the eastern world who told their parents that they had seen a vision of the Blessed Virgin Mary. They would never be seen or heard from again. You must believe Me when I tell you that these nations must be converted, but the greatest vices against human purity occur in democracies, especially here in the West. This is the effect of freedom on people who reject righteousness. This is what our mission is most prominently about. I have said that non-Christian people must come to the Church of Jesus Christ of their own volition, or else Roman Catholics will suffer along with The Christ for their conversion. They are blinded to the power of the Crucifixion, and therefore, they are unaware of the perils of their eternal destiny. The souls in Hell are there because they rejected the Cross of Mount Calvary, regardless of their religion here on Earth, if they had one at all. It is possible to unknowingly reject Christianity if the fullness of its light is not shed on the human soul. The mission of the Church is to share this light; the mission of My Son is to shed it. I pray with you today for the lost sinners who have strayed from the Church, who have abandoned their faith because of what the Church teaches. I particularly pray for fallen-away Catholics who persecute the Church and work against the Seven Sacraments. I pray for people who unjustly malign the Church Hierarchy and the sacred vocation of the priesthood. Those who do these things are most in peril; they are most apt to condemn themselves when they die in their beds. Such people as anti-Catholic heretics like the former Catholic you know who is divorced, remarried, and is now a Protestant minister are more in danger of the eternal fires than the prostitutes on street corners in the nation's largest cities. My Special son, if you think about what I am saying, you can surely understand My point. None of these things is acceptable in the eyes of God, but some actions are utterly more damaging; many are far more repugnant than others. It is the abuse of power and the spreading of heresy that blasphemes the Holy Spirit to greater degrees. Those who are overtly lost in sins of the flesh rarely pretend to represent God.

You and your brother have always known that sin is sin; it is all unwelcome in the mind and heart of God. However, you are also aware that there are various stages and levels of sin, some that are mortal, some cardinal, and others venial. It is more a mortal sin to lead someone away from the Church Sacraments under the appearance of being a minister than for a woman to fail in her marriage to her husband and seek emotional comfort with another man. Again, this does not mean both are not failings requiring repentance and the absolution of Jesus. My message today is that everything I have shared with you for these long years is connected to the other messages that you have seen and heard. And, they are uniquely connected to My apparitions in Fatima and

Lourdes, and all the shrines delineated in the 20th century videos and anthologies. The summit of all these is the Medjugorje messages that are having tremendous success in opening the eyes of the faithful and unfaithful alike. My Special son, their simplicity is what matters most. You are correct that Saint Thomas Aquinas turned his heart over to God in his latter years differently than he had before because he became aware of the crushing of the human intellect that I spoke about a few moments ago. Most all Martyrs were men and women of the heart because their greatest converting influence originated there. Simple souls everywhere understand the genius of the heart when they cannot comprehend the architecture of the intellect. People cannot effectively pray from the mind because they have little control over their thoughts. Satan brings more destruction into the world through the mind than through the heart. It is all about controlling the mind, shaping the consciousness toward fashioning a life of holiness or wickedness. This is the reason Jesus crushes the heads of those who reject His teachings. He allows their hearts to remain intact as the converted remnants.

Here, we have entered February where you shall soon reach another anniversary of My messages to you and your brother. It is not that the years have passed that have made such an impact, but that you have built upon the Kingdom that Jesus handed humanity 2,000 years ago. You have assembled new frameworks where lost sinners can climb to their own dignity in Him. Indeed, this world is bringing ruin to peoples and nations everywhere, but the Kingdom you are tendering to humanity through your work for Jesus cannot be undone. It is being prepared by your lives, and at this very moment, for the new inhabitants that you and I set out to find long ago. You are both on a course to tremendous and overwhelming success in what we together have wished to achieve for the majority of your lives. The dailiness of this world, the pressures of your chores, and the lack of response of your relatives and friends keeps you from seeing this sometimes. I have said that all goodness and righteousness has its costs. However, Jesus has paid the price, and you are united with Him in this Sacrifice. Your lives will change in unwelcome ways once My messages from here begin to circle the globe. It will seem almost too much to bear. I have been protecting you from this so far. It is as though you both will become property of believers and nonbelievers alike. This is an ugly prospect for you, and this again is the reason you have been given your anonymity heretofore. A quarter century of messages is taking its toll on you and your brother. They will soon have your books. This is the power that I am talking about that you will have sooner than you wish. It will be a different life; it will be much more burdensome than you care to believe. This is the cost of the presence about which I speak. I offer you now My holy blessing as we continue to face the upcoming conversion of the unwilling world."

Saturday, February 9, 2013
1:22 p.m.
Submitted resignation from HSHS effective 2/11/2013

"I shall take what is mine and leave the rest."

- Jesus Christ

"My Special son, because you have freed yourself from the burdens of your workplace, the atmosphere in Heaven and on Earth has taken on the air of the Resurrection. We are joyfully celebrating your valued judgement to prevail over evil that you have heretofore avoided. You are essentially a new creature. Thank you for allowing Me to sense the trust you have placed in My Son in ways that few people accord. As your brother has said, you have been vindicated; your place in history as a servant of the Lord has been assured. You no longer agree to compromise with the devil. The stabilities in your life will remain and even grow stronger. I only ask that you perceive yourself as embraced by the new dignity you have inherited. Today, I come to pray with you for the millions who have placed themselves in traps and economic sleeves from which they cannot escape. It is the same worldwide. Those with power, influence and money have enslaved billions of others because they control the wealth. Those under their command do not trust God in the way that you have decided. From My Immaculate Heart, and on behalf of the Sacred Heart of Jesus, we offer you our profound congratulations. You will move forward with peace and a sense of renewal that you have not felt in over two decades. You are wiser than your friends; they decline to trust. Even those with children to feed, house and educate should reach out in trust. This is the only way to behead the beast. This is a month during which you can savor your accomplishments and plan whatever you please, whenever you choose. If it is the Will of God, you and your brother will indeed set out on a new course that will include self-dependence, that will mean that you will no longer be forced into service by malevolent men. It is all about one's chosen standard of living. Here, I am speaking about your potential to hold and effect the wisdom that must be held, that must be nurtured and shared with the whole of humanity. You are a much different individual than twenty-five years ago. What has occurred during the past two days has given you and your brother a new beginning. Thank you for trusting in Jesus; thank you for giving your hearts to Me. I have told you that I would speak more about My life with Jesus as He was growing from childhood to boyhood, and into an adult Man. He made transitions that indicated His willingness to bear more patience on those around whom He lived. These are the same transitions that normal humans make. Did you know that the older people grow, the less they are apt to fight? It is true that Jesus, the Son of Man, the Son of God came home with a blackened eye on occasion. Imagine that! The Savior of the world was the Victim of playground scuffles. And, He was not immune to practical jokes and evoking a sense of humor that made Him so endearing to His friends. This is the same sense of humor exhibited by Saint Pio and Saint Father Joseph Timothy Murray. This humor was made of the composite of their gladness of the conversion of lost sinners and their own suffering to make it come true. If there was any semblance of balance in them, it was surely their awareness that God has positioned in time and space the Plan of Salvation. No matter what devious plots are put into place against the Church and against the redemption of the penitent, the Church and the Salvation of converted hearts and souls cannot be expunged. This has been the thesis of our messages together for all these years. This is the origin of My confidence and the underpinning of your hopes.

This, then, is the way we shall proceed as our conversations continue in the future. And, this is the same foresight that the boy Jesus embraced even as He would come home laughing from the playground with a shiny bright swelling around His eye. I ask that you and your brother, and all My children, carry on this same fight in a spiritual way. Indeed, you and others have already been bruised! You bear this likeness with the Messiah who was bruised and lashed in a corporeal way. You share this distinction with the Martyrs who were beaten, beheaded, burned and consumed for their faith in the Gospel of Christianity. Well, Jesus would tell Me during those earlier years that His mixing with those peers made Him feel more human, even more perfectly human than them. He wrote these things down because He kept a personal Diary that will be found as the closure of the Earth comes to pass. He confided in Me His problems and insights. He shared His determination to succeed, even as He knew from His earliest days that He was the Savior of the lost. I also know that various priests, clergy, nuns and others are saying that I played no part or had any influence in Jesus' life other than to give Him birth. Others are saying that Jesus is one of many biological brothers. Jesus is an only Son. I had no other children. My Special one, when you argue these things, you can readily ask these same people how Jesus could be a sinless person born of parents who had other children that were sinful. This makes no sense. Do you understand? *"Yes."* The point I am making is that those who reject the truth of Jesus' origin and birth are contradicting even themselves. When the Bible speaks of brothers, it is in the same context that you and your brother Timothy are brothers. And, speaking of your brother, he is working steadily toward the completion of his work at the university. The future will be as promising as Jesus permits it to be, based on His knowledge that you are still sharing in His sacrificial Crucifixion. No matter what the course, you will always be victors and conquerors in Him. You will be seeing ominous signs in the months to come around the world. It is all according to the passing of the ages into history, and the passage of men into their eternal rest in Jesus. It is part of the plan that Jesus completed, that He has finished, and over which He presides in this world and the next. I ask that you enjoy your new life of peace and confidence, that you never fear or have anxiety about what the future brings. You have a right to live the dignity that is yours."

Sunday, February 17, 2013
10:06 a.m.

"Faith and Judgement"

"My dear little sons, the loveliness of your trust in God is breathtaking even to those who no longer need to breathe. I am utterly heartened by the way you take seriously your way of life, your walk through the dangers of this world with the courage of lions. It is expected that you would know to do this with vision and a sense of protection, but you have gone well beyond the parameters of faith. You are exercising prudence in ways unbeknownst to your peers, neighbors and friends. We have spoken about this vision in the context of your own resilience. You do not mock the words of Scripture, you personify them. You reach out for Glory and do not wait for Providence to come to you. I speak about Faith and Judgement against the backdrop of Divine Love. Let us consider what this means. Love in the way of God implies that humanity enlists righteousness as a means of viewing life. Love in the way of those who do not believe in Christianity takes on an entirely different meaning. Love without faith is not true love at all. Secular people believe that love means that someone is drawn to someone or something else as a material satisfaction, not a moral or spiritual one. Infatuation is a better definition for their idea of love. However, Love in the way of Jesus implies sacrifice and commitment. My little sons, you have the wherewithal to continue your homeland here in this place as your destiny in Heaven. You wish for Paradise to overwhelm your homeland here. Even as Jesus teaches that you have a future and a place of rest in Heaven, you have this same future and rest in Him today. This is what people outside the Church do not realize. They have no faith, and therefore, they are unaware of the principles of Judgement. They oftentimes believe that 'love' is their faith, the type of love that is not of the Father. This is the same love that makes them do odd things. It is said that human love impairs human judgement. People on the Earth have crippled themselves, taken their own lives, and taken other lives because their version of love is based on selfishness instead of sacrifice. Prisons all around the world are occupied by people who committed crimes of 'passion' that were manifested from their definition of 'love.' Hence, their 'judgement' became impaired by their own misguided definition of love. This is not the kind of love that Jesus teaches. It is not wrong to desire love, but the kind of love most desirable is Sacred Love. It is possible for men and women and husbands and wives to share Sacred Love as defined by the Father. Everything must be decided in Him. And, this is the point of Faith. Love in the way of Christianity is based on Faith, and that Faith apprises the human conscience to make proper judgements, and that Faith also preserves the dignity of the human soul for the Final Judgement. It must all be God-centered in order to succeed, in order to avoid the pitfalls that come when only the human definition of love is followed. And, the concept of concentric circles is beneficial here. If all is centered in God, other circles with the same center of God can coexist here on Earth. The Lord God does not want to be left out. He requires the love of His children not to make Him greater, but to make Him happier. All the praise of humanity in the whole world cannot make God any greater, but it surely makes Him feel happier. Jesus is the only creature in Heaven besides Myself who is capable of being unhappy.

Therefore, when I speak about Faith and Judgement, My children must see that these things rest on the fulcrum of human love that mirrors and manifests Divine Love. This is the sacred element that makes the Kingdom of God engulf and envelop the terrains and domains of humanity in all their characteristics. This is the way that someone is said to be characteristically holy. It is innate to their nature to believe that righteousness is a better way of life than unholiness. To refer to oneself as a Christian without embracing sacrificial love is only a simulation. My Special son, the concept of 'simulation' is what you see in the lives of certain public leaders and impious clergy. Authentic leaders know the difference, but some of them are too busy to know what is happening around them. Let Me give you a prime example of Faith and Judgement. The rhetorical question is in the framework of the utilization of the priesthood to foster a sinful lifestyle. This is the same as the radical priest whose email teachings you rebuked at your workplace, referring to the Son of Man as a woman. Think about this for a moment. The Son of God is referred to by this priest as 'she.' As I told you earlier, it is all about one's knowledge of Faith and Judgement. Priests who mislead Bishops, priests who preach that homosexuality and lesbianism are acceptable in the eyes of God, priests who preach that Jesus Christ is a woman are committing blasphemy to degrees that are patently impossible to sustain before Faith and Judgement. And yet, this is what you are seeing. I wish to not dwell on these types of occurrences during our messages, but they must be made clear between you and Me; and with us together, the whole world. It is not so much that Jesus does not care what happens here in America and around the globe, but that God has given free will to humans to condemn themselves as their last act. If they exercise the Faith to which they are called, they would abandon their error and make way for their own conversion to the Truth. As you and your brother are aging somewhat more now, you realize that humans are given only so many months and years to effect their conversion. Thankfully for yourselves and for the Church, you and your brother are on the side of holiness and righteousness, on the side of the Truth. This is what you should always know about yourselves. This is the focus that you must never lose. And, this is the legacy that you have left your workplace, a business place that is still reeling in shock from your departure. Your decision has been a work of genius and providence. Why else would the Holy Spirit inspire Pope Benedict XVI to announce his retirement on the same day? Everyone is saying, 'This cannot be an accident.' Therefore, you and your brother must continue to accord the Father your trust, and also in your patience and sacrifices should you lend Him your faith. As the modern world says nowadays, 'It is all good.' It is good and proper that you should trust the Will of God. Please know that there are millions of Angels praying for you, and millions of Saints interceding before the Father. It may not always appear this way sometimes, but these same Saints came to Heaven by way of the Cross and the Crucifixion. Their admittance into Heaven has been made possible by the lives that you and your brother are now living."

Sunday, February 24, 2013
9:50 a.m.

"22 Years - The Glory in Your Eyes"

"My cherished little sons, I see the Glory in your eyes! There is change happening here! The world is uprighting itself because of your love for Me, because of your lives of sacrifice and prayer. Indeed, you claim that you cannot see it, but your hearts know. Your eyes reflect the Light of the Resurrection even as you seem unaware. This is the day that the Lord has made, Jesus has handed you a victory and a meaning. Where is it? Why can you not see it anywhere? How big is it; how much does it weigh? These are the questions that human minds are prone to formulate. It is not in the answers to these questions that the Glory about which I speak is found. In your eyes is found the Glory of Eminence; that is right, not imminence, but Eminence. You are the children of God and followers of the Messiah on this day, even as you cannot lay hands on the trophy that is yours. Jesus is placing in your hands the whole of Creation a day at a time, a moment, an ounce, a smile and a touch of consolation at a time. Can you not sense that you are feeling something in the offing that is in many ways already here? *"Yes."* We are the personification of His Kingship in Heaven and on the Earth. Yes, as your brother says, look again at what you have written in your books. Today, it is important that we remember the intentions of Pope Benedict XVI who will no longer be recognized as Pope when I speak to you again. It is imperative that you seek in him the example that has been handed down throughout the ages. I am pleased by and happy with Pope Benedict XVI because his life and mortal meaning have been to the growth of the Faith and the dignity of the Church. This is the man who made Pope John Paul II become John Paul the Great. It is true that these sacred men assumed the duties of Saint Peter in their lives and times; this is the majesty and succession to which you have been drawn many times. Here, I am saying that you will again witness another assuming the Chair of Saint Peter, but I do not want you to live in fear or unease, believing that the Church will in a few weeks be handed over to the devil. Remember that the gates of Hell cannot prevail against the Catholic Church. Even as you have seen My messages around the globe about the number of Popes who will live and die; even as you will see the unfolding of the prophecies that Jesus has made across the centuries, My Son will remain as guardian over His flock. It is clear that you know that these final ages will be filled with hostility, desecration, blasphemy and outright evil works, but you still have Glory in your eyes! You will not be distracted from your mission, the life you have given to the Cross and your souls you have handed to God. Remember the billions before you who have waited through their mortal years and now await in Heaven for the reckoning that is about to occur in your day. This is the Church; it is the reality of the Judgement of the Lord, and it is the essence of the Glory in your eyes. You have given more than the past '22 Years' to this effort. Even before I spoke discernible words to you, we were communicating. I saw your little lives, as I have said before. I watched and listened as you both spoke in the 1970s and 1980s, driving around in your pretty Firebirds, about the way the world ought to be. I heard your assessments of the conduct of mortal men.

I listened with joy when you spoke about Jesus as the example of human life forever to come. And, I did not see anything that either of you ever did wrong! Whatever you did, I saw; but it was not wrong. It is redeeming for other people to know that you have been the mainstays of the Faith as lay-persons. You have both been vessels of the Holy Spirit to the same intensity that I am the Vessel of the Messiah. When we speak about looking back and looking forward, are we not really talking about all time as one? You are permanently united with the Father regardless of the age, no matter the year or decade. This is part of the grand miracle; it is the fact that your hearts and souls never grow old.

O' so many changes come upon the Earth because of the failings of the flesh, so much new that accords you ways to retrain your thoughts and visions. But, the constancy of what you have always believed about your place here in this world has always been the same. Life is what human life becomes. You grow and ponder, pray and fast, walk and run, laugh and cry — all these as the same creatures whom the Father placed in your mothers' wombs. Your identity in Jesus remains unchanged, but your cognitive abilities and your world views change. This is the great benefit of life! Can you imagine what your years here in exile would be like if nobody sinned? Sadly, the world is a sinful and sinning place. You are surrounded by people who defer to evil works for profit, who make other lives miserable because they have not accepted their share of the Cross. You live here beaming in confident assurance, while others who deny Jesus exist here without a plan for tomorrow. Would it be better that I do what I have said, that I would appear to every one of My children in this world so they would believe in everything I have ever said to you? It is an uncertain idea because, given the opportunity, sinful men would search for a way to prove that it is not Me. I wish that you not allow this to make you bitter, but that you become even more joyful that you are not one of them. I see hatred emanating from their misdeeds, but I see Glory in your eyes! How can it be true that the Lord manifests great miracles that the world does not yet see? What can be happening in a Creation that is yet fraught with peril in the wake of the Resurrection of the Prince of Peace? Sinful men get in the way of their own vision. They stand in front of themselves. They do not allow the Holy Spirit to move them; they stand out in opposition to the healing and purification of all who must listen and hear. My message today is more than a reference to 22 Years, it is about the Glory that I see in your eyes. You are refreshment for the Poor Souls in Purgatory because they can sense their dignity before God in your lives. They are like blind men in a dark room, and you are the hands that touch them to lead them where they must go. This is the meaning of Christian discipleship. It is the image of the Saints to whom you have been devoted for decades. I can only say today that 22 Years can be measured by moments or months, or by decades and generations; or it can be measured by countless souls whom you have led to Salvation. It can be viewed as the proverbial end of the beginning and the beginning of the end. It is the prize piece on the mantle of Jesus Christ who looks at the spoils of all the wars men have fought for Him to elevate the redemption of the lost. I am saying here that you have power, even more power than the Holy Spirit dispenses to others who believe. This power may not be readily recognizable to you. *"I can sense it welling me to tears!"* Yes, this is good; can you feel it as well? *"Yes, I feel like I have the full power of the Gospel ready to dispense to a broken world."* My Special son, it is being dispensed as we speak. It is not that you are expending your shots only one at a time because you have sufficient ammunition to launch your final bombshell on an unsuspecting world. But, the power about which we are speaking is being shared right now. You will see this power in the Vatican soon. You will see it in the eyes of your Bishop. I am elated that these 22 Years have brought the Eminence in you that I have spoken about here today. You are upright and strong, poised for action, eager, ready and unbridled in your desire to see the mission through. All the final commendations recorded in the Bible were meant for these days.

My Special son, when I see My children such as you and your brother, I see you more than just individual personalities. I see your dedication to Jesus, but I also see more than this. I see your soul. It has color and texture. It overflows with potential. It stands for something; it stands for everything good. Your soul is the embedded essence of your identity that will appear before Jesus when you die. Please believe Me; it may be invisible to everyone here in this life, but your soul has discernible attributes that distinguish you from all other men. This is the color and texture that I am describing. Jesus can touch your soul like you can touch the shoulder of your brother. The redeemed human soul is capable of movement anywhere inside and outside of Creation. You will be able to pass through walls and inside and outside of expired centuries. You will counsel the early framers of the United States Constitution as though you were there all along. You will be concurrently a Cardinal in a Papal Conclave and the newly-elected Pontiff yourself. You will open graves, restore the lives of aborted children, reverse the flow of rivers, replicate sunsets any time you wish, and walk a mile in three seconds. You will fly high above the broadlands and seas, and you will pluck a fish from the jaws of its predator just in time to save its life. My Special son, these are not statements of a world that has not yet come. It is not something of fairytales or hopes that cannot be made real. This is the power of your soul, and it can and does happen every day. You do not hear the applause because the game is yet unfinished. You cannot go outdoors and stare-down a mountain lion because the process of human conversion has not yet ended. There are sinners out there. There are murderers and thieves. It is to these sinners that the animals look for models of their own behavior. When the 'will' of all men and women is turned to the Christian Gospel, you will in fact take a ride on the back of a tiger and run freely with the foxes at midstream. Now, hear Me. When I speak of all men, I am referring only to those who will eventually reside in Heaven. Those who will go to the netherworld have no effect on the residue of the Earth. These are among the reasons that I still have hope. *"Thank you for this beautiful message of hope."* You are wholly welcome. It is an amazing life that you are living, and yet you seem unaware that those who surround you have so far to go. I assure you, we will retrieve them. Jesus will touch them. Life will befall them. The Lord will Judge them, and Eternity will encapsulate them."

Saturday, March 2, 2013
2:59 p.m.

"As the future rolls on and the great tragedies come, and you wonder why all these things have come upon you, God will remind you of the evil that you have perpetrated here today."

- Timothy Parsons-Heather

"My dear little sons, the Princes of the Church are soon to deliberate the future of the Church amongst themselves, the Cardinals who are spiritually martyred every day for what they believe. They know that they must defy the liberal aggression that is taking hold both inside and outside the Church. My Special one, I have opened My message today with a quotation that I have asked your brother to use as he fights against the pagan environment of the university campus. This same quotation is fitting for many other venues, first impressioned by the great Saint Thomas Aquinas, and given to the world during some of its most grotesque eras. You must believe that the Roman Catholic Cardinals throughout the ages have thought of this quote from time to time. Today, I bring you good tidings from Heaven and the Sacred Heart of the King of the Church. I give you peace from within. I offer you continuing congratulations on your decision to escape the tensions and diabolical means of your previous workplace. Your former colleagues continue to suffer the oppression there. I bring today news that many misfortunes are being averted; many healings are taking place, newborn children are being laid asleep in their bassinets, grievances are being heard, and prayers are answered because of your diligent faith. What you see in your heart is the meaning of beatific love; what you hope for is the opening of the Eternal New World. We cannot speak today without mentioning your countless contributions to the Catholic Church and to the enlightenment of the world about redemptive grace. You and your brother have heretofore contributed to the purification of mankind in ways that are yet unheralded; and believe Me, when you see what could have occurred, you should be pleased to be so anonymous until now. It is fitting that a Cardinal has taken your books with him to share among the other Cardinals who will be electing the new Pope. Yes, 'White Collar Witch Hunt' is a household phrase in the Sistine Chapel. These are among the things you cannot yet see. You are made aware only because I tell you. If you continue to trust, you will see what I have also told you about the immensity of the human soul, about its color and texture that I have mentioned. You will discern the magnitude of Truth to which the converted soul becomes attuned, with which it becomes aligned. If you listen with your heart, you will hear the Holy Spirit telling you and your brother that the human soul also has fragrance; it has the capacity for uproaring during the silence of nonbelievers that the Son of Man is alive. You can point your soul into any direction, and it will go there without moving your body. I am telling you that the human soul is a timeless entity with a distinctive identity, that it has power and wisdom, that the soul has within its purview the capacity for creating uncreated things. This is power that defies the Earth's laws and elements. It is larger than any other contemplative imagining or prospect of paranormal relief. There is no miracle that the human soul cannot conceive; there is nothing about being human or superhuman that it cannot discern. Hence, do you see why the soul is worth saving? It is the priceless gem that the Lord values above all the creatures and horizons.

The soul is the blessing given to Paradise as rain to the earthen meadows' flowers. I give you every reason to believe that the human soul can stand and withstand the tests of time and perpetuity, that it cannot be impugned, that it has the capacity of speed and light, that it never tires, and that it will bend to kiss an innocent child before the child ever knows what is coming. This is the priceless humanity that Jesus has come to save, not human history, not the flesh, not the inventions of war and communication, not even the medicine that prolongs mortal life. Jesus died to redeem the souls of men that, if not for Adam, were perfect from the start, but perfected now. I have said to My worldwide visionaries that the human soul is like honey to the bee, the fruit of the harvest, the way of the world refined, the genius of the Heart of the Father, and the only viable attribute about humanity that will outlive the final holocaust. The human soul has dimensions that cannot be measured, mass that cannot be weighed, beauty that cannot be replicated, and a spirit of peace that can never be subdued. Do you see, My Special one, why the Son of God died to save the human soul? *"Yes."* The human soul stands tall and permeates reality. It speaks of potential and achievements already done. It archives the future before the future ever unfolds. I am simply saying that the human soul-redeemed is like Manna to Jesus. It is what He wishes to devour in the flames of His Love. You will someday see what happens to human souls in Heaven! You will be here; you will live and live some more, and never die. This is the origin of your happiness and the meaning of your faith. If any of this were untrue, I would have told you. I would have never kept going on. Now, I listen to you, I wait with bated breath for you to speak the strains that shake Heaven and Earth with jubilation. I wait for you, for humanity, to awaken like you and your brother have awakened, to peer upward and outward with hope! This is what inspires the heavens and brings rogue nations to ruins. The invocation of the God of Abraham is the balm for this aching world. The Church for whom the Martyrs died is the blessing of the ages for which all generations have pined. They will speak again through the Cardinals before the end of this month. These same Martyrs and all the Saints have been recollected where they bask in the Light of Salvation to tend to the matters in the world they left behind. I have said that Jesus will not turn His Faith Church over to the devil. Humanity shall see what prophecies must come true and which have been suspended by reparational prayer. It is the majesty of the Church that nonbelievers despise because the majesty is a reflection of its Truth. I have spoken of the Church's elegance and eloquence, of its strength and endurance, of its ability to preserve its own dignity in the face of vengeful attacks. This is My Church; it is the Church of Jesus Christ. The God of our fathers will not turn the Church over to the devil.

Thus, I bring you more Good News. I hand you and your brother a new hope and a new beginning that was set in place upon My Immaculate Conception. It was claimed and reclaimed during the Annunciation and the Birth of the Son of Man. This is the same preservation of dignity that I have spoken about before. These are the fruits of the Resurrection. These are among the reasons we waited in joyful hope on Holy Saturday and into the next new dawn. I continue to embrace this hope in My Immaculate Heart because now it is about you; it is about humanity reclaimed and redeemed. I wait in prayer and pending victory with the knowledge that the Second Coming will bring humanity through the veil of its own tears into the presence of the Church Triumphant, where at this very moment, every Pope who ever served Jesus faithfully is concelebrating the Mass of the Resurrection. This time, they see! This time, they shout-out their professions and liturgies with the throats of giants! This time, they hail the Son of Man with the Son of Man standing visibly in their presence! The High Priest is the main concelebrant in the Kingdom you are about to see. Therefore, My children, pay no mind to your enemies anymore. Do not even pity them for keying-in like thugs on their own raw ignorance. Commend them to the Divine Mercy of One Jesus Christ! Hold them at arm's length and tell them that they stink. Say to them that they are damned, and mean it. You have My permission and the latitude of the whole Apostolic Church to speak and write as you will, giving to God what belongs to Him and helping Him dispose of the rest. Indeed, this is what the great Saints believed. This is the Incense of Justice that will soon befall the world. This is the Light that has come to conquer the darkness. This is the Will of My Son; it is the reason for His Bloodshed on Good Friday; it is the reason why God refused to leave Him dead in the midst of His murderers. Before I leave you only by voice today, My children, I ask you to harbor your own self-confidence and internalize ethereal peace. Be certain of your own genius; know that you have breached the chasm of the ages that has only beaten other people down. Please continue to be My sons in every way you have shown; and know that I will always love you. I will love you longer than the suns will shine in the skies. I will love you after all other sentiments have died. I will love you at daybreak and when the seas roll over again. I will love you when the years exist no more! My gratitude for you is immense, My intercession profound, and My determination to make you heroes for the ages is intact. Thank you, My Special son, for allowing Me to speak to you again today. Do you have any issues to discuss with Me? *"I just thank you for everything you have said; your love gives my heart such happiness and peace."* I give you these messages because you and your brother share your love for each other and your love for Jesus. Truth and justice would have it no other way. Thank you for taking such good care of your brother. I will say this, as well, until the finality of the ages arrives."

Saturday, March 9, 2013
1:36 p.m.

"The Tempest Anthem"

"Here come I, the renowned Mother of God, to speak again to your minds and spirits, to raise your awareness of your own goodness, to remarkably advance your joy in the Kingdom of God. This is another day that is both ordinary and extraordinary. It is common that the Holy Spirit is with you; there is nothing new in that. But, it is extraordinary that so much Light and Wisdom are being poured forth into the world because of your continued faith. Untold numbers would have walked away long ago, waiting for a better god, wanting something more for their efforts, demanding their royalties for having invested a lifetime of trust in the Holy Trinity. My Special and Chosen ones, you are that investment. You are the highly cherished and esteemed genius that has come to this city, to an unwary nation, and to a waiting world. You must perceive Jesus looking at human life as though He is taking an object in His hands. He lifts and turns the existence of men as if inspecting a gem for flaws. He examines all the facets. He determines the fineness of human life by the glory shining back at Him. In effect, Jesus looks for His own reflection in the lives of exiled men. And, in making this inspection, He indeed looks for signs of righteous value, of incalculable and priceless goodness that would prove that His mission has been worth the cost. Human life has edges and planes in much the same way that the soul has these things. You are the carpentry in His hands. There are measurable dimensions and immeasurable aspects of human life that are seeable and unseeable. There are dilemmas and paradoxes that can be resolved by the simplest nod of a head. There are problems with solutions that will come only in the next realms of life. There are blessings in human life too – Jesus puts them there. Hence, My Son inspects His own handiwork, looking for evidence that His stewards and caretakers are keeping the Faith, walking upright and straight, and teaching the lost about their destiny in the Cross. This is a divine power that is Jesus' to wield because He is the Father and the Son as One God. I come today to tell you that the Lord reserves as His own principles the right to judge what is right and determine what is wrong because He is the Maker of right. Whatever deviates from this Truth is not in alignment with man's matrimony with eternity, but his enslavement by time. We must pray, My little sons, that humanity and the secular void will come to know the difference between living and simply existing, between dying and living hereafter, and between knowing the joy of love versus the indifference of disinterest. And, this does not even broach the damning consequences of outright hatred. No, the latter is something else altogether. Dare I say that it is true that whomever is damned has already chosen their path? Human volition makes it so. This is not what I mean when I speak about spiritual conversion. Conversion means that the human heart opens wide and allows the Holy Spirit to devour the soul like a nut from a shell. Those who shall be saved are already cracked by now. You can tell who they are; they have a discernible sensitivity to them; they have a flickering light that will soon emit a tremendous glow. The souls who have entered Heaven and those who will eventually get there have been inspected in the way that Jesus has looked at the merits of a righteous human life. My Special one, you and your brother will go to Heaven someday; it is mathematically certain. You have made this choice, and Jesus honors it. The point is that you have handed your mortal existence and eternal lives to Him. He sees Himself when He looks at your lives. He hears the timbre of your faith. He sees the sensations with which you wait in joyful hope for His Second Coming. He understands your motivations. He honors your prayers and sacrifices, and He oversees your days as His own Shepherd for His Father.

Now, we have come to a time in human history when you see certain messages that speak about specific events occurring within discernable time frames. These events are descriptive and graphic; they have definable outcomes, and they are connected to the purification of the lost. Will they all occur as prophesied? As you know, this depends on the intensity and sincerity of the prayers of humankind. Absent those prayers, the prophecies will unfold as told. Either way, it is imperative that the faithful not live in anxiety or fear. Those like you and your brother have predestined your own victories in My Immaculate Heart and the Sacred Heart of Jesus. This is all good news for you, but a boding of misfortune for the lost. The key is that we must share with those who are still spiritually asleep an alarming clarion of global cultivation that will awaken them and hasten the demise of those who will never convert. This is the reason you are seeing the messages elsewhere, Jesus speaking about claiming and reclaiming what is His, and about destroying in no uncertain terms those who have made themselves His foes. These are auspicious times because something is finally happening to separate the sheep from the goats, something in your time and your day that will make way for the King to Return. It is important for you and all My messengers to remember that you have participated in the Plan of Salvation in the same way as the Saints and seers of old. You are one another's counterparts, and you are companions who happened to live hundreds of years apart. When speaking and reflecting in these terms, all time is one. Therefore, is this not the same Year of the Crucifixion? Yes. Is this the Advent of the Second Coming that is portended in the Bible, that began upon Jesus' Ascension into Heaven? The answer is 'yes' again. The original descent of the Holy Spirit placed the Son of Man in My Sacred Womb. The furtherance of this descent alerted the Apostles and Saint Joseph about preeminent events in their lives. Even more examples of this descent are found in the Acts of the Apostles and the founding of the Church at Pentecost. You might say that the whole initiation of human redemption from the mind of God to the plains of the Earth is a descent of His judgement about His priors, about what He thought to be important in prehistory and what imperatives live on to this day. You and your brother were given roles to play in this sublime parade. You have done your work without a glance of help; you have taken on your burdens with courage; you have borne your yokes with obedience for a God whom you have never seen in His full Glory. And, you have the good faith and conscience to realize that the Mother of Jesus Christ is speaking to you now, that it is I who have come forth to change the hearts of the children whom I adopted on Good Friday. Humanity was handed to Me that day, and the burden of incumbency has been real; the means by which I have attempted to touch those who belong to Me has been frustrating and exasperating, to say the least. I have told you many times that I bore no part of the Cross that saved the souls of exiled men, but I have been deeply involved in the Passion, just as all who live according to the Gospel have done. My Special son, we are real human beings. We see by looking outwardly; we listen by being attuned; we give advice based on what we believe; we share the suffering of our friends; we ask the Lord to intervene, and we have every reason to believe that all who are meant to be saved will live one day as a single, glorious collection of happy souls in Paradise with God.

Real human beings understand that you live by transitional grace, the same grace that, as the lyricist said, has brought you thus far. Real human beings do what Jesus does when looking at life. We perceive and measure, examine, inspect and assess. We ponder what will come after this day has ended and another one begins. We see Nature and the natural order of things as gifts from the Eternal Father. Just because I live both in Heaven and on Earth does not preclude exiled men and women from conducting themselves as I live. You and your brother do it, but others decline. And, this is the reason why most of the prophecies you see in My messages and others worldwide will eventually come to pass. I would now like to address the messages from other installations that speak to the suffering of the Church and the persecution of Christians. If you were to write four or five things about what you learned about humanity, the good and the bad, from your experiences at your former workplace, what would some of them be? *"I worked with long suffering, sacrificial, good-hearted people. I had a safe workplace with the freedom to come and go. We all endured condescending 'lords' who thought it was their responsibility to wield their authority over everybody. We endured epicureans who demanded everything they asked for. We received no respect whatsoever for the monumental work we achieved for the organization. I was paid well, even though senior leaders were bilking the organization of everything they could steal from it."* This is an amazingly accurate accounting, and does it not speak volumes about why you left? *"Yes."* Now, I wish for you to generalize or globalize what you just told Me into the greater exercises of human affairs. Do they differ from what goes on in the rest of the world? *"No, it's even worse."* Therefore, you have a framework with which to perceive what Jesus must do to rein-in the horrific acts of the enemies of the Church. I believe that those people at your former workplace are indicative of the worldwide corruption that needs to be addressed, the process outlaid in the content of those other messages. Here is the point of My question. How much longer would you wait before enacting these prophecies? *"I would start this minute."* Then, it shall be. You will see what I mean in the coming weeks and months. I see that I have spoken about 'The Tempest Anthem' as being a song about recollections and reckonings. It is a song about chastisement and submission. Its melody is about eradicating injustice and imprudence. Its cadence is about The Walking Christ approaching the exiled world from beyond the horizon. Its resonance is being heard echoing around the nations and into the skies. It is both gentle and deafening. It will touch child and great-grandfather alike. It will renew fond memories and expunge old vengeance. It will cut deeply into the flesh of the wicked and remove the scars of the innocent. 'The Tempest Anthem' is written by people like you who speak of the God-Song, of the song of bringing, a song of deliverance, a song of justice. This is the sound that you will begin to hear if only humanity will listen, if leaders will bow before their flocks, if preachers will preach, if servants will serve, if bold men will act boldly, if women will defer to the fatherhood of human men. My Special son, I have hope because you yearn for these things; many other seers do not. They cannot wait to take to the streets wearing their pride on their sleeves, boasting that the Mother of Jesus deigned to come to them. I have always sought obedience from My children, and I have sought it gently. I only ask for those who are called to protract their own lives into Creation on behalf of Jesus to begin expanding, to grow and profoundly accept the reason for their lives. They can do this! Those who have power given them by the Holy Spirit, doctors that heal, teachers who share knowledge that is worthy of the Cross, children who strive for purity in the face of the pressure of their peers – everyone must think and act larger than their own selves and lives. The glory about which I have spoken to you for over two decades must come to center stage now; no more cowering, nor more whimpering, no more putting it off until tomorrow. The Roman Catholic Cardinals are assembling at the Vatican for a very important week. I will be there with them, and here with you and your brother. No matter what the world thinks about the successor to Pope Benedict XVI, I hope humanity respects the process and admires the majesty of the Church."

Saturday, March 16, 2013
10:19 a.m.

Jesus Christ can christen any facet of life or form of being unto Himself. Jesus Christ can recount the record of human history in a single syllable.

- William L. Roth

"The Co-Redemptive Dogma"

"Now comes the delight of My Motherhood, that I am able to appear in your presence with discernible words and metaphoric terms. This is the reason you are so blessed, and I am able to communicate to you the priorities of Heaven. I bless you for your future, My little boys! We have together established a state of understanding; you have come to know Me as Mother and consoler. You have learned about the Savior-Teacher, about Jesus the Messianic Victim and Eternal Prophet. I wish to speak to you again today because this is what we do together. Being Co-Redemptrix is not a condition, it is an identity; it is My identity, soon to be set into dogma by the Roman Catholic Church. My Special son, your prayers are the Light of Jesus' Dawn, and you have at your discretion the ability to hand Him the problems and wrongdoings that must be redressed. We are refashioning Creation in the likeness of Heaven, and the inside of your heart has been the situation room. Your heart is the parlour of God's eloquence, that you have written and spoken the strains that your Bishop called to mind during Holy Mass this week. He saw you and your brother praying with him for your new Pope Francis who was chosen by the Electorate Cardinals. And, when I speak of the concept of co-redemption, this has many dimensions. I wish for you to think about redemption in terms of forgiveness and transforming the redeemed into their own state of perfection. You are living as if in a courtyard where all the elements of life come to you; they are available to you, they are near at hand. You are not hidden away; your presence in this life represents a universal exposure to the perpetual meaning of being eternally alive. Hence, you are on a journey that has taken many turns; your prayers and obedience have brought about these turns. Some of them have been difficult, but most have been awesome and auspicious. You and your brother have taken-on your own collective identity as co-forgivers, not in the way of the Crucifixion, but in the way of your own sacrifices in union with The Christ. You are filling the vacuum where others have turned away. I am the Co-Redemptrix of humanity, and those like you and your brother, and all My children who are faithful to the miraculous calling of supernatural belief, are co-forgivers. This has been true since you were handed to Me by Jesus on the Cross, passed from His arms into My arms before He delivered His Spirit to the Father. Thank you for the two passages offered at the beginning of this message. Jesus can christen any form of being, including life itself, unto His own purposes. This is the Spirit of Providence that has taken on the challenges faced by the Church. It is the same christening that makes way for modern Saints to perform their own miracles; it is the strength of the Martyrs to preach the Gospel until their tongues are silenced by death. All these people were christened as co-forgivers beneath My Mantle on Good Friday. Being co-forgivers is an honor, but there is only one Redeemer. No sinful person's blood can save the human soul. Thus, you are honorary co-forgivers whose acts of grace and obedience place you in good favor with the Father.

So, what are some of the examples of co-forgiveness? It begins with the volition of men to proclaim their willingness to allow the Son of Man to live in them, and instead of them. You and your brother are much like Saint Francis of Assisi, after whom Pope Francis takes his name. You can see now the power of the Spirit of God in a Saint who was given to the Cross and to self-sacrifice. The priestly vocation is another means of shepherding the Lord's people toward the Gate of Paradise. You must believe Me when I tell you that an overwhelming number of redeemed souls are not led to conversion by priests and other clergy, but by the witness of lay-people like you. Those with vocations administer the Sacraments, but there is scarcely any evangelism in them. Archbishop Fulton Sheen is one good exception. You have seen this throughout the history of the Church. Indeed, Saint Francis of Assisi brought to light the primeness of Christian discipleship in ways that are unique and unprecedented, but not beyond the reach of ordinary men. I am pleased that this has occurred because it proves the power of the converted human heart. Priests and nuns are expected to lead holy lives. They are accorded due respect for what they accomplish, but their years of service to the Church are no surprise. Hence, you and all My children are co-forgivers, not like Jesus is The Redeemer, but your lives and actions are in accordance with the conversion of sinful men. You have the power to absolve them through the gift of pardon. You have the ability to ask the Lord to heal and comfort them, and He will do it. When you read the Scriptural passages that declare that everyone has his role to play, you can see what these roles mean depending on whom you see. For everything that is true about humanity being the Mystical Body of Jesus, this Body has many parts; all are provided for in the consciousness of God. When you speak about Jesus being about to recount the history of humanity in a single syllable, you are affirming to the world that a single breath, a single thought of God has already preceded and will succeed the existence of humankind and the meaning of being a member of humanity in eternity beyond. This meaning is wrapped around the decision of the faithful to live-out the tenets of the Gospel as best they can from their station on Earth. When I say that you have the power to work miracles, I am not only implying that this is yours to discern, I am declaring that you are already performing miracles beyond your sight. When people say that God has not made Himself sufficiently apparent in the world, they should look more closely at the Roman Catholic Church; they should look toward people like you and your brother for evidence that Jesus' commendations are true. There is validity in your lives in Him because God has mandated your poise and eloquence in the ways that I have said. My Special son, these are among the reasons I keep coming to you. Jesus sends Me here every time. He has in His foresight a vision for this world that incorporates your own willingness to help. When you pray and ask Jesus to look a certain direction, He does in fact turn His head. If you ask Him to dispense pardon upon an individual or society, He raises His hands and blesses them accordingly. And, the crux of knowing the efficacy of human suffering is in the way it amplifies the Crucifixion to a person or people who do not yet realize that He died to save them from condemnation. This is the honor of those who suffer; it is their privilege to reflect and magnify the essence of the Cross. Humanity killed the Son of Man in direct contradiction to the Sacred Commandment, but His Sacrifice redeemed the whole human race. And, there is no logic in this. God decides what He pleases for His own Glory and for the sanctification of humanity. When I look through My Son's Sacrifice at My children, I see beauty, love, confidence, providence, abiding courage, hope and destination. I see such potential that it is difficult to put into words. Can you see the beauty about which I am speaking? *"Yes."* I see all the love that humanity can muster. I see a gift to God and a blessing for the world. Even as you are giving your lives to the Will of God, you are being elevated as Saints. See here what beauty and devotion and love humanity can give Him! This is grand and awesome! As I say, you and I do not see what everyone else sees. We see honor, piety, charity, goodness and peace. We see a hunger for righteousness and a willingness to be a vessel of the Holy Spirit. However, all these things are right now so foreign to others that they cannot take it in. They cringe at the thought of sacrifice because they cannot see the outcome of the world. They shiver and shudder inside because they are afraid of what others will think of them. They cannot accept that purity and faith have any worth other than secular scorn. This is the irony; this is the paradox; this is the contradiction, just as killing the Son of God appeared to be all these things as well."

Sunday, March 24, 2013
Palm Sunday, A Sign in the Sky
2:33 p.m.

"The honor is distinct indeed."

"My little sons, imagine the elation that Jesus feels, knowing that you have come praying to Him, to the heavens for the conversion of humanity, long beyond two decades. If you fathom this; if you can immerse your thoughts in what My Son feels, you will sense that the inevitable destruction of everything that stands in your way is imminent. My Special son, you have trained on My messages for good reason. The conclusion of human mortality is inevitable in them. You are seeing reasons why Heaven is poised to retake this world from the throes of evil battering it into darkness. This is also a time of joy! It is a period of cleansing and bringing to life the dearly beloved faith in God that has been given to all exiled Creation. I have come again today to tell you that My love for you is more than you realize. Just as on Good Friday, I have stood beside the Church for centuries, knowing that My vision has been perfect all along. I have told you what the Lord wants of you. Would you be so kind as to read from My March 24, 1991 message from your Diary behind you on top the bookshelf? Yes, please begin reading My message from that day as it reflects a vision of the ground from where I am poised. *(Bill read the March 24, 1991 message).* Thank you for harkening to the miracles that are still ongoing, and you see that My call for the conversion of humanity is also as strong. My Special son, you and your brother have published My messages for humanity that were mentioned on that day. It is during these recent years and months that you are giving them greater flight by your undivided devotion to Me. I have told you that you are worthy of all the accolades that I give you, and you are seeing the changing world as the preparation for the Second Coming of Jesus, just as I have said for many years. If you and your brother go on, we will usher-in a power yet unknown to any messages ever given through the Holy Spirit of God. And, it will not be by your own doing that this will come, but all the focus and attention by those seeking to learn more about My messages from this city will be upon you. Why? Because you were the first to believe your brother when he told you that it was Me. Throngs will want to know why you did not doubt. They will ask which of the virtues gave you the most courage. They will not seek-out your brother for these answers because he will seem much too secular and academic to know. He will be seen as holy, but certainly in no way as contemplative as you. The reasons are found in the differences in his writings and yours. It is clear that you are more meditative and contemplative, while he is more practical and managerial. Can you see how this condition exists? *"Yes."* I rarely speak about the outcomes of your days or the events of the future because the prayers of the faithful are bringing change to life every day. However, you can be assured that the themes of My messages over the past 22 years remain intact. The mandates from God are still in place. The miracles you have witnessed and the expectations of your effect on the purification of the Church are still true. What has changed is the increased dispensation of Jesus' Divine Mercy because of your lives of simplicity and nonjudgmental discernment. You have not questioned the motivations of the Lord. Your courage has been your strength during times when the battles have been brutal. You may not see them as such, but you have given in ways that are most instinctive to you. I am thankful for your faith and trust that I am crushing the devil's villainy through My children worldwide. I have given instructions and made requests that are private and personal to each one. This process has not been one that will have no meaning for you here in this life or eternally of itself. I have been trying for years to create a venue through which you and I can face-down the devil. Yes, we will defeat Satan.

I also realize that you are aware of the requests that I have made of My messengers through the centuries. I am transferring to you the intentions of the Father that would allow His Only Begotten Son to be crucified as Saint John and I looked on. Nothing could be more grotesque, but it is the Sacrifice that has redeemed the world. I have spoken of ironies and paradoxes before, but the Passion and Crucifixion of Jesus is the most counterintuitive of all. It is the reason Simon Peter said that surely it must not be done. And, what did Jesus say to him? *"Get behind!"* What did Jesus mean by this? *"That He was not going to be deterred from the Truth."* And, what was this Truth? *"That the Crucifixion was going to save humanity."* It has, as you know, done this to the Hallelujahs of the Angels from on high. My Special son, you have seen as God the Father and Jesus stood by with Sacred Love as Christian after Christian was martyred, thrown to the lions, stoned to death, tortured, disemboweled, burned at the stake, carved into pieces, and tossed into the sea. Each of these horrific sacrifices was bountiful in the eyes of God. They served to defeat the prince of darkness; they glorified the Kingdom of Heaven, they lifted-up the Cross as the meaning of all human life. There can be no true conversion without these sacred gifts. I am speaking about the resurrection of the hopeful human spirit that yearns to be like Jesus. I speak about the willingness of Jesus' faithful disciples who desire to walk where He walked, take the insults, bear the bruises, receive the lashes and endure the pain. These are the Saints who have said that, 'The honor is distinct indeed.' They were once like you and your brother are now. They held on to their faith with the grip of lions' teeth. They saw with magnified sight! They rose in the morning laughing at the devil because he can do no more harm than the Father allows. They pondered the destiny of the world and felt its pull toward the Final Judgement – all this while they walked the ground with confidence that their time would eventually come. All the Saints before you wrote poetry that was never committed to the page. They sang songs that have not since been heard. They combed their hair and brushed their beards, chuckling that in Jesus Christ they had found their way to the Land of Paradise. And in them, as in you and your brother and all My messengers, they harbored the same hope for the conversion of lost sinners that I spoke about on March 24, 1991. Each Christian in his own day will see the formations in the skies that will help them believe, that will ensure their comfort, even as the Mother of God may ask them to soil their faces at a grotto or do anything else that seems contradictory to them. New lives and new resurrections will come from everything I have asked My children to do. The Church will be transformed and glorified because the faithful will have done their part here on the Earth. The Poor Souls in Purgatory are released by the hour because Jesus disguises Himself as the poor and goes places where He will be found. He leaves signs everywhere He goes to prove that it is Him.

I know two little messengers who saw Jesus disguised as an old man who just wanted a frosty treat, but he did not have any money. And, these messengers paid the cost to give this man relief. Here again, the sign of Jesus' presence was in the numeric price of the sacrifice. *(This was in reference to a little old man last evening at the ice cream shop who did not have enough money for an ice cream. Timothy and I bought him what he wanted. One of the girls working the counter met us at the door as we were leaving and thanked us for doing something so kind. She was nearly in tears while she spoke.)* A different kind of redemption occurred that day, but the meaning is the same. And, I know messengers who comply with the requests of the Mother of God just because I am the Mother of God! This is the handiwork of the Holy Spirit here in this exiled world that is making Saints of commoners and bringing Light to the inferior realms. Do you know these messengers too? *"Yes."* Soon, humanity will understand what this means to them; their history of disbelief will come unraveled, their questions will not only be posited in their own minds, but the answers will come from within them as well. Responsibility and sacrifice will overcome entitlement and sloth in a spiritual way. Dutiful obedience will be remarkably more attractive than personal comfort. I have spoken about the infiltration of the Paraclete into the lives and hearts of lost pilgrims, but it has not been an offensive movement. This Holy Spirit must be invited into the presence of those who seek the answers to human life. If it is quiet in the heart; if there is deference there; if there is a condition of repentance, the Spirit of God will permeate the heart and soul of a person and remake him or her in the image of Heaven. Once this has been done; once the conscience of the Cross has taken hold inside someone, it can never be removed. It will always remain and linger there. It will always be the touchstone against which all other human actions are compared. The Holy Spirit of Jesus Christ refuses to be evicted from His home. Surely, there may be times when the devil overwhelms someone and tries to drive righteousness out, but the Son of Man always prevails. Jesus becomes the identity of the reborn Christian. It is like lightning striking a pile of straw, igniting a new fire of life, burning-out whatever inhibits the flourishing of goodness from prospering thereafter. My Special son, when Jesus was growing from a child to an adolescent and into a Man, He thought along the same lines that you do now. He gathered information about His surroundings. He took into account the vulnerabilities of His friends. He measured the temptations that lure good people from their faith, and He waited patiently for His time to come. This is the way of you and your brother. It is the way of all who believe in God and practice the Gospel of Christian Truth. Like Jesus, you are warriors for the Church, and you are conquerors in Him. We have given our efforts; we have dedicated these years that you have lived on the Earth to making the difference that Jesus would have made in His own time. All the changes that have come since Jesus lived, died and was Resurrected have not modified or supplanted the simple fact that human nature, no matter the century, remains fundamentally unchanged. There are still thieves and zealots, dishonest tax collectors, rapists and murderers, and thugs and night-stalkers. But, just as in Jesus' day, there are humble servants who refuse to surrender to the secular void. They decline the comforts of the upper-class, not because they cannot afford them, but because they know that they have nothing to do with the Cross.

    These servants personify Wisdom in the way of you and your brother, in the way of the Popes and Martyrs, in the way of the Doctors of the Church who all strived for the same end, and for the same new beginning. You have the honor of living this way because you shall live with dignity in Heaven. You will join the battlefield giants who have fought the good fight. Your bodies will break like all before you, but your spirits will never die. And, for all the books you will ever write, all the testimonies you will give, all the prayers you will say, all the days you shall live, all the college honors that could ever be earned, these things will culminate in the grand reunion of Heaven and Earth when the Son of Man says that the time has come. My messages to you will someday ring around the globe like the pealing bells of Saint Peter's Square when a new Pope is elected. The miracles cannot be mocked; the Truth cannot be ignored, the sacrificial lives of My seers and messengers will never be in vain. I will not allow it, and Jesus would never condone it. Here also, I have spoken to you at length today about God's determination to disallow humanity to get in the way of humanity itself. I have said that Jesus requires unconverted sinners to walk to Him, to lift Him up, to venerate the Cross, and live like princes in the New Kingdom to come. And, I have alluded last week and again today about how you and your brother will continue to play your part, and you are doing well. It is a sacred mystery that God ordains. As I close this message today, I wish to refer to the messages I have given you since December 28, 2008. Yes, I have said that My messages to humanity as 'The Morning Star Over America' have ended, but we have never pronounced My messages to you personally complete. It must be made clear that I no longer speak publically after December 28, 2008, but you must implicate to the outside world that I am very much still speaking to you with messages perhaps more profound than before. Evidence My messages from the past six weeks alone. I do this not only because I love you, but because My mission here is still ongoing. You are willing to listen to the Mother of God speak Her strains to someone with love enough for Jesus to make a difference in this life. We will make the most of what you and your brother have done!"

Saturday, March 30, 2013
Holy Saturday
3:15 p.m.

"The transfer of meaning – Jesus walked within Himself."

"Here, little sons, we approach the dawn of Easter with remembrances of what this means for humanity and the extension of Creation into eternal morning. I am joyful that you are still together as brothers and friends. You are companions in the search for new Christians; you are one in Jesus with Me. I am delighted today. I am happy, even as I see so much heresy and the desecration of sacred relics that has brought so much sorrow to the faithful through the centuries. My happiness rests in the sureness that the Resurrection of Jesus has expunged all these things. In the Light of Eternity, there will be no recollection of anything that has caused pain or sadness in the material world. And to you, My Special son, I owe the greatest gratitude for staying the course with Me on the long journey of the Church through the darkness of the Earth. You have never lost sight of the Triumph of My Immaculate Heart. Your hope is brilliant, your determination is everlasting. I wish to speak today about the mystical 'transfer of meaning' that was spread by the Apostles as they were taught by Jesus in their exile. This is a new subject that I have never spoken about before now because there is a sequence to your messages. What I am relating by the transfer of meaning is that every intention of humanity in reflection of the Cross gives credence to the Church; every act of love and timely divinity makes human beings more than mere mortal creatures. If you consider what it means to transfer meaning in reference to the teachings of the Church, you are naturally summoned to ponder how Jesus transferred meaning as it applies to this world through the purview of Heaven. Jesus had thoughts while living here in the flesh. These thoughts were translated into wishes, mandates and expectations, the lessons and parables that He addressed to His followers. These expectations became needs inside Jesus' consciousness. He explained to those who believed in Him, and demanded from those who did not, that there are certain requirements that are immutable if someone expects to see the Father in Heaven. The next issue is 'agreement.' Jesus commissioned His followers with the willpower and authority to teach the Gospel and spread righteousness in His name. This was not permissiveness in the way of modern definitions, but in the sense that those who spoke on Jesus' behalf were not required to submit their writings and speeches to Him beforehand for approval. This agreement led to action on behalf of those who professed the Gospel; they told their fellows and strangers alike that the New Covenant was personified by the Son of Man. Finally, this action led to change; it resulted in the message of the Bible that was written after Jesus' Ascension, with the help and inspiration of the Holy Spirit. All this was embodied and personified by Jesus the Man-God who walked and interacted with mere mortals in the same framework of time and the same temporal realms. Imagine what it would have been like to stand physically beside Jesus and become a friend with the Man who would redeem the world. Now, when I say that Jesus walked within Himself, I am referring to the same transfer of meaning about which I have just spoken. Jesus did not clash cymbals together to project Himself like someone might throw a spear or sound a horn. His confidence was and still remains in His knowledge that He is perfect in all ways, and this is the comfort and consolation that He gives His followers to this day. 'Go and make disciples of the nations' means that Christians are supposed to live in the image and likeness of Jesus in the same way that He is the image and likeness of God. Even in logical terms, it is impossible for someone to walk outside himself and remain one with the soul that inhabits his flesh. I am calling My children to be comfortable with who they are, once they have inherited and become acclimated to the perfection of the Messiah living in them.

This is where the meaning is transferred – Jesus walked within Himself with the expectation that His life and Crucifixion would draw all men to Him. If He be lifted-up in the way of the Gospel, this shall be done. In other words, Jesus was single-minded in a duplicitous world. He was the One God in Three Persons the same way the Father and the Holy Spirit are one. When a person says that they feel beside themselves, they are undergoing a sensation that is not of the confidence and oneness about which I am speaking. Even the joy, and oftentimes anger, that makes people feel beside themselves must never allow this spiritually-centered oneness to fade. The transfer of eternal meaning cannot occur in someone who is not completely single-minded because of the implication that there are multiple messages. My little son, do you understand thus far? *"Yes."* This opens the discussion to the reasons why mortal men, even clergy and other holy people, drift from the message they intend to relate. They are incapable of transferring meaning because they are not trained on the single sight of righteousness that comes from the One God. This is the reason priests, like one you know, drive Lincoln Town Cars. It is the reason you see such lavish lifestyles by the two Protestant evangelists, the married couple on television, who profess to be so holy. They are not walking inside themselves like Jesus walked the Earth inside Himself, hence they are unable to transfer the eternal meaning of self-sacrifice and simplicity required by the Gospel. You have walked inside yourself your whole life because of your obedience to Me and Jesus; you have matched step-by-step the path of Jesus because of your awareness of the divinity in you. There are other opposite examples that we need not address here, but the meaning and the transfer of meaning must never be divided one from the other. This is the way the Messenger is also the Message. Jesus is the Speaker and also the Spoken Word. Do you understand? *"Yes."* I am asking that you view your life with righteous humility that you have been like Jesus through all your years. This will help you understand who Jesus is. And, your books and writings, My messages and all the miracles embedded in them transfer eternal meaning. The sequence of thought, expectation, need, agreement, action and consequence are all instinctive parts of who you are. This has been the way of all the Popes who are in allegiance and alliance with the Will of God and the 'sense of the Church.' Here again, I have opened the door for you to recognize what your Bishop and others who have seen your books are looking for; they want to know what meaning is being transferred, what the message is, what the sequence looks like, and whether you are walking inside yourself in the way of Jesus Christ. They are indeed seeing these things. The outcome of the world depends on whether all men from every walk denounce the duplicity of a multiple-mind, of relativism and pluralism, to concede that there is but one Gospel and one Truth. You have said this before in many contexts, and you are absolutely correct. When you read My messages from more than two decades, you will see their unity with the teachings of the Gospel and the Traditions of the Church. You will recognize that I was the first to have the Son of Man inspirited in Me. He was likewise given Flesh of My flesh, and all this has been handed to humanity through the Apostolic Church without much more than a bended knee.

You can by now sense the reason I have come to you so happily here today; you know the reason I embrace the confidence that you embrace, and you are aware of the inevitability of the Triumph of My Immaculate Heart. This transfer of meaning has been ongoing throughout the ages since the Annunciation, all the way to this moment as I am speaking to you now. This meaning is seen in the architecture of spiraling cathedrals and in humble people praying the Holy Rosary sitting on a park bench. It can be heard in the chirping birds and the tolling of the church bells in New York, Philadelphia and Rome. This transfer of meaning occurs in words of gratitude, in smiles and wafts of holy smoke. It happens every day in places about which only few are aware, and this is the sort of thing that is rarely broadcast on television or spoken about in the billions of cellular phone calls made every day. This is the transfer of meaning that began with Moses and then to the Archangel Gabriel. The prophets and Doctors of the Church transferred this meaning by their warnings and writings. The Cardinal-Deacons throughout the past 2,000 years have transferred this meaning from their lofty places before throngs to announce in the strains of a dead language; 'Habemus Papam! We have a Pope!' At last, the language is not as dead as humanity believes! Yes, and all this meaning is wrapped around and emitted from the Sacred Heart of Jesus who is the genesis of it all. Every act of kindness and obeisance given by mortal men is in response to this transfer; it is 'inspirited' in the hearts of those who have taken hold of themselves and handed their hearts and souls to God. The meaning of the message is this – that Christ outlives the ages and Creation too. He manifests change and expunges irrelevance. He digs deeply into the human consciousness and exhumes what is left of the happy heart. He grants His peace and Providence to those who will listen. We have said that He seeks deference from the world. Yes, we have! And, this is good; it is tasteful and worthy of the Glory that is now and forever raining down on all who are blessed to be His disciples. I assure you that all these things are part of the process that will lead to the event of the Second Coming, closer now than most meteors that might hit or miss the face of the globe. This is the same meaning that you and your brother have been called to transfer through your surrender. You are being asked to apply your own glorious touch to the meaning of righteousness that will make the Church shine with new joy. There is meaning sailing all around the globe in the skies and beyond, all for the purpose of setting the stage and preparing humanity for the trumpets' last blasts. My Special son, you and your brother have faced ungodly conduct, terrible opposition, ridicule and mockery. Nonetheless, I ask for your prayers for the Church; we have arrived at a juncture in time that will reshape the world for the imminent return of the King. We are awaiting not only the final reconciliation between lost sinners and their God, we are preparing for the Great Reckoning too. I ask for you to pray for the missionaries and priests serving in dark places who have little commodities to share with their parishioners. Thank you for listening to Me today! I will pray for everyone you remember in your own prayers, and I will ask Jesus to grant your petitions as well."

Saturday, April 6, 2013
2:38 p.m.

"In the palms of princes."

"The charming atmosphere you have created for Me is wholly consistent with My Grace, little ones. I love the peacefulness here. I adore the way you honor Me with your prayers and deferential speech. And, your compliance with Heaven's summons places you among the favored of God's children. Today, I have come to speak to you about justice and purity, and about the abundant joy that Jesus holds in His Sacred Heart because of your reflections of His life. You are seeing the world taking shape just as the Scriptures prescribed and according to the prophecies of My messages. This is a wonderful blessing! I do not wish for you to gain the sense that a worrisome life has come upon you because you are elevated in the sight of God. You may well indeed be called to sacrifice in the way of the Saints before you, but this means that you are chosen; you are the elect; you are sacred people in the Kingdom of Heaven. Already, you know what justice means. It is not the same as vengeance or inheriting some type of civil right that should be rightfully yours. Justice is not a nominal way of believing that things will be better after the sun has completed its mission in space. Justice is a living, breathing prospect here in this world, alive and well in the Crucifixion and Resurrection of the Son of Man. What He believes to be justice is not always what mortal men presume. And, when I speak about abundant joy, it is entirely related to the purity that is mandated by the Holy Gospel. Surely, the Lord God reserves the power to join two souls in the paradisial version of matrimony in any way He pleases, but humanity on Earth lacks that authority. Even the Pope in Rome knows that marriage between a man and a woman is wrought by God, and therefore it is a Sacrament dispensed by Him and in His own name. The public debate used to discuss the merits and non-merits of same-sex unions cannot be equated with this Providence. It is not a civil right to break the Commandments of God. Purity demands that everything completed on Earth comply with those Commandments. My point is that all things accomplished on the Earth should be done in communion with the teachings of the Church and the intercession of the Holy Spirit. Therefore, purity is the product of justice, and justice also succeeds purity because of the chasteness of the Christian soul. The Father has placed hundreds and thousands of people in the world to serve as His counselors, and most of these souls are not members of the clergy. They are people like you, My Special son, who understand what it means to open your heart unequivocally to the wishes of the Lord. You make this commitment without reservation; you submit to the Will of God as a matter of course. In referring again to Jesus as a child and growing adolescent, He was like you in this and many other ethereal ways. I am not trying to grow your self-image to inappropriate proportions, but it is necessary that you see this excellence in yourself. Many are trying to get there with you, and they are making substantial progress. Most lack the confidence that you have inside you to know that you can be perfect as Jesus is perfect. So, when Jesus was growing as a child to an adolescent boy, He looked at Himself not critically, but with self-assurance that the phases of His life, His mental, emotional and physical maturation, would only ratify what He always believed. This is the same self-image that you have now, that Jesus wishes all men and women to embrace. You can see in other people's eyes this lack of confidence because they are not willing to take the long steps and steep sacrifices that render their perfection before God. Abraham was willing to comply. Job wondered what was coming next. It took the voice of the heavens to bring Saul to his senses. Even My husband Saint Joseph was led by Angels because he was unsure what the Father expected of him. These are among the same Angels who are counseling you now. I am saying that justice and purity must be manifested from tendering the whole of the human will to the Prudence of Love that Jesus has brought from His conception in My Womb to the Holy Spirit through which He speaks to humanity today. If you look at this on a broader scale, it seems logical that God would ask intense sacrifices of those closest to Him because it was His Only Begotten Son whom He sent to suffer and die on the Cross. It has to be someone like Him, free from the encumbrances associated with guilt. Here again, you live without guilt because you know that your soul is free of stain as a gift of the Sacrament of Penance. While most people are struggling to become this likeness of Jesus, it is because they will not permit themselves to be that person. You, conversely, are willing to embrace your own sacred identity.

I am citing you as an example today because you are representative of the kind of person Christians are supposed to be; you feel the sense of inevitability of the Triumph of My Immaculate Heart and the Victory of the Cross. No one has ever claimed that this is something to be appropriated by mortal men without the intervention of the Spirit of God. You are open and receptive to your own perfections in ways that most human beings are not. This is what you must think about when pondering what testimony you will transfer to others when the time is right. Yes, I see what you are thinking; you could be perceived as arrogant and over-confident. People might see you as pretentious and presumptuous about your standing before the Throne of God. Please remember that this says more about them than it does you. They could not make these kinds of statements if they were incapable of seeing their own deficits in their vision and conduct. All people who are far from God know it. All the unholy ones are aware of their own wickedness. They simply choose to live that way because it is easier; their lives are without sacrifice, and they feel unburdened by the summons of the Cross. This is the attitude of losers; they are losers in the final acclaim. They hope to ride the coattails of their sacrificial friends into the Promised Land because they know their friends are praying for them. The surprise is that their friends' prayers for their salvation will be rewarded, but that salvation will come only after those for whom they are praying crawl through the fires of their own conversion before they see the light of Heaven. Deliverance implies that every soul must awaken from the slumber of sinfulness of their own accord. They can do this by their own inspiration; they can come of age because of the divine infusion of wisdom, or they can ask God for redemption based on their own ignorance of a converting life. No one stumbles unintentionally through the gates of Heaven! And, this is why great responsibility is placed on the clergy, the priests and deacons, and on Bishops, Archbishops and Cardinals. These holy men are responsible for the ecclesial leadership of their flocks at the same time that others in the world, the hundreds and thousands of other representatives of the Cross that I spoke about earlier, are called to personify the identity of Jesus for the whole of the Earth. Most all of My modern messengers are among these thousands of non-clergy disciples. Yes, you and your brother are called. You have answered, and the fruits are being borne. You should know that the calling is different for males because the Father is a Man in His Son Jesus. The Father holds domain over all Creation and everything outside Creation as a Man. God has revealed Himself as a Man. Everything He has created responds to His maleness in the context of His sovereign desires for His Kingdom. Hence, justice and purity are products of this maleness; this is the reason women are not called into the Hierarchy of the Church. They refuse to accept this; they are unwilling to defer to the Wisdom of the Holy Spirit.

The Father desires to nurture His little girls and hold them like gentle flowers in His arms. The justice and purity about which I speak flows from the hands of the Father as a male. His is the seed of righteousness that has refined the world. His are the Commandments that make the Church sacred. His are the hands that have manifested all that is seen and unseen. And, people like you and your brother, and all the sacrificial souls that your brother has been honoring, are the holders of the gentleness of humanity. The Father wishes that those whom He has created to be male lift the poor and all who are yearning to know Him to their dignity like roses. He wants those who desire this same sense of belonging to find themselves in the palms of princes. It is a beautiful and reciprocal gift to the Church and to the redemption of the world that God would wish all men to become like Him, little saviors who embrace His broken children here on Earth. I am not saying that they are redemptive saviors, but they are oftentimes bloodied just the same. Theirs is not sin-forgiving blood, but heart converting blood; it is cleansing in the sense that it washes from themselves all desire to seek a life's orientation anywhere other than the summit of Mount Calvary. Peter, James and John were asked to make sacrifices on the mountaintop that were never recorded in the Bible. These are the ends to which My messengers are called. And, for the record of the Earth and for eternity too, your calling is much enhanced. It is in the life you have already given to Me and Jesus; it is in the happy future that you will inherit here in this place and beyond your mortal days. Your sacrifices are ongoing and quite apparent. When you awaken every morning, you should feel the sense of appreciation that Jesus has for you. With the help of the Angels, you and your brother fully understand what your sacrifices mean for humanity, just as Peter, James and John saw the miraculous ethereal glory of the Messiah that day. I wish to close this message by thanking you for your awesome attention for so many years. You are an avid learner; you absorb what I say with eagerness. You are an exemplary child. Thank you for your delightful heart!"

Sunday, April 14, 2013
9:08 a.m.

"Western Democracy and the Psychology of Faith"

"My little children, here you see an appropriate title for an article or book about the state of American spiritualism in the 21st century. It is not My intention to have you write such a piece anytime soon, but it is something you might consider in the future. The thesis of the title is centered around the proposition that I have previously made in My messages and later in your manuscripts that the Western world is composed largely of free societies, not completely though; and that this freedom is seen as much a means to avoid religion as to celebrate it. The whole concept of democracy implies that the majority of the people rule; they make and even force decisions for the whole society. You have seen the awful repercussions of this so-called freedom in such atrocities as abortion and the removal of religious icons and relics from public places. Democracy is the same framework that makes it permissible to submerge the Crucifix in a tank of urine and smear feces on depictions of My face. These things are the result of the freedom in America to perpetrate evil. Western democracy allows these things under the guise of free speech, at the same time that religious people are not permitted to display religious icons and symbols in certain places. Religious people have no such free speech. The so-called free speech in the Unites States that permits advertisements for abortion but denies the expression of Christianity convicts the United States government as being a society of fascist radicals. It cannot be said any more clearly than this. What needs to be addressed is not only the theoretical and tangible results of this fascism, but that this kind of evil is being bred into new generations of Americans given the absence of opposition. Young people are being indoctrinated to believe that it is normal to celebrate atheism and detest spirituality. All the evidence would seem to be on the side of those who utilize the material aspects of human life to prove their point. It is difficult for someone to refer to a spiritual concept by asking those to whom they are speaking to look at the Holy Spirit or touch someone's interior faith. Hence, the basic 'psychology' of faith in America is biased against the gift of religious belief. Jesus on the Cross is being reduced to someone's idea of a belief system that is among many other belief systems, none of which can be visibly seen or touched. This is the same point that I have always made about encountering My Son's life and Crucifixion from the center of the heart. Therefore, it is time for a little comparison of My own. When an atheist loses a loved one to death, they weep, grieve and mourn accordingly. And when a Christian asks them where it hurts, they say that the pain is deep within them. This is when the Christian should say that this is the same inside depth that contains the religious faith of billions of believers, the same inside that atheists deny even existing until they lose someone they love. The contradiction is stark and repugnant. The hypocrisy of atheism is pervasive. The psychology; and this is the point I am making, is that those who do not accept the Crucifixion of Jesus Christ use their own terms to define their place in time, history and Creation. They choose for themselves what realms they will engage until they are uncontrollably grieved or fall victim to helpless circumstances. The psychology of faith in a Western democracy makes this hypocrisy possible. Faith has become a soiled term in contemporary America. It does not seem to produce immediate or discernible material results. It cannot be seen with the naked eye or held in the hand. It provides no consolation for those seeking a reason to work for the poor; faith in fact binds people to being servants for the poor. Western democracies believe the power lies in giving people the latitude to decide who they are and what they wish their future to become, no matter how counterintuitive these things may be to the language of life. Hence, you are seeing every few months a new kind of perversion beginning to emerge. Perversion has become the new energy behind American freedom in this new millennium. Yes, perversion is defined as anything that contradicts the teachings of the Catholic Church. Make no mistake, some of these perversions are coming from inside the Church itself in the persons of rogue priests and disobedient orders of nuns. Here, the freedoms of secular America have invaded the sacred realms of the Faith-Church on Earth. Look and behold! The actual mission of the Church has come under assault. Secular America is telling the Roman Catholic Church what to believe and practice. Abortion and contraception are two such examples. When viewed on the merits – indeed, I use the term 'merits' loosely – what secular America is struggling to produce is a nation in which truth is relative and all definitions and persuasions of spiritualism are accepted. This harkens to Sodom and Gomorrah! The ideologies are the same. Americans have become so burdened by the strain of a broken capitalist system that they lack the time to see this happening; they are too busy trying to feed, clothe and house themselves and their children. Secular America has deceivingly impressed upon its citizens that their basic rights include cellular telephones and exorbitantly priced tennis shoes. Young Americans purchase these things with haste, and skip meals to do it.

    The psychology of faith in Western democracies is just that – religion has been reduced to a thought process, a mental concept, that makes judgements even about the necessity of believing in God. It has become an option in

America to accept with conviction that God requires something of the exiled sinner. We have said many times that material distractions procured by rampant consumerism is the root of this issue. Pragmatism, entertainment, sports competition and non-committed interpersonal relationships have contributed to the movement of pushing God out of the national debate and evicting Him from the public arena. These things are not new, but they have never been framed in the context of a collective psychology. Religion has long been hailed as an option, as I have said. However, it is the choice that makes for the avenue of evil to travel the byways of America and steal the hearts of the young and old alike before the Holy Spirit has an opportunity to enter. And, as you might expect, this movement of choice will not prevail. It is in its last times; see My messages elsewhere around the globe. It makes Me happy that Jesus has allowed Me to speak to humanity with such urgency, and that Jesus, Himself, has done so as well. We are winning; we have already won; the world is changing, and the enemies of the Cross are about to be annihilated in the same way you watched those napalm explosions on television last night. I am not just speaking of incidents that might occur; they are surely inevitable. You will be reminded of My words here today when you see this happen. And, as I have said on prior occasions, do not mourn for these sinners. Do not pity them or take-up a collection to aid their legacies. Divine Justice is always more powerful than Western democracy or its psychologies, no matter if the psychology is about advancing secular zeal, lording over the forces of Nature, or journeying far off into outer-space. The human intellect has no capacity to comprehend the ethereal excellence of the Son of Man until the soul has departed the flesh. What is written in the Bible and spoken from inspired priests and other religious people is sufficient impulse to activate the pious instincts of everyone who will eventually go to Heaven. I have said that it appears to Roman Catholics that all time is one; this is what the Eucharistic Prayers confirm. It is what the Saints declare every time their names are invoked in prayer and song. The world around you is brawling and bubbling, just like the writer proclaimed. There is noise and noisiness. There are perversions and distractions. There is pride and impurity. There is indifference and injustice. All these things are offensive and unsightly, but they do not matter in the course of Salvation history. They are the skeletal remains of the pre-Messianic age. Time does not yet prove this to be true because time itself is a remnant of the Fall of Adam. Therefore, My Special son, it is the genius in your heart and the pricelessness of your soul that allows you to understand what I have told you. You have the faith of giants, not of psychology, but the trueness of heart that transcends human thought and action. You know that freedom as defined by Christ Jesus has more to do with Divine

Truth than social liberation. Freedom is love, and love is a manifestation of the Will of God. The Father wills to love His earthly creatures because these same creatures were preceded by His love. Do you understand everything about your country that stands in opposition to what I have said today? *"Yes."* As I say, you need not immediately write or speak about this subject, but it is something that is not much broached in today's theologies. There is room for the heart and mind to converge, just as I told you in 1991. The heart must prevail over the mind in order for the human species to live in alignment with the teachings of the Church and the mandates of the Messiah who heads it."

Saturday, April 20, 2013
3:07 p.m.

"The Inimitable Way"

"My Immaculate Heart is the origin of your consolation, and Jesus' Sacred Heart is your resourcefulness for everything you need in life. My sons, plenteous are the memories by which you have shaped your view of the world, but those you have yielded from Me will be your fondest. I always call My children to resilience in this fact because of the perpetuity of Absolution that you find in the Blood of Jesus on the Cross. My little children, please take heart. Be comforted by the confidence that you have found in Me. Store in your minds' archives everything that I have taught you. My words have been priceless during these crucial times. Through the wisdom of the Holy Paraclete, we have generated for humanity the framework of spiritual sustenance that will prepare them for the terrible years ahead. I have come speaking to you again about your Christian identity in Jesus. You already know that each of you shares the fullness of community in the Cross and the Kingdom now bearing down upon the Earth with constant compassion. There is but one Mystical Body of Jesus, with many parts. However, there rests in each soul given the breath of life a single identity, a spiritual signature that is unknown to everyone else. Each person enjoys his or her own oneness with God straight-away; no one can share your birth, and everyone dies as a single soul. Even the resurrection of all souls is wholly united in the Resurrection of Jesus, and yet singly gifted to each soul by the same God who gave them life. Hence, I speak today about the inimitable way of the human soul. It is a way of living and dying like no other; inimitable means that life and the pursuit of excellence is unique to each soul; no one can either steal or replicate it. If you think about someone speaking of 'people,' another person might use the term 'folks' to describe them. The term 'folks' is a more casual way of speaking, meaning that a person has a folksy way of leading human life instead of being more distinctly classical. The greater point is that the self-will that God gives each person is as individual as the person's perceptions. You must believe Me when I tell you that the gift of the self-will has brought many holy manifestations into this world, and they are given through the Holy Spirit because of the deference of the person to the Will of God. You also know that the self-will has been the cause of much evil and acts of horror, terror and destruction. The events in Boston have proved this to be true. I am speaking about each and every creature aligning their own non-replicable identity with the identity of Christ Jesus. We have seen the writings of the Saints, Mystics and Doctors, and they each have a different approach to the same destination for the refinement and conversion of the human spirit. While they are not meant to be contradicting, they are diverse and unique to the persons who write them. The intersection of all the billions of inimitable ways of God's children is where the perfection of life is most readily seen. Your lives in Jesus have become polished. They run like fine clockwork. They keep time with the beatific facets of mortal life that will be taken with you into the realms of sacred redemption. I am saying that it is all right for My children to be different in their ideas and motivations, as long as their ideologies and actions do not conflict with the teachings of the Church. You know what the Lord asks of His disciples. He wants the world to be holy. He asks fathers to give flowers to their daughters, to kiss their sons on the cheek, to ensure discipline in the conducting of domestic affairs, to bring home bread and break it, and to be the master of the house. He asks wives to be receptive to the love of their husbands, and He wants children to work for their wages and be simple of heart. Please think about the oneness that Jesus seeks from His people in the midst of all this. It speaks of playing the roles properly that are given from the Lord. It means accepting one's own crosses so others can bear their crosses more easily. It means allowing God to touch humanity as individuals, and yet as one body of people. All Jesus ever asked this world is that men give Him berth to share His Kingdom. Even as He said that anyone who loves his life would lose it, this life must not be lived in vain.

Embracing life does not mean becoming immersed in materialism or idolatry. It does not pave the way for taking roads and paths that do not lead to sacrifice. Embracing life means facing the challenges that overcome the skewed perceptions of the world being imposed on societies by misguided men. There is a battle in all this, but it need not be a bloody one. There is no certain call to believe that preaching the Gospel must be an act of humiliation. This is the reason that Christ Jesus gives ample latitude for men to be who they are within the parameters of what the Father first deigned them to be. Some men become

Popes, others wash laundry in back-street clothing stores. Some wage war, others make peace. Some become fathers and patrons, which is not always the simpler path, while others make the purpose of their lives propagating the Salvation story from one continent to another. What Jesus despises most is those who fall in between. My Son rejects lukewarmness. There are followers, and there are true leaders, but there are also those who are uncommitted to what they must become. The oft-quoted, 'I am uncertain about whom I want to be,' is an unacceptable proposition to the Man who died for the sins of the world. One does not have to look far to see examples of this. His disciples who fell asleep should have either remained awake or departed the evening. There are no half-hearted Saints. My Special son, this is the underpinning of your life here with your brother. You have been committed to Me and the Holy Gospel with full-throated energy. You were untethered to the bindings of the priesthood where you would not have been able to release My messages to the world, lest a Bishop silence you and hole you up in a monastery somewhere. As I have previously said, you are living in a nation that espouses free speech, so you have not been incarcerated by your government. And, I ask you to take another look at all your forewords, prefaces and prologues. You and the Spirit of God met on those pages in ways known only to you and the Father. Your own inimitable identity in Jesus was placed there in such a way that cannot be replicated by other men. To provide an appropriate comparison, Jesus sees your contributions as unique as your DNA. You have a spiritual DNA that is unlike any other person because this is the beatific relationship that you have with your Savior. If you think about the collective DNA of the tens of billions of souls who have lived on the Earth, you will see the immensity of God's Will to create a body of distinct creatures on their own journey to the same destiny. This makes the prospect of what gifts could have been given to the world by aborted children even more magnified. I speak of uniqueness because Jesus desires all His brothers and sisters to be who they are, and yet remain children of the same Father. This refers to sharing one's self-image and self-gifts with the collective whole of humanity. Do you understand? *"Yes."* Now, this is the first part of My message today. Think now about the nature of these identities spread across the generations and ages. The Holy Spirit has dictated through men the Gospel of Messianic Salvation, and humanity composed of distinct individuals has replied with compliance. Each converted heart in his own inimitable way has said 'yes' to the call of the Cross according to his capacity to comprehend. The levels of this ability come through prayer and self-sacrifice, through living in accordance with the mandates of the Church, and responding to the circumstances that are unique to each Christian's life.

Christ Jesus Himself was the first to live out this inimitable way. He came to Earth and laid down a template for humanity to accept the Will of God. That template was never meant to constrict the uniqueness of each person, but to enhance it in Him. There are as many gifts to the Kingdom of Salvation as there are people who give them. Artists, musicians, writers, laborers, public officials, technicians, doctors and so on. There is a fragrance of righteousness in the lives of each one that Jesus recognizes as their way of glorifying Him. Others like you and your brother are outright visionaries. There is no symbolism in what you have done. You are greater than the sum of princes that I recently spoke about. You are more contemplative in your craft-work; you have placed before the world the words of the Mother of the Son of God that cannot be dismissed. People like you and your brother are born to transmit in your own inimitable way the Gospel of redemption through the prologues and writings that I mentioned just moments ago. I have given you My messages since December 28, 2008 for a purpose, and you will decide what effect they will have. Hence, when I say that Jesus has given exiled humanity a mandate to live in Him, in each person's inimitable way, I refer to examples like you. There are realms and horizons yet to be explored, but there are insufficient souls willing to proceed. You and your brother have made up for what is lacking in them. Your hearts are fine-tuned, and you are on the righteous course. I congratulate you for succeeding, for completing the task that Jesus has assigned to you. *"Thank you."* I wish for you to remember how grateful I am for your complimentary words about My messages. I am humbled that you like them. *"I think they are awesome."* You have prayed them into being! You asked Me to respond to your daily recitation of the Holy Rosary, and My messages are My answer."

Saturday, April 27, 2013
1:03 p.m.

"Here, we have our joy; this is our moment for remembering what our love means. It is through this joy that you understand what the Father wills for you. My little sons, I am filled with this eternal joy on this day as you pray with Me for the conversion of lost sinners. There is no weariness; there is no backtracking, no concerns of prejudice or a lack of justification. We have within us the unified meaning of sacred truth uniting us in God, and you will one day, beyond this exile, hear Me dictate these same words to you outside of time. Every morsel of earthly time measured in minutes and hours is ours for the joy to which I have dedicated My presence. If you think about your life's mission, or own objectives, all the providential 'accidents,' and the fullness of human life that is coming upon you now, there can be no mistaking the prescience of Jesus telling you what to do. It is the Son of Man inside you who reigns sovereign with the Creator, and you are the vessels and vehicles of His righteousness here in the world. You have longed for your share of this providence; you have foreseen the beauty of Heaven and foretasted the sacrifices that will take you there. Your power is in your suffering, whatever you perceive suffering to be. In all that will open the eyes of your brothers and sisters, your lives here become you. You have already inherited yet undisclosed fortunes bequeathed to you by your forebears and the ages in which they lived. It is not, My little sons, that you are not writing new songs. You are creating melodies and marking cadences by which your contemporaries can understand what I have taught you through the years. You are more than you measure yourselves to be. Modesty shrouds your vision of your own greatness. Eloquence sometimes escapes you because you are too humble to speak. The light in which you stand has you wondering why so many others are living in the darkness, and rightly so. So yes – joy is the reason I have come to you today. I ask you to imagine humanity resting in its own peace, laid back and awaiting the Second Coming with gladness and imagining. The world may be writhing and twisting in unsightly ways, and humanity's back may be bowed as if outstretched over a barrel, but the infusion of the brilliance of God ultimately reigns. Reason and justice will supplant agony and fear. Jesus' entrance into His Kingdom here on Earth is the awakening that has yet to instill in nonbelievers the commitment that will take them to His side in Heaven. We have spoken of the conversion of lost sinners as a process and not an event. You are in this process now. You are seeing it with your own eyes, the process that contains ebbs and flows, that will moreover be riddled with old questions and blessed with new answers. Even as you know a man of great religious stature who is authoring his own works, he too has gained insight for his own writings from what he has learned from Me. Yes, it is ironic that he would assimilate what he knows to have come from My Immaculate Heart into his own writings without surrendering to the origin of his wisdom. He, as of yet, refuses to embrace the Morning Star Over America as authentic, but uses My grace to enhance his personal stature as a bearer of the Gospel. This is the way of the world. This kind of hypocrisy will not stand, but you should not be surprised to know that it is happening. We are trying to pray-away the influences of evil from everywhere, and from all time. It is difficult when there is so much upheaval being caused by unbelieving men. It is not yet over. I have not finished saying My piece. My Special son, this is a particular time of grace for you and your brother because of your patience during the process about which I speak. Imagine the yearnings of so many Saints and servants before you who laid down their lives to honor the Cross, and who prayed for the ratification of their actions during their mortal years. There have been millions of them. I know that you are prepared for disseminating My messages in your deposit of works, preferably with the public approbation of your Bishop. I am praying that he will respond to the prayers of the faithful who are asking for miracles such as this, given to you over the past 22 years.

God knows the timing of the crucial moments in the history of this world. Those times have arrived! One cannot wait a hundred years, or even a decade, for a time that may never come. God is not going to wait for any sinner to decide whether it somehow feels right to give to humanity what I have given to you. So, it is in joy that I have come; it is this joy that makes Me say that we will soon pronounce a widespread sharing of My Morning Star messages here in this land and nations abroad. My Special son, saints are tested. Christians are persecuted. Righteousness is ridiculed. Messengers are ignored. Holiness is impugned. The Church is despised. There is nothing new under the sun. It is imperative, however, that you do not lose sight that the ensuing months ahead will lead to overwhelming change in the consciousness of the world, the focus of humanity on things beyond the Earth, and the fact that My messages and intercessions will be at the center of it all. This should make you as joyful as Me. The world has been exhausted by the incivility of its occupants. Lives of little people have been torn apart by the excesses of those in power. We will here together, you and I and all who subscribe to My role in human redemption, redefine the meaning of 'power' so that clarity in all things miraculous will become known. It has a great deal more to do with defeating the wicked than whether a child is healed of a disease. These miracles will be about burning barns and charred flesh. They will open the eyes of the blind that God has allowed such suffering on Earth the past 2,000 years just to prove that He can suspend it now. He can reverse it and rewrite history. He can send those 65 million aborted children back to America carrying swords and scepters to conquer the people who are committing this grave atrocity to this day. Crimes abound here in this land, but so does justice linger near and nigh. You will know when it occurs. It saddens Me when others say that ending abortion will be too late. They are using their worldly minds. They need to remember that the end of abortion will, just as I have said, reverse the tides of time and history. The Lord will not permit this injustice to stand. There will be a reckoning from mothers to jurists to doctors to politicians. Call it whatever you wish – fire and brimstone, the thunder of the Lord's vengeance, the clarion to awaken the dead – but the fact remains that Heaven will have the last word. It will be deafening and decisive. It will separate the sheep from the goats. It will incinerate every soul saturated in the accelerant of unconfessed sins. Jesus will bring His Justice into the world quickly and properly. More people need to pray. This is the way to conquer the evilness of Satan. My Special one, you have been traumatized by your last employer, and you might believe that all employment will leave you similarly so. It is going to be difficult, when you see how so many millions of others have lived in America and nations far and wide, for you to look back at their lives in time. They have been repugnantly beaten, starved, enslaved, physically and psychologically tortured, sensory deprived, exploited, and slowly marched toward impalement, disembowelment, crucifixion and death. When you see these things in the reflection of history, you will wonder why you had such a blessed country in which to live. I am trying to focus My children's vision on the Cross, but so far, humanity will not allow it. I only ask that you and your brother look at the Passion and Crucifixion of My Son without the blinders imposed on you by time. I ask for your acceptance, that what you are enduring in this life is in communion with the Crucifixion, and this is how My messages in your books will be spread. All throughout our time together, you have seen Me respect your feelings, listen to your concerns, offer My consolation, proffer My advice, and beg you to live in the likeness of Jesus. You have been receptive to Me. You have been like Jesus every day you have lived. It is not by comparing your lives with others that you will know that you have emulated Jesus' suffering, but whether you have carried the crosses handed to you with as much empathy for lost sinners as He did on Good Friday. When I say 'you,' I am referring to humanity at large. I will in the future hand you some multi-dimensional messages about Jesus' life and death. I have an entire deposit of messages about what Jesus was thinking during His earthly ministry, what He felt the day He was arrested, what He left unsaid during the trial, and what else He wanted to say from the Cross that was never put in print. I have thus far found no venue to say these things because I have for twenty centuries been consoling the suffering of My messengers. I have yet to find other visionaries who understand the way you and your brother do. This is the reason that I am speaking to you now; the joy with which I have come is complete."

Sunday, May 5, 2013
1:35 p.m.

"Mind and Thought, Heart and Love"

"My little sons, My presence gives you reassurance that all is well in the Lord's earthly domain. You have with you the Providence that gives you peace, that uplifts you beyond your concerns, that proves that the future will hold the blessings for which you pray. I ask that you never forget our engagement, our connection in and through Jesus, our embracement of the power of the Cross, and our mission to remain united with the Will of the Father. You were given a heart before you were conceived in love. You were given wisdom of thought before you were given a mind. You were conceived in this world, but your origin is from the Heart of Eternal Light. I ask that you ponder what the thought of love means to you. It is a function of the spiritual realms that holds its consciousness in your determination of faith. Today, I am calling you to reaffirm your confidence from your youth; you have not lost this confidence, you have flourished in it. You must remember that you are not broken or breaking, you are being perfected in the ways that I have told you through the years. I have always known your fullness of human perfection that you will take to Heaven when you go. It begins in your belief that you will get there. Your eternal thoughts blossom from your eternal mind in the same way that your eternal heart produces eternal love. It is a manifestation of your desire to be seamlessly connected to the Father through the Son and the truth spoken to you, and by you, through the Holy Spirit. My Special son, Jesus is hailing you to not yield to Satan's attempt to convince you that you are old and weary. The whole concept is a diversion. I am not saying that you do not become physically tired or have thoughts reflecting your tiredness, but that these are natural to all Saints. I am saying that Satan is trying to convince you that this should be your natural state, that physical exhaustion should be the way you lead your life. Remember the reflections of Saint Padre Pio. He described this phenomenon in distinct detail. Saint Pio was exhausted all the time from enduring attacks of evil, but he never became incapable of compartmentalizing it. Of course, he bore the sacred stigmata, which even made things more difficult for him. Your scars and those of all Christians are borne inside. You are bleeding in the way of Jesus from within your spiritual core, but this is not a blood loss that will affect your ability to fight for the redemption of men. In fact, it enhances it. If you think in the context of the mind and thoughts with emphasis on the heart and love, you will see that they are not mutually exclusive. This is the essence of the writings of the

Doctors of the Church like Saint Thomas Aquinas. It is as simple as one 'Our Father' or telling someone that you love them. It is only something as mere as these that allows you to overcome any perceived defeatism with which the devil is trying to torment you. Thank you for everything you mean to Me, for all you have given the Lord's Kingdom, for the life that you and your brother have led to honor My Queenship for the advancement of the Church. I have told you about the penetration of Truth into the darkest places in the world. The Gospel needs to be told there. The Sacraments must be administered there. With the force of Divine Love, the Salvation of humanity must be shared with all who have never heard the Sacred Word. So many religious writings from others do little to address the grievous circumstances of sin that are facing the world. Many seem to believe that I must ask permission to appear in a certain diocese. I offer you messages for specific reasons, and no one should stand in My way. You see the reason why the Roman Catholic Church has become so disregarded in America. Most of the worthy warriors have passed into the Light of the Father. You see a celebrated Prelate giving-in to his political fraternities, deceived by the devil into believing that secular politics and the truth of great faith could possibly complement each other. This is the reason that the Truth must come so starkly into quarters where the admonition of the Holy Spirit is often shunned.

The virtues of heart and love, faith and prayer do not enter the realms of the secular void. It often comes down to dealing with the devil on the devil's terms. You have seen this for a long period of time, I am not telling you anything new. This is also the reason I have told My messengers around the globe that it is through My work with them that humanity will convert. I am helping foster the movement of Christianity in the remote places I spoke about a few moments ago. I am stirring the flames, aligning the efforts of My children, driving the Truth into regions previously untouched. I am making sure that you and your brother and all My seers and messengers shine like diamonds amid the grim conditions of the world. You are covered like dew with righteousness, while others are parched like ashes. You are establishing a rhythm by which others will walk toward Paradise. You may see few signs of it now, but your hearts know this to be true. As I told you last week, there is coming in the offing an explosion of Truth that will rattle humanity to the bones. You will not be surprised when it happens. You will remain confident that the Lord knows what He is doing. As the days pass by and you witness the unfolding of My words, it will become clear to you that this new awakening must come. You are neither worried nor anxious because you and your brother have known about the Lord's warnings for decades. Morning Star Over America will accomplish everything that Jesus intended from its inception on February 22, 1991. My messages of love given to you and your brother will be revealed. What is more important at this hour is that old evils have now become new evils. You have seen this in the case of the abortion doctor in Philadelphia. What you are seeing and hearing does not scratch the surface of what is going on. My Special son, you have been prescient and correct all along. I am the Miracle that the Church in America requires. Please do not worry! Revelation and justice are imminent. My Maternal role as Patroness of the United States will not be in vain. This is why the Angels reinforce God's desire that you do not fear. It is the reason I tell My Medjugorje messengers to never cower from the complaints of those who decline to believe what I have said. It is the reason I ask humanity not to judge. Judging does not matter much; prayer and love gain the attention of the Savior of the world. This is the state of mind, and these are the thoughts, that will awaken humanity. Now, before I speak to you again, you and your brother will celebrate his next great accomplishment – there will be a graduation, and there will be a new beginning. All this will precede the judgement of the exiled world and the Great Reckoning itself."

Monday, May 13, 2013
8:54 a.m.

"Reproof the Ages"

"My lovely children, My holy sons with hearts of gold, I wish you happiness on this beautiful Monday morning. We have here with us the Fatima visionaries who aided in the transmitting of My messages held so sacred on this anniversary day. So, with all the gladness I can muster, I tell you that it is My honor to be in your company once again. You enjoyed last Saturday the graduation of many college students, including My Chosen one in this home, where you heard some not-so-lofty speeches about things that mattered little. You listened to stale remarks and canned rhetoric that did nothing to instill in the listeners what it means to mark the ages with achievement. Therefore, I would like to share My own sentiments here. The speakers should have said that winning the fight against any challenge such as education or athleticism, or overcoming sickness or depression, begins not with taking on battles laid out by others. The following commendation is what should have been spoken on Saturday –

'Graduating college is never about fulfilling the requirements for a degree or making the grade. Graduation implies that the inner-self has been changed; it has been transformed to mean that the day commencement occurs opens the door for what will come, not what has already happened. This is the way of the teachings of the grand philosophers and ancients; it is what humanity learned by the great battles for righteousness; it is what Moses inherited from On High, and it is what Christ Jesus gave to a people lost in darkness and drowning in iniquity. Never mind the pleated robes; do not worship the tassels and hoods, and forget about the lights and cameras. Focus not on the issues that will pass into history with the millions of others who have walked to the same anthem, the same pomp and circumstance that dies the moment the final note is played. Indeed, it is all about the inner-self. All that history has borne for modern man is useless now. Heroes and legends who have passed before you have left only skeletal remains of their lessons and teachings. Except One – The Son of God. What makes Him different? He was already born with a perfect inner-self to which all other men should aspire. This perfect inner-self is where the Divine Truth lives. It is where men and women understand that there are no interdisciplinary levels of true human love. There are no theorems or chemistries. There are no mathematical formulas or digital systems in the perfect inner-self. There are instead wondrous imaginings of a world drenched with glory, saturated with good will, shining with the peace that humanity was destined to embrace. Indeed, the Single Truth of a Single Cross. The power of one Crucifixion has eclipsed all the weaknesses that any humanity could possibly suffer in any Creation or time. This is why the ages are so deceitful. Halls of marching men wearing gowns and mortar boards have done little to heal the aching human heart. Unity with the Father, oneness with grace, plenteous piety, and the underpinning of self-sacrifice are the four legs of this table of plenty. So, look at your neighbors and friends. Look into the eyes of your fellow graduates sitting next to you now. Know that this moment has been fashioned from the beginning of the world to uplift you, that it was made possible not by books or institutions, but the Providence of God. Graduation is your clarion for action, your summons to see this day as the opening of a door, a door that leads to the redressing of griefs and the healing of wounds. This can only be done by fashioning the intellect in the ways of righteousness. The true identity of intellectual achievement has the hallmark of superlative genius in the themes of human absolution. This is where the inner-self begins. I am not just speaking about forgiving someone for saying something offensive. It is not about pardoning someone for stealing your shoes. It is about opening your hearts to a fuller, more complete understanding of the way the Earth is being remade in the likeness of Heaven. This is the awakening that must come. This is the cleansing by ice and fire that shatters not the dreams of men, but the nightmares of those who believe that their hopes will never come true. Walking with Christ Jesus not only implies that you are compliant with His Will, but recognizing His Will as your way of life, your reason for reprimanding and reproving the ages for ignoring what I am telling you today. Graduation is not about any one person or a single idea or deposit of thought. It has nothing to do with climbing higher on the economic scale or acquiring fame and fortune before other men get there. These things die! They pass away because they have no true life in them. By all means, graduation is the beginning of the realization that you may as well remove your stately gowns, go out into the streets, and cover the homeless with them in the image of the Saints. Give them your cloaks and your heart-works too! Then, dress their poverty with your hoods and tassels. Tell them that if not for the fate of the world, you would be each other today. Then, come back into this hall, be seated once again, prepare to propagate the divinity of human reconciliation, and thank God that you have inside you a framework to begin afresh and renewed. Thank Jesus that the Holy Spirit is guiding and protecting you. Remember the origin of your blessings with humility. Embrace servitude with the gladness of children. Give everything you have; expect nothing in return, and stand with sureness in the dignity that is yours. This is the inner-self that will change the world. This is the human mission that must shape the future. It is the sign of destination for the whole of the Earth, that peace may come in your day, that plenty can be spread far and wide, that the sun will forever shine, and that suffering will be no more. It all begins inside the human heart, not in models or paradigms, not in fancy dwelling places with ornate fixtures, but in the final understanding of the self in comparison to the Perfect Son of God. May the Lord give all of you here today the courage to achieve it. Thank you.'

My Special son, these are the words that I would have said on Saturday. They are not profound. They are not flowery or eloquent, but the venue was none of these things either. I pray that you understand what it means to Jesus and Me that you attended your brother to the ceremony, that you made his presence there possible. I beg you to remember that it was you who did this. I beseech you to accept that he could not have done anything without you. I am pleased that you are working on your memoir for the reasons I gave you in past weeks. The year 2013 has been a blessing thus far; there have been many changes in your lives, there is much more stability now. There has come a sense of accomplishment. I ask that you and your brother take good care of yourselves.

My Dominion Angels have been talking to your brother through the night and through the day, mostly to tell him what to do better. They advise him of the wishes of Jesus and God the Father, and it almost always has to do with some sort of sacrifice. I am pleased that he is aware of what is being asked of him. Many good things are happening now; the world is unfolding, you and your brother are on course, and there is victory in the offing."

Saturday, May 18, 2013
9:26 a.m.

"Love and Cruelism"

"History will prove that it was here that the great enlightenment of modern man began. Wisdom has been spread in evocative places around the globe; and signs, wonders and warnings have been given, but the celebration of eternal truth has found its third-millennium origin in The Morning Star Over America. My children, you are not the helpless victims that you sometimes appear to be. You are warriors; you are visionaries and prophets. You are disciples, peacemakers and custodians of the culminating ages. Today, I report to you that your Bishop has received your letter. He is seeing an assemblage of signs that align with My Morning Star messages. My Special son, of all the dates for him to choose to cite in his opening remarks upon assuming his episcopate here, he selected January 27th, your brother's birthday. No one can see these things without recognizing the signs of your labors. The mysticism of the Holy Spirit is rising from beneath his feet. It is an excelling grace that has caused this to occur. It is a result of your prayers, the blessings that you and your brother have bestowed upon humanity through the gift of your lives. God will not wait. We shall move forward with the enlightenment that I have heretofore encouraged. I thank you for looking beyond your present-day affairs, your seeming inconsistent success with your books and employment. It is all about the fight between good and evil. When you speak of not having 'lights' in your lives, you should perceive these times as being the opposite. The rest of humanity is burdened by daily strife, properties, materials, distractions and catastrophes. You and your brother are sailing smoother seas. When you speak of the secular world having lights in life, they are not permanent to them. They do not understand love in the way that you and your brother know. There is a shroud covering the eyes of your brothers and sisters that they do not realize is there. It is like the invisible dome that you have seen on the television program; people ram into its dimensions without expecting it. Other people have self-induced parameters in which they reside – not so with you and your brother. You see that I have opened My message today with the words love and 'cruelism.' These are antonyms, having opposite meanings. I use the term 'cruelism' instead of 'cruelty' because the latter implies an act or series of actions. What people suffer who are united with love is more chronic than that. It is a perpetual state of discord with those who refuse to love. There is no such word as 'cruelism,' but you know that I am prone to create new terms. Cruelism is more than a series of cruel acts, it is the daily rush of hatred that overlaps one cruel act with another into a single massive sum. It is an ideology that opposes everything joyful about the Cross. Cruelism crucifies the human heart and attempts to obliterate any semblance of hope. My Special son, when I spoke to you last week, you were elated because of the accomplishments that you and your brother made on Saturday, and none of this has changed. The Lord knows of your advances in defeating His enemies. He wants them defeated as well. This is the battle of love against the cruelism that tries to keep God's Kingdom from flourishing. And, we already know that love has rightfully won. It is as though everyone is born in the middle of a motion picture. You mature into an age of reason and see the battles that rage. You are gently called by the Holy Paraclete to embark on an ungentle journey. But, believe it or not, this is the source of human joy. This is where you find your purpose. It is where Jesus destroys everything that stands against the Cross, the Cross that alleviates all pain, sorrow and indignity. Surely you know that this is where the Victory of the Church and the Triumph of My Immaculate Heart intersect. It is as difficult to explain as the Blessed Trinity itself.

The Holy Cross is the mode of the death of Jesus Christ. I am emblematic of the beauty that My Son's Sacrifice has brought into the world. I am not asking you to dismiss the unsightliness of human sin. I am not saying that it has been neutralized. I urge you to hold true to your joy despite that sin, knowing that it will be brought to ashes in the Blood of My Son's Divine Love. As I speak to you now, I see the world through a different set of eyes, and you likewise see as I see. You see the effects of cruelism leveled against the Church. You see it in the lives of the poor. You know that it makes wealthy people happy and paupers kneel in tears. We are overcoming it now; we diminish the forces of cruelism every time we pray, every time we share My messages, every moment the world itself joins in the conversation between Heaven and Earth. You come to greatness in these things. It is not what you have already given that matters most, but what still remains to be done. Heroes never wave white flags. Christians do not surrender. Everyone needs to adopt your way of seeing life – more fairly, more calmly, more united in the Sacrifice of the Savior of the world. You personify greatness in the way that Jesus asks the Church to be great like

Him. When the world asks what more might be heaped upon them, this is their awakening hour. They will likely never be nailed to a cross or have their flesh pierced by a sword, and they will definitely never find that they were sinless people who died an innocent's death. My Special son, thank you over and again for urging everyone to be holy in the way that Jesus commends. You are always holy; you are good in the eyes of God. You give of yourself in ways known to few other mortals on Earth. You are united with Me. I do not mind that you seek greater courage from the Bishops and other Christians. They have been conflicted throughout the ages when confronted with messages from the Mother of God. It is about revealing the joy of Christ. It is an opportunity for high-ranking men to perform their duties in abandonment to their Immaculate Mother. My Special son, I hope that you can sense My happiness as I voice this message today. I have long known the difference between love and cruelism. I have always known about the battles between them because I am an exceptional Mother. I will never abandon My children. I support My priests and Bishops, even when some of them struggle with doubts and weaknesses of their own. This is the mission that keeps Me coming into the exiled realms to fight for the last lost soul. It is the signature of My Holy Queenship before every wayward sinner. Thank you for helping make this happen. You know that you and your brother's sacrifices aid the transformation of the Earth. It is a blessing that you commit yourselves to these sacrifices; it is pleasing in all ways glorious. It is not just specific to you and your brother, it has been ongoing to the joy of the Son of Man for generations and centuries. So, never be sad about life, and know with every fiber of your being that you live beneath the Mantle of the Mother of Jesus Christ. Do not write a dark script about the closing of the world; feel happiness and lightness of heart. This is when you are near to Me, and you are especially near when I come to you during times of distress and despair."

Saturday, May 25, 2013
Birthday of Saint Padre Pio
10:13 a.m.

"The Lord digs deeply and wins mightily."

"My loving children, My stately little sons, the gentlemen who keep inviting Me here to pray; it is an honor to tell you that Jesus is pleased with you, not just in your ways of faith, but your dedication to the reconciliation between Heaven and the Earth. It is no coincidence that you have given to the organization doing the work of Padre Pio. He is indeed greeting his brothers and sisters at the Gate of Paradise. My little ones, if you remember everything that Padre Pio did for the Church, for humanity in exile, and for the glory of the Cross, you will realize that greatness is truly not in riches. Prosperity exists in the integrity of your beliefs and the eternal moments that you share with God. You have understood for more than five decades that the Lord is one with you. If there seems a vacuum in what humanity is doing, it is because Jesus is waiting for Creation to upheave. He is resting peacefully in the tabernacles of the Church while His disciples do their work in exile on the Earth. You see, even with all the power that God holds in His hands, He transfers this power to humanity, His creatures, who comprise the world where you live. I know that this is difficult to believe. Every single gift that was ever handed to humanity has been the result of someone's spiritual prayer. Every blessing, every peace accord, every healing, every morsel of food, every hope, every grace, and every moment of enlightenment has been God's response to someone's Christian prayers. The believers from past generations have handed you the Church that you magnify today. All the timeless adventures and modern miracles that you have ever heard about were manifested by the calling of the world to the holiness of the Saints. And, the Father sends down these miracles to nations far and wide. Inside His Kingdom, there are many mansions, and most of them reflect the architectures of the Roman Catholic Church. Not the Second Vatican Council ones, but the historically elegant and majestic ones. When the Son of Man takes a deep breath to inhale the fruits of the Church's faith, the Father's gratitude inspires His peace. All that you do, My little sons, manifests eternity. Especially those things that you hope to see with providence are handed to you by the power of your prayers. And, these same prayers, many said when you were still young boys, are the reason I am speaking to you now. When you walked the streets of your small home town, peddled your bicycle, and rode your minibike around the yard, the Holy Spirit was there to know. You must remember that the Father, the Son and the Holy Paraclete speak in consoling overtones, and at their own discretion, and they are always in accord. One God in Three Persons implies that Jesus can see something to which He draws the Father's eye. The Father can ask the Son what He desires about a certain sign, and the Holy Spirit is the voice of advocacy to His creatures on the ground. This is how I have come; it is in their name that I have spoken to humanity over the centuries with such poise and eloquence. My Special son, these are grand years and auspicious times that you and your brother have made possible, and that others like you have brought into being by their faith in the Will of God.

    You often wonder how I can come to you with such joy and anticipation, and the answer is that I have seen the lives of those who accept the Cross. But, what about the rest? Carnage. Complete and utter annihilation of nonbelievers whose plans include their own demise. Their defeat will feed the fires that will keep good souls warm through the blizzards of the Earth. They once belonged to Me you know; they were bequeathed to Me by Jesus on the Cross, but they have chosen an errant path. Please pray for them! It is not wrong to cast out the wicked who will not convert. Some of them may do so in time, but millions will refuse. I trust what God is doing in Creation. I knew it from the moment that I learned that I would be the Mother of the Messiah. Even from My youth, I was deigned to be the Virgin of the Church. I sufficed the dignity of all the virgins on Earth by giving birth to Jesus. He has enlivened the eternal joy of the virgins now in Heaven, these souls who came to their Salvation as such, ones who pray from their lofty place with God, ones who will spend eternity being nourished by the echo of Saint Gabriel's voice. Their sacrifices on Earth have led them to the joy they have gained by remaining faithful to the Church. My little sons, you are the incarnation of their happiness; you are the object of their gratitude, you are the ones still living on the Earth, giving them this joy. And in this, you receive the benefits of the blessings that you have wrought from enduring the world of men. This life need not be a tormenting one; it can overflow with joy, but these things come only to those who have faith and trust in the Father through the Son. Once all souls understand what I am telling you today, no man will ever see another sad face again. The apex of Christian life is about growing, focusing and acting on one's faith in Jesus Christ. When the Fatima sun plummeted to the Earth in 1917, it was never about frightening the pilgrims or parching the soil after the rains. It was about learning that celestial spheres can descend to wherever you are now. It was about the capacity of the heavens to awaken the sleeping world. It was about humanity being gladly victimized by the presence of true love. My Special son, this is the story that you and your brother are revealing through your lives. It is not about oblivion or a ruthless death from sin. It is not to taunt someone who has little self-control. It is a testament of perfection that seamlessly unites humanity with the preeminent love of God. It is not about uprooting apple trees or counting captains' chairs, it is about seeing what it means to please the Father who ordains the way you live. This is the reason for sunbeams. It is why breezes blow and Angels' choirs fill the air. The whole circumstance of human life is reasoned by what Adam and Eve were supposed to do; not to be distracted by a Serpent and a tree, but live and love the way the Father asked them to. The sin they were meant to avoid was the lies from the Serpent's tongue. The devil was trying to divide and separate them, to draw their attention from the reason God gave them life. The Father wanted to see them in the fullness of His sight, committed to their purpose in the way you have envisioned in your dreams. So, being expelled from Paradise was never about dying in ways that are repugnant to the truth, but about disobeying God, straying from His command, and surrendering to a fallen angel who was bargaining for their pride.

My Special son, sin means undoing the grace given to humanity by leaving God behind. He is indeed a jealous Lord. He asks for the undivided attention of those to whom He gave the breath of life. It is said that Adam and Eve had no umbilical scars, but such is not the case. They received them when they severed themselves from God. They were the scars left behind when they descended from His side. And yet, the more intense wounds were inside the Father's Heart, scars that eventually fell on the hands of His Son who died an awful death. Jesus in the Garden asked that the cup might pass Him by, proving Him invaluably Human. His humanity made Him no less divine. Indeed, the Father and all the obedience that pleases Him were glorified by the New Adam in the way the Old Adam had refused. This is why the Father's joy lives in the story of human redemption. It is why Jesus wants to know whether humanity will commit to remaining in the Truth. It is why the Church is asked to suffer in the image of its King. It is the reason children are born with such agony upon their mothers; answering the call about whether fearing childbirth is worth the joy of fulfilling the Father's Will for prospering offspring in the womb. It is all about obedience to Him. Everything required by the Gospel addresses this way of life. All these sacrifices encourage the expectations of Heaven that the world will finally change. When this happens through men and women of faith, Creation begins to move toward reconciliation with its own afterlife. Stenches of arrogance are annulled. Shouts of gladness are heard; sunshine chases out the darkness, and symphonies dry the tears. Crippled children run again; the blind can see their friends; families have new reunions, and empty stomachs are filled. This whole composition of life revolves around obedience to whatever God demands. Abraham was prepared to slay Isaac, and never bat an eye. Obedience, trust and purity, these are the things that matter. My Special son, My words are made possible today because God wants you to know what others have yet to learn. Through Me, He is depositing wisdom in your hands that He is confident you will share with the waiting world of men. Their own disobedience is the origin of their sin."

Saturday, June 1, 2013
1:59 p.m.

"Crumbling beneath its own weight."

"Your Mother is with you, little darlings. The miracle that you have lived goes on. Today begins the month of the Most Sacred Heart to whom you have long been devoted. It is assured that you will embark on a summer filled with joy, a fair amount of consternation, some disappointment, and always accorded to the Will of God so lost sinners can be converted. My purpose today is to remind you that you are blessed. You have vision about the standing of humanity before the Cross. You can discern the distance between the collective consciousness of the world and the spiritual conscience it ought to have. Being open to Truth implies that Truth is welcomed, not just acknowledged. If ever there were a time when two people have been blessed, it is My Special and Chosen sons here in America. I have said this in many places around the world; it is living and breathing in the archives of time. Let us be reminded today about the reasons I have come. First, it is because I am your Mother who loves you. I have promised that if you were the only two souls on Earth, I would still be here, not speaking about how lost humanity is, but how beautiful humanity is. The two of you are so profoundly advanced in your spiritual wisdom and love for Jesus that it defies description. Indeed, I have come because My other children need Me. So, why have I not spoken to them? Because they will not listen to the voice of the Holy Spirit; they have hardened their hearts. I come to you because you are satisfied knowing that Jesus is Lord. This has made you receptive; it has taken you places both inside and outside of Creation where others refuse to go. The content of your hearts and the genuineness of your faith make it so that I can teach the world through My messages about the blessings and gifts that God is dispensing. Never have the issues devouring humanity's joy been because the Father is not making Himself sufficiently apparent. The problem is that lost sinners are ignoring Him, but they grapple with their own reasons why when they hear the story of Mary, the Mother of Jesus, speaking for so long, so prolifically, and so eloquently to two men in the heartland of the United States. Western civilization seems to have no room for this; the United States seems to believe that God has already pronounced favor upon a nation that espouses such freedom and self-individualism. I am saying that I have come to this place because they are wrong. You know the examples that prove what I am saying after the many years that I have spoken to you, and yet for only two decades. I assure you that before all things have come to pass, I will accomplish

My mission. You are too precious; you have given your lives to Me for the conversion of your lost brothers and sisters. Their redemption has been pronounced by Jesus, and it is in this gift that Providence has spoken the strains of enlightenment through the hills and valleys of the Earth. You have served the excellence of this gift. Your lives have become eternal for the reasons I have said. My Special son, I know that you are enjoying My messages dictated since December 2008. Whenever, and if ever at all, you choose to share them is yours to decide. I stand in awe of your humble receptivity. I remind the Angels and Saints often that you stand out in history and in the vastness of Creation as a visionary for the ages; you know the blessings that I have given you. We pray that the whole of humanity will follow your lead, that they will tread the paths of faith that you have cleared. I am filled with admiration for you; the Providence about which I speak today is ensuring the reckoning for which you pray between the wicked world and the Holy Cross. There are billions of lost souls on the line. I have said this to all My visionaries throughout the ages. Being a Marian seer was never supposed to be easy; just watch the suffering to which your brother is often subjected. He does well. He remains loyal to the death for you. He will hear your voice and obey you before he will defer to the Angels. This gives you the power of his discernment, and it is all right with Me. I am saying that you are exemplary of the resounding Wisdom of the Holy Spirit in extraordinary ways. This proves that the world will respond to what I have said here in this home.

Power grows where obedience lives. This is the thesis of My most previous message. It is for those who are willing to reach out, to be strong and vigilant, unique and bold. It is taking the Truth to America in prayer and deed that makes Christians true disciples of the Church. Even as you live in sincere simplicity, you thunder the Gospel across this nation. God is taking it to those who require it; the people who are asleep in sin are awakening with a hangover of regret about the way they have lived. It is to your credit that they are acknowledging what they must do. I can give you no other reason than this that the acres and miles of Illinois and the other states are becoming aware. Your vision is still growing; your obedience remains fruitful. The Church is praying and changing; priests in your diocese are being relocated to suit their better angels; your Bishop continues to read and pray, and the stars and daylight hours dance around you with fire and celebration. Your life here with your brother need not always be about what will eventually come, but what has already happened. The two of you have captured more blessings for the world than can be counted on a million hands. Even if the Son of Man would return today, all that you have given is sufficient grace to bring enlightenment to every last soul.

As I have said time and again, the rest is up to them. Indeed, it is not always about what will come; it is about your confidence that you have won battles too numerous to count in a war whose final victory belongs to the Father. I ask you and your brother to live the dignity that is yours. You are colleagues of the Saints in two separate realms. I hail your names when I speak with them. They beg to be reminded what more they can do from their stately places in Heaven. These are intensely meaningful years for you and the Church, and this is what makes Me weep with happiness. It is the reason I have come today. It allies My response with the many who have always venerated Me. I only ask that you remember these things. And, remember everything for which, and everyone for whom, I have asked you to pray. The Father is listening. You have seen that He has already effected changes in people's lives in advance of the prayers piercing His ears. We have unending joy in this, My Special son; we have everything inside and outside of Creation that reminds us that the Triumph of My Immaculate Heart is unfolding. The world would not be such a wreck if this were untrue. Evildoers, despots, wrongdoers and devil-worshipers know that they are in their last days. Satan himself continues to lie; he tells them that conditions are in their favor. The devil's whole empire is crumbling beneath its own weight, and still he remains in denial. He tells his evil legions that they are on their way to victory – but look, he even believes his own lies! The Blood of the Cross has annihilated anything permanent that Satan might inflict on the Mystical Body of Jesus – even death itself. Humanity will suffer; the good may be saddened and despised, but those who live by the Gospel will prevail.

So, you see a world saturated by its own indifference. There are murders and desecrations every day. Those who decline to live prayerfully are killed in accidents and tragedies of all kinds. This has been the way of the world for thousands of years. You and I and your brother care not about the inevitability of whatever may come. A world seamlessly united to the Kingdom of God would know not of the darkening of the heart anymore. I am simply pleading with My children to believe in the reasons I am joyful. Know that grace and peace have overcome tyranny and sorrow. All attention is on every new moment in history. This is true because all moments are overlaid onto the beatific consciousness that every Christian owns. You are not spinning your wheels. Your arrows are still arching into the skies, reaching their apex, and descending like lightning strikes upon the enemies of human salvation. Your hopes mean something to God. The Cross will always be glorious to Him. These are the elements of life that change the future, of an existence on Earth that is superseded by an eternity in Paradise. My words to you and your brother, millions of them, are yet finite here, but they prescribe and give way to an indescribable joy that calls infinity its home. We shall at long last see each other face-to-face and heart-to-heart in Heaven the way you see other people in your life today. This is as sure as you hear the airship hovering above you now. *(A helicopter was flying over the house as we prayed. It was making a huge noise to the point of almost being distracting.)* I only ask, My Special and Chosen ones, that you do not live out your lives believing that your greatest days have come and gone. They will flourish intensely through the weeks, months and years. You have discovered that the miracle of a lifetime can arrive at any hour. All around the globe, there are people pondering the value of human life, the purpose of being here, the distance of far-off universes, the goal to be reached when an anatomical heart takes its rest. Jesus is that purpose. He has vindicated the need for prayer. His Blood has granted pardon for everything conceivably wrong except rejecting Him. He has mitigated every ill act, thought, role and purpose that humanity has ever forged into being. This is the power of the Cross. It is powerful because it is the ultimate act of obedience. As I told you, the Heart of the Father does not hurt so much anymore. His pain has been transferred to Jesus. The lights above the spires of human morality are powered by the Sacrifice of One Good Man, born with distinction in the eyes of God, but without fanfare in the exiled world. And, My Special son, when you see life from the other side of time; when all the world has the opportunity to look back on itself from eternity unchallenged, then you will know that all Christians, all the Saints, all the Angels, and everyone who believed in simple faith gave the Child Jesus dignity upon His birth. You were all there with Me. Even those yet to be born hundreds and 2,000 years later were there in the mind and Heart of God. Providence united us all the same way we will be joined on the final day of the world. We will understand everything that only the Father knows now. I will wave My handkerchief to you as you ride past in your Chariot. I will be holding the Little King whom you will see again in His transfigured brilliance when your carrier arrives at the portico of Heaven. You will sense the feeling of anticipation, knowing that everything you have ever done and believed will be validated before Creation and all that is unseen. So, where is there room for sadness in all this? Why all the anxiety of people here and in lands far and wide? Why the rush for possessions and pride? And, when that hour comes, you will hear peace like it is above you right now. *(The helicopter overhead had flown past, and it was a quiet, tranquil moment).* You will go with Jesus and see the Father face-to-face. You will hear orchestras playing commencement songs. You will walk past what seems like statues of legends and heroes who will come alive the moment you recognize who they are. They have held their stately poise like sentinels, waiting for the hour when the Saints from Earth arrive in Heaven to tip their caps and rejoice that the Church has become one. Jubilation will flood the palaces like waterfalls; and before this grand scene, the whole of God's intentions will be fully revealed. Evil will be vanquished and forever forgotten. Love will remain, and only love will remain. Therefore, My Special son, I owe you the world for giving Me the venue to say these things so mortal ears can hear them. I have many more strains of verse and poetry to lay out before the King of kings returns. I beg you and your brother to live in peace and confidence that Jesus knows what your dedication means."

Sunday, June 9, 2013
9:13 a.m.

"Jesus lived fully, spoke kindly, loved deeply and fought mightily."

"We give devotedly of ourselves so that lost men can be found, hungered millions will be fed, the unsheltered quartered, and heavenly thoughts can be nourished and shared. My dear little sons, this is the credo that has ensured the trust of the Church throughout the ages. I know that you believe it with Me, that you are aware of the universal purpose that you have lived alongside your exiled brothers and sisters. I began My message this morning with a passage about Jesus as He laid down His life for the Salvation of the world. The most important part is that even though He was only 33 years old, He lived fully. What does this mean? Surely it is not confined to a simple breadth of years. Surely longevity is no presumption of someone's righteousness. Given one day on the Earth, a living creature can suffice the definition of grace in a single moment. Jesus brought more than tenure to the Church. He gave it dignity, majesty and love. He gave to humanity more than His own Divine Humanity. He dispensed to all believers the authority to demand holiness from the world of nations. It is therefore wrong to believe that speaking to a person admonishingly is somehow unkind. I have given messages through the ages about being bold in the face of indifference. Humanity can be reproved by God while God is still smiling. Those who stray from righteousness can be corrected by Christians who retain their admiration for those they correct. Things are not always as they seem to those being persuaded, gently or otherwise, to accept the Cross and propagate the mission of the Church. Please allow Me to describe it this way. My Special son, you are aware of the art of lip reading. If someone is in sight of another person and cannot audibly hear what that person is saying, they can often read their lips to detect what is being said. Many people are well trained in this art. What most people do not know, however, is that if a person is speaking a foreign language, the lip reader can inadvertently translate their words into other meanings. There are only so many ways that someone's lips can move. This has happened many times. It is like transcribing a language into another language with a different meaning. Do you understand? *"Yes."* I ask you to remember this metaphor because it is indicative of what humanity is doing with God. They refuse to move close enough to hear His voice, so they appropriate meanings that are wrong. This is the same way that some people misinterpret the Sacred Scriptures. They reject My miraculous intercession for the same reason. As I have said, the Lord does not amend the Gospel or the pathway to Salvation by dispatching Me here. He does not infer anything different about the Traditions of the Church by what the Angels say. Heaven does not repeal any mandates spoken by the Son of Man just because humanity believes they should be. There is no such thing as an evolution of the Church from the Immutable Truth that has kept the world aright for 2,000 years. The term 'liberal' may mean 'free' in ancient tongues, but this is not the kind of freedom that most modern liberals want. God defines liberal as the freedom to stay the course, live rightfully the teachings of the Gospel, speak clearly to those who must change, and fight mightily for the conversion of lost sinners. Along with these things, I wish to impart to you the knowledge of My overwhelming joy. I see the faces of converted humanity breaking past the dawn of each new day. I see the innocence and honesty. I see the piety and spiritual infinitude. I realize the potential of every man, women and child to stand for something holy, to reach for goals that will reveal to the Father that they are moving toward Him.

It is true that ultimate power can yield to lesser powers with the intention of allowing those lesser powers to come of age. This is what Jesus did during His earthly ministry. He asked pointed questions of those around Him while already knowing the answers. He wanted people to engage the ritual of human life and exchange the miracle of holiness. This was a gift from His humanness; it laid the foundation for Christians to be more like Him. It was their means of knowing themselves, and it is still happening to this day. During the periods between My messages, for example, Jesus waits for hearers to respond. This is part of the growing enlightenment by which the world is being changed, by which hearts are cultivated, and through which evil is being expunged from human affairs. I hear the call of the poor to be relieved of their poverty, and miracles are wrought from their petitions. The Father waits for the response of those who hold the Earth's wealth between miraculous events. This is part of His patience; it is a product of His endless love. It is about dispensing His Son's Divine Mercy based on the repentance of sinners. As you know, this is not a perpetual state; there will come a time when the Son of Man says that all who will hear have heard. He will judge in favor of the righteous, and do it swiftly. He will draw a line in the sand and dare anyone who denies Him to cross it. Mercy is still being heaped upon this world to inexplicable degrees. This is the infinite compassion of Jesus for His disciples. My dear sons, I do not have a lengthy message for you today because this is sometimes what I do. I ask you to proceed through your days with peace in your hearts in knowing that My plan is on course. This is the origin of the joy that I hold in My Immaculate Heart every time we speak. I ask you to place your vision through My eyes and see the admiration that I have for those who belong to Me. Imagine how much I appreciate those who yield to their lesser fellows for the good of the Church. Meditate on what I have said today, what I know about you, the new beginning you have inherited from Jesus on the Cross, how you have responded obediently, and the fruits of all these things now in the hands of your Bishop, the fruits that you will share with the world. I am grateful that you have taken to heart the request of Jesus to remain strong, that you have done so with courage, with smiles on your faces and hope in your hearts. I am the Mother who came to you years ago and watched you threading crayons into the pagoda on your grandfather's desk. I have witnessed the transition of papacies for hundreds of years. I have watched in awe as millions of Christians around the world have dedicated their lives in service to their faith. I have wept with gratitude that you have remained loyal to Me. Please remember how I see the world. It is not that I am unaware of the evil that strikes, I am highly aware of the righteousness that destroys it. I speak at times about the Eminent Eternal Ages, and perhaps they are difficult for men to understand. It is imperative that everyone remember that eternity has already begun, but those still in exile cannot yet see it. They cannot overcome the stresses and patterns of everyday life to realize that each day has a new beginning. Every moment, every hour is another opportunity to hear Jesus, not by reading His lips from a distance, but coming close to Him through His Sorrowful Crucifixion to make His Wisdom their own."

Saturday, June 15, 2013
10:07 a.m.

TimoTHY WILLiam

"Yours will be the last song to leave this world."

"With intense love and admiration, I bring the Grace of God to you. I seek from you the acknowledgment that you are aware of your goodness. My little sons, many have been the generations that I have sought children of the Father who would stay the course like you, but you are the only two in modern times who have remained in allegiance as holy brothers. This remarkable union shared by you and the Lord was fashioned from the foundation of the world. It is in your own ascension to divine understanding that you should embrace the glory within you. This is no reason to feel superior; it is simply the means by which you are living for the Gospel. You are hailing God in all Three Persons to come to you, to awaken sleeping humanity, to go where the Supreme Deity is welcomed, and to cultivate His Divine Kingdom through the continents and ages. Each of My visionaries is given melodies that befit their talents. Everyone plays a part. This is how I have seen you, My Special son, in accompaniment with your brother, raising the strains of I AM for the whole world to hear. The Saints of bygone ages were given their own strains to raise. Two-by-two and in multiple throngs they traveled the miles of this nation and the next, telling the Good News of Salvation in Jesus. They performed precisely as they were summoned. Their renditions of redemption were pretty; their lives were lovely, their faith was indelible. Here, you now see that you are offering your own songs and melodies of human love and Divine Truth communed. Even as the Saints of old have passed into history, beyond the sight of the exiled world, most have taken their works of genius with them. Why? Because the sinners of Earth would not listen to them; millions still refuse to hear. I daresay, however, that the brilliance of your artworks and the glory with which you are adorning the Earth shall never die. It cannot fail. Your faith and love are as perpetual as the Gospel herald itself. You have laid your messages on the altar of human life, and this message will be spread before the ages. Yours will be the last song to leave this world. You already know it; you have felt it for decades. I give you My beatific promise that no human soul living on Earth or suffering in Purgatory will enter Heaven without reading or hearing every syllable I have given you and your brother here in Springfield, Illinois. The Great Emancipator would have it no other way. This is the begetting of your awesome joy and your satisfaction for the legacy of your lives. I give you My sacred oath that you will someday stand before Creation-redeemed and hear the words from the King of kings that you bow to no one. Thank you for your service to the Church, for your long-suffering and life-giving faith. Thank you for being who you are, undivided from your Savior, unseparated from the Glory that has taken you in. Today, I am here in the ides of June to say that many markings are being left by the faithful, by the Church, that will suffer but never know defeat. It is exhilarating as the Mother of God to know that the focus of human ingenuity is being placed on the Gospel message; the emphasis of realistic genius is toward the conversion of the wicked. Even as they are converted, they must act. It will not be enough for them to simply awaken; they must rise and go. They must take to the streets and reverse their error. They must be interrupted in their journeys to Damascus and far-flung cities too. They must reorient their identity to absolve those who have persecuted them before that persecution even occurs.

I ask, My Special one, that you and your brother remember that the Church now stands at the ready. There is imminence in every prophecy ever told. There is anticipation and a march toward the extinction of everything counterintuitive to the fairness of spiritual life. The Man of Flesh has left His mark on this place; the human body need not be a detractor from the refinement of the soul. We here on Earth during this mid-June Saturday have come to understand that everything pious and glorious is always new; and there is ironically nothing new in that. We have also come to know as Mother and children that the likeness that Jesus seeks in other men of His image must take hold during these key moments in history. Mortality is calling, but I am summoning My children to disregard its effects. Live your life, My Special son, as though you would live a thousand more years, but nurture the expectation that you might see the Son of Man tomorrow. This is the progress about which the Scientist should sing. Science and progress; one need not counteract the other, progress in all things righteous can complement the miracle of science. (*Our Lady was affectionately alluding to a song that I was playing recently, 'The Scientist' by Coldplay.*) When people reach into their hearts and memories and say, '...Take us back there, Lord...,' they are speaking to the restoration of their lost innocence. They speak of days when they felt like running through the fields and frolicking in the meadows' tall grass. They yearn for quiet times when they can hear the softness of the rains that I brought with Me here today. They strive for the eloquence that will allow them to describe how the flowers' petals feel freshened from the watery blessings from above. This is newness and 'knowness,' it is movement in the direction of Heaven as Paradise comes to Earth. What practicality can live in the ethereal realms! It is not wrong to be pragmatic about the verses of faith.

It builds and grows like the rains falling in full. It makes the Earth applaud, it causes God to declare that His love for men must be heard. It resounds from beyond and gives reason for men to have hope. There is nothing impractical in this. It reaches into the depths of humanity and recedes again; divinity in the human heart is a constant source of comfort that ebbs and flows, massaging the soul in ways that cannot be undone. So, I am here with you and your brother and all the world today. I see the decisions and actions of mortal men that will change their lives, but rarely conform to the standards of history imbedded. We are not only making history by our service to God, we are supplanting history with a new way of being. We are generous with the Lord's blessings that come through our hands as well. I ask you and your brother to be comforted in everything I have said here today. Think about the fibers of human life. Know that what is upright was put there by God to perpetuate His Kingdom, to conquer evil, to carry-on the fight for true goodness. Men should especially remember that the God who is now unseen will one day be seen, and He can also be touched. He is touched by those who trust and believe in Him. His Kingdom is multiplied by those who take joy in His commands."

Saturday, June 22, 2013
9:39 a.m.

"The Beatific Fulcrum"

"My little sons, wellness, goodness and mercy are emitted from your hearts into your brothers and sisters' lives when you pray for them. We have within our power the ability to amend their lot, to lift up those who feel oppressed by their mortality, and give to the poor a new hope that can come from nowhere but Jesus. Thank you for your perseverance during these difficult days for your nation and societies in turbulence. My Special son, I mention today the beatific fulcrum that I addressed to you in another message dated September 12, 1991. You know what this means; it is illustrative of the veil between Heaven and Earth. It is a way to describe the relationship between the physical world and the spiritual realms. I would like to discuss this fulcrum again today in the context of the ever-changing events and proceedings in private lives and on the intercontinental stage. It is clear that you and your brother understand this fulcrum because you have written about it many times. It is the bridge across which humanity travels when gaining knowledge about their relationship with God. What I have not made clear to you, however, is that the fulcrum is movable. It is mobile; it can be relocated by the prayers of the Church and the response of the Father. I was making the point on September 12, 1991 that the power of the Cross is far greater than the weight of human sins. This will always be true. You highlighted the distinction of the veil and the fulcrum when you included the picture about the shape of the Cross in Heaven and the shape of the Cross here in this world. Do you remember? *"Yes."* The veil is not unlike the fulcrum where prayers are received in Heaven and answers dispensed from God through the intercession of Jesus and the power of the Holy Spirit. The veil between Heaven and Earth when seen in the context of a fulcrum can be moved as if someone is placing their face closer to a mirror. It is as though the Lord is looking from On High more carefully by leaning down and placing His sacred face just above the clouds, much like the sun descended to the Earth at Fatima in 1917. This is not an exaggeration; it is the motion of God into these realms preceding the return of Jesus in Glory. Now, if you think in terms of relocating the fulcrum that I have mentioned, you must also think of humanity moving closer to the veil, and even permeating the veil, without passing through to the other side into the realms of eternity. I have done this today; you cannot see My body, but you can hear My voice. I am present in the world, and also with the Most Blessed Trinity in Heaven. I can see God the Father who has yet to be seen by any exiled man. I can see Jesus and all the Saints who have the same spirit with which they were born on Earth. The movement of the fulcrum, therefore, is about sharing the information I just told you. The fulcrum is moved by the mission of the Church, during the dispensation of the Sacraments, when beatific lights shine from inexplicable origins, and when people sing supernal songs. Think about the song titled, 'I am, I said.' It is as though Jesus is telling Heaven what He told humanity on the Earth. When the Hosts of Heaven inquire what Jesus said to lost sinners, His reply is, 'I am, I said." This is the true origin of your brother's recognition of this beautiful song. He feels in his heart that the fulcrum upon which his perception of Heaven exists has moved. His idea of the sublime attributes of human life are clarified. His senses can better discern the presence of the Afterlife. You have felt this many times too; it is the origin of your melody about the willow tree. One of the most prolific moments of the relocation of the beatific fulcrum is when the Angels helped you write your poem titled 'The Final Colossus.' Hence, you are gaining a clearer sense of what I mean when I say that the fulcrum is moved and the veil becomes thinner. I have told you this today to place a backdrop behind My messages here and around the world, the ones that you know about from other seers and hearers. The purpose of these messages is to embolden the Church to strike out harder against sin, to turn back its enemies by engaging God's intervention, and to gain strength in summoning the intercession of the Church Triumphant. If men can move mountains, they can surely move the beatific fulcrum connecting Heaven and Earth. The entire destiny of the world hangs in the balance. As you know, you have come to the 21st century, and this is the tipping point that will determine the fate of billions of sinners. Every day that you and your brother have prayed with Me during the past 22 years, tens of thousands of Poor Souls in Purgatory have gained entry into Heaven – every time, and that is a lot of days. This is what the Lord does; it is the reason Jesus came to the Earth from the beginning. God said that He wished to superintend the transfer of His people from this exile back into Paradise. Jesus' birth, life, Crucifixion and Paschal Resurrection have committed humanity to this providential process.

What I am saying is that humanity on Earth has power. It is all about the empowerment of the human spirit to effect the changes in this land that Jesus calls for in the Gospel. It is the Church's reluctance to recognize this power that has caused its perception of weakness. The idea of turning the other cheek does not mean that someone should not strike back, it means granting mercy to the ignorant until they inherit divine wisdom, and then rebuking those who gain it and reject it. Inviting you to turn the other cheek allows time for this transition. Do you understand? *"Yes."* The whole concept of human redemption is based on this same mercy, the Divine Mercy, to which all Christians should subscribe and to whom Jesus gives His fullest measure. Do you know the greatest moment of the relocation of the beatific fulcrum in the history of the world? It was not the Crucifixion alone, but the entire New Covenant, beginning with the Annunciation of the Archangel Gabriel. *"I understand."* With this New Promise, God not only took the world in His hands and held it within inches of His Heart, He literally placed Himself here. Why would He come to Earth as His own Son? Because there is no other God. And, how could this God be confined to a physical body on a globe with weights and measures? It is divine logic that He came to Earth as Christ Jesus, His voice and His progeny, to manifest the fulfillment of the Old Covenant through Him. The Father turned it over to Jesus and His Apostles and disciples. He came to Me, the Immaculate Virgin, through an Archangel with the request of conceiving in My Womb eternal life for all who believe. My little son, humanity needs to see this as more of a miracle than they do. When I carried the Son of God in My Womb, He was prescribing everything that would be written in the Bible. He pondered every word I would say to you today. The story began when I said 'Yes,' and it was finished on the Cross. Even though the principal character was crucified during the course, He was raised again; the crisis was reframed but not averted, and the world of men was saved. Jesus died on the Cross. When He did so, He said, 'I love you Billy and Timmy – I love you John and Cindy and Paul and Rebecca'

– and so on, down to the very last soul whom the Lord has placed in your midst. Without human contrition, without those who first believed in the Messiah, the beatific fulcrum would have been permanently placed where Jesus left it on the day He died. It has been moved as His Sacred Heart has been moved. It has been shaken by mortal tragedies and strengthened by human triumph. This is the Heart of the Man. This is the way Galilee would remember their hero. You and your brother have inherited His character. You have seen through His eyes the desperation of long-suffering men. You have witnessed the challenges faced by those who fought for Him, and those who have fought against Him. We realize what this means for a world in peril. We know how the future will be told. All in all, the victory will be worth the fight. This is the reason your brother does not fall into despondence about the way he is mistreated by those who despise him. He refuses to place the blame on people who have assailed him because he does not want them to be stained with guilt. He remembers the Man-God who took all culpability upon Himself so that others could be absolved."

Saturday, June 29, 2013
12:46 p.m.

"Love God, and He will love you back."

"In the Name of the Father, and the Son, and the Holy Spirit. Amen. My darling children, we pray for lost sinners and those who are suffering. We pray for the broken and afraid, and we ask the Lord to bring peace to foreign lands. I am with you during your exile, where your torment can be blamed on people allowing Satan to rule their lives. There will be time to explain the inexplicable when our prayers have sufficed all your needs. Today, I come with the peace of the Holy Spirit in My Immaculate Heart to give you wisdom about life. You are more holy than you believe, and you are making greater progress than you realize. You know that I am a protective Mother, and that I pray for the conversion of the wicked. It is said that when some things go wrong, it is often the effect of good people making bad choices. While this may be true, making bad choices is also indicative of a lot of misbehaved, misguided and misinformed people. If one acts according to what he believes about the world, this is how he will be judged. The parable of the vineyard worker arriving later in the day than his counterpart, and then being compensated an equal amount, does not say that there are not other consequences for being delinquent. You know that I am not asking My children to become perfect overnight, but I wish for them to change in a reasonable time. Waiting until the last moment is no virtue, and demanding holiness from others is no vice. It is virtuous to awaken from the slumber of the exiled world sooner rather than later because so much can be accomplished in a converted life. I have every reason to believe that these virtues are growing wider around the world, else I would not be speaking to so many visionaries. I am pleased that the prayers of the faithful have the endorsement of the Father, even as His Will is done to purge the world of evil and sanctify the indifferent among you. My Special son, I pray for everyone who has been called to accomplish certain goals at the behest of the Holy Spirit. Jesus is elated when priests administer the Sacraments. He is filled with joy watching you write your memoir, reciting your prayers, relaxing at home and enjoying your days. The Father approves your graces given to the world by all you have embraced as His holy works. This has been a wonderful springtime for you and your brother. It has given you weeks to survey the blessings you have received. It has shed light on the condition of the Church. These are the hours, days, weeks and months upon which you will look back and say that you have truly lived in peace. I only ask that you remember to exercise and rest. Do not fall to the temptation to be cynical; have more hope than that. When I speak of peace, I am referring to peace that cannot be given by the world. It is the kind of peace that comes from God. It comes from the inspiration of a life borne in a heart that belongs to Him. This is the reason your brother's sister called him on the telephone yesterday. She has survived her horrific automobile crash, and that gift is now being shared through the Fruits of the Holy Spirit. She wanted to talk to your brother to be closer to God; it was a blessed overture on her part. It is all about reaching out, I have said this many times before. Jesus wants His disciples to reach out to Him in the Most Blessed Sacrament to communicate the needs of the Church. As you see in My second day of the month Medjugorje messages, I clearly state that the Church's priorities must center on the purification of the self. It is within you at all times, that you have the knowledge to understand what humanity must do. My little sons, I will speak at great length in the future about My wishes for humanity and the steps that must be taken to respond to the Lord's warnings about to befall the wicked of this world. As you see in My June 25, 2013 Medjugorje message, I come to humanity in joy. I have said this many times. I have joy because, no matter what happens on the Earth or through the annals of time, Jesus' Resurrection has won the peace that I am asking the world to accept. Approach adversity with a calm demeanor. Think about this peace. I am asking you to be even more like Jesus. You have extolled His righteousness; you have embraced His confidence, and I ask that you have a peaceful spirit in the way of His Most Sacred Heart."

Sunday, July 7, 2013
9:23 a.m.

"This excelling pursuit."

"Where you are, My children, so am I. I wish you peace and good wishes on this beautiful summer day. It harkens to the olden days when I would speak prolifically with your predecessors, when they would ask Me with emphasis what might happen tomorrow. I told them, generations and centuries ago, that their lives would benefit the lives of those in future times, for you yourselves, and that upon you would fall the burden of praying nigher to the conclusion of the exiled world. Here, I have come to keep that promise that I made to your forefathers. I have come seeking your petitions and invocations so that Jesus will be more merciful than humanity expects. This is My excelling pursuit, little sons. I have during years more difficult than these watched the Earth unravel and be stitched back together again. I have seen the Son of Man place His sacred palms around the globe as if to massage its pain away. I have stood beside Him in awesome wonder as if unable to take-in everything He would ultimately achieve. Those ages are not gone; they live on in you. Everything that magnifies the freedom of faith and trueness of the heart is being spread around the world in your beatific prayers. You have already seen what the Catholic Church is capable of doing. Satan cannot destroy it. He uses force, but has no effective power. Preparing for the warnings of God does not imply multifaceted change for those who trust in Him. However, He summons those who are uncertain of their faith to become unequivocal in it. The Father of Truth is still dealing death to the father of lies. These are among the reasons that I still speak to My seers around the globe. No number of miscalculated acts by sinful men can reverse the tides of goodness that are imminent here. Anyone who scolds, attacks, opposes or impugns the Roman Catholic Church will be defeated. Indeed, not one, but two Popes will soon be canonized Saints on the same day, John Paul the Great and John XXIII, and the Lord would have it no other way. It is bound in Heaven as it is bound on Earth. Acknowledging this ascension of human obedience is the beginning of the end of the Earth, not the end of its beginning. My Special son, I am grateful for your heart; you always hear Me well. I yearn for the kindness that you offer the Mother of the Lord as much as I savor God's wisdom itself. You are providential in ways that you do not even know. You are like the New Adam; you are His brother and consoler, you are true and beautiful in the way of the silver streams of Paradise. Your blood flows as majestically; your speech resounds as gloriously. Your trust in God is as triumphant as My Most Immaculate Heart. I wish humanity would embrace the Will of the Father in the way of you and your brother. Jesus came to Earth as the New Covenant, and this is a sacred proposition to which all in the world should respond. You have seen the destruction from the will of men when they act in ways not aligned with the truth of God. Jesus says to His people, 'I am waiting here for you. Come to Me. Let Me love you. Let Me lift you up into the highest realms of My Shining Glory!' Jesus feeds His disciples eternal knowledge that they would never in forty thousand ages learn on their own. He reaches for the lost and pitiable. He holds love in His holy palms for them. And, as He feeds the good on Earth this wisdom with full compassion, He turns away from those who spurn Him. You have seen that My Son does not beg lost sinners to accept the Cross. He invites them to come to Him, but He does not force them to do so. He does not demand them to violate their will to become holy, but He commends them to a pious life. This is the righteousness seeping inside the human heart to nourish the seed of faith that the Holy Spirit has planted there. Yes, Jesus says that He wants their friendship, but He will not steal their hearts to get it.

Soon, there will be signs and wonders, births and casualties, movements and destruction, and light to cast out the darkness. It is clear that these things are subject to prayer; they are not written in stone. You have said that you were raised in America during a more benign time, an innocent and simple time. This is true, but you have likewise witnessed that humanity has fashioned even more distractions that have lured them away from the Church, away from the teachings and traditions of the Apostolic Faith. Do you remember My declaration that the further lost sinners stray, the greater the impact of miracles? *"Yes."* Here, I have prepared you for the future to come. I have said that your books will prosper in your day, here on Earth, even as you are still in mortal flesh, making the case for God. I do not wish to be ambiguous, but you should not expect much applause for what you are accomplishing for Jesus. *"I don't. Most people are going to be enraged."* It is not relevant whether the impact of your books occurs during your mortal lifetime or thereafter. However, I expect that you will still be walking the Earth when that great enlightenment comes. I am saying that Jesus' measures of Mercy are amended by the prayers of men. The more people who pray for the coming of His Kingdom, the more actions are manifested by those who convert. This is one of the reasons why Jesus has not returned heretofore. I am trying to allay the world's concern that Jesus is taking too long. I am telling Him; indeed I am urging and pleading with Him, to waive the sentence of time and bring the exile of men to a close. Yes, as if to say that it is time to make Saints of those who accept the Cross, and cast the remainder into the netherworld. You must surely be surprised to hear this. *"Not at all. I understand how much you love us."* I am praying for miracles from God as much as you and your brother. Even as I am the Immaculate Queen, I feel a sense of holy urgency that I rarely mention to My visionaries and locutionists. It is about the warnings that the Father asks Me to declare. I have said that these warnings need not take the form of chastisements, but they will certainly involve castigations. This is not the kind of power that the Father prefers to wield, but He will not breach the will of men to save them. He will not descend with fiery brands and conscript those whom He desires to live in Heaven. He marks souls as His own when they come to the Sacraments and offer their lives to Jesus. He asks for perseverance during ominous times for the Church – this is the true rewarding path. These spiritual gifts should amend the conduct of the wicked, and they do so when performed in the name of God. Give Jesus the glory by committing to His Gospel, extrapolated into the created realms by a faith so genuine that it cannot be repealed. There are miracles in all things holy. When people pray, the script of mortal life is rewritten, and the final act of the world is changed. This is what I have said to My messengers for 2,000 years; thank God it is true! *"Thank you."* I will help you discern the future so you will know how to fashion your prayers. The Lord is preparing for your work to bear sweet yields and bountiful fruit."

Saturday, July 13, 2013
2:32 p.m.

"The New and Everlasting Covenant."

"My dear little sons, I am so elated today that I can scarcely contain My joy. You are praying to Jesus with fervor, and imploring Creation to respond to Him. You evoke the prayers of the Angels and elicit the intercession of the Doctors of the Church. Remember the patience to which you are summoned. Hope as non-seers hope, and do not worry. You are living in the age of the New Covenant that cannot be destroyed. Look and see what I am saying. Look at the vastness of the hearts of men. Resound with your voices the gracious energies that are remaking the face of the Earth. What must be done is happening. You have spoken about editors that lie and doubters that persecute. You have seen with permeating perspective the capacity of Jesus to reprimand those who deny Him. Here and hereafter, you are enlisted in this grand purpose. You show it in your faces; your instincts are lent to this truth. You arise and stand forward to be counted. You are slain in the Holy Spirit. You have inherited a veritable fortune of blessings and wonders. Is this what suffering is for? Do these things fill the vacuum where human doubt previously prevailed? Has the world sprung a leak in its own ability to question? I say to you again that the Lord is not a God of vengeance solely for the sake of retribution. Truly, you are more like Jesus than you know. You have identical attributes to His earliest disciples and apostles. You have been created only a little lower than the Angels. You have been born in the eloquent Wisdom in whose voice you speak to the world. Your thoughts are implanted in the mind of the Father. Your learnings are being transmitted to the leaders of your faith. Your hearts are sources of fullness; you are opening wide a berth through which the Church walks confident in the presence of its King. And, even in all this, you remain simple. You espouse the gentleness of the Lamb of Love, and you know why righteousness follows your path. Indeed, I come to you in celebration today! I only ask that you believe Me. It is not something you can see with your eyes or track its signature by the hour. Does the date July 8, 2013 tell you anything? It was a day of signs for the future to come. I pray for these signs and blessings to visit this home and touch your lives, as you are worthy of the gifts from God. My Special son, I must tell you about the things I see. They are more than something that can be seen with the eyes, so I ask that you invoke your own imaginings too. I speak about your holiness and aspirations both inside and outside of this world. You stir the Lord to forgive those who have trespassed against Him. You invite His Son's Passion to touch those who have betrayed Him. It is all about the Will of the Father; you are blazing trails and clearing paths down which all who must come will travel. They are behind you now in the shadow of the years. They are calling from Purgatory; others are only now reaching the age of reason. They are being awakened and converted, upended, informed, transformed and welcomed. I see gladness that harkens to those times about which you speak from 35 years ago. Never mind what your bodies may do; keep them as healthy as you can, but do not worry what the passing of the flesh may bring. I see your souls shining in the freedom of the Cross and the light of the Paschal Resurrection.

Life is not only about walking forward to your destiny in Heaven, it is about being carried by the blessings that have brought you thus far. This is not laurel-speech, it is a means by which you can prepare for the overwhelming celebration in the offing. I see imaginings of you and your brother standing at the Chandler Cenotaph, just as I have said. Do you remember all these things? *"Yes."* They were not vague stories about what might have come, they were promises handed down from the Throne of God. Please do not wait for the accolades of your peers or the approbation of the Archangels to feel inside that you have accomplished a great miracle for the Roman Catholic Church, for Jesus its Head, for the Holy Paraclete its inspiration, and for the Most Blessed Trinity its Deity. Do not hold out your joy just because you and your brother seem secluded here as unknown visionaries of the Gospel. You are not holed-up alone! You are in the presence of the ages and the emeriti who have been watching your words and works from vaults not even seen. These are the imaginings that I cherish in My Immaculate Heart because they have become realized in My sight and are imminent in yours. The Mother of Jesus Christ does not make false promises! I ask you to recognize that living in exile can present itself as an illusion of futility. I have said that the sins of other men make it seem this way. But in truth, you are poised with grace and vested with new dignity. Time is not your enemy, and neither is aging. The entire process of transferring this world into the realms of the Lord is dependent upon the prayers of the faithful. I have made this clear at every shrine I have ever commissioned. I have done everything in My power to direct My children to pray there. If humanity will not come to the spring, the spring will come to humanity, grandly splashing and abundantly overflowing. The Earth and Nature will place My messages in the heralded news, if not by beatific strains, by conflict, toil and turbulence. Christians lead lives provided for by the Gospel. It is all in there; all the numbing pain and sorrow, all the needy parables, all the crying and laughing, the rude extractions and gnashing of teeth, the sacrifices, the holocausts, and the miracles. Yes, I am in there too. Everything the world requires to be awakened from its slumber of a million dark and broken ages is written for the righteous and unrighteous to absorb. This is the thesis of My intercession from which My messages flow. My Special son, the most often asked question from My seers is, '...How come you are so happy all the time?' My response is always the same. It is because I already know what My visionaries will discover. I know what you and your brother will see, hear and experience. I admire you for anticipating the joy that you will soon have and hold. It may not be next week or a year from now, but it will come anyway. Your elation will reflect every hope ever known to man. It will place in the annals of history a new generation of peace that can never be deposed. And, why are others not preparing for it now? Because they are being distracted by the world at the same time that their hearts are calling them into the service of God. Everyone who will go to Heaven strives to work for the light of His love in this life. The human consciousness often clouds this awareness. Do you remember the passage that says it is not imperative for men to take wives? This passage is based on the fact that men, and women too, know in their hearts that their first calling is to find Jesus in their day. So now, I commend you to the joy that is to come. I ask you to respond to the Father's voice, that you and your brother will remain in peace as you have for so many years. His New Covenant has kept you apprised – His love has made you whole. The victory of the Church will been won, and justice is near at hand. I ask you and your brother to embrace this vision, and to accept what I have told you about the imaginings that I have shared with you today."

Saturday, July 20, 2013
1:02 p.m.

"It is one thing to be sightless, but quite another to be clueless."

- The Dominion Angels

"Despite the dereliction of most of the world to heed the call of the Holy Spirit, you My little sons, are with Me to hear what the heavens have to say. Yes, there is coming a reckoning from God that precedes the Final Judgement, and it is in the former that wayward sinners will find themselves. I speak today of a new life espoused by the Holy Scriptures, the Commandments and exhortations, and the summons into the service of the poor. My Special son, you see at the opening of this message the statement issued by the Angels to your brother and passed on to you. There is wisdom in this proclamation. No one on Earth has seen the Father, but many know beyond any doubt that He is there. I wish to continue My discussion today about the ways in which My children are commissioned, sent out and dispatched across the lands to personify the glorious sacrifices and Sorrowful Crucifixion of Jesus, and teach the ignorant about their responsibilities to the Church. First, I wish to say that it is not that the Lord is indifferent to such atrocities as abortion, He is commanding those who hear His Sacred Word to end it. This is the way humanity will reshape its identity into the image and likeness of Jesus, and the manifestations that appear to be evil or display the attributes of evil will be conquered. All human suffering has been more an enlightenment and preparation than a punishment or lack of compassion. No one can dispute the erratic nature of the assaults against humanity's dignity and character, but these tend toward the gradual reconfiguration of the Earth and the conversion of lost sinners. Even in your own trials and difficulties, you have exercised faith because there is tremendous love in you. Hence, when the Dominion Angels speak about vision; when they say that someone is sightless, they are not implying that people cannot understand the spiritual dynamic of human purification and redemption. And too, without experiencing the tragedies of life; without knowing that sinners commit such evil acts as abortion and other murders, humanity would be clueless about how immoral the exiled world has become. This is likened to the concept that there are venial sins and mortal sins, even as all sins are evil. There is a principle that applies to righteousness and unrighteousness. All men are caught between them as either perpetrators or victims. Using human logic to understand deific judgement does not lead exiled men to the same conclusions that God has drawn in the wake of the Sacrifice of His Son. Do you understand? *"Yes."* That is why you and your brother have always been trustful in this, whereas others have been questioners. It is not that most of them are unwilling to participate in the refinement of the world; they demand a logical handhold that cannot be found in the beatific realms of Salvation. The rudiments of human redemption are called Sacred Mysteries for a reason. Everyone should remember that they, for the most part, have not been subjected to the deprivations of the millions before them who were either martyred or persecuted for their faith.

You need not hold back from relating what I have said today because many will be receptive to it; they have not heard these kinds of reflections before. It is through prayer and the intervention of the Holy Spirit that such wisdom comes. The world is filled with questioners who are not unsighted, and neither are they clueless. They are trying to apply mortal logic to a vast immortal Kingdom. How many sabers and lashes have the Saints suffered? How many lions' jaws clenched the flesh of the Martyrs? In what numbers were the stakes on which the greatest testators of the Gospel put to death in the name of God? The Lord knows the answer, but how do such numbers measure against the Passion of a single Man? Being clueless, just as the Angels have said, is a bereftness that can only be eliminated through trust and endurance. It is eradicated by the awakening of the heart, mind and spirit. In truth, being clueless is wiped away by accepting one's crosses in the likeness of the King on the Cross. I know this is true because I have seen it firsthand. You are sighted because you trust in the Lord's Will and have internalized the lessons of being a Christian your entire life. What is bereft in other men will come to them in every means celebrated by the Gospel and the echo of its call. The passing of the ages cannot stop it; the objections of sinners cannot impede it, and all the squalls that Nature could muster cannot delay its inevitability. So today, I have told you about vision and wisdom in a world that rejects both. But, hear how you are praying now! You are calling 'Hail Mary' and I have come, for I always do. This is the message that must be transferred to the world from all My shrines and seers. You and your brother have done your part. Whatever else you commit to is a fruit of your generosity to the Kingdom of God and the redemption of the lost. The unrepentant will change from here to the end of the world because of the royalty of your faith. This is among the reasons that I have come to you in joy. I know that you, your brother and all the faithful are assisting the Church to make the Father pleased by the goodness and virtue here in your lives. No one knows better than Me the sacrifices you have made toward these goals. You speak about the mounting number of years that have come and gone since I first came speaking to you. It may seem as though the years have been long, but you knew from the beginning that you would devote them to Me. Your soul sensed it from the moment your feet touched the soil of Medjugorje. On a temporal basis, more than twenty years seems a long time, but certainly not to the Eternal God in whose mansions you shall rest. The Father does not think in terms of millennia or billions of years. He thinks about the perpetuity that you have inherited and the absolution that is engulfing you now. This is a profoundly auspicious happening; the best of all possible outcomes. Your faith is real; your trust in Jesus is alive, your days are progressing toward the grand celebration that you have always desired. This is what the sightless cannot see, but they will soon see that what I am saying here is true. It is also what the clueless do not know; it will come to them in breathtaking doses. You have heard that ignorance of the law is no excuse. If not for the Divine Mercy of Jesus and His desire to console the Church, the punishment for this ignorance in the hearts of defiant men would be an unprovided eternal death."

Saturday, July 27, 2013
9:42 a.m.

"If there is any excellence."

"Now, My venerable little sons, I come to you bearing My compassionate love, praying that you are sensing the divine omnipotence engulfing your lives. We hold ourselves before the Father as His dear creatures, and we bring forth our blessings to humanity to glorify His Son. Thank you for remaining strong during these crucial days of modern men; you are stronger than you know. I ask that you not portend your own sadness by assuming that your daily lives are nondescript. These sensations grow out of frustration and confusion, others are manifested by world disorder. And, still more are the simple product of discontent. I told My children again worldwide in My July 25, 2013 Medjugorje message that I came in joy. There is little way that you might believe that I would have joy, given the condition of the Earth, but My joy springs from the origin of your Salvation. I am the Mother of your Salvation, and Jesus is your Savior. It is by the Blood of Jesus that humanity is reunited with God; there is no other redemption. Writers, poets and dreamers have tried to capture the magnificence of the converted heart. It is spiritual light that they are trying to describe; they are attempting to define in finite terms the glory of the infinite realms. I have come before you as a Woman filled with the blessings of that infinity. There can be no goodness without the invocation of the Triune Truth that comes only from God. There is no virtue in humanity without Him. Here, you see that you have been aligned with this virtue the whole of your years. I have assisted you to recognize the reciprocity between your faith and the Lord's intercession that would have existed even if I had said nothing. It is not the hearable aspects of your relationship with God that count; it is the laudable ones. I opened a message months ago with the words, 'If there is any excellence...' I have done so again today. The reason I repeat this preface is so that you can understand what has existed, what has occurred between these two messages – you have found that excellence. You have drawn the connection between human suffering and the purification of mortal souls. You have watched Heaven inundate the Earth with invocations and overtures, and many nations have responded with a rare and vindicating ascension. But, more people need to participate; not everyone is listening. Hence, it is not just a Phillipian question of whether there is any excellence, but whether the fullness of human repentance is being manifested in the heart. This is the true source of atonement. My little children, I come in joy today as I did in Medjugorje because the potential for humanity to heed the call of the Holy Spirit is being realized. You are simply not hearing about it. It is not popular news to know that righteousness is overtaking the world's loathing, perils and evils. Let the Mother of God write the headlines! I know what should be told in the mediums of men. It is not as bad as it seems. Sin, tragedy and negativity are sold for profit around the world. The tawdry, dark and seedy are popular themes almost everywhere. It is not enough that sinners gather fruit for feeding, they have a scandalous mentality about it. Their curiosity about how misbehaved other sinners have become makes them feel better about themselves.

A Saint named Alta once said that other people should clean off their own doorsteps before complaining about hers. She rightfully asked who can know the content of someone else's heart. How many people can discern another person's intentions without admitting to their own indiscretions? The Holy Scriptures are replete with examples of this hypocrisy. Therefore, if there is any excellence, it will be found to have originated in the heart; it will blossom from there, it will be fed from there. All virtue is a manifestation of spiritual excellence. There can be other excellences too, such as a symphony of harmonic voices and the laughter of infant children. There are sights and sounds of glory throughout the universe in the form of hopes and actions that reflect the genius of God. Going into outer-space to explore the unwieldy frontier of unknown voids is an example of human excellence, given there are no deficits elsewhere. Chants of exceptionalism are wonderful too, as long as the whole world shares in it. It is in connecting the ties between the rich and poor by summoning self-sufficiency that the equalizing gift of responsibility resides. Yes, My Special son, someone can be either too rich or too poor; but if there is any excellence, neither of these will remain. Christ Jesus did not render a socialist approach to human equality, but one that includes hard work, fair aspirations, and all the Fruits of the Holy Spirit. Thus, I have come to share My love with you, to tell you that you are winning the race in declaring that no one can own you, and to reaffirm My commitment as you bear the facets of life in the exiled world. I have said on prior occasions that you sometimes view your suffering and sadness in terms relative to different times of life, when you should see your hardships in light of the Cross. I wish not to downplay your burdens and sorrows, but to repeat that you are stronger than you know. When you pray as you ought, you avail life to all the possibilities that might not have come. You hold a catalogue of all the thoughts and actions of good men in your hands – the Holy Rosary. You now and forever will be inspired with the sacred knowledge of what life is supposed to become every time you say 'Hail Mary.' I am honored that you and your brother have given your lives to this."

Saturday, August 3, 2013
9:00 a.m.

"Some things might be forgotten, but they will never be unknown."

- The Dominion Angels

"For the unification of the Earth with God, My purposes here are apparent. This is another hour of joy, My little sons. My Immaculate Heart overflows with happiness because I have seen the close of the ages. It is here, now and ongoing; all that must be done can be effected on your playing field of life. Heaven can be summoned here. You are assembling the Angels and the proverbial better angels of men as you pray. I beseech you to give the Lord God the opportunity to prove Himself in ways that you have presented yourselves to Him. This is a high cause of truth, My little children. You see today the words of the Dominion Angels that you may attribute to them in your writing – even though it appears rather simple, the passage is wholly profound. Those who have reached your age have already forgotten more than they will ever learn anew, but their deposit of knowledge is cumulative. Something forgotten cannot be unlearned. Something revealed can never again become secret because, once flushed-out, all human endeavors are imbedded in the marketplace of thought. And this is good; it is to the wisdom of the human heart that sacred knowledge is transferred into spiritual power by its own origin. This is the way Christianity has come through the ages, so unique and expansive, so broad in mysticism, so bountiful and beautiful, so original and providing. The Holy Spirit always gives the heart the inspiration to express the Will of God. It is inevitable. This is the reason openness to the Holy Advocate is mandatory within the Christian conscience. My Special son, you speak the strains of love every day. Priests and religious hail the dialogue between God and themselves when they offer testimonies on His behalf. Your manuscripts are premier works of the Holy Spirit, eclipsed only by the Scriptures themselves. At the same time, I have spoken to you so that humanity will realize that the Father can leave the world speechless. He will always have more to say than exiled men, and He always reserves the first and last word. He gives men the breath of life with which to speak, the skill to craft new languages, the intelligence to interpret them, and the willingness to put them down in print. All good things come from God, and everything malevolent is finally crushed by Him. Hence, My message today is about your capacity to be Heaven-like here on Earth in ways that have not occurred to you. You and your brother are living descendants of your parents, of their parents, of their parents' parents, and so on. It is a mystery that all this wisdom has been bequeathed to you, but it is yours to utilize for the propagation of your faith. When the Dominion Angels tell you that a fact or opinion cannot be unknown, they are speaking about your identification in this cycle. All sacred knowledge; everything shared for the advancement of human salvation, streams from the Spirit of God. You have heard that there is nothing new under the sun; this is partly true, but you and your brother have become new creatures shaped by the faith of your forefathers and your manifest pious consciences. Imagine, however, how convoluted life would be if you could remember every single word you have ever spoken. This is why you have the gift of forgetting. Imagine those who have suffered trauma like your brother's sister if they were to recall every moment of their pain. His sister cannot remember the automobile crash or the intensity of her suffering because God wiped it from her mind. Even though such memory lapses come, the subconsciousness cannot 'unknow' what it has learned. And, this is My metaphor for what happens to Christians who stay the course through trial and time. I was humored by your brother telling the committee during his recent interview that he once won a county spelling bee, and was then allowed to participate in state competition in Peoria in 1968. He told them that he could not remember the word he spelled correctly to win the county contest, but has no difficulty remembering the word 'pomade' that he spelled incorrectly to force him out in Peoria. Those who heard your brother say this chuckled with him; they understood what he was trying to say. Human beings often remember more what traumatizes them than what leads them to victory. It seems that the poignant is seared into the soul more deeply than triumph. It is man's unification with the Crucifixion of Jesus Christ. It is built into the heart to search for oneness with the Perfect Sufferer. This is a blessing for human survival and the grace of eternal redemption.

Men walk more steadily on the foundation of suffering than past milestones of victory. This is the balance between mortal life and the immortality inherited in the Resurrection of the Son of Man. Everything you see; all that interests and disinterests you contributes to your identity in realms that change the world. You have learned it through the years; you have lived and known it, but your mental architecture lacks the capacity to recall everything you have done. This is a gift from the Father. It is what brings men to search for something greater. It is the origin of challenges and curiosity; it is the source of man's questioning, and it is connected beyond the universe to the eternal realms of God. Jesus proved it. He was dissatisfied with a world that He tried to change with blessings and miracles, and was crucified for trying to make it holy. He tapped the inquisitive nature of men to search for something greater than what is discernible with the senses. Indeed, it was beyond their capacity for imagining. Remember that Jesus was a messenger from God, not the new Moses, but the New Adam. He emphasized the transformation of sinners by His own sinlessness. He is the Messianic Martyr who was prophesied by the Old Mosaic Law. Hence, Jesus came into the world to remind humanity what they had forgotten, foretold by a bush and the prophets. He was born to reprimand lost sinners for not accepting the truth. He came to fulfill humanity's redemption in humanity's own presence. Creation. This would be the stage on which the actors of human redemption would play-out the script handed down by the Father through generations of time. This is the same stage on which you and your brother are living now; it has been the setting of heralding triumphs and bold miracles. It has seen its share of tragedies and melodramas. Whatever men choose to call it, it remains the battleground where the close of the ages will finally unfold. My Special son, you and your brother have always known everything I have said today. I have spliced dozens of thoughts together into one theme, but you have many images with which to further your contemplations. I do not expect My words to have complete congruity in your understanding as My learning child. I am overjoyed because good men have contributed to the beauty of mortal life and the edification of the lost. Even in their weakness, these men have displayed inexplicable acts of courage for the advancement of the Church. People who are learning to be holy are handing themselves over for persecution. All that spires and heaves has come to them; all that will put them down and lift them back up again is happening as we speak. Their fair faces and strong frames are bearing against the enemies of the Cross. They have a unity with the heroes of the Afterlife. My Special one, you and your brother are among them, but you are likely unaware. You wake every morning with hope as in the olden days. Yes, Theodore Roosevelt and Sir Winston Churchill spoke as eloquently as they did because they suffered in your likeness, as well as you in theirs. They have never said anything that your hearts have not foretold. They gained their consciousness from their parents, and their parents' parents, and on and on, as I said. You can sense the reason why you and your brother are drawn to the archives of human endeavor in a way that is already revelatory to the presence of the Church. What touches you, and what you willfully touch, connects you with God. This is why I say Creation, Creation. You are the Lord's creatures in Creation, and this makes you miracle workers in His Kingdom from above. It makes you ranking members of the Blessed in the vineyard to which the Son of Man will return. I ask you to dwell not on your setbacks, but on the Master who turned defeat into victory by His Sacrifice on the Cross. This is the definition of sacred love; it is this to which humanity is called. I have spoken about such obedience for 2,000 years, but only few among you really understand what it means. I hope that your wishes prevail, that the Will of God suffices what you bind here in the land of prayer. Thank you for the loveliness of your heart and the good will that you hold for everyone who prays. Bless you for remaining steadfast in your faith."

Monday, August 12, 2013
9:02 a.m.

"Erstwhile times and abandoned missions."

"My dearly beloved children, 'erstwhile' means from the past, former, or no longer in existence. I always speak to you about the future, but it is from the past that you remember the Saints and the labors of all who have contributed to the Church through the centuries. There is an interconnection with the 'timeliness' and 'timelessness' of the faithful that cannot be broken because, by the power of the Holy Spirit, there are no weak links. When you ponder religious people living in a secular world, the contrasts are too stark to ignore. There are many missions that have nothing to do with the redemption of man; this is the reason they are ultimately abandoned. This is not to say that someone who builds furniture is not doing the work of God. And, those who gather kindling to keep their children's fires burning are surely servants of the King. The point of My words is to stir your thoughts about what connects you to the past. What did those times hold that brought you to this moment with respect to the mission of the Church? You are unique in this regard because of your station as messengers for Me. This is the summit of righteous service. Hence, I ask you to consider your accomplishments for God etched into history, and in eternity too. Indeed, what about many others? You know what the Popes have given. You are aware of missionaries who have fought for justice around the world. Presidents and paupers can have tremendous impact on the Church because piety comes in many forms. This is how Mother Teresa could rebuke a world leader in any manner she pleased. So, I speak about erstwhile times and abandoned missions to give you pause to consider everyone who has done at least one good thing that replicates the mandates of the Gospel. I once told you about Jesus taking a photograph of someone's life, their best of times, so that this will be the way they will see themselves at the gate of Heaven. The Ancient Crucifixion has proved to be more than the Salvation of humanity, it is redemption's Signature. When someone wears a Crucifix around their neck or on their lapel, they are revealing to the world the Signature and the Author who penned it. Such things as these are indicators of tides of time that will eventually arrive into one moment – the Second Coming. Here, you see that preaching the Gospel or helping the poor are unique designs that will never fade from the history of man. By all means, they ratify the proneness of humanity to be holy. In essence, there are no pious abandoned missions. Prayer is never in vain; it will always be the source of blessings from the Father. Prayer will never be an abandoned mission. When I refer to erstwhile times, I speak of the vast collection of events that affect these present days. Whatever is seen as having advanced the mission of the Church will be likewise recognizable by those whose souls enter Heaven. Memories are made of this. When someone cannot remember where they placed their precious reflections, they will come to the Father's House and say, 'Oh, that's where I left them.' My little sons, these are the reasons why I have always told you that you are more given to Eternal Glory than you really know. People you see at the supermarket or on street corners who are also bound for Heaven see it in your faces. They knew you before ever meeting you. These are the resonant strains of the Holy Spirit that identify you. Yes, that you are lent to Eternal Glory suffices everything about which you are unconsciously unaware. This lending toward Glory assists your knowledge about the End Times and the coming New

World, the righteous frameworks and glorious designs that you will realize in this life and the next.

My Special son, the Father is having difficulty getting people out of the way of themselves. They are preoccupied with secular missions that will ultimately be abandoned. Millions around the globe have their so-called worldly missions; they will pass into history and erstwhile times. They have no lasting effect on the mission of the Church or the refinement of man. On the other hand, we could speak about gunsmiths, chefs, pilots, teachers and on and on; they all have their missions that parallel the reason they were given arts and talents. Still, they must think about their lives in the context of the Roman Catholic Church. They must cling to those things in erstwhile times that brought them to be holy, and they must focus on the Church's mission and abandon all other missions not about the conversion of lost sinners. This speaks to the priests at the Motherhouse about your messages in light of your brother's potential employment there. My Special son, it is the same as I have always said – what could possibly be the motivation for someone claiming to hear the voice of the Mother of God? What would cause a person to spend 22 years co-authoring twelve books for which they do not yield a dime? This is the great paradox with which they are dealing. It is emblematic of the way the Lord sounds the trust of those who believe in Him. You and your brother should remain calm and peaceful. The Lord is being the Lord – I AM – for all the people, during erstwhile and present times, for the future, and for the whole of eternity beyond the last day. The Father teaches humanity through His omnipotence and prophesies which missions should be abandoned. Thank you for praying for the souls who are in need of Jesus' compassion and intervention. Your brother's sister-in-law Nancy Jo Heather will soon be called to Heaven and become a powerful intercessor. She has led a simple life. I ask that you pray for all the broken, sick and dying. I will remember everyone for whom you pray in My intercessory prayers as well. I offer My blessings to the suffering poor."

Saturday, August 17, 2013
9:29 a.m.

"The art, the theater, the pageantry, the eloquence."

"Welcome to My Immaculate Heart, My little sons, where you live at all times and in perpetuity. Your confidence in My intercession is both beneficial and benefactoral. You have the means to tell humanity about the greatness vested in you, about the holiness by which you have always lived, about your faith that is tested every day. It pleases Me dearly that you have exposed yourselves to the grace of wisdom raining down from Heaven. We know among us that we are making a difference in fashioning the Kingdom of the Lord here on Earth to be the likeness of Heaven. How do I know? Because the multiplication of wars tells Me so. The fact that so many are fighting against evil is reason enough for Me to believe it. Today, I come more happy to this place than you have ever heard Me. I am more jubilant, more sufficed in gratitude, and more assured of the atonement of humanity with the Father in Heaven than I could have previously thought possible. It is true that the Roman Catholic Church is under siege from the inside and outside; it is being tested as your faith itself is always tested. My little sons, you are pouring forth into the vastness of the world your allegiance to God in ways that will be ultimately revealed to all. Your prayers, books, testimonies, memoirs, and strength of endurance are all proof that your role as warriors for the Cross is becoming evident to all. Even though the religious Sisters may never overcome their questions about The Morning Star Over America; even though they may turn away the messengers of the Lord, they will eventually proclaim here and to the world, 'Surely this must have been the Spirit of God.' There is no losing here, My little ones. Positions of employment and stations of power come and go, but there is no diminishing the aroma of the Spirit of God, there is no dismissing the Truth. You have yet to become fully aware of the indelible mark you are leaving on the faithful here in this exile, and the impact you are having on those who do not yet believe. My joy is incapable of being measured; My awareness of the success of the Church has never been more pronounced. Remember the writer who said, '...up again, old heart; there is victory yet for all justice.' This is the way I live; it is the way I ask you to live. My little sons, where I place My eyes is where I am given impressions of how this world will conclude. I speak of My physical vision and spiritual foresight. I see people standing tall and proclaiming their faith, their self-confidence, their trust and acceptance of the Lord's proceeding Kingdom, their daring in conquering everything that tries to diminish their faith in God. There is a stalwart erectness of the conscience of men that has been handed-down through the ages to this age, to you and all who believe, to the ones who are willing to look upward and outward in ways that expand the Gospel into foreign lands and mountains. I see smiles everywhere. I see sensations of expectation for the Second Coming in what priorities faithful men embrace.

    My Special son, My joy here today exceeds My previous messages because we are closer than ever to the Return of Jesus Christ, the King. I am not worried anymore that My children will fail. Many of them may fall, but they will never fail. And, it is perhaps not possible that you can see the forthcoming glory with your eyes, but your heart and soul are capable of discerning its color nonetheless. You can sense the streamers of celebrations to rival the Earth's rainbows. And, your spirit can feel the warmth of the Holy Spirit in whose light you are bathed. Indeed, you can touch the immensity of God's power by your grasp on the Holy Rosary. And, as I have said, you can sense the aroma of life beyond death, and even death itself, in your anticipation of entering the final days of this world as it has been foretold. I stand ready with My arms opened wide. The Angelic Hosts have trumpets in hand. The drum corps are poised to strike their first cadence. All of this is nigh at hand, and the world seems completely unaware. Nigh at hand implies that the years do not matter anymore. Today matters. What you do on this day, not what you did yesterday that has already been forgotten, not tomorrow that may open with Jesus descending on a cloud, but today. What happens when you open your eyes on each new dawn is what should matter to you at that time. Do you know why? Because the Lord scripts your existence here in the same way that He prescribed your creation from the beginning. He hands this power to you. He gives you and all people the ability to shape lands of peace and oceans of calm. He does not strike down the wicked in all cases because He wants to see His soldiers fight. He is engaged in the battle for souls in advance of that one final day. Not all of the wicked will be condemned; not all the wicked will convert. The separation of the sheep from the goats will proceed in earnest once everyone has taken their side. This is the motion and commotion of the cyclical seasons of life. Here today, I am again proclaiming that the conversion of lost sinners is occurring in massive numbers; you simply do not see them or hear about them on the news. This grand manifestation is not imbedded in internationalism, not in politics or partisan gain; it is found inside each human heart that is open enough to acknowledge and accept the Will of the God of Abraham. This God mandates that His people espouse decency and purity, chastity and charity, and prayer and penance. This is the Lord who commands that humanity must be baptized in water and purified by fire. Yes, this is the same Father of the blessed who has deigned to hand His own discretion to those who love and believe in Him.

My Special son, all this is a charitable thing. It is about sharing the warmth of Sacred Love; it is about touching others and allowing others to touch your heart. This is the primary essence of My messages that deal with empathy and compassion. This Sacred Love is always about understanding what other men suffer, what offends them, what heals and restores them, what makes them want to live. This is the same Sacred Love that has imparted in Christians the ability to see life beyond its present problems and ongoing obligations. Not all blight is malevolent; some is cleansing, enlightening, and purifying. Not all suffering is what it seems; it is beautiful in its conclusive realms. This is the message of the Cross. I ask you and your brother to remember this. I desire that you see the suffering of other men and your own suffering as the delight of the Angels as they perceive the Calvarian Cross. When the Lord speaks about repentance, He speaks about the capacity for exiled men to become heroes in the likeness of The Christ, like the Saints and Martyrs, like the little people around the world who walk with canes and ask only that others allow common decency to have a chance. Believe it or not, even as you and your brother are conquerors for Jesus, you are among these little people. You do not rage against the darkness like slayers, even though you certainly could. You do not make demands of God as though you are His equal. You do not destroy neighborhoods and cities; you do not burn the devil's barns just because you can. You are like Jesus. You know where and when to stone Satan's dogs. You, like God, are masters of timing. You realize that your prayers are more powerful than most American citizens are willing to believe. So, why would I not come in joy? I see colorful surfaces prepared to receive the burden of the years. I see a breathing, enlightened humanity poised for victory. Yes, and this victory has already begun. It will not spool like data into a queue; it will fall upon this Earth like a billion lightning strikes. It will fall men from their horses before they ever knew it was there. It will lift-up the poor and turn the world upside down; new rules, new priorities, fairer skies, and happier times. This is the victory that I have always described to you, that I have always told you would breathe triumph and elation on you in ways that you could not possibly have foreknown.

This is the same way that I see the upcoming release of your first memoir; genius in the material realms. It is the inscribing of the faith of your fathers in a 21st-century work. It reveals the content of your heart in ways that have been previously untold. I am overjoyed about this! I am here to say on this day and always that nothing can remove your revelations about God and your union with Him from history or eternity, those that you have packed into your extraordinary book. This is the stuff of miracles; it is the reason men throw their fists into the air and dance in place because their soul cannot stand still. You know that this is true; you cannot deny it; you would not try. Jesus feels what you feel, and He touches with His hands everything you have created. He runs His palms across your life and feels gratified that you have shaped your 'being' into the likeness of Himself. He sees as I have told you that I see. And, this makes Him realize that the performance of lordly holiness is emanating from you. I have said this to a scarce number of people in the past 2,000 years. When the poet asked his listeners to heed the call, to embrace the concept of, '...up again, old heart,' he was saying that life's burdens and worries can be overcome by the justice of God.

The daily mantra of negativism is not a true description of what is really going-on in this world. Listen to Me! Hear what I have to say about the actualization of justice happening around the world. There is a sleekness, a newness, a powerful freshness to the Kingdom of God that He is injecting into your everyday lives. If you allow Him, He will internalize this fact into your conscious awareness in ways that has sustained His Christians for centuries onward. Remember, I am not promising that there will be rose petals covering the pathways on which you will walk. The skies will not be wholly shed of dark clouds and thunder. There will be drawn blood and bruising. There will be deficits and disappointments aplenty. But, you already know the outcome of the war. There is a purpose for it all. Thank you, My Special son, I offer you My richest blessings for making My intercession into this world so filled with joy. I will speak to you again. I love you. Thank you for having responded to My call."

Saturday, August 24, 2013
9:42 a.m.

"The wry and the honorable."

"Yes, My little darlings, I am with you today as always. I bring the good tidings of the Lord and blessings abounding. I hold in My Immaculate Heart all the encouragement you will ever need. I promise that My prayers are yours. The thoughts of Heaven are with you; the Glory of God is with you. I speak about the wry, those who tend toward error and contentiousness, those who are devoid of patience. I also speak of the honorable who have given themselves to the Cross, to embracing rightness and goodness, and whose consciences are shaped by the teachings of Jesus. While there are stark differences between the two, My point is to tell you the reason that most people live somewhere in the middle. Everyone who is growing in righteousness undergoes a process. It involves learning what Jesus wants of them at the same time they are learning what they expect from themselves. My Special son, I have come today to share the good news of the changing of the human heart, the amendment of lives and the enhancing of the capacity of men to find themselves on the road to redemption. This is the status of the unseen realms where, deep inside the heart, the evolution of the conversion of humanity occurs. Wryness means that there is a great distance to travel to the admirable life. Honesty and honor are inherent in those who not only know to try, but who do their best to make this change. Now, what does this mean for the modern-day world? It implies a return to simplicity, to peace-filled days, to hours of reflection and consecration to My Immaculate Heart, and to the holier things that I have heralded for decades. I have also said that men are not inherently evil; they are affected by evil in ways that make them commit to unholy works. These are the reasons for the manifesting of ill will and hard feelings around the globe. And, even more than that, some people profit from their distance from the Lord. In other words, they know that their motivations are wrong, but they cannot resist the temptation to behave the way they do. Some see themselves being worthy of the best life; they believe that this is their inheritance, their bequeathal, of being born into the world. What should motivate humanity is their worthiness to be in the presence of God. This, My Special son, is the first question that Jesus asks every sinner when they see Him face to face. He veritably inquires, 'What was your reason for the way you lived?' And, it is from this derivation that one can sense his own life patterns. This is the juncture where Jesus reveals to the nations the intentions of all creatures. And, at that moment, when a man reaches the presence of Jesus, he sees whether fidelity to the Cross and a sacrificial life were imbedded in him, whether they were revealed and exemplified by him. What a momentous event for the human soul to find itself situated before the crucified Son of Man! Indeed, this is where someone ultimately judges himself before the backdrop of the Sacred Life of God Incarnate. My Special son, this is the crucial point of the inspection of the worthiness of a human soul. It seems conclusive; it seems all too factual to be true, even after the burdens of the flesh are lifted. So, I ask you to remember that the appearance of the departed soul before its Maker is a measure of truth and honesty. This is why we pray for the conversion of lost sinners; it is possible to tell untruths to mortal creatures, but it is impossible to deceive the Judge of all men. It is not possible to lie to Jesus Christ. Where there are men who are one with this truth, living day-to-day, just as I ask of you and your brother, who have love in their hearts and the intentions of the Father for a holy world, they live in accordance with the reason Jesus was born. I have spoken about Jesus' birth. I have addressed the events that foretold and succeeded His Incarnation, but humanity seems shorn of interest in the reason He became Man. Why would God come into a world so rife with error, inhabited with such broken people? Because God is sinless – Jesus is free from error, and He came to reveal to the world what human brokenness means. Jesus was a perfect Child in My Womb, a perfect Man and perfect Savior. He was not corrupt like the corrupted, and He proved that corruption cannot change Eternal Love. Sinners broke Jesus' Body the same way a priest breaks His Sacramental Flesh at the Holy Sacrifice of the Mass, but they could not break His Spirit. The Holy Spirit can never be fractured. Jesus' soul will never be undone. Men wishing to become the likeness of the Savior of the Church must realize that their souls, their spirits can likewise never be broken. Hearts may feel pain and sorrow; they may sense breaches in their determination, but they cannot be severed from Jesus on the Cross. When living in His likeness, pain and suffering are unifying with Him. This provides a sense of destiny toward Heaven; it is how son goes against father, father against son, and mother against daughter.

My Special son, you have heard this in other settings having to do with the image of the splendor of men. It means that human splendor takes many forms; it plays multiple parts in the refinement of the earthly experience. The image that I speak about here is the one that Jesus has laid before you; it is honorable and redemptive to emulate His life, propagate His teachings, embrace His suffering, and stand for everything for which He was sent by the Father. This is the image shared by people like you. This is the splendor that pleases the Lord. There is a new way of life when someone understands what I am saying today. Cynicism disappears; negativity and sarcasm no longer make their case. The worthiness of the soul becomes more apparent. Therefore, My little son, it comes down to this. When Paul said that he had become worthy of the crown of a Saint, he was not being haughty or pretentious; he was aware of the providence in his own voice celebrating the power of God's forgiveness before the nations. And, was Timothy surprised to hear this? Not at all. Even Timothy's soul was united with Paul's warrant for humanity to follow his lead. Hence, you see that I have used the term 'wry' in My message today, and similar words might apply – these terms describe lives that depart from the teachings of Jesus. Conversely, it is honorable; it is good and right to recognize the need for the heart to sanctify human life. This is what conversion is all about. It speaks to the reason Jesus was born of My Womb. God addressed the need for men to abandon sin, to become holy and righteous, and to enter Heaven unstained. My Special one, I must tell you again how warmly you are embraced, how much I admire you, how firmly you have built a foundation on which other people can understand the meaning of My messages. I do not say these things to you lightly, but to state precisely what My Son thinks. I cannot overstate what you have accomplished in this life; you have likened your years to an historical papacy for God, for His Faith Church, for the Poor Souls in Purgatory, for all who yearn to live in Heaven. When Jesus tells His flock that He desires all creatures to have, '...much happiness,' He is saying that He wants the Church to live as you have lived. This will make people holy; it will set them free from the burden of their sins, it will rescue them from the chains of their own error. I have asked you and your brother to walk with Me, and you have come. You are like roses blooming in the middle of an ash heap; you are like fine pearls inside a vat of tar.

Consider it this way – when you are driving down a gravel road, imagine coming upon a stretch of pavement covered in solid gold. This is what I see; it is how your lives look to the weary traveler named humanity in exile. It is what Jesus sees as He calls His Church home. There is ruggedness and ruthlessness all around the globe, but there are also silks and laces so fine that one would think them fit for a Queen. You are the essence of these things; you and your brother have come this far. You are the fruits of your own hope that is filling the void wrought by a wretched humanity, made so by its own absence of good will. This is what you and your brother are trying to undo. This has been My purpose with you. I speak about holiness, strength and vision in places where they would not be expected to reside."

Saturday, August 31, 2013
9:37 a.m.

"To Crispen Courage" – Ten Years Hence

"My dear children, here in this land of plenty, many have been your joys, and brief have been your sorrows. It is another important day as we pray for the conversion of lost sinners. It is now ten years since I asked you to help crispen the courage of your brothers and sisters, and to reach out in ways that others have refused. My little sons, you did as I asked, and good fruits have come. When we speak about crispening courage, we refer to the stages of justice that are ongoing, ushered into the years by signs, wonders and miracles as brightly shining as the stars. I come to you today with the same joy that I see in you. You have no way of knowing what this joy implies about humanity. It means that faith can change the future of the Earth. When Jesus told the Apostles that they would be fishers of men, He was speaking forward. He was referring to the power of prayer, which in itself is a way of fishing for the souls of lost sinners. Prayer at the behest of the Father maintains your ability to 'see' what you cannot see, to envision what has been previously unknown. It is not unlike recognizing a face beneath the surface of water staring back at you, but not the reflection of your own face. This is the reconciliation that must come in this earthly domain, that all men become sharers of redemption by this same holy grace. You are fulfilling the charge to crispen the courage of your fellows because you recognize the need for calling the nations into the friendship of the Church. I am also speaking about spiritual conversion and the coalescence of souls beneath the Cross. This, in a sense, is the ethereal transition that precedes all other kinds. It is through, in and with Jesus that you are absolved and redeemed. And, it is for, before and in the Father that you are reclaimed and canonized. The transformation is the same. When I spoke to you on that warm August 31, 2003 afternoon, I made the case for the justification of all that makes Saints of sinners who yet did not know that the Blessed Trinity even existed. That 'magnanimous book,' I called it, yet stands as the culmination of the faith of millions. You will see in time that what I have said is true, what effects this culmination has on the Faith Church and the Church Triumphant in Heaven. You have been told that there are billions of souls already in Heaven, but only two bodies, Jesus and Myself. But, does the latter truly matter for now? Does not the spirit of the ages and the souls of the faithful departed, when united with the Deity in the Lord's Glorious Kingdom, suffice the gladness that is yet to come? This, as I have said, is what makes every day on Earth unique in itself. Humanity and each individual person takes positions that must align with the teachings of the Gospel. When this occurs, the finality of Heaven at the end of time reaches its potential form. This is what Jesus meant when He said from the Cross that His Kingdom is finished. And, equally important is human posture. A position is often a one time opinion, but posture is a long term belief. I am of the position that most all My children in America will accept their inheritance in the Blood of the Cross. My posture is that the Blood of the Cross has the power to redeem everyone on Earth. We must remind humanity that to live in Jesus is to die in Him, and then to live in Him again. Death has no clutches; it makes no permanent claim on anyone given to the Crucifixion of the Lord. The freshness that I spoke about ten years ago, the sharpness that I reflected upon, is based on the fact that those ten years have done precisely that. While Jesus is the same, the world is in turmoil. Everything in opposition to the oath of Abraham is dying in its tracks; it is being killed by the wreck of this world. It is this wreck that you see every day, as though watching a tremendous crash unfold one frame at a time, as if one per day for a thousand years. This is the tragedy of the ages. The joy that overcomes this tragedy is that the wreck has been undone by Jesus' Sacrifice on the Cross. The only death to have redemptive consequences is the Crucifixion of Jesus Christ. This is the death that has reversed the tides of history and made way for the rising of the dead in His Paschal Resurrection.

My Special son, I realize that I am telling you about a Salvation story that you already know, but the context in which I speak is the setting created by your work with your brother for so many years ongoing. It takes a fresh courage for humanity to accept that their deaths will culminate not in tragedy, but in the joy of the rising of the Messianic Son. Yes, the wreck is horrendous, just as the Cure D'Ars foretold. It is possible to be both a witness and a victim of this wreck, but it is not the wreck that matters, but the aftermath; who lies dead? What preceded and will succeed this carnage? Who is to blame? How many victims have been slain? I am speaking about the sacred conscience that makes men convert. I am referring to the motion of history-makers that keeps the world intact as much as it has been heretofore controlled. Such people are everywhere; they speak of the peace and stability of God through the power of the Holy Spirit. Their intentions have resounded through the generations to give rise to the Christian conscience about which the Martyrs spoke. Does this take courage? Absolutely. Can it be accomplished in one lifetime? Not for many. But, the contributions of multiple people comprise this contingent of history-makers. It is all about the common understanding of the need for the intervention of God. Nothing else matters. I have said that motor carriages and flying machines, communication devices and all the rest are here for what they do, but they have little effect on the conclusion of the world. Unless used for the enlightenment of humanity about the Kingdom of God, they are just mere novelties. This is the reason you have freshened the faith of other men; you have stirred their movement toward courage, away from the weak-mindedness by which they have lived. Even some intellectual Prelates will scratch their heads, wondering why they spent so many years in the Church, but never realized that the psychology of Roman Catholicism could be this simple. It is men that make faith so complicated, not God. This is why you stand against roadblocks and gatekeepers. Every time a new invention comes, or some desire of humanity arises that does not comport with the teachings of the Church, these intellectuals would rather reinterpret the Scriptures than disavow their penchant to deviate from them. It takes courage to turn down new vices and devices that seem not in keeping with the freedom of men to actually live freely. This is the message that I hope you will transfer to the world when speaking about your books, diaries and memoirs. Men must stand tall. Young men must stand even taller, those with the strength, endurance and willingness to hold fast to their faith handed them by their elders. Wisdom comes in time, but it need not be a lengthy time. This has been proved over the centuries. Indeed, how old was the girl who conquered the whole of France? *"Seventeen."* But, it requires the willingness that I just mentioned; it takes a specific openness to embrace God's miracles and live sacrificially for years, and often decades. All the signs are here that precede a unique warning that must come into the world. It need not be a devastating blow; it need not take people to their knees in pain and sorrow, but it will because sinners make it that way. What part of 'sacrificial' do they not understand? How far must they travel down dark paths before recognizing that they are lost? These things are being revealed to you now, predicted by the Gospel and the influence of the Church. My Special son, I pray that you know how much I love you. I am proud of your faith and obedience, for your hard work, for the production of your books and first memoir, and for living peacefully here with your brother. This is the essence of your thanksgiving heart. You have vocations that are not heralded by the masses. As September comes, you will see each day with the newfound joy that I mentioned when I began speaking today. I ask you and your brother not to be disturbed by events to come, that you be mature and trusting, that you hold onto Jesus through Me. It is a rare life in which a Christian's faith is not tested. When humanity learns who I am, what I stand for, what I can do for them, and how beautiful is the House of the Father, the procession of the ages will near its culminating joy. Thank you for remembering the poor in your morning, noon and evensong prayers."

Sunday, September 8, 2013
The Nativity of Our Lady
3:03 p.m.

"What does redemption sound like?"

"It is to infinite magnitudes of gladness and suffering that you are taken as Christians, My little sons. The whole world abounds in vindication because you are faithful to the Cross, and the Lord's Kingdom flourishes because the meaning of life has become more apparent to you. I am joyful in the Salvation of men, and I am overwhelmed that you have participated in their conversion. Yes, this is the anniversary of My birth into the world as celebrated by the Church. We have cited what this means in history and beyond it, to the masses and every individual soul, to the particulars that have upheld you as dignitaries in the lineage of the Saints. My children, while it seems a contradiction that happiness rarely comes in the form of discernible gifts, the joy that Salvation brings is itself a gift beyond measure. Please remember that no matter what happens here in this life, it is a happy transition; life does not end, it changes. It is your transfer into the ethereal realms that live in your faith. People who ask why the Mother of God would have an earthly birth have missed the meaning of God's communion with them. They are focusing not on absolution, but the logic of the seas. I was born through the same Grace that has redeemed all souls. I am the personification of Grace. It is through Jesus that humanity is saved, and it is through Me that Jesus was born. While I desire the consecration of My children to My Most Immaculate Heart, I pray for the conversion of lost sinners to the Cross even more. I wish to grow the faith of My children in the Son of

Man. When I see this happen; when I see that the Earth is turning to Him, and being consumed by His Crucifixion, this makes Me happy beyond all else. It emboldens the Angelic Court; it makes the Church Triumphant sing new anthems of glory. My Special son, it is particularly to you that I speak today to hearten you and broaden the scope of your hope. It is not just a lack of faith that makes men unhappy, but when their faith is tested. Your brother loves you; he is your friend for life, and you are good to him. Everything that you have done for your brother is redemptive for the whole Catholic Church. Always believe that this has been another reason for your companionship with your brother. It is part of the salvific plan that God set into motion long before either of you were born. It is in accordance with the Triune Truth that you have lived together, embedded in a neighborhood that has been none the wiser of the miracles being wrought in their midst. My work will be revealed when the Lord ordains, when the gates of enlightenment have been raised, when the Warning becomes its strongest, when the rains have fallen in torrents, when the light will shine anew, when we have worn-out and stared-down the world together. It must be this way, My Special son; these things must come like the rising tide, as arrows pierce the flesh of unwary men, as the dawn of the Great Reckoning breaks over the horizon of the Earth. It will not be long in coming; it may seem so to you, but I promise that it is just beyond the corona shining over the Gospel of the Church. What this means, little one, is that human life is a time for reflection for all men of faith. It makes these times the most powerful in the annals of men because all time is headed for the bay that I spoke about in My first thirty messages here. You have seen that redemption has a face, the Face of Jesus, the face of suffering, the Sacrifice of the Cross, and the dispensing of His Messianic Mercy. You have touched redemption by sharing in the Cross, by your pains and disappointments, by your tears and unforeseen obstacles.

    I am speaking about the growth of your own awareness that being a Roman Catholic Christian who has been made aware of the necessity for self-sacrifice has been clarified by Me. Imagine what I have seen. Put yourself in My place; think about what makes Me pray with such compassion for those who are lost. It is not unlike seeing your drunken next-door neighbor ramming the tree with his truck and staggering unaware to his doorstep. You were like Jesus that night. You saw with pity the healing that he needs. You listened to his voice of confession, of someone who said that he has turned to the Son of Man, but cannot overcome his own vices. He is burdened by low self-esteem, a nation that says he is afflicted, that would rather give him chemicals than the gift of love. Do you remember that you were not angry? Do you know that you saw from everything you witnessed that there was a fragile soul lost in his brokenness? Do you recall? *"Yes."* This is what I saw as well; it is the way Jesus sees humanity on the Earth. Redemption need not sound like the blaring truck horn that night. It does not have to mimic the fright of an alarm, but humanity makes it that way. In all the inebriation of human pride and arrogance, the Holy Spirit is trying to break through. God is attempting to be heard. My message today is not about the subtleties of trickling streams and giddy children. Even though redemption sounds this way, it would be too simple. Nothing either discernible or beyond the senses of sight and mind could voice the sound of redemption. It would be too elementary to perceive the sound of redemption as being like dramatic symphonies or rainbowed fireworks. While these are applicable; while they indicate the same glory for the moment, they are too temporary to describe the sound of human redemption. Indeed, the sound to which I refer has a towering reach, with distance instead of loudness. Imagine hearing something of expanse rather than volume. Imagine hearing the anticipation of something rather than its arrival. It is like a train whistle coming closer to you. You know that the train is approaching; you hear its wheels on the rails, but the matter is of distance rather than sound because the whistle does not change its volume. This is the perfect analogy for when humanity asks why they cannot hear the voice of God, when they want Him to speak through the Holy Spirit more loudly than before. Truly, it is not a matter of God's voice not being loud enough, it is sinners needing to move closer to His Providence. The Father is everywhere, Jesus is everywhere too, and the Holy Spirit is equally with them. It is humanity that is not everywhere; some people are nowhere at all. They are too vague and indisposed, simultaneously infamous and unknown. This is the paradox that keeps the Church from overcoming every obstacle in its way. The sound of redemption cannot be mocked. The words of Salvation are too true to ignore. The sound of redemption speaks volumes that have yet to be heeded in this century, at least by the millions who ignored them in the last.

Therefore, I ask you to hear Me as I tell you about the sound of redemption, the collective summons of God from His Throne in Paradise. Here, I am telling you and your brother that the sound of redemption is an unbridled roar of elation that you feel when you rise to the mornings' silence. It is a prayer that cannot be unsaid. This sound is reflective of beauty in the heart, that makes the soul sing in delight. It is about the Truth shining-forth the reconciliation between the Lord and His people; it can be heard over the din of all battlefield blasts. Even in the dead of the breaking dawn and the pitch black of the night, these battles rage on in this life, breaking past the universe into the parameters of the next. Yes, the fight for justice revels the mightiest among you to come to the aid of the weak. And when they do; when the white stallion breaches the sunbeam at day's first light, you can hear what your own eyes visibly see – the horns of triumph in the wailing of the suffering poor; their cries of vindication when they taste their first feast. I am trying to unite two senses together, sight and touch, to describe the sound of redemption in the exiled world. The sound of redemption can be heard in Angelic songs, inherent in those who believe, while everyone else is deaf. And, as I have told you through the years, the sound of redemption echoes through the birthing of children, through the call of the wild to raise them with love, through the crackling flames in which their mettle is tested. You can hear the sound of redemption when your automobile engine engages to take you to Holy Mass. It is everything that communicates the Scriptures to those who should know. The sound of redemption is the firing of a shotgun aimed at any man who would lure you away from the Church, who would lead your children down errant paths, who would harm any of the innocents. These are not melodies just in this life; they are heard this way in Heaven too. The Father adds His harmony to all things holy, that cultivate His vineyard for the Second Coming of His Son. This is what He meant by whatever will be bound on Earth shall be also bound in Heaven. There is an impedance in the ears of some men that keeps them from hearing the sound of redemption. They are put down by bald-face lies. They turn to quick-snapping fingers instead of the hands of Jesus applauding the Church. Yes, the sound of redemption is about touching the souls of men with the divinity of the Gospel unfurled. When someone asks to be shown their way in life, they are waiting for a sign. This sign, seen and unseen, heard and unheard, is the sound of eternal redemption. It is a flood of sorts, but not just with water. It is an invasion of the heart that comes when the Spirit of the Lord has been welcomed. It is a piercing, peaceful, satisfying, fulfilling presence of supernatural love that heals and makes whole, that elates and cleanses, that enlightens and delivers. It is passionate and compassionate; it is what humanity must know to place itself in the presence of its King. It takes the heart and volition of men to lend their lives to this truth. My Special son, I feel fulfilled by your faith, touched by your hope, consoled by your consecration, honored by your perseverance, humbled by your graciousness, adored by your daring, and comforted by your peace. You are the personification of the perfect child of God, the preeminent Christian, the boy and man who has never once strayed from righteousness; and I thank you for making yourself My birthday gift today and always, from now into eternity. And, bless you for staying so near your family, especially your nephew. He will be a tremendous defender of everything that you and your brother began long before he was born. When I think about My birthday today, I am reminded of the twelve days of Christmas. Do you know what comes in another twelve days?

Yes, your birthday! And, how long have you been living on Earth? Yes, 52 years, but timelessly a prodigy and eternally a statesman before humanity and the Throne of God. I will pray for your prayers, for your petitions, and I will bless all whom you have asked to be blessed. Thank you for remaining steadfast with Jesus and true to your faith in which all good men and women will be redeemed."

Saturday, September 14, 2013
10:00 a.m.

"The Quest of a Saint for a Womb."

"Little darlings, you have found your Mother! I come prepared to speak of the Sacred Light by which you walk, the Glory that invigorates your hearts, the Cross by which you are redeemed, and the peace that comforts you all your days. Where there is the Mother of God, there is forgiveness, there is reconciliation and renewal. Why Me? Because I am the Mother of Forgiveness. I come, My little sons, to make these impressions known to humanity through you. I do not speak about reincarnation; this is not the Gospel message. I speak about a redemption that restores lost innocence and encourages prayer to God against the malevolent forces that tempt you. You have known through your whole lineage that there is plenteous absolution in Jesus on the Cross; there is hope for all who feel the pain of guilt and bear the torment of regret. I do not just speak of symphonies to describe this forgiveness because an orchestra cannot be heard above it. I have said that My intention is to make saints of My children, to foster the conversion that opens the gateways of the Lord to the souls of His creatures. You see the reasons why I am filled with joy, as you should likewise be filled with joy to know that all this has been made possible by the New Covenant Gospel. When speaking about this Salvation, you know that you are like veins of gold here in this land; you are the untapped beauty, the value of the heart that the world is seeking. They may not realize what I am saying today, but you already know. You have within you the infinity that no one's mind can grasp. You stand with confidence that what I am saying is true. Therefore, I ask you not to dwell on the errors of humanity. You know what changes must be made. You would be cynical if you did not turn your hearts to the good that is being done. And, you are not only standing tall in the righteousness of the Lord, you represent the broadness of this faith; you are the visitation of this love on the landscape of the earthly domain. My little sons, what I am saying is that you are exiled here with your brothers and sisters to the extent that you are assisting the

Providence of God to intercede where other men will not go. You have the daring that I spoke about last week, that has been hailed for centuries long before you. This daring is a spiritual dynamic that models the benefits of conversion for the whole of time and space. You have benefitted from this wisdom by your inheritance from the New Adam. You are becoming Saints here in this life, and you are looking for Jesus as He has found you. You have met in Me. You have become friends through Me. You have become companions in the sanctity of My Womb. It must be said to all good men that this is the mission of human life. All sacredness, all purity and faith, all compassion and all humility are manifested within the Womb of the Mother of Jesus Christ. I will pray you into the vestibule of Heaven, and Jesus will carry you in. You are tethered heart and soul, life and limb to Jesus; one with Him, you are! You have the fortune of being the adopted children of the Virgin of Bethlehem. This, My Special son, is a Sacred Mystery that seems one of the most improbable things. Salvation comes through the Sacrifice of the only sinless Man who ever lived. Forgiveness comes through God who conceived Him in My Womb. But, why would it not be true that the Father would destroy humanity and all the Earth's bounty in retribution for the Crucifixion of His Son? Because Jesus made the Sacrifice that proved the Father's Love. Even in the Garden of Eden, God told Creation that humanity had been corrupted. He said it through the strains of Moses, through the writings of the Prophets, through the warnings of the Angels, and through all time, history, energy and nature.

God wanted the world to know that He was telling the truth. And, upon the Sorrowful Sacrifice of His Only Begotten Son, He proved it. He foretold through the Old Covenant that the Messiah of the New Covenant would redeem everyone who believed in Him. He has kept His Word in Me – He kept His Word through Me – and He keeps His Word here still. This is what I wish you to tell the world when the opportunity arises; declare that the veil between Heaven and Earth is being pierced as the sinners whom I am converting in this life are united with the Father by the Crucified Fruit of My Womb. Deep inside My virginity rests the reconciliation between God and man because this is where the Blood of the Cross was conceived. So, let no one approach God without accepting the Cross! This is what humanity must know. He will make Saints of all who are this penitential. And, let no one come unto Me if there are millions of dollars in their pockets and beg Me to take them to their Savior because I will send them away, back to the origin of those millions, until they have learned the difference between richness and poorness, faith and assumption, and foresight and blindness. My Special son, please say this to your brothers and sisters. Remember that I am not saying that the Salvation of humanity was done by Me.

Do not mistake this point to those with whom you speak. I am saying that Jesus is so innate to My Grace, so inebriated by My Motherhood, so devoted to My loveliness that He wishes all who come to Him to feel the comfort of My Immaculate Heart. It is the foretaste of everything anyone will experience at the beginning of everlasting life. Think about it this way – it is the Quest of a Saint for a Womb. Humanity must ask for Me; they must enlist My intercession. Christians in union with the Church, all who are commissioned to become the image and likeness of Jesus, must embed themselves within My Sacred Womb to be reborn. It is the Womb of compassion, the Womb of Wisdom, the Womb of holiness. The Savior of humanity came to the world within My Womb. He knows that purity finds its origin in the Mother of God. My Special son, I wish all My children to come to Me in their quest for meaning and accept My role in their conversion. You must remember that these are miraculous times, but there are forces that oppose miracles on a daily basis. Please remember that I will be with you in future days, and especially next Friday when you will be 52 years old. *"Thank you."* And, you should realize that your soul is still as young as when the Lord placed you in your mother's womb."

Saturday, September 21, 2013
1:55 p.m.

"It is not about invigilation."

"With whom you share your days, My little sons, you shall likewise share your happiness. With whom you suffer, you shall also share the providence of the Crucifixion. This is the reason I have come to you, My dear ones. I wish to share My happiness with you. I wish to connect you with the Cross and Resurrection, that you will know full joy and perfect absolution. I come today to dispel a myth that often keeps sinners from coming to the Cross, from embracing redemption in Jesus' Blood. The myth is this – Who would seek forgiveness of their sins from someone who judges their every move from afar, who never communicates with them, who watches over them for no other reason than to punish them when they make mistakes? The idea of 'invigilation' is attributed to Christianity by those who reject the Cross because they believe that they have no control over their own destiny. Watching over someone with protective grace is the desire of the God of Abraham. However, watching over someone just to castigate them for their mistakes is not the desire of the God of Abraham. My Special little son, I have described to you the reason why so many of My messages are discounted. Many people say to themselves, '...there goes that God again, coming to wreck our lives, to beat our backs with lashes, to punish our errors, to take the best from us and throw the rest away.' It is true that the Holy Scriptures speak of the Lord and His invigilation, but this overseeing dominion is not meant for punishment, but for supernatural guidance. One can be guided without being impugned. A sinner can be admonished without losing his dignity. Remember that Jesus is a loving Savior, a sacred friend in whom humanity has found their dignity. This is more reason to be pleased about your sacrifices; you imitate the Man who has remade the world, who has given cause for the Church to be magnified in Him, who has defeated the doubters of the Cross. My Special son, you know about Jesus and the Father in Heaven being described as deific disciplinarians who command the world's compliance without sharing in humanity's suffering. This is the reason many people take other paths. Let us look more closely at the means by which God intervenes in the lives of His flock. I know that earthbound men are prone to cite the Old Testament trials, punishments and chastisements to refute what I am saying here today. But, I am not contradicting the Mosaic scriptures, I am telling you that Jesus is fulfilling them. He places self-discipline in the hands of those who believe. The New Covenant presumes that lost sinners will also judge themselves. This is a great deal of responsibility for them, to decide their place alongside the King of men. They must ask questions about their worthiness to inherit His Kingdom. They must ask themselves whether they can walk in His footsteps. For sure, they declare, the God of their fathers expects as much from anyone else as from His Only Begotten Son. Remember that Pope John Paul the Great said that the Holy Spirit comes to heal and bless, teach and elevate, and to build peace and instill hope. This is an intervention that gives support and lends confidence to all who believe. It is not punishment at all; it is divine wisdom. It is not punitive invigilation, it is making someone aware of the consequences of their actions. The punishment, if any, rests in the guilt of the unconfessed sinner, in the sinner's regret for the way he has lived.

    Jesus forgives and teaches self-forgiveness through the Sacraments. This is why non-Catholics are so far from the truth. They cannot imagine a God who so loves His creatures that He would come among them Body, Blood, Soul and Divinity. They have no idea what Beatific Love means. The Protestant Book of Discipline, for example, when referring to the Holy Sacrifice of the Mass as a Romish superstition, is blasphemy spewed from the mouth of the devil. You must remind your exiled brothers and sisters that all religious doubt comes from Satan. People who question their own faith, especially what the Roman Catholic Church teaches, are culpable for not upholding what they profess to believe. Humanity must understand the Crucifixion the way I have taught you and your brother, the way the Catholic Church teaches, that the Holy Mass is embedded in human Salvation, and human Salvation is embedded in Jesus' Sacrifice on the Altar. You are correct in your observation that people like your brother know the difference between blind invigilation and miraculous intercession. When you see messages referring to certain warnings, these are not meant to frighten those who have aligned themselves with the Gospel. The Lord watches the Earth from On High, and He does so with vast sympathy and compassion for all believers. The warnings are aimed toward sinners who know about God, but who reject Him because of their own pride. The warnings are for those who abuse their power in the secular and religious realms. They are for those who will not submit to the life that Jesus teaches in favor of a life where only their selfish whims are satisfied. My Special son, do you understand what I am saying today? *"Yes. Thank you."* It is an important distinction because it is the essence of why some believers turn away. This is the primary argument against the presence of God used by atheists. They cannot understand how any God could watch so many billions of people simultaneously, as though He is somehow influenced by the effects of time and space. Atheists also cite the destruction of holy shrines and relics as proof that God cannot be taking care of His Kingdom, even as these atheists are themselves the origin of this destruction. I have always said that irony abounds. God does not teach with fists and whips. He teaches with blessings and Sacraments. Jesus did not come to condemn the Earth, but to save it, to give humanity reason to believe in redemption, to bring hope instead of despair. Jesus came to rescue the world from dying of its own sins. My Special son, you know that He does these things still. You also know that the New Covenant places the impulse for action in the heart of Church. The framework is there; the foundation has been laid in Jesus on the Cross. Here, I have given you a means to respond to those who deny the Will of God because they believe that He is not interested in who they are, what their identity is, who they perceive themselves to be, and what future they hope for themselves. Huge swaths of people cannot seem to connect the Love of God with their daily lives; they cannot understand that the power to change the world is in their hands. God gives it to them. It is written in the Scriptures. It is scrolled in the diaries of the Saints. It is detailed in the intricacy of Nature. It is the handiwork of those who have bequeathed their faith to you.

    Concepts are blessings when spoken in the context of the Church. Things like 'arrival' and 'survival' take on new meanings when pondering the connection between mortal life and the Afterlife. Once the Holy Spirit imbeds in the human heart; once Jesus is present there, the definition of survival means not just getting from one point to the next, but what road is taken and who travels along with you. Forgiveness is not just about saying 'I am sorry' and going on to something else, it means 'I regret what I have done, and I will amend my behavior into a more righteous course.' And here, human life takes on more dimensions as someone learns the difference between just living and moving toward one's glorious new beginning. Do these blessings sound like a Kingdom that practices invigilation? Utterly not. This is the call of the Third Person of the Triune Deity. God issues a heart-piercing love so profoundly through the wisdom and consolation of the Holy Spirit that, if seen with the human eye, it would be too blinding to bear. This is the charge that comes from Heaven every moment of every hour, but still, some people reject it. They must be cultivated; they need to hear new warnings every day. This is what God is doing, and someone without compassion would never give such warnings in advance. I ask you to pray for My messages around the globe, for each has its purpose; each is proof that God does more than just watch the suffering of men from afar without taking pity on their pain. If atheists want to view God as someone who punishes the world, then they have the correct perception when it comes to sinners like them. God will break and defeat them. He will strike down their spirits. He will cast them all, of their own volition, into the fires of the Abyss. They will judge themselves harshly, and Jesus will honor their self-condemnation. My Special son, Jesus will tell these sinners to take their accomplices with them, all of them, everyone involved in the ruination of the Earth; all the idols, conspirators and co-conspirators who will populate Gehenna without a droplet of relief. The point I am making is that humanity has the power to set their own course aright through the mandates of the Scriptures and the teachings of the Church. If there is any invigilation, it should be the ordinances of someone's conscience keeping watch over their own life. Make no mistake; God sees, hears and feels everything that humanity does, but I do not. I have said that I am spared most of the evils that Jesus does not want Me to see. I see all the good things, though. I see the gift of holiness in newly converted hearts. I see hugs and 'thank you' notes. I see smiles and the baptism of children. I see the rainbows that put their seers in such awe. I hear the prayers of those who will be Saints in their time. I am heartened by what I see, the love between parents and children, forgiveness that heals the deepest wounds, confessions that eradicate the most egregious errors, and the light that leads lost sinners to find themselves in the presence of absolving grace. I weep with joy when someone says that they are sorry and will change their ways. I pray in thanksgiving when little children are born. I raise My hands in blessing over those who help the poor and lift the weak. I shelter beneath My Mantle all who are consecrated to My Immaculate Heart. My Special son, these are gifts from God who cares that men not only live, but that they live wholly and fruitfully. They are evidence that the Creator has not abandoned His Creation. They are proof that the God of Abraham and Isaac has kept His promise of generations of peace to those who accept the Crucifixion of His Son. The Will of God and the will of men are connected at the center of these things. God and His creatures are one when men who see their purpose in life as an opportunity to build a world that looks so much like Heaven that no one can tell them apart. My Special one, I live in this hope. It is not just because I am the Mother of Jesus that I have this hope, but because I have seen it in people like you. I have heard it echoed in voices like your brother at your side. I have welcomed in My arms billions of souls who have lived and died in Jesus Christ; He who was so profoundly announced, birthed, reared, crucified, resurrected, and ascended for the Salvation of the world. So today, My Special son, I have given you another beatific message. It sounds sweet resonating back into Heaven from the center of your bountiful heart."

Saturday, September 28, 2013
1:17 p.m.

"Dust off the winner."

"My dear little children, you are heartened by your achievements; you are sanctified by your sacrifices, you are comforted by your sacredness, and you are blessed by God for undertaking it all. I am pleased to be here today because you are always uplifted in My prayers. We are ensuring that the Lord knows of your determination to not turn back. Like My other devoted messengers, seers and locutionists throughout the ages, you are connected to the Divine Love of God's Kingdom without departing the boundaries of this world. When I say the words, 'Dust off the winner...,' you are given an image of endurance and reward. You are aware that your testament to humanity is not just voiced, but also written by your actions, lived to their fullest, and imparted to Creation while everyone observes. Indeed, you have never been alone in anything you have done. It may seem as though you are secluded from the nations, but you have been preparing a grand presentation for the Heavenly Hosts, for God Himself, for Jesus and the Saints, for the Martyrs and Doctors of the Church, for all the little creatures who pine for renewal, and for the permanence of the changes that have come to remake human life. I have kept you anonymous here, but this means that you have had time to prepare your holy works without the eccentricities of curiosity seekers who only wish to be near you to say that they have been here. Most of these people are only shopping around; they want to know what God might say not for the purpose of changing their lives, but to take a whiff of righteousness and go on about their business. My little sons, these souls will never be winners. They will never soil their clothes or step forward to volunteer a journey through the dark corridors of the Earth. They are spectators who refuse to surrender control or their ability to make their own choices. I have always protected you from them, even as I have been protecting you from certain parishioners and other believers who want only to tear you down, to soil your reputation, to publicly rebuke you so they do not have to believe what I have to say. Indeed, they are also holdouts; they refuse to be conscripted into the ranks of those who are willing to enter the arena. Even more, being willing to enter the arena and doing so are two different things. You know by now that when someone says that they would wish that the Mother of Jesus would speak to them, they have no idea what they are asking. This speaks to the acclamation, '...if today you hear the voice of God, harden not your hearts.' The grass is not only less green on the other side, it is often barren and colored green by the devil who lures you there. This is why I ask My children to remain loyal to the Apostolic Church. There are millions of suffering souls in the Church; there are millions who are keeping their faith and trying to finish the race. One must remember that dusting off the winner implies that the winner has fallen along the way. A Christian cannot really come to his feet unless he has seen his faith from the underside. This is the reason I am speaking to you. It is not now, My little sons, that you remain on the ground. You have already been raised by the Church. You have been put down by the world and raised up again in Jesus on the Cross. You are living the dignity that is yours. Hence, I come today to say that the course on which you were placed many years ago is proceeding. Do not be afraid of things that might come. When you see something that must be done for God's neediest ones, remember that sufficing those needs comes through servants like you. When you are hungry, you should say, '...the Lord's vessels need more nourishment,' and the Holy Eucharist will be right there. Yes, you are vessels of the Holy Spirit and sanctifiers of the Earth by your lives. When you need anything that promotes the mission of the Gospel, the message of the Cross, and the Glory of Jesus' Kingdom, you should say that, '...we need this' or '...we need that' so there is unity of your hearts with the Father and the Son. These are your prayers. You are aware that this tethers you to the sacrifices that accompany eternal redemption. Yes, yes, it is clear that you have reached reconciliation with Heaven because you have shed the enticements of the Earth.

My Special son, when you cited the priest's words to Bernadette in your memoir, that she is simultaneously in Heaven and on Earth, this applies to your heart and conscience as well. Your soul is not yet in Paradise, but the wholesale essence of your existence is already there. All you need to do is enter the gate and occupy the Father's House that He has prepared for you. You realize that you must work here in His vineyard until you are called by Jesus to conclude your tenure, pass through the veil of your exile, and enter the Promised Land. Men claim that they have already seen it, but they are speaking metaphorically. It is a great sign of predestination for someone to say that they have already 'seen' the homeland of their soul. It means that they not only believe that their Salvation in Jesus is imminent, they have been bathed in His Blood from the inside. This is what it means to be cleansed in the Blood of the Lamb, to turn oneself inside out and transfer one's self-identity into that of the Saints. This is often a rigorous process. Days and nights can be long; agony and misery are rampant – this is the origin of your joy! It is the shedding of the old self in favor of the new. This is how a Christian becomes a giant among men for the advancement of the Church. These sacrifices are like stepping stones through mine-laden fields. They are like milestones on the journey of truth. They are like indicators on a volume switch, turning up the sound of righteousness so even the deaf can hear. These sacrifices are the balm that soothes the Sacred Heart of the Perfect Sufferer whom I have told you about for decades. They find their origin in one's consecration to Jesus' Most Sacred Heart and My Most Immaculate Heart – the two of us, united and determined, unfazed by the failures of men, devoted to the last millisecond of the world, encouraged by prayer, invigorated by humanity's beginnings, and willing to sustain the buffets that still impact us over 2,000 years after the New Covenant was fashioned inside the ages of the world. My Special son, we have courage because we have made these sacrifices about which I speak. No more sorrowful heart ever existed than the Mother of the Son of Man beneath the Cross of Mount Calvary. I was devastated by Jesus' Crucifixion at the same time that I pitied the soldiers who murdered Him. But, it was that day, My Special son, that I gained My first glimpse of humanity redeemed. It was on Good Friday that I first had the sense that the Child of My Womb would do precisely what He came into the world to do. I was no more prepared for His death than any parent in this life. It was all about Sacrifice, but I discovered that this Sacrifice was the wielding of the weapon that gunned-down the evil in all the ages to come. Satan's reign was not just killed that day, it was forever destined to Hell to never rise again. No other man would have to die for the redemption of lost souls. Surely, I am aware that Satan still wreaks havoc here in the exiled world. He enlists those who do not believe what I have said to you today. This is why I am trying to convert lost sinners to the Cross. I would have already done so if the temptations of this world were not so alluring. Accepting Christianity and adopting a holy life in accordance with the Gospel requires more than speaking nicely about others. It demands the rehabilitation of one's sense of identity and involvement with the mandates of the Church. It requires fighters who are willing to fall down and get back up again. It demands competitors who are unsure whether they will ever see another day. It speaks to the fact that victory seems but an illusion during the darkest hours of the night. It means tasting the bitterness of battle and the flesh-piercing blade of the enemy's sword. It is a promise to the devil that his best days are over, that his threats and poison will never make you turn your back on the Cross. And, it is by not doing these things that your brothers and sisters are failing. Their intentions are lukewarm, even cold and dismembered. They wish to pass through life's uncomfortable moments as quickly as they can. Many lack passion and romance; they go through the motions just to say they did. They take a pedestrian approach to an authentic fight for the justice of the Earth. This is not the way real warriors live; it is not the centerpiece of apostolic zeal. Their lives have nothing to do with the propagation of the Roman Catholic Church. Even still, God loves them anyway. He knows that humanity is afraid, the same way it has always been afraid, too timid to be engaged because they cannot preordain the outcome. My children have been so riddled by the devil's attacks that they seem too reticent for the fight. My Special one, if they become obedient in the way that Jesus has taught you, they will see beyond that horizon. Bless you for praying for them; you are the hands of the Lord in this life with your brother. You are his holy companion, and I am proud of you for reflecting the image of My Son."

Saturday, October 5, 2013
9:39 a.m.

"Repairing humanity's stress fracture."

"It is with deep gratitude that I speak in wholesome strains here today, My little sons, because you remain peaceful amidst the feverish commotion ongoing in the world. My gratefulness is extended to all who call on My help, the millions around the globe who look to My Motherhood for guidance, comfort and wisdom. You can see by My opening phrase today that everything ill that I have brought to your attention can be described as a 'stress fracture.' It is the strain on the human person by the sins of exiled men, by humanity's excesses and overages, by immense acts of neglect and offense, and by the inordinate rudeness that is borne into Creation by those who do not believe in God. I have given you reason to believe that this burden can be lifted, not just sustained, but removed from the back of humanity's soul. It is repairable for sure, and this is the best we can do for these times, at least until the nations embrace the Kingdom of God, destined to annex the Earth into His eternal domain. I wish for you to understand that the expungement of humanity's stress is uniquely possible in this decade, but the will of other men makes this a formidable task. My Special son, you have written in your memoir the reasons for this, obvious and implicated; and you are one of the world's few authors whose vision transcends these seeable and unforeseeable conditions. When we ponder the cause of the world's stress, what has created the fissure between perfect love and humanity's standing, we could speak for hours about it. And, when we speak about repairing the stress fracture or removing it altogether, we know that the solution is contained in the Gospel of Jesus Christ. The first is a litany of errors and omissions that are too grotesque to catalog; the second must come as men sacrifice themselves, their agendas, their materialism, and their impurity and selfishness for the mission of the Church. They must put everything else down and take-up their crosses. I do not wish evil upon anyone. I pray during all earthly times for the conversion of My children away from the paths of devilish works. At long last, My Special son, can you see why the Lord allows the fires and darkness of life's fears to come upon non-believing souls? *"Yes."* He must run them out of the dark corners like rats and roaches. He must impact their consciousness with the prospect of '...what's next?' This is not the injection of trepidation into their lives by anything that God commits, it is the shedding of light onto their own voids and faults. It shows them their standing before the Son of Man in whom they must now claim their redemption. Hence, repairing humanity's stress fracture is about refocusing the world's attention away from its self-induced indifference, which is in itself the origin of such stress, to a new perception about life's priorities and sets of pursuable principles. Yes, you and your brother have extolled My Virginal Countenance, magnified your oath to the Cross, lived your dedication to the Blessed Trinity, and refused to deny My intercessory succor. You are not just reluctant to turn away from Me, you have wept to remain in My presence. There is a difference, and the difference is the same as recognizing that humanity's stress can be either repaired or expunged. Here, you attest your Confirmation into the Church by knowing that every stress in the world is a manifestation of the sins of men, and that you are confident in your work with Me. And, Satan knows it; everything in the secular void is being manipulated by him. This is where he tempts and lures, toys with men's feelings, corrupts their actions and expectations, and distracts them from the teachings of the Church. However, it is also a place where I have focused My attention for almost 2,000 years. Just because something is secular does not mean that it must be unholy – but it commonly does. My mission here is to lead My children who participate in the secular realms for their sustenance to fight for righteousness. You must remember that the Church procures its resources from secular people and secular institutions. This is the reason that it is not wrong or misdirecting for you and your brother to work in the secular void. It is only a void because we have not yet driven the devil completely out.

    We are trying to conquer secularism and fill its vacuum with righteousness; this is what repairing humanity's stress fracture means. Worldly secularism and Christianity will never be amalgamated, but they can coexist under the Flagship of Righteousness that guides the Church through the annals of time. The reason secularism is a failed system is because it is comprised of billions of people who do not subscribe to the teachings of the Church, even as they have no legitimate right to do so. Christopher Hitchens had it backwards; the Chaucerian frauds are sinners who lived like him. He saw the same breach, the stress fracture, in the world, then he blamed it on God. Now he knows that if the nations would have embraced the Church of Rome, there would have been no battles for him to cite. Christopher turned against the Church because his mother committed suicide; he refused to believe in God after that. But, the stress that he saw, the fractured nature of humanity that he so despised, was lost to him because he refused to accept his portion of the Cross. While he is emblematic of this sorrow, we have today discussed the stress fracture with hope, not despair, not defeatism, and not by wringing our hands. Think about the young people among you, those who are only now developing their perceptions of life. Their impressions are being made by what the Church teaches them, how their hearts are opened by the finer things of life – things like love, peace, justice, hope and chastity. They must learn them from the Church because the secular void is absent of them. It need not be this way; the stress fracture can be repaired, it can even be expunged. My Special son, I know that good people like you and your brother might say that this would be a tall order, even for the Son of Man. My response is that if something can be measured, it can be overcome. If there are limits, these limits can be exceeded. If there is any excellence in this life, it can be fostered by this perfection. This is the reason I have given you this message today. I speak about breaking beyond the boundaries of human mortality by humanity before mortality itself arrives. Does this define a miracle? Surely, it does. Have I motioned Christians onto the forefront of the world's stage? I absolutely have – to be servants. To be heroes and boundary-breaking visionaries. To wreck a world that already lies in the same ruins that took Adam and Eve from the Garden. To turn it upside down and kill the repulsion that keeps good men from fighting harder for God. Christianity is an unsightly prospect. It involves battling and bleeding, scolding, reordering the priorities of civilized men, charging against gates and bulwarks, reaching into the depths of disoriented hearts; and yes, even dying in the street. It is an exhausting war against the enemies of the Cross. And, it has only mere time to go before the stress fracture finally disappears.

I have said, My Special son, that you and your brother are being silently persecuted for what you believe, for what you have done for Me. Why, you might ask, do I not remove these obstacles from your path? Because I take My advice from the Perfect Sufferer whom I have spoken about for many years. He does not desire that you lack the aid you need to succeed. He is elated that you are willing to march forward with or without it. Remembering the soldiers who marched with boots made of burlap bags; none of them would have been remembered if they had armored tanks to transport them. Jesus' own death would have been remanded to any other execution if He had not been nailed to the Cross. It was done publicly because of the public nature of human redemption; you will see on the last day that there never were any hidden absolutions. I am speaking about expunging a public stress fracture caused by billions of people whose lives are yet unwitnessed by the hordes and masses. I speak of repairing the breach because it may be the best we can do for now. *Come, O' Jesus, into your Kingdom by way of miracles! Rush them, and slay them! Bring not only your presence, but also your present-ness! Become the true reason why human hearts beat and then fall motionless before the Glory of the Cross! Instill in us, your Mother and your children, the will to endure what You would have us take as another sip of your righteousness.* My Special son, you must realize the opportunity that humanity has been given by the miracles of these years. I know that you are aware of these miracles, but it is in their aftermath that the changes to the lives and identities of ordinary sinners will come. It will occur once the miracles find their fulfillment. It will be an effect of many warnings come and gone. It will be in the silence after the storm, when losses can be counted as in the wake of an atom bomb. I am not speaking about something that will happen many decades from now; places like America are rushing it into the fore. Now, rather than complaining about what you see, rather than becoming frustrated, be thankful that these days have finally arrived. *"I am. Wait until the world hears all you have said."* There, you have uttered the words to describe the Spirit of the Man-God living in your heart. Take seriously the content of this message about the heroic side of being a visionary. Allow Jesus to witness what you shall still accomplish for Him. This is perfect obedience, the precise reflection of Jesus on the Cross. Through your faith and prayers, you were given a sign of power because you perfectly committed yourself to glorifying the Cross, and this is why

Satan strikes you. Your allegiance causes evil men to fall flat on their faces. Your obedience shines the Light of Heaven on the devil's domain of darkness. It raises Divine Love in the Lord's vineyard as the standard for human life. Hence, I have completed My message for today. You are making excellent progress on your memoir. I know that you are not opposed to the assistance of the Angels. It is a profound book; it is a masterpiece of divine revelation in the lineage of the Doctors of the Church. Congratulations! *"Thank you, Mama. I am happy to be your son, and to know it."* Thank you for praying for the Catholic Church, for all who are suffering for Jesus' sake, for the poor, and especially for the protection of all unborn children."

Saturday, October 12, 2013
9:28 a.m.

"From a sewing needle into a skyscraper."

"Yes, My little darlings, I come to this place with awesome graces to bless your lives and embolden your hearts. It is peace, My little ones, that I bring you to soften the gruffness of your days. I wish for you to know that you are changing humanity; you are remaking the face of the Earth by the power of the Holy Spirit within you. My opening remark today is simple to understand; you are indeed growing the Kingdom of the Lord from your home and your prayers as though transforming a sewing needle into a skyscraper. Yes, from a teardrop into a waterfall, from a tricycle into a star ship. These metaphors are indicative of the whole Church, but few see or recognize them because they are distracted by the material world. You have recorded in your books and the longevity of your lives the Will of God for humanity and the intention of Jesus to redeem all who believe in Him. This is why you are attacked by the devil. You are obedient to the calling of the Mother of God; you employ your great works on behalf of My Son, and you deploy everything in your hands to turn back Satan's evil schemes. This is the reason you are so despised by the world's evil legions; it is why you are ignored by citizens of power, it is the reason you are attacked in the night. You embrace and propagate Divine Love in a world that rejects Jesus with impunity. Taking down a picture of Jesus at a learning institution is the ultimate cowardice of the faithful and those who claim to have inherited the legacies of the Saints. Imagine this; the multi-billion dollar education industry did not want to fight to keep the iconic photograph in place because it would cost too much money. This tells you about everything you need to know. It is not about fighting for truth, it is about compromising with evil through social expedience. Why did Jesus not intervene in this case? Because He wanted the whole world to realize how close to His Second Coming humanity has become. Indeed, the end of the world as they know it. There is no question that the suffering of the Catholic Church will go on as long as there are wicked souls like these on Earth. And, why would the devil come to someone in the night with such grotesque experiences of murder, torture and destruction? Because the poor soul undergoing this agony is so close to the Lord. Satan believes that he can break someone's faith in God by proving that God will not stop these attacks. Let us remember the Holy Scriptures. Satan never attacks those who are closest to him. He pursues the innocent, the little ones who have given their lives to divinity and righteousness. Being attacked by Satan for one's devotion to Jesus Christ is one of the highest compliments that could ever be paid to a man. (*In the midst of the routine assaults upon us by the devil that have been commonplace since Our Lady began speaking to us, Satan has chosen to manifest great persecution and suffering upon my brother in recent months. Timothy has been undergoing horrific mystical tortures wrought by the devil himself. There is no way for him to escape them, but only endure them. Their depth would make one question how he has survived them. Imagine the 100 most gruesome tortures experienced in the history of mankind, and being forced to endure each one as if it were literally and physically being inflicted upon you; not as a spectator, but as a victim. I know this will continue for only as long as God allows. Miracles of conversion are being wrought by his suffering. Both he and I know that we have the power to make it stop any time we wish, simply by rejecting our work with our Holy Mother. Imagine that. Choosing all of this because She is so beautiful and knowing Her gifts are so needed by the world. How would the world be changed any other way? Only through our own suffering in union with the Crucifixion of Jesus Christ.*)

My Special son, you know that there are times when I speak at length and others with brevity. There is no certain aforethought in this distinction; it is simply something that I sometimes do. Given all that is occurring in your life with your brother, I have decided today to come sharing My unity with your faith and to bless you. I have come to remind you that I am your Mother. I have come to reaffirm that My sacred duties include watching over you and protecting you from harm. I do this because you live so prayerfully. When I speak about the transformation of a sewing needle into a skyscraper, I am asking you to remember that you and your brother are growing the mustard seed for the rest of the world. I realize that there is no great profundity that you can recognize on a daily basis originating from this truth. Your lives seem the same, but there are unique and powerful graces emanating from you nonetheless. You are so loved! You are admired and raised before the nations of the Earth in the realms of Paradise. God loves commitment! Look at how far you have come. You have expanded holiness throughout Creation. And, this makes Satan angry. He might do things as simple as causing pulled muscles or inflicting intense headaches. Or, as in the lives of the great Saints, he brings tortures and terrors, as with your brother. He does this as much in vengeance as trying to lure you away from the Cross. He mocked Jesus through onlookers on Good Friday, asking that if Jesus was indeed the Son of God, why did He not save Himself from the Crucifixion. The answer is not that Jesus could not have descended from the Cross, but that He chose not to. He still understands above all other knowledge that His Passion and Crucifixion have procured the redemption of the world. And, Satan knows it as well. When Satan begged with overtones that only Jesus could hear for Jesus not to kill him, Jesus responded beneath His breath that the matter could not be reversed. The battle had already engaged; the first shots had been fired, and all and everything evil would be expunged from eternity by this Holy Sacrifice. It was the Will of God that became the Will of Jesus even before He was placed in My Womb. Jesus knew the outcome that He pronounced from the Cross. He said that He intended to ensure the demise of the devil; and with His Bloody Sacrifice and the Glory of the Father in His soul, He said that it was finished. That was the day that set the world on a fulcrum, rocking all humanity onto an irrevocable course of reconciliation with their Creator, and nothing could turn it back. From that day forward, the battles to come would not be about whether Satan would finally lose, but when. My Special son, you are seeing that 'when' is occurring every day; you can tell that it is not really about whether a picture is removed from its place, but the place in which the perpetrators will lastly reside. I ask you to remember that I pray for them, but I do not pity them. Yes, these words came from the Mother of God! There are countless implications to this matter that we will discuss on another day. When one of My children, especially someone born on the auspicious day of February 22, needs help and assistance, I send them aid. I choose to lead them to health and peace of mind. I choose to recognize the intercession of Saint Peter to lift-up those who are born every day, and especially those born on the Feast of his Chair. My little child whom you are assisting is trying the best he can to overcome decades of hurt from his youthful years. Thank you, My Special son, for helping Me assist him. You and your brother are My extended hands in the temporal realms. I am comforted by your prayers. I adore yours and your brother's love. I am drawn here like a butterfly to a flower. My Immaculate Heart, as strong and invincible as it will always be, is given even greater comfort when I see the dedication by which you lead your lives; your dedication to God and Jesus, to Saint Peter and Saint Joseph and all the Saints, to your exiled brothers and sisters, to the Lord's creatures great and small, and to the Providence by which humanity is led to redemption in the Will that has made the Cross the Salvation of the world. To all the sinners who are still lost and to those who have already been reborn, I promise that I will hold fast to everything given to the Church through Me and in My name. Therefore, I remain in defense of My children against every ill-conceived notion under the sun. I will not retreat from My mission of interceding before My Son for humanity's sake. While there is plenteous power in the Wisdom of the Holy Spirit, I have shared this power with hundreds of seers and messengers like you and your brother. I have given you free rein and pronounced blessing over your lives and writings. You must live in faith like everyone else; you must not induce or take advantage of your station as messengers to circumvent your lives. I will help you to the fullest extent of My Motherly guidance. Do you understand? *"Yes, I understand. Thank you."* It means so much to Me that you trust Me. You must make sound decisions in everything you do, everywhere you go. Thank you for your prayers. I promise that I will touch all whose lives you have asked Me to bless. I will complete My purposes here in these exiled realms."

Monday, October 21, 2013
9:18 a.m.

"Discerning intelligence – Seeing beyond the illusion."

"Awesome is God's Holy Word, and blessed are they who believe in Him! This is My message to humanity, My little sons, through you, through the Angels, through the ages, and through all the suffering men and women whose legacies have emboldened the Church. I ask you today to remain joyful in your stations; keep your hearts aloft in the Will of God. I have spoken about His Wisdom, that His Wisdom is the origin of your intelligence. It cannot be the other way around. And today, I have come to remind you that the discerning wisdom of your own humanity is in communion with God, that this is your means of knowing what comes to you in terms adoptive to the Kingdom that is to come. I speak of seeing beyond the dark illusions that impact you every day. I am not saying that your consciousness is built on some paranormal state while you live in exile – your holiness is this miracle. The supernatural facets of your lives come to you from within, not what is around you. My Special son, I am pleased with you because of your reaching out to your family at your mother's birthday party and going for recreation in the country. You are proving that someone can be a messenger and seer of the Holy Virgin and still remain connected with sensible intelligence to the temporal world. This is the balance that My children require. You see before you a life that has wrapped you in the Grace of God at the same time that you are given the opportunity to factualize this Grace into seeable forms. But, the illusion to which I refer is in everything in the world that tries to diminish your faith, that erodes your freedom, that attempts to make you believe that your knowledge of right and wrong are symptoms of excessive rigidity. I am describing the wisdom, intelligence and knowledge 'continuum' by which righteous men live. Wisdom manifests intelligence, and intelligence fosters knowledge. One might think that knowledge fosters intelligence, but this is untrue because false knowledge is unwise; it lacks intelligence. Knowledge is oftentimes neutral too. In order for knowledge to reflect wisdom through intelligence, it must be based on the truth, on God's Divine Truth. Thinking is the processing of knowledge, also known as thought. So, what is this progression? *"Wisdom, intelligence, knowledge and thought."* Yes, and how does this affect your ability to see through the illusions of the world? *"It helps us become more contemplative. Contemplation is from a platform of prayer that places you in touch with God's Wisdom."* Yes, perfect. There can be no illusion in this progression because prayer must come from the heart, and the heart cannot lie to you. There is always truth in the heart, meaning that even evildoers know that they are not righteous. Truth tells them that they are unholy, and they realize it. Even they cannot be fooled by the illusion cast upon them by their own riches and excesses. *"But, they create an illusion as their intelligence; and they truly believe the lie in them, and then begin to think and live by it. The light inside them is darkness."* Yes indeed, and this is the illusion that Divine Wisdom helps you see; the Lord aids in your discernment of others' acts and motivations. Seeing beyond the illusion means that you know the so-called rites and rituals that others use to place men into servitude and poverty. This is one of the most grotesque aberrations of the American capitalist society. This is what you were trying to say earlier about the cost of simply surviving here in this land. You said that they extract wealth from you, and your brother says that they extort it. You are both correct.

Your friend said yesterday that he wants to get his house paid off so at least that part of 'the beast' will withdraw from his door. It is all about the insatiable appetite of the capitalist beast that causes so much stress and dissension here in the United States. Part of the illusion about which I have spoken today is that being indebted to the beast seems to be an unavoidable aspect of life. It has nothing to do with liberty. It is part of the punishment imposed on hardworking people who aspire to have a nice place for their families to live, far from the grime and unsightliness of the city. It seems that if someone aspires to live comfortably like so many you know, they are unduly criticized by everyone else whose hands are in their pockets. The illusion is that this is the way America is supposed to be. The liberal elements in your nation have won the notion that people are not allowed to be self-sufficient without also paying for the slothful; this is the illusion to which I refer. And, when you calculate the cost of everything from food, shelter, clothing, heat and all the rest, the illusion also says that the capitalist monster must prosper if the nation does not want to die. They do their worst to concentrate most of the wealth into as few pockets as possible and to fear-monger the rest into having to purchase insurance for homes, cars, and everything else with a fiscal worth. Illusion, illusion. Do you understand? *"Yes."* What I am saying is that none of this has anything to do with human redemption. It is not wrong for anyone to desire to live in a comfortable home they have built with the sweat of their brow, but what does it contribute to the conversion of the lost? *"Almost nothing."* I am not criticizing anyone for their hard work, but would it not be better to construct a mirror image of this home and save hundreds of thousands of dollars instead? So, My discussion about the illusion is even more contorted when good people decline to live frugally. The twisting and confusion grow even more intense, and the truth has another dimension pushing it further into the shadows. Illusion, illusion. I see it all the time. I see it worldwide. Most of your friends are good people, devoted to God, sharing and compassionate, hardworking and decent. There is nothing wrong with the way they live. I am just making a point about yet another dimension to the illusions that prohibit the Lord from being visible to inquisitive mortal eyes.

I will also tell you that _____ will in his time propagate My messages more than I can explain. He will disseminate your books into far more places in this world than the Church could ever imagine. In his day, it will happen. Make no mistake; we will advance first, but he has the energy, and will appropriate the audience, to take My Morning Star messages into places yet unknown. All the darkness about which we have spoken will be eradicated by the Light of My Son. This is why I have come; this is what you already know. Always remember that Jesus is with you. He makes good use of your apostolic love. There is no illusion in you; justice will come for those in whose arms and hearts the Holy Spirit rests with joy. I repeat here today that the wisdom you require, that all men require, to remain steadfast in your faith is your knowledge that sacrifice is the key to redemption. From this sacrifice, you will discover the origins of intelligence and thought; you will prepare to see the Saints you will join in Heaven. You will be one with the Contemplative Will of the Father. Yes, it is through prayer that you have done this. Through your prayers, you will ultimately see how many souls have been converted, how many have been released from Purgatory while you and I and your brother have prayed here together. Imagine how many hours we have prayed since February 22, 1991. How many minutes, how many seconds? And, a soul for every second has been granted admission into Heaven from Purgatory. I bless you for this, for embracing My messages, for taking good care of your brother, for standing fast in your knowledge of My intentions, and for facing-down the world with courage. You will someday see that all these times have been blessed, even when you have suffered, even when there was nary a flicker of hope, even when you wondered if the Lord was even listening to your prayers. Grand things come from the most unexpected origins. It can be no other way. This is the thesis of the mustard seed. It is the begetting of all the blessings that I have spoken about. Dimensions atop of dimensions. This is the way illusions are overcome. Yes, the world is about standards and wealth; it is about cultures and fashions, but these things are not perpetual. They are illusions themselves. I have brought your vision to the pinnacle of human understanding. And, I have done so by asking that you remain embedded in your society of friends and your family as a faith-based human being. Thank you for remembering all who need our prayers, especially those who will be marching at the Illinois Capitol. May God have mercy on their souls."

Our Lady was referring to the March on Springfield for Marriage Equality.

Saturday, October 26, 2013
9:21 a.m.

"Faith in the abstraction."

"Together we pray, My little sons. Together we mend the world with our love; together we fight off the darkness; together we conquer the night, together we bring back the morning sun. I am with you in this home and through all time. You have nothing to fear, no reason for apprehension, no thought of retreating, nothing that will make you turn back. My children, this is the origin of My joy. You speak about the way human life ought to be; and if not for sinful men, that way would become true. If God spoke of annihilation, beheading, punishments, chastisements, deficits and deprivation, faith would be shorn of hope. I urge you to know that Jesus wants for you the life that you wish. He asks God's people to defer to Him, thereby granting yourselves the lives you seek. It is important that you understand that sinful humanity is the reason for your suffering. This is the message of the Gospel and the teaching of the Church. If you think about the practical aspects of your belief in God, you know that this requires you to walk blindly, but yet sighted, by virtuous faith. The Holy Scriptures are your tangible grasp on what seems to be an intangible redemption. I have broached the topic here that keeps so many societies from believing in God. How can someone see without seeing? How can someone know without knowing? This is the abstract nature of your faith; it is the way good men walk toward the sun without being blinded. It is the way Divine Love enters the world through broken humanity. My Special son, do you suppose that a little ring bearer actually knows what he is carrying up the aisle at someone's wedding? *"No."* This is the same way that God calls on the innocence of humanity to participate in the marriage of Heaven and Earth. Indeed, even the ring bearer is wedded in that moment. Faith in the abstraction means that human beings do things without fully knowing the reason why. It is a mystery to the temporal world, but the redemption of lost souls and nations depends on this instinct. Letting go and allowing the Lord to use oneself is a grand and noble enterprise. I have said that little is preordained in the exiled realms, but humanity keeps making the same mistakes as if to suggest that nothing can truly change. You have heard that time is neutral; time itself has no bearing on the decisions that shape and reshape history. Events and transitions are the markings of people, either by commission or omission, and time is but an onlooker. This is why you must believe that you are arriving at the victories that you seek. I have seen them, and you will see them too. If you consider faith in the abstract opening all the possibilities that you might dream about, you must know that they are forced into being by the human actions about which I speak. These actions must advance the Kingdom of God and extol His Glory before the world in order for them to have eternal consequence. Only the things that have this consequence are sanctioned by the Father; only they have an effect on the outcome of time. The Father also ratifies the self-destruction of sinners who are bound for Gehenna. Heaven does not want them. God casts them out from His presence. This is the ratification that humanity should be terrified to see, but the world cannot seem to transfer their perception of faith from the abstract into the practical. If a man declares that he believes in God, but lives the life of a hellion, what blessings to himself or the world does he impart?

  Faith in the abstraction means that human action and reaction are founded in the 'decent peace' that comes from knowing what God desires. You and your brother have been hounded and beaten back by the devil's dogs because you are practitioners in the real world of a faith that can only be seen in your hearts. It is there that all things play out. The heart is the battleground where faith in the abstract is seeded, and its practical effects are protracted into the physical world from there. As I have said, you cannot see such things as love and affection. You cannot see hope and inspiration. However, you can see their fruits by giving charitably to others or hugging someone. You can see groceries and medicine. You can see artistic works that depict the lives of the Saints. You can touch the relics that they leave behind. All these manifestations articulate realities of faith in the abstraction. Jesus came into the world at Bethlehem to prove that Divine Love can subsist in a world that is devoid of beatific conscience. From the mind of God came the Son. From the Love of God came the Son. Jesus was begotten from the spiritual consciousness of an Eternal Father who has always lived. Here, I have said that the mind and the Love of God are one in being, and this is what He summons humanity to emulate. God desires the existence of humanity, from thought to practice, to be about Divine Love, perpetuated through human love. When this is perfectly achieved, faith in the abstraction will be seen in physical terms in the created universe. My Special son, I ask you to believe Me when I say that humanity is on their way to doing this. Why would I have otherwise come? Why would I have enlisted your aid for so many years? Why would I have put you and your brother through such struggles? All these questions are answered at the center of your success, with reference to your posture of upright triumph that will soon befittingly be apparent to the world. I ask that you recognize that demonic forces around you have become exasperated by what you have done for Me. They are playing to their own presumed strengths; they are utilizing faithless men and women to push you away. They are enlisting an army of faithless flocks to ignore your achievements and make you believe that God wants it that way. Imagine what I think every time you are told that you are not good enough for them. I say that yours is the dignity that will outlast their offenses in any Creation, during any time. You are like the Angels, Popes, Martyrs, Saints and legends. If it were easy, everyone would be like them. If you were not worthy, you would not have been chosen for this battle. If there was not so much truth hanging in the balance, you would have surely been led to something else by now. I have been speaking in paranormal terms about your lives that are stationed in the normal. If there is an agenda to your lives, it is that you are living out the Gospel as modern disciples, the children of Mary, teachers of the unknowing, fishers of men, finders of the lost, and remnants of the same Crucifixion that has brought light and life to the dead mortal world. Yet, much of the world still lies deceased; there are still dead consciences, dead motivations, dead spirits, and dead hopes. I am saying that Christians must live at the convergence of abstract faith and practical faith, to combine what is knowable about God with what is unknown to man. There is power and potential in this unification. Humanity can do it. Just look at all the space flights that have come and gone. They were accomplished as feats of true genius, but all there is to be shown of it now is a spattering of lifeless Old Glories, stuck like needles into the powdered face of the Moon.

I speak about taking this same spirit of accomplishment and exploration into the heights of human spiritual perfection that can be seen and unseen, that will live beyond the history of the universe in dimensions not yet achieved. My Special son, this is the courage that I am waiting to see from My exiled children. This is the thought and action that will raise the Church Triumphant to its feet, to see that I have succeeded, to know that the Immaculate Queen has reveled the Lord's slumbering masses and enlisted them in a faith-induced evangelism that will eclipse the nations and epochs of this world. The whole of human exile is destined for this moment – it is not far away. My Special one, I wish that Jesus would allow you to see your future. You have every reason to believe that your happiness is assured. As I once said, there will be more difficult times to come; people you love will pass away; your country will continue to deteriorate, the Church will be wholly crucified. But, the light will eventually dawn. The enemies of the Gospel will fall not just one by one, but in vast incalculable droves. A wave of righteousness will rise from the ashes of this destitute Creation. You and your brother are exiled men in the lineage of all the greatest and most valorous soldiers to ever defend the Roman Catholic Church. Adam and Eve did not win. Your mourning will be turned to joy; your sadness will be supplanted by your elation. You have read this storybook before. You are aware of the annals of history; you know about the parables of life. You keep pace with all this because you are not even close to exhausting your knowledge of what Jesus always wanted this world to become. Deep inside you is the deposit of sacred energy about which I speak. You grow weary and seemingly spent because you cannot see the visible signs of the abstraction of your faith. I can see it; this is why I am a messenger from God, and you and your brother are messengers for Me. The whole thing makes sense. Time marches on, but it has changed only little. You are yet as innocent as the moment you were baptized. I watch you live your days as those who preceded you fought and scraped their way back to the dignity that sinful men tried to take from them. I have seen the shroud of darkness that sinners have hung above your heads. My point is that such things are real only to the extent that you allow them to be; nothing can hurt you unless you let it. See the perfection of humanity through the lens of the defeat of your enemies in your lifetime. My little son, do you understand everything I have said today? *"How do we defeat the evil that impedes us in this life?"* You find new and more exacting standards that evoke from you a strength that can come only through the resurrection of your hearts. Do not allow other people to decide what makes you happy. You must connect yourselves to the Sacrifice of Jesus on the Cross, that your lives be as ameliorative to the collective human spirit as My Son's Passion, Crucifixion and Resurrection. Adopt an Easter attitude toward life that cannot be put asunder, giving it right back to your detractors by proving that they cannot steal the peacefulness in your hearts. Show your enemies who persecute you how tenacious you are. Retake your power from the devil's fiends by holding to the facets of your own identity that make you so unique. Jesus lends this aid based on how you can best imitate His life. When He decides that you have accomplished this well, then you will know that you have been chosen because of your ability to advance the Church. This has been the case all along. Does this answer your question? *"Yes."* Please repeat back to Me what I have said. *"We must pray and endure until He says enough."* My little son, is this not the way of all who have remained steadfast in Him? *"Yes."* And, please remember what I have said. It is not Jesus' fault that these things happen. It is that those who should be treating you with dignity are more prone to sin than living according to the teachings of the Scripture. *"But, if He is going to allow demons to attack us, should He not enlist the Angels to fight for us to defeat them?"* Jesus has protected you and your brother from more harm and poverty than you could possibly imagine in a million lifetimes. In the abstraction, your question is well taken. In practical terms, you should ponder what Jesus has already given you. Thank you for placing your trust in Jesus, for helping Him mend the divisions between humanity and the Father. Thank you for kindly giving yourself to the sacrifices that have thus far gained you such esteem in Heaven and among the Communion of Saints. Welcome to the Messianic life. I see in your heart that you are wondering where the victory of the Resurrection is. It is the antidote for all malevolent things, along with your determination to overcome everything evil by dwelling on the blessings of today. Your sacred joys will soon flow like rivers. Your books will be spread worldwide, and millions will be converted to the Cross. These things are yours. Your nation will return to the righteousness of its roots. The evil will be vanquished. *"Thank you for helping me understand."*

Saturday, November 2, 2013
10:11 a.m.

"The reach of theological inquiry."

"My holy sons, I come to you in peace with My Immaculate Heart filled with gratitude for your longstanding devotion. Yes, I come as always with the perspective of the Cross and the Church's eternal mission in My prayers. Jesus is mindful of your petitions and the desires of your hearts. I bring you this same perspective, this Glory of the Cross, as you are suffering on behalf of the Salvation of lost sinners. I reecho Jesus' intention of having humanity participate in this process. My Special one, this is the framework of human purification that God has put into place; this is what makes your memoir so relevant, so priceless in its explanation of what Christianity means. It is the conversion of the soul to Jesus and the transformation of the world into His Kingdom. I speak about the reach of theological inquiry in describing the questions that humanity asks and the responses that God provides. I also speak about the reach of theological inquiry with regard to the questions that Jesus asks of sinners, and what responses they give back. I have spoken about this reciprocity many times; as Jesus blesses the world, humanity should bless Him with their own spiritual conversion. And, this conversion must be seeable in the ways that I discussed in the past. My Special son, you cannot imagine how impressed I am with your first memoir. There are no words to describe it; you are far too modest in accepting My compliments for your vision, for your persistence and hard work. Your brother is learning a great deal about your younger years and the intensity of your private thoughts that you have never shared with him. As your brother keeps reading your text, he asks the Dominion Angels to tell the Father that your memoir must be directly from Him. 'Surely this must be the Son of God.' This is what your brother believes as he so humbly delves the depths of your faith. He has no difficulty believing everything you have written, especially about the Protestantism into which he was born. He met you through Me, just as you have said. And, all the instances and parables that you have included in your memoir give it complete relevance and legitimacy as a productive summons for the rest of the world. Congratulations; your memoir is beatific and brilliant; it is timely and pertinent, it is well-spoken and uniquely presented. *"Thank you, Mama."* I wish you could see it from the vantage point of those who have yet to read it. It takes Me back to explore the question, '...what about theological inquiry?' What is its reach? Why should exiled men examine themselves before the standards of the Church? The answer is that any question that a person can ask about someone else's faith must eventually be addressed to himself. The reach can expand around the globe, but the answers must originate inside the heart of the questioner. What does this mean for someone who wants to know the Divine Truth? The fact remains that Truth must be welcomed into a heart that does not doubt the outcome of the world. When approaching Jesus in prayer, it is sinful to harbor contempt for the Father's Will. Jesus' mission has been to purify Creation, cultivate the hearts of man, cast out demons, and to open the future for the flourishing of His blessings across this land. If Jesus is to claim His Kingdom, and there is no question that He will, He must purge the Earth of everything that stands in contradiction to the Gospel.

When we speak about Jesus' blessings upon Creation, I wish for you and your brother to remember that it is a gift to rid the world of anything that does not serve human redemption. This is painful; it is often like removing burned skin, as I told you several years ago. It is about exposing hedonism, corruption, heresy and blasphemy. If it were not meant to rid the Earth of unholiness, it would not be centered upon the purification of modern man. This is the transformation that has been brought to the world in your place and time. If the Lord did not believe that this could be accomplished, there would be no New Covenant. This is the reason why everyone will be brought into the providence of suffering. You and your brother have been suffering all along; you have given of yourselves and your lives for the advancement of My messages to glorify the Scriptures. Contrary to the beliefs of many, My messages here and around the globe have the power of spiritual conversion. I cannot dictate new dogma; this is a matter for the Church. But, I reinforce the Catholic Church's dogmas by telling humanity why they were adopted. Why can I not proclaim new dogmas? Because I am not a member of the Pontifical Succession. How would it have been appropriate for a Maiden so humble to appear in the 1800s and tell the world that I was conceived free from sin? Even though I was, this had to be proclaimed by the Church. I identified Myself as the Immaculate Conception only after it was proclaimed by the Roman Catholic Vicar. Here, the reach of theological inquiry was connected from the Seat of Christianity to the Throne of God and back again. My Special son, this is likely the most divisive dogma ever proclaimed by the Catholic Church because it counterpoints the thesis of the Protestant Reformation that you have upbraided in your first memoir. They have said that the Roman Catholic Church practices repugnance against the teachings of Jesus Christ. They are even more disturbed now that I have appeared by apparition around the world to say that the Catholic Church has proclaimed the truth. Theological inquiry can be based on empirical evidence or articles of faith. This is the reason these Protestants are stained with such shame. Science, technology, psychological examination, and photographic impressions prove that I have appeared on the Earth. The reach of theological inquiry has incorporated these assets into the facets of humanity's faith. They have not diminished faith, but ratified it. Yes, motives of credibility. And, this is the reason that you and your brother are such miracles for your age; you have remained steadfast in what you know, not just what you believe, but what you actually know about what God commends for His people. I have said that your hearts have assimilated through petition and servitude the Will of Wisdom for these times, in all places, to peoples everywhere, and to imponderable dimensions. This is the Lord's gift to you, and it is yours to Him. He claims dominion over the world, and you and your brother have remained beside Him. When He comes again, you will depart in His grace. You will not board a vessel and sail off into a universe unknown; you will be here and everywhere. You will see what the meaning of life has been from the eternal side of time. You will be transformed from mere existence to perpetual life. And, in this prospect, you have already begun. This is your answer; it is how I address your theological inquiry about why this must be true.

Eternal redemption demands the shedding of the flesh. It requires that repentance be made here, that the reunion of all previous generations must occur in the infinite realms, not those you see in this world. The transfer of the human soul must be made in a place where there is no darkness, no sorrow or injustice, no rudeness and no impurity. If the world became like this now, men would not realize their passage from this life into the next, just as I said many years ago. You must employ your faith to believe that all the inequalities of this life will lead to the Final Judgement where everyone who has persecuted you for your faith will be called to answer. The reach of theological inquiry suggests that not everyone whose faces you see through the years will be saved by Jesus' Sacrifice because many will reject Him. Some of them will condemn themselves; please do not pity them for it. The question you ask is which people they are. You have met some of them. You have seen them in workplaces and on television screens. They have appeared to be benign and gracious people, but underneath, they belong in the devil's den. It is your honor to realize that you are not like them. It is your right to allow them to condemn themselves. They belong to the netherworld; they reject Jesus as their Savior and despise Me as their Mother. What you pray about comes from your own inquisitiveness about what damage they have done and what harm they might do in the future. When you pray for them, you are asking Jesus to purify them or cast them from His presence. He will do so forthrightly, according to what mends the world and manifests the victory of the Church. You know that God has not commanded that there be a vanquishing of His enemies without a battle, without the rising-up in large numbers of His disciples to push back their error. And, even as these foes do their worst to punish the children of God, the greatest problem rests in those who claim to be Christians, but are only hypocrites. Your brother was declined the recent employment position for which he was eminently qualified. He was also turned away from the position with the State of Illinois by a man wearing a Protestant collar who saw him as too much a sinner. How ironic. Do you understand what I am allowing you to see? *"Yes."* Above all things, I am asking you and your brother to not be bitter. I am asking you to view other people for who they are, and for what they do, based on their demands and distractions, what threats you seem to be to their financial security and the ideologies they practice. I am not justifying what they do, I am saying that they are more afraid than courageous. You are blessed to be persecuted by them, and they will lose not just in the end, but soon in the future. My message today is about this; it is about what questions must be asked, who must ask them, who must answer them, in what light they are placed, what relevance they serve, and what outcomes they yield. In the middle of this commotion, you and your brother remain stable souls, upright warriors in a world skewed by selfishness, hatred and blind partisanship. You are doing well; your mission is on course, you should feel confident about yourselves and the plans you have laid out. Indeed, the entire idea of theological inquiry is what surrounds the examination of your books by the Church and the others who read them. Identifying the themes of My messages is difficult for them. I have never spoken anywhere in history like I have spoken to you and your brother. *"Thank you so much."* Thus, let us go forward together, completely united for what years remain, if only a few, before the Son of Man comes in Glory. These are sacred times for you; these days and hours are rendering you and your brother primed for pure victory, ordained and inaugurated for admittance into the Lord's Glorious Kingdom. My Special son, if for no other reason than this, you must remember that your lives are a bouquet of love, a gift to the Father, and a blessing upon the Church. You must know that eternity is timeless, not just a long time, but perpetually infinite and unceasing. All who are dying, everyone, everywhere are hearing My messages to you and your brother on their passage into the Light of Paradise. My words are engraved there for everyone to see, especially 'The Final Colossus' poem to which all souls are drawn because of its description of Me. Heaven owes you its benison for this. Jesus is indebted to you for your elevation of the Matriarch of the Church, as the Angels have laid this remarkable text on the floor of Creation through you. In the final score, the Father always issues more answers than questions. It is the duty of exiled men to make the right inquiries, ones that lend to the advancement of the Gospel, that open humanity to all the dynamic potential that comes when the Will of God is followed. He has ordained it from the first. He has asked only for humanity to love Him."

Saturday, November 9, 2013
9:37 a.m.

"The rise of the righteous class."

"Little sons, My presence here is proof that Jesus remains steadfast in His determination to draw all men to Himself. I am evidence of the Father's persistence in retrieving lost sinners from their waywardness. And, you must be confident that everything blessing you is from On High where the lilies never die and the sunlight forever glows. There is no joy that is beyond the reach of God's children; even here in this land where you live, it is buoyantly possible. Today, I bring My optimism to you as you watch the degradation of the American society and the more deeply entrenched opposition to the Church. Every time you see someone elected to public office who promises to broaden the scope of infanticide, you are an ominous step closer to witnessing the wrath of the Father. When you see state legislatures more interested in making homosexual unions prominent in the face of impressionable citizens than tending to the poor, you can be assured that the final journey of democracy has begun. These are eternal decisions for people who will be lost not only to the ages, but as their posthumous fate as well. It is said that there are none so blind as those who will not see. This is what has come to America by its own departure from grace. It is a precursor to the domination of the continents by the righteous, soon to be realized in your day. I do not ask for you to count the days before this arrives, but prepare for them. This preparation induces you to never surrender your principles, to be patient, to watch with holy sanctity what will happen before your eyes. When the leaders of the nations defy My appearances in Medjugorje and expel My messengers from their precincts, you can be certain that the worst battles of human suffering are near. There is a permeating spiritual purification on the rise, led by the manifest righteousness of Christians, that will be awesome to see from My station in Heaven. The Earth is the focal point of God. He reaches out to those who invoke His presence. He summons the sacrifices of the holy in reparation for the unholy. He asks His disciples to emulate the sanctitude of His Son. He heaps upon the righteous the burden of cultivating the Earth in the image of the Saints. My Special son, think about this. How can a pendulum swing to the right if it has not swung to the left? This is the manifestation that you are seeing at this time. It is not like clockwork, but more like striking blows, more like shifting momentum, more like utilizing prayer to offset the diatribes of the devil. If you perceive the news you see every day in this way, you will know that this shift of movement has begun. The Son of Man has come to His feet, with righteous indignation against the wicked and a Scepter of Justice for the ages. He will welcome you and your brother and all the Church into His presence with everlasting gratitude. I do not wish for you to assume that the rise of the righteous class is years in the offing. Look what has happened in the past five years. Look at the content of your memoir. As your brother has said, no Doctors of the Church or theologians have been able to encapsulate the condition of the 21st century world the way you have described in your book. You speak about the deficits and excesses of human life in terms indicative of the thoughts of God. You uplift the heavens in ways unknown. The rise of the righteous class is proved in your writings; you speak of its imminence in ways that everyone should know.

It is not that mild-mannered souls are not trying, but they do not yet know how to proceed. You heard Reverend Billy Graham say that Jesus and the Father were completely separated when Jesus hung on the Cross. I have said otherwise. The Father's burdens were lifted when Jesus redeemed His people. Even as the Scriptures identify the Father and the Son as two Divine Persons, Jesus is God Incarnate, and therefore inseparable from Himself; united with His own Spirit in the Most Blessed Trinity. How can this be a separation? When these things are understood with the clarity of your faith, the righteous class will fly like an eagle and ascend like a rocket ship bound for outer space. It is flying now, as sure as fine stones can sharpen steel. It is happening beyond the sight of most modern men, and you and I know it. Your brother and all like-minded Christians know it as well. Your memoir is a genius manuscript that pulls humanity back from the brink of soiling their lives; it allows the whole world to see the true meaning of human existence on Earth. The real question is whether you and your brother, and all My messengers, have the patience to see this process through. You are living with humility; you are tendering your hearts to the Will of God, and you are perfecting the practice of patience by watching your brothers and sisters' holiness come to life, and their dysfunctional obstinance die. I recently told you that you have met people who will not enter Heaven. As difficult as it may seem, some of them are mainstream people, public officials, business owners and casual secular fellows. I pray for them, but I do not expend My energy wondering why they will not convert. They willfully choose their path in life, uncaring about the outcome, unconcerned about the consequences. They abhor being castigated about their conduct; their pride keeps them from self-obedience. You wrote in your book correctly – I love them, I wish they would convert, but I do not obsess over their rude disbelief. I choose to elevate the distinction of My children who remain with Me through the exhausting of the ages. I look at you every day. I gaze into your eyes with admiration. I have held you in high esteem for what you mean to Jesus since you were a young boy. I am delighted by your gracefulness and sacred life. I am absorbed by your faith in God and dedication to prayer. You remind Me of Jesus during His most tender hours, during His quiet and prayerful times, and in moments when He was playful in the home and around the neighborhood. I know that you are rising; all the righteous are rising, as a class of holy citizens of the Kingdom of Love, here in this place, here in your time. You have written this in your memoir, and it will be well received by all who believe. It reflects your will for all men to be one with Jesus through Me, and united with the Father through Jesus. My Special son, I realize that you are a praying worker and a happy warrior for Jesus and the Church. You are aware that Christianity is about teaching the world what all peoples must come to know, warning lost sinners about the Great Reckoning, preparing humanity for the righteousness that flourishes from the Crucifixion of Christ the King. How can something so auspicious rise from such a Messianic tragedy? Because this is the way of God. This is how redemption unfolds; it is how all that is glorious is manifested from such a passionate death. Jesus was born as Servant and King to humanity in a Bethlehem manger – quite a contrast, quite a stark contradiction. This is how wildfires emerge from slow-rolling streams. It is how your obedience to Jesus comes through the ways He has asked. It is how flowers bloom from the darkness under the soil. How can anything so beautiful be raised from beneath the footsteps of men? This is the irony; this is the miracle. So, I want you to know that I am aware of what you suffer. I hear the content of your prayers, I know the intensity of your invocation of My Immaculate Heart to change the world and make right the intentions of men and their wives. I am honored to receive your petitions; it is My privilege to enlist the intercession of My Son. It is the joy of My Eternal Motherhood to feel your touch of love when you call on Me. We pray for all humanity to become like you. We ask for their obedience that you speak about in your memoir. We hope for the reconciliation of the world's priorities with those you have recounted in your testament. When you mention the Saints in your litanies, when you invoke the Doctors and Martyrs of the Church, you are proving that you have not given up on humanity's future. Your heart is a bedrock of truth upon which lost sinners can fashion their dreams. This is your gift to them; it is your loyalty to God. My Special son, the rise of the righteous class is embedded in your life."

Saturday, November 16, 2013
9:27 a.m.

"...as we forgive those who trespass against us."

"My dear children, your lovely hearts live abundantly in God, and they are comforting for Jesus and compliant with the Truth of His Kingdom. This is a tremendous day of blessing for humanity because I have come to speak to you again. It is here that the bewilderment of the world is expunged, here that I have brought God's love to you. Thank you for praying to receive Me. My presence today is to reemphasize My call for forgiveness in the world, not just for those trespasses that seem accidental, but for the malevolent sins that harm you, that cause righteous people to suffer, that cast a shadow on the journey of men into the Promised Land. I do not say that you must forgive others just because they know not what they are doing, but because your absolution of their offenses is holier when you offer it in unity with the Cross. My Special son, sometimes when I speak to other messengers about this, they pronely say '...Oh no, not another warning about letting our enemies win.' You know that this is not what I mean. It is not a form of weakness to pray for the wicked, and it is not a concession to beseech Jesus to forgive them. When someone prays that their trespasses be forgiven as they reciprocate for those who offend them, it means that all men should become one in God. You have discussed in your memoir that God will deal with those who oppose Him, and I agree. However, I have told you that the further someone has to travel from their station in life, from their obtuse attitude about God and religion, the more impact it will have on healing the world. What is looking you in the face every day is not a monster; human life is not that way. You can sense in your heart and ponder in your thoughts what it means to have honor. Honor says that you are closer to God than people who do not know Him. My Special child, you have noticed through the past 23 years that I have rarely referred to you and your brother as sinners. This is because I do not see you that way. I see some other people that way because they do not heed the Holy Spirit circling the globe with Wisdom and forewarning. In Jesus, you have cast off your sins; and while this does not imply that you will never again do anything wrong, it proves that your esteem before the Father is laudable. You can feel the winds of hope gushing from the skies into the parameters of your consciousness. You know from the depths of your soul that God's plans will overcome everything that stands in contradiction to His Kingdom, to His wishes for Creation, to the peace that lives in the hearts of those who believe. This is the reason you espouse and embrace all these things to the highest of your ability. You uphold your oath to belong to Jesus through good times and bad. Jesus knows that in His honor, you forgive those who offend you. He realizes that you take comfort in knowing that you should never hold a grudge. You have a peaceful heart to forgive those who trespass against you. My mission in this place, My goals for the world have been to instill in My children the ability to look beyond the languishing days and the troubled nights, to see past the distractions of the secular void, to perceive with clarity that the joy of the Lord's apostles is coming to pass. It is like polishing a window that is being pelted with bombshells. Never mind the destruction; as long as you keep polishing the window, nothing can shatter it. This is how the lives of the Saints stand in such contrast to the world wars. It is how the Holy Spirit gives rise to the simplicity to which all men must aspire.

My child, I see these same distractions in the temporal world. I know what Satan is trying to do. I ask that you and your brother find a new sense of peace, realizing that most of the issues that come before your nation and across the media are temporary, if not utterly irrelevant. I live in this peace, and remember that I am a human being too. No one can say that I am not aware of the toilsome nature of human life. I am here and elsewhere during every mortal and immortal moment to ask Jesus for His intercession. Jesus knows that I must touch the hearts of My children, leading lost sinners to His Holy Sacrifice because I am the Shepherdess of the Church. I come calling around the world to share the Good News to a humanity that has gone endlessly astray, that mocks and rejects Sacred Scripture. It does not disappoint Me to know that not everyone has yet converted because I am like you; we are aware of the inevitability of the Kingdom of God, of His claim on His earthly domain, of His triumph over whatever opposes Him. I am not saying that this is an easy struggle, but knowing the outcome should ease some of the pain. Realizing that someone will reach their final destination, without question, makes the journey easier to bear. Therefore, I have given you a perspective about how I forgive those who trespass against the Church, against the Salvation of the souls of men. They cannot win; they will either convert or be condemned. Even as Jesus will judge them, they will also judge themselves. I weep when people who know better do the wrong thing, but you and your brother make Me smile again. Even as you and I speak about the catastrophes of life, we pray with hope and truth in the spirit of victory. I commend you for staying the course. I am rendered speechless by the profundity of your memoir. So, do you understand the impact of your ability to look beyond the destruction and see life for what it is? *"Yes."* Indeed, you see as I see. As for your brother, he is trying to form a way to measure everything that you have done together in light of what life might have been. He is pleased that the two of you have stayed with Me. It happened because you said 'yes.' You are filled with delight and daring; you have foresight and courage, you give Jesus the best of yourselves and believe that He will prevail over humanity's faults. There is no sin in these things. You have an 'immaculate perception' of what life is supposed to be. If we could share this gift with your brothers and sisters, we would be on the way to rescuing their faith from the rubble of the world, from the wreck that has claimed their good senses. I again tell you that My admiration for you is immense. Please remember to pray for all who have died, especially those whose deaths were unprovided."

Saturday, November 23, 2013
9:17 a.m.

"Looking up to God's disciples."

"My little darlings in whom Jesus has placed His worthy trust, you are more consequential than you really know. You have given Me the joy that thousands of millennia would pine to receive. You are the loveliness of men's faith on Earth; you are the personification of the Father's Wisdom. Today, I have come to speak to you about the intersection of miracles and everyday life. I bring with Me the Lord's blessings and the glory that has engulfed you for years. Do you not know that you are as fit as royalty before His Throne? You, who are the princes of light, makers of justice, shiners of truth into the dark corners of the globe, are saturated with His holiness. You have within you the storied excellence only dreamt about by secularized men. I have been speaking to you for decades; and today again, you have loved and given the Father the venue to reveal Himself as Patriarch of the Church. Yes, here you have looked broad and wide, deep and beyond; you have wondered why so many misfortunes have befallen the righteous, and you have prayed for the conversion of the wicked. My dear little sons, you have been raised and lifted yourselves up. Your consciences have become keen and erect; your vision has been made clear; your meditations have been ratified, and your perception of life has been sharpened by the suffering you have known. You are esteemed and dignified in the Cross. Your stature has been elevated in the Lord's Paschal Resurrection. Your peace has been assured in the Bethlehem manger. It is true that human action is a product of feeling, thought and judgement. The decisions of men fall from their lips in syllables. Speech is extolling, eyesight is revealing, pain is hurtful, humor begets laughter, and truth is the scepter of joy. But, what about colors? Colors that do not glorify God are not colors at all. They are only tints and shades.

True colors are innate to the workings of the Church – there are red and yellow, white, gold, black, purple and such, but there are no offsetting hues. The hues that men create by mixing different tones mean nothing to God. He sees nothing useful in pastel lukewarmness. My Special son, when I look at you and your brother, I do not look down in the way that I did above the Ashland Saint Augustine Cemetery in 1991. Even though I am stationed in the skies, I am also down here with you. This is the color of love that many people do not understand. The prominent themes of Salvation history render those who do not accept My Motherhood color blind. This is the point that your brother was making yesterday about the universal nature of Catholicism. The Catholic Church issues the wisdom about the beatific colors of human life. These colors are constituted by God and handed down to His Original Apostolic Church. And, those who practice any other religion have created tints and hues on Earth that are not recognized by the Father in Heaven. They are only halftones and ill-conceived illusions that are not on the Lord's divine pallette. They are reminders of what happens when men are left to their own devices. Although I am always above the created world to bless and intercede, I am with you where you walk, work and pray. When it is said that a mother looks up to her children, this is what I do. I am a Mother who is humbly proud of you and your brother, of My Church and its leaders, of those who serve the poor, of missionaries and field workers, and all the rest. Hence, I look up to you from My station as Queen of Heaven and Earth. You emit rays of divinity that are constant here and in the Afterlife. You have the strength to believe that humanity will change. You make the most of life, the best of the years, activating your most noble aspirations upon which Jesus focuses His eyes. He seeks the flames of justice in you, and those leaping fires are glowing around the world through your prayers. I pray that the Sacrifice of Jesus will be widely known, and I see His Passion in your heart. All through the ages, I have sought these things in those who are devoted to Me.

Yes, I look up to you with anticipation. My Immaculate Heart is filled with the expectation of your victories to come. And, My Special son, you make Me feel like John Paul the Great made Me feel. I know that I am welcome here. I feel wanted and needed. I know that My Wisdom is sought after by someone who cares. And, do you know why? Because you, like Pope John Paul II, are a goal-oriented Christian. It is not enough for you to just know that God loves you. You want to learn the outcome of this love. It is not enough to know that humanity is redeemed in the Cross, you implore results from those who will be saved. Yes, you are like the priests of centuries' past who have made the connection between faith and action. Promises must be fulfilled. Oaths must be kept. Fruits must be yielded. My Special son, this is why I look up to you and your brother. You stand with conviction and confidence; it is written throughout your books, in the depths of your memoir, in the expressions on your face, and in the content of your prayers. I wrap My sacred love around you with the prominence of the Father's Will. I sing to you, just beneath your ability to hear Me. I see the future through the lenses of your eyes. And Jesus watches you, His holy creature, with this same admiration, with equal gratitude. Jesus understands the nature of your thoughts. He mandates the whole world to take notice. Every time you breathe, every time you move, every impulse you have that would usher dignity nearer the heart of the nations, He sees and hears. You have living within you the Glory of the Cross, the energy of the Church, the unity of the heavens, the substance of eternal life. You are not only admired for these things, you are recognized as a prodigy in the lineage of the Doctors of the Church. Yes, you are a faith prodigy and legend of these times; these months and years when the methods of humanity's existence collide, as the secular void and the Catholic Church fight it out, as the best of My children's hearts is pitted against the forces that oppose them. My Special son, you have come of age, and are still coming of age. This is the way of My little children; this is the legacy of My messengers. You have veracity and spiritual courage to your advantage. You are yet younger than you think. Thus, you know from My message today that someone cannot just invent some kind of tint and call it a color. They cannot equate their secular aberrations with the Truth of the Catholic Church. Why? Because when God is asked what those other 'colors' mean, He responds that they are not colors at all. He claims that they are the chaff of deviants; they are epitomes of unsightliness, indicators of a world gone wrong. Fortunately for humanity, however, you and your brother are fighters for a Kingdom that is right. My Special son, I will keep praying with you from My station in Heaven. I will bless you from the vaults beyond the skies. *"Thank you."* Please remember that you are not required to offer a response to everyone who asks you a question. Do not fall victim to fallacious inquiries. You are not required to have opinions about such matters that are not based in fact. The presentation of false choices is a popular ruse used by the enemies of the Church. It is like someone showing you a living horse and asking what color they should paint it. There is no sense to what they are saying. Or, they might ask while presenting a picture of a mountain range, '... do you think these would taste better with syrup or honey?' Men do not paint horses or eat mountains. These are false choices like those used by people who support same-sex unions to justify their error. My messages will help My children formulate their thoughts about upholding the tenets of the Universal Church. We should wait beyond Advent to proceed with the propagation of your books. There is still plenty of time. *"I thank you so much for coming to me all these years and being so close to me. It makes me so happy."* Thank you. I pray that you have a good Thanksgiving. I will be looking up to you! God bless you!"

Saturday, November 30, 2013
2:22 p.m.

"The great American brain wreck."

"My little sons, My compassion and holiness accompany Me as I come into your presence once again. Jesus is glorified by your sacrifices, and I am given hope by your prayers. Today, I have come to ask that you remain strong during your life's work so you will not surrender to the sarcasm of the secular void. If you think about it, you will see that everything that opposes Jesus is trying to reorient your thoughts and make you concerned about the false choices that life presents. I have beseeched My children for centuries not to be lured into these snares. Secularism is prone to force you to take sides, to make you believe that life is supposed to pit one group against another. As I said in early 1991, some people must lose in order for others to win. This is how capitalist prosperity works. It is a movement that preaches that all things mortal need to be dissected. Exiled men search for ways to make capitalism their framework for life, using people as pawns and victims of their self-aggrandizing progress. My little sons, it is a system based on lies, half-truths, trickery and untenable distractions. Your country is working toward the great American 'brain wreck.' It is almost there. The deception of many in the United States is their means of amassing the most wealth in as few hands as possible. This is their concentration of assets into one class of elitists. They even use religion against those who are trying to fend for themselves. On the other hand, American liberals are trying to spread the wealth into the hands of the slothful. You know that Jesus preaches a position different from these extremes. The brain wreck that I am speaking about is the demise of the simplicity that once unified your country. When citing the demonic forces against the principles of democracy as a reason for the diminishment of American freedom, those who speak about it refuse to place the blame on the government itself. The United States' federal government is a behemoth monstrosity that is trying to devour the independent wealth of Americans everywhere, in all classes, even from those who have worked hard and obeyed the rules during their entire lives. There are too many laws and mandates. Trillions of dollars are spent on problems that can be resolved by people being more self-reliant. Your national reputation is in shambles. Your moral framework is in shreds. Your churches are almost empty. Your unborn children are being slaughtered in the womb. On and on, this dismal record ensues. This is the conduct of a nation that refuses to espouse the Holy Gospel of Christianity. The whole democratic idea of self-governance came from Christianity, not the Greeks, not the ancient philosophers, but from the Wisdom of God. They say that if only the world could intellectualize itself; if only man could see himself through the lens of pagan thought, then all these problems would go away. The way to eradicate these problems is to turn back to God and disavow the vanity that has caused such a wreck of human life. Indeed, power and pride are consuming men's hearts. Waste and impurity are eroding self-respect. And still, I am elated that the closing chapters of the old world are drawing nearer. I have said that My Mantle is sacred, My presence is abiding, My prayers and intercession are perpetual. You have seen sin for what it has done to the family of nations. Now, you are seeing sin for what it has done to the consciences of men. It has been fatal. Sin has devastated what is left of the decency of the vast community thoroughfare. There is nothing left for men to do than turn to the Lord for help; now here where there are wars, but not world wars. Today, when the morality of the Earth is at its lowest point, the existence of man is like an alcoholic. It must hit bottom before it will begin to recover. You must believe Me when I say that you will hear the thud. Every day, you see something that seems worse than before. It is true; it usually is. However, you are preached-to about raring up in opposition by people who do not care. They want you to be alarmed so you will patronize their false fears. They are appealing to your brain and not to your heart. They are trying to stir the American people into believing that nothing can be done to annihilate the evils of this world.

My Special son, you have written in your prefaces what they need to know. You have declared in your memoir what will enlighten them. I have given you this message to tell you that keeping up with the propaganda is exhausting. Every day, you and your brother are insulted by what is being desecrated. This is the origin of your fatigue; it is the reason you are so disheartened. It is why you sleep with such burden through the night. It breeds a cynicism that I have asked you to avoid. It forms a circle around itself, and you and your brother must not enter it. It must not devour your perceptions of life or your personal identities. Realize your life in America for what it is. Do not condone or justify the gristmill of your country's immoral march. Be simple, remain peaceful, and embrace your own spiritual intelligence. Reject the paranoia, panic and alarmism. Live your dreams as messengers for Heaven. It is for this reason that I remain calm and placid. I am heartened by the piety of the Church. I have seen everything I have told you today for more generations than I care to number. It is not a concession easily made. But, the will of exiled men makes these things happen. It is in their sins; it is their unwillingness to convert. Some of the most grotesque legislation against unborn innocents has been signed into law by so-called Roman Catholics. And, as you have seen in Illinois, your Bishop has denounced the imposition of a law allowing same-sex marriage, promulgated and signed by Roman Catholic politicians. And, why have they done so? For wealth, power, pride and social expedience. They are frauds and liars. They are unworthy of the Sacraments. They will pay the price when they are judged by the Son of Man. They are among the reasons that there is so much global human suffering. They are the most demanding, the most haughty; and they pay the least wages for those under their employ. And yet, My Special son, these are My children! These are the same individuals who mock Me, who refuse to believe in My messages, who claim to be Catholic for bragging rights, but who do not obey the teachings of the Church. Over half of American Catholics believe that abortion should be legal. More than two-thirds think that same-sex marriage should be allowed. And, these are My adopted progeny? Can you see why they have mocked My divine presence in Lourdes and Fatima, in Medjugorje, and now here as the Morning Star Over America? They have done so because they are victims of the great American brain wreck. They believe the propaganda. They have bought into the scourges of materialism and lust. I am not speaking in alarmist strains or hyperbole. I am stating the truth. And, I am happy. As I said a few moments ago, I am elated that the final chapters of worldly life have come. The ending ages will be sweet for God and treacherous for His enemies. This is the happy ending for which My children have prayed since the days of Saint Dominic. All of us; you and I and your brother, everyone who lives with good will, all the friends of the Messiah – we should be leaping for joy right now! We should toss our fists into the air. We should acknowledge that the human experiment of living against the grace of the Church is a complete failure. It has been a patent lie against ordained decency since civilized men first proclaimed themselves to be advanced enough to govern the world. My Special son, I wish to impress upon you and your brother that you must not fall victim to the overwhelming sense of alarmism that is being peddled here in America. As I have said, it is exhausting you; it is the source of your sense of helplessness. I realize that you want for more ways to fix it; it is obvious that most men do. But, the Lord would have to destroy your country to save it. The will of Americans, the approach of 'public servants' makes it that way. Politicians and politics; these are directly from the playbook of the devil. There are no kings among them. There is no royalty except for those who search for shelter within My Most Immaculate Heart. There is no worthy armament unless deployed in the name of Jesus' Most Sacred Heart. As you know, these are not complicated matters. You must continue to rest, be calm, and do not worry. You and your brother had a lovely Thanksgiving day at your parents' home on Thursday. Your sister hugged your brother because she senses the calmness in his heart, the simplicity of his demeanor, and the steadfastness of his love. I will speak to you at the opening of another new month. Thank you for praying for the unborn, the poor and the suffering. You are reconfiguring the spirit of this world."

Saturday, December 7, 2013
9:35 a.m.

"The eyes of all wait upon Thee." (Psalm 145:15)

"My little sons, your patience is not wasted; your trials are not in vain. See the created world for what it is becoming. The grand aspirations that leapt into My Immaculate Heart upon the Annunciation remain somewhat unfulfilled, but I have not surrendered hope that the conversion of humanity is nigh. Imagine this. How many years since the Archangel Gabriel announced the favor of the Lord? How many decades? How many generations? How many centuries? And yet, here we are; My prayers are about to come to fruition. One thousand years? Two thousand years? Even so, it has come down to your time, your age of men here in the Lord's earthly vineyard. Psalm 145 speaks about the Father giving food to everyone who hungers for His love, grace and pardoning. The eyes of all wait upon Thee! This has been the sacred credo of the ages, as much as the Angelic Salutation adorns the Mysteries of the Holy Rosary. I come to you over and again with good tidings, with comforting words and consoling sentiments. Why? Because you listen to Me when others turn away. You do not harden your hearts when you hear the Lord's voice. You rise to welcome the Holy Spirit in your hearts, yes even as you see the wretchedness of this world and the grotesque errors of the faithless hordes. So many Christians have asked Jesus why He has permitted the catastrophes and atrocities that have befallen the souls of Earth. The answer is that He does not permit them, He just does not preempt them. It is the same principle as not holding to the hands of a child who has for the first time come to his feet to walk. If he falls, Jesus will catch him. But, he must come of age before he can tread arm-in-arm with the rest of the world. This is the way of souls searching for redemption. Each person must take those first few steps, just as Peter was bade to walk on the water. What you have been watching for the past 2,000 years is the maturing of the human race in their trust in God. You have seen the casualties caused by the severities of sin. You have seen the lifeless battlefields; you have seen the mourning; you have heard the dirges, and you have listened to the eulogies. And, so too have I. I have accompanied the Church and its people through joy and sorrow. I have watched the gait of statesmen as they approached their podiums to describe the way human life ought to be. I have welcomed their tones and overtones, their eloquence and their sentiments echoing through the realms of Paradise. I have reverberated their cadences into the hearts of the Angels. And, O' how those Angels have cried! They have wept in jubilation that someone down below felt as holy as them. I need not tell you how awesome are these times that ensure the blessings of God upon His earthly domain. He has not forsaken it, He has ordained it. The Father proclaims, '...Let the will of men lead them to Me! Let them remember My Son's Sacrifice as expiation for their sins! Let all Creation shout-out that Jesus Christ is Lord!' My Special son, I have come on this December day to accompany you in your prayers with your brother. You are living near the final act of human endeavors. Soon, you will know what steps led to this; you will become uniquely aware that Jesus never turned His back on His disciples. Through you and His Church, He has faced down the devil and all evil works. Through your prayers, He has purified the nations. Through the wreck of this world, Jesus has procured its everlasting peace that will live beyond the ages. I ask you and your brother to recognize your place in this. Be pleased by your efforts. The children of your contemporaries will come running to you. Your life with your brother has been a preparation and reparation. You have carried the Torch of Righteousness; and you will give it not just to your mortal successors, you will hand it to the Son of Man, Himself. I have told you about My wishes for many years. I know that they will come true because I am the Mother of God. And, in your unity with Me and our union in Jesus, we have found a future together that cannot be destroyed.

  This is the reason for My joy, not just that the Church is committed to the Truth, not just that colossal numbers of abortions are averted every day, not just that the sun will rise and warm the continents and its peoples everywhere, but that you and I have found ourselves in each others arms. It is the same with all My children. I hold you dearly. I advocate for you before Jesus with intensity. I remind Him at every turn that the world needs more wine. And, Jesus responds with the same joy by which I have come here today. He recognizes the extremes of humanity everywhere. He knows that there are wretches and zealots in every quarter of the globe. He realizes that the hemispheres are withering-away in pain. He has full knowledge that His disciples are being persecuted where they stand. This is the meaning of the Cross. Remember the message that

I gave in Medjugorje on December 2, 2013. To know oneself in Jesus, one must know the Cross. It is a Cross of self-denial, of sacrifice and service. It is a Cross of prayer. You know this Cross because you have absorbed its substance and meaning into your identity and your life. This is the joy of God! You have claimed Him, and He has ratified your actions. This is the meaning of keeping your eyes focused on Heaven with your heart. Indeed, the eyes of all wait upon Him. My Special child, I assume that you know the power of everything you have dedicated to the cause of human conversion. You walk every day with confidence that this is what your years have wrought. You are living in the early years of your sixth decade of life, and your wisdom is growing beyond your age. No matter what anyone on television says, politics is not the touchstone for human virtue. I told you this just recently. Politics is the bane; it is the stench, it is the distraction. Holiness in the way of the Martyrs, the Saints and the Doctors of the Church is the touchstone of human perfection. No one would have remembered these souls if not for their sacrifices for God. They proclaimed to the nations the Glory of the Father, the welcoming genius of the Gospel, the means of forever redefining the purpose of human life. Politicians cannot do this. Scientists and physicists are lost for the origin of their disciplines. They can only measure and examine; they cannot speak to the genesis of Creation's beauty. Indeed, what is in a name? What makes a flower's fragrance sweet? How does rainfall bathe the tiniest creatures beneath the soil? It is all in the hands of the Father; it is His to know, His to share, and His to determine. And, all the determining has been rightfully done. Humanity has been transformed from creation to purification. The Sacraments of the Church are real. They are sunshine and moonbeams. They are the light, the breezes, the glory that keeps Christians connected to the miracles of the universe. It all began with the assent of a Maiden to bear the Man-God into the exiled realms. There was never a question of 'yes' or 'no.' It was all about 'let it begin.' Yes, I responded that it should begin with Me. I am the origin of human spiritual wherewithal. I am the iconic Lady of Grace to whom all who hunger for life must come. I hold in My arms the Incarnate God of Salvation, the Christ, the Messiah, the Greeter of Converts, the Redeemer of Believers. I know who I am. I realize the role I have played, and I am humbled by it. I am grateful that the Lord chose Me because it has led to this day, a day on which I reaffirm to you that you and your brother are My sons. See this through My eyes of joy. You are My children; you are My little ones in whom the Savior of the World has placed His trust. Whether you prosper or suffer, no matter what your lives bring, this communion of souls cannot be undone. There can be no greater joy than this, save your deliverance into Heaven itself. I feel the warmth and gladness of that day to come.

Therefore, I tell My Son at the turning of every moment that, '...The eyes of all wait upon Thee!' He shall giveth them their meat in due season. My little one, there is no telling what this means for the future of men. It cannot be put into words. The agendas and mortal frameworks that you see every day, dealt to humanity by the cold secular void, obscure the truth of the blessings you are receiving. Hear Me now. Humanity is being converted and absolved. Yes, Jesus is doing this, and you are doing it with Him. You are shepherding His lost flock back into His arms. You are warning the nations about the briefness of the years. You are asking for their hands in consecration to Me. I have concluded what I came to say to you today. We pray that the Morning Star Over America does not get caught-up in the same obstruction that has come to My Medjugorje miracles. Where is the faith of men? Where is their trust? Please remember that I have with sincerity spoken today about My admiration for you; it comes to My mind and Heart with truth and genuineness. *"Thank you, Mama."* And, thank you as well for your holy prayers."

Saturday, December 14, 2013
9:36 a.m.

"The esteem of apostolic loyalty."

"Withstanding all the happiness that you could possibly imagine will soon be your great concern, My little sons. You will wonder from where it came; where did the dam burst? How did the skies open so copiously with the grace of God's fidelity? It is here that the Good News began; it is in your obedience that your love for Jesus has been made manifest. And, what about the suffering world? What about healing the sick and those with broken hearts? What of the future of your pious works? They will culminate in and enrich the Church. The void will be filled by the Church and the fruits returned a hundredfold to its members. My Special son, I have in store for all who are faithful to My Child Jesus the whole world spirited and renewed. I have plenteous joy and unceasing victory. I have a Triumph that cannot be annulled. It is in the Will of God; it is the Will of God; it flows and blossoms from the Will of God, not man's will, but the Will of the Eternal Father, the Creator of all righteous things, the Light in the darkness, the purity of the flesh, and the genius who has sought a wholesome goodness from His people. While these words are among the most hopeful you have heard, they comprise a narrative of Salvation and redemption; they ratify the sanctification that converted souls have found in the Cross. It is here that you find your esteem in apostolic loyalty that has been laid on your souls. I know that the exiled realms are not pretty. They are not prone to the sanctification of men. But, they are your battlefield; they are the Lord's vineyard in which those who wish to seek Him find themselves. You and your brother have lived long enough to see the reciprocal nature of this world, to know its glories and downfalls, to see what stirs the hearts and ires of other men. You are aware of the distractions that keep humanity from becoming upright in the innocence in which they are born. If it were not a life of sacrifice that takes the holy to the foothills of the Promised Land, what would? Surely it cannot be found in the outrages and excesses that drive the sinful further into despair. And, it is not in materials and licentiousness because both of these expire in the wake of humanity's conversion. Indeed, sacrifice in the way of the Apostles, according to the teachings of the Messiah, in the echos of the far-flung Gospels – all these have made sincere the intentions of the Father to absolve you. You wake in the morning not knowing what the day might bring; you do not even know its parameters. Each day is another opportunity to ponder your unity with Jesus through Me. It is a moment for you to settle your heart into His peace. I have said that each day is for the propagation of Divine Love, and this you do through your prayers. You find your esteem through this apostleship because of your loyalty to Me. And, you are granted your wishes for those who suffer; you set men free, you reckon with Me what else might come to cleanse the nations and the hearts of humanity before the sun sets again. Evil men are cast aside by what you ask Jesus to affirm. The lowly are lifted up; the weak are strengthened; the blind are given sight, the lame come to their feet and walk. Today, I bring My maternal blessing to your home, neighborhood and city, to this nation and to the world. I bring it to all these places through you, by you and in you. I wish you to know that I am a nourishing and protecting Mother. I have provided for those who are consecrated to Me. I know of the loveliness of your petitions and your call for justice against the wicked. They are taking their last gasps; they are unable to claim any lasting victory over the just. And too, it is here in this place that the origin of humanity's conversion yields its true harvest for Heaven. Those who have opposed you, the people who left in shame and obstinance; they are all coming to know the suffering they have wrought. They have buried children and their dreams alongside them. They have wondered what might have been if only they had believed. They are emulating Job and Jesus in the Garden. It is clear that you are not unaware of these things.

You know when the Lord's justice wafts through the spiritual airs of this world. It is a feeling of confidence that builds in you, knowing that everything you see that opposes the Gospel will perish, and so will the people who perpetrate it. This is not vengeance, My little son. It is rightness. It is the ability of God to watch the perils and outrages in this world and still have the final say. It is His persistence in elevating His Church, raising to their feet all who remain beside Him, and dignifying the suffering that has come in the image of His Son. So, when priests say during the Eucharistic Prayer, '...Give us some share of your Kingdom, Lord...' it will come true in their day, and in yours. My little son, I am weeping with happiness now, tears streaming down My cheeks because I know how blessed you are. I know how good you are. I know how endlessly I love you and how blessedly Jesus believes in you, as you in Him. I bring My Immaculate Heart of gladness and compassion with Me today. I offer you My assurance that the promises of God are true. It is like the mother listening to her child, being asked by that child how much longer the journey will take. And, I say to you, just a little while longer. We are almost there; the Eternal Truth is prevailing here and around the universe; God is in control of His Creation, the wedding bells are about to peal, the Hosts of Heaven are rising to their feet. No one who has ever lived anywhere could possibly grasp how much you mean to Me. It is patently impossible for a human mind to understand what you have done for the Father in Heaven. It is as though you are capable of seeing that far from here, but you only need to look inside yourself. Consider your confidence and self-composure. Remember the eternal genius that the Holy Spirit has implanted in you. Be comforted that the Blessed Trinity has wrapped you in grace and power. You are not just a follower of the Messiah, you are a maker of His dominion in the exiled realms. You bind things here in this world that are justified at the Throne of God. You see what must be done; you call on Jesus to do them, and you will soon see the world that you have dreamed about to come. You will see the bucolic peace and rustic beauty blooming from the lives of the former enemies of the Cross. Conversion is ongoing; the adversaries of righteousness are dying, the dedication that good men must have to the mission of the Church is being solidified. I beseech you to look at the ruins of Earth the same way I have watched them for 2,000 years. Every time a catastrophe strikes, I know that it is caused by the corruptibility of unconverted souls. And, I know the remedy for this. It is more destruction – yes it is true. One way to stop the catastrophes is to allow their self-inflicted annihilation. Imagine that. All that would be left absent the material world would be humanity and their God. Is this not the real journey of human life? Is this not the way to prove to the stars that wretched men can come to their Father and humble themselves before Him? I have hope that righteousness will rise; not more suffering for the innocent, but torrents of justice bringing down the haughtiness of pride-filled men. Saint Michael the Archangel proclaims, 'Destroy the gems and jewels; lay waste to the castles and penthouses. Replace the elitist profiteers with servants of the poor. Knock down Wall Street. Tear up Broadway. Flatten Beverly Hills. Expose the frauds and exploiters. And, most important, protect the innocent victims of the greed of the barons who have lived in marble-lined mansions for thousands of years. Drown the magnates in their beds; do whatever else it takes to ensure that only mankind and God stand face to face in the end.' This is what is coming; it is happening now. And, I could not be more pleased. My little son, I do not wish to give you the impression that I do not have sympathy for philanthropists and those who are generous with their wealth. You understand the wisdom that brings Me to pronounce these things. Be happy in your achievements; be proud of who you are, remain strong in the knowledge that the Father is supporting you. Be grateful that you and your brother are yet strong enough to retain your relevance in the outcome of this world. Yes, these are the things that prove your desire to proceed, to go on and live the responsibility that was bred in you from a little child. Please remember to live one day at a time, one moment at a time. Worry not what will come next week or next month. As you can see from My message today, Jesus is taking care of these things. We will pray in advance of the great Feast of Christmas! It will be a grand commencement for millions of souls in Purgatory."

Saturday, December 21, 2013
9:29 a.m.

"The Mary Christmas"
Renewal, recompense, absolution and exaltation

"With good wishes, gladness and appreciation, I have come today to speak to you. My children, eloquent are the strains that you speak about the Will of God; profound are your sentiments about the condition of the world. I seek peace in you, and I beseech from you happiness in the knowledge that Jesus has saved you. If you had been on Earth when Jesus was born, you would have been among those with sound wisdom, those who said, '...Let us go into the presence of the Messiah; let us look into the face of the little King and tell Him that we welcome the Lord among us. Let us promise our allegiance and love; let the whole world come to realize the Salvation we have found.' It is proper that you consider that you were there on Christmas beyond the effects of time. You can tell Jesus these things now. You can share with Him your welcoming prayers and remind Him that you know of His providential life, death and Resurrection that irrevocably altered the wholeness of human events. Also today, I bring My hope that you will pray this Christmas for the virtues that I brought to open this message. Renewal and recompense are key to the enlightenment of the spiritual heart. Absolution and exaltation are imperative to the destiny of the soul. Hence, I ask My children around the globe to have a 'Mary' Christmas. I ask My messengers to invoke the Holy Spirit in their petitions in a way that dignifies the lowly and brings joy to the sorrowed. My Special son, it is important for your brothers and sisters to remember that Christmas is a time of joy in the birth of Jesus. We have spoken, and you have written, about the reverential component of the holidays. There is tremendous spiritual wealth in the Christian heart derived from the Nativity of Jesus, and this wealth can be redeemed in one's life for new beginnings and endless blessings. When I come speaking to you, it is always My honor; it is My privilege to teach you about your earthly exile and the Afterlife. You have seen by looking at the secular void that just living on Earth is not enough. Growing in years is not a sufficient resource for inheriting eternal wisdom. Indeed, it requires being fixed in Jesus beyond the element of time and the parameters of the world, a station in which My children before you have described as the 'faith parity.' This is how you have lived; it is the way the Saints endured the suffering they found on their journey of evangelism and servitude in Jesus. The entire New Covenant is representative of this faith parity. The Holy Scriptures tell you how to live on Earth, while providing God's framework for eternal redemption. They are inseparable, which means that the faith parity is the connection of two halves into one complete revelation of Salvation. Good people must serve the poor and brokenhearted in the way of the Scriptures while concurrently appealing to the Father for eternal redemption. They are like the east and west hemispheres of an orb, or perhaps the northern and southern. The goal of Christmas is to ratify the exaltation that humanity has for being born, for being taught about life and the hereafter, and for acknowledging that holiness has an eternal effect. It begins here in this life because of the inevitability of your deliverance. It is not just a play on words to allude to 'Mary' Christmas because I bore the Son of Man to the world on behalf of the Father. My Special son, I will lead My children to their Savior the same way that I led you and your brother to each other. This is the Christmas ratification that binds the Will of God to your intentions. Christmas provides the miracles of healing and freedom that you will hear about in future years. This is why souls are released from Purgatory into Heaven on Christmas; people are focused on Jesus more on Christmas than any other time of year. This is a manifestation of the reciprocity between Heaven and Earth that we have previously spoken about.

Therefore, I assure you of My sacred presence again this year during your Christmas hours, not just so you will feel warm inside, but so that you can give Me your most earnest petitions that I will place in Jesus' hands. Yes, Christmas is a time of joy, and a unique opportunity for humanity to exchange heart-songs with God. This is not something about which you have been previously unaware, but it is a prospect for you to think about when considering your ability to bring change into the world. Contemplate this – one of the greatest gifts of prayer to the Lord is to ask Him to induce other people to pray. You might say, '...Make them change, Lord. Give them the signs and wonders to know that their trust in You is well placed. Manifest miracles so more miracles will come.' Praying to Jesus to help other people pray is meta-prayer. You do not hear much about it anymore, but it was common in earlier centuries. And, its purpose? If someone is carrying a load that is too much for them to bear, you can help take the load with them to their destination. This is the way of meta-prayer. You are asking Jesus to accept your prayers and those of your brothers and sisters too. This is the marketplace of mysticism; it is when people from different lands and walks of life assemble for the good of the whole to create a spiritual commonality in the Cross of Christ Jesus, preceded by His birth from the Queen of Love. Here today, My Special one, I have joined My prayers with your petitions, as I do every day. The summit of our purpose is our unity in God. The genesis of our power comes from the same Holy Spirit that made Saints of us both. I have said what I wanted to share with you today. Yes, it is Christmas time; the week containing the Eve of Joy will begin tomorrow. And, the world of believers will look upon My Holy Son with hope, awe and wonder, with reverence and respect, with jubilation and thankfulness. This is as it should be. And, I will remain with you always, even beyond the end of the old Earth, as Jesus is as much in your presence today. The New Earth will come, the Glorious New World, the perfection to which all pious Christians are summoned, and all eternal life will ensue. I remain devoted to you for your purity, goodness and loveliness. I welcome your testimonials to your life experiences. I adore your simple heart composed of complex emotions. I admire everything you are doing for the Kingdom of God. Please remember all who are far from Jesus in your prayers this Christmas. And, pray for the unborn, for those being held against their will, and for the homeless and downtrodden. Remember the little children who are seen as being only underfoot, that they may be elevated to a stature worthy of their dignity in Jesus. We have all seen them; they are like puppies looking for attention, and the exiled world must not tread on them just because they have not yet gained their voices. Some of the greatest Saints ever known to man are growing in these realms! And yes, there will be tragedies and misfortunes during the days of Christmas because sinners are not always careful. Some of them are faulty creatures who are reluctant to embrace the prayerful lives to which they are called. Thank you for your holiness. We have a special bond, you and I and your brother. We have the power to implore Jesus to take Mercy on His Creation. Let us pray that He does."

Saturday, December 28, 2013
Feast of the Holy Innocents, Martyrs
10:03 a.m.

"The Morning Star valedictory, five years hence."

"Welcome, My dear little sons, to the prolific grace of My Most Immaculate Heart. My adoration of your lives is intense because you have so deeply accepted the burden of the Cross into your own lives on Earth. There is an outpouring of sacred love showering upon you from Heaven. There is eminence aplenty filling your hearts with confidence. What can be said of these things? That you are holy and worthy; you are aware and advised; your days and hours are filled with blessings streaming from the Throne of God. Today, I have come to reassure you that I have kept My promise from five years ago. Your messages did not end. I have told humanity what the world needs to know about faith and the Lord's Divine Love. Yes, My Special son, what your brother said yesterday is true. The best way to rebuke atheists is to tell them that they are incapable of love. There can be no true love without the Holy Spirit imbedded in the human heart. And, what I have taught you and your brother has reinforced what God placed inside you in your childhood. He has reigned within you. He has ordained your every holy action. He has ratified your decisions. I have only placed perspective upon the things that you already knew. It is all about living for a God whom you will see once all moments have expired. There is a sacred accounting for which all Christians are prepared. It is where life outgrows the movements of Earth, where men walk through the ages, and time ceases its procession. I am touched by your devotion to Me. I am moved by the immensity of your consecration to Jesus. My Special and Chosen sons, I come today to renew My promise that I will speak to you during 2014. I am unsure how many more ages will pass because I know not the hour of the Second Coming. However, I will speak to you as long as the Lord allows to aid, advise and console you. I will be here as long as your friendship is intact. I will pray with you for the conversion of the wicked. And, I will be your benefactor of affirmation and reassurance during your days in exile. All the while Jesus is dealing life and death, I will be here to tell you how and why. I will speak directly to the Thrice-Blessed Trinity in Heaven to be your advocate in this world. It is said that time is a strange element, and it is mostly irrelevant when it comes to the Truth of God. Billions of souls have passed through the nations, but not all of them have known the reasons why. All will ultimately discover the answer to their questions whether it be in their mortal bodies or in the spiritual realms thereafter. My children, the prayers of the Church are powerful; they are the antidote to the evils of this world. This is why I call My children to remember to the Father everyone who is far from Him. I am pleased to know that our prayers are helping. Today, I also come to reassure you that everything you have worked for will have its full effect. Even as you seem isolated and banished from secular circles everywhere, it is they who are lost. They are wandering the netherworld paths that will only lead them to dead ends. We have in our grasp the answers they seek, but they do not know the questions. I feel the anticipation of their conversion to the degree that I am elated with new joy. I know what this spiritual contact means to God. He gave these creatures life. He instilled in them the will to search for Him. And, when all the world is through, all will see their beauty from within. All will know the tenderness that was always theirs to share. The nations will stand in awe of the mightiness of the simplest human beings. Yes, each was fashioned into being by the God of Abraham. Imagine how Jesus sees them, even in their brokenness. They lay low and stand upright; they interact and touch one another with passions of eloquence. They walk as singular individuals and together atoned. They inspire inside other vessels the means to be even more courtly for God. This is the best of the universe, the perfected human person inside Jesus' Most Sacred Heart, sanctioned for entry into Paradise; liberated and prepared for redemption, freed and freshened for the best of all possible eternities beyond the constraints of human death.

I am with you here, and I will be with you forever. I survey your beauty and weaknesses today, and I embrace your souls both now and then. It is all possible and pursuable. All this grace and blessing, forever wrapped in the Sacrifice of Jesus, is being dispensed rightfully upon all who believe in Him. Is it possible for a genius to be so spiritually feeble as to be blinded to this truth? Indeed, it is. There are governors and legislators who are ignorant as to the priorities they should be seeking. I do not feel sorry for them. If someone is intelligent enough to draft legislation and configure a mathematical equation, then they are capable of believing in God. They have the tools to see better than they are seeing, to remember the teachings of the Church in their laws and decrees. They are surely enlightened enough to know that humanity has not just evolved from some lower species, but that people are supernatural beings directly descended from the hands of God. My Special son, when you think about the messages I have given you since five years ago today, they are more relevant to your understanding of the relationship between man and God than My Morning Star messages. It is all the same vision, but you are learning the motivations of the Father as a father. You are seeing how the Holy Trinity approves of righteous courses and rebukes the ones that are not. And, how does the Lord reprove those who take no time for Him? He gives no time to them. When the young singers poised themselves on a hilltop and jingled the tune '...I'd like to teach the world to sing...' they were unwittingly predicting what I would do here since February 22, 1991. What must be sung now are not just songs of inclusion, but of truth and justice, of peace and reconciliation. Therefore, I ask you and your brother to remember, and always remember, that you have lived at the forefront of the enlightenment of America in ways never known to your country. For the most part, your isolation has been your own discretion. You could have reached out to potential friends and former acquaintances, but you remained prayerfully here instead. What you have done is good and right, but you could have lived another way. There is no wrong life in this regard. And, even as you have not been social characters, you have learned that humanity is in pain. Sinners are lost and misdirected; fashions and materials come and go. I have a great deal of them with Me, the ones that you would have liked to keep. Yes, I have in My presence the brand new 1977 Firebird Formula that I will hand you on the day you enter Paradise, if you and your brother wish to travel those roads of friendship again. The butterflies you saw as a child will touch down on your hands. You will know the definition of eternal sweetness and the grandness of your loftiest dreams. These are from the urging of your soul; this is part of your reward, a portion of the Salvation you have gained in Jesus' Paschal Resurrection. Gifts and more gifts; it is only a matter of time.

What awesome strains you have written in your memoir! And, you know it. You are convinced that it hails from the New Jerusalem. It does; it all springs from your maturity in life's lessons, your command of your own ability to convey meaningful messages by your usage of the English language. I would tell you that I am amazed by what you have written, but I am not surprised because I know your heart. You have a poise and pose that is emblematic of the divinity of God. You have been endowed with His sacredness. You have internalized His Will to the degree that it comes naturally to you. And, for all those fallen priests and other religious who have been stripped of their vocations, you are making-up for what has been lost. You are sufficing their deficits; you are ensuring their commitment to God through what you have done for Me. So, December 28, 2013 has come, and the year will expire in the next three days. It means little in the grand scope of life, but it portends profound blessings for the Church-Militant on Earth. This is all because of the love for the Father by you and your brother. You have heeded the lessons of history; you have stayed awake while your Savior has suffered. You have dressed His wounds and identified with His sorrows. You have preached the Gospel and tended to the poor. I give you My promise that you will be repaid a hundredfold not only in this life, but with prayers from all the Saints who reside with Me now in Heaven. When you see the record of the ages; when you have been apprised of the service of men, you will look back at these days in jubilation that they unfolded as they did. You will wonder why you and your brother have seemed so alone, for truly you have not. You will see with eyes aglow how billions of people have been your right guard, who have stood with you through it all. Remember that it is not always what you see that counts, but what you cannot see that matters most at the last. The goodness and mercy of the Lord have been with you all the days of your lives. Thank you for attending the celebration of Christmas with your family, and bless you for taking such good care of your brother. As I have said on many occasions, nothing can stop the preeminent glow of the Morning Star Over America. Thank you for your prayers. Please remember the homeless, sick and starving. Ask Jesus to bring justice to governments in lands far and wide that convict innocent people. Thank you also for remembering the unborn. I love you!"

The Final Colossus
In the Light of Her Majesty
AD 2014

Saturday, January 4, 2014
9:40 a.m.

"Window with a view."

"My children, your utterances are sacred to Me; they are reverential to God, they invoke the power of love into the exiled world. I ask you to speak from the heart when you pray, and remember that it is through your unity in Jesus that the gift of human conversion is wrought. I also ask you to remember your dignity in Jesus, and the statesmanship you have inherited through the Holy Spirit. Today, I am speaking in the Year of Our Lord 2014. You are closer to Heaven than those who do not believe; you are stationed nearer the Eternal Gate than anyone might ever know. This is why I have come to bless you today and petition your prayers for the people you have described in your books, the sinners who refuse to lower their heads and comply with the ordinances of God. My Special one, you are emotively moved by your first memoir because you have seen that the Spirit of Jesus has written it through you. It is in fact the Lord reproving His Creation. There is a distinction that comes after time when reviewing one's holy works; it is seen in the magnitude of your pious thoughts. You realize at the last that they have all along been manifested by Jesus for you, in you and through you, just as you are redeemed in Him and through Him. If you consider where you have been in your lives, what impressions you have taken from certain situations, what perceptions you embraced, and the lessons you have learned, you begin to realize that you are already seated within the sacred purview of the Father, and you see what He sees in the physical world. My Special son, you have through your faith traveled the Earth, seeking to satisfy your spiritual curiosity. You have done this cognitively and spiritually through the beauty you describe in your memoir. It is a liberating and edifying experience handed to you by virtue of your faith. Simply said, you have been given a window with a view toward the future that is framed by the past. What a grand notion this has been! What a blessing for those who have believed. You have gained power and intuition through your obedience to the New Covenant Gospel. This is the product of your willingness to believe, of your desire to understand the overages and underpinnings of the Creation that God has allowed to unfold. It is a sacred curiosity, not a counterproductive one, that permits you to reveal to the universe the providence that I describe. This power is embedded in the love in your heart; it is revealed to your brothers and sisters in the sanctity of your beatific wisdom. I am not suggesting that you own the power of God without Him, but that your insights of human existence and eternal life are compatible. This is in advance of those who do not believe in God; it is light years beyond the scientists and astronomers who are trying to discover the meaning of life from the stars. It makes Me joyful that the Lord allows Me to speak to you in mutual understanding, that I do not appear condescending to you just because you are exiled on Earth. You and your brother are My children for sure, but you are My colleagues in pursuit of the conversion of the lost. I have always been human like you, but born without sin. I have always been incapable of committing sin. These are not attributes that are lost to you. It comes down to your willingness to be confident in what you receive from the Spirit of the Lord. We have spoken about the aroma and sound of redemption, but it also has taste. The flavor of redemption is brisk and fresh, never stale, always enlivening, and forever strengthening. You have heard the metaphor that life can leave a taste in someone's mouth, and this is what I am saying. But, the taste of redemption is the taste of Salvation; it is always sweet. Even as you live in a world that deals in gall and insult, the sweet taste of Salvation is your redeeming brew. The reason I know these things is because I have lived where you live. I am living here still. I know about the blindness of your detractors. I rest in the assurance that I did My best, and I am still conveying the Gospel message as the Queen of Heaven. As I am the Mother of the Church, the Mother of the Most Blessed Trinity, the Matriarch of humanity, I continue My living presence through people like you. I still remain in My original body, just as Jesus does.

    We are united inside your heart; you are a disciple of the union between My Immaculate Heart and Jesus' Sacred Heart. You said it correctly to your brother last evening; there are forces and diversions that would make you believe that the Holy Spirit has no place in you. However, the Holy Spirit is there because Jesus and I live vibrantly within you. This is the reason that I ask you to take good care of yourself. Protect your heart from harm; do not worry about what others might think. When I saw the sanctity of your composure and presence at the Ashland Village Hall on Thursday, you seemed such a stately man with ethereal vision. You were a trusted adviser with a meaningful message. My little son, this is what the Hosts of Heaven see when you are looking from your window with a view. This is the reason that the Popes of the Church have come to a window to greet the pilgrims at Saint Peter's Square. The Popes have had a window with a view. They have preached sound doctrine from there; they have blessed, healed and consoled their flocks there too. Hence, you see the metaphorical and realistic purpose of the Pontiff appearing at the window. This is likened to the spiritual window that I mentioned at the opening of My message today. And, what the pilgrims have noticed while listening to the Pope's message and receiving his blessing is as much about the taste of redemption as seeing and hearing. They savor the sweetness of their faith, exhibited by a single Vicar in a living Church. If you close your eyes and taste something, you can tell what it is. The point I am making is that tasting something requires you to touch it. This is not true with seeing and smelling. The taste of redemption is present in the Blood of Jesus on the Cross, and profoundly hewn into Creation by the suffering of the redeemed. You can taste redemption in the Holy Eucharist; you can claim the predisposition for accepting the trials, tribulations, gifts and blessings of human life on Earth through your belief in what the Blessed Sacrament does. Do you understand? *"Yes."* This window to the world through which you have a view was fashioned into the framework of life by Jesus and the Church. The veil of your exile, as thin as it is, makes up the glass through which you cannot pass until shorn of mortal flesh. But, you can still see! You can still savor the fragrance of eternal life by looking through this window. Theologians have not written about the mission of the Church this way. They have been doubtful to believe that humanity could be drawn this close to the perfection of their Savior. Indeed, this is the meaning protracted by Jesus when He commended the world to become perfect as He is perfect. Come to the window with an expression of repentance on your face! This is what He meant. Tasting eternal redemption requires a disposition that is receptive of miracles. This is why you and your brother must believe that life tastes good, even if it rarely seems that way. Tasting holiness portends living for redemption. This is what Jesus has promised. Come to the Altar of Sacrifice and taste the freedom of everlasting life; this is what the Church is teaching. It is in the call of the Cross. If you think about all the forms, facets and purposes that compose your life on Earth, the most meaningful is in your recognition of life's blessings in the Sacraments. Now, as we speak, there is perpetual light shining upon you. Humanity is passing through time, while time itself is waning. It is a grand revolution; it is a new beginning and an imminent expiration, and it is glorious and timely. There is no question that you have thought about what I have said today, and you should place more context into your pondering. This context is in the faith that you love. You should see life as a gift, here and in the Afterlife, that can be nothing less than perfect when done in the image of Jesus. I ask that you and your brother come to the window and enjoy what you see. It is a sacred vision, a beatific foresight of the glory that God has prepared for you. My Special son, I have taught you to breathe-in the moment; do not cast your thoughts too far into the future or worry what might come next. Remember the teachings of Saint Pio. Thank you for praying for the conversion of the world, and thank you again for helping the villagers in the town where you grew up. I will be with you forever."

Saturday, January 11, 2014
9:31 a.m.

"Commissioned by their own beauty."

"There are moments when time and eternity seem absolutely aligned, My little sons. When I speak to you here; when we share the Love of God in so many ways, these are among those moments. I have for centuries waited for the past two decades to arrive. Even though I do not yet know the Second Coming of the Son of Man in earthly time, I have always known that I would be speaking here on January 11, 2014. I knew that there would be two-by-two, and that there would be two more who would accept My presence in America, who would propagate My Queenship, who would be both devotional and obedient, who would never surrender to the distractions of the world. Thank you, My little sons, for saying 'yes' to Me the way I said 'yes' to God. The whole of the ages has been bettered by your faith. Today, I speak about the Christian identity that is present in all who believe in Jesus and pray for His Divine Kingdom. Think about Christians this way – you are commissioned by your own beauty. What does this mean? It means the ratification of the hopes and dreams of the Church. It manifests the acceptance of the difficult sacrificial life of evangelizing Jesus' Crucifixion. It means shouldering weapons that may not be fired until sunrise on the last day of the world. There is beauty in this sacred identity; it is the Christian commission, a Messianic holistic commission that takes men far beyond their life's roles. You become more than commoners, more than mere mortals. You participate in the life-giving power belonging to the Father. He gives you the morality that you wrote about in your first memoir, the morality by which you have walked during your whole lives. Commissioned by your own beauty means that you can foresee what things will come whether they are based in previous experience or not. You have the capacity to know the commonalities and differences between cause and effect, and action and reaction. My little sons, you have this sacred beauty; you are accorded this commission through the advocacy of the Holy Spirit. You hold dominion over Creation because of this commission. You are leaders and policy-makers through your spiritual faculties. You shine with the illustrious genius of the Wisdom of God into the dark corners of humanity's being. And, I am with you here, and I go with you there. I only ask that you realize that only few in the history of the world have understood human life through My eyes the way I have described it to you. Only a handful of souls have known the mind of our Creator to the depths of your experiences. Therefore, it is not just a miracle that I have spoken to you for so long, but that those to whom I have not spoken are keeping their faith as well. It is the plan of the devil to rid the world of faith in Jesus; this is what you said in your memoir. However, it is the purpose of the Lord to instill that faith to even greater degrees, deeper into the lives of those who follow, and delving like daggers into the hearts of the many who have yet to believe. Yes, Jesus knocks on the door of your hearts. He will not kick it down, but He can see through it. He can pierce its surface with miracles so profound that humanity will open it from the inside to see from where they have come. Indeed, Jesus has had countless doors opened through My intercession. The commission about which I speak requires more than a sense of destiny between Christian hearts. It mandates that humans touch other humans in starkly spiritual ways. This commission is a venue through which lost sinners are invited to participate in the life of the Church. Christians stand tall; even from here, looking down upon the Earth as servants. You share the Gospel humbly, but confidently. Christians are commissioned by their own faith-beauty, sent forth to invigorate suffering people with the presence of the Lord's sublime peace. Standing tall in this commission makes the human spirit take on a statuesque presence, one that does not defer to the negativity of nonbelievers or the opposition of secular kings. There is true providing in what you say as Christians. There is love, eminence, providence and prophecy.

My Special son, I am telling you today that you and your brother, and all who believe in Jesus, are practitioners in the founding of the True New World, the fashioning of its ramparts, the re-writing of the old history that is soon to be annulled. You are infused by the Heavenly Father with passion and willpower. You are vested with propriety and sanctity. You are allowed to prescribe for the Church in Paradise what the Faith Church shall discern. Here, I am telling you that you are commissioned; you are sent forth to multiply the number of believers until there are no more unbelievers still alive. Imagine what I see as this process unfolds. I have been watching it for centuries. Think about what it means as Mother of the Church to know that My Son's disciples are My children. The New Humanity, spared from the fate of Old Adam's stain, standing before Me in the presence of Jesus to say that they are prepared to begin again, that they desire to be reborn. Theirs is the commission to change the universe into the likeness of Heaven, one soul at a time. It is based on the single most important issue in the existence of man. It is toward the goal of making the Earth like Heaven in the span of a few short centuries. Anything that distracts from this goal is unworthy of God. This is the reason that man was made able to think about one subject at a time. By all means, if someone is adding a column of numbers, can they add another column at the same time? Of course not. If they are thinking about a certain topic, can they split their mind and examine another one too? No, the answer is no. This is the single-impulse orientation that makes Christians one with Jesus. They accept Him and no other. They receive the grace of pure life from no other. My Special son, it is with admiration that I speak with you and your brother today. It is all in the context of My Motherhood that I tell you that the world harbors no ill will for what you have done for Me. It cannot. It will never be eligible for redemption holding any ill will for your years of dedication to sanctifying the visible realms through the righteousness of the invisible. You have taken the oath upon your baptism to uphold what the Lord believes should come of the ages during which humanity has lived. There is beauty in your heart; there is awesome wonder in your faith; there are changes in the offing for the world for which you pray, and there are multitudes of blessings that have been stationed in your life. It requires different gifts from anonymous people. Some will suffer kindly; many will die begrudgingly, others will come and go without so much as a sigh. The world is as much in transition as in turmoil. Millions of people go through it as the days pass by. It is the transformation of the Earth, the evolution of the human spirit from mortality to immortality. Never mind where the flesh will eventually go.

  I am elated to pronounce these things. I commend you for helping God to such degrees. There are people who are commissioned as Christians who are not speaking up as they should. Whatever kind of corruption and perversion you might imagine is occurring somewhere around the globe. I ask that you be patient with all the sinners who have not been speaking to Me, to the billions who have never heard one syllable of My voice. I have said that Jesus' Spirit walks the Earth, and His Truth is welcomed by you, in you and through you. This is the concept of reciprocity again. And, you and your brother, and all My messengers and seers, are doing your best in a world in which you are responsible to take care of yourselves; to feed, clothe and house yourselves, to learn and remain aware of the paths the devil takes to bring the innocent down. Your awareness of the Will of God is your compass, just as you have said and written. I ask you to remember the esteem that you have found in Jesus as His holy commissioners of The Faith. Never lose sight of your dignity in Him, even if you suffer the way He suffered in His final hours, even if you are frail and weakened, even if your life and heart are cast-under by the stockholders of the world. The purpose of your faith is to go to Heaven and take as many others as you can. There is no question that you are accomplishing these things with sterling design. I am urging My children to respond to My messages, to heed the call of the Catholic Church, and to lay down their weapons of war. I have been making Myself available to all who call on Me, regardless of their beliefs, no matter where they live. So, My Special son, are you happy today? *"Yes."* It is good to know that you are happy because it proves that you are aware of your commission in Jesus the Messiah. I have for you a sense of love and respect that you cannot imagine. It is all in the Kingdom to which you are drawn, into which you will soon be taken. These are marvelous times, supernatural times, miraculous times in which you are living."

Saturday, January 18, 2014
9:57 a.m.

Votive - granted in fulfillment of a vow

"Grace bellows through your lives, My little sons, because you have given yourselves to Me. The world makes unbelievable assumptions about God, ones demanding Him to respond; and of all things, ones calling Him to its obedience. However, you My children are steady in faith for Him. You prevail over the world because you are not distracted by its intrusions. You have loved so profoundly that ordinary men cannot take it in. This is your consecration to Me and to Jesus' Most Sacred Heart. I come today with a sense of urgency, that you remember in your prayers everyone who is committed to furthering My Medjugorje messages. Millions of little mustard seeds have been planted there. And, My message today is a call to keep in your hearts remembrances of My Sacred Love for all you have commended to the Father. You have given Jesus the venue to reach lost sinners through your meticulous works, through your life-long devotions, through the vision you have placed before the eyes of those seeking to come to redemption in the Cross. My Special son, you know that a 'votive' is something given to fulfill a vow. It is an accordance, a signature, a means of recognizing that the Father owns your humble heart. You placed your trust in Him when you departed the Hospital Sisters last February, and He has rewarded your faith in response. Your prayers have been answered because God loves you. I wish for you to remember that your new venture will come somewhat delicately at first, and you must be patient. You must be confident during the initial days with a humble disposition. Let them know that you are dressed in the simplicity of a decent man. And, do not hunt for villains. There are people everywhere who are stressed from what they are required to do. You saw this at your last workplace. Be their friend and counsel, but also be their leader. Be the kind of colleague that you always wished your former colleagues to be. The Lord expects mighty things from those who are close to Him, but you are not required to conquer the world. You are among many things a consummate professional, profoundly intelligent, overwhelmingly capable of unmatched kindness. This is how I see you; it is the way Jesus sees you. Please let this beginning create the environment that you always wanted at your last workplace. You have the opportunity to begin anew. Congratulations and good wishes! We have much more to accomplish with our messages; we will not desist until we have yielded the outcome that we have always sought. I again say that you and your brother are blessed because you have welcomed Me here. It is My privilege to speak to you openly and discernibly. You recognized your Holy Mother in 1989, and I asked you to come to Me. You are with Me now as closely as any human being on Earth. Your life is My gift. Thank you! You now have even more reason to remind your friends that I will dispense the signs and graces accompanying My promises to all who pray the Holy Rosary. Here with you, I feel more heartened than when I am elsewhere. Yes, I love My messengers all the same, but you are open with Me; you do not banter with Me, nor test Me. You are loyal to the purpose of human suffering for the conversion of the world. You see the darkness and share the glory of everything that life has ever been. You stand tall in holiness; you pour out upon this land your showering love in the image of the Saints of the Church. You pray with your arms wide open, with the 'Fathom' of your own identity, with your eyesight set on ridding America of the indifference that has lulled it to sleep. It may appear that you and your brother are among the only people who know this, but there are 70 billion others who have lived and died that savor the fruits of what you are doing. It has more to do with the Church Suffering and the Church Triumphant than anything else you see with your eyes. Your life augurs a refreshing stream of consolation to the Poor Souls in Purgatory. It reflects the glistening streets of gold on which the Saints are stationed. Your holiness is the sheen of the footlights before God's Throne. Your honesty, your determination, and your dedication to the Gospel uphold the wishes of tens of millions of exiled Christians every day of the world. It is here that I ask you to look. Be confident that you are willed by the Father to live in this time, to represent Him here, to applaud the good works of your friends, and to respect the dignity of all who are persecuted for the faith by which they walk. These are glorious times and unique moments. I am elated that it is you to whom I am speaking, not the President of the United States, not the billionaires who hoard humanity's wealth, not the elitist next door, and not the most popular person on the national airwaves. It is you to whom I am speaking, and it is My honor to do so. I wish goodness and mercy upon all who accept My Son. I pray for their longevity, good health and eternal joy. I plead for Jesus to be merciful toward the blind and misguided. I ask Him to deliver the innocents from harm. I beseech Him to instruct the ignorant and lift up the lame. I pray for all good things, and no misfortunate ones. Heaven will rain justice down on those who deserve it, just as you said in your memoir. We need not ask humanity to do it. And, it is right that your brother has spoken to his brother's wife Nancy with perspective tones. She is afraid of her imminent passing; she does not see life the way you do, and she does not understand death with your wisdom. She will go to Jesus through Me. She has always been a good Christian. She will join her family members in Heaven when she hands her spirit over to God. This is the way of the Lord. He receives souls into His house with gladness when their earthly lives are through. They are sainted the moment their flesh falls lifeless. This is the process of deliverance through Jesus' Divine Mercy; it is the way mortal creatures are welcomed into the everlasting."

Saturday, January 25, 2014
9:04 a.m.

"Pawners, pundits, peddlers and panhandlers."

"My little sons, flourishing accolades pour forth from the Heart of God for your holiness. Ageless confidence has been instilled in you, that the world might come to know Jesus the way you embrace Him. It is true that I do not speak as lengthily in some of My visits as others. It is like the rhythm of the years, but it is one eternal moment for you. I have not conscripted you into My mighty army of warriors, you have volunteered your own righteousness to Me. Today, My little sons, I think reflectively on what you mean to Our Father God and what you have accomplished for the Church. Dare I say that I lionize My children? Yes, indeed. You are priceless; your hearts are praiseworthy, your gifts to the redemption of humanity are immeasurable. While I will speak to you as long as you wish today, I have brought no lessons or anything profound. I am thinking about how you differ from the people mentioned at the beginning of My message today. When you think about yourselves as Saints in this life and in Heaven, when you see your contributions to the poor, when you ponder what you have shared with the world, you are not commoners anymore. You are becoming Doctors of the Faith; you are holders of your own scepters to which men are being drawn. You are filled with the Holy Spirit in the way that pawners and pundits never will. You are not asking for something in return for your kindnesses because you are assured that Salvation is the path you have inherited. You are not peddling another way of life to foster your eternal redemption, and you are certainly not beggars. You do not approach Jesus with your hands outstretched, saying that you cannot work for what He will bestow. My little ones, imagine what this day means, January 25, 2014. It is not just a day in time, not just another date in the calendar year, but a day of blessing for humanity. You have brought this into being. I have said that you show confidence in the face of the doubts of others. This is why you are courageous. You are not just holding the Lord's goods until He comes back to retrieve them; you *are* the Lord's goods! You are not pawning the future for a world that is in hock; you *are* the future. You need not be hustlers when so much has been given to you. And, most importantly, you do not take to podia around the world and tell humanity what the Father will and will not do. You are not the pundits of the Kingdom of Divine Love. Yes, you *are* His Divine Love. And, I am in love with you. I hold your hearts and souls, your sacred identities, as precious as the Son I bore. You are distinguished and esteemed; you are nobly remarkable before the nations, you are the chosen elect in whom Jesus has placed His wisdom. I ask you to see yourselves this way. Be thankful that you are not only on the right side of history, you are helping God expunge the wrong side. You are not sitting on the fence between rightness and political correctness; you rebuke those who will not stand for the truth. This is My message today, My little sons. You are living a transition in your lives and for the world entire. You are witnessing the recovery of spiritual discretion that has been lost. I have come to share this with you. I have the insight to know what you desire. I understand your hearts, as they are united with Mine. You must not take yourselves too seriously, and you must never underestimate the cunning of your enemies. All men should place the Will of God before their own.

Many people cast off the warnings that impact their consciousness. They ignore the signs; they pay no heed to the perils. They write off beatific wonders as being superstition. They turn their faces away from God's graces, calling them coincidences. They are not only unobservant about what these things mean, they are ignorant about how their lives will be judged. You once saw two companions safeguarding a ring who were watching the cataclysmic completion of the world; and one said to the other that he was glad to be with him, '...here at the end of all things.' The whole of humanity that is not tethered to the Cross of Jesus Christ will not be able to say this to God. They will be shorn of the opportunity to turn to Jesus and say that they are blessed to be with Him, '...here at the end of all things.' They will never know that they could have been seated beside the New Beginning that was destined to be their future. My messages have always been about this preparation, for the unification with the Perfect Man, the Christ Child in whom everything good that has ever existed below the Throne of God resides. It was meant to be this way; it has been about Jesus from the beginning.

Now, you know that you are living in the end times that I spoke about in Garabandal. I ask you to remember that millions of people have already forsaken Me as their Mother because they do not see My prophecies unfolding the way they would do it. Those who remain with Me will be given the fulfillment they desire. And now, we see the Church. We watch as Cardinals, Bishops and priests rebuild what has been brought down by the sins of a few. It is not that the Church will ever be destroyed or even begin to list. No indeed, it is the perception of the Church that must be rebuilt. It is humanity's oneness with perpetuity that should not be overlooked, the ability to survive beyond the centuries and millennia. All those who claim to be enemies of the Church, not just those who persecute the Church, will be found in the end to be as culpable as the rest. It is the same as lusting in the heart. No one can harbor ill will against the Catholic Church and be united with its Messianic Priest. My Special son, you know that there are degrees of contempt leveled against the Church Hierarchy, that it is too patriarchal and all the other things you have written in your memoir. But, all this will be neutralized by the contemplativeness of the faithful ones, those who hold the Church dear to their hearts. You know that there is one 'evil beast' who has been the villain of the ages, for the history of men on Earth, but there are smaller beasts that have been spawned from his satanic error. These evils are everywhere; they are not infinite, but they are apparent in everyday injuries and insults, in slights and indiscretions. You have heard that sin is just a sin, but there are more egregious transgressions that bring harm to innocent souls and fragile hearts.

Just as the Father knows about all the birds, fishes and hairs on the head, He also knows about those little beasts who are committing such wrongs against His disciples. The depravity of every one of them will be addressed, individually and collectively, in the sum of all the ages and the culmination of the Earth. You need not worry that something that you see as offensive against virtuous love will go unpunished. All will be held to account; everything will be adjudicated and mitigated. What does this mean? It means that those who live luxurious and unholy lives will be put in one place, and they will not be able to utter a word in self-defense until they have witnessed every minute of every life of the disciples who were true to Jesus. They will have no recourse; there will be no alibis. The faithful will feel vindication the likes of which you have never seen. The enemies of the Cross will beg at your feet for forgiveness; they will weep for just one more chance. And, you will give it to them; this is what reconciliation is all about. The transition to repentance is theirs to make. It is an old saw that Satan uses against Christians. He causes sinners to claim that they were victims in a world where they could not fight against their own temptations. While this is true for some, many have chosen their devious ways. My Special son, I am not asking anyone to be insensitive to the repentant. You will know who the authentic converts are. You will know by the tone of their voices, the look on their faces, the humility of their posture. You will recognize if they harken to the innocence that they had as children and beg Jesus to give it back again. You will know by their speech about the presence of virtue and whether they have the Holy Spirit in their hearts. My little son, when they begin to weep bloody tears, you will know that their souls are prepared for redemption. It is all a wonderful mystery, a merciful gift from the Father that they will have these moments to decide. I have never told you this, but in addition to My endless love for Jesus, I am righteously proud of Him, not just for the way He lived and what He has always meant to Me, but that He walked the world with a childlike Heart, even as the Victim whose Sacrifice has reconciled all men to Himself. He never shed His modesty, His ability to receive all who came to Him as friends. Yes, the Mighty Savior, the Messianic Martyr, the Man-God whose Sorrowful Crucifixion will forever be the greatest event in human history always wanted to remain just a little boy. This does not mean that He did not shed the things of childhood to become an adult. He simply yearned to be His Mother's Child, playing in the dooryard, asking Me to hold Him in My arms. And, I still do. I carry Him everywhere, even as He stands as the Eternal King in the celestial skyways of Heaven. My Special son, I ask you to remember that you are as precious as Jesus to Me, as are all My children. With My love for you wholly shared and forever constant, I offer My holy blessing for today. Thank you for your petitions. I will intercede for all for whom you have prayed."

Saturday, February 1, 2014
9:35 a.m.

"Love for a lifetime of reasons."

"This is a new month of glory that has come, My little sons, the opportunity to share what you know of life and what I know of Heaven. I remind you that I hold you close and dear; you are the reason I have extended a super abundance of grace in attempt to convert lost sinners to the Cross. Today, it is clear that you have made remarkable progress behind the realms of your comprehension. Your deposit of works was mentioned at a Vatican conference about the messages of Medjugorje. One of the principal theologians wondered whether Medjugorje was a precursor to My Morning Star Over America messages and that, along with the millions of visiting pilgrims there, it is among its most viable fruits. The theologian was speaking about the prescience of the Holy Spirit. It is a time for discernment for ponderers worldwide. We shall see how the good Lord unfurls this prospect. Also today, I wish for you to understand the blessings that are coming. There will be advancements and setbacks; there will be darkness and light, and there will be challenges over which you will prevail. I ask that you do not be disconcerted; do not banter with people about the mechanics of My appearances. You need not reveal anything private about our relationship, its mystical aspects or anything else that might give someone reason to calculate their level of belief or disbelief. Please be prudent in your discretion; remember to safeguard the sanctity of your relationship with Me. My Special son, you have completed a meritorious memoir. You will be rewarded with profound blessings because of the efforts you have invested to exert your faith. Imagine all the people around the globe who are yet unaware; think about what they will feel when coming into first contact with the miraculous intercessions that I have given you. Yes, many would pray a million years for Me to appear at their door and say 'hello.' You and your brother have not lost sight of the gifts you have been handed. My opening words today speak of loving humanity for a lifetime of reasons. Could they be listed on a page? One might cite social unity and inner-peace, the alleviation of suffering, the end of abortion and disease, the protection and preservation of the innocent, and the spreading of the Good News by which all men have been saved. Capturing these blessings is among the reasons everyone should pray. A life completed for these goals is a life of sacrifice with lingering grace, a deferential life that encompasses giving to others the best fruits before feeding oneself. This is the way of Jesus, but it is not a life bereft of consolation. There is no doubt that knowing that your brothers and sisters have a new beginning in Jesus is welcome news. It feeds the human spirit with confidence and paves the way for the future. I wish the entire world were this way. I wish that there were no spiteful words or impatient wills. I wish there were no lust, materialism or vanity; these things have yet to be stilled from the behavior of men. There is unmitigated greed all around the globe. And, I wish that My children would live out My intentions, that they would think about what they are saying and doing, what impact they have on sprawling societies, what impressions they make about God in the world. My Special son, I know that you wish for these things too. I can see it in your eyes, and hear it in your voice. I know that you are among the holy, faithful and dutiful ones, the Christians who understand what it means to be in love with Jesus. Yes, God is all knowing and all powerful, and He has placed in the human will the ability to choose, to make decisions that preserve the virtuousness of the Earth. He gives men the choice not to sin. He has laid out freedom in such a way that humanity can elevate itself to the heights of sainthood before anyone else should die. It is about the holiness that I have celebrated with you and your brother for decades. And, it is about honorable people recognizing that they have a vast responsibility to the Original Apostolic Church, to themselves and their families, to their neighbors and friends, and to their own benevolent dreams.

Being freed from sin is not about advancing superficial life or inhumanity, it is about perfecting what it means to be human. It is about sculpting the self in the likeness of Jesus that matches the natural to the supernatural. This is what you and your brother have been doing for years. Humanity must become worthy of Jesus in the same way that you and your brother are worthy of each other. It is not inappropriate for Jesus to admonish even those who follow Him for leading lackluster lives. Yes, it is about accepting the supernatural, whether human souls are appealing before the eyes of God, whether their spirits are photogenic, whether there is a sense of eternal destiny in their decisions and actions. Fighting against the exploitation of the innocent is one such action; praying for one's enemies is another. Capital punishment itself is based on the false premise that someone is unworthy of prayer, unfit for mercy, ineligible for forbearance or clemency. Even those who order the execution of the condemned say with horrendous hypocrisy that they forgive the criminal, but that the criminal must die. This is not the way of the Gospel. Jesus says that humanity must love for a lifetime of reasons, and this lifetime consists of one's exile and immortal life. The intention of someone's heart over the years determines what decisions he will make at the end of his life. This is the self-judgement that is mentioned when speaking about the value of the soul, the worth of the human person when measured over time. There are alternatives to many things, but not when drawing conclusions about the virtue of someone's life compared to Jesus on the Cross. My Special son, this is the love that must be shared by all My children. The lifetime of reasons must come down to one eternal moment, taking Jesus' hand and walking into Paradise unstained. It is the ultimate discharge of the duties of the Christian to stand united with the Man-God in whom the future of all men is placed. I do not take lightly those who refuse to believe. As you wrote in your first memoir, it is possible that I will uplift those who have turned away from life's sacrifices, but My will is united with My Son that some sinners must face justice. I know what they must endure to reach perfection. It is all about glory, and glory is about self-denial and unification with the Passion of Jesus. I have said that only few men will be martyred in the flesh, but everyone who attains the age of reason will be spiritually slain before seeing the summits of Heaven. There is no sadness in this fact; there is no reason to live with a sense of doom. It is a blessing to join Jesus on the Cross; it is a sign of true destiny. It is a way of learning the difference between knowing something and acting on it. It clarifies the Christian perception of wisdom. It is an avenue down which the Saints have traveled, on the Cross with Jesus, seeing human life from His vantage point, claiming one's victory over the perils of the Earth, asking the Father to accept the sacrifices offered in His Name. My Special son, your brother is filled with anxiety because he does not know how to embrace the sacrifices that he is often asked to accept. I have yet to demand him to walk a tightrope or slay a slithering reptile. I have not told him to tread a gauntlet or kick down the door at city hall. I have said that your brother is experiencing a confrontation with his own fears. This is why his courage is important, and he will invoke it. There is suspicion and questioning all around the world. There is doubt about others and self-doubt as well. There are faults and unworthy judgements. There is reticence and refusal, but the Lord will win at last. God is watching, and Jesus is waiting; the destiny of humanity is at stake. This is what makes prayer so important for many reasons, a lifetime of reasons. My Special son, thank you for offering your petitions that amplify the Kingdom of God in your city and around the nations. It makes a difference in ways not always visible to you."

Saturday, February 8, 2014
9:00 a.m.

"Grouping with the ethereal assembly."

"My little sons, the most relishing observation made by those who enter Heaven is that the sacred atmosphere is sweet; it is rich, it is filled with joy and brilliance. Grouping with the ethereal assembly means living on Earth with those who are bound for Heaven someday. And, it also means joining the Communion of Saints with whom redeemed souls were always meant to be. The Faith Church and the Church Triumphant comprise the seamless life of holy love in those who have accepted the Cross. My Special son, I have always told you about the idea of power with regard to your faith, practicing what you believe according to the teachings of the Church, the means by which you turn back the temptations of the devil. This power is given to you by the Holy Spirit because you are loved by the Father in the Most Blessed Trinity. However, the key reason that anyone is given the power of the Holy Spirit is because you are, in the eyes of God, patently beautiful. Yes, you are pristine and precious. You are divinely and sublimely adorable. Those who reject the Holy Spirit are unsightly; they are repulsive and ugly, even in a physical way. It is through your power given by Grace that you are presently in the honorable society of souls who will enter Heaven simultaneously and conspicuously. You are a member of that society; you are one of many like your brother and all good souls who are enjoying your membership in the ethereal assembly that transcends the created realms and the waning ages, too. The power I speak about is not the kind of power that would allow you to pick up an automobile or throw a 747 airplane into flight as if it were a toy. Indeed, it is the kind of power that matches you with the expectations of the Father for you to be perfect like Jesus is perfect. Yours is the power of kindness and genius; it is an overwhelming sense of self-confidence and self-determination, both founded in your faith and trust in Jesus the Son. The kind of power you have permits you to see with the eyes of your spirit the sacred bond between your everyday life and the Afterlife, to envision what you wish to accomplish tomorrow or the next day, or even at midday today. The power to choose is yours; the ability to benignly manipulate the future lies in the hands of all Christians who believe that religious mysticism is as important to the purification of the Church as charity and service. My little son, it is all based on who prays for what. You have always embraced and extended universal prayer that is supported by the specific circumstances in your life and the individuals you uplift. This is not the kind of prayer offered by some people because they are unaware of the universality of their relationship with God in the Apostolic Church. If grandma is praying for her grandchildren to do well in school, she is not doing so with the hopes that they will change the world, but that they will lead healthy and prosperous lives. Grandma does not really care what happens in China. We see things with more permeating eyes than this. We have our sights set on the whole of humanity, toward making the Church holier through the conversion of single souls and massive numbers at a time. Sanctification, in this sense, means the holy fixation of an entire continent, the union of all peoples under the Cross of Salvation, offered through the Church and at the behest of the Father in Heaven. Your power, and the power of all like-minded Americans, is to grasp this universal purview while you are tethered to the King of the universe.

This is what makes your books so evocative. It is the reason you have blessed the nations with your faith in the Lord. You are tethered to the King with your heartstrings, something that is not shared by millions. They are 'in it' for what they can get for themselves, for their families, for their dogs and cats. They turn blind eyes to the outer edges of human existence where children and paupers are marginalized out of sight. Your power is equatable to the power of the whole Church through the concentric identity of the Holy See in Rome. If you were an outside observer of your first memoir instead of its author, you would plainly see that you have made leaps and bounds in describing this unity to the rest of the world. Your presence of faith is a manifestation of beauty for humanity; you are beautiful, as your brother is beautiful. You have gained collegial status, expert status, with the Doctors of the Church even before you shall someday join them in Heaven. Imagine what our beloved Pope Benedict XVI is thinking these days. He sees his life through the lens of the Crucifixion, and Jesus sees his life through the Paschal Mysteries. Pope Benedict has brought intense dignity to the Church and the ethereal assembly in which you are a member with the Saints. There are identifiable attributes to belonging to this society. You have the satisfaction of knowing that your enemies cannot defeat you. Your victories will rise and vanquish your adversaries. Why? Because of the Resurrection that has restored your life. You must take comfort in knowing that, through Jesus, you will always have the final word. Jesus will give you everything you need to say when these moments come. And, you will know that it is the Holy Spirit guiding you because you will feel a sense of the self-confidence that I mentioned moments ago. All Christians are spread before Creation like a massive blanket of protection of The Faith and the innocent. You have the power of the Love of God within you, and every petition you raise to Him is like another arrow of righteousness pulled from your quiver. In this sense, you can dictate the providences of the world. You can create conditions by which the faithful can flourish in the promises handed down through Moses and Abraham, through Jesus and the Apostles, and through the Church and Myself. You have infinite power through a measurable earthly life. This is what you do when you pray; it is what you and I are doing now. It is said that strangers are only friends that you have never met, but this is somewhat too simple to be understood in the context of your faith. You cannot be true friends with someone who will not accept their part in the purification of the Earth. They may appear to be kind and generous; they may seem sublime and courteous, but they will never cross the bridge that will take them to suffering and sacrifice for the sanctification of the world. This takes courage enough to join Jesus on the Cross and tell Him that you are willing to endure His kind of suffering. Even as excruciating as it was, Jesus' most intense pain was caused by those who rejected Him; it remains the source of His greatest agony. It harkens to the old man who told his wife that she could slap him in the face every day, just do not leave him. As long as the world is called to the Holy Mass, as long as the Holy Sacrifice is offered, Jesus will be reminded of those who are rejecting Him. You have spoken about the times when the Mass will be complete, when Jesus wipes His vineyard clean, when the world is through and all souls are called to Judgement. And, pay attention here; it is through your life that Jesus is living, through your passionate zeal for the reconciliation of Heaven and Earth that Jesus finds His joy. You are His wound dresser, just as many other Holy Doctors who are giving Him reason to believe that even the most wretched sinners are worthy of His Blood. This is the most gracious life that you could live; it is the most endearing way that any soul will greet Him face to face. It is the life of honor; it belongs to you, and you have nourished it well.

I have sometimes spoken to you about human life having surfaces, some that are two and three dimensional, some that are seen and unseen, others that contain more dimensions than capable of being surveyed. The things that they have in common are that they must make themselves as sleek as they can in the themes of holiness. They must be free from the baggage of self-ingratiation and self-aggrandizement. These surfaces of life must be clean and pure, even as they are battered and scarred by the evils in the exiled realms. These surfaces must be like the Kentucky All-State Choir singing your National Anthem in the atrium of that facility. There is a detectible sleekness in their performance that is not only discernible to your eyes and ears, but inside your heart where you hear the voice of the collective ethereal assembly. You can see that they are members of it too. Jesus attaches Himself to anyone who calls Him from their inner-heart, from the origin of their knowledge that He reigns for them. It is the same point that I made in early 1991, the Dove of Peace comes to light where there is peace; peace must begin with those who seek it. This is the essence of the Franciscan prayer, '...let peace begin with me.' I have sentiment for those who understand what I have told you today because it is practiced by few on Earth. I do not mean that the ethereal assembly is small, but the practice of the power is not as fruitful as I would like. In other words, I want My children to know about their power, to be aware of their identification with the Triumphant Communion of Saints. I desire My children to know their own beauty in a humble way, not subservient, but with gratitude. All My children should acknowledge that God does not allow Me to see many unsightly things in this world; it is unbefitting of the esteem in which I am held. But, with this in mind, I always see My little children who are consecrated to Me. I have full view of the lives of the many who are gifted with the conscience to pursue the Gospel through every given means. My Special son, the power that you and all Christians have been given by Jesus is more than a cordial practice, it is a realization that you are sky-bound and ingenious. You are blessed and intensely commissioned. You are sacred in the ways of the Father, and this is why I keep telling you how dearly you are loved. It is true; it is as true as the day is shining, as true as the Crucifixion of Jesus, as true as your imminent admittance into the Promised Domain. You are aware of those who are not living this way, the millions who are spending their days engaging in excess, in the lure of the flesh, in selfishness and meanness. I am certain that you are also aware of their defeat, of their expungement from the manifest of souls who have presented themselves more dignified before the close of the ages. My little son, I advise you to always approach people and problems professionally, with humble confidence, with self-assurance and kindness. Be patient and enduring, understanding and helpful. You have long prayed for a new beginning, for a way to prove that you are the person whom you always wanted to become. And, with your new position of employment, you have that opportunity now. You have been given your new beginning; you have earned this new day. All is well; things are on course. We shall forever be united in Jesus' Most Sacred Heart."

Saturday, February 15, 2014
9:29 a.m.

"The analgesic of linear time."

"Perseverance and wherewithal; these are the symbols that describe your determination to overcome the obstacles of this world, My little sons. You know that the Mother of Jesus has many times made compliments about the lives of My children, but I have issued criticisms as well. I have one citation to relate today, and it is this – you often refuse to accept the accolades that rightfully belong to you. You are champions for Jesus. I hope deeply in My Immaculate Heart that you graciously accept the gratitude that comes from the Father. You are worthy; you are esteemed, and you are loved. My Special son, to say that you are given God's mighty blessing would be putting it mildly. You will be rewarded for your achievements, and you will be asked, even beseeched, to accept the gifts from the Father that are appropriately yours. *"Thank you."* We now have another Saint in Heaven, your brother's sister-in-law Nancy; she has joined her loved ones and all the Saints. Your brother was a sympathetic diplomat at the memorial service, an ambassador for Jesus in ways that many had forgotten he was capable. He was stately and compassionate; he was a beacon in the night. He was everything that I have taught him to be; all that the Father would have asked for His children who are sad, grieving and mourning. And, your own relatives were of the same comfort to Nancy's husband and daughters. All things went well for the service of the faith for Nancy's survivors who remain here in exile. Nancy arrived in the Father's House with her broad spiritual smile; and she was, just as you imagined, grateful that she suffered for the purification of the world in the image of Jesus. This is the happy ending for which all prayed from deep within their hearts. Indeed, it is all about happiness that we live; you and I, all those working for the redemption of lost sinners, the mission of the Church, those who feed the hungry and tend to the sick. For all that is said of the sanctifying gift of human suffering, it is even more sanctifying when people comfort the suffering. It brings everyone close to God, all who live and breathe to a deeper understanding of Jesus' Passion and Crucifixion. You must remember that the Catholic Church emphasizes that the Resurrection could not come without the Sacrifice preceding it. Life cannot come until death arrives. Dawn cannot break until the darkness has done its last. You have seen this throughout your life; you have addressed it eloquently in the lessons and sentiments of your memoir. Today, I have come not only to beg you to accept the Lord's congratulations for your recent efforts, but to tell you that the hungry world is being fed the nourishment of righteousness by what you continue to do. You will set out on a new beginning in the next few days that will be filled with new blessings and challenges. You are a senior fellow in humanity who has learned the lessons of the ages. You have inherited from your forebears a stature that serves you well, that enhances the esteem of your colleagues, that changes the world one moment at a time. This is all that can be asked of anyone. I have said that time is a peculiar element, that it does not move, but that you move through it. Today, I am telling you that your movement through time allows time itself to soften the torment of the years. Time is linear; it can be viewed by past, present and future events. Something that takes away pain is an analgesic, a phenomenon that restores the painless life, the condition of analgesia. It would seem that there is little pain-free life in your earthly exile, but it is sometimes a matter of perception. People like your brother's brother and all who suffer the loss of loved ones are healed by the analgesic of linear time, but the perspective comes through the Holy Spirit resurrecting the joy in the heart.

My Special son, this is not a false promise. The fact that Jesus is alive in you proves that you and the rest of My children are resilient before the backdrop of human suffering, in the face of misery, sadness and misfortune. Life is dark enough without human beings creating their own darkness. I am not speaking about manifesting some flawed sense of joy or ignoring the seriousness of life's sorrows. I am speaking about living the Easter Joy that is worthy of all men who believe in the God of Abraham. I am referring to the entire constitution of your sense of self, poised inside My Immaculate Heart, given to the Wisdom of Jesus' Most Sacred Heart, and handed to God to the ends of the Earth. While there are aging forces around the world, there is still much youth. There are growing and forming hearts and minds that must be told about their destinies here. This is the gift that people like you and your brother share with humanity. How many times have I spoken about the legacies of the Saints and the encyclicals of the Popes that have been handed down throughout the ages? What would become of the Church and its mission without realizing its gift to humanity? How would Jesus feel if He believed that linear time were not an analgesic for the agonies of the world? To be clear, it is not time itself that manifests the easing of pain, but the uninterrupted trust of generations of men that keeps their faith alive. You are living the miracle that I have told the world from ages past. You are seeing the bright, sunshiny Love of God being deposited here and around you, all over the globe and across the centuries. You are inside the dream that has become reality. You have eclipsed even your own sense of genius, touching the outer limits of perfection in everything it means to be a reverent man in the image of humanity's Redeemer. This is how you know that the Father is as thankful for everything you do in His Name as you are grateful for the gifts that He bestows in return. The Father wants you to succeed, but few people know how He does it. Few realize that there is a seamless connection between the sickness and death that Nancy suffered and the Crucifixion of Jesus Christ. It is not talked about on the street; it is rarely mentioned in eulogies, it is not made clear to the mourning and weeping. Even when Nancy told your brother two weeks ago that it is untrue that God will not give humanity anything to carry that cannot be borne in Him, it was obvious that she did not understand. She lacked the vision to see what she might have known, not because she refused to believe, but because she was never taught. Millions of people suffer around the world every day without knowing the connection between their suffering and the sanctification of humanity. But, it is clear to us; we know the purpose, we are aware of the contrast between pointless suffering and redemptive suffering. Whatever is pure and holy, whenever men find their way to God, especially in suffering in the likeness of Jesus, this is where their distinction in life resides. I am not saying that it is easy, but it is true; it is from the days of old, it is prophetic and beatifically designed.

My Special one, I have given you My message for today with overtones of bittersweet harmony and the bourgeoning of love. I know that you have seen the harshness of the winter from your vantage point within your home, where such brotherhood and kindness have been shared by you and your brother. You will have more years to share. I thank you for taking such good care of him. I bless him for loving you with such infinitude. We are moving to the time of making your deposit of works publicized in this diocese, even as we wait for your Bishop to make a statement of approbation about My messages. I promise that you and your brother's efforts have not been in vain; the world is hungry for what I have said, the condition of humanity's spirit demands that My messages be spread with wholesome flourishing. I am heartened that Jesus will do these things soon because of all the matters around the world that call out for justice. Remember that we never despair. It is not to anxiety that I lead My children, but to reason, confidence, serenity and peace. This is how I ask you to live; to speak gently, embrace your own honor, and reflect your confidence in your everyday life. With your new employment, you will enter an era where you will make many difficult decisions. You will fashion them on your intelligence and the confidence about which I speak. You will lead by the truth that you should be good to others, even in their faults. You have compassion for those who are only now learning what they must do; it is about completing a job using common logic and reassuring kindness. I bless all who are close to Me, and weep for those who are not. I ask Jesus to foster more priestly vocations around the globe. I harbor beneath My protective Mantle all who are consecrated to Me. On and on, My work continues the same way your work goes on in your life. Thank you for your prayers. I will speak to you again on the anniversary of the beginning of My messages."

Saturday, February 22, 2014
9:50 a.m.

"The Morning Star and Christian Internationalism."

"My little children, the longer you live, the more you see the transition that humanity must make during these times. It is one thing to view the Crucifixion in the depths of reflection, to see it through eyes of faith, but it is another to touch the Crucifixion with your heart and soul. This is the transition that individuals undergo when they suffer in this life. It is the transformation of agony into glory. This is what your friend felt as she became ill and died; she went from seeing the Crucifixion to touching it with her soul. And, this is similar to what her husband is doing as a mourner; he has transitioned from the sight of the Holy Sacrifice to touching it with his heart. This is yet another example of the difference between being and doing. My Special son, if one considered a minute to be a dime and an hour a quarter, what reference points have been crossed? Time, shape and value. If someone looks at a dime as being a segment of time, it makes no sense. However, if you apply the two coins to the concept of time, it does make sense. You need something in which to frame the value to understand the analogy. This is the same way that the Crucifixion is a point of reference in the exiled realms. *"I understand."* While this is a simple concept, it has tremendous implications. The prospect of touching the Crucifixion 2,000 years ago does not seem possible in this century. However, it is something that humanity does countless times every day. Touching the Crucifixion in 2014 that occurred 2,000 years ago is not figurative at all. This is what makes the Crucifixion the most imperative event in human history. It transcends time; it supersedes mortal life. You cannot count the number of times that you have touched the Crucifixion with your heart. You have suffered intense interior, spiritual distress as well as physical pain. These things have brought you to the Crucifixion during your life by virtue of those events that occurred long before western civilization was ever formed. Now, let us connect this to the Resurrection. It is not until you have laid down your life in Jesus that you will be raised again. This does not mean that you cannot contemplate the Resurrection according to the Scriptures; it does not mean that you cannot see it with your eyes of faith. However, you will not be able to feel the Resurrection until you have fallen asleep in death or when Jesus comes in Glory and exchanges your exile for your paradisial home. This makes men's lives on Earth a product of the Crucifixion of Jesus Christ, at least those who desire redemption into the everlasting ages. So, you can see what I have seen, what all the Saints have seen, what the Holy Innocents inherited, what shall become of these created realms. As a messenger of God, you are stationed in this life and providentially beside Me in Heaven. It is not a Heaven that you can yet fully see, but you know it is there by the truth in your heart. A measure of time becomes a physical shape with monetary value. A minute becomes a dime, and an hour becomes a quarter. Here today, I began this message speaking about the Morning Star Over America because this is the anniversary of My appearances to you and your brother. You have seen that I have spoken in vast global terms about a nation that celebrates its worldly power. There are foreign countries that are built on theological frameworks, such as Islam. My purpose all along has been the unionization of humanity beneath the Cross, the Christian internationalism that must come before the end of time if all who live on Earth expect to be redeemed. While there is a question whether this will come to pass, it reveals how far the world stands from being prepared for the Second Coming of Jesus, the Messianic Head of the Church. I am not saying these things with regret, however, because I have told you that those who believe in Jesus through the Original Apostolic Church will help convert the wicked by the Catholicism of the Cross. Please join Me in this gladness. Elevate your spirit the way you have joyed over the past several days to remember that true change occurs. Even as you wonder when God will spread My Morning Star messages to the ends of the Earth, know that it is preeminently happening now.

One of your greatest detractors in this diocese has been removed. There are no miracles ongoing in his new location to impede. Here, you see that more and more, the ground is being prepared for what we will accomplish. I simply ask that you and your brother live in peace, knowing that you have each other, that the world is being cultivated; humanity is being purified, and the enemies of Salvation are being defeated. The Lord has entered a New Covenant with His people that will magnify the dawning ages and expunge the present times that have been darker than any before. It is good to be Christian. So today, I remind you that the passing of 23 years has done nothing to douse the brilliance of your future in God. I remain the Matriarchal Virgin who approached you and your brother in 1989 and 1991. And, you are the wonderful children who are eager for the Church to succeed, for the Triumph of My Immaculate Heart to unfold, and for the victory of the ages to prevail. I am with you through these things. I have never left your side. I have watched all the hours and days expire; all the weeks, months and years. I have witnessed your sacrifices and long-suffering faith. I have prayed as you have poured out your lives for Jesus. I have consoled you when you were in pain. I have applauded your advancements for the conversion of sinners and your support of newfound converts. Your faith is no different now than when you were a child, but you have energized your faith to incalculable degrees by the opportunities that accompany turning older in years. This is the theme that is common to the Saints. It is the way the Book of Life is written. A seer once asked Me if there were multiple editions of the Book of Life. There are no succeeding editions, but concurrent ones. The Book of Life has yet to be lastly published because the prayers of men have not been completely said. This means that moments on Earth still count; it says that mortal men are empowered. I spoke about your power and spiritual eloquence during the past several weeks. It is My honor to thank you for your continuing trust that it is indeed the Mother of Jesus who has been speaking to you since February 22, 1991. You have done more to alter the course of history during those 23 years than all the cataclysms of the centuries combined. And, it is further My privilege to say that you have blessed the world with the dignity of your service, directly from the hand of Jesus, straight from the Sacred Heart that has enveloped the Church and mainstreamed the consciousness of God's redemptive desires. My Special son, you alone have done this, and your brother has been your helper. He knows what I just said; it was he who first spoke it to Me. He wants it recorded in eternal history this way. He wants the Father to remember that it is you who carried the ring, you who agonized and served, you who at long last had the faith to believe what I first came to say. I have granted your brother's wish, not to please him, but because what he said is true. Your brother knows that he is nothing without you; he is everything with you, his life has meaning beside you. He remarks in his prayers that he is grateful to be in the presence of one of the most perfect personifications of Jesus Christ to ever don human flesh. This is his gratitude for having given him his new life of faith, for believing in his friendship, and accepting his love. It is his thanks for your dedication of your first memoir to him.

So, upon ending our message today, we will go forward undeterred as we have always done. We will pray together for the wicked to be converted and the holy to be uplifted. We will pray for the healing of the sick; and if this shall not be the Will of the Father, for the acceptance by all who are blessed with touching the Cross. I have been described as the eternal optimist because I live perpetually in Heaven. This is what I have always shared with the world, always hoped for My children, always handed those who have called on Me with faith living inside them. No matter if someone lives to be a hundred years old, it would seem that the succession of the Afterlife comes too soon for those who remain. It is only because they do not understand what I have told you today. It is not obstinance or stubbornness, but a lack of vision and knowledge. You will in your lifetime share what I have said with untold numbers of souls. Even as you speak at the Chandler Cenotaph to tens of thousands of eager hearts, your voice will resonate to the world's foreign shores afar. Indeed, that cenotaph may be from the front steps of your home, from the uptown public square, or the porticoes of the United States Capitol. The Chandler Cenotaph will be anywhere it needs to be, not just in the cemetery of a small Cass County village. Your heart is your podium; your wisdom is your lectern, and your love is your message. With all the mystery that comes with your faith, with all the energy and dynamic will, you shall change the face of the Earth with Me at your side. This is the way of the secrets that we have concealed from humanity for so long. They will be revealed; Medjugorje will be vindicated, and lost souls will be found. The bells from Saint Matthew's Cathedral will peal with the crispness of a new springtime morning. My little son, your faith is as strong as a million stallions, and I am piously proud of you. Thank you for the last 23 years of your life and the many before them that brought you to February 22, 1991. It is inspiring and invigorating to see the way you live. *"Thank you, Mama. I am your son who lives in honor of Jesus."*

Saturday, March 1, 2014
9:24 a.m.

"The Cross and Apostolic Catharsis."

"My dear little sons, you are not constrained on Earth, you are temporarily imbedded in it; you are at the threshold of eternity through your future in Jesus. You are not inhibited; you are liberated and empowered. Today, it is the joy of My Motherhood to speak to you again here in this place and new month. I have always spoken about time being relative because, as has been said, it is a neutral element. Things change in your lives, but time expires according to your desire to seek the conventions of God. I spoke the term 'catharsis' opening My message today, which refers to reaching a state of peace, reason and fulfillment through some aesthetic or soul-touching event. Apostolic catharsis refers to the spiritual internalization of the Cross. Nothing inside or outside Creation contains as many dimensions as the Cross on which Christ Jesus was crucified. It is structural and fluent; it is sacrificial and life-giving. The Cross is both timely and perpetual. All who hope that their personal identity will last beyond a thousand lifetimes find it in the Cross, for the Cross is emblematic of eternal meaning. My Special son, I have spoken to you and your brother about Christian daring, about spiritual courage and catechetical foresight. The basis for My message today is that all are capable of this daring. Everyone can transcend their fears and apprehensions by invoking the Cross. Jesus' Crucifixion is the source of all human empowerment because it is in the Cross that humanity is absolved of every inequity, pardoned of every transgression, and purified in heart, mind, spirit and soul. Hence, to be absolved is to be cleansed, to be washed of sin – historical sin, situational sin, and incidental sin. Apostolic catharsis happens when the consciousness of the person recognizes that this transition has occurred. My Special one, I will show you an image that illustrates what I am saying. (*Our Lady presented an image of a boy standing on a beach, leaping up as if to touch the underbelly of a jetliner flying less than fifty feet over his head while landing at a nearby airport in his vicinity.*)

What is this boy doing as he appears to be leaping upward to the landing jetliner? First, he is creating an image that cannot be captured on an ordinary day. He has reached beyond the commonness of life. Second, he is revealing a prospect that transcends the bounds of human power. He looks as though he is attempting to influence the airplane or affect its movement as it lands. Now, we know that the boy can have no effect that is seeable to the human eye. However, in the context of physics, does the boy leaping toward the airplane have any effect on the unseen variables of its imminent touchdown? (*I responded that he does not.*) I believe that he does. Do not the unseen air pressure and force of gravity change below the airplane, wherever it lands? (*I answered that this is correct.*) So, even as massive as the aircraft is compared to the boy, its movements are affected by his presence below it. This is akin to the mustard seed. It is not the roaring jetliner that matters in this image; not even the boy's body mass is most important. What is important is the daring of the boy, the point of catharsis that he reaches with a subliminal sense of empowerment, as though he is aware of the influence of air pressure and the force of gravity.

The image of the boy beneath the airplane speaks more than a thousand volumes; it is timeless and multi-generational. Who is to say that the boy will not someday become an airline pilot himself and truly change the flight of the craft? Governing what you know about the beatific realms, and what Jesus has taught about finding wisdom and genius in the littlest ones, you already know that the boy has as much influence in the unseen realms as his older self. Innocence and implications abound in this scenario. Allusion to apostolic catharsis is massive and momentous here. When Jesus said that He would make fishers of men, He referred to the boy who so unwittingly affected the landing of the airplane. How? Through their own daring, their own capacity to overcome the influences of the world and think in ethereal dimensions. I said on January 25, 2009 that I would give you messages about My private life with Jesus before He began His public ministry. I said that I would speak about the topics of our conversations relating to His worldview, to His casual speech and preparatory state of mind. My Special son, Jesus told Me as a fourteen-year-old boy that humanity would craft massive mechanical flying machines to transfer people and properties. He said that some of them would even be perceived as angels from on high bringing life-sustaining provisions to the poor and refugees. He did not mention what they would look like, but He said that no matter how sophisticated these flying machines became, they would never overshadow the sense of daring that He would one day instill in those who would become His apostles and disciples. This sense of catharsis was originated from the wisdom of Jesus when He was but fourteen years old; it was seeded in His identity as the Father Incarnate in the Son, given to humanity through Me. Jesus further said that men would come to see Me as Mother of the Messiah and Mother of the Church, but that some would decline to accept Me as their Eternal Mother. However, much to the contrary, even the title of Theotokos is insufficient to describe Me because it is intended to mean 'Mother of God' and 'child bearer' in a limited sense. Jesus told Me as an adolescent boy that I should present Myself as Eternal Matriarch for the whole of humanity, as the Mother of

Perpetual Help. Perpetual means infinite and unceasing. Hence, I have told you through our conversations that I am your Eternal Mother, that I would support and love you in this life and the next. I am the Queen of Everlasting Life. I am the Mother of all in Heaven who ask for a mother because they were deprived of being mothered here in the exiled world. My Special son, Jesus pleaded with Me during our evening prayers to assert My Motherhood, even as I was Assumed into Heaven beyond My earthly years. When I reached Jesus in Heaven upon My Assumption, Jesus and the Father told Me that I was welcome there after having come from a worldly domain from which I never fully departed. Yes, I am alive in Heaven and on Earth, just as the priest told Saint Bernadette on the day she passed away. And, this begs the question about what occurs to other souls given to Jesus by their faith and interior solace. Jesus told Me stories about His Birth as Savior and Messiah, even as He was in His early teens. He would often say to Me, '...Mother, please assure Me here today; tell Me that even those who have yet to lay down their lives will become Saints in their day. Implore My newfound brothers and sisters to see Me as the personification of pardon and gentleness, of peace and spiritual accord, of truth and light, and of chastity and sacrifice. Tell them that I lived for them even in My youth, and that I sought your wisdom and intercession as a child, just as they should follow Me in these things.' My Special son, I recognized Messianic zeal in this boy of such compassion. I knew that He desired to share this zeal with those who believed in Him, the many who would come to serve Him. Jesus was never in need of any catharsis because He was the incarnation of peace and life. However, He knew that the Apostles would require this transition, either tranquilly or upon the dictates of war. And, it was true that Saint John found his catharsis long before the others, the Apostle that Jesus loved, the servant in whom the identity of the Church would be vested – not the Seat of Christianity, but the identity of the Church. Saint John would represent humanity purified and redeemed at the Crucifixion on Mount Calvary. And, it is by Saint John that men are called, standing with mourning and thanksgiving beneath the Wooden Cross, receiving grace and absolution from the Father, leaping in timely catharsis to receive their redemption, much the same way that the boy leapt with daring empowerment toward the descending airplane.

Jesus and I had conversations that rendered Me speechless. I was then and remain today His Mother, and this Mother learned from Her Child. The Man-God was teacher and learner, Son and helper, human and superhuman. He once told Me that the whole world would eventually accept what He came to say, what His mandates would be for a world centuries beyond our humble household, and forever different from the early age in which we lived. He often told Me about the immutable effects of our shared human love and Divine Love. He urged Me to pray for the day when His Church would pronounce Me its Immaculate Mother, sinless even before conceived, capable of infinite affection, and enriching to all who would summon Me for aid and consolation. Yes, My Special son, I learned as a Mother from My Child on Earth that I would never die. I was told by My own Son that Motherhood could never be more perfect than Mine, that even as I called on Him for miracles before His time had come, My pleas did not fall on deaf ears. The whole world is awash in redemptive Blood from this Son of Mine; the daring and dignity that Jesus has always sought from exiled souls is engaged and enriched by My intercessory prayers. I give everything to My children that is universally possible. It is not something that floats in the cosmos or confined above the gated vaults. I am a real, living Mother of those who are bound for the Land of Promise, the Eternal Mother of Jesus' Mystical Body; and I search for daring apostles who leap, even if inwardly, to touch and influence the holiness of life from their station here as Christians. I wrap My arms around the souls of My children everywhere, on Earth and in Heaven. I repeat the strains of redemption to all who will listen; from Fatima and Lourdes, to Medjugorje and Springfield in Illinois. I speak of the pardoning mission that comes through prayer. I stand as a beacon of hope for those lost in darkness. In final effect, the Cross has become the apostolic catharsis for centuries of men; it is there that their freedom is won, there that their Salvation is sealed. My Special son, do you have any comments this morning? *"I completely understand your thoughts today; they are profound. Thank you so much."* I have never told another person what I have shared with you today. Thank you for your prayers and intentions for the poor."

Saturday, March 8, 2014
9:28 a.m.

"The etceteras of sacrificial life, expressed and implied."

"My dear little sons, the Providence of God ordains My presence here. We are helping humanity become more holy and the world to be a better place. It is the authenticity of our relationship that fosters this unity between Heaven and Earth. There are too many facets of life to express in a single day or generation, or even a hundred years. You know that the Gospel contains more implications than commands; all this is part of the conscience of a human soul united with the Father. I refer to these extra measures as the 'etceteras' of life because they must be taken into account. Just as all the books containing Jesus' words, deeds and intentions could not be held on Earth, these same realms cannot be examined by one mind in the span of a lifetime. My Special son, you and your brother have come farther than anyone else in your age to understand the synthesis of courage and wisdom into a singular principle of thought. Your lives have become more universal, your vision grander, and your perception of human life fairer than most all your contemporaries. This is your gift from Me, but more important, it is your right as a Christian. All souls have this right because they are consecrated to the sacrificial life and all the etceteras that come with it. When I told you in 1991 that you move through time, I referenced some of these etceteras. When someone travels from one place to another, he must move through physical space to do so. As the days of a man's life pass one after another, he must travel through time to get there. For everything to which you have been dedicated long before I began speaking to you, your heart and conscience have always known that these are blessed times in which you and your brother live. You have been elevated by your sense of faith and morality to study righteousness for Jesus' sake, for the visiting Angels, for the mission of the Church, for the propagation of the Cross, for the accomplishment of your life's work, for the success of your Marian apostolate, etcetera. In other words, one cannot say that they wish to set parameters about leading a sacrificial life. There are no rules defining how self-sacrificing someone should be. Indeed, some men are martyred because they will not set parameters; they refuse to draw lines that must never be crossed. To them, the commands of Jesus are expressed in their faith and implied through their spiritual meditations. While I have always said that doing good works is endemic to the Christian life, it is equally, if not more important, to pray in one's personal life, to be one with Jesus singularly in the heart and collectively with all humanity. I have given you parables and images to which you are drawn, but manifesting your thoughts and writings has come through your relationship with the Holy Spirit. I have given you and your brother for 23 years messages containing words, but their meaning and your reactions have come by the openness of your hearts. This is from where pious energy comes. Today, I wish for you to imagine the seeming contradiction between My station as Queen of Heaven and Earth and the Lowly Handmaid of the Lord who stood with such sorrow and pity beneath the Cross on Good Friday. Imagine what it was like to see not the criminal among humans being crucified, but the King of kings, the Innocent Man, the maker of all things holy, pouring-out His Blood for the redemption of His executioners. Imagine the Truth being slain by a people so filled with lies. Ponder the Incarnation of Divine Love being crucified by a world overcome by hatred. I have said throughout the years that these contrasts are real; they are apparent and speak for themselves. However, millions of sinners cannot see them. They cannot grasp in their mental reservoir that a Messiah so good could be killed by a world so malevolent. Even in light of the Commandment that 'Thou shalt not kill,' sinful humanity did it anyway. To effect the summit of all ironies, they violated this Mosaic mandate and made way for the Salvation of the entire human race.

This is the expressed Gospel of human redemption handed down by the Holy Spirit through the life of Jesus Christ and written in the Sacred Scriptures. It is further expressed that those who wish to be saved must take up their own crosses and follow Him. What can be made of this? That there are multitudes of human thoughts and actions implied by the life of Jesus through the Gospels. And, not all that is implied has tormenting ramifications; many are spectacularly blessed and wonderful. Just last week, I told you many things that Jesus made remarkably apparent during His younger years; and this week, I will reveal My thoughts and reactions. It speaks to the beginning of My words today. Could I have known when the Archangel Gabriel first visited Me that there would be overwhelming suffering for the Son I would bear? Yes, absolutely. What was not expressed in Gabriel's words is implied by adherence to the Holy Paraclete. And, why was something implied? Because the Bible would be thousands of pages long describing all that Gabriel said. This remarkable Archangel told Me that I was to become the doorkeeper of grace for the world, the maintainer of Sacred Love for the generations and centuries to come, retroactively and proceedingly. My Virgin Womb would be the beginning of the reunion between the Father and His creatures. My thoughts and reactions to Saint Gabriel had nothing to do with discernment because I never paused for a moment to calculate what a challenge it might be. The Archangel said that I would become the Lady Gabrielle of the Apostolic Church. I would announce God's favor on humanity through His Only Begotten Son. I would appear for centuries and appeal to the conversion of the masses; the unwitting lost, the forsaken, and especially the wicked. I would rise from the dust of the world's implosion as the Queen of Peace, the Queen of Love, the Immaculate Conception, the Mother of the Redeemed, etcetera. I am saying that the message of the Archangel Gabriel was never in question. I thought about this new beginning that the created world would find in the Fruit of My Womb. I thought of the new springtime that would come to the icy hearts of humanity. I meditated upon the harvest of souls that would begin with Me. Yes, I was the Lowly Handmaid, but I was also the Mother of exiled virgins, the Holy Matriarch of courageous men, the consoler and standard-bearer for the army of souls who would, as the Sacred Scriptures reveal, defend everything that Jesus would know and come to be known. This, My Special son, is what I carried with Me through the moments when Jesus' time arrived. I heard the so-called case against Him. I listened to the liars and hypocrites. I watched in disbelief that a magistrate and Roman soldiers could be so ruthless. And, just as I have been impressing upon you and your brother for decades, I knew deep inside Me that Heaven would have the final word. These were nearly unbearable times for Me; they were filled with the malevolence of secular hounds; they were dark and perilous for the friends of God, they were born in error from the pit of human sin. I knew everything that Jesus wanted Me to know about His preeminent Wisdom. He was the Father and the Son in one Divine Savior. And, I was always aware; this is why My mourning was accompanied by such subtle consolation. This, My Special one, is the same Messianic message that you and your brother have been transmitting to the world through your lives on Earth.

I once told you that My Heart went down with the sun that day, but it came back up again on Easter Morning. Your whole life as a man; your profession as a Christian, all this should be founded on the realization that you know now what I knew then. Heaven is already having the last word. This is why over 70 billion souls have outlived their own earthly mortality. I am saying that I cannot express everything that must be said about the life and death of Jesus Christ. I cannot put in measurable terms the impact that the Crucifixion has on man's endurance. There are too many dimensions, far too many etceteras to Jesus' sacrificial life to record, too many implications to everything He said to bind into a countable sum of books. Yes, My mind contained an amalgam of the mournful and the ecstatic on Good Friday. I was hurt to the core of My Immaculate Heart that My Son was killed, but I was overwhelmed that His Sacrifice meant the end of human death. While My sorrow was intense for His suffering, it was more poignant that I knew that not everyone through the ages would accept what Jesus did that day. And, this is why I have returned, to find lost sinners, to touch as many hearts as I can, to enlighten the ignorant, knock down walls, shake the bushes, rattle the chains of ignominy, and breathe new life into the dying spirit of unrepentant sinners. I would like to say that this has all been a joyful effort for Me, but many things have hurt. Just as in your life on Earth, My life was filled with sorrow and grief that such an awesome Sacrifice would be so disparaged by many wayward sinners bound for condemnation. Yes, My Special son, Heaven is indeed having the last word. You and I, and all those aligned with our cause, are making the difference that the Martyrs could not make. Their voices may have been silenced, but their message lives in us still. The resonance of truth might have been impeded for a while, but it is being reechoed in the annals of your life and times. This is why I keep coming here hour after hour, week after week, year after year. I long for your heart as My child. I am eager to instill in you the same hope that Jesus gave Me. I am pleased to say that everything you are working for will be accomplished inside and outside of time. It is here that humanity is being changed, not that you can see it all the time, but much larger than your thoughts can imagine. Yes, flooding etceteras of triumphs and victories are on course to greet you here where you live, gifted from God to those who believe. My Special son, I have concluded what I came to tell you today. I am happy, effusive and reflective in the company of such esteemed messengers as you and your brother. Bless you for allowing Me to speak to you this morning. *"Thank you, Mama."*

Saturday, March 15, 2014
9:23 a.m.

"The vindication of all your victories; your nonperishable, spirit-perpetuated, life-sustaining Christian faith." - Pope Peter

"My precious little children, My Immaculate Heart engulfs you; the power of the Resurrection emboldens you, the mightiness of Divine Love sustains you, and the endearing innocence of the Child Jesus consoles you. Where there lives the bounty of these blessings in the human heart, the soul belongs to Heaven. Thank you for praying with Me as we ask God to look with Mercy on His people. You are witnessing the vindication of your victories; you are seeing blessings unknown in your lives and around the globe. You are aware of the perpetuity that sustains your faith, the same faith celebrated by Saint Peter for all humanity. All that has proceeded throughout the ages has been sustained this way. Everything good, all that inspires prayer and the unification of humanity with the Lord has been sent from Heaven, poured into the vessels of human life, granting pardon, peace and consolation, and leading to a destiny in Holy Providence that cannot be annulled. My sons, this is the reason your forebears marched onward without ever having first seen where they were going. They were inspired by visions of a better life in an eternal Kingdom. They saw images of higher victories in their future; they wondered what vindication actually felt like. And, what can be said of these images? They were constructed from a medium of miracles. They were perpetuated by a people who recognized the rawness of their own capacities and the richness of their comfort in the Cross. They accepted Jesus' Crucifixion and emulated His grace. They knew that darkness always preceded the dawn. My dear little sons, the early Christians who were addressed by Pope Peter with such invigoration were hungry for the satisfaction of their faith. It was well placed in Jesus; they knew this, but it would have been fruitless if not put into practice. Through the guidance of Peter, they wanted to travel every mile, awaken every sleeper, cut through every forest, knock down every wall, scale every mountain, and embolden every heart. They desired to stand for Jesus with such devotion that every spot on the globe became their top of the world. Their hearts ached to be heard; their voices leapt and commanded; their eyes glowed with divinity, and their tongues dripped with the Gospel refrains. It is different today because the fervor of the early Christians has not been matched. O' it might be seen here and there in various places on Earth, but the generations have not lent favorably to the spiritual zeal of men. All those distractions that we have spoken about have taken their toll. And, the idea of sacrifice has been diminished too. It need not be this way; it will not always be this way, you can tell by the signs of the times. There is an urgency in everything but righteousness during these days, it would seem. My children, just as quickly as a slip can lead to a fall, all this will be reversed by the miracles of your age. I ask you to trust Me, to have hope that those who sleep in sin will be awakened. Their fear will exhaust them; their guilt will haunt them; their life's choices will indict them, and the Crucifixion will convict them. The warnings spoken about elsewhere are precursors to events to reorient humanity to the uprightness of Pope Peter's message. It is good and right that this be true. Indeed, the calling of the Mother of Jesus in Lourdes and Fatima were precursors as well. There, I spoke about the conscience of men, their alliance with the Holy Spirit, the responsibilities of their faith, and their shock when given a heavenly sign that God is serious about their conversion. Those 70,000 pilgrim seers were predecessors to the multiple billions more who will see even greater signs from the heavens before the Earth is through.

My dear Special son, if two things happen in sequence, they cannot occur simultaneously. This is the way of the world. However, sequential occurrences are seen concurrently by God. This is the reason He suffers no anxiety. He sees perpetually every beginning and every ending at the same time. He knows Jesus as the Alpha and the Omega, fully the same Second Person, just as you can see simultaneously from both of your eyes. There is no way for you to know which part of what you are seeing with your eyes is being recorded by your brain until you close one of them. The Lord always sees with both eyes, Heaven and Earth, the created and spiritual realms, the beginning and the end, the good and the bad, and everything else that underlines His sovereign dominion over all He has fashioned. And, you have heard of turning a blind eye to something. There is no such thing as a blind eye to wisdom; the Father can see with His Spirit. It is not that He is just capable of bi-location, He is everywhere all the time and outside of time. He blesses and cultivates His creatures with sanctity, regardless of the time. He can reduce a cosmic sphere into a table saucer with a mere thought. He can proclaim justice over an entire universe without saying a syllable. And yes, He can vindicate your victories by simply saying that He loves you. I am overjoyed that Saint Simon Peter walked with Jesus in faith and anticipation. Pope Saint Peter was a human being, capable of tremendous vision and courage. When he denied Jesus at the appointed hour, it was his humanness that caused it. At the same time, however, Pope Peter was infallible in matters of faith and morals because Jesus made it so. It was Jesus' way of absolving and empowering the Apostolic Church before it was ever given breath. Therefore, you are seeing the images of the early disciples and apostles appearing like apparitions before your eyes. You see them in varying dimensions of mysticism. You imagine the ways you would change the world in your day; these are apparitions of hope that you are manifesting for God. You are allowing Him to see what you would make of the Earth, just as He shows visionaries elements of the promises of Heaven. You already know about the things that I have told you today. You have always been aware that the Catholic Church is a spiritual superpower alive in your hearts, manifested by signs and wonders in earthly places. Every human heart should resemble on the inside the architecture of the Church's most elegant cathedrals. The spirit-perpetuated, life-sustaining faith about which Pope Peter spoke is still vibrant through you and within you; and in all, everyone and everything that magnifies the Gospel that you profess. This is your prefigured stateliness. Please think about it – every image you have ever thought possible to reflect the beauty of God is replicated by the faith in your heart. I cannot describe them in words, but your soul sees them. They have no measurable dimensions or temperatures, but you know that they are enormous and heart-warming. They are neither cold nor caustic, or your Christian spirit would not welcome them there. This is what vindicating your victories is about. It is what it means for your faith to be spirit-perpetuated and life-sustaining. It is the image of the beauty of the human soul living with a single-minded purpose. It is the heart given to the Father through the Son, Jesus Christ.

Jesus was the perfect sufferer on Good Friday. I have told you this before. He laid down His life between two imperfect sufferers, the sinners on His either side, in whose presence the Salvation of the world was accomplished. I recently spoke to you about Saint John, likewise there at the Crucifixion, wishing that the Messiah and himself could suffer as one. However, Saint John knew that there was but one Messiah, one Holy Messenger and Sacrificial Victim, one Mediator between the Father and His Creation. It fell upon Saint John to recognize the voice of Saint Peter as the Church's tenor, the anointed Apostle upon whom the faith of the new disciples would be built. Therefore, it is just and right that Saint

Peter was aware of his part. He spoke the verities that humanity needed to hear. It was Pope Peter's victory to uphold the commission he had been given; it was his victory to be vested as the foundation of the Church. Both of these victories were vindicated by the righteousness of this Proto-Pontifical Vicar of the Catholic Apostolic See. This is not just an illusion. It is not something deposited beneath the echelons of the ages, never to be heard from again. This is the making of new beginnings, the way human life ought to be. It foretells the completion of the exiled realms with themes of breathtaking dawns, with prudence and resolution, with offense and remaking, with darkness and light, with cowardice and courage, and with whispering and calling. My Special son, I ask you not to dwell too much on what this means, but pay attention to your life in the moment. Live for what you must do today; concentrate on what you can accomplish here through prayer and deed, through thought and action, through your own advancing toward the purposes of God during these difficult times for the world. Imagine what it would have been like for Me to have appeared to you and your brother and laid twelve books on your doorstep, asked you to publish them, and then went away. This is not what your life was meant to be. As you have written time and again, we share a relationship that fills the voids of time and suffices the expectations of eternity. When I declare that you walk with miraculous images in your heart, I am not saying that you are dwelling on something that will never come. You are seeing from within what will eventually be revealed."

Saturday, March 22, 2014
9:33 a.m.

"He suffered and died, that there might be heirs, prodigies and crown princes for His remarkable Kingdom." - Pope Peter

"My precious sons, I am with you because you are loved and beloved; you are the incarnate sacredness that the Child Jesus celebrates in His Covenant, you are the crown princes for His remarkable Kingdom. I offer you My gratefulness for being so faithful to your Savior in whose Sacrifice you have been redeemed. Today, I wish to give you some suggestions about your meeting next Saturday, and tell you that great manifestations are occurring because of your prayers. I am speaking to you about your public comments and presentations not just for next Saturday, but in the future beyond. My Special son, you are to lead. You are to share My voice in the domain where there are equal numbers of believers and doubters, where questioners' motivations are to trip you up, where schemers and advantage takers will attempt to posit that it is not Me who has been speaking to you. The entire experience about you and your brother making appearances to share what we have done will not be auspicious unless you understand that such appearances are opening-wide our sacred work to the skeptics and cynics who refuse to examine your manuscripts. This is the reason your brother said that he would rather not appear anyplace in person, because everything anyone would want to know about the Morning Star Over America is published in your books. However, great fruits can come from your public appearances. You can invite your audiences to read your books before sharing anything personal about your private life. This was your brother's impression at the beginning when he alone was being judged, when you were the only one who believed that it was Me. Now that you have long been in this light, you must know that it is for scandal that anyone would want to interview you if they have not read your books; and not just two or three of them, or even ten of them, but all of them. While I say that such meetings are meant to bring scandal to your work, they also foster opportunities to propagate the Salvation of the world through the Cross. Whenever you appear where there are curious minds, you can be like the Great Saint John; you can be an evangelizer, you can share your perceptions of the Holy Gospel with regard to human life. This is why I do not decline permitting public appearances of My visionaries around the globe. You must also know that My messages to you and your brother are among the most lengthy in the history of the Church; and for this reason, questioners will demand to know about the mechanics of My presence. They will want to investigate how you can record so many phrases, parables and messages that are in such great depth while you are praying. Simply tell them that you pray the Holy Rosary. Then, you are able to record My words one time; it need not be more complicated than this. It is a basic, practical explanation for a vast mystical experience. And, it is one that dismisses scandalous questions from anyone to whom you are speaking. Everything that needs to be said is in your Marian codices. If someone asks a question about the early days, tell them that all they need to know is in your Diary. Now, as for your brother, he is not supposed to take the leadership role when speaking during public venues. If it were the choice of practicality, you and your brother would not appear anywhere until the whole world has read My messages. The unbelieving masses will not be upended by you or Me, but by those who do believe. This is the way of the Holy Spirit inside human hearts that wish to flush out evil where it can be destroyed by the Church. If you contemplate it clearly, the Father was genius in mandating that those whom His Spirit christens will become evangelists around the globe. While you and your brother are the receivers of My messages, your brothers and sisters must become co-messengers.

I will speak more today about what Pope Peter said about 'this Kingdom' to which all are called in their day. Heirs, prodigies and crown princes. What do they look like? Just as there are hardly terms to describe the bounty of Heaven, surely even the Mother of Jesus cannot aptly put forth Her vision of how Her children appear. If anyone asks this of you, remind them of what Pope Peter said about heirs, prodigies and crown princes. The first prospect that comes to mind is that the Lord is grateful for His disciples. He thanks you for what you have done, that you have decided for Him in ways that make Him happy. Yes, indeed, making God happy is the most rewarding life that anyone could live. Of course, it is about accepting His Holy Will, and much more. Pleasing the Father means exercising the human will in ways that complement the Father's Will, in ways that resound what God wants for those in exile and in Purgatory. He asks His earthly creatures to be fearless, to be who they are in relation to Him, purely empowered, capable of exhibiting unmatched beauty, subscribers of sublime wisdom, willing to dare the devil to stop them, and always leaning toward the spiritual horizon. Everyone on Earth should know that the Father will finish what humanity has begun in His Name, given that those beginnings are reflective of the teachings of the Gospel. If men on Earth plant the seeds of redemption in other men's hearts, God will nurture, water and cultivate them, protect them from predators and vultures, and harvest them once they have pierced the soil and reached the plinth of His Throne. He will place in those who aspire to His perfection a drive for success that cannot be diluted in this world or the next. He will receive all the desires of mortal men into His welcoming hands that advance His Kingdom, that establish a beachhead against those who oppose Him. I recently said to you that this is a beautiful battle, a bloodbath that creates new warriors and crowns the old ones. It need not be about violence, but a spiritual bloodbath of mercy and unity, of coalitions and celebrations. Killing the fatted calf means uttering the verses of forgiveness and repentance where neither is welcomed. Off with the heads of hatred, wherever they may be! Real men do this with oneness in the Cross and companionship with the suffering. Humanity cannot reach the millpond without first going through the rapids. Here, you share the premise that I am describing, that irony abounds in the conversion of sinners. How do you stop someone who is in a frantic rage about their life's station? You cannot always touch their spirit, but you can slap them across the face. This does not seem gentle, does it? But, during the moment when the flesh is stunned, the spirit's awakening will rise. If the body is numb, the spirit is fully attuned. If the devil is defeated by the heroics of the Christian faithful, evil cannot prevail. If it rains on someone's parade, the true patrons will remain and watch, while the imposters will go home. If a perfect Man is crucified for the transgressions of humanity, then all imperfect men will be absolved through Him.

My Special son, these are the kinds of perfect images that I see every day. There are many things I do not see, as I have said before, but I see all the good things that matter to the mission of the Church, ones that glorify Jesus' Sacrifice on the Cross, ones that make Martyrs of ordinary men, ones that will shine like diamonds when the Man-God comes again. I see meaningful suffering, oneness with Jesus that builds up His Mystical Body, suffering that says 'I love you' to God, and suffering that changes centuries of ill will. But, I see mostly the beauty of the Earth and its reflection of Heaven. I see you and your brother, two souls whose appearance before Me and the Kingdom of Heaven is worth an eternity of joy. I see what you have done for God, what you mean to His Messianic Son. I see you as heirs to what He has given the world. I see you as those prodigies that are celebrated in the Lord's verses and rhymes. Yes, I see you and your brother as two crown princes whose images cast divine revelation into this world and the next. I see the precision of pious power, the functioning of your potential in real time, not just a promise of what you might eventually become, but what you have already achieved. I see your tracks, marks and legacies in the same way of your forebears, of the legends about whom you have written, of the mighty ones who did forthrightly change the course of history and archive its revisions in the halls of Paradise. There are moments when I wish I could touch you more fully in your place and time, that you might feel when someone else touches you. It is all in due time; we are preserving your faith in order to preserve the destiny of billions of sinners, and you know this to be true. Your brothers and sisters do not always strike harmonious chords in human life; sometimes the light is not always bright enough to see the most spectacular blessings. There are obstacles in the way, or someone's perceptions are too small. It is all about progress and maturity; it is about the transition of humanity into the image of its Savior. Now, My Special son, I have strayed from My original message today, but I cannot refrain from expressing My love for you. I cannot stop speaking about how special you are to Jesus and Me, to the Father, to the Angels and Saints, and to the finished Church that God will embrace beyond the dimensions of this world. Do you have any issues to discuss with Me today? *"No, I am just thankful for the beautiful words that Pope Peter speaks. Tell him thank you."* I will do as you ask.

(At that moment, Saint Peter spoke to me by locution. I could sense his fatherly gentleness. I could feel that he was still the simple fisherman. I was touched deeply by this spontaneous mystical grace.)

"*I am Peter, Pope of the Roman Catholic Church. I am with you in heart and spirit. I am the Rock. I am Peter. I am the brother of The Christ and the founder of the Church in which you believe. And, even as this man, I am a child again. I am a little one here in Heaven with the Holy Trinity. I will for you all the greatness that any man could receive. I intercede for you in ways that you cannot comprehend. I stand arm-in-arm and hand-to-hand with all the Popes and Cardinals, all the Bishops and priests, all the clerics and lay people, all who have united themselves with the redemption of the exiled world. I knew Jesus Christ on Earth, and I remain with Him now in Heaven. And, in the gentleness of my heart, I offer you the promise of my friendship in Him. I beseech you to live a happy life, a meaningful life in Jesus, a life that will allow you to someday say you lived and loved in peace. It is all worth the cost; it is fully worth the price; it is all true. And, it is too beautiful for you to comprehend right now. Inside your heart, you can know. Thank you for helping our Mother, for making Her happy and inspiring Her, for making Jesus gladder than you could possibly imagine.*"

"There, My Special son, is your answer. It is your blessing for today."

Sunday, March 30, 2014
9:39 a.m.

"The berth of freedom."

"Resiliency – this is the issue that you have in common with the heavens; resiliency is what makes your faith unique. My little sons, deep inside you rests not only the wisdom required to see beyond the travails of your time, but also embedded there is 'desire.' You have an eminent need to be one with the Creator of all things glorious. This is your identity; it is your trajectory, and it is the story of your time. I am overjoyed that you recognize your part in the movement of all worlds toward One Eternal Kingdom, the universal 'being' of humanity in Jesus. My Special son, when I say the 'berth' of freedom, it is not the same thing as the birth of freedom. I have said that you and your brother, indeed all My children, are stationed in the glorious unity of Divine Truth that circumscribes the location of your soul both in and outside of time. You are positioned here and everywhere because of your acceptance of Jesus' Blood on the Cross. This is the 'berth' about which I am speaking. Let us imagine what this means to those who believe. You are asked to be reborn in Jesus for the sake of your eternal soul. This is your birth into redemption; it is the point where you enter the doorway of the infinite. Once you have entered that door, you have a 'berth' of freedom that is equally infinite. However, your birth into Jesus' Crucifixion is not fully eternal until you deliver your soul to Him in death. Hence, you have entered the doorway, but you have not yet received your crown. You are still unable to measure the berth of your redemption because you remain constrained by the limits of the world. Thus, you have infinity in you now, but you do not yet have Heaven's fullness. You have the beginning of glory in you here, but it is not endless until you have passed through the gates of Paradise. I am not contradicting My earlier messages when I said that you have entered eternity in this place, I am fulfilling them by extrapolating the way you understand it. Now, what of all the constraints and impositions that mortal life places on you? Truly, they are of consequence only to the degree that people let them. I have spoken of eternal wisdom and earthly knowledge before. Earthly knowledge can be a part of eternal wisdom when it magnifies the Gospel lessons; this is the breadth of your beatitudes. It is the origin of the righteousness that you have adopted as your reason for living. This berth is defined by freedom itself, the ability of those who are prone to recognize that they are not tethered to worldly distractions and the allures of the flesh. Those who realize that they are irrevocable candidates for sainthood understand what this freedom means; it implies the freedom to be who they are according to the new identity they have inherited in the Cross."

Parable of Sears (Willis) Tower Glass Observation Rooms

In the Sears (Willis) Tower in Chicago, Illinois, they have constructed glass-encased observation rooms that extend a few feet outside the exterior tower walls. These observation rooms are located 1,353 feet above the base of the building, attached to the 103rd floor of the tower. People can step out of the building into these observation rooms where there is nothing but glass between themselves and seeing over the city of Chicago and out over Lake Michigan. They can also see through the transparent floor beneath their feet, and experience the sensation of vulnerability as if it might be possible to fall to the sidewalk below. It is as if standing in mid-air at a height of 1,353 feet. So, one can imagine the experience people have at stepping out into one of these observation rooms, and the unique sensation that overwhelms most of them. Their minds process a sensory experience that is completely unique in that they are somewhat able to experience standing in mid-air at a height that, if the glass enclosure were not there, it would be impossible for them to do so. They have a 'berth' of experience as they step out of the building through the threshold, but are still contained within the parameters that prevent them from engaging the full reality of their position in space, should the parameters of the glass-enclosure no longer exist. This is analogous to what Our Lady was relating to me today. Our birth into Jesus' Crucifixion opens a 'doorway to the infinite' within us that allows us to step into the infinity that surrounds the expanse of Creation, while the parameters of our exile maintain our separation from Eternity until we have completed our lives in Jesus.

"This is the reason I began My message today with the term 'resiliency.' What is faith worth if someone sets it aside for a month or year and only practices it during hard times? Where is the resiliency in this? Where is there a new berth of freedom, a new means to measure inside them the eternal immeasurable? The eternal part of the Christian soul originates from knowing how to suffice one's curiosity in what makes faith admirable in the eyes of God. I am describing why your presentation to your friends yesterday was so ingenious. You reached into the future as all of you will soon know it, making it relevant in your day. You turned your listeners' words into the lessons that I have taught you and your brother for 23 years. You helped them understand that their eternal souls exist in the here and now, and the perpetuity of their redemption rests in their future lives in Heaven. Jesus was speaking through you by the power of the Holy Spirit. And, what a remarkable sensation as you listened to yourself, when you heard echoing through your consciousness the words of God coming from your lips in utter majesty. It is clear that you know when this happens. You felt a sense of the berth of freedom to which every soul is given when, in you, lives The Christ. It is a type of permission that you give the Lord. It is your heart and spirit saying, '...Come inhabit me; make me your vessel. Bring my soul to be an instrument of your peace.' I am saying that the heart and consciousness are not separated from God, even when things seem otherwise. The Holy Spirit is always in those who believe, during every moment of the day. You need not make inspiring speeches to continue this supernal relationship. When you look at the created world, the same thing happens. This is what your tablemate was trying to say about gazing at the rising and setting sun. He had the principle correct, but not the context. Admiring the sun and feeling as though the sun is feeding you is like sitting down to dinner without saying grace. I mention this metaphor because it speaks to My comparison of the birth of freedom and the berth of freedom. Those who worship the sun cannot see the whole picture; worshiping God who suspended it in the sky enlists the entire view. They feel free because of the awesomeness impacting their eyes, but they are not taking advantage of the full berth of its glory. It is the same as saying that if you give someone a fish, they will eat for a day, but if you teach them to fish, they will eat for a lifetime.

I have been trying to teach My children about their true freedom in Jesus for many centuries now. I want all believing souls to realize that faith in Jesus is not a heavy burden, the yoke need not be a constraining one. Imagine all the possibilities that can come to humanity that becomes one with this truism. This is why your acclamation about prayer yesterday was such a perfect definition. Prayer is always manifested by comparing one's life to their perceived and actual levels of suffering. If there is no suffering, then what is happiness worth? Can there be a true berth of freedom if someone does not feel impacted by their own perceptions and episodes of suffering? I am speaking about self-induced and situational suffering. I am including consequential and God-ordained suffering. Nobody ever said that Christianity would be free from suffering, indeed far from it. Suffering is the nucleus around which authentic redemption revolves. Hence, the Cross is the center of the Christian faith. But, Christians must remember that Jesus did not raise Himself from the dead independent from God the Father who raised Him back to life. It was our eternal God who resurrected the eternal Man-God, even as the Father and the Son are one. The point is that humanity must realize that all that is imperfectly human must die in Jesus on the Cross, and that death is reversed by the Man-God, fully effected on Mounty Calvary. When Jesus was raised from the dead on Easter, the whole community of believers was raised along with Him. It comes from outside the human person; it is a manifestation of the greater berth of freedom found in those who believe, and it is a product of the seed that each person plants in their future. Christians reject Satan and all his evil works upon their baptism, and in doing so, they sign their lives over to Jesus here and for the fullness of perpetuity. They have adopted the infinite, but they are awaiting their own deaths to reach the perpetuity of Messianic deliverance. My Special son, have I confused you? *"No, I understand."* Your presentation yesterday to your friends was all about addressing this transition, while you held them to the point that they can see that far from here. They can focus on where they are going by paying heed to conditions in the here and now. And, this is the greatest lesson of prayer; it is the power that aids believers into generating their own version of life in alignment with the teachings of Jesus so they can be unified with the Teacher, once the lessons of life have been fulfilled.

How can I thank you for what you said to your friends yesterday? How can I convince you to believe that what is happening is a precursor to many more presentations? I also want to thank you for being so kind to little Thomas who, as you know, is especially endearing to Me. He will play a significant role in the assisting of America's conversion through the Morning Star Over America in his lifetime, most likely in the near future, governing the urgencies that are occurring worldwide. The harvest is truly rich, but the workers seem so few. Thomas once told your brother that he is trying to reverse the history of his name. He does not want to be known as the 'doubter.' He wants to make reparation for the Biblical revelation of Saint Thomas by being even more holy during these times, perhaps reclaiming the name 'Thomas' for the record of the years. As I have indicated to you several times, these are supernatural years you are living. You can sense it every day. Thank you for praying with Me today, for listening to My message, for contemplating how it can be presented to humanity for their edification in the themes of righteousness. Do you have any issues to discuss with Me today? *"I had to be very blunt with the young girl about her conduct."* Indeed, you did what you were required to do. Perhaps she will now realize how distasteful her behavior has been. I will bless all for whom you are praying around the world that you mentioned yesterday at your meeting. Your testament to the way I have taught you is a legitimizing factor, and taking your thoughts around the globe to pray for the poor and suffering is the way to induce the Lord to heal them. Your eyes of faith are open and aglow; your heart is right; your love is unconditional, and your future is intact. I will speak to you at the opening of a new month; may the peace of the Holy Spirit always be your comfort."

Saturday, April 5, 2014
9:34 a.m.

"Breathe on me, breath of God, fill me with life anew."

"My little sons, My honor is fulfilled in praying with you in thanksgiving, in gratitude that you have found yourselves in Jesus. We share a mighty blessing from the Lord by our humanity, by way of our adoration of the Providence that created Me as the Queen of Heaven and you its newfound Saints. Today, I feel a wellspring of peace that comes from you, from all who believe in the repentance of the lost and their conversion to the divinity to which Creation was meant to be given. My little sons, we espouse one another; we embrace and extol everything that renders you like Jesus; we make way for the Holy Spirit to inform you in the Truth of righteousness. Even as I was born a sinless Virgin, I have shared your humanity. I speak of the avoidance of sin in My messages around the world, and rightly this should be. And, I also speak of the good My children are doing, what this means for the world here and now, and how much holier the

Mystical Body of Jesus is becoming in advance of the conclusion of the ages. It is that a perfect, living creature called righteousness has come into your presence, descended from the heavens, urgently aware of your suffering, troubles and burdensome ways of life. This Messiah is Jesus the Christ; there is no question about it. And, as The Christ, Jesus' Crucifixion is yours to accept, not just as Savior, but the perfect reflection of the Father through His own preeminent grace. I have said, and you have been taught, that the Child Jesus came into the world as a slumbering Babe. This is the image that the Father ordained. And, you have known that I raised this Child according to the Scriptures to bear out the responsibilities that would fall upon Him. Hence, the image that God ordained is of transition, that you might remember yourselves as children, and that you would be inclined to imitate this image, replicated through your lives and the ages by the purity of humanity, so finely etched into history by the Only Begotten Son of Abba, the Father. Once this transition is placed in the heart, it becomes inevitable that children will grow. After all, humanity throughout time has done so. You come of age in spirit and wisdom, thought and judgement, and perception and reaction. What I see as you pray here with Me is too priceless to describe. You come voluntarily before the Father so that He can bestow upon you a peace that blossoms with spontaneous blessings. In other words, you have placed yourselves in the position to win, and God manifests the conditions that make it so. You needed only say 'yes' to Him, and He has transformed your affirmation into incalculable triumphs. There is, as I have said, a new identity that becomes you, another way of life, a means for fashioning your values as Heaven would desire. You shape yourselves into pious vessels fit for everything that God wishes to dispense to you. My little children, even your desire to be Saints comes through the presence of Jesus in you. There is no other way for you to know. In Jesus, you acquire the sleekness to reflect His beauty in yourselves. You live and breathe His love; this is the same love that I have spoken about many times. It is a combination of youthful vigor and mature wisdom; you have the benefit of both worlds. It may seem difficult for you to believe, but your identities as distinct individuals coalesce in Jesus' Most Sacred Heart. The whole of humanity is collected there, not those who reject the Cross, but those who embrace it. And, this is the source of your vision. The eyes of your hearts are sighted by the way the Lord wants life on the Earth to become. With this new sleekness, with this ethereal beauty, you come upon the function of your faith; you make God happy by the essence of your being. This spiritual fineness distinguishes you among the nations; you are seen like airships soaring above the rattletraps. It is dividing the sheep from the goats. With this spiritual excellence, you acquire a holy sheen that is visible to others, a shiny perfection fit for your esteem. Those who are embedded in religious mysticism are too bright to deny by the wicked who are otherwise blinded by their own transgressions.

My Special son, I am speaking about creative virtue that the Father always intended humanity that is consecrated to Him to have. It is as though human beings spend their entire lives breaking into spiritual crescendoes, begetting a perfection harvested from the teachings of the Church and untold numbers of Saints. And, it is not just the crescendoes that matter, but the process leading to them. Every new hour, every day of life, all the moments and passages, all the struggles and reliefs, all the stories and legacies, and everything else whose origin is the perfection of man pours forth toward this purpose. You and I and your brother are engaging this process now. While I am seeing the finished Church, inside the element of time, you are establishing and ordaining the parameters of My vision. You are helping My prayers come true. This is the primal meaning of the Incarnation of the Son of Man. The Nativity of Jesus was the fulfillment of the promises of the Father. The whole process of Jesus' life was to prove to humanity that men are worthy of redemption, given that they accept the Blood of Salvation and imitate the life of their Savior. This enlightenment continues to this day. Jesus sits before you now as He did long ago, waiting and listening, at the same time He is performing the multitude of miracles that will open the eyes of the lost. He knows of His power dispensed to you; it is not a power that makes you lift an ocean liner or fly across the sky as though you have wings. But, your power comes from beyond the ages, allowing you to crush the malignance of evil everywhere you see it. You have the moral providence to choose rightness over wrongness, to shed light in dark places where predators lurk. You have the ability to foretell what the Father expects from those who believe in Him, even as He seems immune to the throes of the years. Jesus never trembles in fear, but He sometimes shakes with excitement. Yes, He leans forward on the edge of His chair like you did watching Secretariat win the Triple Crown. He is like a giddy little child when He sees His brothers and sisters celebrating Him, when they take pride in their faith, when they dare to accept the rejection that is foisted upon them by the atheists in their midst. Jesus' eagerness is overwhelming when I see it. His cheers and glistening eyes are a gift to behold. He counts the beats of every heart that lives for Him. He stoops to kiss the cheeks of His champions. He raises to His breast the millions who are suffering in His name. And, He watches the process that I have spoken about today with holy anticipation. After all, it is He who has inspired it. Yes, not unlike those young people who were assembling their crafts at the Convention Center yesterday, He knows when something is well prepared. He realizes when victories are imminent – He hands to humanity the opportunity to prevail in Him, and the world must follow this accord. This is not about supernal control, it is about infinite freedom, freedom to be who you are, freedom to bend and shape Creation into what Jesus wants it to be, affirmed by the Will of God. There will come a day, My Special son, when this process will end. I have described it in many ways over the past 23 years, but I have not even scratched the surface of what will eventually come. My little one, I have not the proper words that you might comprehend; there are no sufficient expressions to reveal it. I only ask you and your brother to expect a joy that has never before been seen, not by Pope or prophet, not by servant or master, not by Saint or mortal sinner. This joy will come to you because you are distinguishing yourselves among your peers, transcending the ages and the laws of Nature, too. This process is not so much about logistics as it is intent.

You have always intended to prepare the world for Jesus to return, to clean up the unkept corners, to polish your soul skillfully, and to sanctify what must be made new. This is your gift to Heaven; it is your estate to humanity. I have completed what I came to say to you and your brother today. I am grateful that you are conducting yourself with such professionalism at your workplace; and your witness for Me is as equally profound. I am also asked by the Father to commend you again for the beauty of your memoir, for your honesty and candor, for your admonishment of the wicked, your instruction of the ignorant, and your recognition of the primal nature of the Roman Catholic Church. There is a whole lifetime of truth in your memoir, and you will be rewarded for having authored it. All in all, what I have said to you today reflects the continuance of My hopes that you are bringing to fruition. I ask you to never forget what you mean to Me. Always remember what you mean to Jesus. Never forget that you are poised for Sainthood, along with millions of My children, ready and prepared for life's capstone of the Triumph of My Immaculate Heart. Keep in your heart how much you are loved, how special you are here in these precincts and in the Mansions of Heaven. Know when you see your reflection in the mirror that you are seeing the image of My Jesus. Take heart that millions have come to Me in Medjugorje. Keep in your memories everything I have said about the transformation of the Earth. It is all true. Thank you for praying for the poor and unborn, for those oppressed by dictators in foreign lands, and for the conversion of the lost."

Saturday, April 12, 2014
2:09 p.m.

"Not every position has a contraposition."

"My children, we pray for the culmination of all good things in Jesus' Most Sacred Heart. We hope for health and happiness to overwhelm those who believe in Him. This health, this supernal joy, includes suffering in His likeness, even to the degree that the Saints and Martyrs envy you. I have come to say that not every point needs a counterpoint; there must not be an opposite to everything. There should only exist love on Earth because hatred has no place. Corruption cannot be equated as the contrapose of perfection. This, My Special son, is what you meant when you said that there is no, '...God versus Satan, Round 2.' My message today is to remind you of the single-minded intent through which the Father created Heaven and Earth. God did not say in the beginning that He wanted to fashion Heaven and Hell. Unrepentant sinners created Hell. He formed darkness and light only to bring distinction, direction, dimension and clarity to all created things. Darkness and light were captured and made visible through His Sacred Love for those who would perceive them. I am making the same case against relativism and pluralism that you have outlined in your memoir. Indeed, one cannot equate love and hatred as though they were just polar opposites, even though they are contradictory terms. It would be like flying a Boy Scout flag on the same level as the flag of the whole United States. So, today, I give you justification for not establishing a balance between religiosity and secularism. When someone is not holy, it does not always necessarily mean that they are fully shorn of righteousness. It means only that they have periods of weakness, misunderstanding, lacking comprehension of the virtues that I have described to you and your brother for so many years. Love is manifested; love is made clear, love is self-evidenced through its own fruits. For everything I have said over the past several months about beauty, power, resilience, reaching-out in faith, and seeing human life the way the Lord sees it, you finally understand that there is new life in what you espouse. It grows from the outside in, even as you expand your awareness of righteousness like a seed from within. What I have tried to reveal to you through the years is that Creation is a product of God's motivation to perpetually and consistently intervene, not in a way that precludes the human will, but that guides and complements what must become humanity-refined. Redemption itself is the culmination of His guidance. Eternal life is His gift by your acceptance of this guidance as well. Yes, I am happy when any other mother might be soundly disappointed when looking at the condition of the exiled Earth. I am filled with joy because I often see tremendous perfection blooming from such vile brokenness. When you perceive the contrast between darkness and light that I have heretofore described, you will see that souls wishing to be saved aspire to the light; it is the natural progression of the redeeming process. This is why conversion is simultaneously a process and an event. Jesus Christ is the path and the destiny. Around the world today, there are many hearts awakening to their station in exile; they are seeing that their souls are not yet really home. However, they are homeward bound; they are content knowing that the journey is still underway. This is the motion of redemption; it is their intent for staying the course, their reason for living and praying, their estate bequeathed to the ages they will leave behind. I am filled with joy because this life in Jesus is like a stone rolling downhill; it cannot be stopped. There may be obstacles and idle places along the way; there may be rough patches and hurtful impacts, but the motion toward Salvation cannot be impeded. You have said colloquially that My messages have been 'the stuff of miracles.' I agree. It is true that I have accompanied My children throughout the centuries and generations. I have seen them fall and rise again. I have spoken to the legends, halls filled with them, about their legacies left to their heirs. And, each of them had a different story about the same mission. It was all about protracting the giantness of the miracles about which you have spoken, about realizing that there is more truth in miracles than in every eloquent word recorded in tongues.

Yes, this is the story of your time. It is about rebounding from the impact of humanity against its own fate. It is about standing taller when the wind blows its worst. It is about defying death by your own faith in everlasting life. My Special son, I was hoping that there would be sufficient time remaining on the Earth that scholars and theologians would write reams about what I have said to you and your brother in the latter part of the 20th century and into the 21st. As you are aware, I am unsure of the date and hour of the Second Coming of the Son of Man, so I cannot be sure about what reams might be written. But, think about what I have said here. I have told you that the conclusion of the mortal world is closer than anyone could possibly know. It might be frightening to perceive what signs and wonders are leading to this truth. But, should we assume that there will not be time for scholars and theologians to survey My miraculous works as the Morning Star Over America? The Father in Heaven only knows. I prefer to believe that there will not be sufficient time. And, with that said, I also ponder joyfully an historical record of what has occurred here in this home, in this city and nation. Two young men, they might say, dared to believe that the Lord would deposit more than a few words to a hungry world, feeding humanity not only the Truth from Heaven, but the wisdom to come to the table. I have brought you and your brother to an understanding of both human life and God's Eternal Kingdom in ways that have been heretofore unknown. I have given you lessons and parables that will eventually dazzle nonbelievers. This has been the effect of My visitation to you and your brother, but the effect has come only subsequent to the reason. The reason is because I love you. Please, allow Me once again; the reason is because I love you. I see in you not just potential anymore, but realized spiritual energy that has altered the composition of created time and space. When you listen to the Creation story during the Triduum celebrations, find yourselves in them. Discover your place 'in the beginning' that you were always meant to hold. Find the birthplace of humanity, where the Love of God has tread with peace, where the ingenious process of life-giving energy was deposited in visible form. See how humanity came to be, like a chick from an egg. Watch for yourselves how the very idea of your lives was given form. It all sprang from the reason that I first came speaking to you, to garner the effect of the enlightenment of the exiled realms. It was not God's intent that Adam would fall. He knew it was going to happen, but imagine what a script was written during those formative times. One could not compose a symphony with so many waves. No tides of history could ever crash the shores so providentially. No songs, no sights, no feelings or expressions could ever be so delightfully articulated. Yes indeed, making the Father in Heaven proud of Himself for having such innovative genius to bring to life the imagination of His Heart. This is the power of God that you find in yourselves here in this home and in one another around the globe, those who accept the Cross as their way of life and redemption too. My joy is complete because I have always known that the Father cannot fail. He is the ultimate playwright and composer, He is the most noted author of every strain that glorifies what He forever wanted humanity to become. Adam fell of his own free will, but the whole human race has been redeemed by the Will of its Divine Creator. This is the creed of those who believe not only in what He is, but what He can do, what total and complete Universal Love can bring to the nations and continents who espouse His identity and meaning. It was all written in the Gospels; it is living there still. We savor the fruits of human redemption in its chapters and verses.

My Special son, it is for all the things I have said here today that I beseech you to relax. Lessen the intensity in the way you view the world and the cruelties and excesses of those far from God. It is not your job to command them to convert; it is your gift to them. And, as we know, many gifts are summarily dismissed, only to be sought out later. You and your brother must find a way to shield yourselves from becoming disturbed by life; you must begin to see things for what they are, which ones really affect you, others that have utterly no impact on you at all. This is where you will find your rest and peace; this is how you will finally escape the exhaustion that keeps burdening your days. Live and let go; be aware but not worried. Trust that Jesus is guiding your days and years; it is not a signature of slothfulness to simply allow Him to do His work. Your prayers are sufficient. You have amassed an arsenal in your deposit of works to destroy the most evil influences in the parameters of time. These are the years when you are supposed to be confident in yourselves, relieved of the pressures that so marked your earlier lives. An Italian believer recently came to Heaven and heard the words from his Savior, 'Watch Me!' He had used these words so many times in his comedic routine. If he were to speak to you now, he would say that these two words are the most prolific ones from the lips of Jesus Christ than any others. 'Watch Me.' And, sometimes, just watching Jesus is service enough. I certify your beauty before the Throne of the Father. I accompany your petitions to Him with prayers of My own. I attest to your goodness to Jesus perpetually. He tells Me that He already knows. God says that you are not gods, but you are godly men, the Children of Mary, the ones who have given to His Kingdom more than could possibly be expected from any mortal man. And, these are the hours in which you must be aware of your own goodness, a self-perpetuating satisfaction that proves to you once and for all that you have won your place in the Halls of Paradise. You have left your mark here in this world; you have paved the way for billions to follow you, and you can now live out your years in joy that you are one with God through His Providence outpoured. Please, live twenty and thirty more years, if this is your desire. Or, accept your station alongside the sufferers and Martyrs who served Him in so many other ways. The point I am making is that you should find peace here in this world, not based on the fanatics in the media, not in the distractions that take so many away from the presence of God, not in a constant self-assessment to discern whether you have accomplished something in a given day. Your legacies have been written by you and etched into the annals of the Earth and the Mansions of Heaven. I told you this just days ago. I ask you to be happy like I am happy, if for no other reason than to realize that you are on the winning team; your crowns and vestments await you, the future already belongs to you, the story is being lived out now. My Special son, I hope and pray that you and your brother are finally coming to understand how much you are loved. I beg you to live freely in the light of this love. I ask you to take good care of yourselves as I am shielding you beneath My Sacred Mantle. These are auspicious years for you, opportune times, moments during which you surely realize that you are champions in Jesus' holy sight. It is My profound honor to have been allowed by Him to speak to you."

Saturday, April 19, 2014
Holy Saturday
9:32 a.m.

"Lord, make us towering redwoods; take comfort in our shade."

"You are observing in earthly time that the Lord has found a Sepulcher. I join you in this solemnity of remembrance, My little children. I share your holy reflections. I remember with you what I lived during those times. And today, I offer you My great joy that Jesus eradicated human sinfulness from existence; that He took upon Himself the burden of men's transgressions. We realize that you are invested in what this has meant for the world. Please know that your kind sentiments are comforting to Me, even retroactively as I witnessed the events of human redemption unfold. Also today, I have come to share My own thoughts about what Jesus has done, about how you can envision your unique stature in the shadow of His Sacrifice. It is not that you are unaware; this is not My point at all. You are fully knowing of your mission here; you have proved it time and again. We are doing more than sufficing earthly time during your messages; we are engaging history and timelessness; we are seaming the two together; we are bridging the gap between the first century and this one, and we are connecting the immensity of Jesus' Sacred Love for humanity to the world today. Men have prayed that God would make them towering redwoods. Holy souls have asked Jesus to take comfort in them. This is the ingenious reciprocation that the Father seeks of those who know Him, even though they have never seen His Face. Is it that the redwood is somehow more magnificent than all the other trees? Surely the sprawling oaks are just as beautiful. Beyond doubt, the stately elms are as prolifically expressive, and the sycamores hover with the elegance of the stars. Without question, the evergreens withstand the elements, and theirs is the most enduring gift of all. Yes, they are all trees with strength and grandeur; they are metaphors for the power of humanity in the Grace of God. Is it possible that one can equate the divinity of God with the potential of humanity-redeemed? Indeed, it is possible because the Crucifixion of the Lamb has restored to perfection the identity of the human person. It is not just that the redwoods are so sky-bound and stationed, it is that they are profoundly unapologetic about being that way. They never say that they are sorry for their strength and longevity. They never apologize to the sunshine for blocking its descent to the ground. These are the metaphors for standing in confidence, accepting what they were created to be, recognizing that creatures of all walks gaze at them in awe. The power of a tree. The graciousness, the courage, and the charity of the Man-God who was crucified there. My Special son, I have said in times past that knowing about the Cross and touching the Cross are two different manifestations. One must live-out the meaning of the Cross. It is necessary to mourn the suffering of The Christ before His Paschal Resurrection can be understood. You have lived this endurance with all the humble servants of the Gospel throughout the ages. You are handing back to God His own dignity that has been bequeathed to you from the Passion and Death of Jesus Christ. These are auspicious times. This is the beginning of the courtly age that will usher-in the fullness of awareness to those who do not already know. It is a good time to be alive. And, if men are to become those towering redwoods, they must be capable of comprehension, searching-out the true meaning of spiritual service, of ethereal hope and beatific yearning, of unity with the Blessed Trinity, to be single-minded like the Father, even as men focus on their own relationship with Him, with one another, and with the awkward crassness of the secular void. These are the branches about which I have spoken, the spiritual integration of humanity with the mandates of the New Covenant Gospel in fulfillment of the Scriptures. It does not take a collegiate professor to know that these giant redwoods are not only stately, they are compassionately tenacious. They do not yield to the whims of the world; they do not trade their principles for the ever-changing times. They are there. Yes, they are there, just as 'I Am' is 'I Am.'

All of this is so fair to the prayerful mind; it means more than simple language to God, to those who seek Him while He may be found, to the innocent little ones, to the Angels who watch with such care, to the universe and to Nature, and to the birds of the air and the fishes of the sea. They look up to the towering redwoods; they see that good men aspire to be among them, they know that these are the things of righteousness, of inviting the Spirit of the Lord to inform and take refuge within them. Rolling from the tongues of these great giants are the consoling syllables that Christ Jesus has always sought from those who would accompany Him during these last phases of the olden world. Yes, He needs this comfort. Jesus wants those who believe in Him to ask for His counsel as He, just as Saint John, rests His head on the hearts of His disciples. He lends His power to those who believe in Him. He grants pardon to the many who concede. This is a willing concession; it grows from the hunger of the human soul to reach the Garden once again, to see the Light of Truth without blinders, to touch, smell, and encounter the brilliance of creative forgiveness both now and through the endlessness of innocence renewed. My Special son, touching the Face of God is the gift of God, Himself. There are more perpetual dimensions to this gift than could ever be conceived in the minds of men. Here, I am saying that Jesus is pleased by the endurance of His disciples. He admires the survivorship of the Church, the long-suffering duties that it has sufficed, the prayers that have reconfigured the ages, and the confessions that have reunited the estranged. Imagine Jesus sitting beneath the shade of a towering redwood, leaning against its base, looking-up with wonder, thanking the Father for His tenure in this life. You and I have been there. It is in Jesus that you and your brother live, also and likewise making clear your gratitude for everything the Father has done, for giving life in the first place, for sharing the spoils of His triumph over evil, for keeping watch when you have been resting, for fashioning a plan of Salvation that embraces even those most distant from Him. Leaning against a redwood tree with a blade of grass between His lips; this is the image of a Savior who knows precisely what He has done. Of course, He still goes knocking on closed hearts' doors. He never rests while there remain holdout sinners. But, He maintains confidence in Himself because of His presence in holy people, treading the fields and meadows where His Sacrifice still reigns, scaling the mountains to see across the broadlands below, eyeing and peering, judging and forgiving, counseling and uplifting, adoring and consoling. And, He does these things in the bosom of the Church. Even as His Body is broken during the Holy Sacrifice of the Mass, He reminds the redeemed that He is even more human than they will ever be. It is not a sin to be human, but it is mortally damning to be a corrupt one.

So today, My Special son, I have given you My reflection about Holy Saturday, when the world lay waiting for the most consequential Resurrection that Creation will ever know. I have prayed with you throughout these forty days. I have prayed perpetually since I was first capable of formulating My thoughts. My entire life has been a prayer for the conversion of the world. And, in the cogs of these great events, you and all like-minded Christians have been like lubricant; you have made the way easier for Jesus the Messiah, for the propagation of the Gospel, and for the comforting of My Son during His most disquieting hours. Thank you from the whole of Heaven, and bless you in the here and now. Yes, you and millions of disciples have been like those towering redwood trees; you have been righteously tenacious as well. You have been relentless in your admonishments of the wicked. But, you have also been sympathetic and forgiving. You continue to be a teacher for the Lord; you have overcome what you first perceived to be your weaknesses, before you discovered that they were your strengths all along. My Special son, I will never exhaust My desire to share with you what it means for you to be My son. *'Thank you, Mama.'* I will forever until the last day of time seek-out My children, especially those who have never experienced the joy of knowing a mother, those who have been neglected and abused, the many who have been left on cold doorsteps for someone else to raise. I share the confidence of those redwoods, too. I carry in My Arms the Savior who perches like an Eagle in the boughs of the Father's domain. As I bring My blessings into this world from Him, I likewise hope with you. I am pleased that everything is going well for you these days. You can see that the devil is still trying to impede every move that would advance the refinement of the Earth. I have said that it is all about obedience, but it is also about pleasing Jesus' desire for the unity of the Church. I pray for all who have been involved in accidents of all kinds – in collisions and sinkings, in shootings and in falls. You can see that most every catastrophic event of these sorts is preventable. They are precipitated by reckless lives, prayer-less lives of people who believe that they can tempt fate with victory. We pray for them to come to their senses. It is not like those who genuinely must enter places where they put their lives in God's hands. Laborers who drive to their work sites, pilots who must fly airplanes, those who control traffic patterns; all of these are people simply conducting their legitimate offices of life. They have a merited responsibility to be where they are, and they have the authority to ask their guardian Angels to be at their right hand. Thank you, My Special son, for giving the Lord a worthy Lent. Bless you for asking Him to intervene where innocent people suffer. The indignity of the Earth is sometimes like being the fastest runner, but not being allowed to win. You and your brother often seem like the great Secretariat who could have been disqualified because he had already won too many times. As you say, this is the way of the world."

Saturday, April 26, 2014
9:34 a.m.

"Where they've thirsted for perversion, God has poisoned the water."

"Good morning, My little ones. I am present to give you the sacredness of God's peace. I bring the immensity of the multidimensional grace that becomes you, that holds you in such esteem, that underscores the profoundness of your declarations on Jesus' behalf. My little sons, I have told you about these multiple dimensions that themselves defy the boundaries of existence. This is why it is not so much that Jesus just emits the aroma of raindrops, but that He emits the 'meaning' of rain. This is the transforming of human understanding into the thoughts of the Father. This is how exiled men know the basis on which God makes decisions about what He directly manifests, contrasted with what He allows. Does this make men gods themselves? Definitely not, but it makes them part of the eternal now, part of living beyond the surrendering of life. Therefore, when you communicate with the Lord and the Saints, even with the Angels and Archangels, you are facilitating their decisions by defining to them the exactness of truth in a world that is not yet shorn of lies. You are calling for holy realms to infiltrate impious places. You have in your capacity the ability to prescribe in this age the benefits of resolve for those still searching for ethereal power. And, I have told you that this power rests in your spiritual beauty, in your likeness to Jesus, in your espousal of the holiness that the Catholic Church avows. If anything you take from My messages of the past sixteen months, I hope that you see in them My many references to the link between spiritual beauty and supernatural power. Things that are not beautiful may have force, but they have no real power. Forces routinely fade, but power is often lasting, especially the sublime, unending power brandished into being by the Holy Spirit. Let us apply this to the physical world. Most everyone aspiring to success would like to see their faces on a placard in the public square with a blue ribbon tacked to its border. This is not a vain thing if these aspirations are given to Lord-seeking, to clarifying the meaning of Divine Love to the unknowing. This is what you will witness tomorrow in Saint Peter's Square in Rome. You will see the icons of two people who had the same goals, but perhaps different ways of getting there. You will see Pope John XXIII and Pope John Paul II juxtaposed so that the whole of the world can understand the unity and conformity of the Church with the teachings of Jesus Christ. If not for the Protestant Reformation, there would have been no need for Vatican II. And, if not for God's promise to foster the demise of the Soviet Union, perhaps another Pope would have been canonized tomorrow; there would have been no Pope John Paul II. The point I am making is that the bounty of supernal providence will be on display tomorrow through the majesty, pageantry and constancy of the Roman Catholic Church. And, this sacred beauty all began in Me. Even in My humility, I tell you that the Lord God chose Me as His representative beauty, His way of showing the world that fairness and kindness are embodied in Me. Hence, you will hear My name mentioned multiple times tomorrow. And, you will hear the name of Pope Benedict XVI who is equally beautiful as Me in his heart. This is what he knew about hierarchical succession as he relinquished the Chair of Saint Peter to Pope Francis. He did not cede any power because he remains one with the Holy Spirit. This power is innate to all who believe in God through their faith in Christ Jesus. It is God's gift to the yearning masses, to the collective hearts of humanity consecrated to Him. From all corners of the globe, the pilgrims will celebrate the lives of four Roman Catholic pontiffs. It will be an unprecedented event for these unprecedented times. There will never be another question after April 27, 2014 about the continuity of the Roman Catholic Church as the steward of the Christian Faith. The four servants whose names and identities you shall honor tomorrow are like legs upholding the future of the world. I do not speak in hyperbole here. I am using metaphorical images, but the impact on humanity in practical terms is the same. I will play My role as always. I will impart My blessing upon those who pray. Along with Saint Veronica, I will see Jesus' Face glowing in admiration, beaming to be so venerated, grateful to be acknowledged, looking with gratitude upon all who remain devoted to His Most Sacred Heart. This is how His Spirit reflects the fragrance of flowers, the permanence of the Father's Kingdom, the meaning of fallen raindrops, and the sacred spontaneity of sunbeams, lightning, wind and fire.

The mundane human consciousness does not allow ordinary men to fully comprehend how sainthood cuts across life's meanings, how oneness with Heaven permits the impossible to become realized within the confines of the Church. It happens all the time, but those without true faith decline to embrace it. Is it not an authentic miracle to hear a newborn baby cry just after shedding its mother's womb? Is it not equally as miraculous to see the look on that same child's face aged into adulthood decades later when the Son of Man says, '...Well done, My good and faithful servant (?)' What happens in between is what I have been addressing here and around the globe for hundreds of years. Yes, I am prone to say that the Light of God is beautiful; it wafts like flowers, it harkens to the meaning of roses. My Special son, of all the many themes you might address in your speeches and writings, you undoubtedly will remember the transcendence about which I am speaking here today. You will realize that music looks pretty, that the sound of symphonies is pleasing to the eyes. I am not disconnecting what humanity has learned and what all shall eventually know, I am ratifying and legitimizing the sacrifices of the beautiful hearts who have long lived and hard fought for the coming of the Kingdom of God. I am embracing the Faith-Church as a preeminent element of the Church Triumphant because you are becoming perfected through the Sacraments, just as Jesus foretold. So, when men aspire to have their pictures on downtown marquees, looking at themselves objectively for once, they are actually looking at their own reflection of The Christ. Powerful and beautiful. Comely and courtly. It is not an imposition for good men to strive for high offices when they remember what it means to serve. There are more fruits borne of accidental saints than of those who claim themselves to be already there. When I spoke last week about Jesus leaning against the tree, it would not be improper to assume that His Spirit also rests within all who believe in Him with the same reflective poise. Imagine a courageous war general leading his troops to victory on the battlefield now returning home, cladding himself in street attire, walking to a nearby park swing, and swaying back and forth. These are starkly contrasting images, but this is the way of Christ the King. He remains the Child Jesus in My Arms while He simultaneously reigns as the Sovereign Wonder over the entire human race. He is distinctively your Savior in both roles. And, this is why I have always told you and your brother that you are My dear children; you are concurrently humble servants and decorated warriors in the battle for lost souls. Your greatest weapons are your prayers. They are your armaments and conveyances. They are your shields and configurations. They are your ramparts during the hailing mayhem, your compasses, your strategies and tactics, and your beacons in the night. When you see the body of humankind at the end of time, you will see its collective scars, procured through the fight for righteousness. You will recognize who played the parts scripted for them by the hands of the Father. And, you will see where the beauty remained, the beauty that I have reflected upon today. You will know that the power of the Holy Spirit has been the energy for it all. You cannot see the Holy Paraclete with your eyes, but your most pious self knows what righteousness looks like.

You may not be able to visualize the Transfiguration of the Messiah walking in your midst right now, but you can see where He has tread. And, as I share with you these images, it is clear that you have laid the groundwork in your heart for knowing what I mean. You have beatific understanding within you, even as I speak. All the Saints do. All whose convictions are aligned with the wishes of My Son contain this profundity of faith; not a philosophical treatise as some would have you believe, but a religious zeal for the Will of God so powerful that it can reduce the centuries to dust with the simple blink of an eye. There may seem little logic in what I have said to you and your brother today, but everything makes sense before the backdrop of the ages. Here, you are about to enter the month of May 2014, and the dance of humanity will go on. I can see mourning and merriment in these same village precincts. I see praying and warring, visiting and parting, sickness and health, birthing and dying. I see assembling and dispersing, writing and speaking, rising and falling, drawing and sheathing, doubting and trusting, and foretelling and forgetting. It matters not how many of these things come and go, except for the praying. It is all about speaking to Jesus in faithful terms, in ways that encompass the steps humanity shall take to comply with the sound of His Word. I shall never exhaust My reasons for having come speaking to you and your brother a lifetime ago, it might seem. I will keep returning until you come at last in glory to Me. I will tell all the universes that Saints William and Timothy are My celebrated children, not adopted anymore, but fully blood-related sons within the Sacred Heart that I bore to humanity and the world. *"Thank you, Mama."* I will attest to the times and seasons that you have been Mine, that you are Jesus' friends and companions, that you are in the Cross fully His brothers as well. And, as you enter the new month ahead, I beseech that you trust that the Lord's modern apostles will not permit the Church to be extinguished from the halls of perpetual being. Its light will always shine. Its legacy will forever remain. It is all about prayer – time and time again, I have said this to every messenger ever blessed to see My face or hear the melody of My voice. This is the sacred beginning of the end of these times; it is the opening of the redemptive realms that have already begun in you."

Saturday, May 3, 2014
9:32 a.m.

"...and the effluence of that poison water will purge the nations of evil."

"Hello again, My dear little children. I am your always-favoring intercessor before Jesus, your Mother of Perpetual Help, your Divine Love, now come to pray with you. Thank you for aiding Me in the conversion of so many lost sinners. Yes, My Special one, you are seeing impurity worldwide; you are witnessing the persecution and execution of faithful Christians, new Martyrs, because these dear souls have dared to attest to the Salvation of men in the Cross. They have boldly given lost sinners the gift of awareness in the things that will break them of their insolence and liberate them from their evil ways. When the Lord says that He has poisoned the waters where the perverse come to drink, He is reminding humanity that there is no true life without Him. There is no quenching the thirst for those who do not seek the living waters of holiness, purity and innocence. The opening sentiment of My previous message and this message today comprise a testament to what is now ongoing. I have many times said that the atrocious things you see in these modern times are but remnants of the dying hours of everything that is not of God. Your prayers, the prayers of all the faithful, are bearing out this truth; you are seeing it in many unsung ways. Goodness gracious. It is not enough that Jesus has to fight against the evils of the secular void, He even has to compete with the secular media that celebrate those evils. This, as you know, is why I have appeared so many places around the world for so long; it is the reason why Saint Gabriel, the Patron of

Communication, has been heralding the heroic acts of all who believe in the transformation of humankind into the beatific Mystical Body of Jesus. So today, I come to you and your brother to pray that all who are far from God will seek Him, that mothers will nurture their children inside and outside the womb; that fathers will be men again, taking upon themselves the will to practice the responsibilities of fatherhood, and that children will honor their parents when those parents are aligned with the teachings of the Gospel, and pray for their parents when they are not. You know that I have My part, but I have all parts. I pray for humanity in ways indescribable in linguistic terms. I share the joy of My Immaculate Heart with those who seek My help. I bear the burdens of those who ask Me to carry their sorrows with them. My Special son, it is only a matter of time when all souls will come to Me for introduction to the Son of Man. They will ask, '...Who is the Savior whom you have given the Earth?'... and I will reply that Jesus is their Salvation. They must become like Him in all ways mortal and spiritually immortal. Righteousness pierces the lives of those who believe, and grace permeates their consciousness. God inundates them with forgiveness; absolution becomes their new identity. And, in this sainthood, they will know why they were summoned to believe. You have heard all the stories; we have all listened to the reasons why mortal men turn another way. It is clear, My little son, that these are only excuses and distractions; they originate from motivations having nothing to do with the mission of the Church. And, this is why we pray. You have recently met and spoken with some terribly poor individuals in your nation, in the heated, barren west, in places where most Americans would never go. You traveled from here to Chicago, then to Boston and New Hampshire, then back to Chicago and on to Phoenix. I saw you there, and I prayed that things would go well. Imagine the contrast between what Heaven sees every day with hundreds of thousands of people crisscrossing the United States in fancy conveyance on land and in the air, and those people who live in such poverty in the places where few others go. I am convinced that most people go about their lives unaware; they really harbor no ill will against the poor, they simply do not know them. The description that I have given here is a metaphor for a broader premise, that good Christians rarely think much about those who do not share their faith. This is why there is such a dearth of prayer for the conversion of souls. Offering petitions for these people should be as natural as the ingestion of wisdom from the Lord and the sustenance of physical life. It is all a matter of priorities. The life of the Christian, as we know, should be to the advancement of self-preservation in the way of the Scriptures; this is the means to have natural life and eternal life. Prayer for other souls is like giving them food and drink, delivering them from blind ignorance to visionary enlightenment. Hence, this is why I have called for prayers for lost sinners, and for the cultivation of everything redeemable that humanity will ever achieve.

I must remind you that you are a messenger for the Mother of God. You are not just William Roth, the beautiful human person. You are William Roth the ambassador for the Blessed Virgin Mary. I need not explain the difference to you. My Special son, you are a child of the Father; you are a visionary and lettered Marian son; you are lauded in the realms of Paradise as an esteemed and elevated dignitary. You must never again be driven by anyone to locations where your life and safety would be placed into jeopardy. You and your brother have much more to contribute to the Church. Your own beauty, your own life and passion for holy excellence, your dedication to Me and the Kingdom of God are the reasons I first called you to Medjugorje in 1989. I ask that you be aware that there are people all across America and around the globe who do not consider the responsibility to avoid the wiles of the devil. You are too precious to be exposed to their derelict conduct and vast reckless judgements. They have not the ability to decide for the preservation of life. I cannot overstate what your prayers and petitions have done, and I also cannot overstate what changes are imminent due to the sacrifices of so many young people in the Church. One would have a difficult time calculating the number of young people who attended the World Youth Day events held by Saint Pope John Paul II. They went to his canonization in throngs. They have given the Earth the sweet fruits of their labors, seeded in them by this wonderful Saint. And, this is the manifest unfolding of the new world order under Roman Catholic Christianity that so many around the globe believe to be dying. I assure you that your presence in Denver in 1993 allowed you to see the exuberance that they espouse. This is the foundation on which the purification of many others is being built. You once said that it would take another fifty years to reverse the damage done by the secular minions who are trying to diminish the dignity of the Church. It will not take that long; it will not even take another decade. Do you remember seeing film footage of ice shelves falling like curtains into the seas where the temperatures are getting warmer? This is the sensation you will have when you see such animus against the Church plummeting into the Abyss. It will be obvious, palpable and undeniable. I urge you to recall My words when you watch these things happen. Remember this message of May 3, 2014 when I said that it would come. I am adorned with prescience fit for a Queen. There are around you many people that appear to be benign in conduct, but who are corrupt inside. They look to be passive on the outside, but they are demonically secular within. Liberal Catholics who say that they believe in the teachings of the Church, but who act the opposite, will soon come crashing to the ground like those melting ice shelves. My Special son, thank you for being so charitably receptive to My comments today. I love you."

Saturday, May 10, 2014
9:14 a.m.

"Sounding the depths of humanity's fiat."

"Not my will, but Thine, O' Lord, be done. This, My children, is the fiat that has birthed human redemption; it is the acclamation that reproves the world that is so opposed to change, so averse to righteousness, so unwilling to yield to the holiness given from On High. It is the fiat of an earthly domain that must be willing to be flooded again, to be inundated by the Blood of the Lamb. It is the cry of a world that dares to drown in the repentance being accorded by the many who have chosen redemption. I speak of fiat not in terms of judicial systems. I do not refer to edicts and decrees from mortal sovereigns. I speak of a fiat that cannot impede itself, that comes through the darkness into the light, that overwhelms souls and senses, that mitigates the wrongs heaped upon Creation by human ill will. Today, I am sharing with you a foretaste of the expectations of the Father who knows no need for hope because He has already seen and heard everything that will come to pass. Hear! – but He hopes anyway! He dispenses to exiled humanity the opportunity to please Him time and again, to stir His kind emotions, to summon His presence and beseech His blessings. It is not only said that God has nothing better to do than respond to human prayers, but that He must answer them according to the whims of His people. We know, however, that the prospect of God doing something like that is not as profound as God simply 'being' someone. And, His being is, in fact, His own doing. My Special and Chosen sons, this is the being that has been seeded in you, sewn into the fabric of your lives, given energy through your acceptance of the Cross. It is the Cross that you know to be the purpose of human life, not to the forfeiture of joy, but for the conversion of the lost. And, as I have said in opening My message today, we must think in terms of probing the depths of humanity's collective fiat as the Church, as the unifier of the nations within and alongside the teachings of the Gospel. Hence, while the Earth waits for the Lord as sentinels wait for the dawn (Psalm 130:6), you present yourselves as prepared for His return in glory. You stand upright and fitted with justice, the same as Jesus on this auspicious day, the bringing of His Passion before men and history, and before the future about which we often speak so profoundly. I cannot overstate what this promise means for the world. As I have spoken about the connection, the relationship between beauty and power during the past several months, I wish to capstone this amalgam with My assurance that its product is fulfilled in its simplicity. So, the beauty about which I have been speaking is not about fair faces and evening gowns, not about double-breasted lapels or sparkling blazer sequins. It is about simplicity in holiness; this is where the most eloquent strains reside. Power in the way of the Child Jesus is manifested by identifying with His innocence, matched to His wisdom and charm, given life by humanity's fiat that I have spoken about today. There is a circle of life in this respect, but not a swirling one, not a circle that looks like a greyhound chasing its tail. I am speaking not about a circle of motion, but of connectivity, of unity and completeness – that the soul of humanity discovers itself within the Most Sacred Heart of Jesus. This is the 'being' of human life that calls beyond the ages, from the legacies of billions of Saints, from the fruits of the world that have waited centuries to ripen. My Special son, even as you have reentered the secular arena for your sustenance and shelter, you have never lost sight of your 'being' in Jesus. You will always be tethered to Him from the inside out. I have with Me in Heaven the spirits of untold numbers of your predecessors who are living still, watching you and praying for you; and it is not as though they have nothing better to do either. Their peace is not just in doing, but in 'being' and effecting the perpetual dimensions of joy, of forever knowing with certainty that everything they sought in their redemption was true. In Heaven, they never speak about what claims they had on life or what should have eventually come. They speak about the fullness of eternity as endless and boundless, hardly capable of being described as a noun, more easily defined as a verb. Heaven, the place that is not a singular location, but all locations at once; more a condition, but not a condition that is replicable by anything else.

    I wish today, My Special one, to impress upon you the need for happiness in your expectations, for your patience in enduring the torments and agonies of mortal life, for your understanding that you are on the Earth as one of Jesus' true disciples. You and your brother are His sacred representatives here; you are His thinkers and believers, His mentors for those who do not yet know His merciful Heart. We realize that this intercessory power for His Kingdom is manifested by your obedience, by your pious endeavors, by your holiness – all of which reflect your own beauty, and therefore your power. How many times have you proved this to be true? Too many to recount. You are your own perpetual imitation of The Christ in an earthly realm that is limited by its ages and spaces. You harken the freedom of Paradise that is not constrained by the non-paradisial aspects of the secular globe. You are closer to Heaven than the netherworld; you are more here by Providence than mere happenstance, you are affixed to the

Messiah, and disconnected from His enemies. My Immaculate Heart is a realm of excellence in itself, and you are in this grace-filled domain. And too, we are both inside the realms of holistic excellence in the things of glory, where the fullness of time has met its match, where divinity reigns supreme, where we have dignity and never concede to sorrow or pain. I cannot fathom the prospect that any of My children will turn Me away at last, once the Father has unleashed the secrets of the years. Life need not have an unhappy ending, but this is what will happen to those who refuse to heed My words. I have asked you many times not to pity those who turn their backs on Jesus; this is still true today. It is not that they were unsalvageable creatures, it is more that they wanted things their own way; they wanted to be self-focusing gods of their own priorities. This is not the way of the Father's Kingdom. He wishes His people to fill their throats to overflowing with praise for Him, to speak devoutly about His kindness, to set aside their own penchants in favor of embracing His Son. And, once the message of the Gospel is understood, this is no major feat. It is not a call to self-mutilation that the Scriptures summon from men. It is the benign gift of obedience that creates new beginnings, fresh visions, holy thoughts and eternal consolations. Power. It is the product of the splendorous beauty of humankind saying 'yes' to God. When I recently said that touching the Face of God can be a tactile experience, I mean that the whole of the Church is etched into His image. Fill the universe with love! Kiss the Lord's Creation with righteousness; touch His cheek with virtue. This is done through repentance and forgiveness; offer lost humanity the chance to be found in the identity of the Christian heart. There is no rocket science needed here. There are no equations or counter-facts required because, as I said moments ago, there is no confusion between love and hatred. An arrow does not have two points. A spear has only one head. Repentance and forgiveness are one within the human heart, for surely they are of the same contrition. Hence, sounding the depths of humanity's full-throated fiat to God involves the surrender of the soul to His Will, and it concludes in His presence with the unity of all the redeemed. When Jesus speaks about the winds blowing where they will, about separating the sheep from the goats, about dividing the wheat from the chaff, about recognizing the blessed from the outcast, He speaks about repentance and forgiveness as though they are two peas in one pod. He seeks from His apostles the willingness to open their lives and allow His Divine Kingdom to come in."

Saturday, May 17, 2014
Dayton, Ohio (no message)

Saturday, May 24, 2014
9:33 a.m.

"When history succumbs to human excellence."

"The welcome infusion of the Holy Spirit into your lives, My children, is warming and consoling; it is forever inviting of your prayers to fulfill the wishes that you hold so deeply within your hearts. I am here to assist this infusion as the Lord's signature of love. Your faith is rewarded by these gifts and signs, by these miracles and wonders, because there is veracity in authentic faith. My little sons, you are part of these miracles for the fullness of Creation. I speak about history succumbing to human excellence in the wake of these contributions. It takes a seeming lifetime to realize the substance of your dreams, while pain, agony and disappointment appear to come at will. The history about which I speak is rife with suffering; it is plagued by error and corruption wrought by the hatred and callousness of wicked men. It need not be this way; there should not be such a thing as sinful human pride. But, humanity is reluctant to believe that it can right itself. There seems to be no vision for becoming better than before. History is stubborn; it will not yield to wayward men because there is no reason for it to step aside. All history cries out for virtuous grace! Of course, there are moments and movements that have purified the world, but they have mostly been in response to error. There have been victories of war, if there is such a thing. The Earth has witnessed the gutting of the bellies of malevolent beasts that have preyed on innocent life. What I am speaking about is the call of human excellence for the sake of itself, not just in response to something wrong. The Father is calling the Church to this excellence, and He is a benevolent Lord. Responding to goodness with more pronounced goodness will vanquish human error; history will finally succumb to the future, and the ages will yield to eternity. When human love perfectly reflects the Love of God, history will no longer have a choke hold on the memories of men. Tragedies and catastrophes will be annulled; they will go by way of the dinosaurs. And, My dear sons, it is clear that this process has already begun. If it were otherwise, I would not remain in the presence of the nations, bidding sinful men to change and righteous men to do more good. When I speak about the infusion of the Holy Spirit into the temporal world, I am referring to the protrusion of the Holy Cross into the hearts of its lost inhabitants. The Cross is a compass and handhold. The Cross is the scepter for humanity, that all will see from its radiance the glory that is yet to come. The Father in Heaven holds in His hands this scepter for all to see; it is His Son on Mount Calvary, it is the transformation of the created world in one Crucified Man. My Special son, when I speak about this transformation, I am referring to the demise of your long held enemies. You and your brother are fortunate to have avoided the most gruesome persecutions that have come to many of your forebears. You have been sheltered here with Me; you have had each other for strength and support. It is not just a simple miracle that this has happened, it is a manifestation of Divine Providence that will be spread before humanity before Jesus comes in glory. Time and again, I come speaking to you in joy because everything I have said is true. It seems to take forever in your day, but time is brief; it is expiring as we speak.

So, what does this human excellence look like? It is much more fair than one might conceive. It need not be an illusive heroism celebrated only in novels. And, it is much more simple than the vaunted spires. When Jesus saw you and your brother walking down the staircase from SAM 26000 Air Force One last Saturday, He did not see secular presidents or lauded cabinet men.* (*The jetliner that returned John F. Kennedy's body from Dallas to Washington, D.C. which is on display at the National Museum of the United States Air Force in Dayton, Ohio.*) He saw two, like the seventy-two that He dispatched in centuries passed. He saw Himself within you, clarified to the world by the work you have done. Jesus gave to lost sinners your faith in Him as their means of spiritual conversion, and it shall never be undone. It cannot be reversed; the whole of it shall never be divided. And, when your brothers and sisters ultimately come to know what your lives have been with Me, human excellence will finally arrive. It will live beyond the gateways. It will be so mammoth that history will in fact concede; it will be crushed beneath its own weight, it will fade away and never show its face again. You must know that there are many 'two-by-twos' throughout the ages; some are celebrated in the Mass's Eucharistic Prayers. Saints Peter and Paul, Cosmas and Damian and all the rest. You, however, are valedictory disciples of your time; you are shining and reflecting the Will of the Father for these, the closing ages. I have pronounced favor upon you using more superlatives than one could possibly imagine, but I have yet to breach the surface of what your goodness really means. You are the protrusion of humanity's virtue into the physical realms, into the arena where the Church-Militant continues to fight. And, your prayers bleed into the wounds of the Poor Souls in Purgatory; your righteousness fuels the torches in the dark corridors of the Earth. I am not exaggerating what you mean to Me, what you have done for the Lord's Church, what you have given humanity here. You are leading the charge against the sickness of the world. You are part of the human excellence to which it will surrender its record of itself. My Special son, your prayers for the sanctification of your brothers and sisters are not unlike some of the airships you saw in Dayton last week. You stand so stately in the presence of the throngs. The onlookers ponder their own lack of knowledge about how you complete your work, who commissioned you, how far-reaching is your power, and what they can do to eventually become like you. The soft cadence and awakening sound of humanity-excelled begins in the awareness of these things. It need not be heard in the deafening explosions of ordnance overhead, but the concussions can be the same. The repercussions can match your virtuousness, too. You have been detonating these gifts before the majesties of the Angels for decades on end; you have lit fuses that you did not even know were there. These times are your reasons for being saints; they are evidence that you belong to God, and they are proof that He is listening to your prayers. And, to this end, you are the Father's progeny, not His firstborn sons, but His holy sons nonetheless. There are wakes aplenty in the passage of this vessel through the stale waters of time. Far-reaching are the implications of your life here with your brother and your sacred commission within the Roman Catholic Church. If God did not mean for this to happen, your lives would have unfolded in another place and time. You might have made different choices; your own life could have been defined by clearly contrasting ways. But, you unified your will with God's Will; you decided for the purification of the nations over the excesses of your own American homeland.

And, these are the reasons that the pull of eternity is fixated on you. It will eventually void the whole composite of history, not because it will simply outlast it, but because you have given it no reason to go on. You and all My children are heirs of a Salvation that Jesus has bequeathed to you, and an Afterlife that you have helped shape in His honor. This is the power of the Catholic Church; this is the intensity of your faith, it is the reason that God has never closed His Sacred Heart from the groaning of the world. It is all because of the relationship that you have chosen to pursue with your own redemption and the miraculous works with which we will finally convert Jesus' enemies to His Kingdom. My Special son, the fruits of all this are as ample as the conversion of the created world. It is about addressing the injustices about which human history is still boasting. It is about annulling the vanity of those who have been persecuting the Church. Yes, this conversion is about the vengeance of the Lord, not just setting the record straight, but annihilating it altogether. Who leaves their enemies' bodies on the battlefield without harvesting the valuables from their pockets? God in Heaven does the same. Where His enemies have hoarded gold for their own selfish gain, He will reclaim it. He will restore it unto His Creation from whence it was placed in the first six days. He will make sure that those who have chosen Hell as their fate wail not only because they are forever condemned, but that their condemnation has left them bereft of a sliver of light. So, My Special and Chosen ones, I bid you to expunge the annals of this world! I offer you My prayers and blessings for your journey. I commend you to the grace by which all good men prevail. I pray for you as fervently as I have ever uttered My intercessions over time or eternity. I watch you in awesome wonder as you amaze the Angels by your willingness to go on, by your endurance in the face of human indifference, tormented by the distractions that pull your brothers and sisters in so many other ways, and even the procrastination of those within the Church. Thank you for your holy prayers, for your humble petitions that I take to Christ Jesus, and therefore to the Father, who reigns with such Wisdom in Heaven."

Sunday, June 1, 2014
9:35 a.m.

"What good is the dawn unless the fog lifts too?"

"A new month has come upon you, My children, a new beginning, a new demarcation in time, another opportunity to uphold your values in faith, trust and virtue. Think about it. If your families had fallen at your feet, believing all along that your messages were from Me, would they not also feel helpless to get the rest of humanity to believe? Is it not the great and definitive finish of all profound works for the heroes to have been found telling the truth at the last? Is it not true that the shockwaves of the ages have come during the most complacent times? So, let it be. Let us do here what we have always done. Let them stroll along in their indifference, all the Earth's distracted peoples, everyone who believed that human life was about them and their progeny; let the barons and magnates have their day, allow them to dig themselves deeper into their spiritual misery from where they will all someday cry out to God as if innocent of everything they have ever done. What will become of this great mystery that has lived through the past quarter century? It will be your final vindication; it will reflect the poise and holiness you have invested in their redemption through Jesus, at the behest of the Father, and imprinted in the created realms through Me. You will remember that I told you in early 1991 that we have something they all want, and it will be their big surprise. My Special and Chosen ones, they will want Jesus more than they are willing to confess. They cast away the persuasive overtures of Heaven's gifts in favor of their own desires; they cannot see that impurity, materialism and self-aggrandizement end in themselves. They decline to believe that miracles from Heaven can come so close to them. They refuse to see themselves alongside the Saints in whose shadows they should already be living. I have always tried to lift them up everywhere I have spoken; they are not your enemies, they are your lost brothers and sisters. And, you are seeing that they are becoming exhausted and fatigued not because of their service toward the Salvation of the Church, but by the weight of their own devices, the heaviness of their own chosen distractions. Are fame, influence and wealth more important in life than piety and harmony? Is competition more ameliorative than compassion? We know the answers; they are still searching for them. My dear children, imagine the times to come when everyone who walked beside you through these years finally realizes what has been unfolding in this home. What will they say, if they can muster any speech, about the wasting of the months and seasons doing anything other than helping you? With what confessions will they look into your eyes, if they can look you in the eyes at all, to seek your forgiveness for their error? I truly believe and credibly know that this is what the Father is doing with your deposit of works. And, I also know that it will be like raising up the most diminutive souls among the highest of all to be crowned as champions. This is the future of the two visionaries of the Morning Star Over America. Today, I look forward with ease. I remember what all My children are contributing to the cause of human purification. I see the suffering and neglected, the oppressed, the homeless, naked and diseased. I see the lonely ones who pray in silent agony, refusing to demand that the Lord heal their lives, while quietly hoping that He will do so anyway. After all, it is all about the Will of God; we have known this all along. Is the power of a single Ancient Fiat enough to induce all living creatures to be so deferential? Are openness and charity strong enough to serve as the pillars of a greater faith? Jesus will someday ask the Church what has been given to Him that echoes His love and obedience. He will ask His 'other self' how it feels to take on the cloak of guilt that is not rightly theirs to bear. We know that Christianity is filled with this meaning. Your faith would have no mettle otherwise. It has always been about suffering of the innocents so the guilty can be pardoned. I have said that this will not always be true. It is clear that no sorrow or bloodshed can convince a condemned soul to rethink the evils of their ways. It is all about this comparison in the end.

No, I am not saying that the Faith-Church, the Church-Militant, will stand out as the slayers of corrupt men. But, they will be collectively the Mystical Body of the Slain One who saved them. It is against this sacred backdrop that the most wretched souls will measure their lives. June 2014. This is where you are; it is where I am only because the Lord wants Me to be. God asks that I come to you today so you will know what His love truly means in this land, in this century, during your time here when all things are leaning toward justice, awakening and reconciliation. My Special son, you and your brother should be walking these days with such confidence that it would be difficult to explain. You have built in this life a kingdom within a Kingdom. You are about to release a memoir that cannot be matched by the writings of other men. It is all about Jesus Christ with you and your brother. It is all about rewriting the past, refining the present, and welcoming the future of all pious histories into the eternity that is rightfully yours to claim. My Special one, we have never disagreed about anything during the years that I have spoken to you. We have addressed some dire issues and seen difficult times, but we have always been one in truth. This is the metaphor that I seek from the rest of the world. I cannot expect those far from the Church to instantly understand what Jesus wants of them. And, this is why I have pledged My Wisdom to so many visionaries throughout the ages. I am My children's gift of enlightenment. When I describe these things to you, it is about anticipation. It is about planning and expectations. The seed of this anticipation is humanity's awareness that new birth can come from its own voluntary contrition. Shedding the old self and donning the new Christian life is what conversion is all about. I once used the metaphor that it is like scraping off burnt skin with a sponge and allowing new layers to grow. Few things are as painful. But, this shedding must come through the flames of the love about which I speak. A new way of seeing must come. People reflect upon waiting in the night for the morning dawn to break, but they have done little to pierce the fog of idleness in which their lives are concealed. I am not just speaking about the spiritual dawn that will come to everyone, I am referring to the breaking of awareness that sometimes comes in increments, by the hour and day, during the spontaneous life in which the world is situated. And, as I said earlier, what good is the dawn if someone does nothing to lift the fog from before their eyes? This is what you and your brother have been saying for more than a quarter century. I ask you to remember what I saw during My Son's earthly life. I raised a Child to a Man who is the Savior of human souls. I then watched while He was mocked and ridiculed, how so few believed in Him, how evil targeted Him for suffering from the moment He was born of My Womb. I was where you and your brother are now, and God glorified Me for it, as He will likewise glorify you. Fear overcomes those who do not have sacrificial love. We often make enemies of those whom we ask to deny themselves and take up their crosses. This is in fulfillment of the Scriptures; it is the story of modern men. I pray that you are pleased to know that everything we are doing will soon have its intended effect. It is not whether it will occur, but *that* it will occur.

All the actions, emotions, penchants, preferences and pursuits of humanity through history have ended in the single motivation of redemptive revelation. We are manifesting it now. We are speaking about it today. We are the people of the same God who willed our identities into being from the earliest proclamations of His love. And, we are awaiting the outpouring of the completion of Creation in your day that Jesus foretold on the Cross. It was His artistry, His genius, His revelatory Crucifixion that opened-wide the floodgates of forgiveness to resurrect everyone and everything that He desires to keep in His passel of blessings for eternity. There is a certain finality in all this, but it is also an ageless beginning. My entire being, My whole purpose here has been about Mothering the children of God, teaching on behalf of the Master about preparing to meet Him in person. Is mortal life about preparing for a better fate? Certainly. Is it about denying the greatest joys today in exchange for the limitless ecstasy of Heaven? Without any doubt. What happens in between, My Special son, sometimes does not matter much. It is marking life in milestones and making something of few other things. This is why automobile racing and dance recitals come about, but they are not unworthy if all other men are availed the opportunity to have their needs met; the basic necessities of shelter and food, health and safety. You know the rest. I am simply asking you and your brother to look more closely at your own goodness. See what has become of your humble beginnings; you are just as humble now, but you are giants in the eyes of the Father. Hear, let Me reiterate it from long ago. Imagine the throngs of disbelievers wanting to crucify Jesus on Good Friday twenty centuries back in time. It was all about convicting the innocent, denying the Truth, desecrating the sacred, and executing the Godly. This was some of the most grotesque evil that could come from the world of men. However, it meant the demise of the devil and the Salvation of souls. And for this reason, and as blessed as you are by your faith, I am so pleased that you and your brother have prayed with Me during the past 25 years, that you have remained as one through your youthfulness and maturity for over 40 years. You might find yourselves as surprised as everyone else what your faith has given to humanity. In the future, your brother may need to stay a few nights with his dying brother Bobby to comfort him in his last days. The Angels asked your brother to say in response to this fact that, '...the march of the ages has come upon us.' It will be a sad and painful goodbye. Thank you for your prayers. I pray with you every day – I see you sitting here in your humble home, asking the Lord to intervene."

Saturday, June 7, 2014
9:27 a.m.

"The inviolate anatomy of the sanctified human soul."

"With all the blessings of the Supreme Deity, we have come together to remember our calling. My little sons, many are the ages when I wondered when humanity would rise from the dust of their forebears' error, and these days have yielded the transformation I have sought. The old world will expire where it was first formed, but its inhabitants have emerged from the wilderness. I come with tremendous joy into your prayer room, Saint Joseph's Room, here in your home where so many miracles have been wrought. Yes indeed, the inviolate anatomy of the sanctified human soul. This does not mean that a person is not prone to accidents. It does not preclude the occasional misstep. It does not foretell that someone's judgement will always be perfect, or that premature opinions align with the facts. It means that the soul of a man has been availed to all the graces that God has to offer, and that his perfection, through time, is in the process of being forged. It is not an anatomy whereby one might think of an arm or leg, but of a oneness with the identity of Jesus Christ. Becoming sanctified begins upon the conversion of the soul, a process that leads to everlasting redemption. Here, I am describing the uniting of the lost with the found, the shedding of light into the darkness, the resurrection of the dead, the enlightenment of the ignorant, and the celebration of all that is good. My Special son, it is clear from My messages that I would ask you to refer My children to the potential about which I am speaking. It is more than groveling before one's own weaknesses, it is overcoming them by accepting the Cross. This is the 'Christ' identity. And, it is about utilizing one's maturity and seniority to reclaim their own youth, perhaps not of the mind or body, but the youth of the spirit in the innocence that has been found. As simple as it may sound, the Cross of Christ Jesus could be likened to a great expunger. The Crucifixion has all the power of expungement that could be vested in one human act. Punishment was forced upon Jesus, and He used that punishment to rescind the condemnation of everyone who would hear. Hence, the inviolate anatomy of the sanctified human soul does not imply that a person will never sin, but in their acceptance of the Blood of the Cross, their soul shall never die. Going to Hell for endless ages is deadly to the soul; there is no glorious life there, there is no eternal life to be known. The antidote for death is the Crucifixion and the imitation of Jesus' life by those wishing to be saved. It is this imitation, living in His likeness, striving for those virtues that Jesus always possessed, to which holy men aspire. When we speak about good men becoming great men, this is what we mean. The first is about discovering the princely nature of the human soul, the second is applying one's holiness to lead the lost to the Church. My Special son, when pious men speak about the secular phenomenon of cultural noise, they are referring to politically correct speech and the relativism that you denounced last evening with your friends. But, virtue is about ignoring the irrelevant issues not requiring the response of sanctified men. There is cultural noise everywhere; there has always been. It is the origin of the distractions that keep humanity from seeking and praying to God. It is graffiti on a wall in a room that is lacking three other sides; it has but one dimension. We know that a sphere has multiple dimensions, and this is how we view holy life. Those who generate cultural noise are imbedded in fads and fancies meant only to entrap the greatest number of consumers, but their lives are stuck like mud, slung against a faded pane of glass. This is why the daily newspaper arrives on doorsteps on tissue-like pages instead of being published on cubical boxes. There is only one dimension for recounting secular human events, and hardly any for forecasting their future. No indeed, the sanctified human soul is not like that at all. Piety has no need to be categorized as past, present or future; and the fullness of humane love can be captured in an Immeasurable Truth in the context of the Sacred Scriptures.

This is from where all men should view the world; it is a much larger, more vast existence of life, situated at the gateway of Heaven above. This is the Earth as it should be; it is the solar system and universe; it is the mere thought of the heart, it is a worthy peace in its most essential form. All these elements comprise the intersection of humanity with its potential in Jesus. All of this speaks to the inviolate nature of the sanctified human soul. It splashes against Creation with youth and vigor, no matter the age of the person. It has bright eyes and vision to foresee the power of God. It spreads across the ages like wildfire in the night. It plays like a toddler in the presence of the Father with the innocence of a newborn robin. This nature speaks of times and celebrations long before they occur, that will transpire eternities ahead. You and your brother have inherited this nature; you have sanctified souls that shine through the brilliance of your lives. The soul is your identity in God, and your spirit is the life of that identity. And, when the Father sees you the way you are; when He sees everyone who is like you, He says, 'I desire them. I wish for them, and I accept them.' It is not that He never knew you before you were born; it has nothing to do with being strangers to the God who gave you life. It is more about people becoming prone to excellence in the properties of love. My Special son, I have nurtured within My Immaculate Heart a desire to speak to your brothers and sisters the strains of glory that I have many times shared with you. However, they remain reticent to come to Me. They have heard of Me, but they relegate Me to some faint cult in the history of the Church. They believe that I sat quietly on a donkey's back and lived a serene pedestrian life somewhere in the shadows of Bethlehem. They refuse to accept that the Lord would vest Me with the power to commend the whole of the nations to yield to His Kingdom of Glory. Yes, it is far and wide, much greater than men may know; it is more than a spiritual recommendation, it is an overwhelming commendation. Remember that Jesus answers prayers according to the Will of God alongside the Communion of Saints. What they see is what Jesus sees. What Jesus sees is what they see. And, they perceive the inviolate beings here in this life, where you and your brother live, where the Church fights for the truth, where Martyrs lay down their lives, where children pray and mothers weep, where the sun rises on a world that is still embroiled in its own inordinate choices. You will be with Me beyond the end of time. I am with you now, with Jesus in My embrace, with each and all who are united before the Cross with hope for the joyful conclusion of the world. Think about this with Me. God came to the Earth. He asked Me to bear Himself in His Son. I said yes, as you have said yes. There is auspiciousness everywhere! It is not as though the Creator of everything visible reached up and placed it on a shelf. He loves holding Creation in His hands. He admires those who guide and protect it. He listens to what matters to them now. History has its place, but what is ongoing here today takes priority over those archived times. This is the prescience of wisdom. I have at My disposal the leaflets of history that I can page through and see, adoring in grateful tears what the Saints and Martyrs have done, watching cathedrals being built on their blessed foundations, seeing the Angels caressing little children as they sleep like kittens in their beds, and witnessing the penitent receiving the Sacraments of the Roman Catholic Church. I have seen the outpouring of faith, hope and love – the splashing waves of righteousness that I mentioned just moments ago. There may be upheavals in societies and from under mountaintops everywhere, but none can compare to the surfacing of a soul crawling from beneath the carnage of its own unconfessed sins. It is their first breath of fresh air; there is nothing like it in the annals of the world.

So today, I assure you that everything we have done remains on course. All the things that the Angels are declaring are sewn to what we are accomplishing. Perhaps not all the issues will come to the fore; maybe some of them are options, and alternatives too. But, the point is that good men are still engaging their God, still lifting up stairs and stages on which future conclusions will be drawn. After all, this is the journey of man over which the Lord holds the reins. He watches over it with care, that His Will shall be done. As long as men can stand and raise a prayer, they should lift up their Savior on the Cross. They should not surrender until they lay exhausted and spent, done for the fight, and prepared for delivery to the oft-spoken place where their fathers will not be ashamed to receive them. This is the oath of the Martyrs, of all who fight for Jesus, of the Catholic Church that has withstood 2,000 years of insults and onslaughts for the sanctification of humanity relying on faith. With poise and promise you have lived; with trust and devotion you have prayed, and with joy and thanksgiving you shall die. My Special son, thank you and your brother for your love for Me, for your dedication to everything for which I stand, and for being My children in whose hands I have laid the conversion of the entire western world. I am pleased by your memoir; you know how profound it is. Thank you for praying for the poor, for the mission of the Church, and for the innocent unborn."

Saturday, June 14, 2014
10:02 a.m.

"The matrix (culture and environment) of transformational life."

"My little sons, you have the knack for knowing how God perceives the world, how you connect your lives in exile to His unseen Kingdom to come, and the way you understand what must happen before that Divine Kingdom will be wholly revealed. I am speaking in a way that describes your tangible connection to spiritual things through your interaction with the temporal and material. Time and space – I have mentioned these concepts as being contradictory to engaging the dimensionless realms of the Afterlife. This is what makes your life on Earth transformational; your identity in Jesus in this earthly matrix is the way you live your future in Him that has already begun. This is the culture and environment in which the evangelizing of the Holy Gospel takes place, and your decisions and actions help shape this matrix. It is not a contradiction to teach that it is '...not my will but Thine, O' Lord, be done...' alongside the prospect that you have a human will capable of being united with the Will of God. Indeed, it shall be said that '...yes, my will and Thine, O' Lord, will procure the repentance of men and the ages.' In this coalescence, the Divine Will of the Father and the humbled will of humanity are focused on the same perceptions, the same purposes for human life, the identical advancement of the virtues that will make this world a better place, not just the Glorious World to come. So today, I speak of this matrix, this culture and environment as it refers to a transformational life because you are among the few who understand it. It is the same principle as '...the wisdom of the children.' This also seems like a contradiction in terms. How can children be wise? There are more reasons than

I can recount in this brief message today. (*My brother and I attended a stock car race near St. Louis last evening. During the intermission, the track organizers allowed the children from the grandstand to gather on the track for a footrace around the oval. Their ages ranged from 13 years old to children as young as 3 or 4. It was delightful to see their enthusiasm and energy – until each child realized just how far one-half mile actually is. Some of the small children had to be assisted after a few dozen yards because the effort was too much for them. Our Lady seemed moved by their innocence.*) Indeed, when in Pontoon Beach last night, you saw and heard the speeding race cars and roaring engines kicking up dust with violent force. Was it not a stately contrast to then see the little children running around the same path with such peace and delicateness? Was not their youth and playful presence the impetus that touched your hearts, as it did Mine? The answer is yes, and this speaks to their wisdom. It is a reference to the 'humanity' that, even though fragile in its mortal state, will remain long after the machines have been dismantled and their noise has faded. My Special son, when you looked into the sky last evening in Pontoon Beach, you saw airplanes flying overhead. When you looked to your right, you saw sprawling trains and boxcars. And, when you looked forward, you saw the gaudy race cars that I just mentioned. And, even with the presence of these planes, trains and automobiles, the most living thing among all of them was the humanity of the children, the true power of life and song that not only permeates the ages, but will live long after the ages have passed. The point I am making is that they are not a perishing youth; your own youth has never perished. It is not about the health of the body or physical agility that I am speaking, for they shall surely fall away. It is about the '...permanence of the innocence.' When speaking in less than veiled strains, it is clear that this is where the Heart of God belongs. It is in the renewal of the earthly domain by a Kingdom of Love that never needs renewed. When I speak to you about the culture and environment of transformational life, I am referring to the connection between beauty and power that I have discussed during the past several months. This is what we have been praying for during the past 2,000 years. If this cultivating purification is to take place, it is clear that we must, and already have, revealed to the nations that maturity in faith implies the recapturing of one's childlike innocence.

The fullness of adulthood retains its vigor by adhering to the doctrines of holiness mandated in the Sacred Scriptures. This is the intersection of life and perfection, the matrix in which the redemption of humanity begins in the middle of the night. I hold true hope for this phenomenon to reach its apex before the Son of Man returns. How do you know? Because every time I appear around the globe, I begin My messages with, '...My dear children.' I speak in lofty terms to sinners who oftentimes harbor some not-so-lofty thoughts. I am trying to break the ages-old ritual of men seeing life as just repetitive days, but a combination of times that comprise the spiritual matrix of the transformational life to which they are called. It is clear that this transformation need not be an illogical one. There are practical matters to which all good Christians are called. I am not referring to hermits that hide from society as if cloistered in bomb shelters somewhere. I am speaking about common citizens; these are the ones who are connected with the thoughts of nations, of their cultures and marketplaces, of their leaders and legislators. This is the same transformation that I have sought in Medjugorje for 33 years. And, it is clear that you and your brother were initiated into this frame of thought long ago; as you say, just look at your memoir. Jesus sees you as fair-faced and stouthearted. He knows that you desire for the world everything that He has taught since He was old enough to speak. We have agreed that this is a process and not an event, but the process is nearing its pinnacle both inside and outside of time, in practical terms that cannot be manipulated by human hands. Here again, time and space. They need not be seen as constraints on the ability of men to have an inviolate relationship with their Maker. This is how humanity becomes the 'begotten' people of the Lord, not just those God has made in the same way that He suspended the Earth in space. It has not yet occurred to most people that God not only exists, but that He actually wants something. How can it be true that the Father could be lacking in anything that completes His grasp on the spatial and spiritual realms? Adam disobeyed Him. Adam had different ideas, and this created a slippery chasm between all who would succeed him and the surefooted perfection that is inherited in Jesus on the Cross. This breach is mended when human hearts open and the chasm is closed. As you know, God sent Jesus to reconstitute the union between Himself and His people, and this reaffirms God's handhold on those He loves. It is not that the Father lets go, but humanity lets go. Before Jesus was conceived, God realized that the eternity of His Kingdom and the souls of His people were not yet reconciled.

This is the reason you and I have come to know each other through the Salvation of the world. I was created to be the Mother of this Salvation, and you have become heir to the legacy of My Womb. My Womb is the Matrix of human redemption, and Jesus is the Fruit whose Sacrifice has fed the desire of the Father to return His children to His presence. In the old language, matrix means womb. It is the culture and environment in which the purification of all created souls is happening. I was not transformed because I never needed to be, but humanity has access to this reorientation, this clear and evident fortune in which the perfect world shall come. Therefore, when I say that innocence implies power, that the wisdom of the children is deafening, I am suggesting that old men would do well to heed the call of their younger selves, particularly in the way of their innocence. Brightness that overcomes dullness is living there. Cleanliness that expels the soiling of the years is made manifest. Sweetness that expunges the bitterness of life's tragic turns runs pervasively throughout these new beginnings. It is borne through the sacrifice of the self, by knowing that shedding the callousness of age does not expose oneself to the exploitation of others who do not. My Special son, I am certain that you understand what I have said today. Thank you for giving your brother such friendship and support as he does his part in the wonderful plan in which the two of you are participating. He has a 60-year-old mind and body, and he has heroically endured his ravaging portion of the suffering of 23 years of My intercession. The Lord knows what both of you desire, but He also understands the wear and tear you have withstood in your battles against the evil that has attempted to impede your work. Yes, the people at your brother's most recent interview were amazed by his credentials through which he applied for employment, but they are rattled that they would hire someone who claims to be hearing voices and seeing visions. It makes no difference what profoundness is imbedded in your works; they seem not to care that such a volume of miracles is obviously true. It is all about their self-image, fearing that they will be advancing the mission of the Roman Catholic Church if they hire your brother. We shall see what they decide."

Saturday, June 21, 2014
9:08 a.m.

"The true meaning of evolution."

"My dear little sons, My Immaculate Heart is brimming with joy because we are together, united in purpose for the conversion of the lost. Yes, Archbishop Fulton Sheen knew of My role as Mother and Intercessor; it was in his heart that the hopes of the Gospel fully lived. And, he lives on, as the Gospel lives on. What is the true meaning of evolution? What does it imply for those who are struggling to subscribe to the path of holiness, its origins and history, its ultimate goals? I assure you that men did not evolve from primates, and the redemption of souls did not evolve from something so corruptible as the Earth. Human Salvation is the Fruit of the Messianic Crucifixion that was brought into being by the Son of God. For the whole of your years, you have studied and worshiped the meaning of this Salvation; you have identified with the Lord through your propagation of His miraculous works. When I speak about evolution, I am referring to this kind of transpiring. It is about people making choices that place them not only before the Crucifixion, but within it as well. It has nothing to do with the shape of the fleshly frame, how someone jaunts or alters their gait, or about heightening the dissemination of malignant worldly busywork or its sadistic imagery. It is about humanity broadening its comprehension of the demands of life, those issues that deal with the lessons and teachings of Jesus and the Bible. I am speaking about a process of preparation leading to the human soul entering the Kingdom of God. Let us make clear that this can be learned before death. It need not wait until the eyes of faith are supplanted by an unimpeded vision of Paradise. I have spoken in times past about the innocence of all this, about the lack of presupposition that accompanies the soul's journey to enter Heaven. There can be no true surrender to Christ Jesus if a person always presumes what He will do. Men know what the Scriptures say about Him; they learn what He has said in His time. Jesus is more responsive than some people may be willing to believe, and they should approach Him based upon what His living Spirit places into their hearts in real time. Of all people to know that this is true, My Special son, it most assuredly is you. You have been receptive of miracles that others would have summarily dismissed. So, this definition of evolution, its meaning and implications, is centered in the fact that Jesus finished Creation on the Cross, and its completion is yet unfolding in your time. This comes to the chagrin of those who believe in predestination and others who think that they have no other power than to run out their lives and no longer exist. The eyes of the sighted must be opened to see, but the vision about which I am speaking is manifested by faith on the inside; it comes to those who pray and the millions who have just breathed their last. Yes, some people never see the truth until they reach the other side of life. This, therefore, is the essence of spiritual evolution. It is its speech and purpose, but what does it mean? The answer rests in the enlightening designs of the Cross. If you see a cluster of trees in the country, as you did last evening, you are prone to appreciate only the ones that seem more beautiful than others. After all, you have been looking at trees all your life. If you saw a giant sequoia tree growing here in the Midwest among the pines, oaks and maples, you would have stopped your vehicle and gotten out in awe. This is metaphorically the evolution that has come to you already in your interaction with Me. I have been with you through your entire life, but I have in the past 25 years become like that giant sequoia tree with respect to your sense of My Motherhood. It has been an evolution, but one that you made possible, not Me. I have made this point to say that this is what I am trying to do worldwide through My appearances to multiple seers and hearers. I am relating the spiritual evolution of My exiled children to lead them to a supernatural awakening from the slumber of daily life. I spoke recently about the discomfort and upheaval that comes with forcing people out of indifference. You have seen it firsthand through hundreds of sinners in your midst, those who should instead be knocking down your door to procure copies of your books.

With the exception of the Three Wise Men, few others sought out the Savior of the world. He did not receive the voluntary approach of the First Apostles, He had to track them down. Like Jesus, this is where you and your brother are today. However, you need not track down those who will stand with you in the closing hours of the world; they will come to you. The crucial moments will approach all who have been devoted to Me in the Earth's reckoning times, and so will those with the conscience to follow. Knowing this fact is imperative for the impulses that preserve My joy in the finishing of the years. I have mentioned in My earlier messages the idea of 'the point of contact.' It means that there is an incentive to becoming holy and embracing righteousness, in espousing purity and charitable living. This point of contact is like the touching down of a rocket ship on another planet. However, with regard to the inspiration of the human heart by the Spirit of God, the encounter is not so much that the occupants of the rocket ship come to explore the world, but that the dwellers of the world should welcome their new guests. God came onto the Earth as His own Son not to discover what the world is about, but that the world's inhabitants can learn what God is about. He came to an unwelcoming Earth that still says that if they want to know about God, they will come to Him, they will let Him know. You have seen, however, that the Lord has an agenda. He wants something, as I said last week. The unlimited realms of His Kingdom hunger for the souls of exiled men. His Sacred Heart hurts, and He needs the world's humanity to come to Heaven and comfort Him. He has all the intelligence that any Creation might ever need in a single passing thought, but He wants His brothers to stand beside Him to affirm what they must know. It is this reciprocity that causes the evolution of the collective soul of humanity to leap toward the Afterlife. This is where good men rise up, throw down their hammers and yardsticks, and walk to Jesus Christ without fear or the demand of being repaid. They simply yearn to play a part in the final act; they wish to instill new meaning into their lives; they want to be like Me, just as Archbishop Sheen said, as being far too inspired to turn back now. They want to be in the enviable position of having the Son of Man tell them that they have become a part of the architecture of His Kingdom. They want to be taken to the doorway of eternity, place their hands against its surface, and feel it begin to move. This reflects their spiritual evolution, its true meaning. Then, what the mind has imagined, the eye can see. And, what the eye has seen, the heart has dared to touch. And, what the heart has touched, the soul has wholly embraced. At long last, what the soul has embraced, eternity has completely engulfed. In the final truth, My Special son, it is all about love; it is about recognizing the Crucifixion of Jesus as the reason for human life because those who pray for His forgiveness cannot help it. It is about falling in love with the giant sequoia towering above the sycamore trees. It is about breaking free from the bland ordinaries of life and taking hold of the exceptions. You already know by poring over your published memoir that you have completed this evolution. You are even further aware that you and your brother must bear out the meaning of your faith, and endure the remaining years of your lives alongside those who have not yet made this transition. It is not as difficult as it seems. You are a gift to God because you set out seeking Him too. You have helped redefine the meaning of evolution to rebuke those who believe that it is all about fins, scales, shorelines and ugly crawling creatures. We know better. Evolution has always been about accepting the life of Jesus as the model of human perfection. It is about remaining upright in faith, poised to accomplish the impossible, and being courageous in all things sacrificial to the denial of the self. This is how love and goodness become synonymous terms; they are fruits of each other. The meaning of evolution is about the intersection of offering and acceptance. It is through all this that I call My children to Medjugorje; it is from there that they are to become the disciples of Christ. Thank you for offering your morning prayers for the Catholic Church, for the healing of the sick, for the end of abortion, and for the conversion of the wicked."

Saturday, June 28, 2014
9:20 a.m.

"Doffing the stigma of paranormal fanaticism."

"Glory, My little sons; it is all about Glory. The entire framework of human redemption is about the Glory of God. The matter has always been about God and His Dominion of Love. This is what sustains us; it is the genesis of the world and its eternal deliverance; there is no pretentiousness here. The whole of life is defined by the truth that has founded and encircled the ages. Yes, a singular God in Three Divine Persons, wrapped in His own Providence, opened the possibility that all sinners can enter His Kingdom through the Cross of One Man. There is a certain stigma that comes in believing this, that the

Father could be Himself as a Man, that He could make heavy-with-child a Woman who remains a Virgin, that He could heal the sick, cause the lame to walk, and raise the dead from the grave. Most doubters call it paranormal fanaticism. I call it a miracle. Doffing, meaning removing or taking off, is what must be done with those who do believe. Do not allow unbelievers to define who you are or what you choose to practice. They are irrelevant in manifesting the future. Doffing the stigma of paranormal fanaticism means that you refuse to permit others to categorize you by what you have embraced from Heaven. This is what we are doing, doffing any stigma that might be ascribed to you for accepting a faith that cannot be cultured in a petri dish. You are witnessing inside you what doubters and atheists cannot see with their eyes. You are envisioning the purification of a world that will devour the disbelief of those who mock you. My dear little sons, I have seen visions in My lifetime too. I saw them as a Maiden two millennia ago, and I see them yet today. These visions were, and remain, about the coalescence of human holiness and the divinity of Providential Grace. They are about harvesting what you have always asked from life through the promises that Jesus made on the Cross. Persecution is a badge of honor from the secular world. It validates your company with the Holy Spirit. It reveals to the nations that times and places cannot compete with the majesties of the heart. And, when Jesus tells you that your faith is like a cross, that the yoke is easy, that inheriting His redemption is your spiritual fortune, this is your way of doffing the stigma that is heaped upon you by the secular scorners. You must realize that Christianity is not spiritual bondage, it is liberation from that bondage. Moral truth is a vessel in which your righteousness is contained. You have heard more times than you may care to remember that sacrifice is the key to conversion. But, what is actually sacrificed? I choose to see the devotional life as a means of learning the priorities of a sanctified world. My Special son, this is the buffer that your brother was talking about. It is knowing that there is inevitability in all sacred things, and that new beginnings and happy endings are the fruits of letting go. Letting go validates your faith in God and reaffirms your loyalty to Jesus on the Cross. Men and women who espouse what I am saying are set apart from those who deny it. Getting on one's knees in prayer is a means of showing deference to the Thrice-Blessed Godhead; it is not submissive in the way of humiliation, but a gift of worship and promise. Above all things, the Lord is gentle. He will lift you up from the perils of life, even though it seems that He does not spare you from its wickedness at times. He will beckon you to approach Him in prayer and say what you have learned about the Passion and Crucifixion of His Son. Yes, you will see yourselves anew in Him; the whole identity that you inherit from your union with the Victim on the Cross will be clarified to Creation from deep within your souls. It is like the flame on a candle. You cannot see a candle in the dark unless the wick is burning. It is an awareness that your soul is being transformed from mortality into eternal life in what seems no more than a flicker in a world that is filled with such darkness, pain and sorrow.

My Special son, this is how your letters help your Bishop. Remember that no one can see the volume of works that you have handed him and be certain that it is not from the beatific realms. I hold you dearly for writing such an exemplary codex as your first memoir that takes to task all who have protested against the Roman Catholic Church, those who take Jesus' words out of context, and the billions who are treading outright errant paths. Jesus approaches everyone with His arms stretched wide to remove the stigma that comes with everything I am saying here today. He looks with pity on His people; He dispenses nourishment to those who will receive His Holy Spirit. He whispers to the heart with strains of comfort – all the while using His divinity to change the world, to heal, forgive, cleanse and fortify. The graces that pour from Jesus' Most Sacred Heart are too massive to deny; they feed the poor and deliver the forsaken. They are the gift of peace to far-flung warring lands. I ask that you feel the stigma not only removed from your thoughts, but that you would avoid those thoughts from the first. The Love of God is like a seed planted in humanity, but each person must invite Him in. The heart must open like a flower to a bee. It must succumb to the beauty of His Word and respond with an affirmative 'yes.' As your brother told you earlier, I am not capable of anxiety or irrationality, but I am capable of emotion, urgency and courage. I do not wish this urgency to be mistaken for fear; I am not afraid to wait-out My children while they see their way through the fog of exiled life. I have all the time in the world, and everything eternal thereafter. This is what gives Me such true hope. Men, women and children all die; whenever there comes a time, they find their way into the arms of God. Providence and heraldry underscore the course of these events, the complex details of how people choose to live, and what becomes of the heart and its tenacity. I have watched with My hands folded in prayer; and as you and your brother have grown older, you have seen this transition before you. I am elated that you have remained steadfast in your trust in God, that He has ordained for you and your brothers and sisters a religious faith that keeps you going through the most difficult times. So, living day to day is not like a garotte getting tighter around someone's neck; it is the process of loosening it as the days and months pass. Life is not always an uphill battle, it is a slow journey through the valley where the green grass grows. If you could hold human life in your hands, situated in your palms would be a perfect likeness of your sainted self. And, this is the image of Jesus of Nazareth. I repeat today that I am overjoyed that you and your brother have given yourselves to Me. You have not sought fortune or fame, or stockpiles of gold hoarded in warehouse strong boxes. You have given your lives to God who gave your lives to you. And, for this reason, you are highly esteemed; you are adored and admired, you are distinguished and blessed. You are heirs to all the blessings that could find their origin in the God of Abraham's Heart. And, as these heirs, you are united with His Kingdom to come. My Special son, do you have any words to share with your Mother today? *"I pray for Bobby, that he be comforted."* Yes, Bobby will soon suffer his last agony. He has lived a meaningful life, a peaceful and loving life, charitable and humble, holy and pure. He will soon belong to the ages alongside all who have kept their faith alive, who have executed their duties to God with simplicity, who wanted nothing from the world but the opportunity to live in the shadow of the Cross. Thank you and your brother for making My perceptions of the Church and its journey in Jesus such a joy to behold."

Saturday, July 5, 2014
9:20 a.m.

"See the Victim whose Sacrifice has made your peace with God."

"I am elated to be with you this pleasant day, the Day of the Lord. My precious sons, you have seen that what were once obstacles have now become stepping stones to holier things. This has been true throughout the history of the Catholic Church because of humanity's acceptance of Jesus' Passion and Crucifixion, the world's identification with its sacrificial redemption. When a Catholic priest affirms that a community of believers should pray that they see the Victim whose Sacrifice has made their peace with God, he is reechoing the voice of God, Himself. He is speaking on God's behalf to humanity that finds itself the beneficiary of the Sorrowful Crucifixion that often seems so repellent to nonbelievers. Jesus' Sacrifice is not repellant – it is Glory, Truth, Love and Redemption. The Crucifixion is what God's forgiveness looks like. It is more than what you feel when reflecting upon Jesus' Sacrifice in your hearts, it is the extrapolation of Salvation into your time, its meaning to the generations who are only now being told. How can something so sorrowful be so beautiful? The answer lies in understanding what Jesus' Passion and Death brought into the world – forgiveness forever. My Special son, if someone says that they have written a book, but that you are not allowed to read it until you lay on your deathbed, would you forget about it over the years, or would you keep thinking about it until your final hours? *"I would probably be curious about it."* Yes, you are correct. And, it is this curiosity that is felt when people envision Jesus' Crucifixion. This mental image is like a book that reveals in intricate detail the way redemption unfolds. The Crucifixion is the way all human stories end. The human spirit tastes its own destiny during the Holy Sacrifice of the Mass. Compliance with this destiny is foretold in the chapters of the New Covenant. Repentance is seeded within the heart because this savoring of Salvation is too captivating to deny. When you see the Victim whose Sacrifice has made your peace with God, your soul inherits this foretaste of Glory. The Cross is the image of the splendor of Heaven. All the sanctified impulses that you could imagine are imparted by the Crucifixion. Every spiritual discernment required by humanity is found in Jesus' Sacrifice. Every virtuous thought is there; every righteous moral is wholly defended. The splendor of the Crucifixion is where the Father punctuates the world; it is the vessel in which all sacred rituals are conceived. Priests in their youth subconsciously beg for this mark on their souls like a hunger, only satisfied by seeking their vocation. When you spoke about the Great High Priest in your recent letter to your Bishop, you alluded to your Bishop's own transformation from simple Christian to descendant of the Apostles. This is the testament that touched him the most, that you see him as having the esteem of the Apostles. It harkened to his own sacrifices for the Church. He saw in himself the image of the Cross. He knows where the Lord and his destiny will take him. This is the way of all Bishops, of all souls who will judge themselves alongside the life and death of their Savior in Heaven. The image about which I speak sometimes seems confusing when someone just wants to know who Jesus is, but who is fearful when His Spirit responds to the cries of their heart. Fortunately for them, the Lord always gets there first. He declares to sinners that He will lift them up, that He will keep their spirits warm until they can be rescued, but they must stop flailing about as though they will drown in their own mortality. This is the true meaning of letting go. There is a confluence of courage and submission that overwhelms Christians; this is the way humanity attunes itself to the Will of God.

I have for centuries watched this struggle with billions of souls, and this is the fight that each person will undergo when confronted with My messages to you and your brother. They are too massive to be ignored; they are far too beatific to be impugned. Anyone who knows anything about God realizes that you have laid in the hands of the world through your Bishop the supernatural works that will assist in the reorientation of all times and places. I am trying to tell the world that some people see the Crucifixion as a mutating, evolving and ever-changing obstacle to their life's goals. This is because the summons of the Cross has the power to foresee every facet of the mind. However, it is not that the Crucifixion changes, but their ability to envision it matures. It is not that the Holy Cross evolves, but the wisdom of the heart returns one's spirit to its origin in God. This is the heart's ability to recall what was known from its earliest days. This is why Jesus implores His disciples to become like children again, to see something that looks to be ancient as original in their time. Men must fall and be raised up by the Father; this is the way of the world, but it renders the heart as open as a door. And, as modern Saints fall asleep in death when they enter Heaven, they shake off the burdens of the world the moment they die. The ground shudders beneath them as they hand their spirits to the Father. Their legacies leave a triumphant residue on the Earth because of the way they lived. They go onward to their victory beyond the dawn and see what rests behind the image of the splendor of men and their God. They not only see the Crucifixion before their eyes, they taste, touch and savor the Glorious Feast of the Mass, the Thanksgiving Meal, from the other side of time. So, My Special son, My message today is about seeing the Victim whose Sacrifice has made your peace with God. It is My intent to proclaim that seeing the Cross is more than just opening your eyes. It is an image that makes a beatific imprint on the penitent human soul. It is more than a dusking shadow, greater than the reflection of the ages. It is a heartfelt welcome that unites the fragments of human life inside the Sacred Heart of Jesus."

Saturday, July 12, 2014
9:27 a.m.

"The truest and most majestic measure of a man."

"My dear little children, you have said that you are exceedingly aware of your station before God within the Sacred Heart of Jesus, and I am asking the whole world to come to this same realization. And, it is not only your station before God, but in God, within the grace and peace that knows no boundaries. My Special son, as you read your memoir upon having published it, you are now able to objectively see how others will receive it. Yes, it is profound and urging; it replicates the language of the Lord in whom your writings are always inspired. When I speak about the truest and most majestic measure of a man, I refer to this capacity. I give fullest measure of trust and welcome to what you say through the Holy Spirit. I have always told you and your brother that your lives are a prayer for the Church, a blessing to humanity, a reechoing of the life and legacy of Jesus here across these lands. It is more than your lives that you a leading. You are actually making a deposit; you are investing in the future of humanity by granting to the Earth the gift of God's Will to its nations and their peoples. Your entire life has been the ratification of what the Father desires and expects from the times, ages and events beneath His guiding hands. The deposit about which I speak is a sanctifying one. It is a framework of living righteousness that is not just instinctive to you here; it will always be with you beyond the boundaries of the Earth and into the infinite realms of eternity. It is the same concept as someone being unable to un-ring a bell. Once your life has been laid down in time, not just in your passage beyond the beatific vaults, but for all who live and grow to see and judge, you will have fulfilled the meaning of your birth. You are not yet there, for no one is. It is clear that you still have souls to reach and hearts to touch. As unbelievable as it may sound, the true measure of My own majesty is only now being heralded by men, 2,000 years after the utterances of the Archangel Gabriel. Imagine what it feels like to be Me, that I have had the capacity to speak not only to the people of My own earthly time, but to the whole of humanity for centuries since then. This, My little son, is where I have had My greatest impact beyond Jesus' Nativity. It is the role to which I aspire on behalf of the Church. It is the life to which I call My children; there is nothing errant about referring to you as angels and saints; it is not premature to speak of you and your brothers and sisters in such divine epitomes. An analogy might be appropriate here. The Lord is opposed to abortion for the simple reason that new life should never be destroyed; and that left alone, an embryo will become an independent, reasoned, functioning adult. When you see an older person, this is the fulfillment of that intent. The analogy is that this is the way of the converted human soul. Left alone, that maturity in holiness takes on a form itself; it gains the properties of eloquence and stateliness, it is the truest and most majestic measure of a man. It is a sacred deposit; the life of holiness is a boundless blessing to the Creation into which it is born. My Special son, while you cannot yet see it, and no mortal person can see it; human souls have identifying attributes even after they have departed the flesh. There is such thing as an identity to each individual that is likened to anatomical DNA. In other words, there are no generic souls. When you see a group of people assembled a thousand yards away, it is difficult to distinguish one from another. If you looked for somebody in the group, you would be unable to identify the person for whom you are searching. This is not the case in Heaven because there are no dimensions or distances there. It would be like having the ability to look down the road and see someone's soul approaching you from a hundred miles away, with the capacity to know who that person is. This magnifying power is the presence of human divinity that recognizes everything that belongs to the Kingdom of God.

My Special son, this is why I refer to your souls as sacred; they belong to the heralded domain of God inside the perpetuity in which He reigns. Again, this is the analogy between human souls and children in the womb. Left alone by malevolence, souls will gravitate toward Jesus; they will hunger for the new innocence found in Him. Instead of being born into the material world, the soul is reborn into the bliss of His Eternal Kingdom. This is where the Father searches for you. He looks to Jesus as the Gateway to Paradise for those who thirst for His life-giving mercy. And, once His mercy has been dispensed, it is forever preserved. The permanence of Messianic redemption begins on Earth, in these exiled cities that have so often jeopardized their future by refusing to believe. One's sacred identity, the truest and most majestic measure of a man, is defined by his willingness to become a new creature in Jesus, not departing from His side, but standing tall through the Blood of the Cross. When I speak about the DNA of the soul, I am referring to an entire collection, a whole mass of human DNA inside the Man-God. Within Jesus is the assembled identity of every person, stored and nurtured, sustained and adored. While this may seem more elementary than necessary, I promise that the comparison is appropriate. So, when men stand upright and go forward on their march toward Salvation, they must deposit their lives both before the Cross and within it. They must be willing to enter the Wounds of the Messiah for their own good, not to infest His Sacred Body like parasites, but to rest in Him for the sake of their souls. This must be a penetration of the human spirit into the Sacred Heart of the Most High, so much so that the Son pleases the Father, and the Father blesses the Son. The collective heart of exiled humanity must be lanced like the Flesh of its Savior to pour out its love, compassion, prayer and thanksgiving. This is why My intention here is to remind you, My Special son, that the potential that you seek of men is not unrealistic. The strains that you have written in your memoir are attainable in your day. It depends on humanity's decision to deny the forces of the devil in their everyday lives. They need to come to their feet and take into their hands the meaning of their original birth. It is not that men should be thrust into exile that matters the most, far from the presence of the Father, it is about overcoming the temptation to sin that began in the Garden of Eden. It is about rebuking the errors of the Earth, creating it anew through the Chief Shepherd who sets things right, and making way for the spreading of all things holy and true. It is about denying the lures of the flesh, voiding the effects of avarice and greed, and finally handing, once and for all, the destiny of sinners to their God through the Sacraments of the Roman Catholic Church. And in all this, My little sons, the human soul is never left alone. The Father claims you, the Spirit touches you, and the Son redeems you. You have within your reach today to hope and pray into being this newly converted world like a bride on her wedding day, just waiting to be vowed.

The old Earth is groaning and slowly dying; it is on its last leg. We must be pleased about this, not complaining that little is happening to change it. It has taken billions of suns and moons to reach these crucial times. My Special son, the Lord could have placed your soul into the world centuries before you were conceived. You might have been a caveman or an Indian somewhere in the timbers. But, this was not your calling as a vested human being. Instead, your destiny was to be with Me here today, in this place, during this century of centuries, calling My lost children to awaken, summoning their help, invoking their prayers, and soliciting from all well-intentioned people the conscience to make the world a better place for the visitation of God. You have the strength and willingness to achieve what you and your brother, and millions of other Christians, have been commissioned to accomplish. You have been chosen as disciples of these latter times, of these years and decades that will capstone an entire history of human advancement with the most sacred efforts of all. This is why you are a dignified people and a society of enlivened spirits. The entire deliverance of the Earth into the Sacred Heart of God is being culminated in your lives. So here, My Special son, I have explained to you that these are not just ordinary times; these are moments, hours and years that see the simplest notions becoming the most monumental events. We have underscored what your life has been in this place. I pray that you will remember to live in peace, that you will protect yourself from thinking and speaking in unmeasured ways. The world is a mess; there is no doubt that your country is in pain. There is no question that some of your politicians are mean and distasteful folks. This is why you often seem so tired; it is your perception of life and the uncertainties of the embattled world. These issues can be dealt with through the wisdom in your heart. Above all things, do not fret over these difficult times or dignify the devil's attempts to bring you any torment. Do not internalize the impulses that you know will deprive you of your long-deserved sense of wonder. Please understand that I am trying to help you. "*I understand. Thank you.*" I truly admire the letter you have written to Archbishop Lucas in Omaha. Your book will touch his heart."

Sunday, July 20, 2014
9:31 a.m.

"The Reverend Messiah – Jesus the Soul Hoarder."

"My little sons, ponder an image so overwhelming that you could not possibly take it all in. Think about preserving the most awesome sight you have held in your memory to be spontaneously drawn to mind as if new. Jesus has this ability. He can again and again see the faces of the witnesses to His Sorrowful Crucifixion. He can recall their pity, absorb their compassion, and be comforted by their mourning. The essence of such perpetual remembrance began with Jesus. He has been this way ever since His birth about gathering the Father's flock into His embrace, hefting them into Heaven to satisfy the craving of God for the penitent contrite. This Reverend Messiah, the Child of Bethlehem, Jesus of Nazareth, King of kings, this Melody of Love became the Savior of the world at the behest of God's desiring. Jesus not only loves human souls, He pursues them. He chases them down by day and searches them out by night. They suffice His yearning to know that He has rescued lost sinners from the clutches of the devil. Redemption of exiled men is Jesus' Passion. It is His recital of the final repertoire of the Father's symphony. Indeed, if the concept of hoarding has a welcome connotation, Jesus is a Soul Hoarder, the Man-God whose proclivities exceed those of all other living beings. He is inspired in monumental ways by those who simply pronounce His name. He listens for hints of humanity beginning to stir. He rises to His feet when people shout out to Him. He trains His eyes on them as if staring through the darkness; looking, hearing, wondering from where these calls for forgiveness have come. By then, the doorbell to Heaven has been rung. The Father rhetorically inquires who is calling, and Jesus responds that it is Himself, His Only Begotten Son, bearing the fruit of another soul, no longer lost, but found. My Special one, this is the cause of Jesus' joy; it has been the origin of His happiness since His Divine Ascension. With all His concentration poised for Sacred Love, He sets His sights on those who pray. All around the globe, He keeps vigil for those who summon Him. His Peace and Grace are like lighthouses in the night. He knows of His own power. He has exercised His forgiveness billions of times before, but it is all the more fulfilling with each redeemed soul. And, it is not as though Jesus is leading the converted into the teeth of a thunderhead; it is there that Christians gladly bind themselves. The righteous fix their sights thereto; they assemble there in choirs and sing out resurrection songs. Each of them represents another moment for God to say that He loves them, that He knows they have given themselves to Christ Jesus beyond the lineages of time. Yes, the Father's Beloved Son has a penchant for the pursuit of all who preceded Him on the Earth and who have succeeded His Crucifixion since. God always tells Jesus, '...There, go yonder. Go where you may not suspect them to be. Uplift the ones who do not receive their dignity because their faith is disbelieved.' And, the Soul Hoarder knows what to do. He has taken residence within you now. Jesus' Spirit is tethered to your soul, listening to what I am saying at this moment in time. You can feel Him there, He is your wherewithal, His Spirit is your tenacity, His holiness is your arsenal. As much as the safeguard walks through the night, Jesus senses your fears and lends you the defenses to be unafraid. He gives men the courage to fight the good fight, but the valor must come from them.

God has inspired them through their Savior to become savers in their own right; not saviors, but savers. It is in this purpose that disciples like you and your brother have come of age in knowing what must happen before Jesus comes in Glory; it is the sanctification of the Earth. And, what form does this sanctification take? – just as Jesus is the Victim on the Cross, humanity must be victims of His holiness. Men must be cleansed and purged; souls must be scrubbed and polished. It must be done by loyal supplication. Flesh must be mortified; injustices must be annulled, wrongs must be righted; darkness must be cast out, not like the dawn slowly breaking, but like a mammoth explosion of enlightenment that startles even the most piously prayerful. If death comes like a thief in the night, new life comes in promises fulfilled. Here, you and I know that forgiveness far outweighs condemnation. Jesus is not an impartial jurist; He always rules in favor of the penitent. His anger lasts but a moment, and His Mercy goes on forever. Thus, standing tall before the created realms, in every man with the conscience to know, is forgiveness and the capacity to share it. I have told you of the power of God in you; it is prayer. And, with this power, pardoning is now far flung. The world of belief in miracles ensues. The Crown of My Queenship is the pinnacle that men must strive to see before they die. The Sacrifice that stands before you now, this elegant sign that men belong to God, is forever a forward-thinking gift of the new awareness that is handed to those who seek redemption. All the dangers you might possibly imagine could never hamper this brand of joy. No chains are strong enough to hold back the hopes of those who have set their sights on the Cross. And, even though there will always be time for eloquent speeches, there need not be too many when contemplating the Lord's Kingdom to come. Why? Because the Salvation of the world almost speaks for itself. In all that comes to mind about what the next life will be, the hopes of the beholder are too important to dismiss. Yes, we have said that Heaven holds everything you ever wanted in this life, that it will be yours in full measure, but there is more to the New Covenant than this. Heaven will give you all the dimensions that your exile has stripped from you here. It will transform your hopes for redemption from one silent imagining to an infinite universe of glory. Within your 'being' will be new creations strewn with justice, harvests that keep on giving, smiles that never vanish, laughter to rival little children, and fellowship with all the historic legends you ever wanted to meet. There will be rainbows aplenty, robust celebrations, endless exultation, rhythm when you want it; colors and heights, toasts and banquets, and never again a negative word. There will be no hint of rejection, not a whiff of human vanity; only gladness, light and song, a new beginning overflowing with friendship and accord.

My Special son, all these blessings emerge from the image that I spoke about of the Wonderful Counselor, of the phonics of a transformed language that makes the world say, '...Jesus come get me!' Yes, and there shall He be. The Soul Hoarder striking again, reaching out, kneeling down and lifting up, arms opened wide and palms outstretched, never holding back the tears of joy that He has been waiting to shed since the Father placed Him in My Womb. It was not that He cried at birth because He knew that He was exiled, because He was assuredly not. No, Jesus cried upon His birth because He thought 33 years would be much too long, that it was even a second too far in time before never again would a tortured humanity have to face the fate of being banished into Hell. It was His own image in His own mind that He thought would be too distant in coming. This is the image that He has given to you, the image that all men have if only they will open their hearts. My Special son, the word I am looking for is 'reckoning.' What you see in your soul is the culmination of a lifetime of belief that Salvation should come to the just and condemnation meted out to the wicked. If there were not two sides to this prospect, for what would good men strive? This is why there are choices ahead, roads that diverge, minds taking different turns, contradicting decisions to make, and a vast contrast between knowing right from wrong. The saintly man to whom the Lord gave you as father to son, the elder William Roth who visited this home yesterday, has been the beginning of your obedient faith; not its origin, but the source of your discipline within it. He has been your mentor in all good things; through the intercession of the Holy Spirit, he has done his best. The world is filled with elders like him who, just like you and your brother, wonder why so many young people choose to ignore the promises of faith and the pledges that God puts before them. Never mind, Jesus says. He will reach out to them anyway. Kneeling before the Cross in prayer is man's acceptance of that faith. And, if those bound for Heaven cannot find their way to kneel of their own accord, the

Father will take them to their knees. Make no mistake about it; they will thank Him in the end. At the last, it is the will of men that determines their future. God can help them, He can show them an image of themselves, He can lay their lives alongside the suffering of His Son. He can force them to make this comparison without them even knowing He is doing it. Beyond the Nativity of Jesus, My purpose in this world has been a fostering one, to warn My children what lies ahead. You and your brother have not only committed yourselves to helping Me, you have given the Father reason to bear compassion for the wicked men whom He might not otherwise absolve. He has witnessed His own divine likeness in you. He knows your intentions, your assimilation into His presence, and your desire to find victory on His behalf. Everything that you ever hoped the Father would do to change the Earth is steadily on its way. He knows that Jesus hungers for souls, and He wants to feed His Child. He is poised for the Immaculate Triumph that you and I have prayed to have in hand. The truth is Jesus transfixed to the Cross; you can see the expungement of human sin there with your eyes. My Special son, you are as pretty as a sunrise. *"Thank you, Mama. I am your child. How could I not be?"* I am grateful that you have given yourself to Me. You have said that you would '...go to Jesus through Mary' and this is the Will of the Father speaking through your own voice. So, bask in the brilliance of your achievements! Hear Me now, and hold it true – you have suffered for the good of this cause. You have kept your innocence that you never once lost. I think about your college years, when you worked and studied so hard, when you provided a venue for the Holy Spirit in your words and deeds, when you fed Jesus' desire to pour out your heart to your friends and enemies too, when you stood up and dared the world to dampen your hopes and dreams. Alleluia! You are living this way still. You have within you the spirit of peace and joy; it will be there on the last day too. Everything will be repaid a millionfold by the Man-God on the Cross, knowing that you have been His companion through this world and the next. His Kingdom, grace and guiding hands are touching you now. Thank you for your prayers. I hear every word you say; Jesus hears them too. I shall bless all the children who are coming into your nation from the south. Please pray for them as well."

Saturday, July 26, 2014
9:28 a.m.

"The rationale for harmony in the divine order."

"My precious sons, there is a ligature encircling the lives of Americans who refuse to pray, cutting off their friendship with God. You are breathing-in His Love because of your devotion to Me and your dedication to Jesus' Most Sacred Heart. This is your rationale for living in peaceful accord in the divine order to which you are consecrated. You are attuned to making the Earth like Heaven. You are seeing, listening and heeding; calling and acting, and giving meaning to the summons that renders humanity whole. It is clear that God's Peace and Grace are inspiriting your hearts. When I say that you 'touch' God, I am referring to your unity with Him in your perseverance in all that He wills and allows. In other words, you are more than just affiliated with the Blessed Trinity, you are, through the Second Person, an innate part of God's divinity that Jesus shares with you. There is no doubt that this shall come because the Mystical Body will live with the Father, Son and Holy Spirit in Paradise. As you know, you are more than born of your parents here, you are commissioned to propagate the Kingdom of Truth and Light that is eclipsing the land of your birth. Your acceptance of this fact is seen by the spiritual expression of your souls. And, how do you effect this Kingdom? It is not complicated at all; you fight for what you believe in, and you do not surrender what God wants you to achieve in Him. My children, you have this in common with Jesus. And, not only that, you hold in common with Him the ways you interpret what other people do. You are aware of the trials and tribulations that humanity endures to foster into being the holy excellence to which Jesus' Most Sacred Heart has always been given. This is the reciprocal nature of your lives in Jesus; it is His way of ratifying what you do in His name. Hence, whatever you bind through the Church on Earth shall be bound in Heaven. This is what prayer is for; it is what all good works procure. The next thing that must be done for those who believe, My little sons, is that they must see themselves entering the picture of what you have already witnessed with your eyes of faith. You have joined the inevitability of the Lord's Judgement through your consecration to My Most Immaculate Heart. This is not new to you. It is as though you could stand up and travel about in your own sense of awareness, in your acceptance of the Dominion of God within the exiled world. However, your brothers and sisters, most of them, perceive God as though they are looking at a picture on a wall. They see themselves stationed in another place, exiled for certain, incapable of slightly internalizing what it means to participate in this scene of ordination, in this manifestation of glorious life prior to the death of the flesh. This occurs because of the sins of men. All the poignance and ugliness, the sadness and disorder, the nightmares and violence are the result of humanity holding out from entering the domain of the picture on the wall. Billions of souls do not even know it is there because their focus is directed somewhere else, on some distraction, on issues that will evaporate once the final dawn arrives. And, all the beauty that they would see remains waiting for them there. Behold! – this beauty is no less majestic just because it is not being seen. This beauty waits to be solicited; it is like a treasure trove prepared to be discovered. My Special son, you and I know what those who deny the existence of God will eventually realize. We must pray that they will accept Jesus' Sacrifice when it comes their hour to see Him. They will say that they declined to enter the picture because the Father did not call out their names. Human life is that call.

The questions of mortal men about their origin and well-being, their fate and destiny are sown within them from the Garden of Eden. This was the first moral battlefield. It was where good and ill-intentioned human decisions and actions first came into being. The New Eve who is speaking to you now, the Mother of Jesus Christ, has given you messages that will direct the attention of nonbelievers to the vision they require to repent and convert. This need not be a chastening experience; truly it should not be, if those who must be touched will not deflect the overtures that the Father has put into place. You and your brother have spoken resplendently about your own experiences with Me. You have been honest about what rejection means, and how pleased you are not to be caught up in the calamities of the times. You have led a conventional life in this home. You pray in earnest, live peacefully when you allow yourselves to do so, and shut out the ugliness that is wreaking such havoc on other people's lives. You have stepped off the earthen floor and allowed your spirits to be unified with the ethereal tranquility of Providential Peace that will someday engulf the entirety of Creation. It is as though the Father is pointing the focus of His entire 'being' in your direction, and you are projecting your lives back to Him. This is your acknowledgment that the development and expiration of the world are ongoing, that the process still unfolds, and you and the Lord will see each other face-to-face once the commotion stops. This is the winking sensation between you and Jesus that occurs between friends, as though you are saying hello to them, and you will talk with them in person when the work is done. The passages of life are composed of these things. Of course, there is no distance between you and Jesus. You are not passing in a crowd, and your awareness leads you to see that there is much more to accomplish. You and all who belong to the

Church remain here working in His vineyard. There will be breaks and lulls; there always are, but there are also rifts of intense toil and spiritual heaviness. When someone says that they feel lighthearted, they are referring to their unity with the Will of God. It is a function of acceptance that emphasizes the empathy that He has with the human condition. Complaining may do little when falling on the ears of mortal men, but God hears your pleas. He declares in the quietness of the breeze that He asks for your understanding in the purification of the Earth. My Special son, your brother recently said that he believes that God cares more about the preservation of the human will than the preservation of human life. This is a curious thought, but your brother was incomplete in his statement. The Father wants an absolute alliance between the human will and His Divine Will. Once this has taken place, human life and eternal joy will be conjoined at their most essential point. Adam and Eve marred the souls of all who succeeded them, but the Sacrament of Baptism and the Blood of Jesus on the Cross have replaced these stains with marks of grace. Sadly, however, the will of wicked men still breeds error. The will was sullied by Adam and Eve, but it remains a blessing for those who convert.

    All God is asking is that humanity deploys its best intentions against evil. He wants the Church to help eradicate the malevolent forces that have plagued the nations for centuries. This is what the Father means when He asks His people to be upright. He wants His disciples to recognize their own spiritual stature, to embrace and share what He dictates to them in His stead, and to grow righteousness on the Earth like a billion beds of flowers. I have told you on prior occasions that if this were not possible, exiled men would not have been asked to try. When the collective souls of men set out to do it; once this commitment has been made, the lifeblood of righteousness on the Earth will flow. Material goods will fall from rich men's hands like coals from a fire. Heads will turn to the beauty of the heavens as though men cannot keep from looking to the skies. My Special son, our role has been facilitating this process in the way of the Saints. For every Saint Aquinas or Saint Augustine, there is a Saint William and Saint Timothy; and for every Mary of Bethlehem, there is a Saint Joan of Arc. We have lived a lifetime in your earthly years. We have seen new lights shine and rose petals falling from midair. We have tapped our feet to rhythmic dawns and dusks that said goodnight. The real point is that these things have meant something; they mean something still. There is imminence in each passing hour. There is new growth and maturity, but these things are not running from humanity as if becoming smaller on the horizon. They are evidence that the Kingdom of God is here. Whatever goes away is replaced by something else; but in this case, it is the permanent Kingdom of the Son of the Most High. All the energies of Nature are captured in the Savior of the world. I am not saying that He is not here now, for His Spirit surely prevails. I am saying that He will be welcomed Body and Spirit before the last sundown falls away. The fullness of Eternal Dawn is the goal for these exiled realms. You and your brother have already pierced the veil with your hearts. You know that there must be a symmetry between Heaven and Earth that is not yet close to being formed. The grand inclusion of Heaven and Earth must begin with the exclusion of everything malevolent that could make itself known before the innocence of men. Here, I have given you some profound wisdom that must be imparted to those who refuse to believe, and your life with your brother has been that revelation. You have lived in accord with this harmony; you have provided for its rationale, you have placed yourselves in the position to see the divine order of God's prevalence without departing your home. So, while other men are wondering why their vision is being blocked; while they are trying to decide what their ligatures are doing to their souls, you are living the freedom that they are yearning to attain. They will eventually get there, My Special son; we shall see that they do. I respect and admire you along the same lines as My Messianic Son. You are holy, strong, powerful, unique and identified with the genius of the Church. Your life has poise, reach and promise; you are brightly shining as the sun. This is why I do not believe that you realize the power of your prayers. Take confidence in yourself, in your ability to make decisions, in your grasp on the signs of the ages, your inheritance from the Holy Spirit, and your knowledge about what the Father seeks from His Creation. I am simply requesting that you take upon yourself your own awareness of who you are in the Father's eyes. Your petitions show overwhelming foresight. Know that the Lord holds dominion over this world, that He is aware of everything for which you pray. I will intercede for you before the King of kings."

Sunday, August 3, 2014
9:27 a.m.

"Brother of poets, friend to the angels;
the Prince becomes the Master."

"My darling little sons, you are the face of faithfulness; history kneels at your feet. I hold you as reverential exemplars for the blessings you have gifted to humanity and the Church, to God in Heaven, to those who would not have known Divine Love if not for your prayers. I have trumpeted your capacity for saintliness, and I have given you reason to believe that you are already there. I am not saying that you will never make mistakes. I do not imply that you are incapable of sin. I am pledging that you have within you the foundation for making decisions based on the graces given you upon your baptism. The title of today's message is again about Jesus. He is all things to all people. He has within Himself the ability to resuscitate the bellows of time, to flood the years with joy, and to assert to humanity what shall be judged right and wrong in the eyes of God. What does it mean to be the brother of poets? How can one be friend to the angels? How can the Prince become the Master? My children, it is about miraculous truth. It is about transcending the flesh by resetting one's priorities. You have known that poets can relate in metaphoric rhymes what cannot be captured in prose. Jesus' parables are among the first poetry ever written. They soothe the hearts of those who hear them; they call out the lost to be redeemed in His Crucifixion. This is to the elation of God and the angels. Like you have become, Jesus was before you the first friend of the angels, and they gather at your doorstep to herald His Kingdom. My Special son, you and your brother have said that age is no presumption of wisdom, and youth does not imply indiscretion. You see reason and prudence in Jesus, even from a Child. He is present in every man with the willingness to hear, those who will listen, those who know the difference between having life and rightly living it. The poetic verses of the Lord's New Covenant are found in the things you do for Him while not counting the cost, never looking over your shoulders to see who might be shadowing you, never minding what you could have been doing instead. This is instilling the thesis of truth in the rest of the world from the seed of your hearts; it is the origin of your prestige. My Special son, this is the translation that your brother mentioned moments before I began My message today. There are questions that must be answered, key ones, evocative ones, that seek the motivations of men regarding their perception of the Sacrifice of Jesus. This is the way human life discovers its unity with Heaven. Today, I remind you of the Holy Spirit dwelling in you; the Spirit is calling you to peace here at home, at your workplace, and anywhere you go. There are frameworks that help you deal with other people; the truest are in the Bible, others are in your life experiences; and more are addressed, although insufficiently, in your socialized customs that you practice every day. I ask you and your brother to remember that all these things are situated beneath Jesus' guiding hands. He has given them to you for your facility, for you to realize that no issues are un-addressable when placing them in the context of His ministry. Yes, you are somewhat tending to children at your workplace; this is the persona of the position you hold. I would like to expound upon what this means. It is like what the Father sees when He hears disagreements between His disciples on Earth, the elders of the Church, those responsible for antipoverty programs, and the many who boast of the echelons of their own better angels.

There will always be human dissension as long as the world goes on. This is not the problem. The problem comes when this dissension inhibits the spreading of the Gospel. It is a problem when missions remain incomplete. You have seen disagreements your entire life. Many are the stories that you have heard about dissension between the Saints. God does not mind this; it is indicative of getting things right. Reasonable men, goal-oriented men, find a way to achieve their objectives not by ready compromise, but by sharing in the debates that illustrate the contrasts of the task. This is what moving forward means. And, history has proved this to be a gift. Holy men of old worked out solutions to problems that would surface in latter times so their descendants would not retrace their errors. Can a contingent of Saints reach an amicable conclusion? Of course they can. The point is that this must be done within the halls of spiritual wisdom, with righteous passion and not unchecked anger. I am describing what God can do through those who hold themselves loyal to His Son. Remember Saint Joan of Arc! My Special one, this is how the Prince became the Master. If Jesus would have struck down everyone who offended Him, there would not have been a sinner left standing. If He had spent His lifetime dodging men's rhetorical punches, He would have had little time for preaching. Vengeance and reciprocity were not important to Him because He kept His eyes focused on the treasure of souls. The Prince became the Master because the Father believed in Him. God knew that His youth would not become an obstacle to His Wisdom. This is why you could see Jesus walking to the marketplace at sixteen years old and having the presence of a prophet. He blessed the ground with grace, and the ground blessed Him back. This is how you and your brother walk among your fellow men. It is obvious when you are seen in public places and sanctuaries. This is the way I see you. It is not that you are performing on a stage; you are part of the texture, watching and evaluating what the world is doing. They see you there; the Father sees you there. It is clear that you have learned everything I have taught you about modesty. You are not offended when your enemies mock you or speak ill of you in the newspapers; it has happened many times before. You are confident that your work is having its intended effect. Your books are giving the leaders of the Church pause to consider why the Mother of Jesus has come to visit someone in their flock with mystical graces.

It is not so much that they do not believe what you are saying, it is that they cannot find any precedent for it. They have never seen My manifestations occur like this anywhere in the world. Place yourselves in their shoes. They have been given enough messages from the Mother of God for a thousand lifetimes in thirteen published books. I have said more to you in those books than they have recorded for all My private revelations combined, thousands of times more voluminous. This is extremely difficult for them to comprehend against the history of the Church. What I am saying is that I am not blaming them for being rather reserved to see My presence here. I am, however, laying responsibility upon them for not knowing that the Father can do anything He pleases without their permission. After all, they should remember that it was their faithless forebears who burned Joan of Arc at the stake. My Special son, you recently referred to the sensation where your eyes seem to be deceiving you, like when the basketball player broke his leg. You had the same feeling when the airplanes struck the World Trade Center towers. This is very much like what those who have seen My messages are feeling when trying to make sense of what they have read. I have given you so much content, so many miracles, so many lessons and parables, and so much proven dedication by the two of you that those whose eyes it passes can scarcely take it in. Most are lost for words, including many of the leaders of My Son's Church. Many are trying to help, but some cannot overcome themselves, their sense of conservation of the rigidity of the Church, their penchant for believing that miracles do more harm to the faith of the Church than good. They are afraid that parishioners will set aside the Scriptures and focus their attention on Me. I disagree with those who fear these things. And, this is part of the dissension that I have spoken about in My message here today. Will it matter at the last? Not really. I will prevail. The miracles handed to you will be known to the four corners of the globe. The Morning Star Over America will not be hidden out of sight, beyond the view of sinners, by any man attempting to create artificial clouds to keep them from seeing Me. The breath of God will blow them all away. It is a matter of inevitable truth that everything that you and your brother have done will be part of the Triumph of My Immaculate Heart that will prevent billions of sinners from choosing Hell as their final destiny. I ask you and your brother to rest peacefully in this knowledge. There is nothing that any man can do to impede the progress of the Mother of God. Hence, I bid you to be confident in what I have said we will do here together. It is more than My messages; it is reaching out to humanity in a way that leads the leaders of the Church. These are historic times. I am praying for all the causes that are dear to your heart. I am with you every second of every hour of every day, listening and learning from the blessings you display. I hold you in such high esteem that it would be difficult for those poets to write it into their rhythmic romances. Thank you for your prayers. I will speak to you again soon, bringing the infinite depths of My Sacred Love."

There stands a battle-scarred and honorable warship refurbished and refitted by the mystical refinement of the Queen of Martyrs. It rests proudly at attention, its appointments gently tilted to the heavens and glistening in the sun, bearing on skids in that shipyard, beckoning to be christened with the hopes of a broken humanity. It bears in its rivets and the stresses of its steel the purpose of conversion and redemption. The memories of its mighty victories in time echo through its passageways and corridors; its bulkheads cry out, "Let us go forth again; christen us anew, grant us the commission to engage the battle of free men and righteous causes; honor us with conscription into the glories of Thy Cross to cleanse the Earth of despots and demons who bring damnation to men and grief to the mothers of our progeny all." There She stands in the Light of Victory looming! Where are you, eminences, excellencies, dignitaries and officials? Do you skulk in cowardice, afraid to gavel the champagne of mankind's dreams against its steel-cut bow, fearing your mighty ship might glide down that causeway and sink beneath the fathoms to her doom? Oh, that you would see that this mighty warship will hit those waves like the shores striking back to confine the churning tides. Oh, that the clap of righteousness might strike and your ears be graced with general quarters sounding across the decks and reverberating like rolling thunder between the cliff-lined channels that mark her path. Oh, that your eyes would see through your tears the bow of Reckoning turning like a titan into the desolate winds of wretchedness, serving notice to the ages that this offensive voyage into the theaters of sin will obliterate evil from the history of humankind through the valiant sacrifice of Christianity's saintly shipmen.

Sunday, August 10, 2014
8:47 a.m.

"Surveying the fundamentals of the human condition."

"Now, dear little children, this morning is the making of My joy because I have the opportunity to speak to you again, to make clear the loyalty of God to your hearts and souls, and to remind you that your prayers are sufficing the amendments that the world so desperately needs. When I am pleased, Jesus is pleased. When I am happy, Jesus searches the Earth to discover the reasons why. Today marks another milestone for transforming the world because you are another day closer to the redemption of all departed souls on the last day. I have spoken to you about images in your hearts of the way you want human life to be, and this is reflective of My own prayers and visions. When we speak about the human condition, it need not be about a condition where something is lacking.

I believe that humanity is in good condition. The world itself is a wreck, but God's creatures have all the instruments they require to survive and succeed. There are gifts aplenty to make your way to the Eternal Gate. There is bountiful beauty within and around you. My little sons, many people do not understand the happiness that comes from knowing that the Lord created them. He set them on a path down which they can fashion their own future, enhance their dignity, and deal with their talents in all ways that portend the best for their lives. This is why I say that surveying the fundamentals of the human condition includes all the good things, everything that increases your stature before the Father despite the failings of the world. There is innocence all around you. There is innocence inside you! What has not been touched by human sin is as pristine as the day the Father brought it into being. What has escaped the stain of ill-gotten devices, what yet remains in its virgin form is evidence that the Lord has vested humanity with His own divinity. I look at My exiled children with eyes of compassion not just because you suffer, but because many sinners do not understand the meaning of suffering. Looking upward into the skies for one's connection to God is always a good thing, but it is better to search for Him from within, with one's eyes intently focused on the blessings that I have mentioned today. The word that best describes the elegance of the human heart saturated with the grace of the Lord is 'stunning.' Why is this so? Because My children are so awesome to behold when given to the Cross that they cannot help but shine. Innocence overwhelms the human spirit that has been touched by the Spirit of God. Scenes of common life seem brilliantly new. Whatever gives and receives love has a purpose because it is offered for the finishing of the Earth in the Gospel of Jesus Christ. And, you and your brother will be even more surprised to know what I am giving to the Church and its redemption before you shall pass into Jesus' arms in Heaven. There are plenteous gifts graced to all who are consecrated to My Immaculate Heart. These gifts shall be realized; it is promised, and it will happen. Every time I say something new that you internalize with your hearts, Jesus ratifies your lives in ways not known to many mortal men. There is a quiet grandness that overcomes your journey through life, one that holds you as if in a bassinet. It is your way of knowing that you are blessed both through time and outside of its realms. My Special son, your practice of looking at My messages from 2010 to the present means that you still have hope for the transformation of the Earth into the likeness of Heaven. The visionary messages that I have offered are profound, but they are not as profound as your willingness to pray with Me to receive them. You may do with these messages whatever you please. They are not meant for public consumption unless you wish to reveal them. They can be transferred into other contexts according to your discernment.

As you know, My messages, all of them, are gifts to you and your brother from the Sacred Heart of Jesus through Me. And, do you know why? Because you are so good. Humanity is good. Your appealing presence is a delight for the Father. You are realizing your potential to hold things fast in this life that He will hold fast in Heaven. This is the power of His Triune Love prospering through your faith in Him and your role as a disciple. Looking with one's eyes is not necessarily 'seeing,' but looking with the heart has permeating vision. It is deep, thoughtful and meaningful. It is a sight that cannot be appreciated by making rapid judgements about how you feel once you see it. It is a sight that augments what your faith dictates that the world should look like. This is the penetrating 'vista' of the Holy Spirit that has engulfed and inspired you. My Special son, there are glorious days ahead for the Church. Jesus will not allow His Mystical Body to fail. There is no doubt that men will suffer, but they will not fall victim to extinction before the end of the world. The worst suffering humanity endures in these times is self-inflicted. It shows the vastness of the divide between men's corruption and God's righteousness. And, the only way to bridge this chasm is for men to be holy in the image of Jesus. Holiness is the antidote for a lack of righteousness. This is why I declare that humanity is good. It is not good because it is already righteous, but men have the capacity to be holy; even wretched men have the ability to be good. Righteousness can vanquish unrighteousness with one sincere 'Our Father, who art in Heaven.' Good men can do this, and great men are being made better men because they are responding to My call. My little son, do you remember how delicate young foals appear when you see them in the pasture? *"Yes."* This is how God sees those who are only now coming to Him. They are skittish and often unwitting to the dangers that lie ahead. Well, Jesus transforms these little creatures into tremendous stallions, with power and confidence they could never have known without Him. And like these young horses, converted men become wise in holiness; they grow the Kingdom of righteousness even when they are unaware of the effects of their own acts. They are essentially just being who they are, allowing the consequences and benefits to fall where they may. This is much the same as you and your brother. You are gifting God with so many blessings in this world that He continues to construct a proper response. This does not mean that you will not eventually know. These things will come to you here in this life, and others will be there for your inheritance in the bounty of Heaven. It does not matter which it will be. You are already hailed in the Mansions where your forefathers have gone. This should be sufficient accolades for any Saints-in-waiting! What I am saying is that you are amending the face of the globe and codifying the divine writs of Heaven by simply giving your lives to Jesus. This is another reason that you are good. My purpose here today is to lift you up by saying that God sees you as equally innocent as those foals and rearing stallions. You are filled with the goodness that you are dispensing into His Creation every day. And, what are those colossal princely horses that you sometimes see? Yes, Clydesdales. Imagine what they must think when they prance around with such stately steps, when they assure everyone near them that they will be as gentle as any creature might expect to be. Yes, it is much like one of those Clydesdales walking the woods and seeing a deer in the line of a hunter's fire. 'Where is the bullet,' he might inquire. And, when seeing it, he runs into its path and takes it on the hide; not a piercing arrow, not a lance, but something as obscene as a slug from a gun barrel. 'No problem here,' he declares. He is just fine in the end, and the deer runs off to rejoin his friends. These are the imaginings that you are allowing the Father to feel. This is the strength that He has ingrained in you, even as you are in your heart as gentle as a lamb. You are good, and greatness exudes from you. Your soul is marked with the eminence of a Saint. All you and your brother, and all who believe in Jesus, are waiting for is the transfer of your exile into the presence of the Lord. You need not wait until that day to confess the excellence that you are already practicing. My little son, I offer you My holy blessing, and I will bless your family with good tidings. Thank you for your prayers. I love you!"

Sunday, August 17, 2014
9:39 a.m.

"By the expression on their faces."

"Now, little sons, we have the joy of praying with the anticipation that the Almighty Father will respond to our intercessions. I wish you all the peace and happiness that Heaven has to offer as I come to you today. It is not that I only see mirth before Me, for there are plenty of tragedies to count, but that all gladness and elation are personified by Jesus here in this world. My children, as you see the passing of so many souls into the spiritual realms, feel good that they have been brought into the Land of Light. There is nothing worse than a death that has not been preceded by faith. You are given this faith by the Father's hand, directly from His Heart, and from the prayers of all who have exalted Him throughout the ages. They intercede for you now; they ask God to strengthen your faith in the same way that their forebears prayed for them. This multi-generational cascade of petitions has not only changed the world, it has supplanted it with the prefigured succession of the glorious world to come. How do I know that My children are eager to meet the Father in Heaven? I can see it on their faces. The Lord instills this anticipation in you. He looks down upon you from His Kingdom in Heaven with pity and sympathy, with admiration and exculpation. God stands above you and yet beside you as you tread the stepping stones of everyday life. Today, I have the Saints you know with Me, and they are watching what I do from My side here in Heaven. They see what you have seen from the other side of life and time. Yes, I have with Me today your family friend, Saint Mary Margaret Anderson, whose suffering brought tremendous healing to millions who are sufficing their own imitation of Jesus' agony on the Cross. All around Me, the souls of the Saints sing in joy, reverberating through the Father's House, delighting the Angelic Hosts, and resounding the melodies of love that began long before they died. I speak of them not in sadness that they departed the world, but in thanksgiving that Jesus has delivered them into the presence of the Father. The whole transition into glory is made possible by faith and suffering – they are inseparable. And, this unity must be recognized as such; it must be accepted and immortalized at the center of the human heart. My Special son, I have said that men create unnecessary battles that are either won or lost. We choose instead to dwell on the peace that surrounds you. We excel in accentuating the things that make God pleased to be the world's Patriarch. There is tremendous responsibility in having faith because faith dictates conduct that accompanies the drive toward righteousness. I have told you that spiritual faith keeps you young. It is a way of recognizing that everything about your soul is new, no matter how many hours, months or years pass by. This has always been the underpinning of My messages. Your souls belong to God, and are therefore ageless in themselves. This is the tenor of your being. The content of your heart when given to the Father is replete with vast youthful innocence. You have spiritual vigor that cannot be exhausted when you consider what your faith has wrought. When you see little girls and boys frolicking down the street or tumbling playfully in the park, this is the way the Father sees those who belong to Him. He keeps your spirits aloft and your hearts young because He believes in the newness of your souls that cannot be aged by the perpetuity of eternity. I have been told by many Saints that the most intriguing part of immortality is that nothing is affected by the continuation of infinity. There are no cycles that come and go; there is no linear time in Heaven. All is utter oneness and unity. The whole concept of eternity is derived from the fact that measurements of time serve no purpose there. As I say, this is the most compelling facet of entering Heaven because being affected by time is the only thing humanity in exile can use to measure their lives. So, when I say that I can see on the faces of My children their expectations of eternal joy, it is their acknowledgment that the happiness they desire is capturable by the faith they embrace.

My Special son, you and I know that somebody has to place that look of gladness on their faces. This is the gift of the Holy Spirit in the human heart. You can see this blessing being dispensed by the hand of the Father; through Him, with Him, and in Him humanity walks with confidence. Graces shower down from Paradise and wash away all shades of sadness like raindrops falling from the skies. If the Holy Spirit takes residence inside the human heart, it is recognizable on the face of the believer. This is what Jesus meant when He told His Apostles that the world would know who they were. He did not say that they would not be persecuted or martyred, for this is what comes from the application of faith. If you think about facial expressions, they can in general reveal what someone is thinking. If someone is angry, you can see it in their eyes. If they are sad, their frowns expose their sorrow. When a person laughs, you can see it through their wincing eyes. Sometimes tears accompany sorrow and laughter too. This is a means of discerning the content of the heart, and it translates into actions and reactions that can also be seen by others. The point I am making is that My children must allow God to touch their faces from the inside out. They must be willing to allow the spirit of faith to shape how they feel. It is never hidden under a bushel basket if one is devoted to Jesus. This is why you receive Holy Communion with your face tilted back and your love outstretched. You are saying to the Most Blessed Trinity that you are open to receive the Manna from Heaven that makes the heart a holier place. This is your Thanksgiving Meal that connects you with the Lord in Heaven. It is the place where Divine Flesh touches penitent mortal flesh in a bond of perfection that precedes the redemption of the soul. My Special son, you should see the look on the Father's face as He watches you and your brother living your lives! He knows that you are changing the Earth for the better. You are recording His strains of righteousness for billions of souls to hear. You have never laid aside your holiness in favor of some other goal. Indeed, you are still with Me today, and I am with you so you can celebrate the New Kingdom that God has deposited within you. Yes, it is all about the youth of your soul that has been redeemed by the Child in the Manger. My Special son, do you have anything to ask Me today? *"Why do so many people have such difficulty responding to you? How do they mistake faithlessness for prudence?"* The answer to your question is that they wait for more urgent circumstances to arise, and we will accommodate them. In addition, some so-called private revelations have in fact proven to be false. Many have seen these things, as they have throughout the centuries, but cannot discern the difference between authentic revelations and corrupt ones because they are unwilling to reserve time for the sacrificial elements of their faith. Others believe that private messages, even authentic ones, hinder rather than augment mystical faith. Verily, this is an incorrect assumption. It is the way of the world; as I recently said, remember that Saint Joan of Arc died at the hands of the faithful. And, when we speak of the irony of ironies, some Catholics reject My messages and use their devotion to Me to justify it. I am not offended. My sympathy is not lessened. I feel sorry for the way they will eventually regret their reticence."

Sunday, August 24, 2014
9:22 a.m.

"The sonnet, the citadel, the artworks; it all happened on your watch. Go let them smell the Eucharist on your breath!"

"My little children, your prayers invigorate My hopes that all the world will turn to Jesus for guidance and accept His Blood as their Salvation. Thank you for embracing My Queenship with such devotion, such consecration, and such consolation for My Immaculate Heart. You see My opening words today that celebrate what humanity has done to make the world a better place. All the imaginings that have shaped your lives have advanced the dignity of the human race and preserved for posterity the righteousness that is being won. Sonnets, citadels and artworks are the remnants of your forebears' lives. And, they are your prayers as well for those who have loved Jesus' Kingdom, indeed your gift to yourselves to offer Jesus when you see Him in Heaven. You have in your hands the blessings from the Father that you carry through the years. Once a Roman Catholic receives the Holy Eucharist during First Communion, this sweet fragrance remains on his breath for the rest of his life. This too is your legacy for those whom you meet for decades hence. I have spoken about the expression on your faces, and today I am referring to the darling of your palate, the Most Blessed Sacrament, that fills the world with love as you travel through life. I speak of the sonnets that you write through your unity with the Holy Spirit, the citadels you erect to safeguard your faith, and the artworks you give to Jesus and humanity for their reflection in recognizing the providence of the Father within you. My Special son, when I speak of artworks, I refer to the ways that good men manifest the Messianic New Covenant across the nations. You yourselves are works of art, and you are beautiful to behold. You sing the songs of perseverance; your carols regale the constancy of love. You write the lyrics to sound the Truth of the Cross where you walk. You thrive on common piety and mysticism too. You instill in others the courage to go on. And, you spread these inviolate virtues from your hearts into ordinary places that make others want to be like you. I said earlier, My Special son, that the condition of the Earth would be as it is during these present times. Jesus foretold it. The Gospel predicted it, and the Scriptures are being fulfilled. Toward the goal of teaching you what the Father wills and allows, I am urged to tell you today that something occurred with an American journalist in recent days, an event that I was not permitted to see. I am telling you this to share with you how the Father protects My dignity. I know that this comes as no surprise, but I am confirming what you have previously known. I wish to ensure your dignity as the Father preserves Mine. Conversely, I am gifted with visions of those First Communions about which I speak, of the lilies in the fields, of birthday parties and weddings, of children being born, and the Sacred Sacraments that take all believers to the gates of Paradise. I ask that you focus on what you know to be true, based on the splendor inside your heart. I have spoken of potential and accomplishments, about images and expressions, and today, about the fruits of your artworks that are commissioned to satisfy the obligations of your faith. Do you recall the maxim that is often spoken by wise men around the globe? – 'believe none of what you hear, and only half of what you see.' While this is exaggerated, it speaks to the proneness of impious human beings to lead lives that they have created for the advancement of themselves. They do not dwell on the Gospel Truth handed down throughout the ages by the Church. And, it is by this striking contrast that you can tell the sheep from the goats. You and your brother are the living, breathing excellence of the Kingdom of the Father here in an exile that is well served by your prayers.

My Special son, more must be done to protect the esteem of the Roman Catholic Church. Its detractors and adversaries cast off its teachings because they seem not as inclusive as the masses would have them be. This is because the Church refuses to accept sinful ideologies in its definition of inclusion. I am not telling you anything new today. The evils of secularism are at one of their worst points in history; the influence of wealth is one of its most ungodly results. How did it happen that so much money has been accumulated in so few hands? It is the work of the devil. There is a surplus of poverty! And, this is the focus of our prayers here today. Even as I speak about the sonnets and citadels of good and decent men, other men stain the continents of the world with their own vile acts. They are devious and deceptive; they are ruthless and cunning. This is the reason that I dwell on the artworks of bright and shining souls who belong to the Messiah of the Church. I could speak all day about the evils surrounding My children, but I would rather recount your blessings, inspire your courage, and train your attention on the sacramental bounties of your own best intentions. There are grotesque sights everywhere you look, but they should be judged for what they are. I choose to focus on people who are propagating the Gospel to anyone who will hear. I am still trying because God says that we will succeed. While He shields My Most Immaculate Heart from exposure to many corrupt acts of His creatures, He gives Me the pleasure of knowing what you and your brother do, what all My children do who are given to My Son during their lives. And, this is why I am here. It is the reason I am hopeful, a hope that is replicated by the hope living in you. It is the hope with which you rise from your slumber every morning. I watch this anticipation living within you. I see the vigor of your hearts. I look into your eyes and see your acceptance of what any given day may bring. And, most of all, I see your determination to amend what must be changed through the resiliency of your prayers. This is the innovation of your wisdom in the themes of righteousness. My Special son, there will be many more times of joy to come. You will bask in Jesus' Light; you are reflecting His Light from your souls into the heavens like starbursts in the night. The journalist that I mentioned came to Me with rosary in hand, saying that he offered his last breaths pronouncing My name, and he was saved. He was saved because he believed not only in Jesus' Blood on the Cross, but in My determination to lead him there. And, My Special son, this union of child and Mother, this meeting of sinner and Savior was worth all that preceded it. This happens at every moment during this period prior to the Second Coming of the Son of Man. He only asks that the world strive to reach out to Him, invoke His name, accept His Sacrifice, and imitate His life. Evil is never justified anywhere inside or outside Creation, and I can attest that evil will not escape its inexorable final demise. You are living on a battlefield that determines who, by their self-identity, fights for good, and who fights for their iniquitous ways. The earthen floor is the arena on which this battle rages. All the gratitude in the world, every form of thankfulness and approbation could not capture the Lord's love for those who believe in Him. He is triumphing in His apostles and disciples. His life is exemplified by Christians such as you. This is where His Spirit chooses to reside – within you, through your prayers and acts of faith, along with those good wishes that you heap upon all with the resolution to stand strong for the Cross. My Special son, I have concluded My message for today; do you have anything to discuss? *"Just that I am reviewing your messages from 2010 and 2011, and they are so beautiful."* You should always remember that I gave them to you because you are more beautiful than any words I might share. *"Thank you, Mama."* I told you that My messages after December 28, 2008 would be as inspiring as any before them. I hold in My Most Immaculate Heart all the dreams and aspirations that you harbor for the completion of your work in bringing peace to those who do God's bidding. Thank you for your sacrifices."

Sunday, August 31, 2014
9:36 a.m.

"Just as iron sharpens iron,
a man sharpens the countenance of his brother." (Prov. 27:17)

"My dear sons, glorious streams of heavenly love are pouring forth upon you now. The sacred divinity of God is present in you, and His grace clothes you in His holiness. You are sanctioned to do His Will like all the great Saints, Popes and Apostles so humanity will come running like children into the arms of their Savior. My little ones, along with your Bishop, you are held in utmost privilege by the Father, the Son, and the Holy Spirit. You are elevated and admired. It is the honor of Jesus to embrace you. You have heard the Biblical passage from Proverbs that identifies what your lives mean to the world. Touching, enlightening, sharing, motivating and brandishing the Gospel against those who would deny human souls access to the Sacrifice of the Cross. I have said that there are insufficient words that can describe your station in Heaven, but I am trying. I am doing My best to help you understand your stature, that it is your willingness to build up the Kingdom of Love that makes you so endearing. You surely realize that none of this has been easy for you. It is clear that you have been despised and rejected; this is in fulfillment of the Scriptures. Truly, wherever the Scriptures are fulfilled, life begins anew. The reciprocity between Heaven and Earth is at its highest when men defer to the Will of the Father over their own. My Special one, we have discussed what this means in the arena of human endeavors, together with the expectations of the excelling human spirit. When iron sharpens other iron, when swords and knives cross not for bloodshed, but for enhancing their own potency, this is the touch of preparation for the cruel battles ahead. They are not battles of men against men, but of goodness against evil. I have said many times that the real issues of human conversion are founded here. Satan tries to divide men one from another and create the illusion that the fight must not be against him. He attempts to inject a false divergence into the battle that does not exist. Evil takes advantage of the fact that human beings are weak and temptable, that they can be lured by monetary gain and corruption of the flesh. My Special son, your prayers and the prayers of all the faithful are revealing the devil's ruses to those who do not understand them. This is the enlightenment about which we speak. When good men teach other men what they should know about the New Covenant, this is the propagation of the Lord's Kingdom into places it has never been spread. Iron sharpening iron means that young men inherit the pieties of their fathers. It means that they become aware of their own part in the mission of the Church. It tells them that they must stand tall and righteously proud of being Christians, of what their role is in purifying the Earth. There are multiple dimensions to this process. Times, seasons and years contribute to the growth of the Christian identity. Suffering and failures line the hallways of this undertaking. Before someone can know other people, he should have full awareness of himself. He must light his own conscience with self-edifying fires. He has to know what Jesus mandated from the Cross. Some men spend their lifetimes tending to this task before they have time to reach out to anyone else; they expire from the Earth after leading solitary lives. This is not what Jesus expects from those who embrace His ministry. It does not mean that you must knock down marketplace doors or crash the gates at city hall. It means that you must make the Kingdom of God so attractive that marketplaces and governments no longer have luster.

Why do so many sinners who extol the Christian life want to be elevated in public stature? It surely cannot be to make the secular void more like God's Kingdom. After all, half of American Roman Catholics believe that women should have the right to kill unborn children in the womb. And, these Roman Catholics seek public office to defend this so-called right, to reenforce laws to ensure that unborn children are, in fact, killed. My Special son, these are the same sinners who have defied My messages for the past 2,000 years. They are terrified that they might not be in control. It is unacceptable to them that they defer to the Lord whom they cannot yet see. And, My little son, these are the same sinners whose pride has been inflated by the temptations of the devil. You hear about them every day. My role as their Mother is to rebuke them, to reorient their preferences to the teachings of the Church. This is the reason we pray here, why we speak with such solemnity about the changes that must come. The solvency of the human conscience depends on what we ask the Father to do. As I have said, this is not a hopeless matter; all Christians have the capacity to do something about it. It is not just an urgent matter, for these changes will ultimately come. But, it is a corrective matter, a measure that will open the spiritual eyes of those who are on their journey to Hell. There is no great mystery in what our prayers must do. Humanity is behaving as though the world is more cultivated than it has really become. Even if another 10,000 years should pass before the Second Coming of Jesus, mortal creatures must evolve into the sacred humanity that God has asked them to be. Otherwise, new generations will come and go; they will live and die just as the plants and animals who cannot deign for themselves a benevolent way of living. I have said that the maturity that Jesus seeks is based on what the Father requires of those who believe in Him. He is the God of Abraham and Isaac. There is no other god than Him. There cannot even be the thought of God that has not been threaded through the lives of Abraham, Moses and Jesus. Long ago, in centuries past, Jesus said that if any men attempt to worship false gods, if they pursue some sort of feigned divinity in a deity that is not rooted in His Truth, then they will fight just to be fighting; they will battle only against themselves. They will become the scourge of the Earth and the new enemies of the Cross. Here in this 21st century, you have seen what Jesus meant. Look and behold, they then turn against the Spirit of the true and living God by claiming that His Kingdom is no more than another ideology, some philosophical construct contained in a book that can be laid on a shelf. My Special son, this is the evil against which the Catholic Church is fighting. As I say, you and your brother are officers in My Army of Faith. You are children of the great and only God, brothers of the Solitary Warrior who has won the battle for lost sinners. You are decorated by the King of kings; you have been knighted by the Holy Spirit to serve in the ways that you have chosen. You are truer than any lies that held Jesus' body to the Cross. Your intentions are purer than the driven snow. You are gentle to the touch of Jesus' Mighty Heart. You are more revealing than all the signs of Nature and the cosmos combined. You give Jesus the consolation that He deserved during His Agony in the Garden. You quenched His thirst for comfort on the Cross of Mounty Calvary. He focused His eyes on you and your brother that day, and all who would accept His miracles 2,000 years later. This, My Special son, is your heartfelt gift for the lives and times of the world, for enlightenment and conversion, for humanity to finally see itself as it will be judged on its last opportunity to change.

You and your brother are like fine sharpening tools for the consciences of sinners who must convert. This does not make you coarse or rough, not like grinding stones or sanding paper. It makes you sharp and shining, like the stars in the night, bright and proper, prepared for the worst of battles during the best of times. I ask you to go onward as you have always borne yourselves, and remember your sanctity in Jesus. Expect those manifest abruptions about which we have spoken. Never once surrender to despondence or despair. Be patient while the Father redraws the boundaries of His Creation. And most of all, remain with Me throughout all times and ages, no matter what trials might come. I ask you, your brother, and the Church to remember that there will be great manifestations occur in the swiftly approaching years. The face of the Earth will take on radical changes. Older souls will pass into the Kingdom of the

Father. However, the flag of human redemption will unfurl, given steadfastness by My messages worldwide, and brought stately into the breezes by the provident breath of God. It is true that the content of some of My revelatory messages around the globe is contingent on the prayers of the Church. Some prophecies are amended, and others even averted by the petitions and intercessions that God welcomes into His realms. But, the main point is that the whole matter is complete, in its finest form, by the vision that Jesus had in His Heart when He proclaimed from the Cross that, '...It is finished.' Everything you are seeing through these fateful days is shaping the world into that vision. It cannot be preempted by anything opposing it. And, it can only be brought more clearly into the awareness of men through the recitation of their prayers. This is the image that supersedes all other sights. This is like looking at the location of a treasure on a map. It is the same as someone gaining their sight after 80 years of blindness. Indeed, it is as though a person is seeing a light shining from above into a mineshaft into which they fell six months earlier. You and your brother, and the Church Militant, have not yet seen this vision with the clarity of the Church in Heaven, but you are among the few who realize that it exists. Others do not know to search for it because they lack the faith to believe that Jesus manifested it on the Cross. '...It is finished...' means more than it was Jesus' time to die. And, it is billions of times greater than the fact that He killed Satan outright by His Passion and Death. '...It is finished...' means that death will be no more for those who accept what Jesus has done. It means the end of the legacy of Old Adam and the commencement of the Kingdom of the New. It has always meant that I would come to you and your brother in the pitch darkness of a cold February night in the final decade of the 20th century to speak well into the 21st. My Special son, this is the reason I feel so honored to be here this morning. It was fashioned from the moment I saw My Son surrender His life for the redemption of the world. My presence with you and your brother is more than paradisial, it is prophetic for the deliverance of the dead into the realms of the living. It is the transforming of lifelessness into a new birth of eternity. It is cause for earthbound men to burn their calendars, stop numbering the days, and focus on sharing eternity with the Father. Yes, My presence here is a means for the world to know that raining down upon them now is a plenary absolution that renders them clean of iniquity – not just a reprieve from their sentence, but the permanent expungement of all guilt. This is what the eternal record will reveal; it is certain and inevitable. Please remember that you are constantly under the guidance and protection of Jesus of Nazareth and Me, Mary the Queen Mother of God. I love you!"

Sunday, September 7, 2014
4:00 p.m.

"Gracious Jesus, in whom all eternal forgiveness rests, we beseech your protection during our lifelong endeavors. We ask that you shield us from harm; be our sentinel against the wiles and wickedness of the world. Subdue the forces that would have us forsake our heavenly fortune in you. Grant us the gift of answered prayers throughout our lives, and be for your faithful flock every mercy and pardon we shall ever need. Be our advocate before the Father as in the beginning, and welcome our pleas for good health and joy. We ask this through Christ, Our Lord. Amen."

- William L. Roth

"Today, My little children, it is My tremendous joy to remind you that good fortune belongs to those who trust in Jesus. We have in our grasp the conversion of the multitudes because the overarching power of the Cross has taken residence in you. You belong to Jesus not as property, but as apostles. I am with you briefly today to bridge the past week with this week, to reassure you that the Providence of the Lord's Kingdom surrounds and engulfs you. It is not as though the Afterlife is made of particles like atoms or molecules, but that your soul is filled with spiritual truth from the inside out. You are brilliant like Jesus because you are disposed to His Wisdom. You pray to make things come to Earth that exist in Heaven. You hold in your hands the advancement of men and the passing ages toward the eternal reckoning that the world will soon realize. Thank you, My little sons, for participating in this miracle. And, bless you too for the pretty petition with which you opened My message today. Jesus protects those who take refuge in Him, those who do not treat Him as an afterthought once the terrible tragedies have come. We are a proactive and preemptive people in God; we take to Jesus our concerns that shape the Earth like Heaven in real time, before souls become ensnared in the traps of devilish works. Also, My Special son, you must know that I am propagating the gifts that so many faithful Christians have offered the Church to brighten the lives of those held in darkness, to change the course where innocent victims suffer, and to grow the Gospel into quarters where Jesus is rejected. The offspring of your petitions will mature in your faith. The rest of the world should learn to trust Jesus the way you have trusted, to find their confidence in Him, to stake their fortune in His promises, and align themselves in the future He has laid out. I wish you all the goodness and happiness that could possibly be gifted to a sorrow-weary world. When we pray together for the sinners in your midst, we remake their paths; we reorient their lives to the mission of the Church. We help them see before they open their eyes. We rebuke the evil deeds of Satan and block his path from corrupting unwary human hearts. We know that these are worthy honors. They have come because you have given your 'fiat' to the Mother of Jesus – Praise be to God! As I say, I wish to speak briefly here today because this is sometimes what I do. You and your brother have been giving your honest efforts toward leading your lives with passion for the purification of your nation and the Earth. I cannot make it any clearer than to say that the echoes of your prayers are like massive ocean waves. And, I thank you. The Lord your Shepherd thanks you even more. My Special son, please remember how devotional you are, how tenderly you comfort the Sacred Heart of Jesus, and how fortunate you have become to lead the Church's charge against the indifference of this world."

Saturday, September 13, 2014
9:49 a.m.

"May your kindness, O' Lord, be upon us who have put our hope in you."
- Psalm 33:22

"My precious little sons, you are leading lives of masterful relevance, and your prayers are effecting the changes that the world requires to repent. I wish deeply in My Immaculate Heart that I could explain every bold facet involved in the purification of the Earth, but many are far too intense, too ethereal, too cultivating to put into words. This is the reason Jesus often spoke in parables. Mental images are profoundly more illustrative than mere linguistic phrases. The thoughts, feelings and emotions that help humanity know the Will of the Father are best learned through personal experience, by empirical patience in bearing through the ages of life. This is why I have said that your eloquence is sometimes better expressed by your actions, by your wordless but thoughtful human endeavors, and by the meditations of your hearts. My Special son, the overwhelming purpose of My vast apparitions and messages to you and your brother is allowing you to understand the ways in which the Father looks upon Creation. All of your works, every word in your diaries and anthologies, every preface and prologue – these are the fruits of your prayers in envisioning what Jesus wants His apostles to do. You have accepted and processed His Will for humanity by giving your hearts, lives and intentions to Me. Jesus will come to places where the Dove of Peace is permitted to light, and He has done so here. He has arrived in My holy arms of His own accord. Why? Because the Most

Blessed Trinity is drawn to itself; it is attracted by everything sacred to see an image of Triumphant Love. This is the place where the Father comes to see a reflection of Himself. This is the essential identity of your oneness with Jesus on the Cross. And, it is your prayer to Heaven in return. It is evidence of your love and admiration for Me, the Mother of the Church, the Matriarch of the entire framework of human redemption. My little sons, I have spoken about the permeating power and the presence of the Holy Spirit in many venues and contexts. What is coming to you is new life; it is a pattern of new beginnings that supplants the outdated architecture of the exiled world. You have learned that the Lord wishes to fashion these realms after Himself, to manifest peace and good will worldwide, the same peace and accord that reign within Jesus in Paradise. I am not foretelling that your exile will look like Heaven before Jesus comes again, but it has the potential to be. I am saying that the Holy Paraclete can bring humanity an olive branch from the Land of the Living to prove that a life of righteousness is wholly sparing; it is a premonition not of damnation, but of true renewal and reward. This is not just one olive branch carried by a single dove; it is the entire forestry of graces and blessings that the Son of Man has to offer. Humanity should realize that God will not do things wrong just to induce the world to do things right. It is not about showing the Church so much evil that its own holiness looks immaculate by comparison. The Father does not create evil acts or impulses. Wicked men spread evil; it is those who reject the teachings of the Church that bring sorrow into the world. The Father watches this transpire not in awe, but in saturating sympathy. It is shocking to see how corrupt human beings can be. The most hurtful sorrow is that sin leads to more sin. Yes, corruption is a product of sin, not the reverse. Some people become so anaesthetized by their lack of holiness that sin comes naturally to them. They see no immediate consequences for their wrongdoing, and they calculate that nobody in this world or the next cares what they do. As we know, they are only deluding themselves.

The Lord God has brought a fresh new beginning to the entire concept of life through the Crucifixion of Christ Jesus. This is from where the seed of newness grows. When implanted at the center of the human heart, the Spirit of God finds a place to help men regain the purity that was lost by Adam in the Garden. This is the furrow in which the conversion of sinful men takes root. And, it is the difficult cultivation of this environment that you and your brother encounter every day. Just as the soil is laid bare before the open skies, the lives of human beings are exhumed from beneath decades and generations of man's sin and indifference. I am pleased that the Father has not given up on this redemptive gift because it will finally yield the fruit that He has intended. There is no barrenness in the world that cannot be given purpose by His seed of new life. Indeed, by all means, the Church can see this growth with its own eyes. There is evidence aplenty that holiness and righteousness are taking root in places that would otherwise not speak one syllable of beatific oration. What do you suppose a good word would be to define an environment where this conversion is possible? What do you call ground that is fit for planting? *"Fertile."* Yes, this is what humanity has become in the Sacrifice of Jesus on the Cross. And, this fertility implies the same thing as the nutrients in the soil from which heapfulls of harvests can grow. I am saying that the hearts and souls of men must become this fertile. It is yielded from the breakdown of the material world and shoring up the potential of men to carry out their allegiance to the New Covenant Gospel. My Special son, this must be done through the destruction of everything that impedes the mission of the Church. And, as you know, these obstacles do not move aside lightly; they do not succumb to the power of the Cross without a fight. Hence, you are seeing this fight being waged around the globe. It has been this way since the birth of the Messiah. Jesus' Nativity was like an inoculation to the Earth, but all the evil forces in the world have been trying to build up an abominable resistance against the Salvation of lost sinners ever since. I am saying today that there should be no obstruction to the redemption of penitent souls in the Father's presence. Even as you are watching the march of the ages unfold that the Angels told your brother about, these are auspicious times that portend the Second Coming of the Benevolent High Priest who has promised to return. Of course, there are pains, mourning and sorrow; there is no doubt that faith requires an unalloyed assembling of trust. But, this is what the rise of the human spirit is about. There are heavenly battalions charging gates everywhere on the Earth that are unknown to humanity. There are blitzes, forays, onslaughts and incursions that will not be revealed until the last day of the world. There are conceptions and expirations too numerous to count. But, these things are not really the point; they have never been the reason why God sent His Son into the created realms to die. The entire matter is a spiritual manifestation that is imbedded in sacrificial acts. This is how faith is accompanied by good works. True faith is capitalized by the thoughts, decisions and actions that Christians choose to ordain. This is the reason that I so strongly denounced those who committed terrorism in My September 16, 2001 condoling message to you, your brother, and the world. So here, I am elated by your anticipation of the success of the Church and its ultimate victory in eradicating the evil that you see every day. You are to be commended for trusting that God will guide you through these times. Jesus stands beside those who rise in honor of His Name. He looks through their eyes and sees the plight of the Earth. He shapes the values of His disciples who realize what God wants the Church to accomplish. They are His most compelling instruments, just as the Saints have said. God has given humanity a religious zeal that can be felt by the human heart and shaped into recognizable form by the touch of Christian hands. This is what you and your brother are doing. You have inherited the tools from your bygone forebears to continue their virtuous love, to craft the world and its expiring ages into its most appealing self. You and your brother have lived brilliantly for Jesus and Me, and I will give you a special blessing on the occasion of your birthday next week. I hold in My Most Immaculate Heart all the petitions that you offer in your prayers. I give them to Jesus who hears them as you speak."

Saturday, September 20, 2014
Happy Birthday, William!
9:22 a.m.

"It is here we must begin to seek the wisdom of the children."

- John Denver (1943-1997)

"Age 53. This is when the singer whose lyrics you see here today came to Heaven, when he was 53 years old. My Special son, even as you are also 53 years old, I ask you to live long and prosperously on behalf of this singer. Live the years that he was denied. I have come with the sweetness and divineness of My Immaculate Heart to wish you and your brother well on the occasion of your birthday, and to raise your heart above the workplace difficulties that are grieving you. You are taking the divisions much too personally and seriously. They have no bearing on what we are doing together. Please, on My pleading request, do not allow the sins of others to take away your joy. Do not allow them to steal the gladness of your life with your brother; do not permit them to douse the supernal exhilaration that you have found in Jesus. I am not asking you to prioritize these problems or even compartmentalize them. I am saying that they are not consequential at all; you are making them worse by focusing on them. This is what your brother has done to his own happiness at times; it is impractical and unproductive. Here today, I am imploring you not to do it anymore. I bring you the intense elation of the heavens and the blessings that all men should seek. I hold in My embracing arms the Jewel of Redemption that the Father has given you, to all who seek forgiveness for their sins and omissions, to anyone who bows their head to pray. I often speak, My Special son, about your innocence and the grace of your own charitable heart. This is what I choose to dwell upon because they are eternal. I am overjoyed that you have taken on the vestment of pious prayer, but it is liberating as well. Your prayerful life brings shades of peace and good will where they are needed. It is as though you have elevated yourself above the world and are blessing all who believe in Jesus. Men should not hold mortality in their laps as though it is a life-crushing burden. You see and think clearly, and your hope is founded on the gifts that you have in your hands right now, along with those for which you still deign to pray. I have always prompted you and your brother to see life as Jesus sees it. There need not be darkness; you are not called to take seriously every brash moment or event. You are not expected to have an opinion about everything that happens. You need not judge every slight, thought and action against your sense of emotion. Most things need not be justified this way. There are endless speeches and reams of paperwork that are not even worthy of mentioning in your daily breaths of life. Do not lend legitimacy to lies and distractions by dwelling on them. You are not mandated to detail their lack of merit. There are some things that Jesus simply does not have opinions about because they have not reached a point of relevance within or without the gates of His Kingdom. I give you My assurance that this is true. So today, I have come to accentuate the positive fruits of the Cross and the Resurrection of My Son. I come with a blending of the casual with the supernatural to remind you that your life is a miracle in itself. We hold deep inside our hearts unbounded affection for all who are working in the Lord's vineyard for the refinement of humanity and the advancement of the mission of the Church. These are grand days of unparalleled enrichment. We need not focus on the unspeakable evils that are persecuting the Lord's Church and attempting to take its faith away from Him. Our cause is to uplift in our prayers all who stand and fight, those who do not cringe when they hear an occasional sour note, the millions who struggle against sophistry, illness, poverty and disease, all who are given to the Commandments and uphold them despite their enemies' lies.

Yes, and even as these things carry on largely unnoticed by the secular void, we adhere to the Peace of the Holy Spirit; we respond to the calling of the softness of the Most Blessed Trinity in whom the exiled world procures its angelic comfort. And, there we have found one another. There is no division here; there is no discomfort or allowance for disgust or disdain. We are united by the charisma of the Divine Kingdom in which you believe and are already inheriting. I reign as Queen of this Kingdom. I know that you are aware of what awaits you there, all the glory and tidings that will comfort you beyond any comprehension of what eternity means. This is My birthday message for you today, that you will retrain your eyes on the joys of your life and refocus your energies on taking care of yourself. For some reason, there are people who believe that they must always have something to worry about, something that overwhelms them and fills up their hours with cautioning. This is not the way of the children. Remember the lyrics that I began with today. It is here, at this point in time and location in the world, that humanity must begin to seek the wisdom of the children. This is where the Dove of Peace will come. It is not in the idolatry of the world's fashions and whims. It will not be found in believing that every day must be worked to complete exhaustion. These are not the things of innocence. What you must look for is the depths and solace at the center of your own heart, where you will find Jesus waiting for you there. My Special son, human happiness is in the here and now because the Holy Spirit is perpetually yours. Of course it will be more beautiful in Heaven; this is not My point. I am saying that you have laid claim to the independent spirit of righteous joy since the moment of your baptism. Everything that impacts Americans is meant to bring down the poor and raise up the wealthy. This is the devil's work that never seems to go away. There is prejudice and bigotry against people like you and your brother every day of the world, but these evils do not matter; they have no effect if you place no stock in their forcefulness. What your brother has been facing since he graduated the university in May 2013 is almost too gruesome to describe. Satan has been waging a war against his dignity that would take a lesser man down. Again, this is not the point; it is not about how much opposition someone faces, but how much ground can be covered toward the purpose of purifying the Earth. You can see that this is happening with surveyable advancement. All who are destined for Hell seem to be in the middle of their heyday, and this means that the night is nearing its reckoning dawn. Those who will claim for themselves the flames of Gehenna have already set themselves on fire. They are embroiled in their own demise. Their consciences are as dead as their future will be. And, My Special son, they are creatures who will never be united with the faith to which you have devoted the meaning of your life. They are filled with hatred and the spiritual disease of atheism and the rejection of the Love of God. These evildoers are bereft of goodness and light; they reject the wisdom of the children that I have spoken about today. They are finishers of the devil's work, and will spend the fullness of time beside him, agonizing in the blazing flames. They declined to seek the wisdom of the children when it came their time to act. They rejected God and rejoiced in their own pride. I do not want these creatures anywhere near My innocent children or the beauty of the Church.

My Special son, I am speaking again today about envisioning what the world will look like someday when everything about it becomes as filled with holiness as you and Me. It is not beyond the realms of possibility, you know. This is what must come; it is foretold in the Scriptures. It is what the Father wills for the Church and His Creation. If they all love like you, My Special son, it will happen soon. If they defer to the Savior of men as you have paid Him homage through your 53 years today, then all that is right will be posed for that final photograph that I told you about years ago. Creation is still getting there; you must believe that it is. There have always been wars; there are still wars and insurrections, but we do not dwell on them much. We choose instead to remain thoughtful of the New Earth to come, when everything about human life turns to the way you want it to be. This is a gift that will be given not only to you, but to everyone who holds fast to their trust in Jesus. Good men come and go; the bad ones die too, but all in all, you have a victory in the Man from Galilee that you can begin celebrating today. I am not speaking in delusional terms about possibilities that are too hypothetical to occur. I am referring to the only reality that matters to holy men like you and all who have passed into history to receive their eternal reward. This is the gladness that is of old, of the new birth that comes with remembering the promises of God through the Son. If you hold in your heart all the things that I have shared with you today, then you will overcome the saddening events of this world. You will smile as I have smiled; you will find an entire ovation of approval from the Hosts of Heaven to you here in this land, thanking you for being steadfast in God's sacred love. I touch you as Jesus touches you, and I pray for your strength and perseverance. I plead for you to maintain your perspective, despite the dailiness of life. My Special son, masses and waves of humanity have been born unto the Earth and transitioned onto the glorious plains with these thoughts in mind. Thank you for standing with your brother through all these times. No two human beings could be better friends. "*I love him, and I know he loves me. That makes us one here in this life.*" This, My Special son, has caused the manifesting of My messages here. I hope you enjoy your birthday and the upcoming months and years with the same gladness that I came dispensing to you this morning. It is you who decide what your daily invocations will be. I admire your ability to judge wisely the things of the world. You are mature in your faith, and you do indeed espouse the wisdom of the children."

Saturday, September 27, 2014
9:12 a.m.

"You have the right to say – This is not how the story will end."

"My precious children, you have faithfully joined Me again this morning for the bestowing of human redemption. Yes, we will pray as none others have prayed, rightly through your wisdom as the Lord's disciples, and different in your time because you have not surrendered hope that all things blessed will culminate in the Absolution of the Cross. Too many ages before you conceded to despair and their own impatience. This is not the case with you. There is no dimming the light in your hearts! You pray with Me because you believe in miracles; you have within your grasp the knowledge that God can change the fate of the Earth in an instant. Imagine all who have seen My face for the first time, even the Medjugorje children who had to shake themselves to determine if they were dreaming. Such times are manifest abruptions where the Father intercedes both sightfully and tangibly. And, it is in your faith that He has found beauty like the stars and moons. He has discovered through your lives a means of reaching those who will not believe that He is reigning. This, My children, is the reason I always come in thanksgiving. I ask you to disregard the distractions that have consumed the rest of the world. Never mind the evil holding a grip on your brothers and sisters; your prayers will release the grip, and Jesus will expunge the evil. I have said in My introduction today that you have the right to say that this is not how the story will end. What I mean is not just that your prayers can liberate the world from the devil and that Jesus will eradicate the horrendous effects of evil, but that you can assist in writing the script and postscript for the remainder of the years. You are creators, writers and sharers of the most beatific eloquence that the world has ever known. You do this by accepting your part in the sanctification that must come. You carry your portion of suffering. You assign meaning to your sacrifices by placing them before Jesus' Crucifixion. There is no rising from the dead until death itself dies. There cannot be a mission to cleanse the Earth unless there is a reason for the cultivation. And, the reason is to make way for eternal life; all grains of wheat must fall to the ground. All this seems deeply burdensome to the Church, but it is providentially evocative to God. And, My Special son, all My visionaries who have prayed with Me, all who have collected My words in written diaries, each and every seer and hearer has come to Me with stories of gratitude for what I have done, not realizing that they were the heroes. It has never been a challenge to appear to My children; it is an indescribable delight. The true challenge is for these same children, including you and your brother, to go about your lives knowing that the larger meaning of life in many others is not being fulfilled. This is what you were saying to your brother last evening. And, it is not the way I wish for you to perceive your lives in Jesus. Imagine what Jesus had to endure coming to the exile of men once He was old enough to interact with them. He knew from a child that He was not with the Father in Heaven. His mental images were like those you described to your brother during dinner last evening. And, the difference is that Jesus felt alone; there is only one of Him. He did not want His disciples to be alone, so He fashioned a plan where they would be sent into the world two-by-two. They were never meant to feel isolated, just the pairing of them, but to embark on evangelizing their missions to unite humanity with them. Even these disciples would serve in collegial capacities with the same people they were seeking to convert. This was the interweaving growth of the Church into the corners of the globe.

The manifest issue with them is what I alluded to moments ago. They began to see the world as a mechanical device, a physical mass separated from the Kingdom of Heaven. All along, however, Jesus was telling them that even as they sought His Kingdom, they should realize that His Kingdom had come to them. It is coming still. In the process of securing this pious intent, mortal men have believed that they have become separated from those who have not yet come to know the Will of God in the way that I have shared with you and your brother. And, what have been the drawbacks of this? The first is that the secular void seems wholly impenetrable, that it cannot be changed. One of the second things that arises is that even the most contemplative disciples cannot reach the same meditative state in some settings, including the Holy Sacrifice of the Mass, as when seeing Me or hearing My voice by locution. When I say that Jesus does not want this to happen, I am echoing the Scriptures. He went where He could find new converts at the same time He was asking through the Holy Spirit for Christians to be cloistered in seminaries and convents. I realize that this seems a contradiction, but these conditions exist to this day. So, what do I mean that you have the right to say how the story will end? It is not complicated at all. You have a vision in your heart that I have described in previous weeks to be more than an image. It is not just an elusive hope in the aft chambers of your soul. Jesus feels what you think. Yes, as if to touch your thoughts, He connects with your vision of how He should complete the Earth. This collation of prayers through the centuries was placed into His thoughts on the Cross by the pains of His suffering. We are shaping this collation right now. Here, as we are praying and speaking, we are inside the mind of Jesus as He was dying on Good Friday. You are there now, as was I. And, we are here on this day as at that hour twenty centuries ago. When Jesus looked into the darkness that afternoon, He looked upon the darkness of the present day and saw you breaking as the dawn to make way for His Kingdom. This is what makes you stallions rather than mules. It makes you eagles in flight instead of reptiles crawling on the ground. You are standing on your feet and elevating everything that Jesus ever meant to the Father into larger form, diminishing the forces of the world, and enhancing everything that sanctifies the Church He came to redeem. It is a way of leading lives of saints before the last day of the Earth, before your own mortality arrives, before the Final Judgement is rendered, before any more evil can be perpetrated around the nations, before any more innocents will suffer at the hands of the devil, prowling the Earth seeking the ruin of souls. There are fulcrums occurring around the globe that are tilting humanity's exile to its final resting place. Imagine it; an American citizen is beheaded on your homeland soil in the name of a false religion. My Special son, do you remember when I told you that those who are bound for Hell are already setting themselves on fire? *"Yes."* This is one such example. As dastardly as that deed was, it will manifest a true moment toward the defeat of everything contrary to God. It was such a shocking manifestation to decent people everywhere that it will speed up the transformation for which you have been praying.

As I said last week, I also dwell on the holiness that is overwhelming the world. It is leading to more prayer! I look into innocent faces and smile with assurance that the Father's love has overcome it all. I allow you to rise before My Immaculate Heart and tell Me that you have ideas for the preservation of everything dignified. Jesus has placed these images in you. Your wisdom and loving accord for the faith that you serve are nourishing and comforting to God. We are speaking about Jesus' thoughts on the Cross again. The Holy Spirit beckons you to believe that all the outcomes of life are simple backdrops behind the Lord's glorious grace. If you are disenchanted by dull homilies and boring speeches, remember that this is an awakening for your heart. Take joy in knowing that you feel closer to God than you did in your more tender years. Think about what you might say during any given homily if offered the venue, and write it down later when you get home. My Special son, you have seen in nearly every recent message that I have given in Medjugorje that My children should pray for the Lord's shepherds. This is My way of saying that they need the strength and vision that I have given you. I am asking for prayers that they will offer the Holy Sacrifice of the Mass with such sanctity that they would be nearly in tears. I am praying that the Lord will fill them with the eloquence to reflect My most prolific messages to you. It seems that the rest is according to their thoughts and actions; they must be open to receiving the fruits of our prayers. Everything the Church will ever accomplish can be scripted by those who pray. You have the right to say that the world need not end this way. It need not be left in shambles with its sacred relics desecrated and stockpiled in scattered smoldering rubbles. I can sum My message to you today as follows. Humanity should never surrender hope for capturing its most divine identity until I pronounce that your prayers are no longer needed. My Special son, I have bonded the ethereal with the practical in this message for the purpose of declaring that your wishes and Jesus' wishes are the same. It is another way of attesting that the Church is a living being, determined to propagate its own holiness, and capable of stopping evil legions from marching across the world. You and your brother are durable souls; your spirits and legacies cannot be subdued. Thank you for purchasing the Saint Michael statue; it is an ardent prayer for his intercession. *"I admire him."* I will address Saint Michael next week; and in the meantime, you can anticipate seeing a brilliant autumn this year. Thank you for your heartfelt petitions."

Saturday, October 4, 2014
Saint Francis of Assisi (1181-1226)

"The peril is balanced by our determination to succeed."

"Welcome to the nurturing bulwark of My Most Immaculate Heart, little sons. We together represent the hopes of billions of people who long to see their dreams realized, that they might have peace and happiness in their time. We hold in our hands their future in this world because we love them, more than they have the capacity to be loved by anyone else. When we speak of the dangers of evangelizing the Gospel, you have seen the way Martyrs have been created. This peril remains balanced by our determination to succeed, not just in ensuring the redemption of those willing to accept, but to reach the billions of sinners who are only now coming to know. Today, I speak with the fullness of joy in which I always come. And, I receive your prayers and petitions, unite them with Mine, and give them to God in Jesus. You see the great Archangel Michael whose likeness you have placed before us as we pray. It is good and right that you should do this because this is the sword-bearer who has fostered so much justice in the earthly domain. My Special son, I have told you many times that you should not have compassion for those who reject the Spirit of the Lord, who deny Jesus, who hate everything for which the Church stands. Saint Michael the Archangel is evidence that what I have said is true. He does not approach dragons and beg them to surrender; he slays them outright. He never defers to evil spirits or pleads with them to leave God's children alone. He sends them to the eternal flames of Hell. There are human beings around you now who will never heed the call of the Gospel or adhere to the lessons of the Cross. They will never sacrifice themselves for any redemptive good; they will not yield to the Will of God in any way. They are like the evil spirits; they have malevolence in every portion of their being. They are enemies of peace, justice and holiness. It is for this cause that we pray – to see that they bring no harm to you or your brothers and sisters in faith. I wish to address the urgency that Christians speak about nowadays. I have even implored you to speak about the urgency of human enlightenment to your bishops and friends. This is not the same kind of urgency with which someone might extinguish a fire. The type of urgency to which I refer is a commingling of Christology and the events of everyday life. Seeking the conversion of the world is a process that requires the softening of hearts. There is no doubt that this can be done in an instant, but it usually requires strengthening the heart over time. It is a slow building up that results in the reorientation of the spiritual heart to the gift of Salvation. When you speak of the urgency of the Church's mission, you are speaking about taking the element of time to your advantage. As I have said, you and your brother are doing this well. It is clear that you are succeeding, and this success is neutralizing the peril in which Christians find themselves. When you heard the late President Lyndon Baines Johnson speaking to the Correspondents Club in 1968 (*I was watching a recent video*), you heard him say that the struggle for world peace would, '...ask all of our old faith.' This is a unique summary of what I have been telling humanity for 2,000 years. The faith of your fathers and sons, the grace of the Sacraments, especially the Holy Eucharist, the raising of intercessory prayers, and the obedience of the Church – all these things are needed to ensure that Jesus is allowed room in the lives of those who inhabit the Earth. My Special son, not just anyone can say this effectively. President Johnson did it well because this is who he was. You and your brother have the same ability to capture on a page and in audible voice to the masses the Will of the Father with emphasis; with overtures, gestures and expressions that uplift the dignity of the Man-God who suffered through such humiliating torture and indignity.

I have said this today because your books are fruited with miraculous strains, and you will someday lay out the triumph of Jesus in speech before humanity with the fluency that I just described. I have promised that it would happen, and I repeat My promise today. It may be in this world the way you see it now, or in this world during its final hours, or between the Old World and the New World as they transitionally exchange places. It is not important which of these is ongoing once you take to the podium, but take it you will. You have too much to share for it not to be included in the final echoes of the Church's anthems and the reception of your life's eternal gift. The Mother of God will be with you as I am now, and the whole of humanity will know what you and your brother have done over the course of your lives. Imagine what the Fatima visionary Lucia must have thought about waiting so many decades to see what wars would come, what attacks the priesthood would suffer, what struggles Christianity would face, and in what darkness humanity would find itself during the twentieth century. Now, you have entered a new millennium; I have entered it with you, in which you are watching the grotesque results of what ideological secular extremism can do. The prayers of My children are all that have protected the borders of pious nations from being dissolved. I am telling you of the fruits of true faith. All the while, the peril is balanced by your determination to succeed. Indeed, Saint Michael the Archangel finds himself well traveled these days. He stands in Creation like a prince, sword in hand, listening intently, surveying the earthly realms like a watchman, prepared to respond to the cries of those in peril. Anyone who invokes the name of Saint Michael has a friend. He is valorous and potent. He has the durability of a steed. He knows the Sacred Heart of Jesus. And, he is like you, determined to make the Kingdom of the Father the only reason for the existence of men. I find it lovely to admire you, My Special son, because you remind Me of Saint Michael in all these things. You are just like him when you pray; you are one of Saint Michael's dispatchers. When you beseech him to go somewhere, to protect someone or safeguard their life, he does so because he loves you. He waits for the next syllable to issue from your lips. This is why Saint Michael is an Archangel. He has been given the same power by the hand of God that you have been given through your prayers. I have heard your summonses to Saint Michael, and so has he. When the Will of the Father needs made known to all men, you can call on Saint Michael, Saint Raphael and Saint Gabriel to heap copious enlightenment on these exiled realms. Human life is precious, tender and fragile; and the Archangels know it. At the same time, faith brings daring and endurance to those who believe in Jesus. So thank you, My Special son, for recognizing the beneficial intercession of the Archangels in your life; it is telling of your knowledge about the mystical teachings of the Church. I wish all My children would accept these gifts as well, and that rebels and detractors would stop demanding what the Church should believe.

This brings Me to a brief discussion of Saint Francis of Assisi. He did not just tell his father that he wanted to be a follower of the Cross, he took the clothes off his back and handed them to him. And, even though Saint Francis was perceived as being eccentric, it was not in his own lifetime that he thought he would have his greatest impact. History has proven this to be true. Saint Francis went to the battle lines of crusaders and interacted with the Church's opponents there, and his imitation of Jesus converted many of them to the Cross. Saint Francis of Assisi was accorded the Stigmata not because he was seen as having earned a sign, but because he evinced the pursuit of complete oneness with Jesus' Crucifixion. This is a faith life that everyone should seek. Living in moderation, following reason and practical sacrifice – these are the virtues of the modern day Christian. If everyone can achieve at least in their heart what Saint Francis accomplished in his physical life, this is all the Saint would ask; it is everything that God might require. Therefore, today My little son, you see that My joy is replete with admiration for you. I am determined to persuade you to believe that you are adored before the Father in Heaven, that you hold the esteem of the cherished Doctors of the Church. It is not only that you have been devoted to Jesus and consecrated to My Most Immaculate Heart, but that you have never once turned Me away; you have never turned back from personifying everything God desires from His living creatures. This is the way of your brother, as well. I journey the globe with blessings for the poor, graces for the faithful, and vision for all who have looked out their back doors and imagined what the world might become. It is all contingent on the collective human heart. This is the soil that Jesus seeks to seed. And, as I said in Medjugorje on October 2, 2014, I hold in My hands the water that will help this seed to grow. It is Jesus who manifests Himself throughout the ages and atop the summits of continents unknown. We have realized this all our lives, My Special one. We have a sacred pact of love, you and I. You are the son, and I am your Mother. I will provide the venues that will spread My messages across these lands. Thank you again for remembering the poor and unborn in your prayers, and the incarcerated and ostracized too. The Lord knows that you seek their deliverance from dearth into abundance."

Sunday, October 12, 2014
9:20 a.m.

"Born to us, Son of the Most High, Door to the Sheepfold,
Wonderful Counselor, Prince of Peace." (Isaiah 9:5)

"My dear little children, greetings and wondrous tidings are appropriate sentiments to describe the joy with which I come to you today. Even amid the broiling disasters of the exiled world, I can see the breathtaking victories that are about to overwhelm the Church. My Immaculate Heart is the world's own vessel of annunciation in that I come to dispense your blessings from Heaven. My love transcends your thoughts and prayers, and I give you My benediction. I bring humanity Jesus the Christ, and nothing else matters. When you see someone seated at a piano, ready to strike the keys with refrains of gloria, you know what I am conveying. It is I, the Maestroesse of the Harp, plucking your heartstrings skillfully, allowing the Father to amplify your sanctified melodies, reminding the Earth and the ages that all good things coalesce in the Sacred Heart of My Son. You have manifested the populating of His Kingdom. You have listened to His Will, made no determinations of your own, and rightfully complied. You have foregone banquets and festivals; you have fasted for the purification of the sinful. And, My little sons, we are at the point in time when we shall call your Bishop to rise as a warrior. My Special one, I wish for your brother to write a letter to the Church from his own heart, not just the heart of the Angels, but from his own sweet being. This will be a time for your brother to shine with the Angels who will not let his words go astray, for the Angels to find themselves deeply imbedded within your brother's spiritual soul. Remind your Bishop about the nation being consumed by its own fires of corruption. Your brother will need to ponder the content of this letter. This is a period of pious reflection and engagement. Your brother is compliant with My requests because, just as you, he is My obedient child. Also today, I wish to commend you for your endearing reading of the Scriptures at your nephew's wedding yesterday. Your interpretation of the passages was accented and beautiful. It is all about love; the entire Kingdom of God is about love. You appeared wise and stately at the lectern. Your voice was decided and convincing. You were handsome and poised. All who were there saw you emulate Jesus' oratories as He walked the Earth in peace. And, it is in this confidence that the attendees were drawn to their understanding of the occasion. It was My tremendous joy to attend the marriage sacrament of Curtis and April, and I was touched when they offered Me the pretty rose and sang the Ave Maria. It was also fitting that their mothers were honored at the suitable moment. My Special son, you and your brother, all who have given your lives to the conversion of the wicked, are mentors to the children of God, as well as these converts' brothers and sisters. You have allowed Jesus to live within you as their elder brother, and you have permitted the Spirit of the Father to eclipse your being, revealing to humanity what it means to usher the nations into His presence. Please allow Me to be more clear about this. Great Saints will rise from these times – Christians like yourself and Father Ted Hochstatter, all the souls who pray for peace, and the giants who stand against the enemies of the Church – you are the fighters who will live with dignity before the Throne of God with undivided allegiance and single-minded focus. You have created no distractions to make you take a second look at your life. This is a gift that you not only have given to God, but to yourself and the whole Mystical Body of the Church. I hope that you realize the prestige of who you are; this is what I have been trying to say for 25 years. You are named My 'Special one' for good reason. You have the demeanor of someone like the great Saint John Paul II kneeling before My Fatima statue with passion and humanity. You recite the Holy Rosary with conviction. You realize that I am the One Mother of the Church, Mother of the Redeemed. So today, I come to recommend My blessings upon you to Jesus, and ask God to send miracles to the Earth. I am praying that the sick will be healed, that the unborn will be given the gift of their birth, that the Poor Souls in Purgatory will be granted entrance into Heaven, that all wars will end, and that those who are far from God will find their new identity in Him. Thank you for taking such good care of your brother. He was looked upon at the wedding yesterday as a courtly gentleman, and he sat beside your father with grace."

Sunday, October 19, 2014
9:13 a.m.

"Prayer, apostolic energy, and the ancient catapult;
... this is a stark perpetual instinct."

"My dear little sons, ocean waves of Divine Mercy are visited upon those who repent of their transgressions against God's Kingdom, and holy justice is about to inundate those who do not. The conversion of lost sinners is more about forgiveness than punishment, and the Crucifixion of My Son is proof. I come to you with happiness again today. As the lyricist wrote, I come with a joy that will fill the Earth and last until the end of time. These are tumultuous days that you are living, but you are putting them down; you are surviving with your dignity in Jesus intact. I speak about prayer, apostolic energy, and the youthful purpose of your faith. You have the instincts to be drawn to God because of the gifts you have given Him and those you have received. I speak about the perpetuity of this instinct because it will live within you in Heaven. Prayer gives you this power. You are the modern-day apostles of the Church, and yours is the duty of remaining steadfast in Jesus while others are coming to know Him. My little sons, this is the reason that I say that the lyricist was right. Joy can fill the Earth and go with you into the Holy Arms of God. I wish this for you, My children. I know that you view these times with tremendous hope. You have an awareness that comes from the beginning of the Church, from the Nativity of

Jesus, from the mind and Heart of the Father, from the origin of your existence that has been fashioned from His creative Will. It is clear that there are cyclical revelations that descend from Heaven, good ones, prosperous ones; revelations that indicate how you should live. And, most of them come subtly; they require the enlistment of your patient faith. Others are more apparent, more coopting and contemplative like My messages to My seers and visionaries. The Father gives you this same intercessory power in the way you pray and perform pious acts that heal the brokenness of the world. You know that I hold you dear to My Immaculate Heart and invite you to come in. You have done so because you trust Me. You believe that the Lord would never allow your faith to lead you astray. And here, you reach the center of My Immaculate Heart where I give you Jesus' Most Sacred Heart. Why? Because our sinlessness is from the concentric origin of Divine Love through which God gave us life. My Special son, what this means is that you and your brother, all who live the joy of Christian life, see your sacrifices and patience as prayers themselves. These have become your gifts to the Church through your extraordinary lives. It is as though your every waking moment is a new one, not just a repetition of what you did an hour before, but giving to Jesus all the time remaining in your exile. It would seem that many people faithful to God wonder why His responses are not more obvious. Some believe that He must not be listening. On the contrary, there are plenteous gifts being dispensed to humanity through your daily prayers and petitions, even more than you could possibly know. I will reveal a point of knowledge here today that I have never shared with humanity before. God rarely answers prayers as though launching rockets or grenades against your enemies, but through sequences over time. God is not weak, and there is no puniness in Him. Your adversaries are being destroyed as though you are pelting them with ordnance from an ancient catapult. This gives them time to surrender to the messages you are delivering from Heaven! Hence, you see that prayer, apostolic energy, and the ancient catapult usher into the created realms the meaning of life and death. You deal to them the Will of the Father through your prayers and actions on a level that reflects your best perpetual instincts; your wisdom, courage and perfection that you have inherited in the Cross.

    This is not a complex prospect. You are the hosts for an infinite cache of miracles that are being played out before the modern world. And, when I say that My joy is founded in this, I mean that I can see what you are doing even better than you. The whole marketplace of spiritual discourse evolves around what humanity thinks it can prove, which itself is counterintuitive to what the Gospel asks the world to believe. My Special son, we have been in the process of helping the world not only know what Heaven has to offer, but to interact with its sublime assistance on a personal level. It is clear that you have known this for decades, and this is why your father wept yesterday at the restaurant in Jacksonville. Your brother told him that, '...your children and grandchildren are in the Church because of what you did.' Your father began weeping in joy because he knows that such statements can only come through the Holy Spirit. He believed that it was Jesus speaking to him through your brother, and he was correct. This is an example of the ancient catapult. It was your brother's instinct to allow the Holy Spirit to inspire the words from his lips, and it was your father's instinct to believe that it was from the ethereal realms. You have seen what happens during the transitions of life. People are in the beginning younger and curious; and after the passing of many decades, they appear to be older and disinterested. However, this is not the case with the human soul. You are as youthful today as at the moment you were placed in your mother's womb. In fact, your faith has made you more vigorous. I have called My children to live out this robustness within them, this spiritual strength and stamina, this way of connecting with the youthful Spirit of God. This is what love gives you. Through Jesus, the Father allows you to see and touch Him, to take Him inside your heart, to speak to Him when you are alone or in other company. I am not saying that you should perceive your relationship with Jesus as though you have been awarded a trophy to be carried about in your hands. You have been given a divine human being, a perfect Man, someone in whose identity you should aspire to succeed, whom you bear on the inside. This is Jesus within you, and you should do something or commit something into being that you believe He would like. When you do this in His name, Jesus manifests within you a presence of originality that permits you to enhance His Kingdom in ways that Heaven has yet to reveal. It is the same as allowing you to complete a script for which He has only written the foreword. My Special son, this is what Jesus meant when He said that humanity must become perfect as He is perfect. Be the artists, playwrights and performers, the doctors and visionaries, the virtuosos and charmers that He would have you be. Become humanitarians who have never once lost sight of the innocence of your youth. This is where the true power of the heart most prolifically reigns.

And in this, it matters not how the body ages. I see the converse being true as well; this is what Jesus recognizes. Those who are young at heart, and even those yet youthful in body and mind, can display this same spiritual alertness. Yes, tall as mountains, as mobile as eagles in flight! As powerful as avalanches rolling like waterfalls into ravines below. This is your witness of your new beginning in Jesus. For certain, those who have become old, weak and sedentary will never believe what I am saying here today. They are in too much pain.

They cannot perambulate like they did before. They have become embittered by life's disappointments and the dark courses of human events. And, this is why My messages are key to their comfort. I wish to tell them that spiritually, deep inside where their hearts and souls live, they are only little children around My feet. I have said that Jesus wishes this for them. Inside the faithful human person, He looks in awe at what His apostles and disciples have done. It is humanity viewing itself through the eyes of its Maker. This, My Special son, is among the reasons that I have said that you are divine and angelic; you are replete with competence and mastery. The fullness of your faith stands straight up, perfectly unified with the highest peaks of Paradise, unified with the Glory of God, willing to witness and testify to His Sacred Kingdom that has finally, at long last and during this millennium, decided to devour like a sweet confection every last morsel of righteousness that the world has to offer Him. This, therefore, is a good day – one that in many ways will reveal to the nations what must come from Jesus' hands and the joy of My Immaculate Heart. When young men wrap their fingers around the cruciform of a sword, they do so because something is about to happen. They intend to rectify wrongs and slay the adversaries of their truths. They feel inside the sanctioning that comes from God's justice – a justice that has too long waited in the wings. And, each of these sword-bearers is like a new prince come into being. They wield the providence of a fresh generation of warriors against the enemies of the Church. They express their faces into fighters' poses, and they lash out against evil and insolence. These, My Special son, are those in whose ranks you and your brother still serve, and you will do so even if you live to be a hundred years old. You have your palms wrapped around a shining sword of righteousness that will never be broken, not once needing repair or re-forged. It is in your realization of these things that others will emulate you; you have already shown them. It is written in your testament to the Morning Star Over America."

Sunday, October 26, 2014
9:30 a.m.

"Life is not just humanity's rehearsal for redemption,
... it is Salvation's shriving tempest."

"My darling sons, I have come to endorse your precious values that you hold about human life, to uplift you to Jesus in a most special way, and to pray with you for the conversion of the world. The exchange that occurs between a priest and a penitent during the Sacrament of Reconciliation is known as 'shriving.' To shrive is to either seek absolution from a priest or for the priest to bestow the grace of absolution on behalf of God. In My opening strains, I have said that life is Salvation's shriving tempest. This is the repetitive motion of the days and years during which the storms of human life batter those in exile. All in all, however, life is a sure pattern of excellence that comes to those who pray and seek the Cross. My Special and Chosen ones, you have reached this excellence, and the pamphlets that you are now preparing to propagate My messages are further proof. It is clear that the love in your hearts and the work of your hands reflect the meaning of Christianity in its most essential form. And, My Special one, your labors on Jesus' behalf are building up His Kingdom in ways not known to most men. You know this; your excitement in anticipating what will come is worthy of your virtue. My Special son, you have prepared a magnificent pamphlet, just as I have requested. You can gain a sense of what it will do when placed into good hands. It is imperative that you and your brother not grow too anxious in dispensing your pamphlets because the communication chain needs time to evolve. It would be like a monsoon hitting a wheat field instead of gentle showers. Indeed, evil dogs surround you now; you can hear their barks and snarls. *(The dogs in the neighbor's yard next door began snarling and barking hysterically as if they were in a fight as our Holy Mother referred to them.)* They are angry at Me! They sense that I am here; they are opposed to anything that diminishes their sense of power over your neighborhood. Moving on, however, I wish you and your brother to realize your piety in Jesus' eyes. You should feel humbled that you have come this far, that you have imbedded in Creation My supernatural works for the conversion of lost sinners and the strengthening of the Church. I am saying that you have in your hearts and settled in your thoughts that we are on the right side of history and eternity too. We are on the side of Truth because you have manifested in this world the destiny of what humanity should become. You have the face of innocents and the posture of warriors; saints for sure, capable of enlightening the world through your words and visions emanating from the Throne of God in Heaven. How can such innocence possess the power of giants? Because your faith is as strong as steel and your goodness as bright as the skies. Every fiber of your being, every cell of your mortal frames, every thought in your eloquent minds is given to Jesus. Here, I am saying that you are in the prime of your righteousness. You are steady and determined. You have within you the fulcrum of holiness on which the whole of Creation is rocking, moving and leaning in the direction of absolving love. I speak about life as being a rehearsal for your redemption, but not just that, because you are weathering and sustaining the tempests that are trying to bring your hopes down. You are where the world comes for advice to be directed to the priests because you have been given centuries of wisdom in a brief span of 23 years. You shrive the lost and broken through your deliverance of everything I have asked you to share. This is the pose that men will remember of you. They will look into your eyes and wonder from where came such compassion. They will survey your contributions to their repentance and know that you cleared their pathway to the Cross. They will finally conclude that the sparkle in your eyes was placed there by Me. And, without ever having to utter another sound, they will recognize the God of their fathers in the works you have laid before them. They will be capable of judging the journey they must travel by the expression on your face. They will make no declarations that would lend to their own whims – no indeed, they will know that obedience and compliance are the only two legs on which to stand. It is not you whom they will adore, it will be their allegiance to their Salvation in God. This is the Spirit of Truth that they are finding in your life's work transmitting My messages into the world. I am not saying these things to heighten your sense of self-worth, but to remind you that you are esteemed for all that you and your brother have done. You are priceless before the ages, and genius in light of the world's ignorance.

My Special son, there is a sense of eagerness in what we are doing together, but not one that would create anxiety or impatience. We are not rushing to the finish line just because we can see it around the corner. You are given the ensuing years to savor what you and your brother already know to be inevitable. It is the convergence of victory and comfort in one majestic day. There is a constant assuredness that cannot be diluted by anything opposing your work. I am overwhelmed that you have never once said that you would turn back. It is not that I am surprised by your faith or the clarity of your character, but that you have always stayed the course through good times and bad. Even the likes of Saint Padre Pio and Mother Teresa of Calcutta had moments of doubt when, in their own suffering, they wondered whether their years in the Church would make a marked difference. Now, they can see from their stations in Heaven that you and your brother are making the difference that they always wanted to make. Why? Because they lacked the longevity to reach into the brazen 21st century world where the most abominable enemies of human redemption are running rampant everywhere. You are praying and serving in their stead. You are like their holy extremities into a future that they could have only hoped to know. You look outward with the same vision that they are seeing now. You bring the Kingdom of the Father into the discernible realms because you have complied with His wishes in My presence. And, you will one day know beyond any shadows that the fullness of His light has been with you all along. This has indeed been your rehearsal for redemption. God has provided for your sustainment throughout the ages, for all peoples through all times, so that this culminating joy about which I speak can come through the miracles that He has wrought in you. Therefore, with holy foresight, I look admiringly upon what Jesus will do next through His holy brothers and sisters to bring His Kingdom to fruition. It is only a matter of time, and we are glad to wait for this glorious climax. Do you have anything to ask Me today? *"I am praying deeply for our Bishop to recognize the contemporary urgency of declaring the authenticity of your work. I ask for whatever suffering is required to grant him clarifying light upon your desire for the propagation of your intercession."* I pray with you; we should anticipate that time to come. There will be a manifest abruption if the Lord sees the rightful circumstances to make it so. It will happen in your day and in this place if enough gifts are offered to Him. These are the blessings for which we pray. The devil tries to impede everything sacrificial when you perform your obedient works. This is where beatific power comes in effecting your life's purpose – obedient servant first, Marian messenger second. I ask that you please remember to celebrate the Saints and pray for the souls of the faithful departed next week. I assure you that the Saints are holy advocates for what you and your brother do."

Saturday, November 1, 2014
All Saints Day
9:33 a.m.

"The sovereign domain that vests supreme power
 ... in those of little consequence."

"Today, My dear children, you observe and celebrate those who have been accorded the spiritual accolades due them from a grateful Church and heart-touched world. I come in peace and glad tidings to pray with you for the billions around the globe who should imitate the legacies of the Saints, those who are trying to do so, and the untold numbers of souls who are unaware that they should strive for such holiness. I wish for you to remember that, through your prior works, you are reminding your brothers and sisters that human life in Jesus is not a concession or oppression, but a new beginning of freedom and love. If it is to the Lord that all men are led, then surely let us help this worthy cause to be as awakening as possible. You have heard many times that this path is not strewn with roses and that there will always be thunderclouds overhead. You have walked the treacherous paths where your forebears have suffered, where many were martyred. You know the cost of keeping your faith strong and upholding the promises that you have made to God. It is all part of the plan. I speak today about the sovereign domain that vests supreme power in those of little consequence because it is a fitting reminder of where the Saints drew their strength. Many Saints about whom you have learned were ordinary people who performed extraordinary acts of kindness, compassion, service and exemplary Christian charity. And, most of them were not thinking about being enshrined in the Litany of Saints that the Church recites today. They simply wanted to live as Jesus taught, in a way that reflects the purity of the Gospel, and in a way that provides for those who cannot help themselves. The Saints are the clearest example of the binary purpose of Christian faith, to make oneself prepared for redemption, and to alleviate the suffering of those who are persecuted, neglected and exploited by people who do not believe in God. Vesting power. This is what the Father does best. He adores those who do His earthly bidding by placing inside them the Spirit of Himself. Here, we know that you have done this with eloquence, with temperance, prudence and all the virtues that hold you in such regard before the Heavenly Court. You are as equally venerated in this life as you wish your holy friends to be. Therefore, when I say that you are to be numbered among the Saints, it is not that you must undergo a radical transition to get there; it has already happened, and knowing it is only a matter of time. I have said that time is not your enemy because it has provided a means for those who do not know God to come to the Church. Imagine His gladness when He sees another soul convert; it is a source of extreme jubilation. God pours out His gratefulness upon those who work for Him, and it is often more intense than those in the Church realize. Yes, My Special son, this is how the Face of Jesus can be seen billowing from plumes of smoke. You are so precious to recognize these gifts when some representatives of the Church dismiss them as coincidence. It is you who possess the wisdom to know where the Spirit of the Lord has tread. You have the vision to accept the presence of miracles. And today, I also wish to remind you that your pamphlet on which you are working is glorious; it is bright and shining like the seas, and it has taken on the supernatural identity of your books themselves. I so much appreciate everything you do for Me in the name of Jesus. My little son, there are songs and sonnets living yet within you that you are offering the world as comfort for humanity's journey. You make spirits bright because you are aglow in your dedication to Me. I will not permit you to fail in the life you have given to Jesus. It is clear that your brother continues to be pummeled by Satan at every turn; even as he has built an impressive biography, he cannot seem to generate gainful means from what he has done. Thank you for taking such good care of him, for giving him the venue to be so unifying during these times. It is good when humanity overcomes barriers to gather in conciliatory terms. This is one of the reasons your brother reached out to assist in the mayoral campaign, not that he is just trying to network, but that it is proper for decent people to strive to improve the public domain based on the teachings of the Mother of God.

Thus, I speak about elevation. This is what you and your brother have done here in this holy place and outside your home where so much discussion between yourselves and Heaven has occurred. I weep happily because your devotion to My Most Immaculate Heart is irrevocable. Your dedication to everything for which I stand is timeless and ageless. When I pray to Jesus and therefore to the Father, I couple your petitions with Mine. I ask My Son to touch you with gentle thoughts and healing, with compassion and composure, and with certitude resonating through your reflections. These are remarkable days and years to be alive. You hold in your hands the miracles that America needs to convert, that humanity needs to awaken, and that the whole world will soon rely on for reconciliation with its Creator. I am not trying to build up your hopes that this will happen in the next year, but this is where it is going. I have told you about such spiritual kinetics before. As I said at the beginning of this message, the God of the sovereign domain has vested in you and your brother, and all My messengers, the intercessory grace to change the Earth by your prayers and good deeds. Not a single syllable you have ever uttered was left unheard. Every flash of divine enlightenment that came to you was God's response. Every letter you have ever written, every stroke on your keypad has meant more than you could possibly know in this life. Every breath you have taken, every stride toward another floor, every passage through a corridor, every conception that you might have thought – even in all these things, you are brighter than the sun; you are capable of permeating the veil of your exile into the heavenly realms. You hold in your hands the fate of humanity with all its loneliness and precarious paths, with its darkness, torment and ugliness. You are fixed in the lineage of messengers who have come and gone centuries before you, and now it is upon you whom I depend to help Jesus manifest the miracles that took Peter, James and John to the brink of ecstacy. Yes, it is the Saints whom we celebrate today, but theirs has been an inheritance in the Land of Milk and Honey; yours is to broaden the scope of the Divine Kingdom where the ministry of the Son of Man began. This is the reason I have said that it is all about elevation. Once up there; once humankind understands that there is a difference between highness and lowness on a spiritual plane, they will indeed strive for those heights. They will look up and into the eyes of the Savior who is gratified to have poured out His Sacred Blood to redeem them. My Special son, Jesus is amazed every day by the courageous acts that He sees by those who believe in Him. His tears fall like rain into the parched lives of His disciples who toil in His vineyard on Earth.

I have told you in days past that all these things are endearing to the Father. It is not that God expects something supernatural from His mortal creatures, for He is the worker of miracles. It is only that He bids humanity to welcome them. You and your brother have done this with obedience and joy. And, it is not just because you have no other god; of course there is no other god, but you have acted admirably because, like Me, you realize that the full potential of humanity has yet to be yielded. Billions of souls from centuries ago have waited until these 21st century times to see their dreams come true. They are being realized through you! The innocence on your faces regales the innocence that they never lost. This is the legacy of the Saints, to be relived and carried out by you in their honor. This is why each person who confesses their sins in Jesus' Blood is another facet in His Crown. We hold many things to be true, but there is only one Divine Truth, spread worldwide and beyond the universes by the children of God who cherish everything it means to be righteous like Him. My Special son, I have told you about what this looks like if depicted in a picture. If the conversion of the human soul could be shown as an image, it would be of the pauper praying before the Altar of Sacrifice, begging Jesus to make the whole world as impoverished as him. This is how spiritual riches are dispensed. It is the way humanity will be finally healed and transferred, taken to those heights that I spoke about only moments ago. My little son, do you have any issues to discuss with Me today? *"I pray for my uncle John who died, that he be brought into God's Kingdom with you."* I wish to say something specific about your uncle John. You were absolutely correct when you said that he would see your life with your brother and know himself that your loyalty to Me was worth his admittance into Heaven. He is with Me now and the Hosts of Paradise, with the Blessed Trinity, and with his own elation because of what you and your brother have done. I am asked to tell you that he is not feasting on a cocktail of canned vegetables.* It is the Grand Banquet that he is receiving now, and the fare was paid by Jesus Christ. When the hour shall come that others will join him in this heavenly bliss, be happy for them, for they will have gained their just reward. Your uncle John has yet to let go of your Grandpa Roth, and his mother too. Thank you for offering your prayers for the Souls of the Faithful Departed whose eternity in Paradise has been assured. Your Grandmother Eulah Monica is a tremendous intercessor for humanity on Earth! I will remember your petitions to Jesus in the hope that the Will of God shall come to pass."

We always laughed at family gatherings about the day Uncle John asked me to assist him as he was refurbishing his childhood farm home. I assumed it would be rather easy work, but I was instead tunneling all day through a crawlspace, moving dirt one five gallon bucket at a time, and hauling it out of the basement. At lunch hour, I assumed we would go into town and grab a sandwich at the village diner. Instead, he fished two cans of plain vegetables out of the pantry, mixed them together in a pan, and called it 'lunch.' Uncle John was the one who humourously asked Our Lady to tell me that he was feasting in Heaven. Yes, God does have a sense of humor.

Sunday, November 9, 2014
9:16 a.m.

"From the burning bush to tongues of fire, faith's momentum rule –
God would be no lesser if nary a soul chose to believe in Him."

"My dear little sons, if the world was first blushed, it is now crimson. If the days had sparkle to their touch, they are now bursting with light. We have watched the turning of the ages into the blossoming flower of righteousness that will soon cap the hill of time like the knight on the white horse, so storied and so valiant. This, My children, is the 'momentum rule.' It is the mark of your faith through all times and nations. It is the shining imminence that has eclipsed the endeavors of men. It has color, shape, form, aroma and purpose. I have asked, My little sons, that you lead your lives one day at a time, indeed one moment at a time, because the months and years take care of themselves; they should need no guidance from you. I have sought from you the prayers and intentions that will change the issues of today because this day, as every day, is a hinge on which the story of time swings. I can tell you this morning that there will be a hundred souls bound for the fires of Gehenna, but I can also tell you this afternoon that their souls will all be saved. This is due to the constantly changing facets of the gem of humanity, being configured by God as He receives your daily prayers. He has set the world aright, this fine gem, because He knows of the worthiness of the Church and those who populate it. This is the reason that I have come today with such joy, not simply lived for some unknown reason, but inherent in Me from the moment when Jesus was raised from the Tomb. My hope then was founded in My own faith in the Son of Man to whom I am now turning the world. We must understand, My little sons, that God deigns what shall come of this land, but He assuredly utilizes the prayers of the faithful as His guiding tool. This is why there will never be a reason for exiled men to lose sight of their destiny in Him. What a paradox it seems that the Father is always a constant figure, but His Will is amended by those who believe in Him. How can it be true that He defers to their wishes? Because it is through His own sacred wisdom deposited in them that they pray. This is how we pray, and know for what to pray. You see, My little sons, there are designs in Heaven that are also identifiable on the Earth. I am not speaking of timely or spatial designs, but of triumph and transition. I speak about the comely openness that humanity must embrace among the nations, and this same openness is a provided facet of the Afterlife. I have said that the intellectual approach to one's faith is woefully inadequate in learning all there is to know. This is because the Lord's disciples must make way for miracles to capture their attention and inspire their allegiance. The whole of the world is a miracle! It possesses this supernaturalism not for the sake of itself, but because it is a launching pad for all souls, times and places to be consumed by the Eternal Love of Jesus Christ. I am part of this miracle; you are part of it too; everything you have ever wanted from God will come to you as part of this miracle, and the fortunate resolution of your exile in the Sacred Arms of My Son is conclusively part of this miracle. None of these things can be separated from the others; it is a universal whole of benefaction. At the risk of sounding redundant here today, I would like to reiterate that beauty and obedience are two key attributes to the presence of these gifts. I speak of beauty of the heart, spiritual beauty that the Lord in Heaven recognizes because it mirrors the Glory of Himself. You have this beauty in you not by conceding to God, but through your obedience to Him. There is a difference in the two. Concession would mean that you go into the vineyard as if having no choice. The choice is always with the will of men, but obedience is in knowing that the journey is worth the destiny, that there is a logical framework in your faith that can be measured by immeasurable forces. I do not speak of logic in the sense of two and two equaling four, but in the sense of sacrifice being the deliverance of oneself to the shores of perpetual light.

This beauty is of the self-denial that took Jesus to the Cross. It is a compliant obedience that is gladly delivered, forced by the charity of the giver in a sacramental way that allows others to preserve their dignity and recognize supernal value in themselves. When you say, My Special son, that God's name is hallowed, you are not just telling Him that you honor His Kingdom through your acquiescence to His Will, you are pronouncing it to the universe and all whose ears have never heard. The Holy Spirit shares, dictates, resonates and resounds your pronunciations as profoundly as the Archangel Gabriel came to Me. This is why I have said that your beauty secures inside your heart the power to bend the influences of time; you can change and rewrite what has occurred here in these realms for the sake of the glorification of God. The idea of miracles in the way I have described should not preclude the happening of anything that recognizes God as the ultimate humanity lover. This is what makes Him the Father of everything conceivable by the heart and mind of man – not the evil things, not the issues that take humanity down the paths of sin and misgiving, but of the inclination to repent and be reconciled. This is the momentum with which I opened My message here today. When humanity finds itself lost, God helps men to be found. He is the compass that guides lost sinners to Himself. He has the magnetism to make them come running to His Son. And, as I have said for years on end, this is the choice of the man; not the Maker, but the creature. This is the reason we are praying; it is at the behest of the God who sent Me here today. There will come a time when all the children of God, lost and found, will reach out to Jesus and touch Him in the same way that you can touch your brother sitting beside you now. It will be part of the final miracle, part of the intentions of the Father to remake and restore hope in those who wonder where His mercies have gone – all the glorious mercies arbored by the Divine Mercy from the Most Sacred Heart of His Son. They are all still there, everything that consists and subsists in His Holy Will, such things as forgiveness and convention, new beginnings, putting aside reprisals, the reunion of family members, feeding the least among you, everything that defines the mercies about which you have learned. My Special son, these things are magnified with each Hail Mary you say. It is the purpose of your human reason and the foundation of your defiance against those who persecute the Church.

So, we survey the identity of humanity moment after moment, knowing that love, prayer and holiness are changing it. And, it is not a problem that someone may relapse or suffer recidivism. It is that their lips have touched the cup of suffering and tasted the joy of redemption. It is from here that they see their faith's momentum. This is what the Father designed from the burning bush to tongues of fire. It is the standing, almost motionless momentum that cannot be seen by the eyes of men any better than they can feel the spinning of the Earth beneath their feet. It is turning anyway. This is also the reason why God cannot be lesser just because no one might choose to believe in Him. He sets a table before Creation whether anyone attends or not. You and I know, however, that multitudes have already come. Their souls know of the Promise; their faith tells them the pathway, their thoughts are replete with true wisdom, and their energy is concurrent with the Passion of The Christ. I offer you My deep gratitude, My Special son, because you and your brother have permitted Me to come here and share these things. It is the perfect reciprocation of what the Apostles told Jesus. If not for you and your brother, where else would I go? To whom would I turn? I have always begged you to see My messages in this vein because I can do nothing without you. You are the apostles who touch the Church in many meticulous ways. If I appeared on the downtown square before the eyes of another 70,000 souls, would the rest of the world not cast it away as some deceptive ploy? They surely did in Fatima. You do not see the secular void doing anything to remind humanity about My messages from almost 100 years ago. It is imperative that you remember My sentiments about beauty, prayer, power, design, suffering, repentance and deliverance. You will see all these things take on new meanings as this century goes on. We have spoken about expectancy and expectation; they allude to the gifts your prayers have wrought on behalf of My Medjugorje messages and those I have given to you and your brother as the Morning Star Over America. Please do not lose hope like some of My other children. Even as I have deposited My messages into their hands, they are questioning when all good things will reach their summit. My Special son, thank you for attending your uncle John's funeral and being such a compassionate consoler to your father. You were certainly a blessing to him."

Saturday, November 15, 2014
9:23 a.m.

"From primordial origin, sanctioned by the multitudes."

"My dear little sons, the secular, mortal, temporal world despises that we pray for the Lord's Kingdom to come. Those who are far from God are more angry than disgruntled, more filled with hatred than dismay, more unwilling to see than they are capable of looking. I have come here to make them even less comfortable. It is not a measure of crossing cultures or clashing ideologies that we effect, it is the riddance of the Earth of any mention of themes having nothing to do with the righteousness of men. This is your connection to God in this place. The Father in Heaven has established the primordial essence of His Creation, and He has handed to those who believe in Him the sanctioning power to lead all men to His Son. These are the multitudes to whom I speak. It is clear that everyone owns a share of this essence; every man, woman and child who knows deep inside that they must embrace the Cross and everything for which it stands. These were first identified as Christians at Antioch. I am yet telling the world that only through Christianity can the Earth be perfected; only through Jesus can humanity arrive at the totality of their ethereal 'being' before the ages shall come to a close. And, each man possesses in himself the capacity to be like Jesus because the faith given from God delivers the heart to His Kingdom. If Salvation has a face, it is the face of humanity taking on the expression of Jesus on the Cross. For now, this precedes the sacred splendor that will come when the world is uplifted in the Glory of the Resurrection. My Special son, this does not mean that My children should not be happy here in this life; it means that their happiness must be couched in their awareness of the wickedness of the Earth, that this wickedness is overcome by the Gospel of the Lord. This is where your joy is conceived. God did not tell His creatures that they would remain forever sinful, but that His Son eradicated sinfulness and even man's boundness to sin by His Crucifixion and Easter Resurrection. In other words, the plan is in place, and men must walk through the corridor that will take them to the Kingdom of the Son. There are many ways that this gladness can unfold, but doubters keep getting in the way. The Holy Spirit is the resolving hero to whom men must defer. This is the origin of confession at the center of the heart. Hence, the collective expression about which I speak must replicate the innocence of a child, even as this child is aware that there is recklessness in his midst throughout the passing days. Hope is his nurturer. It is hope that mandates the ideals of faith because futures are built on it. My Special son, for all the exegesis of the Bible that preachers and ministers do, they would better serve the Lord by focusing on the innocence of a child. What does it look like? It is that men are aware of their potential in Jesus; they seek to realize it by serving the poor, praying for the lost, composing symphonies that spread the Good News to every shore, and championing for themselves a new song that echoes the Hallelujahs from the Mount of Olives. At the last, it is not the evangelists who are glorified, but the Savior to whom they lead their flocks. What humanity holds in its hands bears the reason for life. If you take up your crosses in the image of Jesus, you will feel the suffering of other men. This is the transcending compassion that Jesus shares with you. It portends a life of sacrifice and a joyous death that is saturated with redemptive meaning. And, when speaking of the fulfillment of hopes, this is the result of active faith. The multitudes. Every Christian has his own identity within the identity of the Catholic Church. I have spoken about this in earlier times. The condition of the heart is of the momentum that I mentioned last week; it is comprised of new beginnings and new life. It is about exercising the beatitudes that make other people stop in their tracks and marvel at the holiness before them. This harkens to the Fatima miracle that struck the seers with such awe.

On the converse side is what the rest of Creation sees. This is how Jesus speaks to humanity from the Cross and with the Father in Heaven. He refers to the people of Earth as His 'other self.' This is a means of declaring that He has already integrated in Himself the identity of humanity-redeemed because of what the Church has done for 2,000 years. The point that He is making is the same one that I am making here today. Converted penitents must strike a pose of divinity reflective of Jesus' righteousness, and they must be able to see Him by looking at themselves. Yes, it is like focusing into a mirror, as if the veil separating Heaven and Earth is a looking glass. This is the reason the Scriptures say that you see dimly as if looking into a mirror. Hear Me now. If the whole world would convert to the Christian holiness to which men are called, humanity would see the Face of Jesus in real time, not as in a mirror, but as it shall be in Heaven. This is the potential that God has handed the Church through the written Word. My Special son, I wish not to belabor the point, but all this has dimensions that can be collated into knowable acts and sequences in the here and now. The first thing is that sinners must confess that they are indeed lost. They must grow their appreciation for the need for repentance and the amendment of their lives. Once this has been done, the Holy Spirit will take residence in them. I am saying that once the human will is surrendered in favor of the Will of God, cascading blessings from Heaven will rush into the basin of the Earth like an inundating bath. It would make Niagra Falls look like a slow running stream. I have every intention of seeing this process through as the Matriarch of the Church. I am looking beyond the vestibule doors and into the boulevards and marketplaces, seeing where My children are hiding behind their pride and material wealth. It is saddening that they do not recognize where they are, but encouraging that they will someday fall from the ranks of power to the harvest of death. There are worse things in life than this. The societies of Earth must succumb to the singular Truth that demands them to bow to the Prince of Peace before they shall join the procession of Saints entering the Glorious Domain. You and your brother have known this for decades, but I bring it to your attention to remind you that the secularists who believe that they are succeeding in some spectacular way are only deluding themselves. I am speaking to raise you up before Heaven as exemplary souls in the line of salvation-seekers who have given Jesus reason to take comfort in preparation for His Second Coming. How satisfying it would be that you could take to the world stage and enlighten the tightfisted moguls and lost billionaires that the paupers living in the gutters outside their gated homes are the richest souls to inhale the breath of life. This is what the Gospel says. They cannot escape it; they are destined for the justice to which they will be summoned when their hour arrives. This is perhaps little consolation now, but irrevocable reassurance to Christians like you and your brother who have been hoping and laboring in the Lord's vineyard so long and dutifully. There is not a syllable that you have ever prayed that did not pierce the ears of God. There is not an image in your minds that He has not seen. You are shaping the expression on humanity's face that makes life here on the Earth closer to the Kingdom that will supplant your exile on the last day of time.

My Special son, your primordial origin is the Providence of God, made manifest by your acceptance of His Son, and ratified by the way you have led your life. This is the lovely sanctioning that unites you with the Saints of old and servants in the world today. Your life has been given authenticity because you are vested with the Spirit of your Savior in every conceivable way. You are sanctioned by God to live the way you do – all who have come to Him through Me, everyone encouraged by the Holy Spirit to seek the truth in their day, and beyond every other pursuit that you might have otherwise sought. This is the mandate that you, yourselves, have placed on those who have not lived as they should, who have rejected the Cross because of the burdens of faith, those who have lived high and mightily because their comfort and materialism were just too alluring to deny. My little son, the whole matter is based on sharing all the righteousness of the Kingdom that will come in due time. How could you be despairing when you hear these things? I have put this question before every visionary whom I have ever called. I am not saying that knowing the outcome of the world makes mortal life any easier to bear. In many ways, it makes its callousness seem even more difficult to endure. But, this is not what matters anymore. What is important is that you bear life like Jesus the Life-Giver. You hold yourselves in the esteem that He preserves for you. This is what it means to be an impassioned Christian. You are not enslaved by the Cross, you are liberated by it. You are not tethered to the Scriptures like a ball and chain; you walk by its tenets like dignitaries above the dungeons of the world. And, you never suffer one sting of error because you belong to the truth of Triune Love. You take pity on those who are persecuted for their faith, who are exploited because of their innocence. You pray with dignity and speak with eloquence because the Holy Spirit is the dayspring of your wisdom. If this is difficult to believe; if you are having thoughts that your life is somehow otherwise, then you must take another look at yourself. You should see your soul the way Jesus sees you, like a priceless pearl resting on a golden powder puff. Take heart and know that God has implanted in you and your brother a converting love that is brightly shining as the Morning Star Over America."

Sunday, November 23, 2014
9:31 a.m.

"Be still, and know that I am God;
I will be exalted among the nations." (Psalm 46:10)

"My little sons, the joy of the everlasting hills echoes our love; they hold to humanity's collective heart the truths that the ages are still revealing. I am praying with you today because you have invited Me here. Yes, there is but one single Truth, but it is shared in the truths of the heart – those things that you know to be based in the Salvation of the world through the Crucifixion of My Son. I am also here because I simply desire to be closer to My two 'Sons of Triumph' who have placed before humanity the opportunity to know their Savior with more intensity than anyone before. I shall always tell you that your power is based on your innocence. I will forever extol your wisdom before the nations. Never will I cease telling God that you have done what He has asked you to do. Even though He already knows it, He enjoys hearing it again like the repetitive strains of a soul-confirming song. To be still and know that God is whom He claims to be is to celebrate Him always and everywhere; this is the Holy Spirit speaking through you. Your voices tell in this place of the Father who has given life to all creatures, and He has given life-sustaining graces to you through your prayers and holy offices. Now, as was said on the Day of the Ascension, you are commended to speak in His stead. You shall bless and reprimand whomever you please. I am with you today also because we have yet much work to do in His vineyard. All you need is to look around. All the terrible conditions that you see are not permanent, they are not capable of removing from the future the redemption that Jesus has promised. It is just that they seem to sully the dignity of the Earth. They strain the lives of good people everywhere, and yet they give true Christians more reason to pray for change. I ask that you remember with intensity how you are loved. Never forget that you are on the side of history that will consume the times of men. Here, you have walked in peace, spoken with the Passion of Jesus on your lips, sown seeds of righteousness where they have been welcomed, and enlightened the ignorant about the prescience of virtue. This means that you have lived worthy lives, pious lives, lives that have meant something more than blindly wiling away your years of exile. You have been agents for change in a world that clings to its own indifference. This is the reason that I have said that you are My 'pray-ers.' You are the children of the Queen in the lineage of the Saints and Martyrs whose spirits rest with assurance beside Me now. I bring you tidings of the gladness about which I am speaking because you are traveling the paths that will take you to them. Where there is love for the Son of Man, there is eternal life in the lover. Hence, I give you My sacred promise that the fullness of your hopes will not be denied. As it is said, there comes a time. Also today, I roam the hills and valleys of the Earth in hope and spirit to accompany My other children during their formative years, the times when they are growing to be like you. My Special son, I love them. I foresee in My Immaculate Heart the kind of Christians they are becoming. This is a prayer for them as they move and grow, as they turn to the light of righteousness instead of away from Heaven's calling, as they begin to understand what I have been saying to you and your brother all these years. It is a brilliance to which you have become accustomed, so much so that you share it with others without even knowing it. This makes you like the Apostles and Saint Paul, the letter writer, the Man of the Epistles, the converter, the traveler, the celebrant of the faith that has brought humanity to the brink of perpetual peace. And, Saint Peter too! It is clear that Saint Peter has been more especially with you and your brother since the Feast of the Chair of Saint Peter in AD 1991. I wish for you high expectations for everything I have asked you to believe since that time. Truly, it is Saint Peter to whom all Christians should turn for apostolic intercession during the battles that lie ahead.

The Roman Catholic Church will not be moved off its pillared center of primacy upon which the Son of Man has positioned it. The Creator of the world has expectations for humanity that cannot be deferred. The Church will not concede to the abominations sought by radical modernists over the past five decades. The legacies of the Saints will not support it, and the Savior of the world will not condone it. This is what our prayers will secure before the closing of the ages arrives. It is important to focus on what Jesus sees. I have said this recently, knowing that the entire world will eventually connect My words to their future. This vision is not like staring at a sunset or looking at the narrowing distance of a railroad track. It is in many ways more spiritual than seeable, more about wisdom than practice, and culled from the greatest dreams that anyone could imagine. God is no stationary Being. He does not change, but He has no boundaries that keep Him constrained in Heaven. He sits on His Throne and beside you and your brother here in your home. He crosses the universe by simply thinking about it. He blesses you from the inside out. He instills in you those dreams that I mentioned, and gives you the faculties to carry them out. He turns your two-shaded hopes into rainbows of reality with the blink of an eye. He not only diminishes the forces of your enemies, He levels them to the ground. And, men with faith might ask when He does these things; why cannot exiled creatures see this going on? Because you are tormented by the sins of other men. You are fighting in darkness for the coming of the light. You are victims of other people's wretchedness, just as the Son of Man was victimized during His earthly years. This makes you sufferers like Him, but it also makes you conquerors through Him. It makes you His image because you do not surrender to the savages and naysayers who claim that spiritual faith has no place in a world of such intellect. I say that they serve no consequence at all; they have only their pride. They preach hubris for the purpose of hubris itself. The Scriptures are being fulfilled. They will someday discover that they were adversaries of their own redemption, and this rejection will haunt them upon the mortality of their souls. Indeed, not just their bodies will die, their spirits will inherit perpetual death in the pit of Hell where hellions belong. My Special son, it would appear that your Mother seems not very comforting on their behalf today, but I have said that I do not grieve for people who have been cast into Hell. It is not just that I choose not to, I cannot bring Myself to pity someone who rejects the Crucifixion that I witnessed on Good Friday. It is more than casting them beyond My thoughts and sights, it is a deep repulsion that I hold against them because they have laid claim to the fallen angels who have for centuries been the suffering and persecution of the Roman Catholic Church. And yet, even in this, I am the Compassionate Woman who carried the King of Mercy in My Womb.

I wish that I could impress upon My children that life on Earth is not a perpetual period of wanting. It is not the passing of years and decades when nothing is fulfilled. It is not just that you are standing in the wings, waiting for your moment to enter the arena or take your place at center stage. There is movement and motion everywhere because of the divisions and diversities between men. These manifestations need not be seen as counterintuitive to the growth and development of the Lord's Kingdom on Earth. All men must mature in their faith; they must practice their faith with passion and see what goodness comes when they do. They must make young men out of their elder selves while at the same time retaining the statesmanship that the Holy Spirit accords them. They must do what you and your brother have done – kept your eyes trained on the present day issues that affect your lives in reflection of the Cross 2,000 years ago. This is the timelessness not only of the Cross, but your perspective about living in exile now, your drive to make the meaning of life replicate the Love and Truth of the Innocent Victim who was crucified there. We share everything about it in advance of your deliverance into the Afterlife. This is the lesson that the Saints would have humanity learn from them in a posthumous sense. They are still teaching their survivors what survival truly means. This is the exercise of their faith through their loved ones left behind. Generations come and go, but this is the age that matters. Today is the only time for men to act, for tomorrow may bring its end. What you do in this moment shapes eternity to come. This is why you and your brother have been so successful; not only have you perfected the blessings of brotherly love, you have shown Jesus that you can make it matter to a world that you will someday see from the other side of time. And, My little son, these things not only foster My joy, they create and empower it. They are the essence of the gladness that helps Me see beyond the trials that are befalling a world that is still struggling to go on."

Sunday, November 30, 2014
9:22 a.m.

"Jesus' Suffering and the Blood of the Cross ...
Christening humanity with the nectar of redemption."

"My dear little sons, My Immaculate Heart is filled with peace because I know that the Passion of Jesus is being emulated by the poor among you, that they are propagating the message of the Gospel and the presence of the Cross worldwide. You cannot yet see that the truest poverty on the Earth is spiritual poverty, and that western societies are among the most impoverished. Today, therefore, I offer you the Will of God that we are praying for the eradication of greed and sloth even here in the United States. I have told you that capitalism is not an evil system, but the greed of those who take advantage of it makes its practice seem that way. The art of profit-making can offer a benevolent future for beggars who are hungry for food. The problems arise when sinners believe that it was all meant for them, that wealth is their gift from God. It is meant for sharing in the ways that Jesus has prescribed through the Church. I wish to tell you that the whole concept of Salvation is based upon the sharing not just of one's wealth, but one's knowledge and wisdom about the repentance of the heart. I am calling My children through such lovely works as the Morning Star Over America beneath the Cross so that humankind can 'see' the doorway to Heaven. Whether sinners choose to walk through the door is of their own volition. My Special son, you have spoken about the hypocrisy of billionaires who are aware of the problems that plague places like Uganda where Father Ted Hochstatter has served. It is their place, as you say, to stop the suffering there. They have a tremendous responsibility laid before them that they are not accepting. It is obvious that you and your brother have spent the most recent quarter century paying the debt that others have incurred through their indifference to the Gospel. You have been Jesus for them on a level that they cannot yet see. The issues that are occurring in Africa and elsewhere cannot be resolved only by financial assistance, as important as that is, but through the annihilation of the evil that is manifesting them. This is the reason we are praying here today. If the United States of America would look abroad at the plight of those who live there, do you suppose that Americans would alter their standard of living to any degree? I am convinced that those who hold the greatest wealth would not. And, therein lies the core of the evil, not only that criminals, plunderers and murderers are laying waste to foreign lands, but profiteering westerners see it and look the other way. I wish not to dwell on this any further because I have more to say about the joy in which I come. The Blood of the Cross was shed by the Lamb of God who has been slain and raised again so that all men should live. This we have known throughout our lives. It is what Christians preach around the globe. What needs to be further proclaimed is that the Blood of the Lamb is the sweetness to which all souls should be led. It is the nectar that attracts the lost and wandering, those who are not aware that the Afterlife exists. And, just like the bees attracted to this nectar, those who taste its sweetness serve as the catalyst for the growth of other missions, for the propagation of faith in places never before known, for the enhancement of the Kingdom that becomes richer because of their faith. This is the multiplication of the masses who comprise the Mystical Body of Jesus. And, as I have said on prior occasions, it only requires one taste of this sweetness for the human heart to be convinced that the promises of Jesus are true. The whole concept of Eternity becomes real for those who are touched by the power of the Holy Spirit to anticipate it. The great benefit of this is not just that humanity is led to their perpetual discovery, but there is new meaning along the way. The path becomes clearer as the purpose of life is refined.

    I know that My messages sometimes seem repetitive, that they rarely break new ground or reveal anything not previously told. However, there are no restraints on the number of ways that the Gospel can be extolled. In fact, there are more advantages to the human understanding of the New Covenant in which men will be saved than there are directions to run from it. Today, I refer to Luke 24 as this new life. So, I have the responsibility of awakening My children from their sleep, even as they are walking around. It is as though the Holy Spirit is placing the tenets of Divine Truth in their path, hoping that they will stumble over its precepts and finally come around. When people speak about alternate states and parallel universes, they are inadvertently describing the avenues down which they travel through life. They must be touched and awakened, even knocked off their feet, to the point that a flash of light causes them to change course, onto the pathway of repentance. This comes through various types of suffering, but mostly through their awareness that their bodies will ultimately break, leaving them standing spiritually naked before the Lord with no flesh in which to hide. I am describing to you the premonition of the New and Everlasting Life to which they are being led, forced into being by the events of the world, and finally by the end of one's journey through time. My Special son, you have seen all those who have died endure these crucial events. It is where My joy is its grandest because of the reckoning of the human spirit, battling against the final temptations of the devil. My Son's Crucifixion far outweighs Satan's attempts to steal lost sinners from His love. Everyone who holds fast to their faith in Jesus knows that the devil who tempted Him in the desert is the same devil whom they must renounce at the end of their lives. No bread or riches are as attractive as the Cross at that moment. Only the heart of human purpose lives beyond that point – not human in matters of flesh and bones, but human in terms of the spiritual reconciliation sought by the Father twenty centuries ago. One at a time, each man, woman and child must poise themselves before the Cross, beneath its arching branches, waiting for the Son of Man to acknowledge them as deserving of His forgiveness. They will then recognize that John 1:14 sufficed the moment, '...the Word became Flesh...' in advance of the imperatives of their confessions on that day. Jesus was not only begotten as the Incarnate Son of Man, but as ransom for those held captive by their sins. John 1:14 validates humanity's deliverance from imperfection by telling the story about what a perfect man should look like. And, My Special son, as I said two decades ago, it begins by humanity's acknowledgment that spiritual perfection can come in these times. It is not a myth that lives in a novel in someone's desk drawer, it is the pursuit of all good and decent men. It is the requirement of all who wish to feast alongside the King of kings. Yes, and as I have led My children to their place before the Cross, all of them who have given their lives to holiness, Jesus will perform the miracles to which His Sacred Heart has always been devoted. I am delivering one of them here. I am speaking to you and your brother today in ways that you could never have imagined in 1973. These are tremendous years, blessed times during which the reason you were born is being fulfilled.

I am overjoyed that you can see what you have done; that you are, and have been, saved in Jesus' Blood on the Cross from the moment you were conceived. The greatest word ever uttered by exiled men is not love or peace; it is not light or hope. It is 'yes.' With this 'yes' to the Savior of the world, He can do anything with your lives that He desires. He can end wars and heal the nations. He can clothe the naked and deliver the lost. He can come into His earthly Kingdom and ask where all the evil went that was there just moments before. And, you can respond by declaring that you drove it away through your invocation of Him. Even as the Earth is groaning beneath the burdens of sin, the sunlight is breaking the dawn of righteousness every day. I wish you to know, My Special son, that every good thing that I have said here today will happen. And, every sorrow, crime and injustice that you read and hear about will descend to its origin – the gates of Hell will open, and all evil wretches will fall like limp carcasses into its soul-devouring jaws. This is where the contrast between darkness and light will be its most stark. This is the separation of the sheep from the goats; this is where the wheat and chaff will be cleaved through the winds of human suffering, where all that is fruitful will be redeemed in the Sacrifice of the Messiah, and the rest cast away. For these reasons, My Special son, My joy cannot be annulled. I have come to you and your brother because I cannot help it – so much are you like the Fruit of My Womb. Your faces are aglow with the imminence of the Triumph of My Immaculate Heart and the Knighting of the Church. We have endured the disappointments heaped upon us by those who were supposed to take My messages to the far corners of the globe, but we remain hopeful because it will be done anyway. Yes, it will be accomplished by workers who will arrive late into the Lord's vineyard, but not so tardy that our mission will not prevail. I ask you and your brother to remain seated in the same joy by which I live. Know that your brothers and sisters are occupied by their own diversions. Their thoughts are lost and their minds are smeared. They are distracted by modern secularism from seeing what I have told you here today. This is a temporary condition of modern men from which they will be cured by everything that has yet to afflict them. It would seem that the Father must bring them to their knees to teach them to walk upright. Thank you for your kindness. I pray that all who are preparing for Christmas will remember that it is the birthday of Jesus! I will speak to you again soon."

Saturday, December 6, 2014
9:10 a.m.

"Conviction, spiritual courage and organized religion."

"My esteemed Special son, I wish to begin by speaking about the recent events involving your Bishop. These happenings are indeed highly auspicious because your Bishop has a new understanding about the seriousness in which I have come. I wish to make clear that you and your brother should maintain your poised dispositions through the grand accompaniment of Heaven that is engulfing you now. Let Me be clear. It is rare and unique for any visionaries or locutionists to evoke a formal response from a sitting Catholic Bishop about private revelations. One of the reasons they do this is because anything they say or write could be used to justify the visionaries' claims. Bishop Paprocki trusts that you and your brother will not do this unless prompted by Me. What must come in the days ahead is the steady focus by you and your brother on faith and prayer. The Holy Spirit will assist your Bishop into responding for a review of My messages. My Special son, the point I am making is that your Bishop has invoked his faith and is making a concerted effort to place your messages under episcopal scrutiny. This is not something that you and your brother should dwell on. Your lives and souls will not be examined beneath a microscope. You will not be hauled before a court of inquisitors. You will not be treated any more harshly than those who have preceded you into the halls of seers claiming the divine intercession of God. This is the 21st century, not the 14th. I ask that you maintain your composure and carry on as though little has changed. Even as I have said this, your deposit of works has taken on a life of its own. Your messages have inherited a new dimension that they never had before. They have become a living, viable fruit of your prayers and deeds as a thriving creation. This is what we have been waiting to happen for almost 24 years. All your patience has been worth the wait. Your prayers with your brother, along with Mine, have reaped the attention of many. You and your brother share the most consequential friendship in the modern history of the Roman Catholic Church. I reaffirm, however, that you should maintain your poise in everyday life without expecting victory to knock on your door at any moment. I have been waiting for these times to come since I first arrived at the side of the Father upon My Assumption. I am asking you and your brother not to run into the streets and pump your fists into the air because this is not what visionaries do, at least not yet! As My children, you may feel this way in your hearts all you desire. There is a process awaiting your deposit of works that will be shortened by your prayers. Yes, I am thankful, but My gladness is tempered by what people in exile might do. Most frequently, it consists more of procrastination than opposition. My sense is that everything having to do with the spiritual conversion of the world is always twenty centuries overdue. I am convinced, however, that these times will find humanity more pliable than rigid, especially when news of My messages to you and your brother becomes more widely known. It would seem that they will permeate the consciousness of humanity; they will be more difficult to ignore for those wishing to put My admonitions behind them. We have known that this would happen.

So for now, let Me turn to My message for today – conviction, spiritual courage and organized religion. We attest that man's conviction to the Cross of Mount Calvary will be enhanced through My presence with you. It will take a tremendous amount of courage on the part of the American Bishops to wrap their arms around everything I have said. And, they must understand the need to allow the very essence of your life with your brother to be a clear example of the organized religion over which they preside. In other words, they will have to accept as truth what I have done in this place. They will need to belay their uncertainties and grow their trust in My Queenship. They must be cautious that they, the Bishops themselves, do not play a part in inhibiting the progress of the Holy Spirit in their day. I am referring to their realization that any lack of trust in what Jesus has done through Me carries ominous consequences. Many of their advisers are worried that My supernatural intercession might hamper the ability of men to focus their faith on the Gospel. I assure you that the opposite is true. Everything I have said to My seers expands the world's knowledge of the Church and focuses the human heart on its Crucified Lord. I wish to make clear that your 2014 letters to your Bishop are assisting him in understanding the preeminence of My intercession. This is what underscores these times of supernal grace. So, the conviction and spiritual courage about which I speak are being effected during these days, and it is just in time for what we must do for the lost and brokenhearted. I know that you have been wondering what will become of your life in the event that millions of people turn their eyes to your works. This would be a marvelous burden to suffer, and I implore that you comport with the sacred attitude of Jesus during His most evocative years. Think about the confluence of His Sacrifice and Resurrection as though there were no hours between them. We must give the Church time to process what you and your brother have presented its leaders, and they will need time to reflect on your written communications. Your Bishop has given humanity a tremendous gift by asking whether you wish a formal review to begin; it is like the Apollo 13 spacecraft having to enter the Earth's atmosphere at the precise angle so as not to glide off course into outer space. One would have greater odds of winning the lottery twice in the same day. These things rarely happen in the world, but your Bishop has invoked his deepest faith. He has acted because you and your brother encouraged him with the confidence of the Holy Spirit in your hearts. I wish you well in everything you do to bring about the conversion of sinners. I am with you, and I assist you. Thank you for your holy prayers."

Saturday, December 13, 2014
9:31 a.m.

"Relief for the poor, knighthood for the prince, a crown for the Church – ... and a berth of redemption awaits them all."

"Surely, My dear children, you are aware of the esteem in which you are held by God and His Only Begotten Son. It must be clear to you by now that your souls are adorned not only with absolution, but with the makings of kings. You have given the world the blessing of your own humanity, one that excels in spiritual beauty and the graciousness accorded to those of true faith. My purpose in coming to speak to you today is one of consistent gratitude for all these things. It is a sacred beauty about which I speak, the traits that make you like Jesus, Himself. What this feels like – what it means to be transformed from imperfection into complete perfection is a sensation that I never felt because I have always been perfect. However, I realize that it is the same as someone being able to remember their own birth, and to be aware of breaking beyond the Earth into the Lord's eternity, becoming one and single-minded with the Fashioner of the universe, and to accede willingly over and again to His glory. My Special son, your existence here in the exile of men was always meant to prepare them for what I have given you. When I speak about giving relief to the poor, knighthood for the prince and a crown for the Church, I am speaking not only about deliverance from poverty, I am referring to miracles much greater than winning great battles. Yes, I am speaking about a turn of events that heralds the redemption of the world. Why? Because these things are as much about process as outcome. They mean as much in the planting, growing and cultivating as they do during the harvest. This is the reason I have spoken so meaningfully to your brothers and sisters down through the ages, because for you, Heaven begins here. Yes, in many ways, it continues here because the Afterlife entails clearing the battlefields of the world through your newfound 'being' and seeding roses into the soil where the blood of your companions was once shed. Here, I am calling you to see and see again what your faith has meant to God. It is your way of feeding Him at the same time He nourishes your heart. He consumes what you mean to Him. He soaks up your holiness and offers thanksgiving in return. He spares due punishment to those who reject Him because of the sacrifices of those who search for Him every day of their lives. This is the unity of the Savior and the saved. It is your medium for seeing what is innate to the Crucifixion, by knowing what soothes the Father's aching Heart through the obedience of His people. Indeed, a berth of redemption awaits all who believe in Him and forthrightly prove it. My little son, we have meditated on Advent that has now come, and I know this seems a contradiction in terms. An Advent that has already come. This implies that something for which someone is waiting stands before them now. This is the timelessness of your faith. It is clear that you not only believe in the transition of men into the folds of all life's glorious imaginings, but that this is happening as we speak. This is the true origin of man's happiness, and the fruits of it too. The passing decades are bringing you to a wonderful new beginning that you are finding easier to expect. The fullness of your service to the Church is proceeding, and it will not conclude until you have said your last prayer. Even as all who have died speak audibly here no more, their prayers are transformed because they recite them in the presence of the Father as Saints. This is the goal of your life. It is the outcome of your gift of faith to God. It is the best lesson that Jesus ever taught those who would seek Him. Prayer is the crown that you place on your intentions, presenting them to Jesus again and again, asking Him to remember that He is indeed the King. It is impossible for anyone who believes in Jesus to ever turn back. I have told you this many times before. Let Me give you an example. If you see a holy image of something that brings you to tears, this glory is imprinted indelibly in the fabric of your heart. Later, if you see images of horrible scourges, ugly battles, bloodbaths in the streets, children slaughtered, and innocent people battered and burned, you might wonder where all the glory went. It is here that the image of glorious splendor takes its most powerful form.

When a person accepts the Cross of Jesus as their deliverance into Heaven, even as grotesque as this image is, this same person is comforted and enlightened when he sees His Resurrection from the Tomb. Beyond all your life's battles resides images of peace and tranquility. When your eyes feast on the Glory of Jesus in comparison to the battles of the world, your soul goes to Jesus for all futures to come. You are able to see the Stations of the Cross in the woodwork of your eternal redemption. Even more so, you are able to unify yourself with His Easter Resurrection that is much more satisfying to your eyes. Once deceased, forever raised! These are the images that come to all men who find themselves at Jesus' side in Paradise. Humanity must become one with Him, allow Him to live in them and humanity in Him, so that you can stand beside Him in the New Jerusalem. This is an eternal oneness that begins here, even as you and I are speaking alongside your brother, your best friend. And today, I further come to remind you that you have given Me and the Angels and Saints more to savor, more gladness and joy, more hope and inspiration. It is not just about living for tomorrow anymore. It is about now as well. What meaningfulness you glean from hour to hour is a gift to Me and Jesus. We are with you entirely for the purpose of calling your soul to Heaven; you must remember that eternal glory is found in these things. Worthiness. This is the word that comes to mind. You and your brother are so 'worthy.' This is a term that encompasses your service to the Church, your dedication to the mission of the First Apostles, your willingness to pray, your acceptance of suffering, and your prospects for purifying the lives of other men. All these things make you and your brother worthy in the eyes of the Father. And, the synonym that describes your hearts is 'sacred.' Yes, you have adopted a life of sanctity while you have been adopted by Me. You will discover upon the conclusion of the mortal realms that we have always been one. Through the Crucifixion of Jesus, you were never orphaned because the Spirit of the Lord has been perpetually yours. In the eternal, you can attest to the wholeness of Creation that you never left the Father's side, even as you were descendants of Adam and Eve. You would have been advocates for absolute obedience when confronted with temptation by the devil. This is the way you are living now. You would have told the woman that she was turning away from Divine Truth. You would have insisted that there would have been consequences that could last an eternity in themselves. And, this is what you are telling the sinners of the world today. It is clear that you inherited Adam's error, but your oneness with the New Adam has proved your righteousness all along. This is because of your obedience to the Father. You have lived as Jesus has taught. You have given your life to the Virgin Mother of God. My Special son, there is no more favorable way to approach the resurrected Savior of the world. Neither priests nor religious can boast that they have given more to the conversion of the lost than lay people who are consecrated to Me. This is why I pray for all who have yet to accept My role in the conversion of humanity on Earth.

My Special son, I will ask now what you have to say, or if you have any questions that you would like to ask. (*I had recently traveled across the United States and recognized the glaringly different cultures and the more liberalized approaches to human conduct in the American northwest. I referred my observations to our Holy Mother.*) Yes, you have traveled to another state and discovered its more worldly environment. You live here in the heartland of the United States of America where the culture is clearly different. I believe the word that you are searching for is 'radicalness.' Those regions on the coasts and elsewhere that do not espouse the simplicities of life seem in radical departure from what you have come to know. I am not passing judgement on who they are, I am comparing them to the way Jesus wants them to live. You are seeing that today's America is trying to reduce the Holy Gospel to just another manuscript in the marketplace. It seems like an outdated teaching that is separate from their alternative ways of life. However, they only have styles, while the teachings of Jesus Christ have New Life. They are trying to integrate sin into men's way of life, while God is trying to purge the Earth of sin altogether. They wish to ignore the call of the conscience, and Jesus is trying to clarify what having a conscience really means. They aspire to little more than sleeping through the trials of life, while the teachings of the Church are heralding the Scriptures that will eradicate them altogether. Faith to these radicals is something far too complex for them to grasp. Holiness is something they discarded with their dead parents' clothes. And, responsibility to accept and promote the sanctity of life is so foreign to them that they might as well be less than human themselves. I have told you of the beauty in which you were born, given the birthright of being My children through the New Covenant Gospel, and now come to this day as the dignified followers of Jesus, the Christ. Your existence here on Earth could not have taken a more blessed course. I have completed My message for today – for all the poor, for the princes waiting their knighthood commission, and for the Church that stands poised to inherit its crown. She is indeed a beautiful sight to behold. Thanks be to God! And, bless you for saying such holy prayers every day and being one with the Sacred Heart of Jesus. I hope you have a meaningful Advent, as Christmas will soon arrive."

Saturday, December 20, 2014
9:26 a.m.

"I have noticed that when God wins, He does not just win handsomely, but with outright shocking overwhelm – inundating the soul, sight and senses of the human person with a veritable super-blast of triumph that could never be contained."

- William L. Roth

"My Special son, this is an extremely beautiful and truthful sentiment that you have shared to begin our message today. It is true because it extols the revelation of unexpected victories that come along the way, the many that are manifested by humanity's bold and spontaneous acts of faith. We share together the hope that My children in every state of this nation and on every continent of the world will turn to the Lord in trust, not caring whether they will have the ability to sustain their current lifestyles, wishing only to enrich the old Earth with the sacredness of God's love. When you speak of outright shocking overwhelm, you refer to the ability of Heaven to be apparent here in this life through human holiness so profound that it can scarcely be seen as merely of this domain. I give you My solemn promise that this is what every person experiences at least once in his life, and some people secure this level of mysticism for decades at a time. Still, this gift must compete with other less ethereal forces on the Earth that tend to shear the spiritually-enlivened soul of its elevation. I have said that the sins of other men are the greatest opposition to the peace of the human heart. It is clear that there must be a new deference grown in the exile of men that allows for the propagation of such things as My composite of messages to you and your brother, and indeed in all lands. There is an attempt by humanity to conceal their own blindness from those whom they would have believe that they are aware of the teachings of the Church. There were actor portrayals in the motion picture that you recently watched where the main character was driving an automobile down the back streets of a city. He was stopped by a policeman; a conversation ensued, the driver's credentials were produced, and the policeman issued a verbal warning and drove away. But, what was the irony as the motion picture continued? The policeman never realized that the driver he stopped was blind. This is the same way that secular men are pretending to fool God into believing that they can see their own way. And, just like the unwitting policeman, the Lord allows these lost sinners to proceed until they crash into their own fate. It is not that God is unaware that these sinners are blind, but He wishes them to discover it themselves. My Special son, this is the origin of the lessons that humanity encounters every day. Those who are not committed to Christ Jesus through their acceptance of the Cross place themselves behind the obstacles of their own faithlessness before they rise from their morning beds. Then, when they do arise, they look into the mirror and see a skewed depiction of what they are supposed to look like; not the living, breathing essence of human holiness that is embodied through authentic consecration to the Father who gave them life. Today, you are awaiting the arrival of the celebration of the Birth of Jesus, a grand high feast that you have observed scores of times. It is not that you have repeatedly celebrated Christmas that matters most, but that you realize what Christmas means. Here again, this places you among the minority of the world's people who engage the Spirit of God in beatific terms, your willingness to comply with the Will of the Child, Prince and King who owns the universe. Your exchange of gifts is that you accept the Lord's presence that, as you say, often comes with shocking overwhelm, and you offer your own gifts of prayer and uprightness to Him in return. This is what is happening between Heaven and Earth every moment of every day. It is the oil that keeps the lamps of the Catholic Church shining so brilliantly. It is the energy for your propagation of My Morning Star Over America messages. My Special son, this action does not happen just naturally, it is requisitioned through the prayers of holy men. This is what you are doing with Me now.

We have not stopped the movement of human life to do this; we are feeding the righteousness of the world while it remains in motion. My little son, this is a source of tremendous joy to the Father and the Hosts of Heaven! Surely you can see this in your heart when you realize that nothing tethered to His Son will ever be lost again. Everything that contributes to the refinement of the Earth and the success of the Church is safeguarded inside and outside of time. We are blessed as Mother and son, you and I, along with your brother and all who believe in the Holy Gospel. I am the only Creature celebrated in the Scriptures who was a perfect participant in the life of the world's Savior. Everyone else spoken about in the Salvation of the world is in need of the Blood of Jesus to be resurrected from the grave. I have no grave because I never had a need for one. I have never died, but was assumed alive into Glory. And yet, I have witnessed the deaths of My children with awesome mourning and celebration too. I have seen the Father's Will protracted through the ages with unparalleled sympathy, especially during times when men and women agonized over their final days. Their childlike innocence was reborn through their own suffering. Their ability to see themselves anew was accorded them through their imitation of the Christ Child in the Manger who set the example for what all earthbound kings must do. They must be true, simple, honest and charitable at the same time they sacrifice for their people, even to the point of death. This is revealed in the heroism of great warriors on the battlefield. It is exemplified by anyone who commits to living like Jesus to the diminishment of their own well-being and comfort. You have by now noticed that one of My favorite passages from the Bible is the suggestion that those who follow Jesus must become like little children. They must have the sacrificial innocence that accompanies the acceptance of Christian life. This does not mean that mature wisdom must be shed or shelved. After all, a twelve-year-old prodigy can have the courage to throw the money changers out of the temple. The point I am making is that this is all a grand and splendorous mixture of gentleness and poise, of vision and virtue, of reaching out and pulling in. It is knowing that the Father will provide – He will set forth the venues and dictate the language. He will hand down the settings and stipulate the courses. He will lead all who believe in Him through the dark corridors in which they find themselves while flushing out their brothers and sisters who are still living in sin, as blind as the driver whom I mentioned moments ago. The key is whether someone knows that he is blind, and whether he is trying to conceal it from his Master.

My Special son, there are more people denying themselves the joy of the Christian life who are fully aware of what it holds than there are those who have no clue of what Christianity is about. This is the arrogance that Jesus has been battling for 2,000 years. And, it is the reason I keep appearing here in the twilight realms, still speaking and blessing, still touching hearts and changing minds. There is no measure to what I have done, but a matter of longevity. I am not subject to the constraints of time or space, so I never tire from My role as Queen of Heaven and Earth. What is troubling, however, is watching My children continuously turning away from the Truth in favor of the falseness of the world. Riches are too compelling; the allures of the flesh are too gratifying, and human endeavors are too inebriating for them to stop what they are doing and see themselves standing still, naked and penitent before Jesus at the foot of the Cross. I have always believed that feasts like Christmas and Easter take hold in sinners who would otherwise not understand the spiritual life. Sadly, while these are great opportunities for the awakening of the human heart, they seem not enough to offset the long days of the year. My children require more miracles and reasons to believe. This makes the case for My presence here. Even those who cannot see Me know that I have come; it is My countenance shining My love where there is looming darkness. It is My perfume of holiness that they detect in the air. It is My calling to Jesus that they can hear echoing in the night. My Special son, you and your brother are participants in this gift; you are attendants for the Mother of God in the same way as the Angels. You are priceless and indispensable in the conversion of lost humanity to the Cross of its Redeemer. And, this is the reason you are so pleased. Yes, it is true that you and your brother are joyful to be together, but the focus of your happiness is knowing that you have made such a difference in the mission of the Church. Your hearts know this to be true! It is based on your prayers and the Lord's gratitude for your lifelong obedience to Me. There is an awesome framework of labors unfolding as the new year is about to begin."

Saturday, December 27, 2014
9:24 a.m.

"I have learned from the Blessed Virgin Mary that human conversion is not so much a punishment device as it is sympathetic behavioral modification, clearly less about retribution than reorientation. It is before this backdrop of healing and virtue that the Roman Catholic Church stands idyllically pleasing in sight of the Father, that He beholds His Son's Mystical Body with His own sense of gratitude, compassion and welcoming."

- William L. Roth

"My precious little boys, it is My sincere honor to be here again today, speaking to you of your redemption in Jesus, telling of the glorious Kingdom that is overcoming the Earth. We have spoken about this life and the life ever after, and we have captured for humanity a means of new awakening to rival no other kind. We have proved that life makes up in elevation what it lacks in longevity. And yes, we have said that the greatest problem with pain is that it demands to be felt. You must realize that Jesus' Passion was His endurance of pain for the glory of love. It is for this reason that all men should accept this gift. I have come today to offer My concluding message for 2014 and say that you are no longer running through life as if passing through a corridor. When you received the letter from your Bishop, you emerged from that kind of life's narrowness and are sailing upon the lofty crests of the Triumph of My Most Immaculate Heart. You will live the proceeding years, but they will not have the same constraints as past decades. The ensuing years are to be lived by you with profound confidence and joy. Instead of showing you as two stick figures running through the corridor of time, I am now pressed to say that you are like two eagles in flight that time itself cannot impede. This makes you much like the Angels themselves, and as the Saints who live in Heaven and on the Earth as well. We are saying to the world's constitution that nothing can hinder you from overcoming its barbs and lances. I have said that your approach to Jesus is with sureness and brotherhood, that your life's expression is of certainty and inevitability. In essence, you have given yourselves so wholly to the Cross that you could not turn back now if you wanted to. All the bridges that connected you to your previous lives have been destroyed. You are lighter than air and unimpeded by gravity. Why so? Because you see through the eyes of Jesus Christ with the vision of the Father. I am saying that you are mature in faith and youthful in compliance. You are like the children who are eager to learn, but who have already mastered the true lessons of life. And together, we have asked humanity to never let the devil leave fingerprints on their faith. We have requested that they be determined to deny Satan the opportunity to sit at his table in the fiery pit and say, 'Please pass the souls.' My Special and Chosen ones, we have done this because you have concurred with God in all things penitential, in everything to do with the redemption of the Church. Today, therefore, I am telling you that I intend to speak to you long into the future, into 2015 and further, if this be the Will of the Father. I will remain with you forever beyond this world, giving you strength and succor while the old Earth withers away. This is not something that I have reserved just for you, but for all who have preceded and shall succeed you. The Child in the Manger has made humanity a bed not made of straw, but of love. He has willed that you should be dignified in ways that were denied to Him. He has forged into being a placid life of harmony through the suffering that He willingly endured. Also today, I am with you in unity and prayer for the Roman Catholic Church and all who fight on its behalf. It is more than an honor to be a member of the Church, it is the ordaining of the future of the exiled human soul. We have seen its elegance and pageantry, its long standing poise in the shadows of the ages. We aspire to flourish its beauty across the nations and seas because it creates for the human spirit a sense of living destiny.

This is what the solemn Feast of Christmas leaves in the thoughts of those who believe. It is giving, and giving even more. It is a commencement of the new beginnings that I spoke about in 1991. Yes, My little sons, it is more than a mere mentioning of the Nativity of Jesus, it is the internalization of what it means that God took on the flesh of Man, and everything it implies about what sinners should believe. It is not possible for someone to refuse to think about something unless he thinks about what he is trying to forget. This is man's ultimate paradox. This is how God pierces the human consciousness without saying a single word. Atheists must consider that there must be a God whose existence they have chosen to deny. Is this a trap set out by the Creator of the universe? Yes, it is. And, it is one that all men must face before they close their eyes in death. What is not a trap, however, is that wicked men have the ability to choose their own fate. They have the choice to either accept or reject Salvation in the Blood of the Cross. And, every time someone accepts, they offer themselves the benefaction of eternity, and they offer God their gift of genuine homage for the life and Crucifixion of His Son. Any time someone rejects their Salvation in Jesus' Holy Sacrifice, they set themselves not only on the pathway to condemnation, but a path that begins the moment they refuse. The Mystical Body of Jesus is growing in this earthly domain larger by the day through the conversion of lost sinners, but this marvelous strain of repentant souls is living among radical evildoers whose ruses and plots they must avoid. It is clear, however, that the evil acts of the devil are making themselves more apparent as time passes by. My Special son, you and your brother are living the remaining days of 2014 with the same sanctity that you entered it. I am here with you; it is obvious that you are spreading your messages given so carefully by Me to the heartbeat of your prayers. We must be thankful that you have placed yourself in a position to do the most good for God. This is the life you have chosen; it is your gift to Heaven for everything Jesus is giving to you. We cannot deny those who are still trying, can we? We cannot say that they will never get there. We must remember that some workers will come into the vineyard at the final hour of the day. This is the reason we pray for them; it is the purpose of our hopes in the outcome of the world. And, it is here that we find our satisfaction in all our labors, in what we anticipate for the future of the Church, in what we expect through the christening that Jesus has bestowed by the miracle of His Paschal Resurrection.

My Special son, one does not have to hold a priestly vocation to advance the Kingdom of God. It is all about whom the Holy Spirit touches, and how those who are touched respond. I have spoken about reciprocation before; it has always been about what God has done for man. You and your brother are evidence that the Father binds things in Heaven that were not bound there before, and He will loose things in Heaven not loosed at the beginning of your lives. He hears those who defer to His Kingdom in ways that could never be anticipated in the annals of exiled men. You are enlightened by your Christian obedience, and humanity is blessed because of your prayers. So, as this year 2014 passes into history, I ask you to remember those who have come to rest in Jesus, your uncle John Roth and all who have died in the Lord's friendship. Always know that they are praying for you as you fight for righteousness in their stead, that you serve where they once struggled for the advancement of the Church. Perfect they were not, but they knew to try. They forfeited untold comforts so the conversion of the lost could be widely advanced. This is their legacy, and it is what Jesus appreciates most. What AD 2015 brings has yet to be revealed, but it is well anticipated by Me. I live in Heaven and on Earth with the benefit of knowing that manifest abruptions do happen. This is the spontaneity of the Kingdom of the Father, and it will remain this way until Jesus comes again. It is the reason that My messages here and around the globe foster so much hope, so many prophecies yielding to prayer, so much expectancy in seeking God's favor in exchange for manifest faith. There are millions of exiled men who are breaking and broken, and there are millions more given the capacity to believe. This is what I seek from My children. My Special son, proof that this is all bearing fruit is that I am yet appearing around the globe. If there were no possibility of humanity's repentance, confession and amendment, I would not be here speaking to you now."

The Final Colossus
In the Light of Her Majesty
AD 2015

Sunday, January 4, 2015
9:32 a.m.

"Your honor is truly glorious, your purity is precious,
your heavenly gait becomes you."

"My precious sons, the words you just heard describe you with profound accuracy, so much are you cherished and admired by God the Father. I am here with you as we pray for the conversion of lost sinners. Also today, I am elated that 2015 will bring so much progress toward the propagation of My messages of the past twenty-four years. My Special son, I will speak briefly today because this is sometimes what I do. We think about what blessings have already come for the prospects of change. You are not connected to those who desire change for the sake of change; you pray for the world to transform into the Kingdom that will eclipse life on the Earth as humanity has always known it. The power brokers and profit seekers around you do not want this to happen because it will mean the downfall of their ill oppression against the poor. I am overjoyed that there is coming a new invigoration of the Catholic Church in America, to the tremendous surprise of its leaders. This is part of the miracle that I told you would come by the prayers and sacrifices of the humble Christians whose names are never heard on the airwaves or published on outdoor placards. We must, My Special son, never lose sight of what this means to us. It is the culmination of what I have done in America for the past 250 years. It is a connecting value to My miracles throughout the Republic of Mexico. Yes, it will bring new energy to the entire western hemisphere through the Spirit of God in places that have been unsung. What causes all this, My little one, is the Father responding to what He sees in people like you, servants who give without reward, who pray unnoticed, who devoutly turn to Heaven for divine assistance without being prompted. This is what I have been saying to My messengers for generations, particularly in places where My apparitions have not been recognized by the Church. It is clear that everything for which I have prayed will come to pass without the great battles lost to those who must fight them. This is what I want you to remember, My Special son. It is not that the battles will or will not come, but that they will be won when they do arrive. This is what My prayers have always meant to Jesus. I ask Him to intercede before the Father as I intercede for you before Him. This is the reciprocation that unites us as God's people, that connects Heaven and the Earth in the spiritual provinces, that precedes the mending of everything that still lies broken at your feet. My Special son, I will bless everyone for whom you and your brother are offering your petitions."

Saturday, January 10, 2015
9:33 a.m.

"Let this be your new beginning; make this the reason for your lives."

"Dear to My Immaculate Heart, conceived for the well being of humanity's future, praying for the conversion of all lost souls, you are part of Me, and I am part of you. We have copiously shared through the years your commitment to wholesome change here in this land, the change that I spoke about last week. What must come for your brothers and sisters is their understanding of everything I have said to you for more than two decades. And, My Special and Chosen ones, this is what makes your communication with your Bishop and others so refined. You are excellently approaching the task of teaching the world about the Cross in the process of My long-living interaction with you. It is clear that not all new beginnings happen on the tops of mountains. True change is rarely like lighting a candle; it is about making subtle alterations in the way people think by allowing them to see themselves in different ways. My Special son, you would agree that My means of awakening the sleeping hearts around you has not been to make them feel unworthy. It has not been My plan to walk into the created realms and tell your brothers and sisters that they are 'really in for it' when their Father gets home. I have highlighted the benefits of self-preservation through the alignment of the human soul with the teachings of God. And, I have explained that progress toward this goal is measured by each person doing his own aligning. No one is dragged into Heaven against his will. We have been in the process of explaining what Salvation means in comprehensible terms. What good does it do to hope for something unless a person has some grasp on the outcome? What good is a product if its purpose has not been explained? This is why I have always led My children onto the landscape of redemption that has had previous care already instilled. In other words, I am taking My children to an ethereal neighborhood where they can choose to share the Lord's eternal mansions. When they awaken before the gateway of that Kingdom, they recognize they must for all futures be satisfied knowing that they had a voice in their destiny. Jesus never promised a Heaven that could never be understood. While He did not articulate the full description of what eternal absolution looks like, He allows each Christian to conceive what Heaven might be through their own reflections. This has many reasons, and chief among them is that Heaven cannot be described in words. We have known this all along. But, the second reason is that Heaven keeps changing every day, here in the time that you are living. It never loses its glory and beauty; it never adds or subtracts any truths. Heaven changes based on what humanity's prayers might be. These changes are in reaction to the ways that good men and women find to overcome their temptation to sin. Heaven changes as the eternal record is amended to capture the new blessings that come. Prayer changes the future of men, and changed humanity enriches the character of Heaven. It is a revelation of the ongoing new life of exiled men that grows in wisdom and virtue day after day. It is not just that Christians want to touch God, to see and engage Him, but that God desires with the infinity of His power to touch His creatures without seeming oppressive. The Father is the Lord. He can enter any room He pleases and nobody can stop Him, but this is not really His plan. God wants to be invited where He goes. He wants to be seen as the Benevolent Shepherd who admires the voices and honors the decisions of His flock. He stands as the most beautiful origin in all the universes combined. He is absolving and evocative. He is ordaining and contemplative. And, He wants everyone pursuing a relationship with Jesus to do so in their own way, as long as this way concludes in obedience to His Divine Will. This is the miracle that He has been seeking since the Fall of Adam. He is imploring humanity to become miracle workers for Him. He asks all who believe in Him to say why, even though He already knows.

It is a voice of acclamation that God wants to hear, that His creatures are being assimilated into His Kingdom of their own accord. Hence, if it is true that God is more interested in preserving the human will than preserving human life, this is the way it must be. This is how much of His own energy and sovereignty that He has dispensed to His disciples, that they will be known even by His own genius because they believe who He is. They will have the virtue and willpower to bless the lowly and uplift the poor. They will know whom to strike down and when to strike them. They will know that their prayers and pious reflections have the power of earth movers, the authority to reconfigure the chambers of Heaven and make way for the deepest hopes of those who have believed. My Special son, this is the faith that I have been describing to you for twenty-four years; it is not just that you are holy and pretty, not just that you comport with what a Christian is supposed to do. It is that you have accepted your part as fashioner of the life that lies beyond. You are aware of the nature of your own destiny, the invaluable essentialness of your perpetual worthiness before the Cross of your redemption. Hear Me now. It is not just that Jesus wants to remake humanity like Himself, but that He wants to preserve everything about you except your brokenness that has been so pleasing to God. He wants to wash clean your beauty stained by Adam and place you alongside the treasures that He has accorded the Father in Heaven. My Special son, you and I know that this is no ordinary endeavor. It was not that human beings had been exempted from damnation before Jesus came to live among you. He wanted to make the Cross the only redemptive instrument, the restoration of the divine nature of a fallen species to which this species should aspire to return. And, while Jesus does not create evil, He came to be its nemesis so the human will about which I have spoken could sense the perfect likeness of itself. Yes, Jesus came to Earth to tell His disciples what they are supposed to look like. He did not want you to see your eternal image until He helped prepare the way you should appear. This has been an exercise in success and futility as well. Some sinners do not want to be converted, either on the inside or outside. Others seem unaware of what it means. But, Christians are particularly well informed about what spiritual conversion is, how one's soul should be cleansed and dressed, what makes them more appealing in the eyes of God. This is how the Gospel continues to be the priceless medium for preparing human souls to see their reflections at the end of their days. And, knowing to view the Kingdom of God through its teachings and tenets is His gift for those who will confide in Jesus at that moment. We speak of landscapes and beauty, of potential and possibility, of touching and conversion, of supernatural truth and beatific loyalty, and everything else that unites Heaven and Earth through human obedience. It is the Lord's prescription for conceptual perfection, made manifest by those who love Him, and is propagated by people who collectively agree that God's Kingdom must 'Be.' It is advanced by their collaboration in helping it prosper because this is what Church-inspired faith does. It flourishes inside and outside Creation to suffice the billions of souls who will inhabit its plenteousness after the final story has been told. This is the revelation of the Messianic City that was chartered with the Annunciation of the Archangel Gabriel.

My Special son, I hope My words have not been too abstract to explain what I have been trying to say. It is not just that humanity is exiled, but that men have a deliverance from exile. It is that mortal souls have a more consequential role than standing idle while the ages of the Earth pass away. As righteousness transforms the Earth into a new kind of being, the imminence of perfection takes deeper hold. It shapes the new identity of the world. All the shootings and mass killings can never impede this process. Cultures and countercultures cannot soil the primacy of the Roman Catholic Church. This is where you and your brother find yourselves. You have been provided for; your futures have been sealed. Your esteem before God is assured. And, as I have said on many occasions, you will see what I am saying as the years expire. I commend you and your brother for the letter you are preparing for your Bishop. It contains precisely the words to advance My wishes. It will highlight his standing before Me, and give him reason to believe that his life as a priest is having eternal consequences. My little son, thank you for remembering all who have no food or shelter during the wintertime months. I shall bless them all as you wish."

Saturday, January 17, 2015
9:23 a.m.

"Let this Kingdom stand sure, let this Truth devour its beastly enemies; let this message be heard once again; imparted, fixed and undefiled."

- Jesus Christ, on the Third Day

"My little sons, these are among the most profound and lovely words that Jesus said upon His Resurrection, meant to reward the faith of all who believe, given with the promise that His Kingdom will never die. My Immaculate Heart is elated to speak to you here again and give you comfort and assurance that your labors are never in vain. I hold in My words a means of enlightening you about the inevitability of the future, one that is bright and shining as a city on a hill, one that cannot be reversed or expunged by the vileness of men. Yes, Jesus said on Easter morning that His message shall be heard once again, and for all times and seasons. The Gospel shall be imparted, fixed and undefiled because it lives on in Him. And, it likewise lives on through those who do His bidding in this world and the next. My dear children, where does a Mother begin to express what this means to God? He has propagated life where humanity has taken refuge in Him. He has implanted His supreme Spirit in those who open like flowers to the sun. Why does He do these things? What meaning in Creation does the manifestation of the perfection of the world accord the ages that might have come? It means that those ages are being transcended today. It says that the intent of human beings to become like their Creator in all things righteous is validated through their faith. Life is forever beginning and growing, but it never wholly dies. It surely changes from one century to the next, from glorious morning until moonlit night, and from mortality to everlasting life. But, life is given permanently to those who accept its origin in the Will of God. I have said that this miracle can be observed and touched; it can see and hear you. It can sustain you through the darkest moments of your exile on Earth. It gives you the ability to perceive with perspective the redemptive power of suffering. My purpose as your Matriarch and Divine Intercessor has been more than just to pray for you, as paramount as that is, but to teach you how to live. I am the Woman who beckons all who are awaiting the Lord's last summoning call. I have been the Queenly Clarion for everyone who will eventually join the Saints in Heaven. I have imparted My messages to those whom I knew would never turn their backs on Me. I have lent My listening ear to the petitions of My children who are in need of strength from above. My little sons, these are not extraordinary gifts that I have offered to you, they are routine measures that come because I love you. Someday, someone may ask what the Mother of God does every day. Your response is that She searches for ways to break through the indifference of the temporal world to reach the deepest recesses of Her children's spiritual hearts. I make it the cause of My Queenship to awaken the sleeping, soften the way people think about life, and offer a new vision for the future that they could never have gained on their own. Today, My Special son, I come with accolades and appreciation for you and your brother. I bring with Me the hopes that I have always shared with you. Yes, there is focus and momentum to the way you live, but there is also perspective and eternal design. You are to be commended for this, for seeing life coherently and making the choices that will spread the Gospel worldwide. All around the globe, people are infighting and battling across great divides. There is bloodshed and mourning, revelatory new beginnings that bring some to reassess the meaning of their lives. There are chasms to close and endings to reckon. The whole matter seems senseless in the grand view of things because there is so much futility in it. What is the war against terrorism if not the battle against the devil? Those who follow the lie of a so-called faith not originating in the Father of Jesus Christ are no more than atheists of another stripe. They shame the true meaning of faith and stain the purpose of giving oneself to a higher being. This war on terrorism is no more crucial than the war to preserve unborn human life ongoing here in the United States of America.

  What does it mean that an unborn child cannot cry out that his birth is the Will of the Father? It means that those who are charged with protecting his life have been deluded by Satan to believe that there is no human life there at all. My Special son, this is why your conversation the other day with the young man was of such perfection. No one had ever laid the desecration of your nation at the feet of the U.S. Supreme Court in his company before. He had never drawn the connection. And, your comments and advice were the substance of prayers to God; this is how Jesus heard them. Many have said that even if Roe vs. Wade is overturned tomorrow, it will be too late to have saved the 65 million children who have been killed in the United States alone. The Lord's response may surprise them. If prayers to end abortion are sufficient to save the life of at least one unborn child, then the prayers of an entire nation over a span of forty years will have served their purpose. Yes, and let Jesus then rewrite history in the way

I have said. Both the motivation of men and the momentum of the years must lean toward the direction of preserving human life. I have said that Jesus was a child prodigy and boy genius; that even in His youth, He understood the workings of mature men. He was aware of the forces of the world and the alignment of the stars not just because He was the Son of Man, but because He allowed His Sacred Heart to survey the tortured ground on which He lived. This is what He practiced to perfection; and He still does. This is what He has always asked from those who believe in Him, those who follow Him. This surveying of the moral makeup of the contemporary Earth must begin anew, to measure the agonizing immorality of humanity against the teachings of the Church. To say that mortal men are found wanting is putting it mildly. The whole application of the New Covenant Gospel in today's world is to indict nine out of ten sinners for treason against the Lord's Kingdom. This is not just something I am saying, it is being declared by celestial forces every day; by the moon and sun, by the winds and rains, by the axes of east and west, north and south that must endure the ravages of human sin seemingly without end. You and your brother stand beside Me and kneel before Me. You have the capacity to see as Jesus sees what is perpetrated against His Kingdom in these times. It is the reason that the word 'appalling' was spoken from the beginning. The good news is that we are seeing the death of human iniquity as we speak. We are witnessing the defeat of those who prefer to live without God. By all means, they shall get their wish. They will go where the life-giving waters of love and relief never flow. They will reside where flames and brazenness accompany their every hour. Yes indeed, they will receive their dark inheritance according to the fate they have procured on their own. This is the war that we are watching unfold. It is the battle that ensues in every nation of the world. It is the fight against evil being waged on every continent and in every precinct of exiled humanity. So, when someone asks what the Mother of God does every day, remind them that I do the same thing as you and your brother. I assure Jesus that His Sorrowful Crucifixion was not in vain. I tell the Angels that everything will be fine in the end. I invoke the supplications of the Church in all things righteous and forgiving.

    And here today, My Special son, I recount the blessing that you and your brother have been to Me. I extol your holiness before everyone to whom I speak in Heaven and on Earth. I celebrate the tenderness of your hearts and the ever-present distinction by which you live. It is My honor, yes, My privilege to be your Mother. I cannot imagine ever being more pleased than I am to come speaking to you and listening to the sonnets of your soul-rhyming hearts. I am overjoyed by hearing about your vision of what the lives of men ought to be.

There are billions of people on the surface of the globe, but most of them cannot bring themselves to accept their origin in the God of Abraham about whom I spoke just moments ago. They decline the overtures that would take them to the pinnacle of human faith. Even if someday the sun would plummet from the skies again and parch the soil on which they stand, they would write it off as some kind of happenstance having nothing to do with God. Yes, even if the number of seers was 70 million instead of 70,000 they would find some way to hold on to their obstinance out of pride or habit, or something else. Not so with the Children of Mary! This is not the case with those whose hearts are affixed to the promises of Christ! We know what the faithless will eventually come to realize, that false gods run rampant around the globe, that these false gods are manifestations of the devil, and these false gods have the impudence to lure innocent people away from their destiny in Heaven. It is through Jesus' Crucifixion that they are rescued. It is through the suffering of His Mystical Body in the confines of time that they are awakened. My Special son, you know that I am not a wagerer, but I am placing My stakes on the fact that everything the Roman Catholic Church teaches will ultimately come to pass. All for which Christianity stands will be vindicated before the backdrop of the ages. Blood and art, truth and honor, work and reliance, gift and sacrifice – all these things constitute the manifest miracle that has always defined the lives of decent men. And, it is with this sense of victory that Jesus spoke on Easter morning. He speaks this way still. He invites and consecrates. He assures and confirms. Yes, He administers oaths and delivers on His promises. My Special son, do you have anything to add to My message today? *"It is awesome. I could listen to you talk like this every day, all day. I just want to find some way to transfer this to the world with a megaphone."* The way is coming; it is being manifested by everything you do. I assure you that all you accomplish for God will be repaid a hundredfold. Thank you for praying for the Church and the birthing of unborn children."

Saturday, January 24, 2015
9:13 a.m.

"Brothers, if this be our dance; if this is a measure of our excellence, if this be the cause for which so many brave men have dared to die, then let it find its victory in us; let our courage commemorate their sacrifice."

- William L. Roth

"My Special son, you have uttered profound words here that you will someday deliver to the masses of people standing beside you in defense of the Church. It is My sacred gift to you and your brother to be here speaking to you, although My reflections cannot match the holy eloquence of your heart. I bring you the goodness of the Lord and His commending Will for you to prevail through the blessings that you have been accorded. How can I explain what you mean to Him? You are surefooted in your station alongside the Saints who have preceded you. You are unwavering in your defense of the Cross. And still, you show patience and indulgence toward those who are yet learning about the faith of the First Apostles. With all this keenness wrapped up inside you, there is no question that your life has been a blessing for the Father who first gave it to you. Today, I have come speaking to you about the misgivings of others that cannot be overlooked. People have certain choices in life, not false ones like choosing to preserve life over taking it, but choices about approaching their responsibilities in building up the world's righteous bastions and taking care of the poor. These are choices based on alternatives, not the converses of right and wrong. We hold that all poverty is heaped onto its victims by those who hoard society's wealth. While this is true, some paupers remain that way because they will not advance themselves through responsible action and self-development. Some of them are slothful and dependent because they have never been taught any better. Others prevail on people because they harbor a grudge against those who have worked hard and followed the rules. And, in all this mix is the righteous way, the Gospel way that says that anyone who is capable of working must do so. And, those who work should be given a fair wage. My Special son, this is where the argument about dearth and excess begins. The whole matter comes down to the human conscience; it refers to how lasting someone wants their poverty to be. I make this point because the greatest poverty known to humanity is the spiritual poverty that has fomented this argument from the beginning. Why would someone not want to market his wares and offer his labors to remain self-sufficient? Yes, this is a rhetorical question. Everyone who is capable should make their own way. On the other hand, why would the wealthy not take care of the poor with their financial excesses that would last them a thousand lifetimes? Here again, the answer is that they should. I am saying that those who refuse to help themselves and those who refuse to help others are opposite ends of the same stick. They are extremes that cannot be condoned in a marketplace of benevolent men. It is based on the responsibility of the person not only in the eyes of the world, but in the reasoning of God. If the Lord provides good health, He provides opportunity. The nation in which you live advances these opportunities to those who will try, to those who do not hold ages-old grudges against the many who have tried and succeeded. The crux is in the outcome. Do people who try and fail believe that they hold a claim over those who prosper? How many more times must they try again? What conditions are prohibiting them from succeeding? Are the rules skewed against their favor? Do prejudices work against their efforts? Are there sufficient resources for them to advance? These questions go on and on, but everything depends on someone's willpower to overcome adversity and achieve what they know they must do. My Special son, the strength of conviction is far more earnest than bodily might. This is how Jesus lived His earthly life.

Conviction is a spiritual element; it cannot be seen with the eyes, but its results can be examined. This is what your quotation at the opening of today's message reflects. Your eloquence comes from your conviction in faith, to take Jesus as your Brother in Love to have and hold. Yes, it is much like a dance, just as you say. And, this is your dance; this is your time. You have emerged from the darkness and the wilderness too. There is nothing more that you and your brother could be doing that would further prosper your cause. You lend Jesus your acts of obedience. In the presence of your prayers and good works, you and your brother are living valiantly and respectfully. Everything you have done and are now achieving is being recorded in the eternal register. Your gifts to God will never be lost. You have already imagined what it would be like for someone to unearth your Marian deposit of works 10,000 years from now, if the exiled world should linger that long. This is what the impact would be to your contemporaries who have never heard of what we are doing. Continuing your humble labors and applying ample patience, you and your brother will realize in your time what this means to Jesus. Unspeakable beauty. Unmatched intelligence. Inexplicable perseverance. Unimaginable courage. Undiminished faith. True allegiance to the Son of Man. What more could be asked of the life of a disciple? What efforts could be more exceptional? What better news could be given to the poor? How could the rich have been more soundly forewarned? My Special son, this is what you and your brother have committed to the history of the artfully rotating world. Human forces cannot stop it. Adversity cannot impede it. Hatred cannot violate it. The universe could never contain it. These are things of super-nature, of gifts and blessings so advanced that a Pope praying for a revolution would be only its speck. I cannot place into words how reckless humanity has been heretofore, but you are ushering-in a reckoning for their recklessness. Grand detonations and flashes of light will stop them in their tracks someday soon. The day has already begun. It started the moment you and your brother first met. It was capitalized on February 22, 1991. It shall be the delight of the suffering and the uplifting of the innocent long beyond the ages, utterly eclipsing the sum of eternities that will kneel before the presence of the Father. It is beyond all envisionment in this life and the next. So, please do not bother bringing a calculator or measuring tape when you get to Heaven; they will have no purpose in the vastness of the glory that you shall inherit there. Limits mean nothing in the Light of Paradise. Yes, this has begun in you, here with you, because of you, and by virtue of you. You are a child of Mary! Think about what this will mean to everyone whom we will touch before the ages are through. The final epilogue that God has promised the Church is being written here; it is a testament to your immeasurable excellence. The eternal register will reflect that given the venue, when handed the reins of knowing and seeing, you and your brother brandished the Cross of Jesus Christ against the enemies of the Church with the valor of kings, with the courage of warriors, with the invincibility of stately galloping steeds. It will be said that you were mighty and pretty; you were kind and complete, you gave everything you had so the Kingdom of Heaven could yield all the Father sought from the Blood-soaked souls whom Jesus handed Him on the Cross.

So here today, My Special son, I have come to say that I love you. I have prayed here with you and your brother in thanksgiving for the tremendous impact that you are having in the world. I have brought with Me constellations afar and courts of Angels nearby to hear what I have said to you today, not just as a fond memory of what we have accomplished, but to witness to two heroes and what is still to come – much more greatness, far more pageantry and prayer, and an unlimited resource of grace for humanity here on the Earth. It is with gratitude and emotion that I commend you and your brother for remaining true to your promise to Jesus so He can take His Promise to the world. My Special son, I see things that matter intensely to My role as Mother. Of course, I see all the little children and trees and flowers; I see gladness and hear the gleeful chatter. But, I also see other things that have far more depth and dimension. I see intentions in those who would prepare humanity for their final hour. I see in My visionaries a desire for conquest, a means for retraining the focus of all men toward the Lord of the Church. I see despondence being supplanted by the efficacy of hope. I see charity expelling selfishness where people are starving in the streets. And, I see the fulfillment of the Profession of Faith in the simplest and least notable souls. I see the rare challenges against the forces of evil that come from the little ones, like that nine-year-old boy who began crying when all he wanted to do was sing. Malaki Paul* was taken down once by the forces against him, but he summoned the courage to stand up and try again. Why? Because his mother was there. She rushed to his side and dried his tears, and gave him courage to sing once more. Yes, this is what I am doing for humanity in your day. I want My children to sing like jetliners taking to the skies with the melody of the Spirit within them, calling out at the top of their voices that they have found their way back home. I want them to dance, just as you say. I want them to look upward and outward beyond the lurks and evils that would turn them back into the wings. No child of the Blessed Virgin Mary should ever cower in fear. None will hide from the battles of this life. None will retreat into darkened corners, believing that no one is with them. Their Queen will not let them down, not just because I love My children in ways that cannot be described, but because I give them the greatest power ever known on this side of the Father's domain, either within or without Creation – the Son of Man, the Babe of My Womb, Jesus the Christ. Thank you, My Special son, for allowing Me to speak to you and your brother today. Bless you for everything for which you pray that will help exiled humanity and the Earth itself enlist the blessings of Heaven."

This is a reference to a young boy who performed on "Britain's Got Talent." He began singing on stage before several hundred people and a television audience, and became overcome by nervousness and stopped in mid-performance, unable to continue. His mother ran from the side of the stage to hold him and give him courage and comfort. It was a profound moment in television history to which Our Lady referred in describing Her love for Her children.

Saturday, January 31, 2015
9:52 a.m.

"Through all the turbulence of these times, amidst all the spinning, confusion and gutted ambitions, we have finally jarred loose our time-honored traditions and ripped apart the very fabric of our lives, leaving us exhausted and tattered, windblown and destabilized – making us vulnerable prey for the devil to complete the divisions from which shattered worlds and fragmented societies rarely recover. There is some question, after all, with what identity we will answer when history finally calls out our name. We falsely believe that our transgressions against God's Holy Kingdom are akin to some kind of benign appendage that can easily be lopped off like a skin tag without addressing their true origin from the inside of our being."

- William L. Roth

"My dear little children, we offer our prayers at the Lord's behest because we know they will procure the awakening and conversion of the nations. Thank you, My Special son, for the passage that you have spoken to open our message. I am grateful that you and your brother are able to realize that ruthless ways and malevolent works are being neutralized by the Roman Catholic Church. I have come to you this morning to speak about your Bishop and your letter of January 27, 2015. Your letter allowed him to see Me as a Mother in ways that he has never known. You, your brother and I have raised his dignity through your inspiring words. He will administer with fairness the *Norms of Proceeding* to review My messages. Can you imagine what it is like to serve as Bishop of the diocese in which these messages have been dictated? Can you see as Bishop Thomas John Paprocki sees that the entire framework has been accomplished beneath the title of 'The Immaculate Conception?' This is the same sacred archway under which My Lourdes messages passed, and tremendous healings are being accorded to those who still believe. In the beginning, there were few who came to Lourdes to discover whether My messages were authentic, but rather how they could invoke the miracle to come closer to God. Those who seek out the Morning Star Over America from around the globe will find Me here where I first began identifying Myself as such, here in the prairie capital where the mortal remains of the Great Emancipator are reposed. I am hopeful that your Bishop will not only expedite the examination of My messages, but that he will pronounce to all who must hear that they should be heeded. Now, you have a commission that I told you about in years past. God is deeply in love with you. Jesus cannot imagine what it would have been like without you walking at His side, and the Holy Spirit in your heart always harkens to the moment you first drew the breath of life here in the Lord's vineyard. You are a gift to the Father, to humanity, and to the world. So, today I remind you that your faith is always new because you have accepted your part in propagating the Covenant of the Gospel in an old millennium and a new one too. You walk with humility because you are a child of the Lady of Grace. And, when someone's faith is new, he has the presence of wisdom and supernatural poise to conduct himself like Jesus. As a Morning Star Over America seer, you have the responsibility to other creatures of kindness and advocacy. You know inside your heart that the great battle between goodness and evil has already been decided, but this is not the way of anxious men. They are still unsure whether the devil will devour everything beautiful in this world. Like Jesus, you have in your hands the destiny of many because you live within Him, and He in you. The future of human souls given to Jesus has been augmented by you; this has been your gift of the past quarter-century to the Heaven that will someday eclipse the existence of the entire created world.

Even as Jesus said from the Cross that His Kingdom and the Salvation of sinners is complete, He weighed the suffering of His Mystical Body that is being spiritually crucified to this day. I ask that you be gentle with yourself because you are deserving of the adulation of the heavenly hosts. Never mind what new dimensions may be discovered in science and technology, whatever new ways to travel will be found, what becomes popular or antiquated across the span of the years. These things cannot escape the times in which they are formed, but your faith in Jesus will transcend the ages. I have commissioned you with the help of your brother to be the steady hand of sacred truth in the heartland of this nation. You have done well to take up the tools that will see your labors through. There is a movement in every generation to discover what threads run through it that are common to previous societies. Your thread with your brother is that you have proved it possible to live a true miracle in the face of rampant indifference. You have created a model for life to which all men should aspire. You have redefined the meaning of obedience. And, you have allowed your friends and peers to see the heart of a lion, the tenacity within you that comes from God. These are the reasons that I tell you that your persistence is laudable. It is not that you are contrarian, but that you hold as nonnegotiable those principles that must remain in place if the blanket of propriety beneath which the United States has been sheltered will remain unfrayed. You rightly said with your opening words today that certain traditions and the fabric of your lives have become unraveled. There is no question that this is true. However, with all the assistance that Jesus has to offer, the goodness and stability about which you speak will be restored as sure as the resurrection of the human soul is being bestowed. There is so much vision in you, so much foresight and knowledge. You hold focus on the right things; you have loosed the arsenals of war against the devil's dogs and strived to upend the complacency that is devastating the lives of impassive men. You are negating the misgivings that might damage the impressions of the Church because you are participating in one of its grandest miracles. And, My Special son, this makes you a cynosure of this land. It is often said that men are never called to become great leaders of flocks and nations, that they rise to the apex of service because of sheer coincidence. This is not the case with you. From the moment you first became a flame of delight in God's Heart, He knew you would be different. He wishes to instill in humanity and the world a new meaning of what life ought to be, and He does this through Christians like you. He commended Jesus to be all things before you – He sent His Son to die for the Salvation of men, but He also summons apostles of spiritual passion like you and your brother, Christians who would live twenty centuries later, to show the world how to recapture its identity through the preeminence of divine life. My Special son, you have done this with the dispatch of the Angels. You have given new life to the Earth that has rarely been witnessed since the Resurrection of the Son of Man. And, thank God you have! I thank you. Jesus thanks you. We bless you for the difference you have made for the Church. Thank you for your prayers and reflections; for your holy labors, good works, faith, tears and love."

Saturday, February 7, 2015
Thomas Wilmer Heather Sr. 1914-1988
9:04 a.m.

"The way we deal with questions of barrenness and sufficiency reveals who we are – the criteria we use to categorize our successes and failures, the indicators that determine our givenness toward conformity and independence, knowing when to sense danger and sound the alarm, the choices we make to avoid stumbling into error, the means by which we prioritize our emotions in the presence of the Lord's divine power; all to worship, extol, perpetuate and glorify the Father's Eternal Kingdom that purifies and cleanses us."

- William L. Roth

"My goodness, My dear little son, you have created a comprehensive view of who humanity is in this quotation. There are indeed untold ways to consider the discernment and choices that men must make during their mortal years, but none is as important as their acceptance of the Cross of Salvation. I have come today to speak to you in unison with the entire heavens because you are praying for My intercession. I am moved by your own inspiration in God. I ask for your prayers for all who are only now coming to know Jesus, that they will grow in their faith as His Kingdom on Earth takes hold. It is here that this transition must begin. Thank you for being persistent in your hopes and prayers, seeking the conversion of lost souls and the eradication of sin. I have not left you since you were conceived in your mother's womb. I have been beside you because I know that the Spirit of My Son lives within you. I have traveled the world where My children are calling. I have seen inside the hearts that Jesus desires to touch. I have heard the excuses that men have used to avoid their responsibilities to the First Apostles. You have seen the effects of their indifference, and their violent works too. You have witnessed historical events where the Holy Spirit was not invited to attend. There is nothing righteous about what the enemies of the Cross are perpetrating against the humanity of men. Do you remember the Scriptural passage that warns against doing anything to mislead the little ones? "*Yes.*" You must remember that this is one of the most prominent mandates in the entire Bible. These little ones must be raised in the Light of Truth that shines brilliantly upon their future; they must come to bask in it. They must be schooled in purity and rectitude. They must never believe that the Cross of Christ Jesus is just another option, but the only true bulwark known to the created world. My Special son, the wisdom that has reproved the ages remains relevant in your day because it has been handed down by those who first solicited it. It is a righteousness that is of old, yet new and infinite to you and your contemporaries by the power of the Holy Spirit. So, we pray on this day on which your brother's father died in 1988. It would seem that he has been in Heaven for 27 years by now, but he has no idea that he ever left there upon his earthly birth. The only thing he knows about life on Earth is what he hears from those who pray. He cannot see what is happening unless mortal men seek his intercession. He knows nothing of the tides of horror overcoming the world until his name is invoked in prayer. This is the way of everyone who has come to Heaven. This is not to say that Thomas does not realize that there is cleansing occurring in the exiled realms. He knows about suffering because he lives in sight of Jesus' Crucifixion. However, the gruesome details are omitted from his consciousness because there are no tears in Heaven. And, there is no sense of the past or the future, just the presence of eternal love. There is light, and no darkness. There is no repetition of days. There is ultimate freedom and ecstasy; and for your brother's father, he always wanted to relive that tragic day in December 1959 and have someone tell him that his little daughter had survived. (*Timothy was walking home with his sister from a school activity in 1959 when she was struck and killed by an automobile.*) This fills him with abundant joy as together, father and daughter, they have witnessed the rewriting of history from the other side of time.

There is a sense of collective satisfaction for all the Saints in Heaven, just as there is a collective cohesion of Christians around the Cross on Earth. The parallels between the Kingdom of God in Heaven and His earthly domain below are striking. You are capable of conceiving the glory that is growing in you every day. It distinctly reflects the passage that you spoke to begin our message today. There are chords striking comparisons and contrasts throughout your words, and they are incorporated into the comprehensive vision of well informed men. You have the capacity for impermeable strength that hails from the vaults of Paradise. You are sacrificial in the way of all the Martyrs. You have the gentleness of the

Angels and the foresight of the most prolific prophets. All of this is a gift from the Father to be shared in your time, just as you have said. I have told you in recent weeks, rather effusively, what you mean to Me, and what your life and soul mean to God. You are of the stately genius with which He created the mountains and seas. You belong to the same beauteous serenity that He has given the birds and fishes. He has given you dominion over them; this is your gift and responsibility. Therefore, as I have journeyed the world since I last spoke to you, I have seen the passion with which people live in practicing their faith. I am not speaking about passion in the way of Jesus' suffering and death, but passion that evokes strong conviction about matters of truth, hope and love. I have blessed the prayers of children and the places where they sleep. I have seen their parents taking them to be baptized. I have witnessed souls given over to the Gospel while being slain in the Spirit of the Messiah. I have walked alongside priests and nuns who have begged for My assistance. And yes, I have accompanied your Bishop on his first steps in celebrating My presence here in this diocese as The Morning Star Over America. Every day, I look at humanity being changed and conformed. I see generations of wrongdoings being reversed by what is being done right. I see the commitment of acolytes to their service, the lending of their birthright for coming of age in holiness. One would think that a world like this would charge full-breast against the evil that is trying to consume it. Like the Angels and Saints, I am not privy to all the gruesome details that are unfolding in places you have seen, but I know that suffering and killing are horrendous. You are seeing before your eyes the atrocities of villains whose souls are destined for Hell. Even in the light of Jesus' Crucifixion, they may never forgive themselves for what they have done. What would it take to muster their self-forgiveness? This remains to be seen; it is clear that there is not much of such resolve here in this world. You speak about catastrophes and barrenness in your quotation today, and this must surely be where evil spirits now lurk. What is barren in them is that they are bereft of love. They belong to Satan's fiery dungeon. They are visible evidence that evil is trying to devour the Earth. They have no life in them; they feed on hatred and revenge, they are deluded by the father of lies. I know where they are going, and I have never pitied them. My prayer is that they will be quickly defeated and sent by the Sword of Saint Michael to their destiny in flames.

And yet, here in your land, I find flowers and fragrances of new beginnings, of pureness and absolution, of holy love and humble life. I sense the perfect light of divinity in you and your brother, in the Church and its people, in Nature that you have sworn to protect, in God's ordinances you promise to uphold, and in the way you embrace the broken and downtrodden. This is the consummation that you have come to know through your faith in God, and it is the reason that your writing speaks with veracity. You know right from wrong and truth from error. You belong to the collective conscience of My Son's Mystical Body that fashions good things, that has the capacity for living along the lines of virtue. You speak to those who are trying to decide what kind of life they should lead. You have the face of compassion to which suffering people look for consolation. Yes, you are in many ways as beautiful as Me because you are consecrated to Me. All who have reached for My hand and called on the comfort of My Immaculate Heart are part of the 'sacred divine' to which all baptized Christians belong. This is a grand revelation for humanity in exile. It foretells great triumphs in future months and years. It is relieving to the touch of the human spirit, not of recognition that you are not yet in Heaven, but a kind awareness that you will eventually get there. It is the same as the day My Son was raised from the Sepulcher and rejoined Me on Easter. Yes, I will tell you what we spoke about that day, but you already share the meaning of what we said, perhaps not the words from our lips, but the aroma of what was voiced. You must be aware that by giving yourself to Christ Jesus, you have already inherited His Promise by which all faithful men live. The Great Reckoning will eventually come, and you know what will occur at that juncture. Separating the sheep from the goats and the wheat from the chaff is only the beginning. Oh, but the songs, speeches and testimonies! The recounting and reflecting! The relief and embracing! The applause and celebration! It is in this spirit that all Christian men and women should live."

Saturday, February 14, 2015
9:31 a.m.

"Where there is life and its origins, we owe its entire age and our own posterity the promise of this truth – If faith be our energy, then prayer must be our nourishment. This begets our release from spiritual catatonia. Christianity is not a demeaning religion. Redemption is the way God sums it up, and sacrifice is the way Jesus breaks it down. The world has yet to fashion an instrument that the Divine Lord cannot play. This is why broken humanity will never mock Him transcendentally, developmentally, analytically or philosophically. We must be cautious about how we allow ourselves to mature, and not commit acts in our vigor that we will regret at our mortal hour. There must be genuine purpose in everything we say and do – no artificial heights, no feigned allegiances, no awkward abstractions, no haughty prejudice, no hollow desires, no wringing out our neighbor's joy, and no great push to delve any deeper into the earthen realms than Jesus first intended."

- William L. Roth

"My Special son, you speak like this because you pray the Holy Rosary every day. And, you meditate on the meaning of your own writings because you share in the abundant wisdom of Jesus through your daily holy hours. What can be said about what you have spoken here today? It is more than visionary, higher than the cosmos, and still it is told to humanity who can understand what you mean. You own a 'practical transcendentalism' that unites Heaven and Earth at the center point of your heart. I ask all My children to become like you and your brother. I seek from them the awareness that My Maternal Divinity is a source of knowledge and consolation. You have borne witness to what God wants His Church to be by becoming someone to be emulated. Your holy heart is clear and concise; there is no confusion in what you seek from humanity in the shadow of Jesus' Crucifixion and Resurrection. My Special son, if the whole world knew what you have come to learn and embrace, there would be no hatred, hardship or suffering. There would be no plight or poverty; there would be no weeping or doubting. You work here with your brother with valedictory poise, but you have certainly not reached the end of your days. You have done enough; please do not misconstrue what I am saying. I am simply confiding that you can work at your own pace at whatever you choose to do. The Morning Star Over America deposit of works is imbedded in human history, and there is no removing it from the pathways of men. It will be a liberating work for many, and a stumbling block for others. It is to those who must fall before they can walk that I have come, those who know only rationalism and secularism, the ones who see religion as some abstract cult for people who have no foundation in life. We are still winning; we shall win at the last, and we will take everything with us to the Kingdom of the Lord in His time. Thank you for being My Special son. As the many will receive untold miracles from the experiences of a few, a question will arise as to why certain visionaries were chosen and other people were not. What will you say to them? *"I will say that you used the material elements that were offered to you for your efforts."* Yes, this is an excellent response. It should be noted that I asked you to say that I have come to those who are unattached to worldly things. *"Yes, that was to be my next point."* My Special son, you are applying your permeating vision to the utmost witness for the Lord. *"Also, you chose the ones who would put their hand to the plough and never look back."* By all means, this is what I have done. You and your brother were young and eager when I first approached you in 1973. You are not yet that old; even now, you remain wholly courageous. You and your brother have avoided being caught up in the intangibles of life that have nothing to do with Christianity, and you have shunned the extremism about worldly matters that have distracted many others from their responsibilities to the Church. Let us examine the prospect of holding elective office. Is it not true that it begins with candidates seeing themselves vested with certain levels of power, and with a binding self-esteem? *"Yes. They have a craving for power and being elevated by others while wrapping it in a seemingly noble shell of service that is quite thin and brittle."* This is the way of the whole of it. What they do with this power is an indication of the types of people they see themselves as being. Jesus never sought to hold elective office, and He did not allow Himself to be hoisted before the masses as a secular king.

Having said this, in order to ensure civilized societies, their leaders must be chosen by the people. There must exist the freedom to choose who will enact laws to establish stable precincts. There must be safety and security in cities and neighborhoods. Leaders who do these things must do so within the teachings of the Gospel. Jesus did not seek public office because He came into the world to manifest the Kingdom of God. Politicians must be self-assured that everything they decide ennobles His Kingdom. This includes fairness to the poor, equality of taxation, and the preservation and protection of all human life. All those who serve in elective office do so in an arena that should reflect the virtues of Jesus' ministry and the levels of compassion that He speaks about throughout the New Covenant Gospel. My Special son, there has never been a public officeholder in the history of the world who has done this well. You have seen those who use the Church as a springboard for partisan advantage, but they never translate what they preach into discernable action. This reflects what I would like for you to say whenever a person asks you how the Mother of God deigns to speak to someone with miraculous parables, signs and wonders. I speak to those who do not exploit their religious faith for secular advancement. I speak to those who decline to see their faith as a means of improving their standing in mortal life. I speak to those who know what it means to have humility abounding. I referred recently to the collective human spirit that lives in the presence of the Father, that transcends both the nations and ages. It is in this vein that most great men approach their responsibilities. Some wish to know how they will be judged after the passing of the years. The problem is that they are concerned about how other men will see them, not how Jesus will judge them in the end. They worry more about the lines in history books than the intensity of their prayers; and sadly for them, it is the latter by which the Lord will judge them. Even though they may be unaware, this is also the way they will judge themselves across the chasm of time. Your Bishop, however, cares not how the secular mavens will judge him; he is focused on his standing before God. The process includes the other men in the Catholic Church who will examine the content of your Marian works. Your Bishop needs them to have faith along with him. My Special son, your Bishop is seen as a theological expert on exorcism, and is highly versed in the procedures surrounding expelling Satan's demonic spirits. Truly, he is a successor of the First Apostles.

For today, I am focused on the joy that all this is happening while you and your brother are still praying with Me in this place. I am pondering what must come when you are approached by those whose charge is to effect the provisions of the *Norms of Proceeding*. There is nothing to be afraid of. You and your brother are confident about what I have told you. There is light shining around you because it is emanating from within you. I hold you dear and precious. I see your historical legacy as one of God and not of men. There is power in everything I have said, but not the kind of power that sets you apart as elitists in the world. I ask that you from this day forward remember what you have given to humanity in the span of 25 years. Think about what you have done for God as exiled men yourselves. Never forget your prayers and sacrifices, that they are foundations upon which the Father has built holier lives for your brothers and sisters. It is in this reflection that you will discover your own humanity, that you have knelt and prayed before the Cross, that you have given Jesus the blessing of your lives in exchange for His Sorrowful Death. We have every reason to know that the years have meant something to the world because they are leading to the redemption of the Church. We believe that your dedication to the conversion of lost sinners supersedes the ages and gives life deeper meaning. Yes, mystical purpose and holier resolution. Thank you for loving and praying, for dreaming and imagining, for taking unto yourself the burden of shepherding the Earth to the folds of Jesus' Most Sacred Heart. It is making all the difference in this life and the next."

Sunday, February 22, 2015
The Morning Star Over America
Saint Jesus the Christ, Savior and Martyr
9:32 a.m.

"Surely the Son of God is not demanding humanity to quell our desire for personal achievement, but He should always be the cause and reason for our excellence and triumphal dynamic, rendering us still of heart but extremely moved – charging, driving and pledging our way with courage toward the exit of this world and into the vastness of His eternal Kingdom. The romanticism of our cities may be dying, but its touch of legendry lives on. Their vision is still there, staring and weeping at what we once were, but celebrating as we depart in the vessel of death for the morning shore, awaiting the echoes of our voices from the hallowed halls of redemption. If the memoir of the created world is to be written along that journey, let its cruelty and callousness be softened by humanity's last confession. Let us hold Jesus close when we get there; let our tears of penitence roll down His cheeks and wash away the sting of Judas' kiss with the outpouring of our heartfelt love."

- William L. Roth

"Here now, My dear little sons, I have come bringing the eternal joy of Heaven to you while you pray. I offer you the compassion and gratitude of the Lord in whose grace you have been saved. I also come today to begin year 25 of our messages about Holy Love, and I tell you that this is the soothing of your wounds. You have seen that the Earth is breaking in violence, pain and sorrow, but you are assisting Me in creating a spillway of relief in Christ Jesus that keeps it from imploding altogether. Why would the Father not make this so? How could He stand aside and pretend that human sin is not destroying His dreams? Therefore, as you delight in your own achievements for Him during the 42 years since 1973, be assured that you have reached for His righteousness, and it is for righteousness that you will live out your lives. My Special son, you have accorded humanity some extremely eloquent passages as we opened our message today. Everything you have said is true. It is imperative that confession and penitence be on the lips of humanity as men say their final words. I have told you that one 'I am sorry' has more power than a thousand nuclear bombs. It can annihilate centuries of hatred from the face of the Earth and erase its stain from the history of men. These are the words that Jesus yearns to hear from those who believe in Him, from the many who pray to enter Heaven and be with Him beyond all time. We have shared the wisdom that is of old, the knowledge that teaches even the wisest men that the world is far too complicated for its pursuit of purity, holiness and redemption. These are among the reasons we pray for the simplicity of the heart and the lightness of spirit that raises human souls above the mortal frays. Today, I have said that Jesus is a Saint. Any person in Heaven is a Saint. 'Saint Jesus the Christ, Savior and Martyr' would be a fitting solemnity for Good Friday. It has not been declared so because it would relegate the memory of Jesus' life to one day instead of all the months of the year. We know that He was crucified on Good Friday, an observation that shall come again in the passing of a few weeks. And, we will celebrate the anniversary of Jesus' Easter Resurrection with like intensity, and pray for the conversion of all wayward sinners along the way. So, I come today, My Special and Chosen ones, to remind you how beautiful you are. I speak about the resiliency of your goodness, the sightliness of your hearts, the dignity of your prayers, and the wholesomeness of your love. What you mean to God cannot be spoken in words because you have given Him your indescribable allegiance. The genuineness of your good works is not unlike your faith itself. Jesus knows your love for Him. You are worthy of His blessings as He turns His eyes toward your march in the battle for lost souls. He inhales the fragrance of your friendship. He listens to the symphonies of your souls. And yes, He tastes the sweetness of your sacrifices offered in His name. This is a savoring of the virtue within you that you raise to Heaven like a cup overflowing.

My little sons, I have said that there are hardly words to describe what this means to Jesus because words end; what Jesus feels never does. This is why your hearts are honored in Heaven as though the Lord is looking at your lives framed in gold. He sees the constancy of your love for Him. He knows what it is like to walk in your shoes. He has been here before you, and is yet beside you today and forever. My Special son, you have seen the image of Jesus carrying a lamb around His shoulders. I wish to add to this vision by what I am about to say to you now. If you were to see through Jesus' eyes, as though you were inside Him instead of being carried like a lamb, you would see more clearly what it is like to be His beloved disciple. It would be as though you were a cloak lining Jesus' shoulders from the inside. Every time Jesus takes a breath, you can feel it too. Whatever direction He turns, you go there with Him. Whatever He says to someone along His journey, you can feel the vibration of His voice inside you as well. When He bends over and rises back up again, you can feel the descent and elevation of His body. This is where Jesus asks His sheep to follow Him. This is what it means for you not to just live, but for Jesus to live in you, and you in Him. I have said that humanity has a collective sanctity by virtue of your faith in Jesus, and this is where the world must go. This is the evolution that men should pursue, not in genetic elements or physical features, but spiritually maturing in Jesus' Most Sacred Heart. This is the way men become successors themselves. You inherit through Jesus your own sense of ownership in His Sacrifice on the Cross. He gives it to you every time you suffer, whenever you reach for something holy instead of materials or the flesh. So today, I am describing what you have done for Him since you attained the age of reason, even when you were a young boy in the photographs that you looked at yesterday. You may have been wearing peculiar bow ties and awkward dress hats, but your heart was beating beyond the boundaries of time. Your presence before the Father was majestic and elegant. Your posture reflected the innocence of your baptism. I assure you that all this remains within you now, obscured by the responsibilities of adulthood and the difficulties of common life, but there at your center nonetheless. You grew into adolescence and manhood in the likeness of the Child of My Womb. You have spoken comprehensively about your identity in the Church. You remember those who have taught, guarded and mentored you. You celebrate in your 2014 memoir the sunrises and sunsets between which you have glorified the Kingdom of the Lord. This comforts Jesus in light of the Crucifixion that has redeemed the entire civilization of exiled human souls.

My Special son, how could Jesus not have saved you? How could He see what you have become 2,000 years hence and declare you unworthy of His Blood? How could He turn to the Father and say that your soul looked better in death than in the Light of Everlasting Life? It was in forgiving Adam that He pardoned all who followed him. It is not that you learned sin from Adam, but you inherited it without knowing what he had done. Now, however, you do know because God has told humanity by His Word. Yes, you have been a victim of the Garden. You were born into the world through the grace of the lovely woman whom you saw on horseback in those pictures yesterday. I am the Mother of your mother, but I am not your grandmother. There is a New Eve who is nurturing the world from a Kingdom that you have yet to see. But here, it is not about Me, but the Son of My Womb whose Sacrifice has stilled the wailing masses, who has given rise to the assurance that humanity can be perfect once again. You can obey the Will of God by accepting the Love of God, made manifest most profoundly through the Crucifixion of His Son. And, I live with you in seamless harmony with the Holy Spirit in our hearts. I nurture the Catholic Church and cherish its every prayer. I safeguard what the Church teaches, and know deeply what it will become. My Special son, the prayers of the Mother of God are never in vain. Jesus will not deny My Immaculate Heart the miracles that He knows to be the ushering of lost sinners to the Cross. This is one of My gifts in Medjugorje, that the language there would reflect the first three letters of the word 'miracle.' I desired that the world would seek peace this way. It would not be obstacles that humanity would face, not chronicles or even ancient oracles, but miracles. You have come of age as Jesus' brother, and you have personified the wisdom that God has placed in you. This is why you are held in such stature in Heaven. These, yes these are the sentiments that I came to share with you today. Thank you for your prayers and the reflections that began our message this morning."

Saturday, February 28, 2015
9:44 a.m.

"Fixed in visible Creation, we are God's Christians. Through the forces of evil, our lives are often strained and our dreams revoked. We endure a rejection that demands everything of our religious faith. The world goes out of its way to despise us for everything we believe. Our holiness becomes our burden and our suffering the price we pay to remain united with Jesus' Sacrifice on the Cross. Yes, this is the way of it; this is our spiritual indemnity. This is how we watch the glories play out; it is humanity's way of letting the music be heard – on and on the trumpets report with our hands to the brass and God's wisdom on our lips. This is the blaring pronouncement of joy and confidence that we find in Christ Jesus that reveals our dignity in Him and feeds our defiance against His enemies. It is the sound of victory amid the groaning gasps of slow-dying men."

- William L. Roth

"Dearly and auspiciously, I come to pray with you today, My little children, for the precise reasons that you just stated. My Immaculate Heart pours forth the Glory of God into your lives, not only because He loves you, but because Jesus needs you. Heaven is attracted to you because you are aglow with holiness in the darkness of the world. As I have said, you not only emit the light of God that falls upon you, but you welcome His holy dawn from within your hearts. It is not the same as phosphorescence because you have a self-gifted brilliance by virtue of your baptism and surrendering your will to the Father. It is clear that this is what Jesus said when He asked His Apostles to follow Him, to become fishers of men in an ocean of godless indifference. My Special son, you have seen what became of these fishers of men. They were the original Christians who would prosper the Gospel message around the world and across the vastness of time. It is in their descendants' hands that Jesus has placed the Catholic Church.

What we have seen of their faith is the making of redemption for the centuries, that they would lead to Jesus all who desired this Light of Love that I spoke about moments ago. It has been said that there is gravity all over the floor. What does this mean? It is certainly something that you cannot see. It cannot be felt by the body, but you know its force is acting upon you. You can sense its effects when something slips from your hands. This is the way to enlist the righteousness that God would have you preach. When you speak about such things that other people rarely mention, the issues of morality and responsibility; when you call someone's attention to their outward conduct, you are soliciting their self-judgment, an evaluation of the way they are viewed by the heavenly realms. It is on this perspective that their deliverance is based. No one will ever go to Heaven against their own consent. My Special son, the letter that your brother wrote to those who are displaying such reprehensible conduct accurately depicts the conditions of the matter, and the response he received is typical of unrepentant sinners. Yes, as your brother says, the world is upside down. This is the way it has always been in the exiled domain. This echoes the Gospel message of slaying the Innocent Lamb. You are a visionary man, and you understand what this means. I cannot tell you that the resolution to every issue will end with the repentance of the guilty, but I promise that it will happen here. These people are not unholy. They are caught up in the tangles of the world, trying to ply their skills where they can, making the most of their talents so they do not rely on other men for their sustenance in life. Their personalities are shaped by their lack of focus on the Cross through which their lives must be cleansed. They are loving people who have become embittered by the gauntlets of western capitalist life. They will be fine; they will do better for themselves and everyone else as a result of your brother's letter. They are not key antagonists to the problems that you face in these modern times.

Also today, I wish to tell you that all the sacred beauty, power and majesty that is built into your mission remains strong. Your apostolate reflects the grand imaginings of the Church. A path of openness always accompanies miracles that are filled with sacred mystery. Your work, as majestic as it is, is approachable to anyone who wishes to learn. This is the work of the Holy Spirit in a world that is afraid of its own shadow. I desire to heap due praise on you and your brother for everything you do, but I do not want you to believe that I do so lightly. I come to all My children with hope. I appear in places that Americans have rarely seen. Yes, the Lord places My image in regions where His Church is being persecuted too; it is surely terrible where these Christians live. They uphold the valor that was handed to them upon their baptism for being slain just because of who they are. This kind of martyrdom, as worthy as it is, need not be the way

Christians should die, not at all – warm in their beds in peaceful sleep, this is how they should deliver their souls back to God. You have seen the battles play out in far-off places, and sometimes closer to home. I pray that you and your brother will not be subject to this kind of persecution as news of your messages spreads. I have said that you did not know the sacrifice you were making when I first came to you. There is little reason to assume that you will suffer much, but you will be subject to ridicule and disdain. This is the way of the Gospel; it is the way Jesus was treated during His ministry on Earth. There is no basis for believing that it will offend you any more than it offended Him. Never mind, He once said. They were forgiven because they knew not what they were doing. I am overwhelmed that you have remained with Me in the company of the innocents in the Triumph of My Immaculate Heart. My dear little son, it is an historic time for you and your brother to live; you will see this more clearly as time marches on."

Sunday, March 8, 2015
10:31 a.m.

"We are summoned by God through Jesus Christ to establish not world nation states, but like-hearted apostleship states. This is the modern challenge of propriety and order – the charge of the Roman Catholic Church and the human firebrand. We have a commission to ignite a torch of light and faith, periling our lives for love and truth, illuminating our way beyond the scourge of hatred to the sanctity of universal peace; not flames just for the sake of fire, not a blazing inferno of discordant voices, but a means to unify the Earth and be poured out and molded as one humanity in the Heart of the Mount Calvary King. This is the way holy empires and divine kingdoms were supposed to rise. It is what the New Covenant teaches beyond any creature's doubt. We have seen it through all the old times and new; revelations that defy the whole network of human thought. We should never concede to death with any other residue on our bones. We must remain standing even after our days are done. No man need fall just because his spirit sheds his body."

- William L. Roth

"No conciseness of literary instruction has ever been more true! Yes, you are the herald of the intertwining relationship between God and man in your time. The story of human life, My Special son, is encapsulated by what you have said. Thank you from the depths of My Most Immaculate Heart for remaining so attuned to the poetics of the Lord's professions. Here today, I have come to pray with you because I love you, and because you love Me. There would need to be no other reason than this, My precious sons, but we also know that there are yet billions of people needing conversion to the Cross. (*Our Lady spoke to me about our efforts to propagate Her work and the impact it is having. I also enjoy knowing that what we are doing matters in the course of events.*) Now, it has come the time for your patience a while longer. I have said this before as well. All good things are transpiring because you have been patient. You have waited for the timing about which I have spoken. I will have the Angels assist you with the unfurling of the vast propagation of My messages. For today, I have come to pray with you and thank you over and again for what you have done. And, My Special son, your stomach and intestinal virus are simple discomforts that Satan hopes will diminish your joy. When Satan begins attacking you for your work for My Son, it will be more along the lines of social hostility, rejection, ostracizing, ridicule, and impugning your good name. But, you will not be in jeopardy. Why? Because you pray, and because you and your brother trust Jesus more than your enemies can possibly know. They will learn it in time, but they are unaware of how fast you hold to His Truth. There are difficult times ahead; make no mistake about it. But, you have borne such difficulties before. Always remember that you are hearing and seeing the Mother of God. I am the Mother of Jesus Christ. I am the Mother of the Savior of humanity. You can receive no wiser counsel or truer compassion than this. I heard you praying for those around the globe who have no health care such as that you recently received. My Special one, imagine what this looked like to Jesus. There you were, in agony at the hospital, hardly able to hold up your head. They took you into an emergency room and began to nurse you back to health. And, My dear Saint William wanted to know about everybody else who was sick. You asked what would become of those half-way around the world in need of medical care. Yours is the heart of sympathetic love. Through your suffering, you personified and emulated Jesus on the Cross.

Also today, I remind you that everything for which the Church stands is fortified by your practice of what it teaches. You have within you the presence to safeguard the Church because you know what prayers are required. You see the atrocities of the Earth, and you know the vices of the secular void. Every kind of evil in the world tries to take down the Catholic Church. It is now more than ever the devil trying to convince everyone that he is the victim. He is asking for pity because he is being treated so poorly. Yes, and he does this knowing that Jesus has already killed him on the Cross. Evil no longer has influence over those who repent and accept the Blood of Jesus' Sacrifice. And, it is for this conversion of lost sinners that you pray. Also, My Special son, you have seen and read other messages around the world that speak to horrific prophecies and consequences if sinners do not repent. You are seeing this precisely as you should. Some of these prophecies are avoidable based on the prayers of the people of the nations. One should think that it would be a good prospect that many of these events are precluded by prayer. All God wishes is to be loved. He does not want humanity to shut Him out of their hearts. He begs to be included in the lives and afterlives of everyone who breathes. It is not that He cannot survive without you, but that He has so many blessings to offer. He is the Father of charity and love. He is the center-person of prudence, peace and joy, and He allows righteous leverage to be appropriated by those who obey His laws. This is what it means to be bound in Heaven once bound on Earth. And, My Special son, it is clear that your brother is more determined than ever to accentuate his obedience to Jesus because he has seen the reaction of your pamphlets in the Church. It is clear that your pamphlet encapsulates your mission more than any other document you have published. It reveals faith and foresight to those who read it. It is more humble than even you really know. It lays out the truth of what you believe because you have never turned away from Me. The Holy Spirit has infused this within you. My Special son, I ask you to understand that you have fewer enemies than you realize. It is true that the whole world is in need of a miracle. Your apostolate is entering into the public forum from so far out of the mainstream that people will wonder what struck them. It is the melodic waltz of their age. Your work will lead multitudes to Fatima and Lourdes because those shrines preceded the Morning Star Over America. All this will happen because Jesus says so. You will not see it in the news every day. People may not summon you by telephone or request a personal audience, but it will come true anyway. It is part of the groundswell of grace that will accompany the Triumph of My Immaculate Heart. You will feel this touch inside you because of the Love of God. You will sense its midsummer breezes on your soul. You will recognize its energy of faith. Yes, you will know that you are achieving the divine mystery of your life because you will hear more about Me. It is all to Jesus through Mary – do you remember? "*Yes.*" I ask you and your brother to remain confident in what we are doing, as confident as you have been for the past 42 years. It is humanity's choice to respond. My peace is upon you, and the Spirit of God lives within you. Thank you for your prayers. I will present your petitions to Jesus."

Saturday, March 14, 2015
9:30 a.m.

"The forward-thrusting, revelatory, surging velocity of apocalyptic wisdom abounds in our present day. It requires us to pause and wonder about patently unimaginable things that seem almost too peculiar to understand. We must be capable of connecting casual life with extraordinary human excellence that fully transcends the external limits of our colossal mortal experience. We must heed the cautions of the ancient missioners, and listen to the winds of change and the rhythms of Nature's spontaneity. We must be wary of the pressures, restrictions and responsibilities that life heaps upon us that try to dissuade us from spiritual insight, that would have us pursue other avenues that have nothing to do with our proximity to God. We must energize our penchant to proclaim His Kingdom, to rebuke doubters who approach us with mouthfuls of sarcasm about our tenacious desire to sacrifice our comforts for the Church. This elevated passageway to the eternal unknown brings us to question what we thought to be beyond our inquiry. After all, how loudly do the mountains really speak? How far down the path can we move the night? How much precipitation can a good brainstorm produce? Not a letter of this is vague abstraction, and neither is it knotty symbolism. For all the exuberance we possess, all the intellect and proficiency, do we really know what must be learned to find ourselves worthy of even living in the same universe as the gallantly majestic Jesus Christ?

- William L. Roth

"My precious little son, your intuition coincides with the creative genius of Jesus. You have certain allocated dreams that make you feel stronger through the night – I always dreamed of days like this with you and your brother, with all My children who seek the Providence of God. I wish you to remember that from the very beginning, what we are doing here was prescribed by the Father. There will be contrasts and metaphors to enhance the dimensions of human understanding, but the simplicity of it all is sustained by your devotion to Me. Thank you more than I have the means to explain. It is on engendering your faith that I focus; it is about knocking down walls and blending the miraculous with the ordinary. As you say, how many languages can a meadowlark speak? It is not just a matter for God and Nature anymore. I completely agree, this is where humanity chimes in to reveal that intangible things have personalities, that their beauty influences the thoughts of men. My Special one, until they have seen this beauty in its most essential form, nobody can imagine what it is like to be redeemed. However, you have already heard. You are one of the few who has been given a foreshadowing of the Great Divine that resides just beyond the perceptions of this world. My Special son, what would be a synonym for power? One might equate power with influence, persuasion or comfort. Others might link it to certain levels of freedom and mobility. My definition of power is attuned to wherever the Lord chooses to instill redemptive bounty in the created realms. All good things beneath the glory of Heaven are fashioned into being because they are gifts from God's hands. When Creation stands tall in this design, it reflects the righteousness of its Maker. It is possible to sense it through the innocence of a child, in seeing a Crucifix, or when someone prays the Holy Rosary. It is more than mass or friction, it is like saying that you can walk into Heaven although your spirit is the only part left of you. True beauty is animated by the redeemed human soul that is poised in the Father's reach, not that the soul does not wish to be touched, but that it soars about so freely and joyfully that it cannot contain itself. This is the righteousness about which the Gospel speaks. You have the strength of eagles and the wings of butterflies. God soaks-up the holiness that His creatures exude. He kisses you when you arrive in Heaven, and He sips your confession like a fine wine. Yes, He absorbs you as you allow your soul to be consumed. These are figures of speech here and now, but they are wholly accurate beyond the bonds of time.

As the Catholic Church is a brief period from observing Good Friday and Easter Sunday, you will focus on the Crucifixion and Paschal Resurrection of the Savior of the world. Men have known for ages what this has meant to Creation and the vaulted realms. I have said that My faith was required as well. I saw My Son hand over His Spirit to the Father, a Sacrifice that I witnessed with My tear-soaked eyes. This was the most sorrowful experience that a mother could endure. When Jesus' Body was spread across My lap, I was scarcely comforted knowing that He would be raised from the dead on the third day. I kept wondering how a perfect Man could enter an imperfect world, and He be the one to die. This required all of My ancient faith, every slice of meaning that I could place into the reason I was born. This is the way the Church awaits the Return of the King. I am aware of the suffering of humanity, the plight of the poor and the agony of the innocents. It is not lost on Me that life is drenched with pain and sorrow. I have been there with you, and I am with you now. Once Jesus' Sacred Body was laid in the tomb, we prayed not just that He would rise again as He said, but that the world would understand why. My Special son, I will tell you what I did on Good Friday evening that I thought would be a portent toward that end. I sat in silent prayer with Jesus' sandals on My lap. I looked down at them and thought about the warrior who had walked so graciously about. I wondered whether the world knew the weight of charity that He bore into their lives that they would somehow try to match. I petted His sandals like kittens, knowing that a lionhearted Lord had worn them on His feet. And, My Special son, I promised Myself that I would hand these sandals back to Jesus on Easter Morning. I would say that they were waiting for His graceful stride. And, I did just as I had promised. When I went to carry them to His side, I discovered them overflowing with flowers in a place where most people did not know what flowers meant. My little son, I have never told this story before; it is not recorded in any history books. It would seem too maudlin, some might say. It would have no bearing on the fact that the King of kings was alive again. They might likely be correct, but it was meaningful to Me. It was something that helped Me through the night. It was a way for Me to see Jesus still alive beyond His mortal passing. I ask you and your brother to realize the grace that you are to humanity, much like those sandals waiting to carry the weight of Jesus' Resurrection to a world so lost in sin. You too have tread in holy places and upheld the same tenets of truth. You have left your footprint on paths to places that would never have an inkling of what God is seeking of the Earth. These are among the reasons that you are cherished in the Lord's Kingdom, not just that you are precious in His sight, but you have distinguished yourselves by demanding that the Gospel be heard. Yes, you have loved. This is the purpose to which My messages are given; it is the reason the Son of Man was born of My Womb. My Special son, it is clear that you and your brother are sharing a miracle because you have said 'yes' to Me. You are My heralds here in this land. You share the gift of peace that Jesus has given to His disciples. I ask that you realize your part in the conversion of the wicked, in restoring the decency that has been lost to sin and hedonism. You are blessings to your brothers and sisters as much as I am the Lord's blessing to you."

Saturday, March 21, 2015
9:31 a.m.

"Dear Jesus, Lord of consolation, hope of widows, hue of rainbows, origin of fire, texture of the woods, balm of the lashed – sing us through the darkness. Usher humanity into the world's most golden hours. Reign sacredly over the guardians of your Church; preside in truth before those who would know you – the comers and goers, your dutiful lot, the poised and innocent, your bright and shining champions. Excise our loneliness with the fineness of your joy; swathe our bruises with your suffering on the Cross, sanctify the pillars of our lineage, safeguard our faith, hold us deep within your care, grant us peace in our day, and lift us to your pleated breast. This we ask through Christ, Our Lord. Amen."

- William L. Roth

"My little sons, it is our mission to assemble here in your prayer room and seek the Lord's blessing upon those who love Him. As has been My inclination, I wish to paint a picture through My words that articulate His desire to transform the world into the righteousness of His Kingdom. Please do not be dismayed by the time required to change human hearts because their newfound holiness will be in itself a timeless gift. We have as our purpose the responsibility of ensuring that humanity finds Jesus through Me. We cannot be impeded in this work. My Special son, thank you for welcoming your helper into your home on Wednesday to address your envelopes. His handwriting upon each one has the power to bless the recipients because of his sacrificial human heart, his suffering and pain, his identification with the Cross, and his devotion to Me. It is his participation as an element of sacred love to what you are doing. Your brother is highlighting My role in human Salvation with those with whom he interacts and through his prayers. There is no question that your brother is unflappable when it comes to politics. Raw criticism and inordinate scrutiny render him unfazed. In fact, he invites it; he welcomes it. I have never known any other messenger who laughed in the face of ridicule and yawned through someone else's mocking as does your brother. It is inspiring to behold. He gained this confidence from his parents; they were always supportive of what he did. They stood by him when others were critical of his conduct. They told him to pursue his goals with even greater clarity when it made important people feel uncomfortable. This will serve us well as we proceed through the nighttime ages engulfing the exiled world. I wish you to remember that the devil is trying to impede our efforts. It is a mystery to those who do not understand it, but it is becoming more clear to you and your brother as My work moves on. You are united in wisdom with Me. You have seen the saber pierce the realities of human life. You know the function of breaking past the difficulties imposed by your faith and marching onward to Heaven in your fellowship with the Saints. My Special son, I wish to reveal something that is not yet known to the Church. It is not dogma, because only the Church can declare dogma. It is about the human person in the face of God's judgement and in the shadow of Jesus on the Cross. The point is this. Whenever someone hands their soul to God, their sense of awareness is equivalent to the age of reason, around seven or eight years old. In other words, when someone dies, they stand before their Savior with an identity that measures their age to be around seven years. Why? Because they have at that age the ability to know right from wrong, along with seeing their lives before the backdrop of their innocence. They will then in the complete Light of Love be able to assess their decisions against the holiness of Jesus, alongside His peace, grace and charity, so they can know that they were not inherently evil as a person, but that evil influenced them to commit wrongful acts in their incapacity to resist temptation.

Do you understand what I am saying? *"Yes, but how can a seven year old ultimately condemn himself?"* The answer is simple. As that person reviews the record of his life, he is capable of knowing when he or she made choices that they knew to be in contradiction to the Gospel. It gives the person the vision to see where his development from his youth was corrupted either by himself or by the evils and exploitations of someone else. It all comes down to culpability. By appearing before Jesus at the presumed age of roughly seven years, the departed person does not begin his self-judgement with all the guilt with which he last inhabited the flesh. There are other dimensions to this phenomenon. A person can deny this gift of consciousness if they ask it to be done. They can tell Jesus that they would rather face His Judgement without the benefit of knowing about their original innocence. The choice is theirs, but it must be requisitioned. Their appearance when they first stand in judgement is to be innocent as in their youth. *"Are some people afraid of comparing their innocence to whom they are now so they choose their current selves?"* Obviously yes. And, who might some of these people be? Abortionists and other murderers. Those who deny the existence of God during their years on Earth. Predators who abuse children. Those who steal from the poor, and many other sinners like these. *"So, most of the people who condemn themselves reject seeing through the eyes of their seven-year-old self. And, unless you become like a little child, you will not see the Kingdom of Heaven."* My Special son, you have just spoken My next sentence. Thank you! Is this discussion clear to you now? *"I completely understand."*

People will do at the Throne of God what they consistently do now in mortal life, and for the same reasons. Those who deliberately lead lives of sin, refusing to call upon the innocent vision of their youth and engage conversion, will likewise refuse to view their lives from that station of innocence at their judgement before Jesus. It is far too humiliating for many sinners to admit the depths of their sins, hence they reject what innocence even means. They live in a sinful dystopia that they are convinced is honorable and accomplished, and they will be crushed nonetheless because the Divine Truth of their lifetime of rejection will confront the immovable reality that they disdained.

"I wish to add more to what I have told you here today. It is the option, as I have said, for every departed soul to decline his own youthful identity when he stands in judgement. These are the souls who are likely to blame themselves for everything they have done. This is not the way an impartial judgement should begin. Do you see the connection in that I come to you and everyone on Earth referring to you as My little children? *"Yes."* And, why do you suppose this is true? Because I want to prepare you for your hour before the Lord, and for you to affirm with humility when asked for whom you have lived, you can say, '...But, my dear Jesus, for you and our Mother, of course!' And, Jesus will reply with His endearing response, '...Correct answer! Well done.' I have today been trying to explain how vindicating the Father's divine love really is. There is no doubt that He requires holiness and prudence. He charges humanity with complying with His Word. However, He is completely aware of the vices that tempt you and the ways that the world tries to draw you away. There are many roads, but which one should a person choose? The answer is knowing what lies at the journey's end. The Church gives you this prefigured vision. The Gospel is your blueprint for Salvation. These are the themes by which those who have not been as dedicated to Christianity can see themselves as members of the Communion of Saints. My Special son, if human redemption could be compared to a substance, it would not be one that could be touched with the hands, but that is indivisibly present in the love of the heart. It is not just proper conduct, but a complete possession of the virtues that generate one's behavior. It is more than seeing with the eyes, but processing one's vision through the lens of God's Will. And, if a person does this well; if there is a scintilla of desire to become obedient to what God expects, that person will understand before they die that a better soul will be present before the Lord than they actually realize.

My Special son, God wants to sanctify His people not because it makes Him greater, not because He simply does not like sullied things, but because He manifests the purity of heart from which all good things come. This is where you and your brother have already been; you have broached the topic and mended the breach that others have yet to experience. This does not make you better than them, it makes you more whole. Wholeness does not imply a stage of perfection on a continuum of sorts, it makes you more capable of unifying yourself with the purpose of human life. This is the life that God has given you, and it is the same life that you must offer Him in return. My Special son, do you have any questions about anything I have said today? *"No, it all makes complete sense."* You are always so open to receive My messages. How can I thank you? *"Just being here is my gift."* Thank you! *"Can there be people who appear at judgement with whom it does not matter either way which disposition they choose?"*

This is a fair question. The answer is that the Divine Mercy of Jesus is available to all who pray. Pleading to see oneself through the eyes of innocence is a gift to the self. Some people, particularly those who have shunned the Sacraments, have already given their response to Jesus the moment they see Him face to face. The core of your question is logical, but those for whom you say the choice will not matter is according to their own self-judgment. *"Or, a Saint who has remained childlike their whole life, the choice would be moot because they see clearly through both dispositions."* Yes, these Christians believe that they are seeing themselves when they see their Savior in Heaven; and vice versa. The Saint and the Savior have the same sensation of seeing a reflection of themselves. *"I understand, that's why suffering allows a person to stand as an image in the mirror."* Yes, you are correct again. I have completed My message for today. *"Thank you, Mama."* Bless you for saying your prayers. I will speak to you next week as we move toward Good Friday and the Feast of Easter. Remember that you are God's greatest gift to your brother; this is what he tells Me every day."

Sunday, March 29, 2015
9:38 a.m.

"The human amalgam – matter, spirit, thought, energy and function."

"With overwhelming grace, I pray with you for the conversion of the world. My dear children, My darling little sons, My purpose here has always been for the propagation of the Gospel message, but it has also been to make clear My love for you. I would still have come to you in 1973 and 1991 if every soul on Earth had already been converted to the Cross. It is infinite that the Father loves us, and it is beyond understanding how He expands the universe to prove it. I wish for you to recognize the opening words of My message as not having any new meaning than that you have known. I am saying that the composite of the human person and the family of man is measurable to every extent that is not spiritual. This is why I have always mentioned the spirit in the traits of your identity, to grow its meaning beyond what you may accomplish in this world. And, energy is often limitless because it is a function of the spirit. Mass and matter come and go; they are residuals of where the Father's wisdom has interceded, and evidence that He has been there. This means that thought and function must precede what you conceive yourselves to be. The whole matter of being human is recognizing that time and space cannot affect you. There is no question that you physically defer to them; this is the way of all the Saints, but you shall ride in victory above them. You will place them in their perspective in such a way that elevates you among the stars. I tell you these things because God has revealed them to Me. I share My Heart with you because you are My adopted children. I am the Mother of all the living. My Special son, you and your brother are already enjoying the fruits of Christendom in this world and the next. You have become widely known in this diocese by virtue of your pamphlets to the priests. And, the Lord holds you close to His breast for not surrendering to the material world. You have remained with Me, encouraged by My words, strengthened by the power of the Holy Spirit, sanctioned by God's Providence, and consoled in the Sacred Heart of Jesus who has prepared you for the fight. There is some indignation in the things that you see, and rightly so. However, there is joy and confidence in what you have done. There is vision that you are sharing with those who are blind. There is inspiration for the masses that is just now taking hold. Please remember that the composite of the human amalgam that I mentioned today is a portion of your identity. Some of its elements will be shed in the fullness of time, while others will grow beyond measure. You will flourish through the miracles that you, yourselves, have helped manifest. You will someday stand beneath the azure skies and remember with fondness everyone who is fighting alongside you. It is difficult to see them now; they are here and there along the way, many in number, prayerfully private where they live, cheering you on and adoring you, giving everything they have in prayer that our whole sacred endeavor will succeed. Billions more are in Heaven with Jesus and Me, keeping watch on what you will do next, praying to God that He will relent in the punishments of the world for the faith you have shown. It is real, all of this. It is happening as we speak beyond your sight and senses, just like you told your Bishop months ago.

There are two perfect human bodies in Heaven right now, Myself and the Savior of the world. We stand as co-witnesses to what the Church has done. We are the identifiers of whom should be praised. We see the Earth in turmoil as you might look down toward a hurricane from high above it. It is not all that daunting, you know. While the happenings around the globe are grotesque and horrifying, they are never infinite. Evil cannot escape the justice of Jesus Christ. It has its force against the nations, but God will not let it bring the righteous down. And here we are, My Special son, you and I, your brother and family, and all who believe in the Kingdom that is drawing nigh. We have never relinquished the vision of what humanity must become. There has never been a moment when we thought that wretched sinners would prevail. Why? Because we are Heaven's eternal people living freely beneath the hand of Almighty God. We hold dominion over the beasts and fishes. We reflect on the holiness of the Church. We stand in the present here in this land, you and I and the Messiah and all the Saints who desire to reside in this world and the next. There is more than enough joy to go around. There are multitudes of reasons to begin this celebration anew. As Jesus entered Jerusalem as the Son of the Most High, He pondered His role as the Redeemer of converted men. My Special son, on more than several occasions, Jesus thought about what I have said today about the human amalgam. He thought about it as He tread over the palms. He kept it tucked in His thoughts when He sojourned the desert, and especially when He carried the Cross. Jesus looked to the Father the same way righteous men look to Jesus now. He thought about all the mass and energy, the miracles and providences. He contemplated what His earthly successors might do with His legacy, what life they would give to His teachings, what would be said of His Sacrifice for the Salvation of souls. Yes, He thought about the energy that He had given the Apostles and the power of the Holy Spirit by which they would be led. My Special and Chosen ones, you have heard that prudence is written into your faith. It is heralded through your voices in terms about which you are unaware. It shines from your faces like beacons in the night. You are the living personification of the goodness that the Lord envisions in His dreams. You are esteemed for this; you are honored and dignified, and you have as your right and left guards His nightly sentinels of grace and peace to usher you through the darkness. The whole idea of human redemption is a replication of itself. You are to become the image of Jesus at the same time you allow Him to reign within you. This is not a contradiction of terms, it is God's ratification that He accepts your faith in Him. You are melded into His likeness by the Eucharist from the altar. You are sanctified by the way you respond to Him. I am telling you nothing that you do not already know. I am giving you measures to consider your worth, greater ways to imagine how the world will end. No matter what the future may hold, you should live without fear. There may be pangs of hesitation about this idea or that, but you will never stray from your certainty that Jesus has ordained it all. It is written in the Covenants, we are prone to say. Give the Lamb your heart, and He will give you legendary lives. He will laud your faith while you praise His Holy Name.

    My purpose today is to restore what has been lost to many in the Church – its sense of duty and destiny, its place in the grander meadows of the created realms, its simple belief in the higher echelons of truth. Listen here – the Roman Catholic Church in Rome has just received a pamphlet from the United States of America proclaiming that its Morning Star has come! These are among the blessings that your faith has impressed upon the Church. Pope Francis has been handed an English-published testimony from two seers in Springfield, Illinois confirming what they have seen and been told by the Mother of Jesus

Christ. This is the mastery of the Crucifixion. It is the lasting testament to the miracle of the Easter Resurrection. It is what the whole world was meant to know, and it is happening now as we speak. So today, My Special son, I am telling you these things because of your decades of devotion to Me, the Mother of God. I am saying this because of the prayers of the Angels and Saints. It is the Will of God to remain your constant guide. This is what I came to say, My Special son, about faith and morals, about your station as a resilient human being, about the role of your messages, and about the fact that we shall win the hearts of men. I would like to close My message with some comments about your brother's relationship with the leaders of Springfield and his stature in public management. Yes, he is seen as a dutiful professional in the opinion of those he meets. This is in stark contrast to 1991 when he was being held in handcuffs on his knees on the floor at the Sangamon County jail, being mocked by jailers for something he did not do. It is because of your love that he has been raised again. You have supported him heart-in-hand while others walked away. You defended him against the lies that wicked sinners told. I wish for you and your brother to embrace your lives; recite your prayers, watch what happens in real time, enjoy the sunsets, and remember that you are loved. My Special son, I am elated that your petitions are so fitting to what the Father desires this world to become. You pray from the heart; you know what must change. Please remember that I am your advocate in unison with the Holy Spirit. I will ask Jesus to bless all for whom you pray."

Saturday, April 4, 2015
Holy Saturday
9:34 a.m.

"Embrace what perfects you, exalt what redeems."

"My children, this is the music that soothes your aching; this is the drink that quenches your thirst. I am here with you for wholly benign reasons. We are praying for the lost world of humanity to find itself once again. It is found where you have said, here in 'The Christ' who has risen, above and beyond the squalls of wicked men, here where the brightest stars of holiness arch across the skyways of life. Today, it is clear that there is a new spiritual awakening coming to the Earth. It is being forged into being by the miracles you have wrought. It is being precipitated by the long, hard battles that good men have fought to manifest the righteousness that God summons through His Church. I am with you in prayer because this is what matters most. I am alongside you as you accompany My Son through the journey of life. My little ones, you matter to Me more than you can possibly know. This is why the Father has sent Me here, not just because He has laid out your commission in linear time, but because He knows how much I love you. Therefore, if you embrace what perfects you and exalt what redeems, you will have accomplished everything that Jesus has handed down. You will have come full circle from the thoughts of the Father and back to His kind reflections again. Easter is all about these things, My little ones. You have known this your entire lives. I have relayed its meaning in more parables than you might number. I have spoken of softness and resilience in the same metaphoric verses. I have referred to the light not only as the absence of darkness, but the conqueror of everything that casts a shadow across your souls. The Kingdom of God becomes you, His Spirit empowers you, His Providence sustains you, and His divinity inhabits you. The final destination of the Church is in these things, My children. Embracing what perfects you means not only taking joy in being dignified in the Son, but also taking heart in the suffering that was forced upon Him. You must accept these gifts as your own; you must learn the lessons of His pain even as you suffer yours. You must realize that the agony of your own life's battles should be united with Jesus' Passion on Good Friday. Only in this unity will humanity understand passing through the needle's eye. My children, the more the Earth groans and suffers, the greater the glory to come. It is like fire consuming a cord of wood. The flames emit tremendous light, but the wood must perish for this to be done. You must give everything you have to God, and He will do the rest. He invigorates the precincts where you live. He supplants anything that other people demand from you with an identity of His own. They see Him in you because you are willing to be reduced to ashes to light the path for lost sinners. My Special son, this is not what I refer to when speaking of the enemies of the Church. Their being consumed in the fire of the Lord's justice is not about emanating light, but ridding the world of scandal. These sinners are not sacrificed for any good cause, but to curse, destroy and damn them. They are not fireside logs; they are chaff to be crushed underfoot beneath the layers of the ages. We hold the truth that all good men will prevail. We attest to God's power to cleanse the Earth through the destruction of its own making. This is the grace of the Easter Resurrection. My Special son, I desire that you always remember the part that you and your brother have played. You are igniting the flame that has brought wisdom to the Church. You have lit the fire that will rid the world of the enemies of the Cross – you and the Saints who have gone before you. As your brother sang from the song 'Pieces of April' that you heard yesterday; it must be them that stand beside you now. Indeed, it is. We all stand beside you; we laud and celebrate you. We dignify you in ways that are scarcely comprehensible to the thoughts of impious men. And, when all this is through; when the battles of the Earth have reached their pitch, whenever the Lord pronounces the great commission of the Church complete, you will see what reformation is. Just like reviving a drowning man, out with the old and in with the new. The hooks will be removed from the fishes' mouths and manna put there instead.

All the crosses of Jesus' disciples will be hoisted before Creation as the mainmasts for humanity's righted ships. Goodness and gladness will prevail, just as the New Covenant says. When men declare that this is the promise of God, that He will nullify the effects of death and destroy its existence as well, they will attest that they have claimed their share. They will stand with humility before the Man-God who has already set them free. They will fall into formation with songs of compliance on their tongues. They will feel the force of the world's commotion being stopped like a clock running out of time. They will raise their hands in the air and repeat the oath of allegiance that they took upon their baptism. They will hear the echoes of their own voices in solemn acclamation saying, 'The Lord has come! Let us go out and greet Him! Let Him touch the purity of our baptismal gowns, kept unstained by His Sacraments, refined by His forgiveness, and pressed into perfection by the suffering that He asked us to bear." My Special son, this is the imprint of Christian greatness. It is the spirit of all men assembled into one humanity. This is Eastertide at its best. You, My Special son, and your brother have been participants in a grand procession of life. Not only you, but the great Saints before you who have charted the course to which the Church has subscribed. You have shared your hopes in endless ways with passionate souls whom you have yet to meet. This is the reason we have been working so long. You have been sheltered and cloistered so the world would leave you alone. You could never have accomplished your work with curiosity seekers hounding you every day. You would have been overrun and overcome by people who care not about how to please the Lord, but to find out whether He really exists. You have maintained your lives in the secular void with your hearts focused on Me. You have said to God that He is your Master, that Jesus is your Savior and friend, that all the mansions of Heaven will ultimately supersede the gated communities on Earth. You have shined and reflected; you have taught and admonished, and you have commended to God through the Divine Mercy of His Son all whom you cannot reach – the stubborn ones who refuse to listen, the haughty and arrogant ones, those who denounce the moral choices they must make, and the multiple millions who are addicted to ill-gotten money, sloth, vice and temptations of the flesh. When you pray for the conversion of lost sinners; when you ask Jesus to remember their redemption with yours, He will do it. I resound your petitions in prayer. I offer to Jesus My own sentiments about the way the world ought to be, how its people should behave, the way its children should be taught, and what must become of everyone and everything that is precious in His sight. This is the culmination of prayer, My Special son. The whole thing comes down to the revelation of Easter. It is the finishing of the faith of men.

My Immaculate Heart is filled with energy and emotion because the Light of the World has come, not unlike previous generations and centuries, but that it has arrived in you. This is the making of My joy that will outlast the Earth's societies, spaces and times. It is true that the vastness of eternity is but a brief moment from now. It may not seem so in the eyes and minds of mortal men, but history should teach you, if nothing else, that everything earthly passes away. All that is of this world that has nothing to do with the Kingdom of God and the divinity of His love will be annulled when He finally says the word. My little son, My Special one, you and your brother are sparking a new sympathy in God. Your obedience has capitalized what this renewal must mean. It is about what Jesus did on the Cross, conveying His agreement with what pleases God and setting His creatures free. It is the factual truth. (*Our Lady revealed to me future events and massive constructions that would flow and propagate from our obedience to Her cause, if Jesus does not return to preempt them and take us all to Heaven.*) These are the promises from God about which Jesus has asked Me to tell you. They echo your humble sacrifices; they hail the blessing that you have been to the Church. They stand as hallmarks for everything you have meant to the Father. So today, I invite you to soak your souls in this Easter joy, in this foresight and imagining. I ask you to smile at the same time you pray and suffer with Christ. I ask for your hearts and hands for all the reasons that the Church must succeed – and it will. All for which the Cross has stood will command not only the times and lives of men, but the conversion to which they are called. I ask you to remain in this joy no matter what might come today or tomorrow, or why and wherever. I am with you as your Mother. I wish these things for you, and I promise that I will pray them into being."

Saturday, April 11, 2015
9:35 a.m.

"The Lord of the Ages has revealed His Will."

"My little children, there is no such thing as a world in which everything is 'all good.' Whenever someone says this, they ignore the realities of human life. They have disdain for those who would chastise them for their heartless apathy. Their purpose is to dilute the need for the holy sacrifices that cleanse the hearts of lost sinners. This term 'all good' has become the slogan for many branches of the Franciscan Order and other liberal ideologies that would diminish the effects of sacrificial love. My Special and Chosen ones, we have in our midst the means to purify the Earth through My intercession and your willingness to help. There is some ambiguity in the thinking of those who are reviewing My messages as to the difference between 'intercession' and private revelations. We know that the two gifts imply the same thing, but some theologians hold that intercession only means lending My assistance through My prayers. You have rightly referred to My messages here in Illinois as My intercession. Please do not be disconcerted. I am telling you this in advance of what you will eventually hear. I implore My children to ask Jesus through their prayers for the divine assistance they need in addition to My Maternal intercession to My Son on your behalf. This has also been confused with the intervention that Jesus provides to guide and strengthen individuals, families, and the community of the Church. Here again, intercession and intervention cannot be separated. The entire grace stems from the Love and Wisdom of God. We know one thing for sure – when we pray for Jesus to help, He renders it according to the Will of the Father. Everything having to do with His Kingdom is given to those whom He blesses because of their holiness and compliance with the mission of the Church. My Special one, I realize that there are multiple avenues of grace by which your life is enriched, and you deserve it. You are praying with Me because you believe in the miracles that amend the lives of sinners who will inhabit the New Jerusalem with Jesus and Me, and all the Saints of Heaven. You and your brother have sanctified not only your decades in exile, you are setting forth the record to prove it. It is not about power, fame or fortune with you, it is about reconciling humanity with God. There can be no more charitable gift than this. Nothing is better to redress the grief of men that burdens their daily lives. You are too modest to recognize the profoundness of your gifts to the Church. Sadly, others believe that power for power's sake is the reason they should rise from their sleep in the morning."

Our Lady initiated a discussion about worldly authority and the phenomenon of family dynasties in positions of leadership and political power. She referred to our city and the family names that have come to define the political landscape for decades. On the national level, two family surnames have been prevalent, one since 1980 and the other since 1992. The politics of the city of Chicago is another example of family dynasties. Because of their politically-ingrained influence, many representatives of state and national government routinely pass the torch of leadership to family members upon their retirement or death.

"This has happened for generations all across America. These families are distracted from the nature of sacrifice, and have lost their focus on the meaning of faith. I am not accusing them of being ill-intentioned or that something is wrong with their conscience, I am saying that they have a distorted view of what public service is. It should be said of all who seek political office that they must do so because they are humbled, not because they feel entitled. This is rarely the case. This custom of familial succession is more pronounced in other countries than in America. The designs of men should not be that they reach out to others to renown their family names, but because they see problems that only they can solve, and that they will make sacrifices to do so. There is no sacrifice in being hailed as worldly kings. My Special son, you know that I rarely speak in this vein about the minutia of the earthly realms, but I wanted you to see the larger picture about what you and your brother are encountering. *"I understand."* I have told you these things to say that your brother's application for the position for which he applied has been denied. The people reviewing his superior credentials have their own relatives and circle of friends from which they would like to make their choice. These things will not matter in the end. So here, I have come to say that you are blessed, that your brother is doing well, and that you are about to grace the Church with your pamphlets. Absent fervent prayer by the American people, you have the correct assumption about what will happen. The economic system of the United States will collapse, and assets and liabilities will no longer matter. The infirm will not be healed; food supplies will be shortened, there will be no electricity or running water, and suffering will proliferate across the states like an ancient plague. This is not an inexorable prophecy, however. I am saying that the greed in your country is leading to this end.

Hence, My message today has not been about soaring eloquence or images of peace and glory. I have spoken about practical matters that must be measured against the need for prayer. Humanity will someday see that the entire existence of men and the beauty of the world have been supernatural from the beginning, that what seemed so fragile was far more durable than men could have imagined.

And, the designs that were meant to endure the test of time and the force of abuse will be the weak ones, the goals and actions that have all along been held together by the tenderness of God alone. The world is not upside-down by anything God has done or failed to do, but because of the negligence of the stewards in whose hands the nations have placed its care. You and your brother should be otherwise heartened by what you see – the gifts and graces that you have procured through your petitions, the witness that comes from those who are devoted to Me, and the presence of God's Kingdom without end. All of this is for your discernment. You have not only the capacity to judge what is good and wholesome about your lives on Earth, you have the right, and you have the commission. You are sanctioned to prefigure, judge, speak and act according to the Spirit of God reigning in your hearts. This is the holiness that has taken root in you. It is the making of Saints of two babes in due time. My purpose here has always been about making you self-evident ones; and more than that, to say that I love you beyond all imagining. Wherever you step, you leave an heroic footprint. Whatever you pray for thunders across the skies above Mount Calvary. Whenever you make a prediction about whether a certain sign may come, the Son of Man will set it in stone. This is why I have asked that you and your brother not only embrace your suffering, but live knowing that God harvests your pain to yield the conversion of sinners."

Saturday, April 18, 2015
8:58 a.m.

"Because humanity went missing."

"My dear little sons, you are listening to your Mother who was conceived without sin. I am the Queen of Paradise to whom you have given your decisive years in exile. I ask that you never forget that My love for you cannot be repealed. It is an immortal flower that shall never die. The Archangel Gabriel came to Me at the Lord's behest because humanity went missing. Adam was cast into exile because of his sin, and the sin of Eve, and their disobedience made all humanity inheritors of their corruption. My mission has always been about lifting you back to your dignity in Jesus. I did not come to castigate the world for its fallen nature. My Special son, I did not come here speaking to you because I thought you were corrupt; you were created beatifically by God, and you have remained that way. You were born into the exiled realms to help your brothers and sisters know their salvation, to understand the redeeming gift of self-denial, and to lay themselves open to be sanctified by the Holy Spirit and nourished to holiness in Jesus. When something goes missing, it creates a void. Imagine what it must have been like to see the first two people fall. It was their own error, their inability to maintain their goodness because of their pride. The Father says that the world should live like Him. This has never been in doubt. Men should emulate the fullness of His Divine Love; there is nothing to impede their progress. It is not that the Lord was opposed to Adam and Eve being in Paradise, it is that He asked them to '...stay away from that tree.' They chose instead to disobey Him. Hence, My Special son, it is by disobedience that humanity has suffered the loss of God's grace, not just that men hunger to have His power. Indeed, it is not that exiled men wish to become like God, but that they want to become gods themselves. You see the distinction that has brought such suffering into the world. Lay aside the fact that the Earth is being overwhelmed by the violence of false religions, these so-called religions have nothing to do with 'The Faith' in which the redemption of sinners resides – the Holy Roman Catholic and Apostolic Church. All souls outside its grace must be delivered through the Cross of Salvation and the sacrifices of the Roman Catholic Church. You have spoken and written about this matter many times, and I am speaking about it now to make it more memorable around the precincts of the Earth. You need not do anything more to make it clear, but you should remember it in the future when you are called to defend the foundation of your faith. It is because humanity went missing that you have been asked to do so. It is for your brothers and sisters to learn of the sacrificial ways to lend their obedience to God. They are not beyond Jesus' reach. They must train their focus on His call for piety, and exercise their ability to render their belief in Him. If you could imagine all the avenues down which men could travel to show their faith, do you suppose they might burn their midnight oil and write them down? The answer is yes, but they remain distracted by their own druthers and devices that send them down other paths. There needs to be an orientation to what Jesus desires from His disciples. Surely it has everything to do with the theological virtues and taking care of the poor. It is about remembering the Nativity and yielding to the lessons that have been shared in Bethlehem. But, as I have said, even though Jesus has availed His plan of Salvation to the Earth, humanity still remains missing. Many are wandering around without an inkling of what they are supposed to do. I know that it is about self-preservation and taking care of one's family, but there must be more than this. The Providence of God must be their reason for living.

My Special son, you have always had a sense for knowing where the Holy Spirit is found as though you can orchestrate its flight. This has been one of your most endearing traits since you were a boy. You are also aware of conditions that represent a departure from God's Kingdom. This is, as I say, one of your unique qualities that puts you in such good stead before His Throne. Having said this, you are also prone to being so self-examining that you often concede to your own criticism. You discovered this week at your workplace that you are a dynamic leader of men. You are a writer of compromise. You can recognize other people's motivations before they say a word. And, like Jesus, you tend toward unity rather than division. I am citing you as an example to make a point about the opening of today's message. Humanity went missing, and Jesus is trying to accomplish with them the same thing you did at your workplace this week. My Special son, it is not that someone was severed from employment that makes the point, but that the contrast between rightness and wrongness is more articulately defined. The mix of personalities and dispositions is important, but they have less effect on problem-solving than the actual facts. These facts include the completion of a mission and increasing productivity. I make this point because the conversion of humanity should be less about personalities and dispositions as well. It is all about obeying the writs of Jesus' pen and speech, and entering into a spiritual contract with God that defies the logic of men. This contract includes suffering for the sake of the Church, teaching by opening one's conscience to the Holy Spirit, praying for things that one may never see in his lifetime, and feeding all the needy elements of the human constitution with the Sacraments so graciously dispensed from the hands of God. I have always spoken about progress in these things, not being 'progressive,' but progress in the sense of likening the world more closely to the Kingdom of Heaven. We have spoken about this progress when a man who falls to temptation climbs back out and never falls again. It is when a nation realizes that evil lives in a woman demanding the right to an abortion. It is when a murderer stands before his judges and says that being locked in a prison will do nothing to bring back the lives of his victims. Progress can mean smoking one less cigarette per day until a person quits. Yes, and progress can mean people not waiting for the opportunity to reveal their obedience to Jesus, but to go out and commit to it themselves. There must be something more prolific that demands a response from the slumbering herd. It requires something greater from those who are about to be touched, something beyond normal, something less pathetic, something that lights up the night like a blazing inferno. My Special son, I ask you to remember that I am not referring to you and your brother. Having leapt out in faith so many times during your life, accepting the gift of My messages twenty-four years ago, and sharing your sacrifices with your brother proves your intentions. It sets in stone the means by which you have proven your love. I ask that you reflect on everything you have given Jesus with tremendous confidence.

You and your brother live in the shadow of other great Christians. Remember the call for Bernadette to spread the moistened soil on her face. I have related to you the requests that were made of Saint Joan of Arc that christened her mission. It is not the substance of such things that matters most, it is that something itself was requested. This dates to Abram and all who came to obey God's voice when they heard it; they who themselves became trustworthy in His eyes. My Special son, one of the greatest questions that any Christian should ask is, '…how does a man become the father of someone's faith?' Truly, the revelations of obedience are found in simply pondering the question, not just finding the answer. Abraham knew the answer because he personified its meaning. And, should not every man become like him, as though all human beings need a faith-based father? Should not the decisions of Popes and presidents be made through this same obedience to the Lord of all life?"

Saturday, April 25, 2015
9:11 a.m.

"The correlation between faith's strength and spiritual energy."

"It is clear that your prayers are more urgent than before, My little sons; not that you have failed to offer them sincerely, but that they are being applied to the world's sorrows more than ever. We must believe that our praying is ameliorative because many crises are being averted. Prayer is the intersection between what humanity needs and what the Father wills. There is a relationship between faith's strength and spiritual energy in the same way that the heart lives and loves. It is the same as being and doing. Faith's strength is given to you by God. Spiritual energy is manifested by those who believe in Him. This juncture is allowed to thrive because the Church seeks redemption. The whole concept of believing in God is that those who accept His Kingdom put it into practice in ways that draw souls into His presence. My Special son, this is the same way that My Queenship engulfs you; everything you do for Jesus is reposed within My Immaculate Heart. Why? Because the center of My Immaculate Heart is the Seat of Jesus' Sacred Heart. When you live in Jesus and He in you, your soul is founded in the grace to which the world is summoned. I am the Mother who is overflowing with these redeeming graces, given purpose by Jesus' call for human faith, and instituted in the earthly domain by the spiritual energy of the Church. I come to you today in tremendous joy because we are fulfilling the wishes of the Father in ways that I have described, and in many ways still untold. You and your brother have lived for Jesus; there is no question about it. You are moving, living and breathing by your emulation of who Jesus is and what He stands for. There are causes yet to come for which you have already commissioned your response. This is the vision that you have acquired. My appearances in your home are not just My descent from Heaven, but My assent that you are in communion with Jesus. My Special son, how does it feel to be in such good stead before God? *"Peace, confidence and strength; it is a feeling of invincibility. It is like knowing the exact point on the horizon where the sun is going to come up, and rushing directly toward that point."* Yes, and you have stature and esteem that your modesty will not allow you to recognize, but I see it and Jesus sees it, and the Father sees it. We know with gratitude that you have accepted your role of living for the sanctification of the world. It seems, as most of My visionaries through the ages have confirmed, that setting My messages before the nations is an exercise in patience. This is their most common observation. I do not call it waiting, but the manifesting of the Kingdom of God in the hearts of men is not a swift endeavor. I have come to humanity as the Queen of Heaven for 2,000 years. I have appeared as the Queen of Peace for decades, and I have come to you as the Queen of Love for a quarter-century to overwhelm humanity's consciousness with a call to actionable prayer in accordance with the needs of the world. It is the same as I have been telling My children since the Annunciation. Obedience. It is not what humanity wants, it is what the Father would have you do. As I told you last week, this is as ancient as the Edenic Garden. We pray because God desires His people to communicate with Him. He solicits the allegiance of men because He loves you. He does not demand love in return or in contradiction to the will of men because offering love should be a voluntary act. And, when God says that something should be willed, He means that it must be done with aforethought and truthful judgement. The Father says that Jesus will judge the living and the dead not just at their best or worst moments, but what they have consistently done to reveal their compliance with the mandates of His love – His Messianic love. My Special one, God knew from the beginning that men were capable of becoming the likeness of His Son long before Jesus was conceived in My Womb. If He had thought otherwise, the Nativity of Jesus would have never come. This is faith's strength; it is given to mankind by way of sublime spiritual wisdom.

The response of the Church, as I have said, is to grow this strength and put it into practice. The latter is the energy about which I am speaking. There are different levels of energy drawn upon by men in exile. There are as many levels of spiritual energy as there are citizens on the Earth, and it is upon high-energy Christians that Jesus depends. These are not necessarily the people making all the noise; they are not shouting out evangelical manifestos from the rooftops.

They are most often simple disciples like you and your brother who are about to break through the barriers of human lethargy with a consciousness-bursting revelation of your own. This will be a tremendous victory not just for humanity in exile, but for the Lord in Heaven. Composers write entire symphonies about triumphs as monumental as this. So, I am saying that you must wait and see, just like all My messengers through the ages. If it does not happen here, you will see it on your transition from this life to the next. The Lord always suspends time for My messengers and visionaries to feel the goodness of their lives before they see His face. It is a heartfelt gift to those who have served. Now, many cannot draw the distinction between this spiritual obedience and the ordinary life of Christian economy. This is the same struggle that I previously spoke about that burdened Abram and thousands of others through the ages. The reason that I have told you this is to repeat that we see beauty in this purpose, while others see only fear and repulsion. When the world begins to see as we do, they will know the Providence of God; they will recognize the beauty of humanity, power, promise, majesty and splendor. When someone knows God the way we know Him, they will be grateful that He has given life to such apostolic souls, that they reflect His greatness and alliance with truth, love, hope and honor. This is the bridge that many have yet to cross. I am encouraging the world to accept the evidence from God that His sovereignty and peerlessness will always be there. You are not shocked because you know what we are seeing. I see such beauty that I cannot put it into words, while multitudes hide their faces because they cannot see it at all. My call for their obedience will perfectly align them with this Providence, this presence, this intuition and artwork of God. This, My Special son, is what makes Me so happy. Your heart, spirit and faith are elevated beyond the point that you might place your palm over your mouth as though astonished over the beauty of what God has done. You know that the Father is instinctively perfect and lent toward handing you in a thought's width the meaning of the existence of life. I have prayed for centuries that My children would come to recognize blessings from what others might only see as coincidences. Here now is the purpose of My telling you about the unfolding of human redemption with its gravity of burdens and elevating triumphs. The human heart cannot be converted until its eyes are planted in faith on the Sorrowful Crucifixion of Jesus Christ to see the eternal destiny of every man, woman and child ever given the breath of life. We have spoken about irony and contradiction many times before. You see the Salvation of humanity when you see the Twelfth Station, and you see the beauty of God's design when you see the visions that I have described here today. Unfortunately, nearly everyone on Earth looks at the Twelfth Station and sees only torture and murder. And, they look casually at everything else because they know that they are like Adam and Eve in the Garden without any clothes.

My Special son, My message today finds you and your brother clad in faith and promise. It is to this resolve, to this awareness and comprehension, that you have been drawn, while billions of other men remain outside its purview. All the Popes of the Church have had it. Mystics and visionaries have had it, but not all of them. All the Angels revel in what the Crucifixion means in the perception of the world's long history. Seeing the Cross according to men's faith is the reason that you have not required other visions to believe everything you know. It was not necessary for you to see the sun spinning in Medjugorje as did your brother who was standing next to you. God did not wish to insult your faith by proving that He can do anything He desires with celestial spheres. To the contrary, your brother saw the rotating and disappearing sun because he did not have at that time your envisionment of Jesus on the Cross. Do you understand this contrast? *"Yes."* This is what makes you united with the Doctors of the Church who are sewn into the fabric of God's love that is being spread over Creation. My Special son, you will be hailed by the whole of humanity for advancing your faith to such degrees. It is strong because God made it that way. You are living it with intense spiritual energy because, like Jesus, your heart is seated in Mine. So, this is My message for today. Do you have any issues to discuss with Me? *"I am so proud of Jesus when I look at Him in those moments of His Crucifixion. I can barely describe it."* He knows it; your Savior is utterly aware of the love in your heart. This is why you and Jesus are one. Please be assured that you are one of few who have lionized what Jesus did that day. Your brother is with you. I love you, and I pray that you will help Me invoke God's blessing on everyone; that humanity will accept their lifeblood of Salvation in the Cross."

Saturday, May 2, 2015
9:37 a.m.

"The Virgin Mary told me that humanity has gone missing. She speaks about the missed opportunities, vacuums and vacancies we have created because of our unwillingness to make the connection between the origin of virtuous truth and the Father's Testament of Salvation. It sometimes makes me wonder what happened to humanity's participation in the Lord's divine suffusion and the true recognition of His Son's Christological imprint. Where did the world go wrong? Why have we become so cowardly in the wake of our forebears' courageous fight against the evils of this world? It is certain that we must acquire a new taste for great reckonings again. We need a new beginning and a vast reconnection with the civilizing dreams that once made America so strong. We need a more keenly calculating vision and a resuscitated national conscience that saw the western world prevail in the two great world wars. We need new drums to march by and heartbeats that sound like thunder, as deafening as dinosaurs stomping across oceans of glass. We need to drive our sabers of love so deep into the gut of the world's hatred that our slashes pierce the universe's hull. We need to reclaim for our children America's halls of decency from the so-called progressives who are trying to block their path with outright lies and false impressions. This should become the focus of our presence, the efficacy of our days, and the reason we reach for our share of human life. Sadly, however, rather than jump in the middle of the fight against Satan's armies, we timidly heckle him from the galleries. We are far too mum and afraid. We are still missing the mark. Instead of delivering death blows to the world's unchecked evil, we only pitch around the edges with softballs and pious platitudes. We measure the heat of the battle with quicksilver instead of our enemies' fatalities. Then, to our shame, we boast in public forums about our daring, and pray about a justice that may never come."

- William L. Roth

"My Special son, this is the most lengthy prelude that you have ever spoken for My appearances here to you and your brother, and it is clearly one of the best. Never mind that people might think that you are dwelling on the negative all the time. It has nothing to do with that. It is sure that Satan will move to attack you for trying to correct humanity's errors; this is what evil does. Your words to begin My message today make for excellent lessons to those who need to hear. I wish you well in making your feelings known in your writings and speeches that you might find the venue to share. We have seen that the fight against evil is often as much about indifference as the onslaughts of the devil. I will speak directly here about serving-out your obedience to Jesus. Blessings will occur. The fullness of the light will shine; healings will be innumerable, and the world will be set aright by all that we have done. Without your obedience, the sword would have been drawn, but not stained. Every man's determination would climb to the top of the mountain, but be too afraid to look down. The gift of courage has been perfectly humanized, personified and exemplified by Jesus on the Cross. And you, My Special son, have emulated them all. You have made known the Kingdom of God here in this world; you have held nothing back, to all the ends you have gone. All in all, you have marked for the human family the blessing of Christian sacrifice. You have lived the marvel of holiness.

You have done your part with excellence. And, most of all, you have not been hypocritical in your call for others to live out this same faith to which you have dedicated your life. There is such contradiction in the way some Christians live. Could it be true that someone who seeks public office would call on another person's help solely to keep that person from joining forces with his opponent? Absolutely yes. Could someone be this cynical in these modern times? You just saw it happen, and your brother was the person thrown into the gutter. And yet, it does not matter; it is an exercise in irrelevance, it is about nothing more than secular pride. I admire you and your brother for seeing it this way, for realizing that your hold on the everlasting blessings of life places you in the company of the Saints whose icons and images have adorned vestibules and prayer chapels for centuries. You are part of the giantness of the Christological miracle. Your hearts and lives are imbedded in the spiritual realms that overcome everything superficial about the ages of men. In effect, you have eclipsed your existence on the Earth, even as you have labored on its soil.

My Special son, you know this to be true. You are fully aware that you have given the decades of your life to Jesus in ways that few ordained shepherds have provided. God will not allow your work to be trampled underfoot or shelved in history's archives. Jesus will glorify the messages that I have given to you! As I speak about trust, virtue, courage and wisdom, I call for prayers for the purity of humanity. I ask for My children to be pure of mind, heart and body. I seek from the world a vision that not only includes a life with Christ Jesus, but consecrated to His love. This is why we are praying now. When you hear of springtime rains and flowers, this is the setting in which the resurrection of the human soul lives. And, My Special and Chosen sons, it is not only about those who know Me, it involves sectors and societies much larger than any one nation could sustain. It is about transcending the thought of existing in a world of strangers; it is about causing men to become recognized and well known inside the Sacred Heart of Jesus and the Providential Heart of God. This is what our prayers are doing. So, when I ask for obedience from My messengers, I am summoning humanity's realization that all good things come through faith. I have accompanied the Popes and Cardinals in the election of Pontiffs through the guidance of the Holy Spirit. I have spoken about the sacrifice that Abraham conceded to God, not just that he was obedient, but that he did not know that he would be elevated to such stature in the history of the Church today. Abraham who? I do declare that the people of Springfield are celebrating the wrong Abraham. It is not about looking to profit from someone's good name, it is about glorifying the reconciliation between God and man through the offering of near-miraculous faith. It is about Abraham and Moses, Isaac and

Jacob and so on. It is about rectifying what has gone wrong with humanity's identity in the Passion, Crucifixion and Resurrection of one sinless Man. My Special son, I have said this before; everything I have told you today, you already know, but I needed to tell someone. I wanted somebody to hear Me say it again. I have invoked your regard, prayers and participation in unprecedented ways in these times. Why? Because I love you, and I need you. "*Thank you, Mama. I so love you too.*" There is grace running freely through your life. The Blood of Jesus is keeping humanity strong, and your prayers are the veiny fruits through which it flows. You and your brother are adorned with virtue, the likes of which will not be seen again in the history of the world. There is a triumph in the offing that will take you by surprise. My Immaculate Heart consumes you and consoles you. I will ask Jesus to bless everyone for whom you have prayed, and all in your future petitions. I especially ask that you pray for the leaders of the Church."

Sunday, May 10, 2015
9:38 a.m.

"Welcome, one and all, to exiled human life. There may be side effects – enchantment, bassinets, hearts full of platinum, sirens, prodigies, crooked teeth, eclipses, eulogies, aromas, alarm clocks, tongues of fire, arching rainbows – and much more than these, but there are no sequels."

- William L. Roth

"It is in true indebtedness that I come speaking to My two sons who are so endearing to the Father. My children, you complete the miracle of the Descent of the Holy Spirit. You welcome and harbor within you the splendor of the Lord in whose stead you are tracking world events, teaching the lost, and lauding the Kingdom to which you belong. My Special son, thank you for your quotation to begin this message. It is clear that you have a pretty heart and poetic spirit. You see the global realms before the backdrop of its ethereal counterpart. If you could only imagine what you mean to God, you would weep tears of joy. Today, I have come amidst the massive enlightenment that your pamphlets are bringing to the Roman Catholic Church. They are reaching the Bishops with the fullness of the grace with which they were prepared. The Bishops are conferring in corridors, on street corners and in parish halls about this grand miracle that has unfolded in your home. And, their response has been, '...Let us see what the Mother of Jesus wants.' It has been made manifest in your deposit of works. Now, you have a letter from your Bishop stating that he has given you and your brother vindication for your faith. My Special son, do you realize what a tribute this is to Me, the Mother of Jesus, to have a Roman Catholic Bishop pronounce that My messages are so inspiring that he has sanctioned a commission to examine them? My goodness! Imagine how this makes Me feel. It means that through you and your brother, I have touched the hearts of humanity. I have uplifted the souls of the leaders of the Church. I have reached the people who need to know. I realize that this is a tremendous affirmation of your work and your longevity of devotion to My Immaculate Heart, but think about what this means to Me. I am saying that there are Bishops and Cardinals in the Church who are willing to read what you have published, handed down from the Mother of God, inspired by the Lord's Holy Kingdom, and placed at the feet of the universe for humanity to consume. There is no way to thank you enough for being My messengers on Earth as well as instruments for God in Heaven. You have shown what true beauty looks like compared to the ugliness of the temporal void. You have proved that sanctity and obedience can bring about the conversion of entire societies of souls. Yes, the Prelates of the Church are sitting in their armchairs, reflecting on what you have sent to them. Some are reading while eating their meals, pondering the prospect that the Mother of Jesus Christ could have so much to say in the span of twenty-four years. And, My Special one, they are even more amazed that two adopted sons of the Immaculate Conception could persist so long in faith and endurance without the Church knowing about it. They are planning their own thanksgiving for the gift that God promised would come. Every person who receives your work will know that the Mother of the Church is the Queen of the human heart. I do not wish to preclude the events of the next few years with more comment about what is happening, but for you to know that your manuscripts are being reviewed in ways previously untold.

My Special son, this has come about because you have believed. I wanted all along to reach you, and I was given this wish from whence you were a boy. So now, you have received a letter from your Bishop indicating that the Church has taken on our cause. I told you in 2003 that there would be nothing so opposed as your love for the Mother of God. I told you about the claim that the poor have on the rich, as spoken by then-Bishop George J. Lucas. These things will always be true, My little son. It is not that the Catholic Church will look down upon you or despise you for being so focused on Me, but that you have inherited in your own right a relationship with Me that most others do not share. You have rightly told them in your books and prefaces that they can have this relationship with Me by extolling the sacred mysticism that I have articulated to you. They can, through their lives in the Gospel, come to the same feeling of being 'special' just as you are special. Everything you have instilled in your Morning Star publications will restore humanity's faith that is being overshadowed by the illusions of the world. How could any mother be displeased knowing this to be true? We have every reason to hope that what Jesus wants from His people will be given to God. Yes, My Special son, the magnanimous nature of your deposit of Marian works is what makes your testimony so believable. This is not something that just happened yesterday or last month. It was not a year or two ago that you and your brother began your journey toward the enlightenment of the nations. It has been ongoing for a quarter-century now; it has a life of its own, as I said before. You have given your Morning Star Over America messages life and liberty because you said 'yes' to Me. This is what I have been saying about your spiritual impressions on the secular landscape. You have poured out your heart along with your brother for the conversion of the multitudes, and you have rebuked those who asked you to live another way of life by remaining steadfast in your labors for the Lord. You hold in your hands a sacrificial legacy that will last forever. It is not effusion that I speak this morning, I am saying how proud of you I am. I am expressing Jesus' joy that you are one with Him, that you are His modern disciples who are making such a difference where others have failed. We speak so eloquently about what Jesus desires from His brothers and sisters because we wish to reach them in a spiritually conducive way. We have spoken about adages and maxims, bluffs and berms, and gifts and confections, but these are only part of the story to which the Earth's sinners should listen. This is the celebration of who we are and where humanity is going. So today, I come to offer My gratitude, to bless and honor you, and share this extraordinary day in a way that highlights the grace of the times that you and your brother are living. It is more than providential that you have held so long to Me; it is worthy of the great Saints of the Church. Thank you for fighting with fervency for the preservation of human life. It is clear that such compassion has redeemed the prayers of Christians through the centuries. It is truly a blessing for the world."

Saturday, May 16, 2015
9:33 a.m.

"The human spirit was never supposed to be about soot or ashes, empty wells, smallish dreams, broken promises or upside-down masterpieces. We were meant to strive for the gift of perfect love, anticipate new beginnings and benign consequences, reach out and touch the Lord's face in His simplest humanity, and without swallowing the Moon whole, gobble up life's toughest struggles with an appetite for redemption and our sights set on enduring joy."

- William L. Roth

"My goodness gracious, My Special son, what a beautiful passage. Thank you for sharing it. I come with the peace of the Lord to pray with you, that we may be united in the Sacred Divine, that God may realize His holiest intentions through us, and that humanity will be the better for our love. Today, I wish you the best of all days because we have gathered in your prayer room to change the world. My little sons, there is greater faith among the Bishops than there was a week ago. They are more spiritually inclined to believe in miracles. I pray that you will understand that you do not simply occupy a place on Earth and in the Catholic Church, but that your identity in Jesus is becoming as overwhelming as His own being. You are still tethered to the flesh by virtue of your birth, but your hearts are fasted in the Heaven to which you will be taken. My Special son, I have read the content of your pamphlet to the Bishops and the media, and I am inspired to go back and read it again. It draws in those who appreciate what you have said. It is the remarkable summation of extraordinary grace for your age and in this old world's shadow. If you please, allow Me to thank you again for your gifts to Jesus and the Church. You have seen the condition of the Earth from your perspective, and I have seen it from Mine. If not for Jesus protecting My senses from many of the more grotesque sights, I would view your exile in the same way as you and your brother. I am saying that you have the capacity to know the world in ways that I would rather not see, and I have the discretion to share the knowledge of Heaven not known to most other souls. It is not that others do not wish to know; it is that they lack the perseverance that you and your brother have given to Jesus. They lack the spiritual tenor that has marked your lives with such foresight. This is why I say that you are blessed, and that you bless God and His humanity in return. You and your brother are Special and Chosen because of whom you have grown to be both here in the Church and the Kingdom of the Sacred Divine. My Special one, there are 'stories' and there are 'histories.' These things are shaped by the ability to know the purpose of human life, as you have shared through your books and years' works. You have an appreciation for the majesty and eloquence of living in accordance with the teachings of the Gospel – yes, even the dark and unsightly things that you endure. I pray that your brothers and sisters will come to realize what this means before the grand assemblage of human events. Living without this perspective is what leads to injustice and the persecution of those who know what everyone must eventually believe. The issue is not just disbelief, but disdain for the truth. It is the rejection of miracles that causes the downfall of men's faith. My Special son, what they do to you is inconsequential. It matters not what they say about Me or the manifestations I have shared through the ages. I daresay that most pilgrims who travel to My shrines do not go there to enhance their faith, but to find out whether God exists at all. I am speaking around the globe because I was given permission. I was dispatched and commissioned by the compassion of God, and Jesus sends Me where I go.

I have dictated to you and your brother a blueprint for living, a means for knowing who I am, and a way for humanity to discover what faith in the heart looks like. My love for My children is in constant vigilance. It is a rainbow in full bloom. It is about teaching the broken world to recognize the curves and slopes of spiritual renewal in ways never before known. When someone says that they have converted, this may not be enough. Converted to what? Just because they may have abandoned their previous habits does not mean that they will not adopt worse ones. This is why I am calling out to authentic Christians. My Special son, I pray that you do not anguish over the difficult decisions that you are making at your workplace because they have no effect on who you are. As your brother said on Thursday, people make their own way in life. They make choices for which there are ramifications. Meanness is not acceptable in the workplace setting, and neither is mockery or contempt. You stand for the right, as it is said, as the Lord gives you the might to see the right. I am with you, as Jesus is Himself. I urge you to take precautions, whatever you may deem them to be, to ensure that no retribution brings you harm. There is prudence within you; there are thoughts and motivations to which you aspire that usher in an age of spiritual light. What you are doing at your office is no more complicated than this. Those who impede your progress are not worthy of being in your company, let alone being paid for driving your mission off course. What has Jesus done with those who have stood in His way? He tells them to turn to God and devote themselves to the Gospel that He has fulfilled. This is what you have done as well. I congratulate you for not allowing your emotions or pity for the wicked to make you hesitant about what changes to make. What do you suppose to be the final words from the lips of Jesus to a sinner who has been condemned to Hell? '*Out of my sight.*' Yes, it is as simple as this. There is a certain measure of this same sentiment that you and your brother have expressed. When the full potential of goodness inside a person is put down by everything malevolent about them, this is something that the person himself has manifested. It is his drawing more on hatred than love. It is his way of aspersing God and collaborating with the devil. Jesus' final words to those who reject Him at their final hour are these – 'Let this be the fate you have chosen because your wickedness is more present in you than My redemptive love.' The whole matter is summarized by the fact that someone's obedience must be offered in return for God's forgiveness. So, My Special and Chosen sons, I repeat how grateful I am that you have lived for Jesus, that you have remained tied to My heartstrings, and that you have refused to be deterred by those who do not believe. I am elated that your courage remains strong, I am honored that you are dedicated to humanity, and I am uplifted that your consecration to My Most Immaculate Heart has yielded so many miracles for the Church. I give you My blessing for taking to task those who would impede your work. My Special son, the gift we have given the world is before them. It has a stately constitution that will touch those for whom it has always been intended. I ask that you never worry that your lives and gifts to Christ Jesus will ever be in vain. Thank you again for writing the wonderful passage to begin our message today. I have not forgotten anything for which, or anyone for whom, you have asked Me to pray. I will enlist the kindness of Jesus in response to your petitions."

Saturday, May 23, 2015
9:38 a.m.

"Contents – one repentant human soul; some assembly required."

"My dear precious little children, often do I come speaking to you because you reflect the Light of Jesus in this world, and I am drawn to you because of your stately brilliance. My sons, I have said that the journey of life is as much about process as outcome, and you are foretelling the shining welcome of the Lord's Second Coming. May the Peace and Light of Christ Jesus and the fellowship of the Holy Spirit be with you always. My Immaculate Heart is filled by your daring faith, that you are willing to risk the wrath of the devil whose evil minions you are defeating. My Special and Chosen ones, I have said that your lives in Jesus seem like the ebbing and flowing of waves against a shoreline. This is the rhythm of the Christian song. There seem to be major advances and minor setbacks. This is the living spirit of the Cross by which you are endowed. My Special son, you are doing a stellar job attesting to My witness of the extraordinary graces from Heaven. You are speaking the truth about what I have come to do. You should feel a tremendous sense of accomplishment in this. My Special child, I want you to remember that I identify with you in everything you suffer for Jesus. I know that you become tired, and sometimes you manifest a reluctance to rest. This is the same with all My messengers; it is not just you and your brother. So, I have said upon coming today that the conversion of humanity is not unlike a package; your allegiance to Jesus is presented this way. The content of this package is one repentant human soul, with some assembly required. What does this mean? It is rather simple. Once someone has converted to the Crucifixion of Jesus for their redemption, that person begins a journey leading to the destination about which we have spoken. Living the Christian life is a rolling process; it must be nurtured and enriched to remain alive. It must be fed spiritual awakenings and faith-based knowledge. This is a perpetual springtime for the human spirit that lives beyond one's passing from this world into the next. It begins on Earth and never ends. Therefore, I say 'thank you' My Special son, for complementing this process. You are a teacher and mentor for those only now beginning to understand their absolution in their Savior, Jesus Christ. You are innovative and insightful. Your heart is the bearer of Good News for the rest of the world. This is not something that I have seeded in you, it is a gift that you have owned since the day you were born. I have helped you grow in faith only because of your willingness to learn. You have prayed long and listened well. You have seen the imperative nature of the Earth's transformation from secular extremism to Heaven's Christian eternity. So today, My little sons, I pray with you for all the reasons we have known for centuries. There is a building up of the love of the human heart from the love that was inspired in you from the first heartbeat of your forebears. I have seen this love because My vision begins in God. We have reams of wisdom to dispense to those who are unaware of the Lord's Kingdom, and we do this best through our prayers. As I have said, we pray for all the reasons we have known for hundreds of years. The cyclical nature of men's consciousness, the cleansing of their spirit, and the communion of one generation with the next causes societies of creatures to safeguard the holiness that is handed down through the ages. Yes, this is what I mean to say; it is not as complex as it might seem because the whole matter is centered on the multi-faceted kingdom of the heart. If the nations are attached like links on a chain, or if one thread weaves through the millennia of time, it is the cyclical nature of men's consciousness that is common to it all. This is what fosters the growth of the eternal conscience. If you believe that every generation is constructed on the accomplishments of its predecessor, then you must believe that you are laying the groundwork for the final age of men. You are building this foundation on everything we have achieved since August 1989, and we are laying it in its rightful place.

It is obvious that this is not easy; it has never been a simple task. However, what matters is that it must be done – it should be done, and it shall be done. Your strength, perseverance and tenacity are blessings from God to the precincts of the exiled Earth. You should see yourselves and your lives this way. When you look into the mirror, be thankful for what it reflects. Yes, you can see the faces of the Doctors of the Church. You are seeing in your own innocence the poverty of the Lamb of God. You are seeing the reflection of sacrifice itself. What I ask of you, My Special and Chosen ones, is that you innoculate yourselves from the barbs of cynicism that have bruised so many messengers before you. After all, this is the reason that so many visionaries have not written diaries and renderings of their own. This world is so opposed to My miraculous appearances and the New Covenant Gospel that it would have burned My seers' books at high noon on the downtown square. This could happen to yours; it would be a tremendous validation that your work is a product of your allegiance to God and your witness that the Cross is the way to everlasting life. I am not saying that it will bring you harm, but you must live as though it could happen. This is being prudent about what you say and where you go. Tell your detractors to read the books. Read the books! Every time My Immaculate Heart is impacted by revelations that My messengers are being persecuted on Earth, I remind them of the Cross. I see the Victim whose Sacrifice has made men's peace with God. I see the reconciliation between the Father and His people in the flesh. I see all the beauty and strength that an exiled incarnate soul could possess. I see the fullness of suffering that any human being could endure. I have said that the future of the Earth is contained in this, My children. Everything that humanity will ever say or do is superseded by what the Son of Man gave to the world and the Kingdom of God on the Cross. The Cross is the center of the universe of humankind and the providing of many blessings to come. This is also, as unbelievable as it sounds and painful as it is, where I find My comfort too. Why? Because the Seed that fell to earth grew to new life. The Rose who slept in death was awakened by the command of God to rise again on Easter morning and beatify the Earth once more. For those who doubted, it was the same as the sun coming up on the second morning of the Genesis world. The horizon was as surprised as anyone else to know that this sacred moment would happen again, but God did intervene.

My Special and Chosen ones, it is what happened between these dawns that made all the difference to the inhabitants below. Yes indeed, everything within and during the repeating darkness waited for the dawn. I have seen this recurring process from the other side of time, and I am pleased to pronounce that your hearts have ratified your faith before its glowing presence. You are good and truly faithful in the eyes of God; you bear fruits with which you are nurturing the innocence of His people back to health again. Standing tall – this is what you are doing. It is not that you just have potential to foster the miracles that will modify the heretofore-mentioned consciousness of men, but you are accomplishing it in your time. You see through eyes of love the delectable Feast waiting for you upon the completion of your years. You have foreseen what it will mean sitting next to your Savior in Heaven. I am humbled by your obedience to Him, I am grateful that you have listened to Me, and Jesus and I are aware that it is only a matter of time before you see everything you have done in this life in light of your finished faith. I promise you that every moment of your lives will then make sense. Every insult, every pain and suffering, every question and untimely consequence will fit into the picture of what you will come to know. We cannot escape, nor should we desire to escape, the grand possibility that your brothers and sisters will animate the legacy you have given them. It must be their own will to begin this journey, to walk where you have gone, to engage the same challenges and emotions that have brought you to this day. Please give them that chance; let them fall down and rise to their feet again. Let them see the horizon about which I have spoken as though they have never seen it before. This is the echo of the new beginnings that I spoke about in 1991, applied to this century in which most of them will die. All this is good news; it is more than just auspicious because it hails from the Kingdom of God. It is glorious and resurrecting; it is sheer beauty manifested in a world of men whose destiny resides in their own faith. As I have said, this is the assembly of the repentant human soul that is pleasing in the sight of God. My Special son, I hope you have enjoyed what I have told you today. I will remember on this Memorial weekend all the faithful departed, that they may rest in peace. Thank you again for your love and thoughtfulness."

Saturday, May 30, 2015
9:26 a.m.

"The prospering of Christian awareness."

"My dear little children, the echoes of the Genesis age remain with you in everything you do for Jesus. It is in this creative light that you retain the strength of your tenacity in Him. Today, I have come to tell you about the global warming of the world through the Spirit of God. This is how ice floes are fashioned; it is the thawing of human hearts. Yes, the Earth is breaking from its sleep, and this is a worthy omen for you. These floes in your lives are your gifts. They come to you when you have peace of heart and when you are rested. They can be instilled in you when you realize the closeness of the Lord in all you do, in everything you have become, beyond all you could ever aspire to achieve as citizens of the world. My Special son, Christians must maintain their razor-sharp faith through their lives, but this can be dulled through time and the ravages of pain. There are so many distractions – I keep telling you this. The western world must place these things in perspective before the backdrop of the teachings of the Church. The world began on a spiritual basis not unlike the ice ages. Prayers have brought the warming of humanity's awareness that God lives in Heaven, that He stands for something more than mere human existence, that He brings you wisdom that delivers the Church to its fullest enlightenment. It is men's responsibility to take themselves to their new beginnings in the Child of Bethlehem. The floes about which I speak today have stropping edges that sharpen your lives in Jesus, that keep your path open to the Holy Spirit in which your life's wisdom is found. If you see human life this way; if you recognize that your life need not be a constant battle to guard the sanctity of your faith, you would be seated atop the floes, and your days would be more meaningful. You would see them as ships instead of icebergs. Behind every act of beauty, there is someone's holy heart. Every sunset has a personality, culled from the infiniteness of God's Holy Kingdom. I have said that the Father requires something from humanity. He would never have intervened in the domain of exiled men if it had been otherwise. And, what the Lord wants is for the souls of His creatures to survive the wreck of this world. He desires that men come to the fullness of righteousness in a way that draws them to Jesus on the Cross. My Special one, this is sometimes done through suffering. Suffering breaks through the world's indifference; it spawns the deliverance of men's thoughts from not knowing to completely understanding. It is awareness, truth and light. Suffering scatters the darkness of sin in which humanity is lost. Suffering is redemptive because the suffered-soul reaches for peace that it knows through faith and hope to be present in the Three Persons of God. Suffering does not breed character as much as it excavates the heart from beneath the centuries of unknowing. But, when the Church speaks of those suffering in Hell, it is not the same kind of suffering. Condemned souls do not have redemptive suffering, but punitive suffering. Nothing they endure will enhance the love of the Church. On the other hand, those who suffer on Earth and in Purgatory carry the light of the Cross. There is transcendence in what they suffer. And, when I say that you might perceive your participation in human life as though you are seated on ice floes with stropping edges, I am saying that your experiences are productive, even in your agony. My Special son, I am describing a phenomenon that hardly anyone understands. Many persons ask why innocent people suffer, why little children become bedridden, why beautiful designs are desecrated. The answer is because the created world is called to live inside the Crucifixion of Jesus, within the grace and power that purifies the souls of men. The innocent have become those strops as well. They are like pillars against which the evil of other men is shattered. And, all who have suffered for Jesus' sake have come to envision His Kingdom before they depart the temporal realms. There are remnants of this gift to the Father all around the globe.

Billions of graves contain the relics of this sanctifying ceremony. Syllables of praiseworthy speeches echo among the mountaintops for the Angels to hear. We can hear them in Heaven, as do the birds of the air. If the skylarks and eagles could speak human languages, one might turn to another and ask, '...What was that beautiful sound?' And, the second would reply, '...That was the imparting voice of Pope Peter himself.' These strains still remain. They can be heard by those who listen with their hearts. Why are they often difficult to hear? Because they are overshadowed by humanity's bombs bursting in the air, train whistles blowing, atheists wailing in the night, screaming harlots, charging race cars, and terrorists blowing themselves up for a belief system based on a lie. This is why I call My children everywhere to peace. Pilgrims wish to know the reason for My role as Queen of Peace, but the answer should be obvious to them. One can look on every continent and before all the nations. Many do not want God in their lives anymore. I appeared in Fatima ninety-eight years ago and heard petitions that said, '...God help us.' Today, I scarcely hear petitions at all, and many of the ones I hear are to the effect, '...God where are you?' Humanity has driven away the Dove of Peace because they have shunned God's love in favor of the turmoil of the secular void. It is an inheritance from the unwillingness of little girls to see their part in motherhood as a means of glorifying God. It is a manifestation of men and boys who have turned their backs on holiness in favor of the exploitation of the Earth's resources for fame and financial gain. It is a product of humanity believing that those who hold the most power and wealth when they die somehow ultimately win. My Special son, you can see why I keep returning to speak to you and your brother. You do not subscribe to the wrongs that I have spoken about today. You share a relationship with the Mother of God! You harbor deep in your hearts a hunger for the truth to which all souls must be drawn. You refuse to be distracted by the shambles of the world's sin. It is clear – you heard evidence of this last evening from the man with whom you spoke. He was speaking about his wife who has become so embroiled in secular life that she seems exhausted. This exhaustion foments frustration, then frustration into anger, and the entire matter descends into the destruction of vows. Then, when one looks at their marriage from the sacramental grace of their wedding day to the present, the times hardly resemble each other. This is the treading of water that you and your brother have refused to engage. Instead, you have lived for Jesus in the lineage of the Doctors of the Church. This is where reality is. This is where the emollient of the human spirit prevails. I pray that you never tire that I lavish you with accolades, but you understand what your lives have meant to Me. Imagine your standing before the Son of God. Understand what your contributions will bring to the finishing of the Earth. This is why I have said that you remain in the moment, but all moments will culminate in the great reunion of redeemed humanity and their glorious God. The birds of the air and fishes of the sea can sense the fragrance of your beautiful oratories that will regale the finished world of what we have done in this place. You never get full-chested about this because you are so humble and modest, but what I am saying is true. You are too close to your work to realize its converting power. I will speak to you at the opening of a new month, a time dedicated to the Sacred Heart of Jesus. Thank you for your prayers."

Saturday, June 6, 2015
2:27 p.m.

"Redemption is encrypted in the fidelity of men."

"You are the heralds, My dear sons, of the truth and love that are overtaking the world. It may appear that the evidence is lacking, but Jesus commands the existence of humanity. He ratifies the lives and actions of the good. He rebukes and disarms the evils of the bad – not in a way that is transparent, but with means to ensure the triumph of justice beyond the ages. My little sons, it is in your life's choices that you find the translation of redemption; it is in your hearts that people will eventually see. The whole composition of the faith on which you have based your lives is in your intentions. The final question to ask every man is to inquire about their fidelity to the Church; not just do they know about its teachings, not whether they will stumble and fall, but whether they have been faithful, even in the presence of self-doubts. No man will ever comprehend the full convention of what everything in life means; it was never supposed to be that way. What is important is that everyone comes to perfection in what Christ Jesus calls you to do. This is how to rediscover yourself in the Kingdom of God, the way you dress yourself in righteousness and conduct yourself in the Church. My Special and Chosen ones, you have during the past days attended several secular meetings where you have met people you have never known. And yet, you know about what they think because you are citizens of the same country. This is a metaphor for what Christians do to evangelize the Gospel. You are known in these places by what you believe, by the way you communicate a particular aspect of human life through the common canons that connect you with the world. You are not strangers here. It is as though these people have known you all your lives by your inheritance of identity that you were given by those who raised you. In your case, this is cause for celebration, a way to personify My messages. I have high hopes that everything you are doing to reach out secularly and through your Marian apostolate will grow the awareness of My role in your redemption. My Special one, it is inevitable. I am peacefully overwhelmed that you and your brother are sharing the content of My messages at these events, even before these souls have completely welcomed them. You are nurturing the mission of the Church in ways that you have never recognized. Hence, I ask that you remember the importance of setting the example that you are practical human beings. You are not odd or eccentric; you are balanced and self-sufficient in your oneness with the orthodoxy of the Church. This gives Jesus not only reason to believe that others will listen, but that they will understand that you have no other motivation than to induce the world to turn to Me for help. I come today to explain what stands behind the ability of good men to succeed. I have used the word 'encrypted' not to suggest that the Will of God is shielded from the sight of humanity, but to say that the mission of the Church is clear. Speaking to others about the extraordinary graces from Heaven is a way to lift up the poor and enrich the faith of believers. I take hope from My successors, Christians like you and your brother. You often say that God could reach more lost sinners if He allowed more miracles to happen. I agree with you; it is for this that we are praying. I spoke the word 'miraculous' in My June 2, 2015 Medjugorje message knowing that we would dwell on it here. I have always believed that miracles have converting power. This is the reason I approached Jesus at the wedding feast. Jesus agrees that these miracles do not diminish the faith of those who would be just as faithful in their absence. Blessed are they who believe without seeing. My Special son, you spoke two evenings ago about 'transformational leadership.' This lends to the purpose of My presence as the Queen of Love. I appeared in Medjugorje in June 1981 to grow the faith of the children and the world, and I have come to you and your brother to beseech you to lead humanity's conscience to the mystical realms.

This is the energy that I have lauded for the past twenty-four years. It is about the capacity of men to be transformed into Jesus' likeness by shedding the old life and donning the holiness of the new. You have given Jesus your attention and participation in ways that are unprecedented in the western hemisphere. You do not view it as a sacrifice because you have moved so close to Me. I have said that you are too close to your work to know its converting power and contribution to the finishing of the world. This is based on what someone might attribute to the miracles about which I speak and the sacrifices that ordinary men make in their everyday lives. You will not be surprised to know that God sees the latter as the greater miracle. He sees you and your brother as miracle workers because, even here in the United States with all its secular allure, you have not strayed onto another course. My Special son, we look upon this from Heaven as supernatural itself. The people on Earth who hold the greatest power do not know they have it. I am not referring to the power to purchase sparkling diamonds or hold high political office, but power that makes a difference in the deliverance of the world. These people change the Earth in increments by doing simple things, offering gifts and sacrifices that glorify God while others are not paying attention. It is like beginning to clap in an auditorium filled with people. After a while, another person claps, then two, then a dozen, and soon a hundred. In a few moments, the entire audience is applauding without saying a word. This is what you and your brother have done underneath these American skies. And, it is heard in Heaven just as you would hear it in some amphitheater where you live. There is one thing for certain. When the Son of Man returns to claim the Earth for His Kingdom, humanity will break into a thunderous ovation. It will be a welcoming sight of thanksgiving glory that will last ten thousand years. Those on Earth when Jesus returns will hear the same response from the Saints in Heaven. The celebration will permeate time and space; it will be heard in every universe and beyond the mysteries of love. I am speaking about Jesus' face shining on those who accept Him, looking into every heart and soul. What will be different, My Special one, is that Jesus will not raise His hands and ask the audience to stop. He will not intervene during this spontaneous accolade to deliver His remarks because He knows that infinity is on His side. It is true – Jesus will stand on the floor of the Earth and acknowledge the applause of men for twenty centuries if He has to. He will raise the Cross and bless the masses. He will smile with admiration on those who have suffered for His sake. His light will shine on the many who were freed from the burden of their sins. And, Jesus will not just say 'thank you' for the applause, He will say 'thank you' for believing in Him. He will know that He is in the company of Saints! So, I share with you the magnificence of what this will mean to everyone who has lived before you. They are all out there, you know. Most of them have entered Heaven; many are mitigating their transgressions in Purgatory. Millions more are in eternal turmoil in the flames of Hell. But, they are all still somewhere.

I ask you to remember that the interfacing arena of Christian redemption begins where you are kneeling right now. You live on the Earth where Salvation and condemnation intersect. Of course the Saints in Heaven pray for you, and this is an auspicious grace. But, faithful Christians in exile have said plenteous prayers to send some of them into the heavenly realms. You are living the thrice-willed gift of God's blessing that has been manifested through the Crucifixion of His Son. You have mourned His Passion. You have prophesied and consoled in His name. You have healed the brokenhearted and fed those who would not have thrived by other means. You have walked by faith and not by sight, all the while imagining in your heart the way the world ought to be. You have accepted the yoke and your portion of the Cross with humility, eagerness and a smile on your soul. All these things are more than elements of a good life on Earth. They are pillars of righteousness that you have invoked from God and His Creation. They are verses in the most beautiful epic that will ever be written in the history of the world. They are the salutation and cadence of the demise of the enemies of the Church. And, My Special little son, they come from you and your brother, from millions of men and women who have accepted their part in the conversion of lost humanity. This is what I am referring to when I speak about divine power. It is prescribing on God's behalf what eternity will become. It is written in the Word. This is the fulfilling of your commission. It is where man's sanctification begins. There was never a question about whether you would drive a dagger deep into the gut of the devil, but a matter of when. The Cross has yielded its mortal victory! The devil is taking his last gasps; the world is only now seeing his final flinches in these horrendous times. It has been a bloody battle. It has been one that the ages cannot describe. The single Hero has won the fight – Jesus the Christ. And, just as timeless as His Holy Sacrifice has been, you are remnants of that victory here. All you will do in this life and in the world reflects the defeat of the devil by Jesus on the Cross. Please imagine what He envisioned on Mount Calvary. He looked into the coming centuries and saw everything you would do for Him. He saw the pageantry of the Church. He was inspired by little children kneeling to offer their bedtime prayers. He heard with gratitude all the rites and litanies that would be written to persuade nonbelievers to convert. Jesus heard the homilies and saw the rituals that would proclaim Him to be the King of the world. And, He drew His strength during the Crucifixion from knowing that humanity would be saved. He was inspired by the sacrifices of suffering, chastity and kindness that this same humanity would offer to their Sacred Lord whom they had not yet even seen. My Special son, this is the miracle; this is the way that redemption is encrypted in the fidelity of men. You and your brother are helping this message to be conveyed. You are breaking the code; you are allowing the world to see the miracles of God in your time, not just in the aftermath of history, but now when good men and women are not only struggling to go on, but do their best to even live. Thank you for everything you mean to Heaven and to God – Three Divine Persons in One Supreme Deity."

Sunday, June 14, 2015
9:01 a.m.

"The depth of His Wounds is infinite, the degree of forgiveness untold."

"My dear little sons, you and the whole of humanity will someday see Jesus tearing reality in half as if ripping a piece of paper. It will make the same sound; it will have like impact on the consciousness of the unwitting world. And, this tearing apart will coincide with the final build-up of the Father's Kingdom here in this place. You will see the previously unknown miracles for which you have prayed – ones that cannot be denied, manifestations that will have no earthly basis, incidents that will have the hand of God written all over them. Deafening will be this tearing apart to those who are unsuspecting of Jesus' ability to do anything He desires, and a welcome riddance of everything that has impeded His disciples from succeeding. My Special son, you have seen the 'Lord of the Rings' trilogy where certain characters are shown in odd camera angles to make them look like hobbits. The exact opposite is true for those who find themselves in the good graces of God. He will prove to the nations that giants have lived in their midst all along. You and your brother are among these giant men. Your hearts, lives and legacies will tower above those who have impugned what I have given to the world for 2,000 years. These camera angles exemplify the ways that your gifts to the world have been magnified, not only because you have believed, but because you have acted on your beliefs. There are many people who look at My works and simply say, '...that's nice.' My Special and Chosen sons, this is not the reaction that makes the most of what the Father has ordained. These people should be rising in acclamation and conceding that there is more to Salvation than nodding off on the sidelines. Your enduring contributions to the Church and to the faith of believers is as immeasurable as absolution itself. In order for this ripping apart to ensue, Jesus has to say 'enough' and begin the process that will reject the world's disorder in favor of the new reconciliation with the Spiritual Truth. This is the reason I have said that the depth of His Wounds is infinite, the degree of forgiveness untold. Within each man of God is a means to generate holiness based on the Gospel precepts. This implies something different to many people, but it is founded on the same elements of life and the Afterlife. Oneness with the Supreme Deity is the purpose of living on Earth. Creating a life of love is the goal of humanity in exile, even as the battles about which I speak seem so unsightly and abusive. God asks the question of the created world – who began this fight? Who fell? Whose decisions wrought the corruption of the human condition? We know the answer to be Adam and Eve, but we also know that the reversing of their error is imbedded in the Wounds of Jesus on the Cross. Jesus' Wounds are the beauty that has supplanted the ugly record of humanity's demise. This is why the Cross has already begun the shredding of the world in favor of the building-up of the Domain of Divine Love. And too, the forgiveness about which I speak is untold, not that it has never been written, but that it is too massive to measure. It is as endless as one might imagine the constellations to be. No calculus can decipher what will eventually come. Only the hands of Jesus Christ, guided by His ethereal thoughts, will reveal how this breaching of reality will unfold. In whose brash precincts will this severing begin? These things will be determined by the prayers of the Roman Catholic Church. My Special son, you know that I speak symbolically about a great many things, but the tearing apart of reality is not one of them. I am speaking here in literal terms that reveal how the presence of Jesus' Second Coming will commence. And, it is not just that this reality will be torn, but that what lies beyond it will be revealed. It is more than an exposition, but a revelation, an infusion of sacred wisdom in the hearts of the faithful that they could never have found on their own.

    God bless you! – you will know what all those books about Jesus' life have said that were too numerous to hold in the created realms! I know what they say, but I cannot explain them because they cannot be conceived by the human mind. There are no languages to describe this revelation. It is as infinite as the Wounds of Jesus and the Mercy that His Sacrifice has wrought. But, this joy of everlasting life will be handed to humanity on a platter, basted by the Blood of the Crucified Lamb. This is what makes your faith more than the miracle for which millions have prayed; it is the conclusion of the faith experience. It is Jesus and Salvation united in a single thought of God, ordaining forgiveness for His creatures and His Creation. The whole momentum of human existence has been traveling this path. The focus of the Catholic Church for 2,000 years has been on clarifying this image. The meaning of life and suffering are encapsulated in what will be heard, seen and felt upon the tearing apart of the reality of the world in which you live. My Special son, this is a good prophecy; the Faith-Church on Earth has imagined what Heaven will be like, and rightly so. Through the Body and Blood of Jesus, a beatific gift has already been bestowed. The Holy Eucharist is your sanctifying plateau overlooking the valleys in which your soul will rest. You will fly and sail, run and laugh, sing and dance, and thank God that the days are finally done. You will move your spirit in Heaven without caring whether your body will be in tow. You will capture everything you ever wanted in this life, every gift and wonder, every new breath and awakening, on a canvass larger than any universe you could possibly envision. Yes, all this is because of the depth of Jesus' Sacred Wounds and the untold forgiveness He has offered. Miracles? Yes, everyone needs them. And, God can ordain them to happen at the same time every day for the rest of mortal time if it should be His Will. No one, infallible or not, can stop Him. This is the message that you know I would tell you back in August 1989. It is the same message that you and I began with your brother in February 1991. I simply wish to know why anyone would have a 'Judas moment' about My apparitions. Why am I so divisive? How can My contributions to the redemption of lost sinners be the subject of so much controversy in light of this Pope's liberalization of the Church, now 2,000 years old? The answer is that the devil can attack anyone who allows it. All seeds of doubt about the purification of humanity are manifested this way, and for all the reasons I have told you about unwarranted fear. It does not take a weak mind to believe in miracles; it takes a weak faith to dismiss them. There is such fear in this world that it has infiltrated the thoughts and decisions of those who should lead. I ask you and your brother not to look down on anyone for defending the Deposit of Faith through which humanity is redeemed. Most are doing the best they can. Remember that they have not for twenty-four years been listening to My wisdom about the way life ought to be.

So, My Special son, you see the reasons that I come to you and your brother as a happy Mother with few exceptions. I offer you the joy of the redemption that you have already found. I come with the knowledge that we can proceed with our plans to propagate My messages in the United States and abroad. Yes, the media representatives received your pamphlets. And yes, they were shocked and awed, but they were put off that anyone should believe that they must do God's bidding, as this is not whom they profess to be. They are the rioters in the streets for every cause except the advancement of the Church. They are water carriers for every secular abomination that anyone could imagine. But, when it comes to the miracles of God and the manifestations of the Blessed Virgin Mary – well, those are things of cults from the delusions of people who have lost their grip on reality. My Special son, we have a surprise for them. Yes, you have let go of their reality just in time to see it be ripped into shreds by Jesus on the Cross. Yours is the new reality, the reality of Christianity, the only reality that matters in the eternity to which you belong. These media outlets might make a mention of what you have done a time or two, and some might even contact you and write a critique, but they would not dare place Me anywhere near a priority in what they do every day. This is not who they are. We have reached them anyway; they cannot claim that they do not know. And, My Special son, whether they choose to act or decline – the entire issue does not matter to Me. Their faithlessness is irrelevant to the final expression on the face of the redeemed Church. If their hearts are closed, if what they claim as their life's work has nothing to do with the Cross, then this is who they have chosen to be. Shame on them, but do not pity them. We have something they all want; it will be their big surprise. My Special one, I will ask Jesus to help those for whom you pray. It is My honor to speak to you again."

Saturday, June 20, 2015
9:38 a.m.

"The sunrise always understands."

"Good day, My wonderful little children! How inspiring for your Mother to remain in your presence, and even more joyful to speak to you in ways that you can comprehend. There are so many dimensions to the word 'beauty' that I find it difficult to narrow its description into one meaning. You are the seed of beauty because you are creations of God, and I am beautiful for the same reason. My children, there can be no beauty without purpose. It is the same as notes being struck into a melody. I wish to impress upon you that inanimate things like the sunrise and sunset have the capacity for empathy; they have emotions that can engage in dialogue with the human spirit. It is here that Creation becomes your counselor. Nature is a mentor and consoler whenever you need to hear the voice of God for the alleviation of pain. Yes, these are more than figures of speech, they are the Lord's means of telling you that He is here with you. Hence, the sunrise always understands because it is at the break of day, it is at the cusp of dawn, that your heart imagines what the coming hours will bring. There is both providence and uncertainty in these things because you are prompted to script the events you enjoy and endure. The whole notion of spiritual conversion is imbedded in your ability to discern what must be confronted and overcome. These seem to be contradictory terms because there is a contrast between the beauty and ugliness of the tormented Earth. I also speak about the sunrise in your hearts, little ones. This is more powerful than any natural sunrise you might see with your eyes. There exists in the human heart a sense of perpetuity that can be found nowhere else in the world. You are the scorers and writers of the future of the nations. By the wisdom in your hearts, you hold in your hands the capacity for eradicating the evils in your lives. You are vessels of the Holy Spirit in which God transfers His sanctity to the earthly realms. I am saying that whatever you deign in His name, it will come true in accordance with His Will. Whatever prospers the Gospel and leads lost humanity to the Cross, the Father will allow. Anything that makes the Crucifixion of Christ Jesus more apparent to the Earth is always sustained. And, My children, it must become not only more apparent, but more appealing as well. How can this be true? What could make the Crucifixion of Jesus Christ the most auspicious sight to behold? This is a property of the Sacred Mysteries to which humanity is called to celebrate. As I have said, pain for the sake of pain is not redemptive, but pain for the sake of righteousness is forever absolving. However, when you are in pain for reasons not intentionally redemptive, you can offer this pain as a prayer for the conversion of lost sinners. God has proved that sacrifice and suffering lead to the reconciliation between Himself and His people. He has made way for the beneficial purpose of self-denial and the uplifting of the poor. My messages have been about this blessing since I uttered My first words from Heaven twenty centuries ago. It is not that self-denial must be founded in the diminishment of one's dignity, but that it be fashioned from the same denial that Jesus offered in the desert. Therefore, when I proclaim that the sunrise always understands, I am saying that the beauty of Nature and the quietude of Jesus' divineness should be absorbed into your lives as an analgesic for pain. This is the sunrise within the human heart. What must be seen, whatever the human spirit endures, wherever the thoughts and prayers of a converted soul travel – all this is a manifestation that the Lord is present here. Omnipresence means that there is never a lacking, never a moment when the Father abdicates His holy office. It is as certain as the rains saturate the soil and the sunshine provides visible light. And, the aspects of your friendship with God must bear the innocence through which the Earth and skies were first formed.

My Special son, what does this innocence mean? It is the absence of sin. One can see both innocence and corruption in the world based on the issues at hand, but in order to be innocent in the way innocence is described in Heaven, one must have no desire to sin. There must be an absence of guilt because there are no scales in the Afterlife – there is no balance between good and bad. There is no darkness to challenge the light. There is no evil to lure someone off the path of righteousness. And, this is what the human heart knows. It is what the sunrise and sunset foretell. One blanket of holiness warms everything inside and outside of Creation. My Special son, I have told you and your brother that this fullness of love, this unstained, unbridled, uncompromised perfection lives and thrives in you. Why? Because you have given your existence and identity to Jesus through His Spirit in your hearts and the actions of your lives. What you find appealing proves your innocence to Him, fully and wholly absent the corruption that can be found elsewhere. This is what makes you rare among the nations. Innocence. It is possible to defer to the sacrifices that God asks you to make and still retain your innocence. My Special one, can you think of anything in the Holy Scriptures that might not be considered innocent that the Lord asked from His creatures to prove their loyalty to Him? *"Abraham and Isaac."* Indeed, Abraham and Isaac. Anything else? *"Yes, Jesus' Crucifixion."* There, you have said it rightly. And, Jesus did absolve all who were involved in His Passion and Holy Sacrifice. It is likewise true that hundreds and thousands of anonymous souls have been asked through the power of the Holy Spirit to make sacrifices that would seem less than innocent in the eyes of the world. The Scriptures are replete with examples of this sacred tender. I have mentioned this topic because I desire you to know that everything having to do with innocence can also have the element of fire. The holy flames of human obedience can annihilate centuries of disobedience from the annals of history and the face of the globe. My Special son, this is what most non-Catholics do not understand. They walk around gleefully boasting that they are led by the Holy Spirit, but they discount and deny the power of self-denial in the sanctification of the world. Christianity in its most essential form is knowing that the Cross preceded the Resurrection. Without the Crucifixion, Easter would never have come. This is why I ask My children to pray the Holy Rosary, to teach the world the sequence of events that wrought the redemption of sinners. These gifts do not come in pretty wrappings because of their poignance to the Church. The Son of God had to die. This is what is taught about the whole economy of Salvation. This does not mean that

God Himself died and had to be raised from the dead, but God the Man died and was raised on the Third Day.

God Himself, in His Only Begotten Son, proved that the Salvation of the human race was worth the death of the Savior who redeemed it. This is a Sacred Mystery as much as the Most Blessed Trinity. The lost innocence of humanity was restored by His Blood. It is not that humanity is innocent; it does not mean that there was never a stain of corruption there, but that the Father has removed these sins from the 'eternals' of His memory. Now, in this land of humankind-redeemed, you can see what this instinct does. You see not only that the sunrise always understands your plight and joys, your vigor and vision, your desires and destinations, but that it communicates with you the honor and respect that the Lord holds for your faith. This innocence is the origin of the Church's power to bind things on Earth as God binds them in Heaven. You are reminded of your innocence any time you attribute to Him the beauty that you see and the love that you feel in your heart. This is the sensation that is elicited when you attend Holy Mass or say a silent prayer. It is your capacity for knowing what is still unspoken by the heavenly domain. It is a way for you to permeate the silence between the exiled Earth and God who created it. If you are trying to add a number with two to yield a number of four, you can rest assured that the second number is two. Hence, if you hold a two in your hands, and the other number is somewhere in God's presence that you cannot see, you know in your heart that it is also two. This much humanity can do. And, My Special son, this is why the work that you and your brother have done is so uniquely connected with the Kingdom of God compared to those who only appear to be there. For example, the two people to whom your brother referred this morning both believe that abortion should be a personal choice. They cannot see the sunrise because they are blinded by their sins. The sunrise knows their motivations, and it does not shed its spirit, warmth or light onto their souls. They do not believe that humanity can be innocent in the way that I have described it here today, and this same disbelief causes them to consider an unborn child to be less than a human being. My Special son, it is a matter of vision and understanding, moral intelligence, spiritual conscience, and the determination to preserve the lives of people they do not even know."

Saturday, June 27, 2015
9:32 a.m.

"Not just a series of events, but a sequence –
The waters pine for parched lands, the winds call out for idle sails."

"My dear little sons, holiness is always more powerful than wealth because there are many things that money cannot buy. The events of this past week, the Supreme Court's decision to legalize homosexual marriage, is an attempt to buy off the truth of God by cloaking this sin in so-called social justice. There is no holiness in what the Justices ruled. There is pandering and corruption; there is repayment for being raised to the high court. There is grotesqueness in their lack of righteous bearing. There is bias against the teachings of the Church. There is disobedience to the Word of God. My Special son, it is not about inequality, it is about those who refuse to listen to the language of Creation. I confirm that equating homosexual relationships with heterosexual marriage is a dictate from the scrolls of Hell. I began today's message with the idea that certain functions might appear in a series, but they must be sensitive to time. There is a sequence to events. This is the way of the unfolding of the world. The same U.S. Supreme Court decided on January 22, 1973 that there is no need for little children. And, they decided this week that there must be no need for the sacred union between a man and a woman. If there is no desire for children, then why safeguard the institution of parenthood? This is an example of the sequence I have mentioned. It is like the sequence you examined in your writings about sensing the shadow of the Lord. There has to be a sequence of events that allows for the relocation that you discuss. My little son, these sequences do not necessarily flow with this same logic in the thoughts of God. This is the reason I have said that it is not so much parched lands that come before the rains, but that the rains seek out the lands. The rains preexist the conditions on the ground all the way back to the beginning of the world. And, so it is with the winds calling out for ships' sails. The destiny of the breezes was forever fashioned over the waters long before any sailors launched their ships there. Humanity is reluctant to see this because they misunderstand the sequence of events preceding their needs and predicaments. It is as though the winds and rains have the capacity of forethought. Just like the sunrise and sunset, even though they are inorganic, they are capable of reason in union with the Scriptures of the Lord. Indeed! They obey Him – the storms calm down at His command. They are in many ways more capable of recognizing right from wrong than the creatures on Earth. They know what God would have them do on His behalf. They are bountiful and priceless; neither good money nor ill-gotten fortune can buy them. They uphold the providence of God in their duties around the globe. They speak in metaphors about life. Their sounds are musical; their gales are divine. They have the gift of prescience that no human being can match. And, when the winds and rains twist the landscapes into knots and shout down manifest fortresses, they speak of the destruction of the world. They are a premonition of what the Father can eventually ordain. And, why will He do these things? Because sinful humanity will not accept the language of Creation and obey their God. My Special son, you recently said that you thought it unfair that the innocent should suffer the destruction of your country because of the edicts of a few. This is where you should remember that the righteous among you are sitting idly by and allowing it to happen. If Christians would invoke their power, the decision by the Supreme Court would never have occurred. God will ratify the destruction of a nation if that nation acts in contradiction to the teachings of His Church. Hence, their decision this week is not only a reflection of the corruption of America, it will usher-in further destruction for the future in sequence. This is the snowball effect that I spoke about before.

  I ask that you not worry about what has happened because the decision will accelerate the breaking of America, tearing out its dead soul and replacing it with the Kingdom of Life where God deems to appear. Do you remember what your brother wrote to the evildoers at the secular university two years ago? He said that, "...someday, perhaps years from now, when the great tragedies come, when you are suffering so much pain, sorrow, destruction and agony, you will look back and be reminded of what you have done here today." This was the Word of God pouring from your brother's lips, and the same can be said to the Supreme Court. My Special son, it is not so much that you are lambs led to the slaughter, but that you are imitating the Passion and Holy Sacrifice of the Savior of the world. And, what happened once His death was done? He prevailed. Jesus Christ was raised from the dead. This is what is happening to the righteous. Those who know in their hearts that what was pronounced by the U.S. Supreme Court this week to be an act of evil will stand in vindication beside Jesus Christ. Your elevation in Him is the consummate outcome; it is the sequence. It is not that you are being defeated; it is not that the Church is losing the war. It is that the alleviation of pain cannot come until pain begins; a seed cannot grow until it is buried inside the furrow. A lantern cannot drive away the darkness unless it is lighted. Health cannot be restored without sickness. Glory cannot be found in the world unless humanity confesses its own sins. These things are elements of the series; they are happening in sequence. My Special son, I am trying to help you and your brother envision these things as I see them.

I realize that I have an advantage in that I am not subject to the influences of time, but you can have the sight about which I speak at this moment. You can have the perspective that everything for which you are fighting will eventually come true. It is as sure as the sun rises in the east in the morning. I ask you to see all lost imaginings this way – everything that bears heavily on your mind and heart is being lifted from you now. The process is slow, often days at a time, and hours and minutes, but the sequence began with Jesus' Sacrifice on the Cross. This does not make you lambs led to the slaughter here in your time; it makes you conquerors in Him. *"Then, why did God raise up Saint Joan of Arc?"* Because Joan of Arc was burned at the stake, and this was her cross likened to Jesus. My Special son, you are using a rational argument to explain sacrificial Christianity. There is a contrast between what I said and the logic that you are applying. It is not that humanity cannot understand the basis for the radical injustices that Christians and the Church face, but knowing that there is a recognition of the fragile core of injustice, that Justice itself will have its final resurrection. *"So, the Church will go as sheep to the slaughter because there is no one to accept the Martyrdom that will save us from it."* My Special son, the Church is already going as sheep to the slaughter in Jesus on the Cross. Where are some of these would-be Martyrs now? If they come forward, if the hundreds of U.S. Catholic Bishops, for example, would camp themselves on the doorstep of the Supreme Court, if they rushed the gates of city halls and abortion clinics everywhere; if they confronted with determination the enemies of the Church, if they excommunicated its radical renegades, then their Martyrdom would offset the particular leading to which you have referred. But, there is a distinctive fear to manifest this righteousness that has been ongoing in the United States for the past sixty-five years.

My Special son, how do you think this makes Me feel? Secular societies do not wish to adhere to anything I say; and at the same time, many in the Church take the stance that My apparitions are not necessary for the Church's mission. Where then, do I go? *"I am here. I will accept you."* My Special son, I know that you are with Me. I have always believed it. I ask you to understand the sequence of events that is unfolding prior to the culmination of the Earth. *"I understand the perspective of those events, that sequence. I'm simply praying for a manifest abruption."* You are doing the right thing, but what does a manifest abruption mean if used every day? There is no impact, no enlightenment, no revitalizing thunder to alter human events. God decides the facility of these blessings based on the glorious drama that you see unfolding. The song has not yet ended. Many strains are still being played. The arpeggios have not come full circle. The wand is still waving in the air. The drums are still beating. The trumpets have not yet reached their pitch. And, as you are seeing, humanity has not yet placed itself in the shadow of the Cross where all that is contradictory to the Will of the Father will be exterminated on sight. Sadly, as you are seeing in the process, there are innocent victims everywhere. It is happening to children in the womb, to hungry paupers beneath railroad trestles, to impressionable souls that have never heard the truth, and yes, to warriors like the great Saint Joan of Arc. The assembling of humanity in that shadow is almost complete. I ask that you and your brother wake every morning knowing that the Lord's Kingdom lives here, not that you see it with your eyes or hear its bells pealing everywhere, but inside your hearts. You have the faith to believe that what I am saying is true. You have the intuition to trust that all this is happening now. *"Mother, I simply wish God to know that here and now, in this life, through my faith, I stand at the ready to engage the fight, endure the sacrifice, give myself to His cause. I leave to Him whether to use me or not, but I wish for Him to forever know that the definition of my life was that I was standing with courage at the ready to serve and to save; that He heard my voice in time say that I stand with my ear inclined to His Word, and to join Him on the Cross in vanquishing evil both inside and outside the Church. St. Joan of Arc, intercede for us!"* I understand your heart more than you believe. I am your Mother, and I am one with you in love."

Saturday, July 4, 2015
9:28 a.m.

"The sophistication of faith –
Love, compassion and a strong right hook."

"I love you, My little children. My Immaculate Heart overflows with tender admiration and affection for your being, as well, the adopted fruits of My Womb. When we speak about the imperatives of your faith, it is clear that you must see yourselves as nurturing the promise of the Afterlife in your hearts. You are poised to get there. Through your own baptism, you are wearing the vestments of your resurrection. You are indeed fit to become Saints in Heaven in the same way that you have sanctified your journey on Earth. I come today with wholesome joy and everlasting peace. I know that you may not yet understand what this means. I speak about the sophistication of faith in your ability to discern right from wrong, a power you have held since you were old enough to believe. And, it would seem that My reference to love and compassion along with having a strong right hook means that there are some people who refuse to accept what Jesus teaches until they are waylaid by their disasters. I speak without apology in this because of all the reasons you know. You are witnessing their stubbornness and obstinance; you have seen their pride, disobedience and recklessness. You have for decades watched humanity take the wrong courses and make the wrong decisions that make life in the earthly realms more taxing. Here now, you will soon see how secular laws will further intrude into the arenas reserved solely for the voice of God. He will hush them, indeed He will crush them, at the behest of those who pray for His help. (*Our Lady spoke to me of certain individuals to whom She was referring. She mentioned their self-promotion and enjoyment of seats of honor in contradiction to the Gospel. She spoke about their missed chances to glorify their Savior through their speech and pen, and how they dismiss Her Immaculate assistance. She was sorrowful for what they will someday see about their lives.*) When I speak about the sophistication of faith, I refer to a full frontal assault against the evils that are so denigrating toward the mission of the Church. When I speak about sophistication of faith, I am celebrating the love and compassion that accompanies Christians, and I am referring to the strong right hook that will knock unconscious the hubris of people like those I have just mentioned. In this sense, they are no different from those whose pride prevents them from believing in God altogether. It is the same self-promotion. My Special son, have I told you how lovely you are? "*Yes, thank you, Mama. I am your son.*" I know you are My son, and you are so lovely! You are pretty and compassionate. You have Jesus' sacred love in your heart, and you extol the righteousness that He shares. I wish you to know that you are beautiful in every way that I have ever described beauty as being. And, when I speak about the strong right hook of the truth, I am telling you that Jesus is defending you against those who refuse to believe what you are saying on His behalf. There are others that Jesus is defending whom you and your brother have yet to meet. There are hundreds-of-thousands of them. It is not that you would not know them, for you do. They possess the same beatific identities in their hearts and souls. You would not recognize their faces if you saw them because you have not yet laid eyes on them. But, you know them on the inside; you have coalesced in like beliefs. You adhere to the same Kingdom. You aspire to the same love. This is what you and your brother have in common with all the Saints throughout the ages, everyone who has invited the Holy Spirit into their hearts, who have deferred to the Will of God and relinquished their own, all the good people who realize that these earthly realms will eventually give way to the New Heaven and New Earth prescribed in the New Covenant. And in this, the world will never outlive eternity to come. It cannot, in fact it should not. It was never meant to be so permanent; it is a preparation place for Saints to enter Paradise, a superstructure where the entire economy of human Salvation must be magnified by those who believe.

There is sophistication in all the suffering; there is poise in the commotion; there is peace amid the screaming turmoil and lines of destruction. Those who come to Jesus have the ability to avoid everything that might push them away, for it is within them that the magnetism of God lives. My Special son, consider what a library would look like if it held the life stories of every person who ever lived. Imagine having 70 billion biographies archived in one place. This is what the Sacred Heart of Jesus looks like. He knows the histories of the souls He came to save. He knows the reasons why so many have denied Him. And, those denials are all based on the same pride that felled Adam and Eve from the Garden. They are a product of the resistance of humanity to live and suffer in Jesus' likeness. Jesus has an infinite Sacred Heart. His disciples with the largest hearts are those that contain the most suffering. This is what is said of all who are persecuted for their faith. They are burdened with suffering because God asks them to carry it for Him in the image of His Son. When someone says that they have a heavy heart, it is because their heart is overflowing with sacrificial love. There are many different seeds of righteousness being planted beneath the earthly soil. And, this is the reason why their stories must be told. We have discussed the disastrous course that the globe is traveling – Christians being martyred by the thousands, little children hacked and burned to death because they do not accept the lures of the devil. The world over, and even in the United States of America, the Word of God is being impugned and rejected. 'Surely these must be the End Times...,' millions of people are shouting. And, My response is that they are correct. The End Times began generations ago, and yet it would seem that they are only now beginning. The reconciliation between these perceptions is that Jesus told the world in His final earthly days that everyone should live as though the end of time will be tomorrow. My Special son, you once said that the Lord must enjoy a good fight. God must like the heroic drama of humanity, fighting for the repentance that must come from all. Yes, you are a visionary in this struggle. God does not enjoy the suffering of His people, but He takes heart in knowing that Jesus does not suffer alone. Jesus is not only the Savior of the world, He is the teacher of the faith that took Him to His death. Casual Christians can speak all they desire about Jesus suffering so that His disciples would not have to suffer, but it is more true to declare that Jesus suffered in order that those who believe in Him would have a model for their own martyrdom. When children say that they want Jesus to teach them how to pray, they are asking Him to teach them how to suffer. The latter is the prayer of deliverance for the many who cannot find themselves taking to heart what God wants them to believe.

My little sons, you must realize that you can see the top of a rainbow. Yes, I know that this is a rare occasion. You often can only see one end or the other arching to the ground, and sometimes both, but you rarely see its apex reaching high in the sky. This is what God wants you to do. He asks that you believe that somewhere up there, beyond the vaults where those 70 billion biographies are stored, is a connection between the past and the present that includes His arms wrapped around the Church. He desires that humility and simplicity supplant the hubris that is so prevailing in your time. And, the Lord's hands providentially precede the past, present, future and everything else that will be consumed by the truth of His eternity. Everything that extols the Glory of God is preserved for this extemporaneous domain. This is correct. All the Saints retain the artwork of their life stories and the capacity for writing new ones too. There are no limits in Heaven. There are more instruments than humanity on the Earth could possibly play. There are wing-shaped winds and strings, and percussions aplenty. They sound harmonies like waterfalls that have not been heard in the annals of men. There are flowers and sweets, precious metals and silk-laced summits, birds and fishes that glow and leap, animals with pelts of gold, and oh! – the suns! How many suns can a soul imagine across the span of a billion eternities? How many brooks? How many mountain ranges of streaming joy and love-sustaining peace? Those who have entered Heaven do not have to reach for anything. Salvation means that what one desires comes to them, that everything delightful is in their grasp before their thoughts ever come to mind. And, did I mention the suns? Oh! – the suns! This is what you will come to realize beyond your final years in exile. It is not that you are now unaware, but staying the course and fighting the good fight will yield a fresh acknowledgment that the promises of God are true. My Special son, you have permission to tell My children about this message. Tell them about the insignificance of human endeavors, that the entire record of world history could be fitted on the point of a pin. Warn them about the indecency of their lies, that they cannot hold a candle to the shining truth of the Son of Man. Do this because you are the holder of My confidence, and you and your brother have esteemed yourselves by living with Me in a way that most men could have only dreamed. I wish to close today by reminding you that you are beautiful. Did I already say that? *"Yes. But, thank you, again."* And, I ask that you share with your brother and the whole of humanity that I love you, that I love all My children with a sacred devotion that cannot be laid out in words. This is My message for today. I suppose that it is about independence on this July 4, 2015, but it is more about the freedom to bask in the Kingdom of Divine Love. We are opening men's eyes to the future, those who are only now asking what the past has meant. Please know that your prayers and labors are never in vain."

Saturday, July 11, 2015
9:36 a.m.

"Hope comes in crates that are unpacked by God, not in pursuing or demanding anonymity or priceless objects. It is not imbedded in spontaneous currencies of triumph, urgency or abundance; and perhaps not even spawned from judgement, character or reason. Hope comes from grace alone. Yes, Our Divine Lord bestows this hope upon His spiritual faithful; the humble, doctrinal and contrite – to all repentant sinners, knowers, heart-feelers and melody makers who render in return an echoing of His sacred love and the sweetness of our own confession. This is the rite of the created world. It is the clearest summation of God's hope too!"

- William L. Roth

"Today, My precious little sons, I come speaking about the wholesome lives that you are leading in Jesus, about the manifest sacrifices that you are offering through your prayers and actions that propagate the Holy Gospel around the globe. My Special one, your words to begin today's message are among the most beautiful I have ever heard. They originate from the comforting of your soul inside Jesus' Most Sacred Heart, and they resonate with the Angels in whose company you are welcomed. You and your brother are giving humanity on Earth the gift of awareness – it may not appear this way right now, but I promise that it is happening. Good men tend to think of it in the presence of Jesus worldwide. Those who believe in Him know that He is in command and control of His earthly domain; there has never been any question about it. However, those without faith demand proof; they wonder how God could allow all the fighting, perversion and destruction that hinder humanity's pursuit of righteousness. Yes, unbelievers do this while disregarding the fact that it is they themselves who are causing the perversion and destruction. Here again is another stark irony. It is as though someone poisons a well and complains that there is no drinking water. I have told you that the rectification of all this is the inheritance by humanity of the holy vision of God. And not only that, it is in men's ability to recognize this vision once it is seen. What good does it do to highlight the beauty of a sunset unless one knows the rarity of each one? If every sunset looked the same, do you suppose humanity would stop focusing on them?

This is likely and undoubtedly the case. My Special son, such things as fingerprints and DNA are indicative of the individual identity of a world of men who are all, themselves, only men. They are unified as one people under God, but you see that He has created them with contrasts to make them unique. This is the way of your thoughts and writings; they are as rare as the sunsets and profoundly more awe-striking. There is never any question that the Holy Spirit inspires this beauty in you, and there will never be a doubt that you are aligned with the Kingdom that clarifies your role in the conversion of the lost. I have said that there are some things that words cannot describe. It is difficult to put into symbols of language what love actually means. It is the same as the hope that you spoke about at the beginning of our message today. Attempting to use words to describe these gifts can be as nonsensical as asking how much life weighs. How far can hope be thrown? What device would someone use to measure an ounce of light? Even still, it is in this poetic tenor that Jesus calls His disciples to approach and understand Him. This has been the essence of My calling for 2,000 years – not that humanity should refrain from addressing the practical matters of mortal life, but that these issues should be placed before the backdrop of the glorious mysteries. Here, joy and fear can be captured in quantities, such as responding to God's voice in prayer. You may not hear Him audibly, but He always hears your pleading. This is the facility of faith to which all believers are called.

    Of course God speaks to the universe in understandable ways. He does so by watching the motivations and actions of His flock. If He says nothing on any given day, then He is waiting for the world to proceed. If He ordains an earthly event that divides time, then humanity must know that they have reached Him. It is a senseless calculation to ponder when, where or how the Lord might speak with His exiled creatures when Wisdom has been dispensed from His tongue heretofore. This is what it means to celebrate your statement, '...Hope comes in crates that are unpacked by God.' He feeds your hopes and answers your prayers because He loves you, and hope is realized in the acceptance of humanity that you are participating in the purification of the world. Time and time again when I have said this to My messengers through the ages, they hold that these kinds of responses are of little comfort amid the scourges and tragedies that accompany the years and decades of life. I always direct their attention to one point; and I will ask you, My Special son, about it here. Is there a place in Sacred Scriptures or in Church tradition attesting that humanity has apologized to God for killing His Son? *"Not that I know."* This is the design of the Father because He wants the ages to remember that it was His gift from Heaven. The Crucifixion of Jesus Christ is as awesome to behold as the brandishing of a sword when someone's life is at stake. How many hidden weapons has Jesus placed in your backpack, in the arsenal of all who have believed in Him? How many arrows in someone's quiver? How many censures and rebuttals to those who take His name in vain? It is all countless, My little son; it is to the blessing of the Church and its Doctors. It is about magnifying the love by which you live. Knowing God and interacting with Heaven is like focusing a camera lens; there are some good days and bad days, depending upon what a Christian suffers during the hours and minutes of each one. If God seems far away, He can be pulled back into focus by reinvigorating the spirit, realigning one's faith with the Holy Cross imbedded in the heart. This is how everyone living in faith knows to stand tall in Jesus' Sacrifice, especially those who suffer at the hands of others. The Father chooses to dwell on what men do well, what uplifts His Kingdom and downplays things that distract men from sharing compassion and seeking peace. It is Jesus' Divine Mercy that has taken to Heaven your one-time enemy who recently passed away. There is little more to which his redemption can be assigned; it is by the prayers of people like yourself and your brother who know that there is some good in everyone. At the verge of non-understanding; when men seem to be at their most desperate, and when the darkest dark has befallen the consciences of those who would believe, this is where the Crucifixion scatters all doubt. It is the point where the human soul says that he or she has erred, and asks for pardon, and Jesus says again with the offerance of forgiveness, '...It is finished...' My Special son, I have given this discourse today in light of your opening reflection about hope. It is as enduring as the human heart will allow it to be. Yes, these crates of hope are unpacked by God, but it is the repentance of wicked sinners that urges Him to act. He cannot be prompted by regaling man's accomplishments. He cannot be bribed by citing every dynamic thing; it has to be a heartfelt confession before the Sacrifice of His Son and the soul's immersion in His Blood on the Cross.

This is the most intelligent decision that anyone, intellectual or otherwise, will ever make. The rising and falling of the hours, the passing of days, the light and darkness and everything in between – all this is supplemental to the human heart's conversion to the Sovereign Kingdom of Holy Love. It is something that you and your brother did before you wept your first tears. It is also something that many people who have written thousands of books, even about Christianity, have never offered. I have asked you not to pity those who choose condemnation for themselves, but there is still time to reach the millions who are teetering on the brink. These are the lost sinners who have the farthest to travel. Their future resides in their willingness to be persuaded by the Lord's response to our prayers. He reminds them every day that we are praying for them. In His own unique and providing way, He makes sure that their conscience is touched by what we offer on their behalf. If this were not true, there would be no need for the intercession of the Saints. I am elated that this supernatural communication has proven to be the deliverance of so many sinners to the foot of the Cross. It has brought to light their lacking, not necessarily to others who may wish to know, but to themselves in their own ignorance of their standing inside or outside the Church. My Special son, these are the gifts to human life that you and your brother have provided. All the Saints have given the same. All the glory and providence about which I have spoken here today, the invitation by the Holy Spirit for the lost to be found, the acceptance of repentant sinners into Heaven, and all the rest – is contingent upon the petitions and sacrifices that the Church is offering. It is not wrong to feel a sense of triumphalism about this grace; it is not a matter of misguided thought or resting on one's laurels somewhere. It is about spiritual deduction as clear as solving a math problem. It is about measuring light rays in such a way that can be calculated in beatific terms. It is about someone whom you would never have expected to accept Jesus' Sacrifice doing so upon seeing Him when they die. My Special son, these are the blissful portraits that I offer when I speak to you and your brother; you have colored them well. You have become the impression in God's Patriarchal Heart of the kind of hope that He invokes, just like you said. The Father knows what must be done, and He will provide. He will apprise and motivate the world in your day and time. He will propagate His own good works. *"Miracles are the answer."* I have said that this is true. We must pray that this shall be the Lord's response; it is happening through us as we speak."

Saturday, July 18, 2015
12:26 p.m.

"Well, we look and listen for the crispness of the changing times – how swiftly those ages roll! And, our thoughts are filled with gladness; even when things seem contrary to the veritable purpose of life, humanity keeps walking along. We take comfort in the clopping of leather shoes on a hardwood floor, the faint echo of ladies high heels in a distant corridor, and even the rapping of our neighbor's knuckles against our front porch screen door. There is newness and commonness there, always the structure and safety of life's paternal framework. But, there exists too the familiar fragrance of pain, torment and suffering. And, this is where our faith comes into its fullest form. We tackle the world in the way Jesus wants us to win, marching onward and embracing with confidence the trust, chemistry and kinship of our spectral conquest of the secular void."

- William L. Roth

"My Special son, now these are some words to encapsulate the ages; voices and sentiments that draw all men to the virginal nectar of the Roman Catholic Church. Here, you see why it is such an honor for Me to come speaking to you; in all that you do, wherever you go, whomever you meet, you are rightly seen as a true messenger for the Lord. This is the stature and esteem that you and your brother have won. Why? Because you are My children. You have handed all the years of your lives to the labor of human conversion. You have laid on the Earth's floor the essential meaning that all must have and hold to understand My role in the redemption of the lost. My little children, we speak of the spectral conquest of the secular void because you introduced it to Me. You have proved that your hearts, in communion with the Holy Spirit, are destined to push back the forces of evil that are attempting to corrupt the lives of your brothers, sisters and friends. I speak about sacred energy because this is the invigoration from which Jesus draws His own desire to respond to your prayers. My Special son, some people believe that Jesus is not making Himself sufficiently apparent in the everyday world. They claim that Jesus is not wielding His power enough to snuff out His enemies where they stand, but I respectfully disagree. There are so many graces being bestowed on the Earth during these days that it would stifle the knowers' imaginations. They cannot see them because they belong to the unseen realms of human life about which we have spoken. They must instead refer to the so-called sub-levels of life in the fullness of God's eternity. Moreover, they must also invoke His thoughts about everything I have said about the beauty of the human heart. Jesus works in the created realms by enriching the Christian conscience; through the spirits, lives and good works of those who believe in Him. Hear what I would like to say now. God created a world that would allow problems to arise. He also has accorded enough resources in your lives to solve them, to eradicate sin, to make smooth the rough places by emulating the holiness of His Son. It is humanity that is not doing its part to bring peace, harmony and purity to the nations. Jesus has provided the template for the sanctification of the Earth in the Cross. The entire teachings of the New Covenant are based on this. Hence, the question, '...where is God' is answered by the response, '...God lives in the hearts of men.' I urge these sinners to meditate upon all the issues that they believe to be confronting humanity, and then ponder which of them could be resolved by the righteousness of men's intentions. Evils can be eradicated if everything good conquers them. What I am saying today, My Special son, is that you are correct when you claim that the conquest of the world's darkness must be accomplished on a spiritual level. After all, what good does it bring; what purpose is served if all wicked men are slain on the battlefields of the world? Is not the mission of the Church, indeed the essence of the Cross, to convert them to the Lord instead? In this, Jesus provides signs and venues every day.

The handhold for grasping the solution to life's problems is given through the artwork of prayer. It is not Christ Jesus who has denied the solutions to evils like abortion, it is wicked men and women who reject His Word. I have told you and your brother on numerous occasions that there will be justice for all things wrought from error. There will be light cutting through the darkness to expose the wretches and evildoers. However, it is obvious that Creation already knows most evildoers. Nothing seems to be done about it because of the 'relative' view of human life by people who are elevated to power by the enemies of the Church. Yes, this includes the radical secularists in the United States who are more interested in freedom 'from' religion than freedom to practice religion. It is as though leftist elements here and around the globe want to be provided a new and untouched canvass on which to paint their own rendition of the meaning of life. They are lost in sin; they are exploiting the innocents who depend on them for sustenance; they are making victims of those who turn to them for knowledge, and they are light years away from the truth to which all men must be led for the clemency in God that they will ultimately require. Here again, My Special son, I refer to your words with which you opened today's message. This is not the first time you have alluded to the means by which Jesus wishes humanity to win; and this is a good thing. Winning means more than fatally crushing one's enemies, but in such a way that the survivors of these enemies know why. There must be such a vast conquest of the secular void that no one would dare to again tread the paths that brought the annihilation of their forebears. This annihilation, the same reckoning that you mentioned in *To Crispen Courage*, is precisely about claiming victory for Jesus on the spectral level. I defy anyone alive to cite an example of a passage from the Old or New Testament that says any of this would be easy. I do not even know what 'easy' means. Is it a reference to skipping the difficult aspects of human life? If so, this stands in contradiction to the Passion of Jesus Christ. Does 'easy' imply that the spectral conquest of the secular void will occur without opposition? Not in this lifetime. None of this is easy because the Father requires humanity to make the difficult choices of self-denial, repentance and a steadfast loyalty to the Cross. This is not something that Jesus expects humanity to suffer lightly. He asks for the energy of faith to be set free, to share with the poor and broken everything required to satisfy their needs. This is the way of the Cross and the mission of the Church. Righteous men must not stand idly by and watch evildoers devour the world. The solution to these problems; the power to exterminate the onslaught of evil around the globe is vested in Christians who lay down their lives for the Messianic message.

My Special son, you recently recited a quotation from Dr. Martin Luther King Jr. about the silence of the good people. This is essentially the point I am making. You and your brother exhibit your genius given to you by My Son! You also spoke about lifting your voices against the institutions of government and its judicial systems to demand the return of Americans to righteousness. This is the movement that we have been trying to effect. This is what the Morning Star Over America is all about. And, I promise that we shall succeed. There is an ongoing battle about this as we speak. It is one of priorities in the eyes of the secular void, but it is about mandating compliance with the Commandments of God in the eyes of Heaven looking down. I wish that you not worry whether you will see the end of this conquest in your lives here on Earth, but it is My plan that you will see it before you come to Heaven. As I just said, this is My plan, but so was the 1917 miracle of the sun over Fatima. God provided the venue and the miracle – Jesus did what He promised to do, but it was humanity who stumbled in response. So-called experts said that it must surely have been a mistake by some 70,000 people who claimed to see the blessing. Others said it was the work of the devil because God never permeates the veil between Heaven and Earth through such things as celestial realignments. And, it was completely illogical to those who study the stars. My Special son, you will someday see that something as mammoth as the miracle of the sun in Fatima will finally break through humanity's indifference and prove that the Morning Star Over America is Me. I am not saying that it will happen tomorrow or next week, perhaps not even a year from now or before you come to Heaven. It does not matter when it arrives. What matters is that it will come, just as the permanent sign in Medjugorje will come. Who is to say that this sign will not turn the world's attention to the same nation whose Patron Saint is Mary, the Mother of God? Who stands to declare that this permanent sign will not cause humanity to focus on the nation that saw fit in July 1969 to travel to the pedestal in full bloom beneath My feet? These are the miracles that Jesus designs according to His good intentions and the prayers of those who believe in Him. My Special son, this entire phenomenon is imbedded in the conversation about hope that we recently conducted; it results from the sacred energy that vindicates the beauty, power and innocence to which all humanity will ultimately be drawn – even those who will deny themselves the forgiveness from God for which their souls still yearn, hunger and thirst.

This is the reason men like you and your brother remain the Children of Mary. You walk upright in your leather shoes and prove to the world that you are masters of the art of living. You speak in parables of glory about the fate and destiny of the created realms, and still remain on the playground of holiness in your hearts. You see with your eyes everything the secular void has to offer, but always know inside you that, as the Children of Mary, you will never betray the Gospel; you will walk with the Saints into Heaven. There is nothing better in human life than to know the destiny you have chosen. You are aware of the truth, chemistry and kinship of this spectral conquest because the Father's Spirit has forged the strength of your own virtue within your souls. I could not be happier because I have seen your victories and triumphs from the eternal side of time. There will be much suffering to come; make no mistake about that. You will see further desecration of everything holy; you will witness the destruction of the institutions that have manifested such civility during the annals of linear time. You will never see the destruction of the Church, but the effects of the Church will wane in places where the Gospel was once read aloud. It is to the alleviation of these things that you have always lived; you have sustained your portion of the Cross for which you will be rightly rewarded. I am saying today that you should live in peace every hour; you should say your prayers knowing that you have already won. It is like giving a medicinal injection in the flesh of humanity – it will hurt in the beginning, but the inoculation will be worth the pain. I promise that this is the way of life; it is the inspiration that keeps Me coming back to you, along with the profoundness of My love that is too intense to relay in words. My Special son, it is clear that you and your brother are sweet, endearing and pretty. You are everything that I ever wanted My children to be."

Saturday, July 25, 2015
9:37 a.m.

"Synthesis and coalescence – in the end, all humanity owns is the Gospel message with all its august and incendiary facets, brimming with discernment, burgeoning with vindication, all too brief but divinely perpetual; dominating, liberating and irrevocably full of life."

- William L. Roth

"My Special one, you write some of the most profound and simple passages about Jesus' Book of Life, and you remain in His admiration for your wisdom.

You and your brother will always be My little children. You have within you the message of eternal redemption; you live and breathe this message to others by your voices and actions. When one thinks about aligning the purpose of life with life's actions, he knows the unity that Jesus preaches to the masses. Yes, it is a combining of the hearts and minds of different people in far-flung places. It is the pooling of values and cultural resources to propagate the Gospel Word. This is the synthesis about which you speak. Verily, this cannot be divided from the coalescence in unity and excellence that connects humanity to the miracle of the Cross. I wish to again make clear that human suffering is not the purpose of life. People suffer because there is rampant sin in the world. But, with this suffering comes the resilience of men to be united in spirit with the Father in Heaven. You describe the Holy Gospel accurately when you say that it is brief but perpetual. It is an eternal message with infinite consequences. After all, one can hold the Bible in their hands, but there is no way to contain the eternity that the Scriptures make knowable. And yes, there is plenteous vindication because all who believe in Jesus have found their new beginnings in Him. My Special and Chosen sons, it is what happens in between that we are dealing with today. This is what some have called the 'now platform' upon which so many life issues are resolved. You work in the 'now' arena to eradicate ills, foster forgiveness and dismantle grudges. You pursue the future from the 'now' to avoid repeating the same errors and build relationships that will last long after the world is done. Let us look at the words you have spoken – incendiary, dominating and liberating. There seems to be a contradiction in this that can only be explained by the Sacred Mysteries of the Church. This is rightly so. You have captured what I have been saying for 2,000 years. You are underscoring the challenges that come with men's faith. It is clear that you have made manifest this phenomenon in your letter to the newspaper editor about so-called Planned Parenthood and their marketing of dismembered unborn children for profit. The women at the newspaper where your brother sent the letter are in favor of aborting unborn children. And, they are still deliberating whether to publish your letter because, as you say, of whom your brother is. My little son, these people are saturated with socially-imbedded evil. Their minds are corrupt; they have no conscience, and their spirits are dead. You hold as much claim on their future as the unborn children whose lives are being stolen. They will suffer the consequences that are due against them; their punishment is not My concern. Please let it be made clear if the opportunity arises that the Mother of God does not suffer well those who reject the teachings of the Church. My Special son, many in the Church itself have an errant vision of who I am. Most of these sinners believe that I am supposed to be some meek woman sitting in a corner somewhere, remanded to silence because I made few attestations in the New Covenant Gospel, and peeking from beneath a veil like a choir girl. Well, you have heard what I have said to you and your brother, and you know what I have decreed to other messengers throughout the ages.

It is not My fault that they deny that I have divine authority given to Me by My Son in Heaven. Yes, I am a humble intercessor, and powerful to the extent that the Father wills, but I am also a disciplinarian when it comes to My adopted children's holiness. Even during these times, I never cease loving them. I am forever filled with grace, teaching what grace means to the Earth, providing and delivering to humanity the wisdom of the Holy Spirit the best I know how. I have spoken to you more in 2015 about power, beauty and sacred energy than during all the previous times. This is because I would like for My children to learn what you and I and your brother have laid before them in your books – humanity is more beautiful and empowered when people recognize their own responsibilities to embrace the Gospel and live the way Jesus has commanded. And to do this, it requires the sacred fervor that comes through prayer. This is the supernatural exchange of thought and action that flows from humanity to God and back again. Yes indeed, the Father is capable of emotion. He has proved this through the lessons and decrees of His Son. It is not counterproductive emotion, there is no question about that. But, it is an emotion deeply imbedded in the maturity of Jesus' Most Sacred Heart. He knows what it means to win and lose. The Son of Man is aware of the obstacles that must be overcome to conquer the evils in this world. This is why Christ Jesus is so close to you. It is the reason the Holy Spirit enlivens and strengthens your faith and vision to see beyond the perils trying to impede the mission of the Church. This is the humanness of the Man who wants to be included in every decision that humanity will ever make. My Special son, Jesus looks at the world as though He were inspecting a fine piece of furniture. He examines the lines and elements of the created realms that are themselves shaped by the people who believe in Him. You can tell a tree by its fruits. This is what humanity can do in an early attempt to judge itself. Is the world a better place because of man's actions? Is there enough evidence to prove that goodness is prevailing over malevolence? If there is not, and it appears to be obvious that there is not, then one must look at the makers of the furniture to determine why that furniture is unfit. If it is built with righteousness, it will sustain the weight of the world. This is the process that humanity is in. Jesus has found deep flaws in humanity's work alongside the grand goodness that is there. These flaws must be addressed because of the metaphor about one bad apple. Here too, good men must detect the motion to which many sinners have become blindly acclimated. There is another analogy to this as well. When you see headlines crawling along the bottom of your television screen, they seem to move too quickly until you try to read them. And, when you walk on your treadmill, there is a trademark on the conveyer belt that passes like a blur until you focus on what it says. It is not until one contemplates these things that they take on new meaning.

I first told you about this motion in the spring of 1991 by way of a prolific message given to you in Lincoln Park while you and your brother were seated at a picnic table there. I talked about motion being a matter of the mind. And, the ability to reduce this motion, such as focusing on a headline crawler or the logo on your treadmill, is a function of the heart. This is where the origin of '...be still my beating heart...' first arose. One's heart, as I have said for centuries, is the center of wisdom and the origin of one's thought having to do with the cultivation of the world. Secularism cannot live inside the human heart because it needs the commotion of the physical realms to survive. It is a simple concept based on the fact that all things heartfelt can overpower casual thinking. My Special son, you and your brother are fortunate not only because you have the Holy Spirit in you, not only because the Mother of the Lord has spoken to you for almost a quarter-century, but because of the gifts you have deigned for yourselves. You have come to certain conclusions about the breadth, length and purpose of human life based on your decision to follow Jesus. You have accorded God the same dignity that you have claimed because He is honored to accept your faith. I am asked to tell you directly from the lips of the Father that He knows that you and your brother, '...stand at the ready.' You made this statement a few weeks ago, and Our Lord wants you to remember that He heard what you said. Indeed, He knew it before you made the claim. This comes from the fire in your heart and the sacred energy that you have generated out of love for Him. It is the beauty and power that you have owned since you were placed in your mother's womb. It is the communion between Heaven and Earth for which God has pined since Adam and Eve first fell – yes, yielded to Him at the Crucifixion of His Only Begotten Son and the Resurrection that manifested Creation's first sky-borne miracle. And in this gift, there may be some sorrow and unrepentance in the world; there may be rampant destruction and outright evil, but none of these things can harm the sacred pact that you hold with Jesus in My Arms. Nothing can breach your unity with the Holy Spirit and Heaven. There is no such thing as a holocaust so catastrophic that it could sever your oneness with Jesus on the Cross. My Special son, this is why your words to begin our message today are so apostolic. There is no doubt that there are consequences to what the New Covenant proclaims, but these are for humanity's good. The sacred brand of this work; the entire Gospel message is meant to reach humanity from all walks of life, from every precinct and quarter, from all minds and cognitive cantilevers, and from any other instinct that a man could possibly exercise. It is all there; it is finished, as Jesus said. And from what we are seeing during these days, this finishing is the deafening wail of the devil dying more every day. You have won in Jesus; you are warriors and conquerors in Him. This is how I see the created world. Be joyful that the Lord is with you. My little sons, the beauty and holiness of the righteous people on the Earth will prevail over the wickedness of these times."

Saturday, August 1, 2015
9:27 a.m.

"If something challenges secular norms and sends humanity reeling to find the meaning of life, then God's hand is in it. If it fosters peace, resolves the dire, syphons morbidity from the bloodstream of the wicked, and makes atheists question their own motivations, then man's heart is in it. It should remain this way from the crests of the seas to the cleavage of the mountains, into the depths of this century's tears. Sometimes we lapse or fall backward, or we tell Jesus we cannot hear Him; we are unable to reach Him because our way is blocked, or we are waiting on a train or something and cannot get there. When God says there are overpasses, we say no, we are waiting as passengers – anything to evade the point, backtalk or apply doublespeak so we can excuse ourselves or obfuscate, whatever exempts us from what He wants. It is clear that we are making the whole thing much too complicated. The Father does not really care that much what kind of syrup we like on our pancakes in the morning. He rarely inspects our lives on any sort of molecular level at all. He is simply trying to touch the center of our spiritual hearts. It does not hurt like being mauled by a wildcat. It does not involve ripping off our flesh or being branded by fire. It is an utterly benign relinquishing of our selfishness in favor of His own vision of the future."

- William L. Roth

"My Special son, the truth well spoken will be one of the legacies of your life. This is part of your contribution to humanity and to the world. You do this because you pray the Holy Rosary every day. This is how you have tapped into the genius of God and drawn His Wisdom into the material realms. I must make clear – all of your thirteen books that you have written so far were founded on the sacrifices that you and your brother have made, in particular the blessing of May 28, 1995. Worthily, you have erected a mansion of triumph atop that foundation. Some people wonder why there is not enough sweetness in this earthly domain. The sweetness for which men yearn comes from God. It is His gift to those who accept it. The Father wants that all people will come to believe in Jesus by what we are doing here today, what we have accomplished heretofore, and everything we will do in the future. The Lord truly sees it this way. He is waiting for all the nations' peoples to accept the Cross as their Salvation; and once in that vessel, He will sweeten the mix with thundering redemption. It is somewhat akin to putting a teaspoon of sugar into a glass, rather than in an entire ocean. All who shall be saved will eventually find themselves in this cup; they will have their fill of light and life. But, they must first be fished from the seas; they must be placed inside the repository of life. This is what our prayers are doing, My little sons. Thus, I have come today to pray with you. I ask that you recognize your own stature as statesmen in this cause, but I also ask that you never relinquish your vision of your inner-child. You are upheld here in this world and in the Afterlife by your standing as My children. There will be naysayers who will try to make you bitter. They will attempt to force you to hate them, but you are not capable of hatred. None of My children know enough about hatred to hate. And here too, you will meet people who will try to lure you away from Me because of promises of riches and fame. We already know that this will likewise fail. Hence, we will hold one another through everything you might endure. And, My little ones, as I have told you about piety and countenance, I will remind you that these are not an end in themselves, but a means to the end that we have been seeking all along – the redemption of lost sinners. Purpose. Purpose implies intuition and direction; it speaks to achieving an outcome. This is what prayer and holiness are for. They always stand side-by-side with you because they are dependent on what you hope for. The heart can be destroyed if it does not serve virtuous ends. Power corrupts if it is not embedded in spiritual benevolence. This is the reason Jesus came in purpose, and on purpose, to seek humanity's participation in the purification of souls. My Special son, I will attempt another metaphor here today. Imagine the concept of humanity being a symphony orchestra, playing-out the strains of life. This is what each Christian does; everyone has an instrument in their hands. Indeed, every individual 'is' an instrument toward this end, just as Saint Francis told. And, each person plays his own song. There are as many different melodies as there are individuals to sound them. The beats and cadences are as diverse as the regions of the Earth. However, when God waves the final wand ending the echoes of the world, all these instruments will fall silent at once. No matter how far, near or astray people may go, there will be no more intonations once the Father cuts the air with His final word. This does not mean that the people who have already died are not part of the song. It simply means that they are at rest during the remaining refrains of the Earth. The entire matter is perfectly clear. There are awkward and errant sounds circling the continents every day. Some sinners would have the orchestra disband altogether. But, as long as God stands before these wayward souls who are assembled on the stage of human life, they cannot escape His direction. There will never be a moment when Jesus will not be here; all the world is subject to His voice.

I wish My children to know that they are not only players; they are not just instruments and sounders, they are composers too. You and your brother have scored and underscored My wishes for humanity for decades and more. You comprehend what it means to change the Earth for the better, to heal and remake it. There is no question that you are Jesus' hailers and modern-day disciples; you are the extended hands of the First Apostles in your day. They reach and touch you, and you sense their embrace. They identify with your suffering, and you can feel their compassion. This is part of the reciprocation that prevails in the Church and throughout the world, handed down through the ages by the advocacy of the Holy Spirit. It is the unity that begins in timelessly believing in Jesus on the Cross and the miracle of the Resurrection. My Special son, the most important gift that the Church will ever espouse and preach is this – the Easter Triduum. The whole idea of believing in God is founded in one's resurrection. And, this is what will come not only for the world and for the exiled Faith-Church, but more specifically the country in which you live. There will be a returning to the ages-long dignity that America deserves, and it will be poignant in arriving. The scourge of abortion will be obliterated by the prayers of the faithful. Everything contentious that darkens the hopes of the righteous will be stopped and turned away. Remember that I am the Patroness Saint of the Americas! I am reminding everyone whose hopes are being dashed that the Lord can resurrect anyone and anything through His own designs. I have not come this far to see a good nation die. I am not suggesting that it will not suffer some degree of annihilation. It has never been My intention to declare that the United States is all that blessed. I am simply saying that something with as much benevolent potential as your country deserves a second chance. It is all about starting over with the Lord, you know. So, the appealing sense of goodness that Jesus represents provides promise for all who are praying. The 'purpose' is about the triumph of goodness over evil; this is the point I am making. While you imagine what the world would look like if only its people would come to Me, this too will likely be the result of the expiration of the ages. Truly, all men eventually will. It is all about Jesus; there is no other king, there is no other redeemer. I have said that this is the reason for you and your brother, and all who have accepted My Son, to celebrate every day of your lives in the knowledge that you have won. This is what you spoke about at the beginning of our message today.

When you speak about the depths of the centuries' tears, you are likely referring to ocean-size basins of sorrow. You are relating to humanity your sense of the hugeness of the battles to come. My Special one, imagine a scenario where there were no battles against evil. What would it be like if the Spirit of God never shouted the cries of victory? You are blessed; your entire nation and the world are blessed that He has deigned to be your guidance and inspiration. It is God's way of touching His Creation, of petting and caressing the lives of those He has given to His Son to forgive. If there is a moment's peace in this thought; if anyone on Earth gains a new purpose in life, then it has all been worthwhile. Imagine what it must be like to be the Head of the Church. What must Jesus be thinking when He sees the unchurched traveling the globe speaking about everything but Him? It is all about the distractions of the secular void about which I have repeatedly spoken. They are either dead already or dying by the hour. It is a vacuum with restrictions, with dimensions and a mortality that will soon befall them, every one. You could not have guessed in February 1991 when My intercession to you began that the 21st century would have ushered forth such grotesque sins and lifestyles. It could have been worse! It could have meant that there would be no Catholic Church in the United States at all. Your prayers and those of all the faithful have ensured that Jesus is still welcome here. Therefore, I ask again that you and your brother take heart in the promises that Jesus has made. Never mind the radical secularists who make idle threats on the television every day. Jesus will not just subdue them, He will conquer and destroy them with outright overwhelm. And, I do not wish to overstate My feelings about the matter, but I do not pity those who will not change. They are the enemies of everything I believe, of all that God has tried to do through His Only Begotten Son, of the very gifts that He has dispensed to persuade the wicked to convert. It is not difficult to recognize who these people are. Now, My Special son, do you have any issues to discuss today? *"I was going to ask if any of the actual furniture that Jesus and Saint Joseph made is still in the physical world, and where it is."* Yes, it is found all around the globe in hidden places, but few people know its origin. There are pieces of furniture handmade by Jesus and His stepfather in the vicinity where Jesus was raised; some is in Jerusalem; other pieces have made their way by the intercession of the Holy Spirit to remote alcoves at the Vatican. It is a good question because you have highlighted the historic nature of these relics. God has not placed a great deal of emphasis on them because He does not wish these artifacts to supplant anyone's focus on the

Cross. "*Do they have any identifying marks or signatures on them, like artists put their names on paintings?*" Yes, they have Jesus' initials on them, but not Saint Joseph's. They are S.O.M. – Son of Mary. Yes, and these are your initials as well. Thank you for saying your prayers today. I will deliver your petitions to Jesus as I have always done."

Saturday, August 8, 2015
9:24 a.m.

"Thinking through life's goals, effects and dimensions; the truth be told –
Speak divine intention until your lungs give out!"

- The Dominion Angels

"These are the Angelic strains that still echo through the corridors of the created world, My children. It is the reason that I hold out hope that all who will come to Heaven will fully participate in their own purification. At no previous time when I have appeared here to pray with you have I had more joy than at this moment. Why? Because even at this advanced juncture of the years, you are still willing to hear what I have to say. You have not strayed from My presence; you have never once been lured onto another path. Your focus has been on the Cross, and we are making a difference that has not been accomplished elsewhere in the history of the world. We have written songs that will be caroled for the fullness of eternity. We have given humanity reason to believe. My Special son, I have always spoken about the capacity for lost sinners to be found in Jesus, and they must be! They must search for the Lord while He may be found. And too, I have dispensed blessings that have bolstered and resulted from the good faith of men. It is always reflective of one's faith in God to know that sacred energy, spiritual beauty, righteous power and divine purpose are the fruits of your prayers. They are indeed good ones. And, their taste of sweetness is inviting to those only now beginning to realize their station on the Earth. Hence, the Dominion Angels say that the Gospel must be told until the voices of humanity give way. It is true that the throat-clearing that began at Pentecost has resulted in the hymns of ancient choirs sounding the praises of the heralded Messiah. What has been given to Creation through these lofty melodies has a sense of piety and reflection. It is to this that I have called My children throughout the ages – Imagine this! All My little ones gathered in their white stainless baptismal gowns before Me, waiting to receive the blessings of the Baby Jesus in My Arms. What the world needs to remember is that this is the goal of

My intercession. Yes, it seems difficult today for sure, but I will succeed without question. Come here! – I say. This is what I have been calling to My children for hundreds of years. Come to Me! Come to the Church that has made your peace with God. My Special son, I have the high honor and distinct privilege of introducing every one of My children to the Father through Jesus. I could spend the fullness of eternity emitting this joy throughout the universes, but it is here that it must begin. Here in this country and a world that begs for its redemption, even as it does not often know it is uttering a word. And, just because Jesus may seem speechless during these times, this does not mean that He is not here. He is with you and I, with your brother and all who are willing to believe, standing with poise and amazement at what we are capable of achieving through Him. It is His grace that has saved you, My children! – and, it is My grace that has taken you to your Salvation in Him. Today, My Special and Chosen ones, I speak of poetic righteousness because these are your glorious times. They are not 'the' glory that you will inherit in Heaven someday, but the begetting of your knowledge of Glory, of your initiation and commencement melded into one. My Immaculate Heart is aglow with love for the people of God. This is what He assigned Me to do, and it is more than this. It is an embarking that I have taken on as your Mother. I work for your maturity by feeding you the Wisdom that comes from the Heart of My Son. There may be some levity in the assumption that the Mother of God has nothing better to do, but there is truth in this as well. I live for the sake of My children! I was born in the ancient times to Saint Joachim and Saint Anne so Jesus could come to humanity as its only hope for redemption. I am sinless and pristine, and I am perfect in love. I give to the world the ability to stand full-faced and confident before their Savior in whom all good things come.

My fair little sons, the words and stanzas of My voice and speeches are those that have been inscribed for the children of God to refrain. It is an infinite source of gladness in that we have come this far. I have watched everything that God has allowed Me to see. As I have indicated more than once, there are certain errors, wrongdoings and slaughters from whose visions I have been spared. But, I know about them by the way I feel. It is not the same as someone describing a catastrophic event, but I have an infusion of knowledge about what happens on Earth. Jesus does this because He knows that I have already witnessed the most painful event in the history of man – His Crucifixion on the Cross. This was Man at His most divine. Jesus destroyed the whole essence of sin on Good Friday. He severed every soul from its bonds to imperfection. He made giants of diminutive creatures by elevating them to Himself. And, My little sons, the echoes of this gift still resound across the acreage of the Earth.

This is what speaks for Jesus when He seems so silent to Himself. And, it permits Me to see the righteousness of My children instead of the mournful grotesque. I see pardoning and forgiving. I see peacefulness and the cohesion of tender hearts. I watch the same sunrises that grace the morning skies. This does not mean that I get lost in them, because I am aware that beneath these same skies lives untold suffering and torment. When I watch the trees softly bending in the breeze, I am reminded that this is the way God asks His people to change – to be deferential to that which cleanses you. He would rather not be a storming force against Creation, but you have seen that this is necessary too. And, I watch people praying collectively and alone in their quarters. I see them dressing their gardens and tending flowers along the roadway. My Special son, it is all a trending toward expectation, that everything I ever wanted from My children occurs a moment at a time, in minutes and hours, and in days and years. This is what President Lincoln meant when he said that it will become all one thing. Everything about human life, all the thoughts and actions, the craftsmanship and constructive glee are destined to rest in the palms of God. They will do so after He allows the resentful among you to slip between His fingers and descend like burnt embers into the netherworld below.

Yes, it is all about redemption and unity with God. It is rightly a means for those who live on the Earth to rethink their priorities. It is a way for humanity to approach their passing from this world into the next with dreams as broad as galaxies. These are the sights and sounds that fill Me with joy, My Special son. I have been gifted to be part of this too, to augment and facilitate it, and to record in My own diary the same joys and benedictions that you and your brother have written in yours. And, O' I so enjoy the launching of the pretty fireworks about which I have spoken, and the fragrance of cookies in the oven, and the birthing of infant children, and the ringing of church bells on Easter and after weddings and feasts. I am filled with peace because I know that these things are the effects of human life lived well. It is part of the same joy that I receive when I hear one of My children whose voice has become hoarse from preaching the Gospel all day. Yes, as the Angels have said, until your lungs give out as well. Here, I have told you that unity and tenderness are gifts of the Christian life. I have said that when done according to the Sacred Heart of Jesus, your acceptance of the Cross does not deny you the dignity that I have described here today. Indeed, it births and magnifies it. I see all these saintly things as though they are stars lining the heavens. When you and your brother took your parents to Jacksonville for supper last night, Jesus opened the doors of Purgatory and allowed tens-of-thousands of souls to go free. This is the reason your father began to cry when you told him 'goodbye' as you were leaving. He is so close to

Heaven himself that he felt the energy of its liberation soothing his heart and soul. As your brother said, it is all about good will, a manifestation of human decency. It is peace and harmony that make the Angels sigh in relief. And, it proves that you and your brother are the sacred princes of the Son of Man, in whom all Christians are set free."

Saturday, August 15, 2015
Feast of the Assumption of Mary
9:30 a.m.

"Love, loyalty and the way life echoes."

"My Special and Chosen ones, you have given the Lord your whole hearts and lives, and you have blessed Jesus Himself. You have accorded the Father the opportunity to remake Creation through you. And, this attests to your goodness, the benevolence of your intentions, and your imbeddedness in everything divine that will ever be manifested in the earthly domain. Today, it is My sacred honor to speak to you who have been so holy for so long. My little sons, I speak about love and loyalty and the way life echoes in light of the proceeding days because they are ebbing and flowing. This is the propagation of your identity in Jesus as you sustain the years. There is awe-inspiring and overwhelming joyfulness in this fact because you remain aware not only of the issues you must address every day, but your destiny in My Son through My Most Immaculate Heart. When you are praying, you can see the immensity of this joy. When you are speaking in rhymes of repentance, you resound the intentions of God for the world. My Special son, God knows that you love Him. Think about that. He knows that you love Him, and He trusts that you always will. Everyone whom you have met through your life, you have blessed. You are the child of God who has always been giving and never taking. You have shed ennobling sunlight over the world's darkest places. You have been unique and obedient to My requests, to the call of the Father to labor in His vineyard, and in your willingness to go on when some paths seemed unsure. This is what I have always sought from My children because it is the way Jesus teaches. It is possible for human beings to replicate the grace with which Jesus lived as the Chosen Son of God. Why? Because nobody is random to Him. All are priceless and brilliant. My little sons, it is often spoken that the greatest people on Earth are the ones who do not know it; they do not seek esteem before humanity. They do not sit in open meetings, point fingers and scream into other people's faces, '...I have a Ph.D.!' The ones who do have an agenda; they believe that males are inferior and must be subjugated. Your brother believes that he has nothing to lose by taking these people to task. He is truly surprising to Me. You should hear the Angels cheer when they see him rebuking people such as these. It is an amazing sight to behold from Heaven. What impresses the Lord is that your brother does not back down, even after he has accomplished his mission. He has the fire of Saint Timothy within him. He is not just mimicking the strong personality of his mother, he has come upon this in his own right because he can detect a charlatan a mile away. My Special son, would you like Me to tell you the reasons why you and your brother have such a distinct vantage point about the truth of the world? "*Yes, please.*" You see, you are visionary and beautiful; you are holy, breathtaking and awesome because I have made you this way. I have wrapped My arms around you and held you in your quietest moments, and also when the world seemed mad and reckless, and you were searching for what to do. Remember what it means to ponder holding Jesus during His Sorrowful Passion and Crucifixion. Imagine being alongside the road to the Cross, and Jesus stops and looks you in the eyes, and you reach out and hold Him. Yes, you just hold Him there and give Him love and affection. Well, this is what you did only days ago when you began to cry because I, your Mother, am so beautiful. Please, I beg you, think about how you have comforted Jesus by declaring your love for Me – the Woman Clothed with the Sun, the Matriarch of the Roman Catholic Church, your Intercessor and Queen of Love. You have lauded and elevated His most beautiful creature, His Mother. You have listened to Me. You and your brother have been obedient. You have given, and given, and given, and given. You have no way of knowing the greatness of what I am relating to you at this moment. It is larger than all the suns and moons combined. It is more meaningful than all the triumphs in world history. I am speaking about the collection of all victories assembled into one.

Jesus with tears in His own eyes came to Me and said that you were crying because I am so beautiful. How can we thank you? How can Two Sinless Souls sufficiently touch your life in your earthly exile that would impress upon you the grandness of what you have done? As your brother is prone to say, this is no small thing! We will continue to embrace and admire you; we will hold your life in our Hearts, and we will ensure that you are accorded the highest, loftiest and most meaningful station in Heaven that any redeemed soul could reach. If the whole of humanity were like you, My Special son, there would be no need for the exile of men. Yes, and I say with endearing joy, we see your brother with equal love. These are among the things that you will hear as the ages march forward. It is in the end not about how beautiful I am; there has never been any question about that. But, it is that you know it and see it. You celebrate the beauty of the Mother of God! I am the Humble Handmaid of the Lord; and you dwell on this correctly, and even more on My Queenship in whose honor the Saints have died. And, you are so charitable and fair that you realize that My speech here today has nothing to do with hubris; it is about the Gospel. The Salvation of humanity lives within the Crucifixion of Jesus Christ. This is the Gospel that the New Covenant message has told. And, the presentation of humanity to this same Jesus Christ is stationed inside My Most Immaculate Heart; this is the other foot of the ladder to the registers where the Saints and Angels now reside. While it would seem that I have been telling you this for the past quarter-century, and that your messages might be interpreted as being verbose, effusive, eloquent and sometimes stark, the whole matter comes down to this ladder's two feet. They are attached to the legs of humanity. They leave footprints where others should strive to walk. This is the essential nature of My messages to you and your brother, not that they may be eloquent, majestic or otherwise, but that they focus on the simplicity of what we have been doing. In the final account, do exiled men touch the Face of God during their mortal lives or not? If they live according to My messages, they will. And, does anything from the ethereal realms have the slightest bearing on what judgements and actions take place on Earth every day? It does if humanity heeds the summons of their Mother. We have made it happen here, My Special son. You and your brother, the Dominion Angels, the Holy Spirit, the Providence and Will of God, the fathoms of your prayers, the light that has overcome the darkness – all of this has manifested the cultivation of the created world here and now. We once reflected that it is not like ripping off one's flesh or being branded by fire, but it is awfully close! It will feel this way to those who are dismembering little children's bodies in their mothers' wombs. It will certainly be the fate of anyone who speaks or acts disparagingly against the Queen of Heaven and Earth. They do it at their own peril. Here again, you know that this is the truth, and all about the truth. So, My dear children, thank you for your prayers, and bless you both for remembering Me on this Feast Day of the Church. I love you!"

Sunday, August 23, 2015
9:26 a.m.

"One difference between love and hatred is that love cannot be destroyed. One difference between light and darkness is that light allows you to see where you have stumbled. One difference between the truth and falsehood is that the truth eventually obliterates lies."

- The Dominion Angels

"Here today, My little sons, I pray with you for the transformation of the world into the Divine Order of God. This has been our prayer all along, as you have more than convinced the Father that you are steadfast in His grace and aware of His determination to redeem repentant sinners. My little ones, I cannot overstate the reasons for My joy. You make Me so happy; you inspire in Jesus tremendous inflection to dispense His Divine Mercy upon those who do not yet know how to ask for themselves. I have told you that you are Children of Light. While you are deep thinkers who meditate on the Sacred Mysteries; you are also aware of the heartfelt ways that Christianity should be lived. It is good to think about Jesus' Sacrifice, and benevolent to take this gift to humanity around the globe. I am trying to teach that light travels faster than thought – light patently precedes thought. We have multitudes of reasons to believe, My little sons, that we are succeeding in this mission. I have focused My prayers and attention on three words that all must consider in their conscience. 'At what point.' These are the words. At what point does the world begin to realize that humanity is on the brink of destruction? At what point will errant men come to understand that a life without God cannot be sustained? And, My Special son, you can apply '...At what point...' to any other ill or wrongdoing men might conceive. There surely must be some place on the continuum of mortal time where intelligent life concludes that it can neither conduct its affairs nor redeem its purposes without the Providence of God. It must be known by all with the capacity of reason that all things good are dispensed by the Lord's beatific being. It is Truth that ushers all peace; it is Wisdom that overcomes iniquity. We have been speaking about this, My Special and Chosen ones, since your messages began in February 1991. Your hearts and souls have known about this greatness since you were formed in the womb. Does the Mother of God ever beg? This question has surrounded the Church since the Immaculate Conception. Well, the answer is that I urge and beseech. I am not a hungry beggar, and I never ask for something that I can acquire on My own. However, the conversion of My children must be manifested of their own accord. I pray and invoke the power of the Holy Spirit, and God knows that I do. And, I appear in the world at the behest of the Father, but My children must be willing to see; they must be prepared to pray. When I come speaking to you here, My children, I know that I am conferring with two men who are already aware. You have made yourselves not only available to Me, but to Christ Jesus and the Father through your willing obedience. I have been reluctant to 'stave' things as though someone might force something into being or prevent something from occurring. My little sons, you have witnessed My ability to enliven the Earth in the ways Jesus prescribes, but the whole idea of Christianity is to require the participation of those who believe. This is more than putting life down on paper; it is turning the world upside down and redefining the meaning of change. I do not fear the changes that come to humanity because upheavals, reversals and disruptions take My children closer to the foothills of Paradise.

When the Gospel message mandates that believers depart from the routine into the extraordinary, it means that comfort will not be taken there with you. Sacrifice does not imply that both feet remain on the same ground. Taking flight as a Christian means that spiritual wings must be spread to get there. This is more than transformation and acclimation, it is inheriting a new identity in the Crucifixion of My Son. I am not telling you anything that you have not known. My Special one, when I speak about something being bright and shining, I am referring to its readiness, its preparedness, and its determination. This is the faith that I have solicited from those whom I have blessed. And, humanity in the world will not respond to this call until they have invested assets in the fight. "*I have always thought that there must be consequences.*" Yes, there must be consequences; mankind must be not only made aware of these consequences, but realize that doing nothing will not work this time. The world has for tens-of-thousands of years believed that problems will be solved if onlookers simply turn their heads and walk way. This is the age-old means of letting God be God to the diminishment of man's participation in the fight against evil. While letting God be God is a good idea, it is better to become God's instruments while there is still time. This is a responsive way to live; it is the holiest gift that a mortal being can offer Jesus on the Cross. These are among the themes that I have spoken about to My other messengers as well, but the dominant segment of the Church and the entire secular void choose to ignore them. Yes, the willful of the Church say that one is not required to believe what My messengers relate, and the heathens of secularism say that they do not believe in God at all. This is the metaphor about which I was speaking about the narrow path required for the stricken Apollo 13 spacecraft to gain reentry into the atmosphere of the Earth. It worked for them during that time, and it will work for us in this new millennium. I am saying that all that is unlikely will eventually come to pass. It may be a narrow corridor, but so is the gateway to Paradise. As you have seen, there have been instances where tough thinking has been required to take the Church and its messengers this far. There have been moments of anxiety and frustration. There has been drama and the influx of emotions. And, there will be a period of silence when the whole of humankind will wonder if God will ever speak again. This will be the passing of the Church through the final fires. It is a manifestation of the stirred conscience of collective humanity that will never fall asleep again.

My Special son, we have seen this play out before. We know all the ins and outs that must befall those who fight against the teachings of the Church. You have witnessed the 'form' of the Catholic Church on the battlefield against the 'anti-form' of the secular void. Yes, there is drama and death and destruction in this. There is question and uncertainty. However, there is also confidence in the outcome – Jesus has won. I have said this countless times. And, He has given His victory to those who believe in Him, but even more to innovative giants like you and your brother who have gone the farthest miles and given your whole lives to Me. I have said that I cannot overstate the Lord's gratitude for your devotion to the conversion of the world, but this does not mean that I cannot try. There are simply no words to express the magnitude of your sacrifices or the unlimited brilliance of Heaven. This is why we pray. It is that you and your brother and all believers have come this far by your own determination to see the world renewed. And yes, your brother has been obedient, as well. He has proved himself capable of surrender – of allowing God to be His Master without your brother's will taking hold. I assure you that you will both soon see the fruits of your tremendous gifts. And, it is not that you just accomplished this faithfulness, but that you provided certainty that it was not a casual exercise to satisfy a neutral request from some apathetic culture. One cannot undergo a journey unless their feet begin to move. Everywhere we look these days, there are people only now taking their first steps. They are being stirred by the power of the Holy Spirit. We must pray for them to proceed as well into the heights. We should invest in them prayers and petitions that are worthy of the Father to receive. This, My Special child, is what you and your brother do best. When the distractions abound where you live, you remain focused on the purpose of life. It is not about race cars or stage performers, it is about asking God to wrap His hands around this world to squeeze the evil out. And after that, it is about feeling the embrace of His arms taking it back again, purged of everything He opposes, cleansed and remade, given a new beginning that cannot be exploited by the enemies of His Son. We shall see this come to pass. I am the Immaculate Mother of Jesus for a reason; not just so He would have any mother, but this Mother. God chose Me to become the Mother of His Son because of who I am, because of My sacred identity in union with His Will. I am not speaking in hubris today, but in truth. No humbler mother in Creation will you ever find. I am simply declaring that what Jesus has said must be told. I have the capacity for undertaking this mission because the Father has deigned to come to Me. And, My Special and Chosen ones, God has come to you in ways that you cannot see; they are all propitious and foretelling. You have gained your sanctity in Jesus because you have allowed Him in your hearts and lives. This is the way you shine and glow, your way of reflecting what redemption means to those who must be saved. It is a blessing that you have given to God."

Saturday, August 29, 2015
9:19 a.m.

"In reflection of everything we do in life, there must always be meaning. Especially during our idleness, we must cling to our momentum in pursuing spiritual holiness. Despite the times when we feel disregarded, star-struck or even mystified, we must stand confident on the underlayment of our faith. And, we must promise to never let go of one another's hand. Even more, we have to strive for virtue. There is often a vast difference between being ready and being prepared. This is what human love is for – not taking for granted all the grand potential that Jesus has given us, but standing smartly tall, speaking clearly and unreservedly fighting for everything that matters beyond the sights and sounds of the waning years. We must not allow ourselves to arrive at the doorstep of the Eminent Kingdom in shattered pieces. We must have hope. We have the ability to make choices that will ensure our peaceful transition from the gullies of the Earth onto the summits of the eternal mountains."

- William L. Roth

"Amen, My Special son. This wisdom that you have spoken resounds the Gospel Truth. It is clearly unity that I am seeking from My children, but not just unity for any cause. I beseech My darling children to learn about their union in Jesus because they will otherwise have no future. Today, My little sons, I come to pray with you in remembrance of the loveliness of Saint John the Baptist, and I ask you to join Me in invoking his intercession for the world of exiled men. There can be no true sacrifices on behalf of Jesus unless those who profess to believe in Him are willing themselves to be spiritually purged of all that separates the Earth from Heaven. My Special son, the most evocative thing you said today is that humankind must not reach the doorstep of Heaven in shattered pieces. While it is seemingly true that each soul through the years reaches Heaven one at a time, it is a mass-entrance outside of time. I see the world in the same way as you, but I also see the latter procession because of My presence with Jesus. It is clear that we must pray for the many who are yet exiled on the Earth for all the reasons we have spoken about for decades. I have said that the preparedness about which you have spoken is more than being ready, so your comparison is well taken. Being bright and shining for Jesus is about glowing with the radiance of the same heavenly brilliance in which I bask. This is not just the origin of My joy, it is also an essence that I factually manifest. It is a function of the beauty of those who have given themselves to the perfection of God that existed long before the Creation that He formed. How long? There are no parameters to measure it because the Lord's omnipotence and providence have always been timeless and perpetual – a difficult prospect to ponder by human beings who encounter spacial and timely boundaries every day. And, the meaning about which you speak also reflects another of My recent messages about love and sanctity. You have taken the purpose of your faith to another level, that of meaning, because you know that intentions are defined by what they produce. Good intentions are the fruit of a holy life, and ill intentions are not. As we continue praying together, your brother should write a note to your Bishop to tell him that I have said to contact him and ask if it would be improper to publicly mention that the Church has begotten a commission to examine My messages. This will mark that I am inclined to defer to him as the head of this diocese. It will reinforce as well your previous respect for his kind direction and leadership. And, it will communicate that I wish not to propagate My work outside the hierarchy of the Church. This communion is what I am seeking; it has rarely been paralleled in history. You have an honest Bishop who defends the dignity, doctrines, traditions and apostolic orthodoxy of the Catholic Church. There is no question about that. He is a constant guard of the Church's teachings, even steadfastly when certain issues arise. I assure you that Bishop Thomas John Paprocki's sense of the Gospel will prevail long after his detractors are gone. Many people believe in playing on the popular emotions of the secular void in order to gain favor with their peers. I remind you that this approach has never worked in the history of the Church.

I am seeing the preparedness that you referred to in your heartfelt prose today. There is a stark contrast in the way things used to be, even in your own country. There is a movement afoot to recapture the moral spirit of the United States from the socialist ideologues who are trying to tear it down. This is why you are seeing plain-spoken individuals becoming popular around the nation who have never held public office. The framework of this trend includes all the issues that we have discussed through the years, and all the new movements that bring shock and horror to the consciences of decent people everywhere. How in the world can someone equate the barbaric abortion of unborn children to opening someone's chest for heart surgery? These kinds of blasphemies are directly from the tongue of the devil. It is Satan-speak. It is devoid of anything having to do with the Commandments of God. It is evil and wicked. It is shorn of truth. And, My Special son, while I am not telling you anything that you and your brother do not know, I wish for you to understand that the Lord sees and judges much the same way as you. You and your brother are in accord with what Jesus believes to be the wreck of this world in which all people will eventually die. It has come to the point that Americans are becoming so desensitized to the works of the devil that they do not know to speak against it anymore. This does not mean that Jesus has left you! It has nothing to do with the Father turning His back on the Church. It is much more than the sum of all human actions combined. Why? Because you are closer now to the final reckoning than any time in history. This makes logical sense; it is obvious due to the expiring years. What does not seem as obvious is that Jesus will exact retribution against those who scorn His Holy Sacrifice. He will vanquish the evildoers who stand in His way. He allows the wicked to judge themselves as harshly as they will. There is no lack of Mercy here; Jesus' entire framework of forgiveness remains in place. It has always been true that human beings judge themselves before the Crucifixion far more harshly than Jesus ever will. This is the effect of the translocated spirit. Jesus will ask these sinners if there is any place in their conscience that reminds them of Him. If their answer is not affirmative, these souls will decide their fate for themselves. Vengeance belongs to the Lord, and all redemption is meted out by the call for mercy. My Special son, all the greatness to which you aspire is being manifested. Your gifts and contributions have been intense and far-flung. I ask your brother to not be despondent about his inability to break through the employment barrier because the Gospel of the Lord is being fulfilled. Like you, your brother remains prepared; you are like bright and shining knights on white steeds at the break of dawn. You have your dignity in Jesus that will never be diminished. Each new day should be met with hope and courage, just as you have said. It is with Me that you pray, in Jesus that you love, and for God that you live. Thank you again for sharing your prayers with Me. I will speak to you upon the arrival of a new month; it will be a time when you will celebrate another birthday! I love you and your brother with endless joy."

Saturday, September 5, 2015
8:59 a.m.

"Righteously true, endearingly calm, humbly appointed, divinely assured, exceedingly disciplined, forever gracious, hued with honesty, seasoned in joy, constantly wise – these are the marks of the worthy Christian; always impeccable, sweet and kindhearted, uniquely benign and apostolically adorned."

- The Dominion Angels

"My dear little sons, I hope you always remember the description that the Angels have offered for your souls. It is accurate and befitting of the lives you are leading. Today, I invite you to know that even though we often speak about the past and the future, it is the present that is our focus. You learn from the past and prepare for the future, but these are the times that will determine what is to come. You are blessed here; you are shaped and uplifted during these present hours. I also have come to remind you that the Kingdom of God is with you. This is what I said in My September 2, 2015 Medjugorje message about My children speaking for the Father through the power of the Holy Spirit. Christians can make claims that cannot be told by those who reject the Cross. You have the ability to assess the world conditions that are causing such strife and struggle. You can take upon yourselves the cloak of wisdom that must be handed down to those who betray your faith. You can renew life by conducting yourselves according to the Gospel. Yes, and you can spare lives as well; you have this faculty through your unity in Jesus. The whole endeavor of the world must be to comply with My Son's wishes in ways that advance His love. All life, the completeness of your journey in exile, is given purpose by your compliance with the Sacred Scriptures, even when it would seem that logic evades the moment. (*Our Holy Mother then described a recent incident where a female public official conscientiously objected to participating in the validation of same-sex marriage. She described how the clothing of a Christian as the Dominion Angels have described it would have persuaded a nation. If the woman would have communicated as one of Our Lady's little girls with humble deference, all people would have followed her in defense. Instead, her angry delivery, her dismissive tone, her inability to reach the hearts of those who approached her made the strength of the truth she professed come across as just insensitive isolationism.*) My Special son, do you understand? "*Yes.*" It is not that this woman was wrong to take a stand, but her demeanor overshadowed her message of God's truth. Where were the traits that the Dominion Angels described? She will be blessed anyway. Her courage will be rewarded. However, the larger meaning will be lost because her message was concealed beneath her crudeness. It is all about telling the story of love the way I always do. Sensitivity means that there is a joining between hearts and minds. This is the product of such matters as public officials holding to their Christian beliefs. On rare occasions did Jesus speak sternly, and then to those who were trying to make a marketplace of His sanctuary. It is about welcoming the sinner that His teachings are about. One can scold someone gently by massaging their conscience with the truth. I am not speaking here about My messages where the enemies of God's Kingdom will be crushed; these antagonists will determine their own future. I am referring instead to those who are '...only now being told...' that must make the transformation from error to righteousness. If they will only still themselves; if they will only stop fighting and careening, if only they will reach for the Cross, they will understand what I am saying. It is about being obedient to the Lord's Will and cultivating the fruits that will grow thereafter.

There are so many gifts in humanity's hands that must be transferred to God. The Father has implanted in the world within men's reach the resources and opportunities to transform the Earth into the likeness of Heaven. I have said that if only My children will live as I ask, they will not realize their passage from this life into the next. This seems a far distance from what you are seeing in this new millennium. My Special son, it will happen because Jesus says so. I am still speaking to you because God has not given up. You also have learned that the Lord's lent ear awaits the prayers of His people. He will amend the world and the circumstances in societies according to the way His children solicit His graces. It is a confirming and conforming obedience that allows humanity to reach the summit of spiritual understanding. It is obedience on someone's lips that speaks about the Kingdom to come. I am saying that God yearns for the constitution of humanity to reflect the image of His Son. If prayer is sufficiently from the heart, and if the intentions of the world are in accord with the definition of Divine Love, then God will sustain the way human life is being lived. This, My Special son, is what I mean when I say that the present is the most important time of all. I have always told My children that prayer from the heart is the penetrating gift that permeates the gates of Heaven and reaches the King seated on His Throne. It requires faith, sincerity, authenticity and commitment to induce the Father into reigning with absolution. All of this has been given to the world by Jesus on the Cross. It is a matter of wise men seeking Him again, living this faith, declaring this sincerity, and embracing this authenticity. Given this, My Special son, do you see how even well meaning people fall short? *"Yes."* They oftentimes make correct statements about the cause of their faith and the truth of the Father in Heaven, but their delivery does not reflect the way Jesus would speak. This is the picture of change that God is looking for in Heaven. His eyes are focused on His disciples on the Earth, but it is humanity's responsibility to bring Him to fix His vision on certain causes; something virtuous must be done to draw His gaze. In other words, He looks at the world like a watchman in the night, but something must stir to remind Him of human hope. This is embodied by acts of love and charity that seem rarer by the day. Sometimes God figuratively squints His eyes to see the slightest movement that imitates the lessons of His Son. But once He sees it, He sends fair spiritual skies and life-giving waters to nurture its growth. For example, God saw great movement when the Ohio Bishop sent you his letter. Do you remember the name of that diocese? *"Yes, Steubenville."* This is also the site of other Marian events to which they have become devoted. As your brother, being ever the politician, has said many times, '...you cannot succeed unless you win Ohio, you know.' (*I laughed at our Holy Mother's humor because Timothy has been a student of politics since his youth, and during every presidential campaign, he reminds me that the one hoping to be elected must win Ohio.*) All of this speaks to the intonation of the Lord's Will in your time. We are praying; the Lord is manifesting, the world is maturing, and the Triumph of the Cross has been revealed. There must remain this mutual cooperation between the Lord and His people; men must take charge of their faith. Faith is a gift from God, and it must be received charitably by the spiritually converted heart.

My Special son, there is a notion that humanity plays an active role in the relationship between Heaven and Earth, and that God the Father plays a passive role. While this is true to a degree, we have long known that God can be stirred into feats of great splendor. He handed humanity the Church at Pentecost. This was the bequeathing of the future of billions of souls back to Himself through the passing of time. However, when the priest pronounces the Consecration of the Most Blessed Sacrament, God must respond as well. The priest's hands on one level reach into Heaven for Jesus' Sacred Body, and Jesus defers to his summons. The Eucharistic Prayer explicitly requisitions the Body and Blood of Jesus from the Father's Altar in Heaven, and God responds. Jesus is 'dying' to make His appearance on the altars of the Roman Catholic Church. Jesus is obedient to the Cross out of love for sinners in compliance with the Will of God. This is what the sensitivity is all about that I mentioned at the beginning of this message. Jesus has always been sensitive to the needs of the weak and brokenhearted. He has known that sinners need a Divine Savior. This is not something that He learned apart from God because Jesus is the Second Person of the Blessed Trinity. It was something that Jesus knew upon His conception in My Womb. It was as natural and everlasting as the Father, Himself. So today, I speak about the furtherance of this wisdom, the protraction of this knowledge to the inhabitants of the Earth. In other words, God is asking the Church to remain as it was in the beginning, at the moment the Holy Spirit descended on humanity in the Upper Room. This Fire of New Life was permeating and permanent. It was wholesome and whole-making. And, this is the Spirit that dates to the undeniable origin of the Salvation of the lost – the Love of God for everything He created and all that He deigns to come. All the worlds, all the creatures that could have been, all the majesty and incarnations, all the secret mysteries and reciprocity – these things God reserves for Himself. He can be induced to reveal them by the means through which the soul has been saved. He can light up the night with flaming new stars. He can detonate exhaustive new bursts of genius. He can turn everything that makes up lions and snails into vapor in an instant. Why has He not done so with the Earth on which sinful men live? Because He loves you. God believes that He got it right the first time. The Father is pleased by His sons and daughters who are doing their best to find their way back to Him. He enjoys the fragrance of human obedience. He ratifies the declarations of the Saints of the Church. All in all, this is His purpose alongside the needs and pining of His people struggling to survive in a world that has not yet yielded its entire acclamation that Jesus Christ is its Lord. This is the sensitivity to which Creation is being drawn.

My Special son, if it were ever true that the coattails of human exile swirl and glitter, then the swirling and glittering are coming to an end. God wants all men to be aware that what they see every day is more of men's will than His. He wants them to see beyond their whims, druthers and accidents. He desires that His creatures spiritualize their existence and deposit their future in Him. I am not saying that the essence of human life is a distraction, but that this essence must be a product of what God seeks from His Church. Feeding and housing the poor? Of course. Teaching the blessings of the Beatitudes? Beyond any doubt. But, there is more about the meaning that we spoke of last week. There must be a new holiness that blossoms around the globe, that does not so much accent the diversity of men, but the similarities they must advance as one people beneath the Cross. It takes chapters and verses to lay this out, but it also takes individuals such as you and Me, and your brother, to give life to what they mean during the passing of time. I am not saying that our voices can globalize at once the words of the Holy Gospel, but that the commotion of the secular void can find its peace in the constancy of the Church. This is the Kingdom that has been given to your brothers and sisters who have discovered themselves lost without the power of the Sacraments to sanctify their lives. I am pleased that the Father's pronouncements resound through the corridors of human life with such commanding distinction. It is My honor to facilitate this process through My messages here. I find beauty and happiness in seeing the courage that My children display. My Special son, through your Marian works, I have laid one of the most heartfelt gifts ever seen in human history at man's feet. The Morning Star Over America reflects your love for Me. Leadership and obedience are the fruits that this gift conveys. Imagine what else you can do through your passionate prayers!"

Saturday, September 12, 2015
9:01 a.m.

"Life is a work of art – or is work the art of life? Either way, the point is this – the masterpiece of human redemption is priceless to those with the courage to pursue it. The seas become quieter, love abounds, healing and light chase away the darkness, and good will feeds the starving masses. This is the knowledge that manifests true wisdom in the world, that accrues our actions inside one dramatic Gospel that defers to no other design."

- William L. Roth

"Here today, My dear little children, I come to pray with you more joyfully than at any prior time. What we are doing to convert humanity is accomplishing its goal. Jesus is elated that we have accorded Him the opportunity to permeate the hearts of wayward sinners, and they will be reconciled with God through our sanctifying prayers. There is great light in the world today, My little sons. Yes, there are other dimensions too, even ones with tremendous drama, but none as forbearing as the Holy Gospel. As you say, none other fosters the good will that feeds the starving masses. Not one other speaks to the redemption of the human race. My Special and Chosen ones, we have lauded the artworks of the Messianic Truth in many ways, and you have personified and reflected them. This is the reason that you have not only been blessed by God, but that you have in turn blessed humanity as well. Many people around the globe have yet to discern the facility of prayer – what it is about humbling oneself in prayer that pleases the Father so. It is about the coalescence of the Church beneath His guiding hand. It is not that a fawn is drawn to a stream. The thirsty fawn was always destined to be there. God placed the rolling stream in the path of the fawn. Desire comes along with Creation; this is the reason God suspended the world in space. He was hungry for new life, and He manifested through Himself an Earth with which He could interact. He wished to devise a tangible fruit of His wholesome love. He desired a people whom He would love with the same infinity with which He has forever existed. Yes, the Lord God can imagine things too. He is the original thinker. He has always believed that life is a work of art, and humanity helps Him remember that work is also the art of life. What does this mean? It not only implies that good works preserve life, but that holy life builds upon itself. The love between creatures is the bond that unites Heaven and Earth. When God said in ancient times '...in the beginning,' He was speaking about the communion of the origin of the seeable realms with His own unseeable omnipotence. Yes, always powerful and always present. Omnipresent. And, inside every converted man lives these same blessings. The heart is touched, warmed and sustained by the fruits of these gifts. It is by the seeding, nurturing, cultivating and harvesting of these fruits that human life is ultimately preserved. What better way to live than this? My Special son, I have brought you the good news that our prayers are having a beneficial effect not just to make you happy, but to prepare you and your brother for what the future will bring. Your works will be ratified by the Church. Countless legions of repentant sinners will be brought before the Cross. Jesus is weeping in gladness instead of sorrow. The light before the dawn is donning its brightest sheen. I realize that these things seem like abstract imaginings right now, but they will take on greater meaning in later years. You and your brother have traveled to Medjugorje to witness the miracles that have occurred, but the miracles thus far revealed are only seedlings of the great ones to come.

I would like to speak to the phenomenon of pilgrims going to Medjugorje ten and twenty times, sometimes even fifty and a hundred times. Once or twice is enough. Those who continue to travel to Medjugorje do not yet understand the point. Medjugorje is a place to drink, much like the fawn partakes of the stream. The truth and holiness ingested there are to be taken with each pilgrim to their place of origin. This implants My messages of the Lord's Salvation all around the globe. However, some people believe that what is learned in Medjugorje is for consumption and depletion there. Of all the millions who have prayed at the Saint James parish and on the hills and mountains there, a sparse few retain this light once they return home. My Special son, I am not complaining about this today. I am making a statement about the impact of the daily world on humanity's faith. You and your brother have done your part to maintain what you gained during your pilgrimages to My Medjugorje shrine. It has assuredly been helpful that I have come to you and your brother here in the United States. And, while this is important to God, it speaks more about you and your brother than about the Father, Himself. There was always meant to be a Morning Star Over America. I have forever contained in My Immaculate

Heart the messages that I have dictated to you. And, I have always known you and your brother from the inside out. It must be made clear here today that you have been dedicated to Me and the conversion of humanity to unprecedented degrees for two individuals who have not lived cloistered lives through religious vows. Hence, God the Father, Jesus the Son, and the Spirit-Advocate witness in you and your brother a level of greatness that supersedes the world's definition of great. You are heroes to God not just because you have lived for Jesus, but because you have helped build a framework of love that reflects His house in Heaven. You know the shapely lines and curves of Paradise long sought in centuries past. You can discern even the warmth of the beating Heart of God from your stately poise here in this world. The rhythm of your thoughts and actions is attuned to the heartbeat of His Son. You are given wisdom that you not only internalize, but that you multiply like loaves and fishes to help lost sinners to know the reality of their fate without the Cross. I have told you on a number of occasions that this is Providence in you, that you have instilled in your identity the ability to see the connection between having life and living it. This is the reason why your brother once wrote about the human will being orphaned until it unites with the Will of God. Spiritual might and willpower are enhanced when handed to the Father through the humble and contrite heart. This is the drive of Christian mobility. Here, it is clear that God maintains control of the throttle of human affairs, but He figuratively sits His children on His lap and allows them to gauge the twists and turns by which they live. Like the Sacred Gospel itself, the whole matter is a spiritual design. (*When traveling to my grandfather's house in the country when I was very young, my father used to allow me to sit on his lap and steer the car while he would run the gas pedal and brakes. I had reminisced about these times recently and Our Lady used them in Her parable.*)

My Special son, it is not that God wants to make the message of Salvation the most painful alternative for exiled men, but that it be the only choice in the pursuit of everlasting life. It is not a matter of taste, but a fostering of sustenance. There is no other life outside the Gospel of Jesus Christ. And, even though there are bitter moments in fulfilling the mandates of the New Covenant, there is no living bread elsewhere. The Gospel speaks about the Manna of Absolution that is found only in itself. There are many distractions that would lure the world from this truth, but they are as short-lived as an inhaled breath that one might exhale. Sacred beauty is not only more appealing than the appearances of the world, it is intrinsic to the final destiny of the soul. All life given to God cannot be destroyed because it is placed in the perpetuity of His hands. This is perhaps His greatest gift of all. And even further, you and your brother have lived in this motivation because I have placed you there. The Morning Star Over America was conceived when the Father placed you both in your respective mother's womb. I prayed for centuries that God would give Me two saints who would never once decline the invitation of the Lord to stand their ground. I always wanted two beautiful sons who would complement each other in the ways of strength and virtue. This does not mean that you are different, but that you have the capacity for wisdom and prudence alike. You are aware of your standing here on the Earth and your union with Jesus at the right hand of the Father. You pray because you understand its power. You look to Heaven for answers not only because you know it to be right, but because you cannot help it. You recognize fact from fiction the moment it impacts your senses. And, I wanted two sons who would stand tall, yourself as a giant of faith, and your brother who would be true to you, to Me and to Jesus without counting the cost. This has been a most beneficial relationship that the three of us have maintained in communion with the Most Holy Trinity in Heaven and on Earth. We have more than uplifted the designs of God, we have helped inform His prerogatives for judging the things of the world. We have told Him that we have tried, and He has responded that we have succeeded. My Special son, I have also said that your sacred works would impact the Earth in multiple ways during your lifetime, and I have told the truth. However, if ever it appeared that it was not until you and your brother joined Me in Heaven, that would be equally as blessed. Nothing, not even time itself or the cleavage of life and death, can impede what we have done on God's behalf. There has never been a moment wasted or a midnight candle that burned in vain. All we have done, you and I and your brother, has been united with the gifts of My other messengers throughout the ages to transform the world into the likeness of Heaven. You do not see it all right now – history is still being written before you. The shadows of bygone ages are being cast across your century today. But, when this shifting of the seas and the parting of hours occurs one last time, we will see together here in this place the miracle for which millennia of men have prayed. This is the promise that God has made that I am relating to you today."

Saturday, September 19, 2015
12:46 p.m.

"One need not renounce his own humanity to accept the Cross."

- The Dominion Angels

"My dear little sons, the Church is, itself, within you. It inhabits you as we speak, recognizing the Will of the Father for Creation, manifesting the glorious righteousness of your predecessors' faith, savoring the Fruits of Divine Love, and protracting into the future what it means to be virtuously human. I have come speaking to you again in prayer because this is the way we communicate with God. I have known that there can be no true communication without the transfer of meaning, and this is therefore what we are accomplishing now. It is not just through thought and reflection that this happens; it is additionally through your labors and sacrifices that you speak with the Father. This is what you see from Him every day. You have witnessed that human fulfillment is His blessing, as are Nature and life itself. Meaning consists of these things. My Special son, I know that you and your brother are somewhat travel weary, but you are feeling quite better now. You had an eventful journey to the Islands of Hawaii where you, yourself, proved to your workmates and friends that you are more visionary than some had known. Even as you realize that I heap accolades upon you for what you deem to be unapparent reasons, I am today telling you that you have touched other hearts in ways beyond your understanding. Your presentations during your sessions are being spoken about with respect. I do not mean that they are just being casually mentioned, but outwardly admired. Your open leadership, deep thinking, affable personality, sense of humor, and capacity for team participation are lessons for everyone who attended. Yes, they are comparing your efforts with even greater ideals that move beyond your workplace operation. It is about being human and applying your humanity to the completion of your mission. I have told you this not to flatter you as you might believe that I have done in the past. I am not heaping undue praise on you just because you are My Special son, but because you have affected your peers and counterparts in the ways that I have described. And, your brother in his kindness has also given your coworkers a sense of the type of people you choose to be your friends. I thought your brother was not the burden that he confessed to have been, but this is who he is. There was talk among some of the conveners and travelers that you and your brother are among the most peaceful people in the world. I have made you this way. And not only that, your friends are taking a close look at your website and the Morning Star Over America manifestation in which you have been involved since 1989. I am saying to you this afternoon that there are good outcomes of your mission to Hawaii, and I ask that you always remember your travels this way. Everything you wanted to accomplish by leaving your book with your friend in Hawaii will flourish the lives of himself and his children. Then, it will grow in the ensuing years like an echo of light. All of this is because you are so good. *"Thank you, Mama. It is because of you."* I have told you in years past that one does not need to destroy his identity to become like Jesus, and I am telling you today that one need not relinquish his humanity either. Being human has countless dimensions, even though you live in a world of restrictive boundaries. Everyone is prone to speak of the limitless power of the mind, but even this is a subpart of the human heart in communion with the Spirit of Love.

Life on Earth does not need to always be about potential being transitioned into substance. Being human in the way of Jesus means that the whole definition of potential is transformed into sacred energy that can permeate time and space. There is not so much a continuum on which time and space reside, but a multi-dimensioned perpetuation that transcends the origin of man. This originality is as spaceless and timeless as the Father deigns it to be. Why? Because as I said in recent messages, there has never been a time when God did not exist. And, there has never been an instant when the love of God did not prosper. Humanity is part of the latter. The idea of conceiving and growing are parts of eternity in the same way that Jesus has always been the Second Person of the Holy Trinity, even prior to His Nativity from My Womb. I am not trying to blur the lines about the Salvation history that men have been taught for ages, but to, in some way, implicate the timelessness to which your bygone forebears have gone. They have all seen what I am describing to you now; and the most faithful men on Earth, those like you and your brother, are likewise so informed. This does not mean that you do not see the same sun and moon every day and night. You are not separated from the Faith-Church in which you are members, but you have a sense with which you can envision the gloried Church-Triumphant in Heaven. This, in reference to the quotation of the Dominion Angels to begin our message today, is the humanity that you need not renounce on your journey in the Cross. My Special son, only a sparse few Christians have ever viewed their faith the way that I am describing to you now. But, it has not been their fault. There have been too many monotonous days, too many distractions, too much earthly commotion that keeps them from entering into such deep spiritual meditation. So, I am asking everyone to enter it the way that I have described it here to you and your brother. My little sons, I have not told you about sanctity, power, meaning and purpose over the past several months just to indicate to you that human life is greater than what you see. I share these things because I wish to heighten your hopes. I have never once in any location on Earth asked My hearers or visionaries to become disengaged from the practical aspects of daily life. I have not requested them to become detached from what they must do to remain self-sufficient and capable of logical thought. I am offering a design of preparation for what will eventually come into the pious heart. There is a certain consciousness that accompanies the 'conscience' with which humanity encounters the passages of life. These must work together to compose the holy architecture of the Christian soul. Nowhere has Jesus ever asked you to renounce your humanity. He says that He would like to reside in your heart to help you to love. He desires to take you aloft when your thoughts and actions descend deep into dark valleys. He is your Godly wisdom when men are burdened by both benign and malevolent ignorance.

    Christ Jesus asks His disciples and apostles to allow Him to permeate their being to perfect who they are, not to eliminate who they are. This does not mean that it is wrong for someone to say that, '...it is not for me to live, but for Christ.' Assimilation into the glory of the Father means that the self-will comports with the Will of God in every way so that human beings become His holy likeness, but not gods themselves. This proves that the Creator and His creatures are capable of coexisting as in the first moment when the Father breathed life into Adam. My Special son, there has always been a romance between God and His Church. The Father does not desire that men renounce the humanity to which they were given because He created them with distinction. Indeed, it is on the inside that God has been yearning to deliver His children unto Himself. They must acquire the holiness of Jesus, no matter their race or place of life and death. It is upon this summit that the mission of the Church has stood; it is here that I have focused My sights. All the anonymous faces that you mentioned when sitting at the Kona, Hawaii airport are those whose spiritual identities you will eventually know. This is a gift for everyone who believes, all who comprise the family of man who will be reunited in the Messiah to whom you have dedicated your life. It is not about turmoil or wars or grievances between nations. It has never been about profit, currencies or bartering or exchange. It is about fusing the human with the Divine in Jesus on the Cross; and the world is closer to this blessing now than yesterday, last week or millennia ago. It is to celebrate the grand procession about to come, people assembling as one, forming a sacred movement to redemption that began the moment Jesus was conceived in My Womb. As Moses gave way to Gabriel, I am your advocate commissioned by the Holy Spirit; and Jesus of Nazareth will have the final word. My Special son, you must believe what I am telling you here. What you and your brother have said and written during your lifetime has foretold what the Son of Man will pronounce when He finally comes again. He will avow your faith and distinction. He will resound what you have declared about peace, justice and virtue. He will smile the same way you have smiled with love inside your hearts. I have said that nothing will be wasted; there will be no good deed done in vain. As I am the Virgin who walked the Earth, who still lives here and in Heaven, I know what perfect human creatures are like. You are as much like Jesus as anyone whom the world might imagine."

Saturday, September 26, 2015
9:17 a.m.

"Transparency, propriety, accomplishment and consequence – donning the chasuble of Christian virtue. These are the things we must examine, or we risk remaining just mysterious, anonymous, elusive creatures to God."

- William L. Roth

"Good morning, My dear little sons. What you are speaking about is your awareness that humanity must become saturated in the Lord's Divine Grace. It is clear that a well-thought approach to Christian life is that it is self-examining, not counterproductively, but to calculate the deficits and excesses that must be measured against Jesus' suffering. This is the reason that Christians, especially lay-persons, put on Jesus like an invisible chasuble. It is a spiritual immersion in the beauty of the Cross, overlaid upon the glory of Easter Morning. My Special one, it is indeed correct that men must make themselves recognizable to God in the form of transparency, as backward as it sounds. There must be propriety to one's holiness by equating it with the mission of the Church. Yes, there must be an examination of the consequences of all these things so that virtue becomes the overriding aspect of the converted soul. One cannot exemplify something unless he understands what it is about. This is the sacred chasuble that you wear every day, and it is this chasuble that the Father looks for in those who claim to be His. It is a light in the night, a beacon in the darkness, a flame in a world lacking holy fire. Imagine if you would have seen a spiraling cherry blossom tree along the road when you were driving at the desolate lava-covered foothills of Hawaii. This is how the Christian soul is recognized by God. It is the way that He is drawn to His disciples. I have spoken about the reciprocity between Heaven and Earth many times. Even while speaking in parables, the truth about Jesus' mandates was transparent to those with faith to believe in Him. He called all who would be saved to make a difference in rendering the world more righteous. And, Jesus overwhelmingly told humanity what the consequences would be if they rejected His Sacrifice as their eternal redemption; we are seeing this play out today. The universality of the role of exiled men in the transformation of the Earth cannot be overstated. It is the reason that I keep speaking to you here. It is the reason that I have given My Medjugorje children their secrets to share when Jesus says the time is right. It is the reason I spoke about Saint Matthew's Cathedral and the signs from Mexico to Billings to Canada. There will be a recognizable revelation of these things when the fullness of My earthly messages has been revealed. My Special son, if the proverbial image of the splendor of men is to include their own contributions, then they must do more than just pose for the final portrait of the world. It must be true that humanity makes your own brush strokes to instill into that eternal image your own gifts to God. These are among the accomplishments that you cited at the opening of today's message. Also today, it seems fitting that I speak about the visit of Pope Francis to the United States. Let us pray for him, for all who must hold to the teachings of the Church, for the many who stray from these teachings, and for the millions who will be touched by what the Papacy represents. I believe that this is what your brother was sharing when he said that he has fallen in love with the Papacy. He sees the miracle and the majesty of the Vicar of Christ. He is touched by the response of the hundreds-of-thousands of pilgrims who wish to be blessed by the Pontiff. Papal visits always do this. The Vatican is called the Holy See because it is through the Roman Catholic Church that one's foretaste of Heaven is preserved and clarified.

I am the Mother of the Church, and you have heard Me speak about trying to keep all the little kittens in the box. A United States senator said yesterday that it was like trying to tend to a wheelbarrow full of frogs. The point is that people will not hold still long enough to listen to what the Holy Spirit has to say. They are much too ego-stricken and fooled by their sense of self. They believe that whomever reaches the end of life with the most possessions is the winner of the game. We know differently because we see 'value' through a different set of eyes. We are capable of knowing what the most important issues should become, and we know that there is not an infinite number of years in which to address them. Our prayers unearth what must be cleansed. It is not that a seer's predictions might be accurate or inaccurate, but that humanity realizes the evolution of world conditions based on the service of prayer. This is the real message that must be conveyed. I have promised that nothing said from the

Kingdom of Heaven will ever be untrue. It is simply whether the world responds or does not respond that determines the future. My Special son, I believe that your brother is doing better with his contemplations of obedience. However, the devil keeps getting in the way because of the power that would be unleashed against him. Your brother has not conceded defeat. He will continue this fight until he draws his last breath. It is all about giving Jesus the joy of knowing your love and trust in the ways He has prescribed. Your brother continues to be rejected for employment because of the good that you and he have done. We pray and watch the world; we soften human hearts, become aware of the forces and issues that might bring you and your brother to danger, and we move day by day closer to the Second Coming of the Son of Man. All in all, it is a good life that you share here together. What I see is more moving than anything capable of relocating a planet in outer space. I see such providence in the actions of men that it defies the imagination. I am privy to the insights of the great ones like you and your brother. I know what builds up on the inside of the human spirit that grows the potential of the whole world. I see universes unknown at the same time I see atoms and specks. Given to Me is the capacity to alter the perceptions of My children if they would only recite a single 'Hail Mary.' The Lord is good and powerful. He is capable of bringing life to statues and glorying the simplest thoughts of a child. My Special son, Jesus has this power and providence. He is the incarnation of Wisdom and Truth. He is the pureness of consoling compassion, golden from the heart, not just gilded like those who would mock Him. And, this is Jesus who shares your journey here in your time and place. I carry Him in My arms and pray beside you before the Cross. This is the ultimate effect of mortal time. Goodness and mercy follow you not because men have earned them, but because God loves you to degrees incapable of being known. Seamless is the garment with which the Lord has covered you in His care, and this is where you find yourselves. My Special and Chosen ones, it is not a matter of visiting Popes or angelic choirs singing in the background. It has little to do with motorcades glistening in the sun with banners flapping in the breeze. The human heart is the vital fundament among these signs. It is what comes from the inside that changes what is seen with the eyes. There can be harmony if men will read from the same score. There can be peace if warring factions vow to embrace it. These are the blessings for which I pray. And, My Special son, any more books that you wish to publish containing My messages from 2010 forward will be continuing gifts to the world, but not necessary for what you and your brother have accomplished for Me. They would be bombs atop of arsenals, and additional layers of grace. It is true that all who give themselves to Jesus will see the Promised Land. What must be endured are the inevitable and inexorable struggles that are faced along the way."

Saturday, October 3, 2015
9:40 a.m.

"Are we actually waiting for the exiled world to somehow right itself of its own accord without the cooperation of men? Do we still question the fact that Jesus Christ can correct it through us? Denial about these things is like believing that a bygone Christian soul cannot be resurrected. We are far more intelligent people than that. The revitalization of humanity is all about nails, lashes, bloody thorns, sacraments of purification, voided vendettas and purged transgressions. It is about the total abandonment of worldliness and dying to the self – sacrifices that never imply irrelevance or separate us from being wholly alive. This is how Christianity transforms the Earth, preserves innocent life and propagates the dignity of the human person."

- William L. Roth

"More than anything else I could ever express to you, My little sons, is that I love you. I have spoken about the issues that you mentioned in your quotation this morning, My Special son. I have given due time and full course to all the sacrifices, purifying Sacraments and forgiveness accorded to all believers. I have drawn the distinctions between darkness and light. Yes, I have even expressed the urgency with which all men should align themselves with the teachings of the Gospel to give their hearts to God. Even still, beyond all this, the most important of My proclamations is that I love you. I have come on this beautiful fall morning to share with you My gladness that we have come upon these days. Every time I speak about the peoples of the world being patient in the pursuit of the refining chords from Heaven to be heard here on the Earth, I refer to the same patience required by the Lord on His Throne in Heaven. It would seem that the people of the nations keep asking the Father what He is waiting for. Why does He not intervene in more prevalent ways? And, this is the question of God in Heaven. What is humanity waiting for? Why have they not accepted the Son of Man, borne into their own identities the Fruits of His Crucifixion, allowed the Holy Spirit to burden them with freedom's strains of righteousness, and caused the human heart to open for the coming reckoning dawn? It is not a stalemate; it is a process of recognition. Men must learn to know their Creator through His New Covenant Gospel, and the Lord must recognize the presence of His Son within those who pray to be redeemed. This is not as though two strangers have never met; it is about reconciliation. It is what we have been praying for all along. My Special and Chosen ones, this process of recognition is occurring now; it has been part of your lives from the beginning. Where there is prayer, there is potential. Where there is potential, there is growth. And, where there is growth, there is change. I am not disheartened by what I see because I have witnessed My Son's victory over sin. It is this vision that I am sharing with you now. Nothing can dampen the spirit of hope that I have dispensed through My messengers whose prophecies are wrongly claimed to be untrue. The whole matter is meant to make evident that prayer can change anything. It is to right the wrongs that you have mentioned in your petitions. And, My Special son, I will tell you that your deposit of Marian works has not reached a stagnant place within the Church, it is just that there are those in the Church, as you know, who are like boulders we must push uphill relating to anything having to do with My maternal revelations. I realize that you have always accounted for the timing of these things.

And, I know that you and your brother wonder how someone like Father Gobbi and other messengers' lifetimes of work could be cast aside because of questions about an insignificant series of words. This happens because people who doubt always look for reasons to defend their doubt. But, those who believe in My messages use ambiguous moments to strengthen their faith through the nourishment of the Holy Spirit. I refer you to Jesus' Agony in the Garden. He never entertained a single thought about not being crucified the next day, but He still reflected upon why the world did not believe who He was. Where was their faith in their own day to trust Him, even in light of the endless miracles that He performed, that He was the Son of God? I am not saying that My messengers are like Jesus' Agony in the Garden. The Earth is living in the aftermath of the worst tragedy and greatest miracle in the history of the world – the Crucifixion and Resurrection of Jesus Christ. This is the year in which you live, that encourages belief, one that provides the right-of-way to cite the Crucifixion and Resurrection as the backdrop for everything divine. You and your brother, and the hundreds and thousands of others throughout the ages who have communicated the Gospel to the nations, are among those who are informed and sustained by Jesus' Agony in the Garden. It was a period of anticipation for sure, but also the precedent to the victories and triumphs that are happening today. The point I am making is that lost sinners might still continue to disbelieve, but you are standing on the shoulders and the Cross of the Crucified One who tread before you the very steps that seem so difficult now. Any authentic messenger who may seem to have become disgraced will regain the footing about which I am speaking. And, it is not so much about the messenger as the messages relayed. It has been the same for generations. Many messengers have not built-up a tenure of sacrifice and a sufficient deposit of works to foster belief among those who were doubters from the beginning. However, you and your brother have given to God through Me a sufficient library of writings that cannot be dismissed. I wish for you and your brother to recognize that the fruits of your lives have in themselves their own lives. I have said this before. The Catholic Church has established a commission to review My Morning Star messages. This is a great advancement, an outright miracle itself, but the boulder is still moving uphill.

My Special son, you and your brother may be getting a little older in years, but you remain valiant and strong. You are determined and capable of judging which matters should gain your attention. There are so many distractions during these days that are affecting the secular realms that it would seem impossible for the Gospel of the Church to be heard. The leftist progressives of the nations are trying to equalize the religions of the world, if not pool them all together. They believe that every form of faith has its own standing. We know differently. There is only one Savior, and His name is Jesus Christ. When you and your brother say, '…take us back there Lord…,' you are praying for the coming of Jesus in Glory. Never mind what the seculars think, for they are irrelevant. Jesus is standing beside you. He lives within you. And, He looks down upon you with compassion and encouragement. You follow Him on the path that He cleared for humanity centuries ago, and He walks alongside you in everything you accomplish in His stead. You often tell Me that it will take miracles to alter the face of the Earth. God believes the same thing. These miracles will come; they are being stored for revelation at the appointed time. I am only saying today that I pray that you and your brother will never lose heart. With Jesus inside, beside and above you, how can you lose? I am not saying that it never gets dark in the world and in your spirits; there is assuredly providence in that. But, it is then that you are closest to Jesus because He needed you retroactively with Him during His darkest times. My Special son, you know that I would never be a political partisan, but I am agreeing with you in everything you say about the way your country ought to be governed. In light of all the evil that is ongoing with radical violence, shootings and the rest, now is not the time to be taking away anyone's self-defenses. I even told you and your brother in your New Millennium messages to keep protection close at hand. The devil must be shown that his own tactics can be used against him. There are too many issues to discuss in our time about what all this means, but another example is the woman in your nation's capital who did everything she could to wrap herself around the Pope during his visit. She is another lost soul who is on track to deny her own redemption before the Son of Man someday. We must pray for her, but not show pity if she does not respond. (*The woman to whom Our Lady referred is a powerful member within the United States House of Representatives who is a rabid advocate of abortion, who publicly professes her Catholicism at every politically beneficial occasion. She is under the influence of the Antichrist.*) I am asking you to pray for these souls, not despising them, but despising what they believe and do. I have given one message spanning many years, but it would seem that it has been millions of syllables long! Bless you and your brother for your enduring love."

Saturday, October 10, 2015
9:23 a.m.

"The Lord's divinity rests within us, not hidden somewhere beyond the arbors on the farthest side of the skies. The Father reads like classics what the sunbeams have to say about the disciples on whom He depends to share His holy word. We live together not just where the lofty eagles fly or decorated soldiers stand out like wildfires in the night. This is whom we have become within Jesus' Sacred Kingdom, our hearts holding out hope like crystal vessels rattling on broken humanity's shelf, poised inside our Savior miraculously raised from the devil's fatal assault. This is the pinnacle of our faith. It is our reason for dancing in the streets. It is the integration of our vision, hope, love and freedom. It has fostered the resurrection of our souls. And, even with all this stateliness, there is more than simple meek and mildness here. There are more than shifting embers of wisdom burning in the bellies of the High Priest's devoted flock. We who are consecrated to the Cross are capable of mounting a torrid defense of the absolute biblical truth. We are indomitable characters and unyielding conquerors who are witnessing God vouching for the signature of the Church. Never mind the lion herds; their courage cannot compete with ours. These are our principles; they are the songs that keep our lives attuned to the timbre of the years. This is the way we live because piety becomes us; unity is our purpose, and our oath to the Cross is our final battle cry."

- William L. Roth

"My Special son, your sentiments today are likely the most beautiful and meaningful than any you have composed. I give you My Immaculate Heart, My eternal being, My motherly affection, and all the blessings for which anyone might pray for your devotion to Jesus. This is not just some simple 'thank you' that I am offering today, it is a response to your invocation of the Holy Spirit to heal the world. I know Jesus more than anyone else, and I have seen what He can do with meditations such as yours. He will sustain life and preserve peace because of your prayers. The divineness in your heart and the civility of your intentions are like calling cards at the doorway of everlasting truth. The Father hears you, and the whole world will soon hear from Him. I am today speaking to you and your brother because the Lord still wills it. While we have this time together, it is clear that you are taking to heart everything you are learning from your faith in God. This is the way of all the disciples who have taken up their crosses in the image of His Son. You and your brother are rendering to this world the vastness of light that will open the eyes of millions. You have already done what Jesus asked of His Original Apostles. That is why this is a good day for Heaven; it is a propitious day for the exiled world, and it is an extension of the miracles that have thus far carried the Church through tumultuous times. My Special son, are you familiar with the phenomenon that occurs when someone looks at a sight or ponders a vision that they have not seen in an extended period of time? *"Yes."* You have the capacity for always seeing something new – a trait or seeming motion that was not apparent before. It is not that the sight or vision has changed, but that the seer's ability to discern what he is seeing is enhanced. This is what the Omnipresent Lord does of His own accord. Why? Because He renders the world more sightly by allowing humanity to be transformed through its own pious acts. God does not change. He will never change. However, while maintaining constant vigilance over His earthly domain, He softens His image of the created world, focuses on the effects of His overwhelming love, and looks back upon the exiled realms of men to see what they are doing. In other words, the Father sees humanity's world in a different way than the early days of ancient dungeons and stalking dinosaurs. He is more focused on the lands where you walk today than when it was just wildlife and prairies. This is somewhat like the way humanity engages God at times, but it is not an inappropriate thing. People on Earth face the pragmatic realities of life in a material world. Problems must be solved, and children must be fed. It is natural to be responsible in these ways with the gift of Jesus' eternal love always present in the heart of the believer. You know that Jesus did not become separated from the secular world when He lived on Earth. Jesus made His way into the secular precincts because He always looked for those whom He could touch in His ethereal way – practical for sure, but devoted to the Spiritual Truth that was incarnate in Him. This is part of the give and take between humanity and the Father that I spoke about in our recent messages; this is the fine tuned relationship, the smooth running vernacular that powers humanity's interaction with Heaven above. Men must solve the world's problems with uniquely divine solutions.

Turn the face of exiled men toward the Light of Divine Grace, and they will see their lives, their sights and visions, in new ways every time. This is not just a recycling of previously exposed envisionments. It is the remaking of the human perception of life in a way that sanctifies the identity of the perceiver. This is how Jesus' identity suffices the human identity in such a way that amends the will of men in favor of the Will of God. My Special son, I have watched this process for 2,000 years. It is never easy for intellectuals or those who hold positions of social power and public influence. We know this from our conversations about certain Christians, especially Roman Catholics, whose secular thoughts and actions are not aligned with the teachings of the Church. There is too much temptation to concede to the offering of social, personal, psychological and monetary gain to remain in a life of humble discipline. However, this is where the image about which we have spoken arrives at the portico of the heart. The entire Gospel is a picture of this – all four accounts describe in thousands of words what one image reveals. You know that My favorite Gospel account was written by Saint Luke. Yes, there are multiple, even innumerable renditions of the same image that can be drawn from the words of the four Gospelers, and this is the way it should be. This is humanity's response to the Father taking countless views of the same world. Time does not move for God; there are no Big Bens in Heaven. However, each moment, every hour, all the days and nights combined are like snapshots that God sees of Creation below. This is an effect of His Eternal Will because He deigns it to be. It is not that He is lacking in memory or that He cannot refocus on something that has passed before His eyes. There is no sequence of events in Heaven because everything is eternally present. The good Lord does these things not to change Himself or reset the architecture of Heaven. He does these things because of what exiled men on Earth commit to Him. When you pray, God takes another look. When you are in pain, He sets out to ease it. When He sees too much darkness for wicked men to see where they stand, He sheds more light on their cold-heartedness and allows them to see it for themselves. If there is a great divide between someone's soul and the Hearth of Heavenly Fire, God is more prone to allow the soul to make the leap of faith than reach out and grab him. But, if someone's conscience trends in God's way, He will never let them fall into the divide. If they lean in His direction, His breath alone will keep them upright. This is how the human person is responsible for accepting the Cross of Salvation and deferring to the Gospel to the diminishment of their own desires.

My Special and Chosen ones, prayer is made up of these things. It is taking a serious look at humanity and the world, and imagining it appearing another way. It is more than just wishing, it is willing along with Jesus that His Kingdom will become more wholly revealed. The responsibility for conversion rests inside the human heart, but once conversion takes place, the Dominion of God does the rest. This is how people who fall in love with Jesus cannot help it. They are so identified with the Cross and the Church that they become the two legs on which they stand. This is where the flowering garden of reconciliation begins to grow – reconciliation between men on Earth and with God in Heaven. How eloquent this is! What words might I use to give you a concise picture of the story of the Prodigal Son? There are no means to describe it. It is a vision that must be seen with the heart, that renders speech irrelevant. There is a glimpse of this glory within you when you see acts of love on Earth. Yes, when the fastest runner is indeed allowed to win. When the skies above are brighter because of the spiritual dawn than munitions bursting in air. If a little child can understand these things, My Special and Chosen ones, why cannot leaders of nations make it their pledge? The answer is that they are filled with the same pride that felled Adam and Eve. I find Myself always talking with My messengers about what the future may bring, as if to say that the future is the only thing that matters. I mentioned this to you in another recent message too. It is during the here and now that faithful men should pray. I am not saying that you must take today's message and begin dispensing it on the street because telling you what I just said is prayer enough. Asking God to mend this sorely broken world is sufficient to invoke His response. Here, at this moment, is when the Father is looking at you anew. He never stops seeing what we do. He never has. His perpetual gaze shall forever be upon us, but the intensity of His watchful eye is heightened when we invoke His Holy Name and summon the intervention of the Son of My Womb. This is the origin of the glory for which men seek. It is the balm for all wounds, the enlightenment for every question, the resonance of every sacred syllable, the gift for all who ever yearned in any way to be given something blessed. My little sons, it is the love of God and everything He Wills to the infinite degree. It is the power of the Holy Cross that is immeasurably deposited within the open human heart. It is the rescuing of a nation from the clutches of evil that has been trying to devour it for 240 years. It is joy and faith and power and invincibility – all the unseeable things that could never before be known by the human mind, let alone laid breadth and length on a roadway bed or tabletop. This is the limitless wisdom that humanity holds in the palm of its hand, richly waiting to be taken from atop the cliff beyond that spiritual divide.

My Special son, you once heard an eloquent speaker say that this was his faith; this was the faith that he would return to the South with. It would be a grand day and rightful moment that a nation would live out the promises it had made. This is the only thing that God asks of His Church. God begs, beseeches and desires that those who claim to believe in Him live out their profession of faith. It is not something that is 'just there.' It is not another issue that must be resolved before nightfall today. This is the faith that must be lived and protracted into a world that is fraught with peril and under the influence of outright evil. It transcends night and day, awakenings and sleeping, the daily musters that are plied to bypass due responsibilities, and the politics and policies that serve only those who write them. I have said that humanity must take another look at God by reevaluating the substance of its heart. It is right because it gives new life. My Special son, I will respond to the question you have for me now. *"Why is Timmy starting to be attacked with these horrific visions and translocations again?"* Because the world is sinful, and your brother is doing his part to cleanse it. Satan abhors someone's allegiance to the Lord Jesus Christ. Your brother needs to go forward in confidence that love will always be his constant companion. He has said during these attacks that you and Jesus are his strength – and in that order. Jesus believes this to be an admirable poise. The Lord will respond affirmatively to your prayers to stop these attacks on your brother. Jesus loves you."

My brother, in recent years, has been enduring horrific mystical attacks by the devil. They are literal, real and horrific. He has been translocated by the devil into alternate states of existence where he has had horrors of unimaginable magnitude thrust upon him. I have found him writhing in bed, covered in sweat, shaking in terror, but not awake or yelling out. I have watched him experiencing these horrors, and comforted him after he is released back to the world. He has told me that when he is in these places, it is as real to his body and senses as if he is present in normal life. It is not just a dream sequence. During these times, he does not have any sense of his life in the normal world in which we live. He has not only been forced to witness inconceivable atrocities and slaughters against men, women and small children, but he has been physically tortured as well. He has been boiled in oil, thrown into fires, beaten and scourged, run through with swords, placed on the rack, disemboweled, thrown off cliffs, as well as many other tortures and horrors that I am reticent to mention. It is only by the supernatural grace of God that his mental constitution remains intact after being subject to these experiences. I have encouraged him to record all of this, but he asks me what purpose it would serve; and he tries to hide it. It is all about reparation for the sins of men, the continuation of our work with our Holy Mother, and protecting the Church's ecclesial discernment from Satan's demonic influences. Oh what a price that must be paid! The Power in the Cross is the firewall that Satan cannot push through. Mystical gifts come and are maintained only by the diminishment of the flesh, and the grace of God flourishes throughout the world through suffering in union with His Son.

Sunday, October 18, 2015
9:32 a.m.

"Verily, we cannot question God's desire to plant within us the seed of the Church, the Lord Jesus Christ, Himself. It is not possible that a crop of this magnitude can remain unattended in our hearts. We must depend on the Holy Eucharist to be our fresh and fervent nourishment if we expect to weather the vile elements, cruel nature and undue punishments of the dark secular void. It is incumbent upon us to do this as God's endeavoring explorers; growing in faith, maturing in love, and reaching for His hand. This is the way we will inherit His Glorious Kingdom. I adore the idea of sainthood. I find tremendous peace and joy in it. There is a rare anti-catastrophic tenor of new majesty in realizing that we will someday sit beside the Son of God and talk about the inexhaustible eternities that prevailed long before the Earth and organic life ever began. Yes, Saint Georgette or Robert or Lennie or Loretta or Wilhelm. Saint John XXV or Saint Galaxy or Saint Saber – anything that identifies us as people of Heaven situated alongside the most grand skies, assemblies, constitutions, contexts and geographies that the good Lord Jesus has to offer. This is not just hope on our part, it is the expectation of a just and due reward that rightly belongs to us. It is the reason we must nurture our conviction, stand sure in battle, and continue singing our songs of repentance that Jesus first fell in love with. This is when our melodies of life sound their best, when humanity rocks the night with sweet confessions of victory that appeal to the Father's most forgiving ear. He listens and hears us shouting out from the rooftops of the Earth, sending down from beyond the sacred vaults an occasional gift of confetti upon our symphony of prayers, anointing us with His promise of redemption just as sure as the world's lighted lamps burn as one in Him."

- William L. Roth

"Thank you, My Special one, for writing another spectacular meditation about the Love of God, about your role in the proceeding ages, and about the wishes of Jesus to be your intervener between this world and the next. It is your spiritual hearts that glow, My Special and Chosen ones. This is the way that all will come to know the Father, to realize that a drop of submission is worth His Ocean of Mercy. I have come today to further our prayers for the conversion of the lost and ask your brothers and sisters to prostrate themselves before the Cross in the submission about which I speak. This is not in any way meant to diminish the dignity of man, but to increase man's awareness of the power of the Cross in the redemptive cause. You must believe that redemption does not take place in this world, but your preparation for redemption does. My Special son, this is what your writings always make clear. You are a contemplative Christian who, like many, are struggling against the elements of a non-spiritual Earth. The very nature of the world stands in contradiction to the Spirit when humanity ignores its origin in God. My little sons, I remain vigilant for you against the evils that are attacking you. I pursue gladness and justice on behalf of My children by asking Jesus to set things right. When it seems that this is not happening, it is because Jesus wants to draw you closer to Himself by sharing with you the throes of the Cross. It is not that you are called to be co-messiahs; that will never happen. But, He wants the world to recognize His eternal love within the boundaries of time. It could be done no other way because human sin requires the cleansing of humanity itself. Yes, Jesus has made you perfect in His Crucifixion. By dying, He has destroyed your death. These are the simple rudiments that children learn from a quite young age. And, what men on Earth must know as they grow older is that the framework of exiled life must be placed in the doorway to the next life; and this is indeed the Crucifixion. When we speak and write about Jesus being the Way, the Truth and the Life, we tell all the universes that their immeasurable expanse is not intimidating to you. In Christ Jesus, you have already conquered time and space. They are creations, but not creatures. They lack the adaptability that you as new creatures inherit in Jesus on the Cross. It is the same for the sun and moon, and all the stars. Even though you are not their maker, you have inherited them and all their storied facets by virtue of your faith in God. They belong to you because you hold dominion over everything that the Father has given in your allegiance to His Will. My Special son, these are the verities that you and your brother have always known, but they seem like foreign languages to those who are far from God. When I first came to Medjugorje and greeted the children there, I arrived to speak 'with' them as much as to speak 'to' them. I solicited their responses. This is not so much an inversion of the conversation between the Lord and His people as an inclusion of the participation of humanity in redefining the Earth. You and I have been articulating this definition because of the very defining moments that we have shared since you were both little boys. The first thing I recognized about humanity once I was assumed into Heaven is not how much pain people are in, not how blind they are to what they must know, but that lost sinners seem unwilling to ask. The world lacked curiosity about its spiritual beginnings. There were plenteous questions about how the Earth and the universe were first formed, and men for thousands of years have been trying to answer them. But, there seemed a complete lack of wonder about the spiritual setting within which these spatial realms reside.

The setting about which I am speaking, My Special son, becomes lost in everything else to which humanity is exposed. You may remember through the years that I have asked you to listen to various melodies to make My point. I have one ready for you now, and I want you to specifically listen for the broaching symphony in this song. Hear the strings that support the voice. Please listen for the majesty about which you spoke in your opening meditation today. (*Our Lady had me listen to a song that exemplified Her discussion. It was a rendition of 'The Power of Love'*). My dear Special son, it is clear that the strings in this piece are the purpose for the song. The singer, the lyrics and the harmony have limited dimensions without the underlying orchestra. This is the point that I have been trying to make to humanity for 2,000 years. There is sacred beauty in everything that supports and reveals what is seen with the eyes. If someone understands this, My Special one, then they have more than just a vague comprehension of the purpose of life. They are capable of seeing the 'location' of life in the Father's divine plan. All good things are drawn to Him, and He implores all goodness to be reasoned by Him. And, where within the realms of human existence is this accomplished? In Jesus! This is where the identity of man becomes fashioned, finalized and reconciled with God. I again ask you, My Special son, to remember that I realize that I am not telling you anything that you do not already know. I am taking advantage of the sights and sounds of everyday life in attempt to make it clearer to your friends, peers and even your enemies where they stand in the vastness of Creation. I am sharing My knowledge with you so that you will know more about Me. You came to Jesus even before you reached the age of reason. This occurred when you were baptized. I am simply giving you and your brother deeper insights about who I am, and how I see My children in the Faith-Church still struggling to live out their lives. I am aware that Christianity is often a hard fought peace because nearly everything on Earth stands in contradiction to what the Gospels teach.

I am speaking about the combination of sight and sound culminating in someone's perception of God. It is a product of the senses for sure, but it is more a matter of handing the human will to Jesus in exchange for the supernatural aspects of the earthly experience. As we have known, human existence does not end here in the world. It cannot, nor should it, because the whole idea of living cannot be contained in the limited depths of the universe or vague expressions of human thought and action. Simple love the way you know it is a subpart of the extraterrestrial love to which all men are drawn when their hearts and sights are invested in God. He can make the human heart grow in truth and wisdom not by inflating it with the innate secrets of the world, but with divine knowledge of Himself. This is beauty and divinity on a miraculous level. You and your brother have known this for decades, but others have been distracted by human voices over the background symphonies of the beauty, power and relevance of the Will of God. I have told you in many messages how you have been admired for this. And, when you reflect profoundly as when you spoke the meditation with which we began our message today, you share your grasp on this underlying warrant of faith to which the world's people are being called. It is the ending of someone's worldliness and the beginning of their identity in God. I will expound on this in the future, but I wished to tell you about it today. This is My way of sharing with you My loyalty to the Father. We are one in Him through the power of the Holy Spirit. I am appreciative that you are praying with Me for all the wrongs that you see every day. It means more than I can relate in words."

Saturday, October 24, 2015
No message

Saturday, October 31, 2015
No message

"Her ways are ways of pleasantness, and all her paths are peace."
- Proverbs 3:17

"Everything comes down to authenticity. God sees worldly fame the same way we see someone rich with Monopoly money."
- William L. Roth

Saturday, November 7, 2015
9:10 a.m.

"Detractors, critics, cynics, naysayers and doubters."

"My precious little sons, the poverty of the English language prohibits Me from sufficiently expressing My joy and gratitude for the way you have lived.

Jesus is righteously pleased by your service to the Church and humanity because He has always been inherent in you. Your views and judgements are fashioned by the Holy Spirit. My Special son, I am filled with admiration because of your persistence to accomplish your goals with complete and utter excellence, not that perfection is required, but that you have been willing to seek the best in everyone beneath your charge. I wish for you and your brother to remember that none of the individuals we mentioned as we began speaking today will inhibit our ability to finish our work. It is to this work that you and your brother have diligently set your hands; and the Father, Son and Holy Spirit will ensure that you prevail. Any opposition in the form of those outlined at the beginning of My message will be overwhelmingly put down. I am calling My children to the Cross with concise vision despite that they are embroiled in such secular controversies. It is much like examining the solar system. My Special son, when humanity ponders the solar system, what is the first thing that comes to mind? "*That it is bigger than them.*" Indeed, but the answer that I am looking for is 'planets.' The bodies and spheres in outer-space are the first image that enters the mind. In other words, they tend to look at the system before considering its point of life-sustaining light. The planets circle the sun. What is taught about the solar system is that it consists of a certain number of planets, and then these teachings grow further from there into other universes unknown. Mankind examines the solar system and what lies beyond; scientists' momentum of thought flows away from the sun. This is what exiled humanity wrongly does with God. The Lord is most prevalent because He is the brightest star in the heavens. I know that you will extrapolate the remainder of the story from here. I would also like to share with you a certain anthem that I have never told you about before. There is a uniting factor between men and God in the anthem that clarifies the focus that men should follow. I will share the anthem with you now." (*Our Lady presented the song, 'I Vow to Thee, My Country' sung by the British people at the Festival of Remembrance*).

> I vow to thee, my country, all earthly things above,
> Entire and whole and perfect, the service of my love;
> The love that asks no question, the love that stands the test,
> That lays upon the altar the dearest and the best;
> The love that never falters, the love that pays the price,
> The love that makes undaunted the final sacrifice.

And there's another country, I've heard of long ago,
Most dear to them that love her, most great to them that know;
We may not count her armies, we may not see her King;
Her fortress is a faithful heart, her pride is suffering;
And soul by soul and silently her shining bounds increase,
And her ways are ways of gentleness, and all her paths are peace.

"My little son, they speak of another country that they heard of long ago. They are singing about the Kingdom of God. They are referring to their loyalty to the country in which they live and the new 'country' in which they shall forever rest, the Kingdom that is slowly growing one soul at a time. I simply wished to share this beautiful anthem with you because it is a prayer for the United States of America, the nation to which I have dedicated the Majestic Love of My Most Immaculate Heart. It is clear that you and your brother have given your hearts and prayers to your country and your God. If it be the Will of the Lord, I will speak to you long into the future, beyond the historic 25-year mark and into your senior years. *"Thank you. You mean so much to us."* If we continue into that quarter-century, do you suppose that I will have spoken to you and your brother for 300 months and 1,300 weeks? It should be a dynamic event in all accounts of human endeavors that the Mother of God has come to this world with such words and images to awaken the sleepy hearts of exiled men. There is a stirring that has been ongoing outside the awareness of billions of people worldwide. None of it shall ever be in vain. Fame and fortune cannot eclipse the responsibilities that all men have to their God in Heaven. Fame, as you say, is as useless as Monopoly money. There may be quick-wittedness and imaginings afar, but these are no match for the miraculous gifts from the Kingdom of Love. There may be the launching of a million more ships upon the glassy-top seas, but none of them dare approach the stateliness of the Mansions in the Promised Land. We have miracles to share here; they have only memories. We practice the redemption of the whole of the Earth; they seek its conquest. We own all the breezes that keep them cool, and we wrap our wisdom around the arbors under which they sit. We encircle everything they ever knew about living on Earth with songs of eternal life that they have never once imagined. This is the love of the Mother of God! Here then, My Special and Chosen sons, I have committed My prayers to the nations, especially this one, that all men will open their eyes at the behest of the Holy Spirit trying to find its way into their hearts. There is yet time to reveal everything that must be known – all the messages and secrets of Medjugorje, the brilliant volumes of love and eloquence in your Morning Star books and anthologies, all the meaningful new beginnings that have yet to unfold. We shall bask in the advent of these things knowing that the final word will be ours. It will be spoken by us to reveal the Will of God for the passing ages. A New World will come – a New World must come! The old world is broken. It is tarnished and exhausted. It is lacking in luster and imagination. Humanity does not have the capacity to resurrect its own history. My Special son, after so many years and hundreds of messages, you and your brother have full knowledge that you are riding the wave of beatific justice on which you were placed decades ago. You are at peace, and you are being carried on the wings of the High-Flying Paraclete throughout your days. Your destiny in Heaven has been assured, there is no question about that. Who else will join you there? This is the prospect that is not yet fully known. And, My Special son, I cannot sufficiently express the gratitude that I have in My Immaculate Heart for your allowing Me to provide to your nephew the miracle that he was seeking. This gift shall rise like the mustard seed and flood the Earth in charitable grace! It will be soon, and you will recognize it as being founded in your prayers of love this week."

Saturday, November 14, 2015
9:27 a.m.

"The brash and the beautiful, the notable and notorious, celebrity gone awry, needless fallen tears, ragweed forests, weary travelers, knighted warriors, birthing rooms and fledgling families, untold questions, tons of belly laughs, cosmic flares, fractured limbs, cordial greetings, friendship pacts, laudatory speeches, sour bourbon twists, blackberry syrup, roadrunners, something called freckles, and a thousand hidden jewels."

- The Dominion Angels

"I have come speaking to you again while we pray for the conversion of lost sinners. You, My Special and Chosen ones, are the reason why the thunder still roars through the valleys of human affairs. Your prayers and righteous actions give Jesus further inducement to travel the world, seeking Christians who will remain with Him until the end of time. I love you, My little children! I ask that you hold within you this knowledge, that you commit it to your memory as I will forever be committed to your lives. My Special one, do you remember when I once asked you to show Me the contents of your top dresser drawer containing your childhood artifacts? *"Yes."* Well, this comes from a long held practice of asking the Dominion Angels what is in their 'top drawer.' I inquire what they may have seen on a particular day in time as they sail around the world and back to Heaven again. The list of 'items' at the opening of this message is what they said they saw just yesterday. These are the things that they reported to Me. It would seem that they really do not know what freckles are! Nonetheless, their list sometimes continues almost endlessly; it would take a hundred years to speak it aloud. The point of this is that everything they cite describes the deep intricacy by which humanity lives on the Earth. Most are not dreadful things; they are just things. In perspective, they allow you to see why it is so difficult for men to take time for their relationship with God. They do so at the behest of the Holy Spirit when they are inclined, but the distractions that you often see cause them to look another way. There are endless signs and wonders to draw them back again. My little sons, please do not lose sight of your first Diary because it is where the seed of everything that follows was planted. It is overflowing with grace, wisdom and enlightenment. I ask that you go forward in knowing that God is manifesting the miracles that shall come from your devotional work to Jesus on the Cross. Jesus loves you so much that it cannot be described. His tenderness toward humanity is greater than anything imaginable. There is time for everything we have set out to do, indeed only a matter of time. My Special son, while you and your brother tend to your work, God is tending to His lost sheep because of your trust in Him. The term 'spiritual proxy' was generated to describe the way you speak to others in prayer whom you have never met, and will not meet in this life. You speak to God, and God speaks to them through His intercessional Spirit. If this were not true, there would be no multiplication of prayers or the inspiration of the heart. When we think about all the things that the Dominion Angels tell Me that they see every day, it is miraculous that as many lost sinners are drawn to the Cross as there have been.

I urge you and your brother to have peace in knowing that this sharing of prayer is one of God's great blessings; it is as though someone in an auditorium holding 200,000 people whispers and a second person hears it completely on the other side. This would seem impossible in human terms, but it is utterly casual in the Kingdom of God. His Will includes the ability of men to change the lives of people on far-flung corners of the Earth. There is a more overwhelming world unfolding now in which the one you see is merely a portion. It is for the human domain that we pray, that this domain will be connected with the Kingdom of Heaven so ardently that all distractions will fade away. Yes, this is the plan, but plans sometimes fail. You are witnessing the destruction of lives and property around the globe because of the evils of radical ideologies. It is not just that these outlaws need to be converted to the Cross that matters, but that they should be annihilated if they do not. They are bound for the pit of Gehenna because this is where they will ask to go. Their wish will be honored by Jesus on the last day.

Please do not presume that I am suggesting that not everyone can be converted to the Cross, but that these evildoers will judge themselves against the Crucifixion of Mount Calvary. Jesus will offer them the fullness of His Divine Mercy, and they will even further see the chasm between their lives and His Holy Sacrifice. Does this mean that not all evildoers will be cast into eternal perdition? Yes, because they will hear the prayers of the Roman Catholic Church at the moment they die. This is the reason I implore My children to pray for nonbelievers. If we convert just one soul standing before Jesus in judgment on the last day, then our prayers will have not been in vain. I cannot overstate that dying and deceased men and women ultimately judge themselves beside the Sacrifice of Jesus on the Cross. While the Crucifixion is both grotesque and beautiful, the sins of those who reject Him are infinitely more unsightly. Disobedience is the cause of sin. The capacity for accepting Jesus' death on the Cross is given to all mortal men. And, likewise given to them is the will to decide whether they are worthy of being forgiven. Hence, it is about the Mercy of the Crucifixion that My messages have always been. It is true that I have described horrible events and circumstances, but we rarely dwell on them. We spend the hours, days and years focusing on what must be the way of humanity, come the end of time. There is a sense of expectancy that surrounds your lives as Christians that enlightens you about the focus, content and outcome of every human event. This is the leap that men must take to accept the Will of God in the eternal realms. Going in a straight line may not be the shortest distance between two points in the mind of God because there are exceptions that are taken into account based on the degree of human contrition and one's willingness to repent.

You will never hear anyone say that the Crucifixion of Jesus on the Cross is an accidental bridge between the souls of sinful men and their destiny with the Father in Heaven. It would have been simpler for the Father to ask Moses to tell humanity that He alone would return in a few hundred years to judge the living and the dead. And, the world's tendency would have been to ask Moses that they would be judged against what. The Father preempted this question by having humanity judged against 'Whom.' This is Jesus, the fulfillment of the Mosaic Covenant and the Savior to whom all men must turn for redemption. My Special son, it would require everything that Jesus could muster, even His death on the Cross, to prove that He came into the world at the behest of God to save the souls of sinners. Truly, this is what the Church knows. It is the awareness of everyone who will find their absolution in Him. It is their inheritance of the Love of God that unlocks the door, their ability to see the truth amidst a barrage of lies, to walk upright when everything else seems so crooked. Jesus did not ask humanity to lay low out of fear of the unknown, but to prepare for His final judgement being brought upon them. He asks humanity to this day to get out of the way of God, to come to eternal understanding that the world as they know it is passing away. This is the substance of holiness. I am with you and your brother in every way, in this world and the next, by all means that would have you dancing with joy in knowing who you are. Your lives are eclipsed by the Dominion of the Father. It is not something that you can always see, but it is happening because you are so loved. You are pious, prudent, prayerful and virtuous here in this land. I will tell you these things until the entirety of humanity understands. I will always be with you, and I ask that you join Me in praying for the people of Paris. *"Please protect our country."* I will ask Jesus to favor your request and all the intercessions of the Catholic Church."

Saturday, November 21, 2015
9:32 a.m.

"Jesus taught the intricate details of leading the sacrificial life by speaking in swaths of symbolism. Appropriately, many of His more poignant parables were spoken in the rain. If men would listen to His voice today in convocation, trust and ardent prayer, the world would learn that peace in the heart can be just as quieting during life's most turbulent storms as when the skies bode well overhead. Joy in faith must become a priority of the 21st century Earth. Among all the frustrations humanity will ever face, struggling against spiritual darkness is one of the great battles of this century."

- The Dominion Angels

"Innocence is fully matured from the moment it is conceived."
- Jesus of Nazareth

"Today, My children, we harken to the beginning times, when we first began our messages two decades ago. We do this because I wish to reassure you that your peace, confidence and expectations remain the same. The years have not taken these from you. It would seem that there is so much turmoil around you and even within your lives, but there is only a different kind of turmoil, not a higher degree. You are living well into the 21st century, and the rancid secular squalor of human hatred and desperation are taking another course. I am with you just as Jesus prevails within you. You must remember what the Dominion Angels and the Son of Man have said to begin our message today. My Special son, there is peace among you that is as inspiring as ever before. You and your brother have remained together with Me throughout the years. Please know that what you are seeing in your lives and around the globe are only different versions of a world that denies the sacrificial life in Jesus to which the Dominion Angels have referred. We pray because we know that it will procure its intended effects. There is more to life than what you see with your eyes, and you are assisting Jesus in making great headway into places where His Spirit has been denied. There are some things that boil down to mind over matter, and this is the way you should view the turmoil surrounding you. I am not asking you to become callous about everything as a means of coping, but to adopt the mind of Jesus and discern what is worthy of your solicitude. If you place your thoughts around the globe, all the evil catastrophes, public attacks, disasters and destruction, you will be able to see the whole of what Satan is doing to shatter the lives of innocent people. I have told you in recent weeks what will become of these wretched souls if they do not repent. I am praying that Christians of good conscience will rise up against the demonic forces that are committing such atrocities around the world. My Special son, I wish that I could come to you and your brother and speak only about the tender things. It would be a miracle even greater than My presence here now if My messages were about the flourishing goodness that overwhelms the globe. You can see that I am like you – I simply desire that humanity share their lives with the touch of gentleness everywhere, waiting in joyful hope for the coming of the Lord. I have told you about the excellence that rises from the righteousness of those who believe in Him. It flows from inside the heart where the Kingdom of God rightfully lives. It is a manifestation of this excellence and the innocence that Jesus teaches. When someone becomes innocent upon their baptism and confession, they reach the fullest innocence that they will ever know because the Sacraments restore one's innocence to its original form. This is what Jesus has said; it is what must be maintained through the life of the believer. Bringing your baptismal gown back to Jesus unstained means that the exiled soul remains pure. There may be dark times and pitfalls here and there due to human fault, but the integrity of one's innocence through the Sacraments remains intact. And too, a fault is not always a sin. Imagine all the people through the ages who have cried, '...O' holy innocence! Please come back! Please come humble me! Give me your company and blessing once again!' It is this calling to which Jesus responds. He restores the innocence of the penitent and wipes from the record any residue of a life being anything other than sanctified. This is the Will of the Father; it is the way of the New World, and it will come here and now, and through all future times, because of the prayers that we are offering here today.

My Special and Chosen ones, I beseech you to not allow the secular void to diminish your joy. I know that it is often a daily struggle because not everyone thinks like you. However, millions of Christians do. The two of you are not alone in this world. There are souls around the globe who believe that they too are the only people who know what God seeks from exiled men. You do not speak with them because you do not know where they live; you are unfamiliar with their precincts and not privy to their secrets. Your unity in Jesus is being perpetuated nonetheless. You are working for the same Kingdom by establishing yourselves as one Church within His Most Sacred Heart. I realize the depths of your pain and frustration, and I ask all like you to allow Me to 'Mother' them in the way that I have wrapped My arms around you. I have come in your day. I have made this My pledge to you here. My Special son, I wish to close today by reminding you that you are the image of human clarity. You signal to the nations the Will of God by your obedience to His Son. What the Father desires for Creation is concisely articulated by you. The Kingdom that will annex the world in which you live is being expanded and adorned by your life of holiness with your brother. I have said that there are insufficient words to describe what this means to God. I can only say 'thank you' and 'bless you.' I can only offer My assurance that you must take heart in what you have learned, and try to live with peaceful thoughts as the future unfolds. Please do not allow lost sinners to dictate your level of happiness. Above all, please exercise the trust and confidence that you have shared with Me through the whole of your years."

Saturday, November 28, 2015
9:24 a.m.

"Truth, grace, peace and synthesis."

"My little sons, yesterday I saw two dozen people knocking one another unconscious, another several hundred stampeding, and untold numbers spending their borrowed money to purchase material items in the department stores and malls of America. This is what has become of the consumerism in your country. However, I come today in peace because those materials will surely perish. It is not unreasonable to say that those people will turn to the blessing of God's grace through their own suffering. My little ones, I come speaking in happiness today about truth, grace and peace because I knew that this is where I would find you. While there is a hierarchy about these things – truth leads to grace, which leads to peace – they cannot be separated. And, this is where synthesis is manifested. Recognizing the Glory of God must be accomplished by examining the fruits and virtues that He gives humanity, and it involves the combining of these gifts that comforts the souls of Christian men. It is a matter of what the Father chooses to do on Earth. It is much too beautiful a place to disassemble at the end of time, so it will remain within His sights forever. However, what new forms will it take on? What makes the world so corrupt at this time that will be sifted from it later? To answer these questions, there must be a distinction drawn between the Earth and the world. The Earth stands alone and predates man. The world is the Earth filled with exiled men. And in this way, the New Heaven and New Earth will be populated only by what is perfect in God's eyes and in Jesus' judgement. This is where you are going with Him now, and you are among those leading the charge against the cold corruption that stains the world. It is said that God will someday judge the Earth, and this is correct, but He will judge the Earth according to the deeds of men. Most importantly, the world will also judge itself. This leads into synthesis again. Everything you have ever known about the kindness of God and your relationship with Jesus has been a product of this synthesis. He beseeches His disciples to join Him in the Glorious Kingdom the way it should be. The life of Jesus bears out the fact that God invites humanity to be like Himself through His Son; and if this is not what Christians are doing, they have not gained a full understanding of the teachings of the Gospel. This is the mixture of spiritualism and physicalism that accompanies the blessings of truth, grace and peace. My little sons, everything you have known about the life of man has been imbedded in this synthesis. The Holy Spirit is the Advocate whom you have enlisted to help you recognize your own place in Creation; this is prayer in a global setting. The question would be to ask whether you are agreeable to this power vested in you, and your response would be affirmative. The second question would be if you are satisfied with the world the way you see it; not the Earth, but the world in which you live. And here, you would relate a negative response. In these two opposites, you are witnessing the energy for your synthesis. My claim for 2,000 years is that humanity refuses to practice reparative prayer because they are too distracted by everything else. Knocking people unconscious and trampling them underfoot proves this point. These sinners lack the ability to know the purpose of life, and it indicates their inability to understand the Will of God.

 My Special son, it is in you that I carry My hope because you are inspirited with the wisdom to envision the synthesis about which I am speaking and infuse it into the Church. This was your gift from Heaven long before I began speaking to you, and years before you first laid eyes on your brother or knew who he was. You were born with this special grace that has made possible on Earth and for the world the spreading of peace, reflecting the Cross from where you have derived your holiness. I am not saying that there are not other grace-filled people in the world, I am declaring that you have been called in your willingness to participate in this Gospel synthesis. Only few others in the world ever knew this – barely a cohort of Popes were aware. And, the fruits of your writings prove that you have superseded the mere understanding of God by exchanging miracles with Him. According to His Holy Will, you have persuaded Him to heal, remake and amend the world in such a way that exemplifies the bounty of the original Earth. You know where the nonsense lies that diverts groups and individuals from the faith that I have been discussing with you for over twenty-four years. I have called you Special not just because you were given life this way, but because you have fashioned an identity that is patently Special in the eyes of the Father. You have been a synthesizer in themes of holiness to which God is asking the Church to subscribe. What does this allow the rest of humanity to see? What is it that you and the Church, Pope John Paul the Great, and the Doctors of the Gospel share in common that sheds such daylight on what must eventually be revealed? You have given Jesus the proverbial best of rooms, your heart, in which to dwell with distinction in these tempestuous realms. You have learned lessons that He would have every Saint eventually know. And, you have personified everything that He addressed in His pastoral parables, spoken in stirring rains and garish sunshine alike, so that there would be a living example of His holiness during the past fifty-four years on the Earth. I know that you are humbled to be described with such robustness, but it speaks to the divine power of God as much as your willingness to participate. You will recall when we turned to your Bishop to speak about My messages to you and your brother, and he established a commission to examine them. My reaction was to say what this meant to Me. I excerpted this response from My words to Jesus when we were discussing your role in the conversion of the world in these times. Christ Jesus, My Special one, has described you as one of His apostles and avengers, in common with Saint Gabriel and Saint Michael. Your compliance with His Will is the result of your synthesizing the Apostles, Saints and Martyrs' identities into the individual you are today. From the cradle that first rocked you, I caressed your life within the palms of My hands. I prayed that you would allow Me to speak these words to you now. I joined with Jesus at your side as He watched you looking around the room. He cupped His fingers across your brow and proclaimed that a brave new warrior had been born. It was a blessed day because the demise of hatred would more swiftly arrive.

My Special son, as Jesus was Himself enriched by the gift of your birth, He asked the Father with emotion to spare you from the devil's snares, to ensure that you would come of age in a nation that seeks the renewal of its heart. The Son of Man received His wish, and the writings that you have been completing prove that God handed down the most epoch-making decision since Easter morning. My little one, all this happened because I asked it to be so. I desired a child who was so much like My Messianic Son that any difference would be impossible to measure. I have not inflated My description about who you are. I am telling you these things because you are too humble to conceive them on your own. If your brothers and sisters hear about My testimony today, they will want to be like you as well. Many are doing their part with honesty and service, but they have never really known why. As I have said, it is about the synthesis of truth, grace and peace. I am speaking about the joining of God's divinity and the holiness that He has instilled in you. The rest of the world has hardly begun, and this is why your writings are so premier for these modern times. I ask you and your brother to recognize who you have become beneath My stately Mantle in the presence of My Son. You have inherited My wisdom through the Holy Spirit, and you have been helped by the intercession of the Dominion Angels to feel the Heart of God. My Special one, I ask that you remember all the glory that you have given humanity through the years, everything that resolves spiritual dilemmas, all that flourishes humanity's devotion to Me and their consecration to the Most Sacred Heart of Jesus. Even with all the darkness and commotion in the world, life is beautiful when men lay their future in the hands of God. The Crucifixion and Resurrection of Jesus should be the bookends by which all men live. I will speak to you at the opening of the final month of 2015. It has been a year of glory and tasking, of learning and teaching, and of starlight and wonders."

Saturday, December 5, 2015
9:46 a.m.

"The Lord always has His finger on the pulse of the trans-located truth to measure the sanctified actions of men. We are prone to make mistakes because ill-willed people are constantly equating corruption with freedom. For a world that is supposed to be drenched in virtue, fortress humanity is often barely even damp, let alone wet. We far too often fight against ourselves with procrastination, incompetence, mismanagement, sleight-of-hand and spiritual apathy. And, we focus on too many wrong things. Rather than searching for solutions to global conflicts and overt evil works, we seem to concentrate on nonsensical issues like worrying about why our time clocks run so slowly, what penny stocks will best return our investments, and why gray aardvarks suffer from asthma. We owe the Gospel much more honesty than this. It is our irrevocable duty to maintain our oath as Christians by pledging the Son of Mary our undivided loyalties, diligence, submission, gallantry and endurance. There is evidence to believe that God may not assist us through our suffering and social upheavals until we do. Sometimes it appears as though Jesus would have us do more. By all means – it is not the fear of retribution from God, but the threat of the loss of our freedom that keeps good and decent people who want a more peaceful and moral society from taking matters into their own hands. This in itself may be the most notable testament to faith-based restraint. And, it is our prayer that good will and brotherly love will eventually win."

- William L. Roth

"My little sons, My presence here today praying with you for the conversion of lost sinners is a remarkable contrast to the vile, detestable and disgusting acts of violence and evil that are happening here in America and elsewhere around the globe. There is no question that this is always the case when the Holy Gospel of Jesus Christ is ignored. And, My Special son, your writing to begin our message today is straight from the Heart of God. I wish for you to know that these types of essays are like everything else you have written – they are prayers for changing the issues you write about. It is for the purpose of this prayer that you and I and your brother are together this morning. I ask that you forever remember My deep and abiding love for you. My Special son, I wish to commend you for the way you remain close with your brother – you have been this way for forty-two years. You give him the dignity that the rest of humanity denies him. You are his strength and help; you are his 'Jesus' here in this world. I lack the words to tell you what place you hold within the Sacred Heart of Jesus for everything you mean to your brother. I ask the two of you to remember that I have promised the effectiveness of your works on My behalf during a time when you will witness its effects. I have been reluctant to say that it may be beyond your passage into Heaven because I have always had more hope than that. Hence, I keep telling you that everything you have desired of your books will occur in your lifetime on Earth. This, too, is My prayer to Jesus. If it has been commitment that He has sought from you and your brother, He has already found it. The world will bend more by what we have done in the past twenty-four years than it would ever have bent under the pressure of secular indifference or outright evil works. My Special and Chosen ones, the fact that you are both living in this world is a testament to the Mercy of Jesus. Today therefore, I ask that you remember that there are practical issues that have always existed in the preparation of your books and anthologies. You have laced your lives with the bright and shining reflection of the sacred divine. You have given humanity reason to have hope as quietly as the sun rises in the morning. You have refused to surrender your lifelong hopes and dreams to the desperation that afflicts so many others. You are led by the Holy Spirit in your place beneath the Morning Star to whom all the nations must come for peace.

I have attempted on previous occasions to describe the fact that humanity is living backward – the way it should be. You are going back to the days of your innocence, even though you are growing older by the moment. This is the reason why good people feel strengthened by the beauty of flowers and the giddiness of children. It is the reason why pipe organs and jet airliners seem so stately. It is the desire of the human spirit to retain what beauty it can see and reclaim the innocence that has been lost. I am not saying that you will ever be babes in the crib again, but that you will have in you and between you the purity of the origin of Creation, directly from the hands of the Father in Heaven. I am saying that you will someday, and sooner than anyone on Earth knows, see the arena in the Lord's Kingdom from which all holy things come. I am saying that positioned inside Jesus' Sacred Heart is the seed of your beginning that will take the whole world back to the holiness in which it was first imagined. There are trellises there bearing more roses than a body can count. There are flittering creatures in such numbers that their commotion whips up a breeze. There is the expungement of sorrow, suffering and torment; and the reason they are taken away is inscribed on the door. This, My Special and Chosen sons, is why I ask you to hold onto your hopes. It is all about tomorrow you know, but all the tomorrows that could ever come cannot take their toll on the love that you share in your hearts today. The sacredness of your love for Jesus transcends the ages and all the spatial elements combined. It is the source of your wisdom and the generation of your energy that drives you to succeed. My dear little sons, it is this love that makes the Father so attracted to you. It is your scent of legitimacy; it is your glow in the darkness of the secular night; it is the way you never concede to those who would have you slain for your faith. It is your connection with the truth. My movements about the Earth are evidenced by locations in which most miracles are attributed. The Angels rejoice when they see Me embark on new earthly ventures. They gather around Me like explosive blasts of colorful wildfire. Why? Because they realize that the world as humanity knows it will never be the same again. I follow those who are devoted to Me. I echo the prayers of My children directly into the Heart of their Savior. I move within inches of babies' breath and make sure that their first word will be 'Jesus.' I hail from the Kingdom that not only knows no end, but that manifests by its lovely existence the holiness to which all men are called. I am gentle and caring, moving and inspiring, seeking and finding. I wish that sinners would surrender to the Cross and claim Jesus as their Redeemer. Yes, I know that sometimes wishes do not come true, but this one really matters to Me. My emotion is constructive. I have in My Immaculate Heart the bounty of the life of forgiveness. I hold in My arms the Incarnation of Absolute Salvation. And, My Special and Chosen ones, this is the reason why the Father will never forget anything we have done. We hope, live and breathe together in Him. We find our solace there. My sinless perfection and your imminent sainthood are fruits of His wondrous love. All the sights, sounds and aromas that we have ever known are gifts from His holy parlours. We are loving human creatures together, My Special and Chosen ones, because God has deigned us to be. The fullness of who we are and why we were given life is encapsulated by the Easter joy that never wanes in you. This, My children, is the way I ask you to live. It is the reason that you rise in the morning more hopeful than on the day before. Never mind the stubborn darkness, I say. Forget about the distractions that lure nonbelievers into walking wayward paths. These things have no effect on you because you have been given the greatest life imaginable – the life of Divine Love blooming with stately poise inside your hearts. My Special son, thank you again for your lofty speech to open our message here this morning. Never believe that your writings are too negative, sarcastic or brash. You are awakening a nation with words as sharp as swords. Thank you again for your holy prayers."

Saturday, December 12, 2015
9:32 a.m.

"When the human soul aches: the application of the truth –
fishbones and bread crumbs."

"My precious little sons, I have come praying with you as we anticipate the compliance of humanity with the mandates of the Gospel. It is not that we are naive that we pray for this, but that we are aware of God's ability to amend the Earth according to His sovereign designs. It was the miracle of the loaves and fishes that procured the hopes of thousands, but they seemed more focused on the nutrition than the miracle. Humanity has been this way ever since. I have been telling you for twenty-four years that it is the spiritual nourishment of the heart that will satisfy the world long after its emergence from the ages. I have given you venue through which to ply your works in reaching them, and you have seen the fruits of your prayers. Yes, and these fruits are far more nourishing than loaves and fishes – they remain with you forever. I have said that the human soul has the ability to ache, not that it has nerves or flesh, but that it yearns for the Salvation that God dispenses. It is willed into those who accept the Cross; it is a product of the relationship between Heaven and Earth, it is the blessing of acceptance and obedience, it is the poise of life in the heart of the believer. As I have said, it is a process more than an event. I would never expect My children to awaken some morning and say, '...Oh, I get it!' This is not how the human will moves aside; it is not something that can be captured in a photograph. I have said that the spirit may bend, but it is incapable of being broken. It is not absent anything that connects humanity to God because the spirit is transcending in ways that objects will never be. When someone says that their head is bowed, it gives the impression that there has been a defeat. The spirit, on the other hand, may bend, but it never bows. It is the heart that defers to God as the human will is handed to Him in palms outstretched in prayer. So, what does the application of the truth look like? How can lost sinners find what they have been seeking for so long? It is more than conceiving their relationship with God as though the two are separate entities. It is uniting the Spirit of God with the spirit of men. The human destiny is neatly positioned among the two. I have given descriptions of images of what God and man can do when men confess their sins and live in accordance with His teachings. Hence, when someone says that Jesus is the mediator between God and man, they are saying that Jesus is the 'soul' between God and man, between Heaven and Earth. It makes sense that the world would enter their relationship with the Father through the Son who knows Him best. My Special one, many people lack the understanding that their friendship with Jesus means giving more than taking. It is the investment of their faith that Jesus evokes, even as He has dispensed so many miracles to help them believe. It is beyond just accepting that one's faith in Christ Jesus travels. There must be a desire to be so in love with Jesus that those who believe in Him are consumed by His suffering. Moreover, it is clear that the altars of the Roman Catholic Church are the feast tables from which the faithful receive their sacramental nourishment. This is the foretaste of the Grand Feast in Heaven. Christians must come to Holy Mass knowing that Jesus' Sacrifice feeds the soul the innocence for which it hungers in anticipation of that great eternal banquet.

    The Cross and the Eucharistic Liturgy cannot be separated any more than Jesus' Body could be deposed before handing His Soul over to the Father. This is not some symbolic magnetism that I am speaking about here; it is placing the human spirit within Jesus on the Cross, and Jesus placing His Body, Blood, Soul and Divinity within the thanks-giving communicant during Holy Mass. I am referring to the agency between Jesus and the Church in the same way that Jesus is the agency between the Church and the Father. Jesus is the unifying, cohesive

Victim who connects humanity with Heaven while removing every remnant of sin. We often speak of the impact of history, about what the record of the ages will look like at the end of time. Where will their weight be shifted? How will the balance between the Earth and Heaven be reconciled? However, these two questions do not apply. It is not like sweeping dust from someone's home into the street as though the dust has just been moved. I am saying that the impact of history and the record of the ages will both cease altogether. What must be reconciled is each person's perception of history, their role in shaping it, their pattern of truth and error, the measure of their loyalty to the Church in all three forms, their compliance with the ethereal virtues, and their own judgement of whether they remained faithful in every aspect of love. This is the only history that will matter. This is where the examination of life and dying will take place. And, the record of the ages? What relevance could this have once the souls of humanity take flight in Heaven? My Special son, I am speaking in terms that highlight the Afterlife that is heralded through the rites of Christianity, but I do not wish to stray from what is expected of humanity today. I have made reference this year to the relationship between faith, sanctity and prayer. I have said that divine help is a product of the obedience of God's people and their accession to His Will. It is in these things that conversion is found. It is a movement that leads to unity inside the Sacred Heart of Jesus. If it is the soul that aches; if it is possible that someone can suffer pain not just of the heart, mind or flesh, then it is the building up of the power of the Cross here in this world. One can hear the sounds of joy beyond the crying of humanity in the same way that new life follows the wailing of a mother giving birth. Clarity, purpose, glory and reason are like newborn offspring to converted men. It is about the monumental passing from this sinful world into the Eternal Heart of Heaven.

My Special son, life need not always be about pain and torment. Through the vestiges of the call of one's true faith, anything converting can be sustained. Any suffering can be placed in the perspective of the Cross. The transformation of the world into the likeness of Heaven often comes in increments. This is the reason it makes sense that the Father would place saints-to-be on a spatial planet that provides the rhythms of labor and rest. As daylight comes, so do the hearts of men make the most of their years. When night falls, it is their time to rest and reflect, to measure their lives against the backdrop of truth, and prepare anew for the reward that is forthcoming. It is not just a final reward, but a commendation of their love for God to hope and redemption. My Special son, I have also spoken to you and your brother during the past several months about the senses by which the intensity of love can be discerned. You are saturated with grace and peace; you have within you the desire to remain inside My Immaculate Heart. This is what we seek from your brothers and sisters, for the billions who do not even know that I have lived. And, this is the reason I have spoken to you in 2015 about eliminating the distractions that keep the world from seeing what they will soon come to know. I have said that we have something they all want; it will be their big surprise. What they are looking for, My Special and Chosen ones, is freedom from their captivity to sin. They cannot put it into words just yet, but they hunger for the breaking of the chains that bind them to this world. We have never been so hungry because we are satisfied; we are fed through our relationship with God. We are attuned to His Sacred Heart. We subscribe to His intentions in ushering good men back to Himself. I knew this long before the Archangel Gabriel came calling on Me. It was within My soul before I was conceived in the womb. Many theologians have wondered how I could have been born of a woman who would herself be the mother of the Mother of God. Well, she was in fact a woman, and My mother, and the priceless soul to whom I turned for guidance and help. Yes, I became My own mother's Mother, another sacred mystery of the Church in the same way that the Sacrifice of the Innocent Lamb expunged the sins of all the guilty. Yes, My Special son, it was a great miracle that touched so many souls all those centuries ago. The pilgrims feasted on Jesus' holy plenty; all that remained were the fish bones, twelve baskets and bread crumbs. This – yes this is what I am asking humanity to do in these times. I hope you have enjoyed My message today, and bless you for taking such good care of your brother. Your sacred love, friendship, and brotherhood will live long past the conclusion of this world. I will remember all for whom you are praying in My intercessions to Jesus."

Sunday, December 20, 2015
9:39 a.m.

"People pass away all the time from quirky accidents, headlong leaps, car wrecks, rattlesnake bites, gunshot wounds, knife attacks, and even alone in their beds from old age and exhaustion; and they enter the presence of God as ready saints or instant converts, each and every one heirs of the moment. So, why not take on the battle against the devil as martyrs before we go? – staring down the heaving throats of a thousand fiery mountains, scoffing at burning stakes, eluding charlatans' swords, bearing the assaults of abomination and thuggery, dodging assassins' bullets, fighting off an occasional onslaught of demonic beatings, and showing up before Jesus Christ as legends of the Cross."

- William L. Roth

"This is the day, My little children, another day on which we are calling on Jesus to defend His Church openly and ardently, when we are asking God to bless humanity with peace and wisdom, when we are taking care to remember in our prayers those who have no one else to pray for them. This is the beginning of the week that will usher in the remembrance of the Birth of Jesus Christ. It is our way of reminding the lost that the Nativity of the Messiah signals the conversion of their souls. Yes, their Salvation is at hand, and it is our role to ignite the fires of their awakening. We need to put out the world and inflame the Earth. It is in our hands to remind the lost that they will be found in Jesus as they become more conspicuous to Him. They must tender their exiled lives to Him for refinement, renewal and reconciliation. I have tremendous hope that we will reach them in time so that their lasting eternity will be filled with joy rather than torment. Here, My dear sons, is where we begin the week of Christmas. And, as you reach the Feast of Christmas a few days from now, I ask you to feel the blessing from My hands and from Jesus' sacred touch that will give you anew the peace for which the world has long languished. My Special son, men might look at the Earth and humanity through the lens of disdain, but I ask them to remember what everyone will eventually become. The human definition of love is sometimes, '...I love who you used to be.' However, the eternal definition of love is, '...I love who you are now and who you will always be.' I realize that humans are prone to selfishness, that they look for love based on what they can profit from relationships. We know that Divine Love does not work that way. It is a measure of arms outstretched enough to accept all the failures and weakness of those whose problems others would rather not know about, and attributes that do not reflect the beauty of the heart. It is not just for the lost that Jesus was born, but the ones who claim to be found but live as though they are not. It is a Christmas spirit that must come to humanity through the ages and around the globe that must live, always live, in the hearts of those committed to Him. Jesus would have it no other way. Grace comes to the Earth like a welcoming rain; it is cleansing and cooling, it fills the air with the fragrance of unity. The term used to describe this phenomenon is 'petrichor.' This is the aroma in the air after rain falls onto soil that has been dry for a long time. It is the sweet odor of life, the re-creating that comes when the oldness of the world has been supplanted by the new. Although it has rarely been seen as such, this is the way humanity should accept the soul-bathing Blood of Jesus on the Cross. The pouring out of Jesus' Blood was the rain that cleansed the souls of humanity. What would it have been like to be there that day? The revelations are in your hearts, My Special and Chosen ones. You have been in the presence of the rains that have flooded the streets in front of your home. This is a sequence of events that began with God's command at the beginning of time that there would be rainfall on those days. It required an atmosphere conducive to shedding moisture from above, an environment of cleansing and rejuvenation. What humanity does not realize is that this cleansing not only makes new the soil on which the rains fall, but it revives the whole concept of life and time. This is the petrichor that is detectable to the world, the Father's sign that life will abound despite the withering of the Earth.

I have come speaking today about petrichor from the eternal side of life. My purpose is to tell you and your brother what happens in Heaven when it rains on Earth. I would like to discuss what it was like where God reigns in Heaven when His Son was crucified on Mount Calvary. Hear Me now – it was the one and the same glory that was given to the Earth on the Feast of Christmas. This is the reason the Eucharistic Celebration is held on the same day that the birth of Jesus is observed. What began with the Annunciation of the Archangel Gabriel culminated with the words, '…He is not here. He has risen, as He said.' From conception to Resurrection – these are the bookends between which all human love is sustained. Hence, the sensation in Heaven's Eternal Domain upon the Angelic Annunciation, the Nativity, the Crucifixion and the Paschal Resurrection of Jesus was precisely the same as the fragrance on Earth after a cleansing rain. The petrichor is the same. When the Lord says that it shall rain, the elements and atmosphere take their appointed shape. This is the same as when the Father sent the Archangel Gabriel to announce the Salvation of the world. Jesus' Blood on the Cross provided lost sinners with the petrichor that they recognize to this day. When someone lays on their deathbed and says they can smell the aroma of rain, this is what they are experiencing. They are entering the vestibule of redemption where the waters of God's love flow – embodied and empowered by Jesus' Blood on the Cross. The Feast of Christmas provides this revelatory scent because Jesus was born to die for the sins of the world. It is the reunion between Heaven and Earth through the Crucifixion of the Man-God on the Cross. My Special son, I would like for you to always remember that Jesus has lived and died, and was raised again, but the most comforting place He ever laid His head was inside My Womb. No matter where else you might imagine Him to be – even at the right hand of the Father, He has never inside or outside of time felt more consoled than when He was placed in the virginal sanctum of My Womb. My little son, Jesus has told Me this time and again. This is the Savior who came into the world at the behest of the Father to instill in humanity the holiness of Himself. This is the anniversary that you will celebrate this week. Can you imagine how it makes Me feel to know that the Son of the Most High has said that His favorite resting place is inside My Womb? This is the reason

I am blessed – it is the reason I am trying to convert lost sinners to His Most Sacred Heart as the Child of Bethlehem and their Savior nailed to the Cross. Yes, given asylum within My Immaculate Womb to be sheltered there beside Him.

But first, the darkness of the Earth must be eradicated. It is all about the Light of the World vanquishing the devilish pit of men's sins. It is about making Sacred Truth more appealing than their lies. We have seen the boundaries of this struggle thus far; these boundaries may grow even wider. I call on you and your brother to refrain from anxiety. You said it rightly at the opening of our message today – staring down the throat of a thousand fiery mountains. What eloquence! What courageous vision! What concession to the Son of Man that victory is yours. These are the things that humanity should ponder on the Feast of Christmas. It is not about strengthening the American economy by giving birth to surplus, but remembering that all materials will eventually return to dust. Christmas is about issuing the promise of eternal love in ways that alleviate human suffering and make workable the instruments of world peace. It is about summoning the Child Jesus to make new the Earth in His likeness, to cleanse the world and rewrite history by His life, Death and Resurrection – to provide the new and eternal glory to repentant men in the same way that the petrichor makes them aware that a different day has come. This may seem too altruistic for many people to believe, but it is real renewal in an age of exhausted histories. It is, in fact, about trading an old death for a new life. Our commission here, My Special and Chosen ones, is not only to foster this exchange, but to help Jesus define it inside the hearts and minds of those who will come to Him through our love. My Special son, what this looks like from the Father's purview is the same as when you see rainbows, waterfalls and skyrockets, and hear the sounds of orchestras making music with the symphonies of your lives. God is positioned on His Throne where I have always seen Him, but He is also here beside you now, standing with gratitude in every inch of your home and through all the moments of your life. He is providing for you, receiving the content of your prayers, reshaping and clarifying His Kingdom, and blessing and nourishing the confines of the Earth in all the benevolent ways that you have asked. May His Christmas peace be upon you now."

Saturday, December 26, 2015
9:47 a.m.

"The maximum exertion of redemptive power involves prayer, cannon fire, golden vaults, exculpating tears, profiles of believers, the synchronization of life and truth, good will deeper than the oceans, the wisdom of the ages, humility in suffering, and the optimal conveyance of sanctifying grace."

- William L. Roth

"Maximum Capacity"

"My darling little sons, I have not finished transmitting the sentiments of My Immaculate Heart to you, and often to you alone, that have brought Me here so many times before. I beseech you to remember that I am as human as you are human. I am simply watching you alongside Jesus as you tender to Him the gift of your lives. You have seen the organic and inorganic creatures and substances that make up the Earth, and I have taken you to the ethereal realms where your hearts actually live. I have asked you to dismiss the darkness of the world in favor of the Divine Light that shines in Heaven and on Earth. If your lives are to be their most meaningful, you will realize that you were created by God to be united with Jesus. I hold in My presence the Sacred Man-God who is your wisdom and peace, just as you have spoken in your words beginning our message today. My Special one, if you consider all the assets that you have cited when pondering the power of divine life, and about the ways that your holiness is shared around the globe, it is clear that they are manifestations of your oneness with Jesus through all times and places. Exculpating tears and the wisdom of the ages are the two pillars on which humanity stands before Jesus. Sinners are forgiven when they accept Jesus on the Cross and confess that they have fallen short of His example. There are some who have not been required to do so because they have been more 'perfect' than others. All the Saints, including the Popes, and little people everywhere; the servants of rightness and justice, and you, My Special one, are examples of those who have been perfected through your faith in Jesus. It is clear that millions of others are still struggling. You have struck a place where all those who are far from God can begin their journey back to Him. It is no secret, as I have said, that this is more a process than an event; it is a long journey toward a destination. It is more about enlightenment than evolution. The wisdom of the ages about which you speak involves rewriting the conscience, and it summons the endurance of suffering that often accompanies this transition. What must be accomplished for a Christian to be perfected in the Cross is truly as much about abandonment as enlightenment. Old habits are hard to break. Some people fall short of reaching the grandest hope to which they aspire in becoming like Jesus because they are not supported by others. Sometimes they relapse because they become distracted or predators exploit them. The entire matter revolves around knowing the difference between being righteous and just being different. As you review My messages since December 28, 2008, you see that I have brought you even closer to My embrace because I am speaking more directly to you than to universal humanity. In other words, I have shared with you during the past seven years more of the aspects of My life, My perception of the Church and the world in which it propagates. It is My honor to tell Jesus that you and your brother have earned a grand place in Paradise, even as you remain exiled in the world. Jesus sees what you have done with the gifts you have been given. And, this brings Me to the point that your brother was making recently about the 'maximum capacity' of someone or something that exemplifies the reason they were created. This maximum capacity is perfectly aligned with the perfection of the world and the redemption of humanity in its fullest form. When your brother spoke about the race car driver running the final lap, he said that the man and the machine were uniquely one entity, operating optimally, just as you have said that redemptive power is exerted through the optimal conveyance of sanctifying grace.

My Special son, this is hardly seen because it rarely occurs. But, it happens every time you and your brother assemble to hear My messages. It is a fruit of your prayers whereby you write such beautiful literary verses. It is like a shaft of light cutting through the darkness of an underground mine. It is the composition of your meditations that are transferred into communicable form. This makes the grace that you have received from God not just sanctifying, but edifying as well. You have chosen this life, My Special son. You have knowingly given ownership of your life to the Son of Man, to Jesus Christ, who is your new identity. This is the call of God to all creatures great and small who inhabit the earthly domain. Hence, the maximum exertion of redemptive power includes the maximum capacity about which we speak. It is about potential and ability – righteousness given venue. I have said this long ago. The openness of humanity to hold access to this venue is held back by all the sins and omissions that are spoken about in the Holy Gospel. Yes indeed, it is as much about what is lacking in humanity as its contents, substances and actions that do exist. Holding out an empty hand to Jesus is hardly giving Him your heart. This is what the world has yet to learn. The heart must be present in the hand – and in the case of you and your brother, it is much more than your deposit of Marian works, it is your gift to Jesus in that you were willing to manifest them. Your love and labors lay heavy on your palms; you hold them to the skies like sweet fruits to grace the lips of the Son of the Holy Spirit. My purpose here has been to instill in you not just the capacity to become messengers, but the inspiration to maximize your effect in the exiled world. I will tell you today that there has never before been this kind of immersion or this level of supernatural detail given to humanity. I had to wait until there were such recording and publishing devices as the ones you use to even consider saying as much to two messengers as I have to you. It would have taken another thousand years. This, therefore, broaches the subject that you mentioned yesterday in your discussion with your brother. It refers to the reason why God and Jesus do not strike-down evil legions that are wreaking such havoc in the world. They are prepared to do so, and they have previously done so, but what about the role of humanity? Is not the Messianic message about converting the nations sufficient energy to reverse the evils that are consuming them now? After all, the Mystical Body of Jesus is not a bedridden invalid. The collective mind of humanity has not yet come to the conclusion that Jesus is not going to stop the march of evil against the purity of the Earth while good men stand idly by. This would be a proxy conversion by a Man-God who is already perfect. And, what about the spiritual weapons of war – what about praying the Holy Rosary that can bring total destruction to any demonic ideology?

My Special son, how many more spiritual signs does one nation need? It is not about the Father's reluctance to act, it is about leaders of nations coddling other 'beliefs' as though they can be equated with the Church of Christianity. It is about suborning relativism and pluralism. Exiled men on Earth are fighting, struggling and dying because these men refuse to collect themselves as Christian nations beneath the Cross of Mount Calvary. It is no more complicated than this. Jesus has not given up hope, and I have not given up hope, because the unifying effort to which I am referring is rising as we speak. It may be difficult to see from your position here, but all the holiness that Jesus has bequeathed the Church is ripening in the hearts of believers like fruits on the vine. This is the transition to which I am referring in My message today. Yes, an atmosphere that is conducive to this ripening must be prevalent for a long period of time; these fruits cannot ripen if men's faith comes and goes. And, these fruits cannot flourish if hatred poisons the air. They cannot reach their harvest sweetness if the skies above are darkened by sins and transgressions. Please, My Special and Chosen ones; please understand that good people have been given the venue to spread the Gospel far and wide, but they are more prone to seek profit from their faith than share the Sovereign Truth. They are too entangled in politics to worry about the mission of the Church. They placate distractions and entertain illusions because they find it more appealing to sit in armchairs beside their fireplaces than pray for peace before the Blessed Sacrament. So I have just come, My little sons, to tell you that Jesus is aware of the conditions in the world. It is that He has given good men access to the maximum exertion of redemptive power to end the wars, stop the famine and turn the hearts and faces of sinners to the Cross. My gratitude is with you, My Special one, for welcoming Me into your home that I have visited for so many years to relate the impressions of God and share My own visions about the way the future ought to be. I ask you and your brother to realize the gift that you are to the Church and to Me, and to the billions of souls whose lives and fates depend on what they know about the calling of the Holy Spirit. Like this year has been, the next will bring many soul-searching events from which humanity must reevaluate its perception of itself. When a new year opens around the globe, it is indeed an event for the ages. Thank you for being such a Special one in the eyes of the Father, in the Sacred Heart of Jesus, and in My arms in which I hold your heart and soul forever."